Organizational Change and Redesign:
Ideas and Insights for Improving Performance

Organizational Change and Redesign

Ideas and Insights for Improving Performance

Edited by
George P. Huber
William H. Glick

New York Oxford   **Oxford University Press**

Oxford University Press

Oxford   New York
Athens Auckland Bangkok Bombay
Calcutta Cape Town Dar es Salaam Delhi
Florence Hong Kong Istanbul Karachi
Kuala Lumpur Madras Madrid Melbourne
Mexico City Nairobi Paris Singapore
Taipei Tokyo Toronto

and associated companies in
Berlin   Ibadan

Library of Congress Cataloging-in-Publication Data
Organizational change and redesign: ideas and insights for improving
performance / edited by George P. Huber and William H. Glick.
p. cm. Includes bibliographical references and index.
ISBN 0-19-507285-5; ISBN 0-19-510115-4 (pbk.)
1. Organizational change.
2. Organizational effectiveness.
3. Performance.
I. Huber, George P.
II. Glick, William H.
HD58.8.07287 1993
658.4'06—dc20 92-27456

9 8 7 6 5 4 3 2 1

Printed in the United States of America
on acid-free paper

PREFACE

Top managers are preoccupied by change, both the changes that they must react to, such as new and important threats and opportunities, and the changes that they initiate as a result of their beliefs and aspirations. To increase organizational effectiveness—for instance, to improve efficiency, gain market share, or simplify the organizational design—managers are constantly creating new programs, streamlining procedures, evaluating proposed courses of action, and scanning their environment for new problems or opportunities. Such activities lead to organizational change and redesign.

Partly because of its practical importance to management and to society at large, and partly because organizational science is tending more toward the study of organizational processes rather than static relationships, organizational change is increasingly capturing the attention of organizational scholars and researchers. Incongruent with its importance, and with the increased attention given it by scholars and consultants, is the slower development of a body of knowledge concerning organizational change. Organizational changes can best be studied across time, but the proportion of systematic studies that are longitudinal is small. Further, organizational research is typically small science—large teams of investigators or developments of large primary data bases are uncommon, so whatever benefits might accrue from larger-scale investigations are only infrequently obtained. For both of these reasons, the development of credible descriptive and prescriptive theories of organizational change has proceeded slowly.

The program of research that led to this book was designed to address these problems. Our goal was to generate new knowledge about when and how different types of changes occur, and what their effects are on organizational performance. This ambitious goal required, in our view, obtaining information from the top managers of a large number and variety of organizations across an extended period of time. The associated workload required that we recruit a research team of highly capable organizational scientists. This we were able to do.

The members of the research team, in aggregate, played three roles. The first role, taken by the two of us, involved recruiting and coordinating the team and designing the central study to be conducted in collaboration with four other researchers. The second role, adopted by us and four other researchers, involved designing and conducting five separate studies that would contribute to the development of theories concerning organizational change, redesign, and performance. The four collaborating organizational scientists initially invited to fill this role were Dr. Kim Cameron of the University of Michigan, Dr. Richard Daft of Texas A&M University, Dr. Alan Meyer of the University of Oregon, and Dr. Charles O'Reilly of the University of California at Berkeley. When Daft went to the University of Michigan and then on to Vanderbilt

University, Dr. Kenneth Bettenhausen, then of Texas A&M University, was asked to step in and help keep the A&M study on track.

The third role was that of consultant to the study. Five distinguished organizational scientists were invited to help in this way: Dr. Arie Lewin of Duke University, Dr. Peter Monge of the University of Southern California, Dr. John Slocum of Southern Methodist University, Dr. Andrew Van de Ven of the University of Minnesota, and Dr. Karl Weick, then of the University of Texas and now at the University of Michigan. The fact that no one turned down our invitation to participate reinforced our belief that there was a widespread feeling among organizational scientists that studies of organizational change were important and timely.

Organizations are now more numerous and more necessary than at any time in history, and they are becoming even more so. Their importance, and particularly the importance of their effectiveness, has caused some of the country's most prestigious science-funding agencies to support research on organizations. We were fortunate in receiving full support from the first agency to which we applied. In 1985, the Basic Research Program of the U.S. Army Research Institute for the Behavioral and Social Sciences agreed to fund the program of research. All of us on the research team, and especially the two of us as the principal and co-principal investigators, greatly appreciate the unique opportunity that this provided.

This preface has briefly sketched how it is that this book came to be. We put the detailed description of the program of research in the Appendix ("Studying Changes in Organizational Design and Effectiveness," reprinted by permission from *Organization Science*) because this book is not about research. It is about the changes that top managers must deal with and the changes that top managers choose to initiate. It is about redesigning organizations. It is about the causes and consequences of different types of change and redesign. These are important matters for managers, for managers-to-be, and for organizational scientists.

One of our goals was to make our findings relevant to the managers and observers of a wide variety of organizations. Accordingly we chose to study many, varied organizations. We studied over 70 organizations involved in the production of automobiles, steel, electronics, software, and printed materials. We also studied over 70 organizations in the service industries—organizations such as hospitals, banks, and business schools. In all, we studied 153 organizations.

To help make this book reader-friendly and broadly useful, we asked the authors to specifically spell out the implications of their work for managers and for organizational scientists. We also asked them to avoid academic jargon. They responded with good grace.

A primary goal of the research team, since its inception, was to write a book that would provide organizational scientists and upper-level managers with fresh insights into the nature of organizational change and redesign. This goal was in mind when we, as the principal investigators, chose the collaborating researchers and consultants and thus, in effect, the principal authors of the book's chapters. The chapters written by the principal and collaborating investigators are influenced by the findings developed in the course of the empirical studies they individually conducted as part of this program of research, but their chapters reflect just as much the broader knowledge base that these investigators brought to their empirical work and that justified their inclusion in the research team. The chapters written by the consultants reflect the combination of knowledgeability and insightfulness that characterizes each of them and that warranted their assuming the consultative roles that they did.

In Chapter 1, we review the contents of each chapter. It seems useful, however, to note here just a few of the book's features, to help frame readers' expectations.

- Each chapter deals with organizational change or redesign.
- Each chapter explicitly sets forth a new insight—an idea or conclusion not currently available in the organizational science or managerial literature.
- An editors' summary begins each chapter, except Chapters 1 and 12. These summaries highlight the key issues and contributions of the respective chapters.
- Chapters 2 through 7 are based on multiyear longitudinal studies of multiple organizations. These features of the studies helped the chapter authors assess the causes of organizational change and also achieve high levels of generalizability in their conclusions.
- The authors of Chapters 2 through 7 draw on a series of interviews with the top managers of dozens of organizations to gain insight into the causes, correlates, and consequences of organizational change.
- Chapters 8 through 11 are tutorials on how to think about, manage, or assess organizational change or redesign. They, Chapter 12, and the Epilogue are each based on the authors' years of reading and study. Individually and collectively, these chapters contain and organize a wealth of accumulated wisdom.

Even though the authors of all chapters were selected because they had outstanding credentials, each chapter has gone through multiple revisions and rewrites as a result of reviews from a total of 16 referees who, like the authors, are authorities on the topics of the chapters they reviewed. (These referees are acknowledged in the individual chapters.) These reviews sharpened the chapters, in both content and style. Our goals were to make the chapters not only authoritative but also reader-friendly. We hope that the results will meet the readers' needs and aspirations.

As we noted earlier, much of the content of this book followed from funding by the Basic Research Program of the Army Research Institute (ARI). It may be that without ARI's willingness to support a multiyear multi-investigator program of study, this book would not have come to be. Nor would the book have come to be without the willingess of the several research teams and consultants to focus on creating an integrated work and to respond to our requests for consistency of thrust and style across chapters. And certainly the book could not have been written without the information provided by scores of top managers who volunteered their time and information.

The editors greatly appreciate the help of the very constructive suggestions made to the authors of the book's chapters. Those colleagues who contributed their talents in this way are: Kenneth Bettenhausen, Joan Brett, Kim Cameron, Laura Cardinal, Prithviraj Chattopadhyay, Richard Daft, Alison Davis-Blake, John Delery, Harold Doty, Eric Eisenberg, James Fredrickson, Janet Fulk, Connie Gersick, Donald Hambrick, Gary Hamel, John Huber, Dileep Hurry, Ellen Jackofsky, K. Michelle Kacmor, Tommy Lasseigne, Arie Lewin, Reuben McDaniel, Alan Meyer, Raymond Miles, Peter Monge, Jennifer Monohan, Charles O'Reilly, Richard Osborn, Dru Pagliosotti, Robert Pappas, Robin Pinkley, Everett Rogers, Deanna Schwarz, Steve Shortell, John Slocum, Andrew Van de Ven, Karl Weick, Frederick Williams, JoAnne Wyer, Raymond Zammuto, and Robert Zmud. To all the above, we say thanks, and more thanks. Finally, our greatest debt is to Libby and Rhonda, whose tolerance and support during this six-year endeavor made it all possible and whose patience and understanding are immensely appreciated.

Austin, Tex.   G.P.H.
February 1993   W.H.G.

CONTENTS

PART III   Conclusion

CONTRIBUTORS

CHAPTER 1 *Sources and Forms of Organizational Change:* Chapter 1, "Sources and Forms of Organizational Change," and Chapter 12, "What Was Learned About Organizational Change and Redesign," were written by the book's Editors, George P. Huber and William H. Glick. Dr. Huber is the Charles and Elizabeth Prothro Regents Chair in Business Administration. William H. Glick is Associate Professor of Management. Both are at the University of Texas at Austin. Together they designed and directed the program of study that led to the preparation of this book.

CHAPTER 2 *Downsizing and Redesigning Organizations:* Kim S. Cameron is Professor of Organizational Behavior and Human Resource Management at the University of Michigan. Sarah J. Freeman and Aneil K. Mishra were doctoral students at the University of Michigan during the period of this research. Dr. Freeman is now Assistant Professor of Management at the University of Wisconsin at Milwaukee, and Dr. Mishra is now Assistant Professor of Business Administration at Pennsylvania State University.

CHAPTER 3 *Organizations Reacting to Hyperturbulence:* Alan D. Meyer is Professor of Management and Edwin E. and June Wolt Cone Research Scholar at the University of Oregon. Dr. Meyer is a Consulting Editor for the *Academy of Management Journal.* James B. Goes and Geoffrey R. Brooks were doctoral students at the University of Oregon during the period of this research. Dr. Goes is now Assistant Professor of Health Care Strategy at the University of Minnesota, Twin Cities, and Dr. Brooks is now the Anheuser-Busch Term Assistant Professor of Management at the University of Pennsylvania.

CHAPTER 4 *Implications of Top Managers' Communication Choices for Strategic Decisions:* Richard L. Daft is the Ralph Owen Professor of Management at Vanderbilt University. Dr. Daft is Associate Editor-in-Chief of *Organization Science* and was Associate Editor of the *Administrative Science Quarterly.* Kenneth R. Bettenhausen is Assistant Professor of Management at the University of Colorado at Denver. Beverly B. Tyler is Assistant Professor of Strategy at Indiana University. Drs. Daft, Bettenhausen, and Tyler were all at Texas A&M University during the period of this research.

CHAPTER 5 *Effects of Executive Team Demography on Organizational Change:* Charles A. O'Reilly is the Lorraine T. Mitchell Chair in Leadership and Communication II at the University of California at Berkeley. Richard C. Snyder was engaged in postdoctoral work at the University during the period of this research and is now Assistant Professor at the California School of Professional Psychol-

engaged in postdoctoral work at the University during the period of this research and is now Assistant Professor at the California School of Professional Psychology. Joan N. Boothe is a doctoral student in Organizational Behavior and Industrial Relations at the University of California at Berkeley.

CHAPTER 6   *The Impact of Upper-Echelon Diversity on Organizational Performance:* William H. Glick is Associate Professor of Management at the University of Texas at Austin. C. Chet Miller was a doctoral candidate at the University of Texas at Austin during the period of this research and is now Assistant Professor of Management at Baylor University. George P. Huber is the Charles and Elizabeth Prothro Regents Chair in Business Administration at the University of Texas at Austin.

CHAPTER 7   *Understanding and Predicting Organizational Change:* George P. Huber is the Charles and Elizabeth Prothro Regents Chair in Business Administration at the University of Texas at Austin. He is former Editor of *Management Science*'s Department of Information Systems and former Associate Editor for *Decision Sciences.* Kathleen M. Sutcliffe and C. Chet Miller were doctoral students at the University of Texas at Austin during the period of this research. Dr. Sutcliffe is currently Assistant Professor of Strategic Management and Organization at the University of Minnesota, Twin Cities, and Dr. Miller is Assistant Professor of Management at Baylor University. William H. Glick is Associate Professor of Management at the University of Texas at Austin.

CHAPTER 8   *Managing the Process of Organizational Innovation:* Andrew H. Van de Ven is the Vernon H. Heath Chaired Professor of Organizational Innovation and Change at the University of Minnesota, Twin Cities. Dr. Van de Ven is Senior Editor for Innovation and Change for *Organization Science* and is a Co-Editor of the Harvard Business School Press series on The Management of Innovation and Change.

CHAPTER 9   *Designing Global Strategic Alliances: Integrating Cultural and Economic Factors:* John W. Slocum, Jr. is the O. Paul Corley Professor of Organizational Behavior and Management at Southern Methodist University. Dr. Slocum is former President of the Academy of Management and former Editor of the *Academy of Management Journal.* He is former Associate Editor of *Decision Sciences* and the *Academy of Management Executive* and is currently Senior Editor for Strategic Human Resource Management of *Organization Science.* David Lei is Assistant Professor of Business Policy at Southern Methodist University.

CHAPTER 10   *(Re)Designing Dynamic Organizations:* Peter R. Monge is Professor of Communication at the University of Southern California. Dr. Monge is currently Editor of *Communication Research.*

CHAPTER 11   *Organizational Redesign As Improvisation:* Karl E. Weick is the Rensis Likert Collegiate Professor of Organizational Behavior and Psychology at the University of Michigan. Dr. Weick is former Editor of the *Administrative Science Quarterly* and has received the Academy of Management's Irwin Award for Scholarly Contributions to Management.

CHAPTER 12 *What Was Learned About Organizational Change and Redesign:* Chapter 12 was written by the book's Editors, William H. Glick and George P. Huber (see Chapter 1).

EPILOGUE *Designing Postindustrial Organizations:* Arie Y. Lewin is Professor of Organizational Studies at Duke University. He is Editor-in-Chief of *Organization Science.* He is former Editor of *Management Science*'s Department of Organization Analysis and Design and former Director of the National Science Foundation's Decision, Risk, and Management Science Program. Carroll U. Stephens was a doctoral student at Duke University during the period of this research and is now Assistant Professor of Management at Virginia Polytechnic Institute.

APPENDIX *Studying Changes in Organizational Design and Effectiveness: Retrospective Event Histories and Periodic Assessments:* William H. Glick is Associate Professor of Management and George P. Huber is the Charles and Elizabeth Prothro Regents Chair in Business Administration. Both are at the University of Texas at Austin. C. Chet Miller, D. Harold Doty, and Kathleen M. Sutcliffe were doctoral students at the University of Texas at Austin during the period of this research. Dr. Miller is currently Assistant Professor of Management at Baylor University. Dr. Doty is now Assistant Professor of Management at the University of Arkansas. Dr. Sutcliffe is Assistant Professor of Strategic Management and Organization at the University of Minnesota, Twin Cities. This appendix is reprinted by permission from *Organization Science,* 1(3): 292–312. Copyright © 1990 The Institute of Management Sciences.

Organizational Change and Redesign:
Ideas and Insights for Improving Performance

1

Sources and Forms of Organizational Change

> May you live in interesting times.
>
> Ancient Chinese curse
>
> Interesting—a word we often use to signal an uncertain mix of danger and opportunity. If we wish to enjoy more of the opportunity and less of the risk we need to understand the changes better. Those who know why changes come waste less effort in protecting themselves or in fighting the inevitable. Those who realize where changes are heading are better able to use those changes to their own advantage.
>
> Charles Handy, The Age of Unreason, 1991: 4

During the 1980s it was tiresomely fashionable for the popular press and the business literature to report on business's turbulent environment. We were bombarded with stories and statistics informing us of events and trends different and faster moving than ever before. We were inundated with advice and admonitions about what organizations and their managers should do to cope with these changes. "Think strategically," "computerize," and "eliminate layers of management" were some.

Looking back, it is curious how void were the media and literature of truly thoughtful analyses of fundamental issues and questions. What are the root causes of the increasingly rapid rate of environmental change? Are there consistent patterns in how environmental change leads to organizational change? Assuming a state of continuously accelerating change, what should managers do? What should organizational scientists do that is different from what they've done in the past? These are the questions of sophisticated executives and forward-looking scholars. Answers to these questions are in this book.

Organizational changes are departures from the status quo or from smooth trends. They are almost without exception the products of an energizing force. There are two such forces for change: the organization's top managers and the organization's environment. The purpose of this introductory chapter is to delineate just how it is that these two forces, individually and interactively, cause organizational change.

The chapter has four parts. In the first part we undertake the task generally and unfortunately left undone by writers for the popular press; we identify and examine the fundamental causes of the environmental changes faced by today's and tomorrow's organizations. In the second part we make clear the nature of the organizational changes that must inevitably follow from the forthcoming changes in organizational environments. In contrast with this focus on the impact of environmental change, in the third part of this introduction we focus on the impact of the top manager. We examine each of the four roles through which top managers influence change—as independent sources of change, as constraints on change, as interpreters, and also as manipulators of their organization's environment. In the fourth and last part of the chapter, we delineate the importance of studying organizational design and change.

ENVIRONMENTAL CHANGE

The fast-changing nature of today's organizational environments is largely a consequence of two factors: (1) the increasing effectiveness of information technology (both communication technology and computing technology) and (2) the increasing effectiveness of transportation technology. For example:

- Global markets could not be what they are if information, products, and people could not be moved as easily as they can.
- The decline of manufacturing employment in the United States is directly a consequence of automation (read "information technology") and across-borders manufacturing and importation (read "transportation technology").
- The social issues that today affect organizations have much of their force because advances in communications technology (1) make social injustices and environmental tragedies vivid and widely known and (2) enable many separate entities to communicate, coordinate, and cooperate in confronting organizations on such matters.

What appears in the popular press and business literature are primarily vivid descriptions of particular changes in certain organizational environments and portrayals of particular consequences of particular changes. What is lacking is an analysis of why these changes in organizational environments are occurring and what will be the general nature of their effects on organizations. Let us turn to this task.[1]

We begin by noting that observing current events is a poor way to predict the future and is an even poorer way to identify the root causes of environmental change. When living systems, such as humans and organizations, find themselves in a changing environment they eventually engage in exploratory, testing behavior. Parsons (1977) and Boulding (1978) remind us that the ratio of tested alternatives to adopted alternatives is generally large. In their current turbulent environments, organizations are exploring many alternative strategies, structures, technologies, and business practices. Which particular alternative(s) will survive is difficult to say. Also, of course, alternatives temporarily rejected may later be embraced, as changed conditions enhance their viability. Clearly, *forecasting long-run future conditions on the basis of current events or even transition-related trends is certain to result in adopting a large number of false assumptions.*

When forecasting future organizational environments, rather than simply extrapolating from what we are observing we must look at longer-term trends. We must select trends that are logically antecedent, perhaps even causally linked, to the changes we wish to anticipate and understand. There are strong reasons to believe that growth in scientific knowledge is the long-term trend that best explains the changing nature of organizational environments. And it is both long-term and antecedent.

Available Knowledge—More and Increasing

From 1965 to 1980, the number of scientific articles published per day rose from 3,000 to 8,000, a 160 percent increase (Huppes, 1987: 65). This increase is only a snapshot measure of the long-term trend in the generation of information and knowledge. To get an idea of the longer trend, consider as a pattern in the rate of knowledge generation the accelerating increase in the number of scientific journals recorded by De Solla Price (1963). The first two scientific journals appeared in the mid-seventeenth century. By the middle of the eighteenth century there were ten scientific journals, by 1800 about 100, by 1850 perhaps 1,000. Somewhat later, Bell (1979) reported that estimates of the number of scientific journals ranged between 30,000 and 100,000. This pattern of growth cannot change in the intermediate future. Knowledge feeds on itself; knowledge is its own raw material. As a consequence, the absolute *amount* of knowledge can only continue to rise. That is, even if the rate of increase in knowledge diminishes, the existing knowledge base will be so large that absolute increases in units of knowledge per unit of time will remain large throughout at least the first half of the next century and very likely far beyond that. We are observing a long-term trend.

Of equal importance is the fact that the growing number of advanced communications technologies will greatly increase the *availability* of whatever knowledge is produced. Even a lay person's reflection on the advances in communications technology during the last 50 years makes clear that (1) such technologies are actually in their early stages of effectiveness and adoption, and (2) other, better, technologies are in the making. Consequently, we must anticipate an increase in the availability of existing knowledge as the technologies mature and become more widely used. The increased adoption of these knowledge-distributing technologies, superimposed on the geometrically increasing knowledge base, will result in a knowledge environment that is dramatically more munificent (or burdening) than that confronting organizations today. The generally unconsidered combination of increases in both the level of knowledge and the availability of knowledge lead to the conclusion that *in the future the amount of available knowledge and its absolute growth rate will be significantly greater than in the past.*

Increases in available knowledge have important practical impacts. For example, globalization, which may be the most important economic phenomenon of the 1980s and 1990s, is possible only because of advances in information technology and transportation technology. Advances in these areas, in turn, are possible only because of increases in available knowledge. Increases in available knowledge are, then, a root cause of change in organizational environments.

We just discussed causes of environmental change. However, we are interested in organizational change and redesign. What are the features of an organization's environment that, when they change, force changes in the organization itself? It seems to us that there are two: environmental complexity and environmental turbulence.

Environmental Complexity—More and Increasing

Organizational complexity has three key characteristics: numerosity, diversity, and interdependence. Examination of these characteristics and their relationships makes clear why organizational environments are becoming so complex. Consider, for example, the number of entities in the environment, such as the number of competitors, clients, or suppliers. Whether or not such entities in general will become more numerous is unclear. If they do, our conclusion that organizational environments will be more complex will be confirmed. Aside from whether or not the actual number of entities of any one type are or will be increasing, however, improvements in communications and transportation technologies cause the "effective" number of entities to be greater. For example, as noted above, improvements in these technologies have facilitated the globalization that is increasing the number of foreign competitors faced by producing organizations and the number of foreign supply sources available to consuming organizations. Thus knowledge-based improvements in technology have increased the complexity of organizational environments.

Increases in environmental complexity do not, however, arise simply from increases in the number of societal entities. Instead they follow from increases in diversity and interdependence. Increases in knowledge enable individual societal units to identify and exploit diverse technological, economic, and social niches, much as genetic changes enable biological organisms to exploit ecological niches. Thus, we observe more and increasing societal specialization and diversity—that is, environmental complexity—as a result of more and increasing societal knowledge, whether or not there is an increase in entities.

Finally, let us turn to the matter of interdependence. Specialization results in interdependence because, as organizations specialize and focus on core competencies, they give up certain capabilities (or do not achieve commensurate growth in certain capabilities). They then rely on other organizations for the resources that they themselves can no longer provide. Thus, increases in specialization necessarily lead to increased interdependencies among organizations and then to the increased complexity of any one organization's environment.

In summary, it seems clear that increases in knowledge lead to increases in the effectiveness of information and transportation technologies, and, partly through this means and in other ways as well, increases in knowledge lead to increases in the number and diversity of environmental entities and in the complexity of the relationships among these entities. Thus, we can conclude that *the level of environmental complexity and its absolute growth rate will be significantly greater in the future than in the past.*

Turbulence—More and Increasing

Today's high level of environmental turbulence follows from increases in the speed of individual events. More and increasing knowledge results in many technologies becoming more effective. An important consequence is that individual events are shorter in duration. They transpire more quickly. One type of ever-shortening event is the product life cycle. Another is the duration of an uncrowded market niche; improvements in R&D technology, in advertising technology, and in transportation technology enable competitors to steal markets more quickly than in the past. The role of geographical distance and cultural differences as "time buffers" diminishes rapidly as improved communication and transportation technologies are implemented. Since shorter events permit more events per unit of time, the eventual effect of increasing knowledge is increased turbulence. And since available knowledge is increasing at an increasing rate, we can expect that *the level of turbulence and its absolute growth rate will be significantly greater in the future than in the past.*

Let us take stock of where we are. We have discussed why organizational environments are, and increasingly will be, characterized by higher levels of knowledge, complexity, and turbulence. Without exception, the same reasoning leads to the conclusion that these trends will continue at an increasing rate. "Interesting times" are here, and more interesting times are coming. There can be no question that today's "turbulent times" are not a transition to a new era, a new environment for organizations and their managers. To the contrary, these *turbulent times are the new era;* they are the long-term future. For good and noble reasons managers may feel or hope that these times are a period of transition toward some new steady state of greater stability. But the reality is that, in the foreseeable future, organizational environments will become increasingly less stable. Given this unavoidable fact, the task of thinking managers and forward-looking scholars is to think about and learn about the organizational consequences.

ORGANIZATIONAL CONSEQUENCES OF ACCELERATING ENVIRONMENTAL CHANGE

What are the consequences of organizational environments being characterized by more and increasing knowledge, complexity, and turbulence? Organization theory and managerial wisdom tell us that for an organization to survive it must be compatible with its environment. When the environment changes to a state incompatible with the nature of the organization, the organization has available the following strategies: (1) adapting to the changed environment; (2) moving to a different environment; (3) managing the environment into a more compatible state; or (4) temporarily relying on slack resources, loose couplings, or other buffers. These or other coping strategies require that organizational decisions be made. Tomorrow's faster-changing environments will demand that these decisions be made *more frequently* and *more rapidly.* The greater complexity of these environments will also cause *decision making* to be *more complex*—that is, managers will have to consider more variables and more complex relationships among these variables.

Many of these decisions will concern changes in what the organization markets as its goods or services and in the infrastructures it employs. Heightened environmental turbulence will require that *decision implementation be more rapid.*

Managers require both information to decide when decisions are needed and information about which choices to take. The increased turbulence of organizational environments will require *information acquisition to be more continuous* so that key events will not be missed or noticed too late. The increased complexity of organizational environments demands that *information acquisition* also be *more wide-ranging.* At the same time, however, the information richness of the environment may create problems of overload, both on the organization's sensors and on the receivers of messages from these sensors. This requires that organizational *information distribution* be *more directed.* Finally, the increased need to acquire information and to exploit it through effective interpretation, distribution, and storage leads to *organizational learning* being *more managed.*

Increases in available knowledge lead to increases in the effectiveness of information technology and also to increases in the effectiveness of transportation technology. In combination, these three changes are leading to the increasing complexity and turbulence that characterize today's organizational environments. Thus *environmental change has as its most basic source, as its root cause, increases in available knowledge.* Since knowledge is possessed of its own generative material and power, and therefore serves as its own source of dynamism, we can expect future organizational environments to be characterized by increasing knowledge, complexity, and turbulence. These changes in today's and tomorrow's organizational environments will require changes in organizations themselves. The organizational consequences of accelerating environmental change are that (1) decision making must be more frequent, more rapid, and more complex; (2) decision implementation must be more rapid; (3) information acquisition must be more continuous and more wide ranging; (4) information distribution must be more directed, and (5) organizational learning must be more managed. These ideas are portrayed in Figure 1.1.

It is important to recognize that changes to these processes cannot be one-time or fixed-cycle changes. Because organizational environments will change at an increasing rate, the redesign of organizational processes must occur at an increasing rate. *Organizational redesign will become more and more commonplace and critical.*

Up to this point, we have been emphasizing the effects of environmental changes on organizations. We want to turn now and examine the impacts of top managers on organizations. Top managers are a key determinant of when and how organizations change.

CHANGES IN ORGANIZATIONAL ENVIRONMENTS   CHANGES IN ORGANIZATIONAL PROCESSES

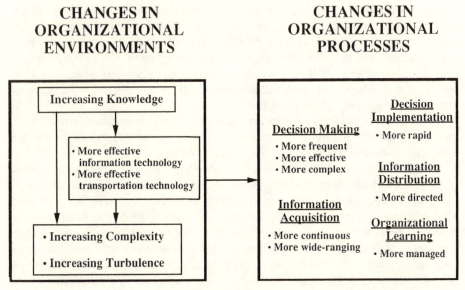

Figure 1.1.   Effects of environmental change on organizational processes.

TOP MANAGERS AS DETERMINANTS OF ORGANIZATIONAL CHANGE

Environmental change leads to organizational change.[2] But what about top managers? Don't top managers make a difference? Don't they influence organizational changes?

> This literature is quite consistent on at least one aspect of effective system-wide change—namely, executive leadership matters. The executive is a critical actor in the drama of organizational change. Nadler and Tushman, 1990: 77

Top managers influence organizational change in four important ways. The first way is through their belief systems—their values, ideologies, and mental models of cause-effect relationships. Top managers' beliefs determine the organizational strategies, structures, and cultures they prefer and seek to create in their organizations, and in this way they cause top managers to be *sources of change.* Values, ideologies, and cause-effect maps are not entirely fixed, of course. Managers learn and unlearn, and their beliefs sometimes change. But even if top managers don't change their beliefs, organizations change top managers. And there are differences in beliefs across top managers. Consequently, when new top managers with belief systems different from their predecessors enter an organization, organizational changes often follow. Frequently these changes are direct internal interventions, as when the CEO replaces the other top management team members or increases the R&D budget. Occasionally the changes follow from the top manager choosing a new environment for the organization, such as a new market niche or a new relationship with suppliers.

Top managers can also serve as *inhibitors of change.* Their beliefs and their competencies can cause top managers to serve as constraining agents. For example, a manager might not be capable of recognizing when changes are needed, or might not be competent in implementing the necessary changes. In these ways, he or she serves as an undesirable constraint on change. [Garbarro (1987) and Hambrick and Fukutomi (1991) suggest that this problem is most acute when a top manager's tenure begins to exceed some industry-related duration, generally about seven years.] Of course, in other situations, appropriate levels of decisiveness and perseverance cause top managers to keep an organization on course in spite of environmental buffeting, and thus to serve as desirable constraints on dysfunctional change.

The third way top managers impact their organizations is as *interpreters of the organization's environment:* "Strategic-level managers formulate the organization's interpretation [of the environment through] the process of translating events and developing shared understanding and conceptual schemes among members of upper management" (Daft and Weick, 1984: 285–286). Top managers label environmental stimuli as "problems" or "opportunities" (Dutton and Jackson, 1987), and these labels affect organizational actions. Through their role as interpreters, top managers mediate the influence of the organization's environment.

Finally, top managers are *manipulators of the organization's environment,* at least to a degree. Top managers advertise, lobby, and educate to make environments hospitable for their organization. By influencing their organization's environment, top managers affect the flow of environmental demands and resources. Lee Ioccoca's success in influencing creditors, unions, and the U.S. government exemplifies a top manager as a manipulator of the organization's environment.

In summary, within-individual changes and across-individual variations in belief systems cause top managers to be sources of organizational change. Differences in beliefs and competencies also cause top managers to serve as constraints on change. And managers affect organizational changes by interpreting their organization's environment. Finally, top managers manipulate the organizational environments that contribute to and influence organizational change. These ideas are portrayed in Figure 1.2. Asserting, as we have, that environmental changes lead to organizational changes is not to deny top managers a major role in organizational change.

Much that we think of as organization change is intentional, managerially initiated organizational redesign. Let us turn to this important topic.

ORGANIZATIONAL CHANGE AND REDESIGN

By an organization's design we mean the aggregate configuration of its technologies, processes, and structures. Systematic research documents the validity of current managerial thinking—an organization's *technologies, processes, and structures* must be well suited to each other and to the organization's *environment*. If these four factors are not well matched, if there is not a good fit, the organization's performance will be less than it could be, and it may be insufficient to sustain organizational survival.

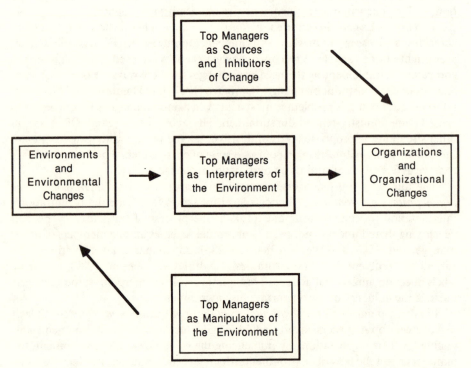

Figure 1.2.   Relationships among environments, top managers, and organizations.

Organizational designs are not wholly and consciously controlled by top management, but they are intentionally and successfully controlled to a sufficient degree that we can speak of *organizational redesign* as the set of managerial actions intentionally used to alter organizational technologies, processes, and structures. These changes are frequently associated with changes in strategy. Indeed, it is difficult to imagine implementing changes in strategy without also changing the organization's processes. Changes in organizational culture are also, of course, forms of organizational change. Experience shows us that changes in culture can be created more effectively with a combination of words and deeds than with words alone, and such deeds often appear as redesigns or reconfigurations of the organization's processes, structures, and resource allocations. Finally, to a great extent an organization's design determines the nature of the personnel required, and changes in design frequently require changes in personnel. Organizational design, then, is so central to what an organization is that we give it special attention here and highlight the importance of changes in design by including "redesign" in the title of this book.

Why Study Organizational Design?

- To a great extent, the design of an organization determines the distribution of resources, authority, and information. As a consequence, it directly impacts the ability of individual managers to make and implement timely, technically and economically sound, and organizationally acceptable decisions. The ability to make and implement such decisions in turn affects the effectiveness of the organization.
- The design of an organization directly affects a manager's ability to coordinate and control the activities of subordinates in order to enhance organizational performance. Proper organizational design can therefore make the difference between having an effective, well-run organization and having recurrent crises and organizational inefficiencies.
- Organizational environments are changing more rapidly than ever before. Because the effectiveness of an organizational design erodes over time as the environment changes, the organization must be designed to fit current and future environments, not the environment of the past.
- Innovative technologies are being introduced into modern organization at a rapid pace. The effectiveness of different organizational designs depends on the technology and the processes by which work is accomplished.
- Modern communication and computing technologies facilitate the process of coordination and control and make new organizational designs feasible. New communication and computing technologies can also increase organizational effectiveness in current or previously abandoned organizational designs.
- Changing organizational designs to meet new challenges and opportunities involves a dynamic process. The effectiveness of an organizational design is partially a function of procedures established in the past and the training and experience provided to organizational members by the previous organizational design.

Why Study Organizational Change?

Three reasons stand out:

- Our society depends on organizations to provide goods and services to its members. The health of a nation or other societal entity is directly related to the effectiveness of its organizations and, hence, to the effectiveness of processes through which they change. Better understanding of the antecedents, processes, and consequences of organizational change will enable organizations to choose and implement changes more effectively.
- Our personal economic well-being and quality of life are greatly determined by the actions of organizations. Much of our lifetime is spent in organizations that either educate us or employ us. Changes in these organizations touch us. Even organizations where we spend no time control resources of direct importance to us, such as our retirement benefits, licenses for our occupations or automobiles, and parklands for our leisure. Obviously, changes that these organizations make also affect us. If we can understand and predict changes in and by organizations, we are better able to plan ahead, to invest our resources wisely, and to construct appropriate contingency plans. Further, if we can influence the direction and magnitude of the changes, we can create a world more to our liking.
- The singular goal of science is to understand humankind and its environment. From a scientific point of view, the study of organizational change processes is attractive because organizational change is not well understood. There is much to be learned relative to what is known. Only a small fraction of existing organizational theory is change related. There are fertile fields to be plowed.

About This Book

In this introductory chapter we examined the fundamental causes of the environmental changes faced by today's and tomorrow's organizations, and we identified some organizational changes that must inevitably follow from these environmental changes. We then reviewed the ways that top managers influence changes in their organizations and in their organizations' environments. Finally, we made explicit the importance of organizational design, redesign, and change as phenomena worthy of scientific investigation and managerial reflection.

Chapter 2 reports the results and implications of the most comprehensive study of organizational downsizing and redesign yet published. Not only did the study track, analyze, and evaluate the downsizing processes of 30 organizations across a period of over four years, but it drew upon the considerable knowledge bases of Kim Cameron, one of the foremost authorities on this subject, and of Sarah Freeman and Aneil Mishra whose doctoral dissertations both deal with organizational downsizing and redesign.

Chapter 3 is one of the very few systematic studies of hyperturbulence. Hyperturbulence, the situation in which the changing demands of an organization's environment exceed the organization's adaptive capacity, is occurring with increasing frequency. This chapter reports the unusual pattern of strategies and revisions of strategies employed by 27 top managers as they attempted to ensure the survival of their organizations. The research leading to this chapter can be described as "radical." It departed from "normal science" conventions in several important respects. Fortunately, for the sake of its credibility, it was directed by Alan Meyer, one of the most respected scholars in the study of organizational adaptation, and resulted in the doctoral dissertations of James Goes and Geoffrey Brooks.

Chapter 4 describes the results of the only available study of the communication choices that top managers make as they acquire information to formulate the organization's strategy and as they disseminate information to implement this strategy. The researchers, Richard Daft, Kenneth Bettenhausen, and Beverly Tyler, brought a combination of talents to this study, and Daft in particular has published highly regarded and frequently cited works in both organizational communication and organizational strategy. The chapter concludes with insightfully derived guidelines for designing organizations in ways that ensure that the information needed for formulating and implementing organizational strategy is available through the most effective medium.

Chapters 2, 3, and 4 deal with the actions of top managers as they attempt to make their organizations thrive and survive. In contrast, Chapter 5 deals with the traits of the top management team and how the nature of the team as a unit affects organizational change and innovation. In it, Charles O'Reilly, a leading authority on the effects of top management teams, and his colleagues Richard Snyder and Joan Boothe, creatively combine qualitative and statistical analyses to determine how change and innovation in Silicon Valley high-technology organizations are affected by the makeup of the top management teams.

The configuration of top management teams has become an increasingly central issue in management practice and organizational science. Chapter 6 also deals with this important aspect of organization design, but the focus of Chapter 6 is on the organization's financial performance rather than on the organization's innovativeness. The chapter is based on two extensive studies of top management teams, one employing primarily questionnaire and archival data and the other employing interview data. The senior authors have a long history of research on the design of organizations and on the role of cognition in organizations, and the research team of William Glick, Chet Miller, and George Huber has recently published three articles on organizational change and design. The results from Chapters 5 and 6 together have important messages and implications for CEOs and boards of directors as they attempt to design effective top management teams.

Chapter 7 provides an encompassing analysis of the determinants of organizational change. Drawing on their extensive backgrounds in organizational science and on several of their published literature reviews, George Huber, Kathleen Sutcliffe, Chet Miller, and William Glick set forth a variety of assertions about what causes and constrains organizational change. They then draw on data from a series of interviews with the top managers of 119 diverse organizations to further enrich their understanding of change in organizations. Finally, using the interview data and also mailed survey data from these organizations, they develop and test statistical models that are highly valid predictors of these changes. This study draws on data provided by the four collaborating researchers mentioned earlier, as well as by the authors. It is unique in the organizational science literature both in the range of change-determinants investigated and in the variety of organizational changes investigated.

In Chapter 8 Andrew Van de Ven describes the variables that affect innovation and how managers can manipulate these variables to create innovation. Van de Ven draws on two imposing sources of knowledge. One is the work and model of Everett Rogers, a leading authority on the diffusion of innovations. The other source of knowledge is the insight and understanding gained while participating in and directing the multi-investigator Minnesota Innovation Research Program.

In Chapter 9 John Slocum and David Lei make a unique contribution by combining knowledge about national cultures, organizational cultures, and the economics of global strategic alliances, and bringing it collectively to bear on the task of organizational design. In this chapter the authors provide authoritative suggestions about how to solve problems that managers and organizational scientists alike have only haltingly articulated.

Peter Monge, one of the foremost authorities on methods for studying change across time, is the author of Chapter 10. The chapter deserves to be read at two levels. On one level, it is a carefully and rigorously crafted tutorial on how to analyze and use historical data in the redesign of organizations. On another level, it is a collection of considerable insights about how to think about the use of managerial experience in the redesign of organizations. Filled with graphics, the chapter asserts itself as an essential component of a book on organizational change and redesign.

In Chapter 11 Karl Weick shakes us free from whatever complacency we might have developed while reading the previous chapters. He challenges and enriches our understanding of organizational design by suggesting that the process is less like the process engaged in by an architect than it is the process engaged in by the actors involved in a theatrical improvisation. He calls our attention to the fact that initiatives for organizational redesign have widely varied origins, that they do not generally emanate from the minds of top managers, and that at any given moment the organization's design is a complex and changing interpretation, not a simple and fixed chart. The contributions of Chapter 11 are its fresh insights and its well-argued challenges to conventional wisdom. Chapters 10 and 11 stand in sharp contrast to one another, and they will provoke readers to consider whether and how these disparate perspectives can be reconciled.

Unlike most editors' closing chapter to a multiauthored book, Chapter 12 does not review the previous chapters. Instead its authors, the book's editors, start afresh with the basic, bottom-line questions "What's new about organization change and redesign?" and "How can we change and redesign organizations to be more effective?" It is not a review, not even a summary. It is an integration.

This book has an epilogue. It deals with a serious matter, the problem of transferring the knowledge useful for redesigning organizations from those who generate it to those who use it. Its authors, Arie Lewin and Carroll Stephens, thoughtfully examine three provocative questions. The first has been a concern of many organizational scientists and a challenging criticism from management practitioners: "What do organizational scientists have to offer managers?" The second question is a source of wonderment or frustration to many organizational scientists: "Why have managers been so uninterested in the body of knowledge that organization theory has to offer?" The third question is of interest principally to the more reflective members of these two constituencies: "Will this state of affairs in which organization theory and management practice operate independently of each other persist in the postindustrial era?"

Enough introduction. Let us move on.

NOTES

1. Much of this analysis of environmental change and its consequences is taken from Huber (1984).

2. This is less true of organizations whose nature is sustained by a society's culture or cultural values. Examples of such organizations are the Roman Catholic Church and the U.S. Bureau of Indian Affairs. Also, although the discussion in this section focuses on an organization's external environment, nothing here is contradictory to the notion of internal environments such as cultures, climates, or constituencies.

REFERENCES

Bell, D. 1979. The social framework of the information society. In Dertovos, M. L., and Moses, J. (Eds.), *The computer age: a twenty-year view* (pp. 163–211). Cambridge, MA: MIT Press.

Boulding, K. E. 1978. *Ecodynamics: a new theory of societal evolution.* Beverly Hills, CA: Sage Publications.

Daft, R. L., and Weick, K. E. 1984. Toward a model of organizations as interpretation systems. *Academy of Management Review,* 9(2): 284–295.

De Solla Price, D. 1963. *Little science, big science.* New York: Columbia University Press.

Dutton, J. E., and Jackson, S. E. 1987. Categorizing strategic issues: links to organizational action. *Academy of Management Review,* 12(1): 76–90.

Gabarro, J. J. 1987. *The dynamics of taking charge.* Boston: Harvard Business School Press.

Hambrick, D. C., and Fukutomi, G. D. S. 1991. The seasons of a CEO's tenure. *Academy of Management Review,* 16(4): 719–742.

Handy, C. 1991. *The age of unreason.* Boston: Harvard Business School Press.

Huber, G. P. 1984. The nature and design of post-industrial organizations. *Management Science,* 30(8): 928–951.

Huppes, T. 1987. *The Western edge: work and management in the information age.* Boston: Kluwer Academic Publishers.

Nadler, D. A., and Tushman, M. L. 1990. Beyond the charismatic leader: Leadership and organizational change. *California Management Review,* 32(2): 77–97.

Parsons, T. 1977. *The evolution of societies.* Englewood Cliffs, NJ: Prentice-Hall.

I

THE CHALLENGE OF CHANGE

2

Downsizing and Redesigning Organizations

KIM S. CAMERON, SARAH J. FREEMAN, and ANEIL K. MISHRA

> I can't remember exactly what percent of the total cost direct labor is, but it's about 5, 6, 7 percent. It's peanuts. You know 85 percent is material cost. We concentrate like hell on the 7 percent, when there is more opportunity for cost savings in other places. I personally think that we have overdone the emphasis on headcount. **Automotive Product Team Manager**

> The most cost savings can be generated by improving coordination, collaboration, trust, communication, and information sharing. Most of our costs reside in these soft factors. **CEO, Auto Supplier**

> Downsizing led people to look at the appropriateness of what they were doing. It brought more activities together that make sense.
>
> **Stamping Plant Manager**

EDITORS' SUMMARY

In this chapter, Cameron, Freeman, and Mishra present findings and conclusions from the most extensive and systematic study of organizational downsizing that has appeared in the organizational literature. In addition to reporting and interpreting the results of their multiyear, multiorganizational field investigation, the chapter makes important conceptual contributions by distinguishing organizational downsizing from related constructs such as organizational decline, nonadaptation, and growth-in-reverse.

Three questions are addressed, each important to both top managers and organizational scientists. The first is "How is downsizing implemented?" Cameron and his associates found three implementation strategies used: workforce reduction, organizational redesign, and a systematic strategy focused on changing the attitudes, values, and organization culture. Detailed descriptions and the relative frequencies of these strategies are presented, along with information about their combined use. The researcher also found two general orientations toward downsizing: a convergence, or reinforcement, approach involving incremental changes and a reorientation approach involving radical departures from previous conditions.

The second question addressed is "What are the organizational effects of downsizing?" Statistical analyses are presented that show the managerial practices that are associated with each of three organizational performance measures: (1) overall organization effectiveness, (2) improving performance over time, and (3) the presence of some common dysfunctional attributes in troubled organizations.

The last question addressed in the chapter, and one of great importance to managers, is "What are the best practices in organizational downsizing?" Here the authors use both statistical analyses and qualitative analyses of interview data to identify the managerial practices associated with highly effective firms. The rich discussion of these best practices amounts to the offering of a number of practical guidelines for managers faced with the challenge of managing organizational downsizing.

Given that the study of organizational downsizing is in its very early stages, it is not surprising that the authors end the chapter with a list of questions in need of investigation by organizational scientists. It is clear that by empirically addressing these questions, organizational scientists could contribute to organizational effectiveness and could extend the domain in which organization theory has been validated. ■

The 1980s marked a dramatic change in several fundamental assumptions underlying organizational performance and change. At the beginning of the decade, a perusal of organizational studies literature led to the conclusion that (1) bigger organizations meant better organizations; (2) unending growth was a natural and desirable process in organizational life cycle development; (3) organizational adaptability and flexibility were associated with slack resources, loose coupling, and redundancy; and (4) consistency and congruence were hallmarks of effective organizations.

By the end of the decade, each of these assumptions had been challenged, not because new theories were developed, but because of the changing dynamics observed in U.S. organizations. The replacement assumptions were opposite of the original assumptions as well as supplemental, namely: (1) smaller (as well as larger) also means better; (2) downsizing and decline (as well as growth) are also natural and desirable phases of the life cycle process; (3) tight coupling and nonredundancy (as well as slack resources and loose coupling) are also associated with adaptability and flexibility; and (4) conflict and inconsistency (as well as congruence and consistency) are also indicative of organizational effectiveness.

One reason for this transformation of assumptions has been the emergence of a particular type of organizational change that heretofore was viewed as an aberration from normal organizational functioning—namely, organizational downsizing. Shrinking, retrenching, or consolidating the organization was viewed as a last-ditch effort to thwart organizational demise or to temporarily adjust to a cyclical downturn in sales. It was almost always targeted at blue-collar or hourly employee layoffs, and it was always viewed negatively (see, for example, Hirschorn and associates, 1983). However, with recessions at the beginning of the 1980s and 1990s, coupled with the decade-long deterioration in global competitiveness among American businesses, a potential weakness in U.S. organizations was highlighted—namely, many firms were over-staffed, cumbersome, slow, and inefficient. Fundamental ways of organizing and man-aging were thus reexamined. Downsizing became a strategy of choice among many, if not most, large organizations. This was evidenced by the fact that nearly all the For-tune 1000 firms engaged in downsizing between 1985 and 1990, and a majority indi-cated that they would engage in downsizing in the future (Heenan, 1990). In 1990 alone, for example, three times more employees were laid off in the United States than in 1989, and 1989 far outstripped 1988 in numbers of layoffs.

However, despite its ubiquitous nature, the study of organizational downsizing is currently in its infancy. Very little empirical work has been completed to date. When research is conducted on "hot" topics, as downsizing is likely to become, it often pro-ceeds without a commonly accepted definition of the concepts and the domains involved, making it difficult for cumulative knowledge to develop. The topic remains a fad rather than a framework upon which other concepts can be built.

The intent of this chapter, therefore, is to define organizational downsizing pre-cisely, to address conceptual issues associated with the phenomenon, and to report the results of a four-year empirical investigation of downsizing designed to answer three questions: (1) How do organizations downsize; that is, what processes are employed to make organizations smaller? (2) What is the impact of downsizing on the organi-zation; that is, what organizational outcomes are associated with downsizing? (3) How do effective downsizing organizations differ from ineffective downsizing organiza-tions; that is, what are the "best practices" that organizations use as they downsize?

Specifically, we try to lay a groundwork for future investigations of organizational downsizing by, first, reviewing why downsizing has become such a pervasive organi-zational phenomena, especially in U.S. organizations; second, discussing precisely what downsizing is and is not, mainly by contrasting downsizing with related concepts such as organizational decline, growth-in-reverse, nonadaptation, and layoffs; third, describing the empirical investigation of the 30 firms, including the methods used to collect and analyze the data; and fourth, reporting the findings that emerged regarding the three main research questions. The last section of the chapter summarizes both scholarly and managerial lessons learned, and it offers some prescriptions for the best downsizing practices for managers.

PRACTICAL IMPORTANCE OF DOWNSIZING

Ginzberg (1985), summarizing the conclusions drawn from a conference on the topic of downsizing, asserted that a tendency exists in almost all organizations to acquire more employees than are needed, especially managers. This is partly a reflection of the "bigger is better" ethic found in most Western cultures. More employees and larger units have been traditionally defined as an indicator of effectiveness, as a reward to successful managers, and as a measure and source of power and status.

After World War II, for example, corporations grew rapidly and, in particular, developed an appetite for more and more management staff. Many firms adopted a divisionalized structure, leading to the duplication of corporate staffs at the division level. Geographic and international expansion led to expansion of management ranks to coordinate an ever-expanding set of activities in diverse locations. Technological advancements more often resulted in hiring additional staff than in replacing workers. When profits were high and growth was easily attained, managerial featherbedding frequently occurred because additional staff were easily absorbed and hidden. Whereas blue-collar layoffs were typical when cyclical downturns occurred, the white-collar workforce was seldom touched. [For example, of the firms that laid off blue-collar workers as a response to the slowdown of the economy in the early 1980s, 90 percent did not lay off a single white collar employee (Thurow, 1986).] Thus, ratios of managers to workers steadily increased. In U.S. manufacturing organizations, for example, 19 percent of the workers were nonproduction employees in 1950. In 1960 the figure was 24 percent, in 1970 it was 25 percent, in 1980 it was 30 percent, and by 1987, 32 percent of all manufacturing employees were nonproduction workers (i.e., managers, support staff, overhead) (Tomasko, 1987).

On the other hand, the 1980s brought about conditions that made unacceptable the continued expansion of managerial ranks and overhead costs. Factors such as recession, the entry into U.S. markets of low-cost competitors from offshore, merger mania that led to inefficient agglomerations of businesses and management redundancies, the emergence of new human-replacement technologies, especially in services, noncompetitive cost structures and inefficient organizational designs, and international events such as the unification of Germany and the formation of a European common market in 1992, all created redundancies and inefficiencies that combined to make downsizing an alternative that could hardly be avoided. This was especially true of managerial downsizing where, for the first time, white-collar employees became the target of cutbacks.

By way of illustration, U.S. white-collar productivity decreased 6 percent between 1978 and 1986, whereas blue-collar productivity increased by 15 percent. U.S. auto companies still have more than twice the number of hierarchical levels as their Japanese competitors. Japanese producers sold the same number of cars as General Motors, 50 percent more than Ford, and twice as many as Chrysler in 1990 with less than half the number of employees (Womack, Jones, and Roos, 1990). U.S. auto manufacturers still hold more than a $800 per car cost disadvantage to their Japanese rivals, mainly because of larger managerial overhead rates. Moreover, U.S. auto firms take twice as long to design and build a car as the typical Japanese firm, at least partly due to excessive management, cumbersome communication systems, over-attended meetings, and multiple sign-offs and required approvals.

This has led many U.S. organizations to turn to downsizing as a solution. Large reductions in workforce have occurred in such name-brand firms as IBM (almost 30,000 employees, or 7 percent of the company's workforce), ITT (over 100,000 employees, or 44 percent), AT&T (32,000 employees, or 10 percent), Kodak (14,000 employees, or 10 percent), K-Mart (45,000 employees, or 21 percent), and Sears (50,000 employees, or 12 percent). Over half a million American managers with salaries exceeding $40,000 lost their jobs in 1990, and between one and two million pink slips were handed out each year between 1988 and 1990. More than one-half of those employees took pay cuts of 30 to 50 percent to obtain new jobs.

As implemented in U.S. firms, however, it appears that downsizing has not significantly improved white-collar productivity. A 1990 survey by Right Associates, an outplacement firm, found that 74 percent of senior managers in downsized companies said that morale, trust, and productivity suffered after downsizing (see Henkoff, 1990). A survey by the Society for Human Resource Management reported that more than half of the 1,468 firms that downsized indicated that productivity deteriorated from downsizing (Henkoff, 1990). Wyatt Associates surveyed 1,005 firms that had downsized between 1986 and 1991 and found that only 46 percent actually reduced expenses, only 32 percent actually increased profits, only 22 percent actually increased productivity, and only 17 percent actually reduced bureaucracy (see Bennett, 1991).

One explanation for these trends is that downsizing has not been managed effectively in many firms and, therefore, the intended cost reductions and efficiencies have not been achieved. Another is that downsizing has created resentment and resistance in firms, so it has hindered more than helped U.S. competitiveness. Unfortunately, not enough is known about the implementation processes associated with downsizing to reach a conclusion, to identify best practices, or to improve organizational outcomes. Despite its frequency of implementation, and its potential for harmful consequences, organizational downsizing has rarely been investigated by organization and management researchers.

THEORETICAL SIGNIFICANCE OF DOWNSIZING

From the discussion above, the question arises: Why has there been such a dearth of research on organizational downsizing among organization scientists? Few empirical studies have been published of the precursors, processes, and effects associated with downsizing, and little theory exists to explain what happens when organizations get smaller. Except when it is used as a proxy for organizational decline (i.e., as an indication of failure), downsizing per se has been largely ignored. A few studies have appeared on the effects of layoffs and firings on individuals and groups (e.g., Brockner, 1988) and of plant closings and exit from mature industries (e.g., Harrigan, 1982; Hambrick and Schecter, 1983). Studies by Freeman and Hannan (1975), Ford (1980), Montanari and Adelman (1987), and McKinley (1987) related decreases in workforce size to changes in structure, particularly the relative size of the administrative component. A hierarchy of layoff and attrition strategies was proposed by Greenhalgh, Lawrence, and Sutton (1988), and one study used their model to investigate relationships between the strategies and various organizational attributes and performance (Rosenblatt and Mannheim, 1988). But in no study has attention been given to the *processes* employed in organizations to downsize nor their effects on organizational effectiveness. Thus, unless it is equated with decline, downsizing has seldom been studied.

One possible reason for this is the past growth bias in organizational theory. Most of the models that have influenced current thinking in organizational design and change assumed, either explicitly or implicitly, that growth and expansion are the main predictors of effectiveness, especially when organizations are faced with a turbulent and increasingly complex environment. For example, the structural contingency models of notable authors such as Woodward (1965), Thompson, (1967), Lawrence and Lorsch (1967), Blau (1970), Pfeffer and Salancik (1978), and Huber (1984) all suggest that system elaboration and augmentation are required to cope with an increasingly complex environment. Increasing boundary spanning units and environmental scanning activities are advocated as the best adaptation strategies in turbulent environments. Similarly, most models of organizational life cycles assume that continuous growth and increasing complexity are the natural path that organizations follow (see review by Cameron and Whetten, 1981). Information-processing theories of organizational design (e.g., Galbraith, 1977) also assume that, as the amount and complexity of information increases, an expansion of the information-processing mechanisms in the organization (e.g., additional monitors, vertical loading) is required. Even ecological theories suggest that in turbulent or unstable environments, generalist organizations (i.e., those that have evolved into complex, expansive entities) are more likely to survive than specialist organizations. Structural complexity is viewed as an enhancement to inertia, and inertia leads to organizational survival (see, for example, Hannan and Freeman, 1984; Carroll and Delacroix, 1982). Most organization adaptation theories (e.g., Miles and Cameron, 1982), adhere closely to Ashby's (1956) "law of requisite variety" in explaining successful adaptation strategies. In short, the organization must develop a comparable level of complexity to its environment if it is to cope effectively.

In sum, these major models of organizational design and change have not traditionally acknowledged the possibility of organizational downsizing as a desirable process. Instead, they have perpetuated a view that assumes a norm of growth and expansion in order to achieve effectiveness. However, current organizational practice demands that more systematic attention must be paid to organizational downsizing and its effects. The increase in downsizing activity has underscored the value of smallness and minimalism in organizations, the value of reductions in size and resources in order to achieve effectiveness, and the value of continuous downsizing as an ongoing and unavoidable organizational strategy.

Because downsizing is often confused with other terms in the popular and scholarly literature, however, a first step in identifying how downsizing is effectively accomplished is to be clear about its definition.

DEFINITION OF ORGANIZATIONAL DOWNSIZING

Organizational downsizing consists of a set of activities that are undertaken on the part of management, designed to improve organizational efficiency, productivity, and/or competitiveness. It represents a strategy that affects the size of the firm's workforce and its work processes. Downsizing is a term that has arisen out of popular usage, not precise theoretical construction. On the surface, downsizing can be interpreted simply as a reduction in organizational size. When this is the case, downsizing is often confused with the concept of organizational decline, which also can be superficially interpreted as mere reduction in organizational size. Yet important differences exist that make downsizing and decline separate phenomena, both conceptually and empirically. Several important attributes of downsizing also make it distinct from other related concepts such as growth-in-reverse, nonadaptation, or layoffs. These attributes of downsizing are briefly explained below, then a direct comparison is made between downsizing and each of the concepts that are sometimes confused with it.

It should be noted, parenthetically, that a discussion of definition and conceptual uniqueness seems more relevant for theoretical purposes than for practical ones. That is, Cameron, Freeman, and Mishra (1991) found that the terminology used to describe downsizing strategies was by no means consensual among practicing managers. Because of the negative connotations associated with decline (i.e., no manager wants to implement a decline), downsizing activities are described by managers with an amazing array of alternative terms, such as compressing, consolidating, contracting, demassing, dismantling, downshifting, rationalizing, reallocating, reassigning, rebalancing, redesigning, resizing, retrenching, redeploying, rightsizing, streamlining, slimming down, or even building down and leaning up. Many of these terms were found by Cameron et al. to be used interchangably, even though each has a different connotation. For scholarly purposes, on the other hand, precise conceptual meaning is required for organizational models and theories. Without this precision, research findings remain noncumulative. Therefore, four major attributes of downsizing are identified that help define and separate it from related concepts.

Key Attributes of Downsizing

Downsizing is not something that happens *to* an organization, but it is something that organizations undertake purposively. Thus, downsizing is, first of all, an *intentional* set of activities. This differentiates downsizing from loss of market share, loss of revenues, or the unwitting loss of human resources that are associated with organizational decline. Downsizing is distinct from mere encroachment by the environment on performance or resources because it implies organizational action.

Second, downsizing usually involves *reductions in personnel,* although it is not limited solely to personnel reductions. A variety of personnel reduction strategies are associated with downsizing such as transfers, outplacement, retirement incentives, buyout packages, layoffs, attrition, and so on. Downsizing does not always involve reductions in personnel, however, because some instances occur in which new products are added, new sources of revenue open up, or additional work is acquired without a commensurate number of employees being added. Fewer workers are then employed per unit of output compared to some previous level of employment.

This relates to a third characteristic of downsizing, namely, that downsizing is focused on improving the *efficiency* of the organization. Downsizing occurs either proactively or reactively in order to contain costs, to enhance revenue, or to bolster competitiveness. That is, it may be implemented as a defensive reaction to decline or as a proactive strategy to enhance organizational performance. In either case, downsizing is usually designed to contain and lower costs.

Finally, downsizing affects *work processes,* wittingly or unwittingly. When a workforce contracts, for example, fewer employees are left to do the same amount of work, and this has an impact on what work gets done and how it gets done. Overload, burnout, inefficiency, conflict, and low morale are possible consequences, or more positive outcomes may occur such as improved productivity or speed. Moreover, some downsizing activities include restructuring and eliminating work (such as discontinuing functions, abolishing hierarchical levels, reengineering processes, and merging units) which lead to some kind of work redesign. Regardless of whether the work is the focus of downsizing activities or not, work processes are always influenced one way or another.

Distinguishing Downsizing from Decline

The combination of these four attributes helps clarify the difference between organizational downsizing and decline. Because there is now a well-developed literature on organizational decline (see, for example, Cameron, Sutton, and Whetten, 1988), it is important to identify the contribution that downsizing might make to that already established literature. Moreover, the misconception that downsizing is simply a special case of decline is quite pervasive and inhibits scholarly attention being directed toward downsizing.

Decline has been variously defined in the literature as shrinking markets and increased competition (Porter, 1980; Harrigan, 1982), budget cuts (Krantz, 1985; Levine, 1985), loss of student enrollment (Freeman and Hannan, 1975), loss of legitimacy (Benson, 1975), maladaptation to a changing environmental niche (Greenhalgh, 1983; Cameron, et al., 1988), stagnation (Whetten, 1980), and deteriorating organizational performance (Hirschman, 1970; Kolarska and Aldrich, 1980). In each case, decline is viewed as a negative consequence of maladaptation to a dysfunctional environmental condition. That is, decline happens *to* an organization; it is unintentional on the part of the organization or its managers. Downsizing, on the other hand, is intentional and can be functional.

Decline also differs from downsizing in that it may not necessarily produce a reduction in personnel, in either relative or absolute terms. Many organizations have experienced a decline in market share or revenues, for example, with no reduction in the workforce (see, for example, Hall, 1976; or consider Donald Trump's empire), and others have reduced the workforce only in proportion to losses in revenues or production (for example, consider Chrysler during the late 1980s). In the former case this is not downsizing at all, and in the latter case it is downsizing as a reaction to decline. Some authors have viewed personnel reductions (downsizing) as inherently connected to "fiscal stress" (Levine, 1985) or have used decline and downsizing interchangably (e.g., Greenhalgh, 1983), but these authors mask rather than clarify the distinctiveness of these two concepts. Unlike downsizing, decline is not a targeted improvement strategy. It is not aimed at enhancing efficiency, but instead it often results in deteriorated efficiency as overhead rates escalate (see findings by Ford, 1980, and Sutton and D'Aunno, 1989). Similarly, decline may not necessarily affect work processes, as downsizing does, because individuals often persist in the standard ways of doing tasks while they wait for organizational demise (see Sutton, 1983).

In brief, downsizing and decline are distinct constructs. Organizations can downsize without declining, as when downsizing is used proactively to enhance competitiveness (see Tomasko, 1987; D'Aunno and Sutton, 1987), and they can decline without downsizing. Downsizing may be a response to decline, but cause-and-effect relationships should not be assumed.

Distinguishing Downsizing from Growth-in-Reverse

Because the opposite of downsizing is growth, some writers have assumed that downsizing is synonymous with growth-in-reverse; that is, it is associated with the opposite dynamics of organizational expansion. When organizations grow, for example, the development of a predictable pattern of stages has been identified, as have a number of organizational outcomes such as decentralization, specialization, and increasing the number of boundary spanning units, (see Blau, 1970; Greiner, 1972; Quinn and Cameron, 1983). Some writers have suggested that downsizing implies the reverse dynamics—that is, a reversed sequence of growth stages—and the opposite of growth processes—that is, more centralization, less specialization, and less boundary spanning (see Behn, 1980; Gilmore and Hirschorn, 1983; Krantz, 1985). However, neither the stages nor these organizational outcomes are necessarily associated with downsizing. The intentional nature of downsizing means that an organization may get smaller in order to decentralize, to specialize, or to become more externally connected through boundary spanning activities—the same outcomes that are associated with growth. For example, downsizing may be accomplished by cutting back corporate functions, leading to decentralization; by establishing specialized units to serve multiple corporate locations (specialization); or by involving external organizations in the downsizing planning and implementation, leading to more rather than less boundary spanning. Similarly, organizational life cycle stages do not reverse themselves, as with an Alzheimer's disease patient who deteriorates in exactly the reverse stages as a child develops. In brief, downsizing and growth may, theoretically at least, create the same organizational forms and structures, and effective downsizing may lead to growth.

Distinguishing Downsizing from Nonadaptation

Some authors have also defined decline as the reverse of adaptation and have placed nonadaptation as a central concept in the definition of decline (Gilmore and Hirschorn, 1983; McKinley, 1987; Weitzel and Jonsson, 1989). Greenhalgh (1983), for example, suggested that the opposite of decline (as defined and measured by indicators of downsizing) is adaptation, and that decline occurs in conjunction with nonadaptation to an environmental niche. By implication, therefore, Greenhalgh linked downsizing to nonadaptability. This implied association obviates the difference between these concepts. Downsizing per se indicates neither maladaptation, failure, nor poor performance. Instead, it represents a strategic move on the part of the organization to increase its performance relative to the environment. That strategic move may be proactive, reactive, or creative (a distinction made originally by Miles and Cameron, 1982), but even in reactive downsizing, ineffectiveness or nonadaptation is not implied. Downsizing can be a reaction to certain missteps or environmental constraints, or, in proactive and creative instances, it can be an anticipatory action to improve organizational performance.

Distinguishing Downsizing from Layoffs

A common manifestation of downsizing is the layoff of employees—that is, terminating workers with or without advance notice. Because layoffs have traditionally been (and, unfortunately, continue to be) the first alternative used for downsizing, some authors have treated layoffs and downsizing synonymously (for example, see Gilmore and Hirschorn, 1983; Brockner, 1988). McCune, Beatty, and Montagno (1988) found in a survey of 100 manufacturing organizations in the Midwest that few alternatives to layoffs were even considered in any of the firms, and 94 percent of the managers planned and implemented their layoffs in less than 60 days. Layoffs were the default option overwhelmingly selected for downsizing.

Downsizing differs from layoffs, however, in being a broader, more encompassing concept. Whereas layoffs refer to a single tactical, reactive operation used to implement a downsizing strategy, downsizing may be both strategic and proactive. Downsizing includes an array of options for reducing the workforce other than layoffs. In fact, layoffs may not be included at all in an organization's downsizing strategy. Investigations of downsizing focus on reductions at the organization level of analysis, whereas investigations of layoffs focus at the individual level of analysis (for example, see Brockner, 1988).

In summary, downsizing is a concept that should be treated separately from other concepts associated in the research literature with the dynamics of decline, ineffectiveness, layoffs, or mere shrinkage in organizations. It is a concept worthy of investigation as an independent phenomenon because of its growing practical importance in organizations and because of its unique dynamics that remain underdeveloped theoretically. However, it is because of the underdeveloped downsizing theory that investigators should first adopt a theory-building approach as opposed to a theory-testing approach. That is, because no current theories exist regarding organizational downsizing or its association with successful performance, an important first step in research is to identify patterns, relationships, and dynamics rather than to set forth a theory for testing. This is the approach taken by the study described here.

RESEARCH QUESTIONS

This investigation focused, first, on trying to identify how organizations went about the task of getting smaller. The first research question was: *How is downsizing implemented in organizations?* This question was motivated by the lack of information about what alternatives are used in addition to layoffs. Since reducing headcount is generally the strategy that gets headlines, and because it is the alternative of first choice for many organizations, we were interested to see what other types of reduction strategies were in widespread use. In particular, what actions did organizations take that are not related to employee cutbacks?

Several writers have proposed alternatives to layoffs, but none conducted an empirical investigation of their effects. For example, Perry (1986) suggested alternatives to layoffs such as job and work sharing, leaves of absence, decreases in paid time off, pay cuts, and performance-based pay systems. Tomasko (1987) differentiated between "push" strategies and "pull" strategies for downsizing where "pull" strategies include incentive buyout packages, early retirement programs, or outplacement services that make it attractive for employees to leave voluntarily. "Push" strategies such as spinning off departments or businesses, eliminating levels in the hierarchy, and outsourcing help push employees out of the organization, but without across-the-board layoffs. Levine (1985), Greenhalgh (1983), and others identified additional cutback strategies, including decreasing overtime, terminating programs, attrition, hiring freezes, and reorganizing programs. In each case, these strategies were identified in single case studies, but no analysis was done of their relative dispersion over multiple organizations.

A related issue embedded in this first research question was whether some predictable patterns of downsizing activities could be identified in organizations. One hoped-for outcome of this investigation was to determine not only what kinds of downsizing alternatives were used by organizations to reduce their size, but whether archetypes might be present in their downsizing activities.

The second research question followed from the first, namely: *What is the impact of downsizing on the organization?* One aspect of this question is whether downsizing has the same negative effects on the organization as does decline. For example, in their studies of declining organizations, Cameron, Whetten, and Kim (1987) and Cameron, Kim, and Whetten (1987) identified 12 negative attributes of organizations that emerge in conjunction with decline. They found that when organizations unwittingly lose employees, revenues, resources, or market share, a variety of dysfunctional consequences emerge, labeled the "dirty dozen." Table 2.1 summarizes these 12 dysfunctional attributes.

In brief, these authors noted that when organizations experience decline, the threat-rigidity response tends to occur. Organizations become rigid and turf-protective, and they react with conservative, across-the-board directives. Communication

Table 2.1. Negative Attributes Associated with Organizational Decline (the "Dirty Dozen")

Attribute	Explanation
Centralization	Decision making is pulled toward the top of the organization. Less power is shared.
Short-term, crisis mentality	Long-term planning is neglected. The focus is on immediacy.
Loss of innovativeness	Trial and error learning is curtailed. There is less tolerance for risk and failure associated with creative activity.
Resistance to change	Conservatism and the threat-rigidity response lead to "hunkering down" and a protectionist stance.
Decreasing morale	Infighting and a "mean mood" permeates the organization.
Politicized special-interest groups	Special-interest groups organize and become more vocal. The climate becomes politicized.
Nonprioritized cutbacks	Across-the-board cutbacks are used to ameliorate conflict. Priorities are not obvious.
Loss of trust	Leaders lose the confidence of subordinates, and distrust among organization members increases.
Increasing conflict	Fewer resources result in internal competition and fighting for a smaller pie.
Restricted communication	Only good news is passed upward. Information is not widely shared because of fear and distrust.
Lack of teamwork	Individualism and disconnectedness make teamwork difficult. Individuals are not inclined to form teams.
Lack of leadership	Leadership anemia occurs as leaders are scapegoated, priorities are unclear, and a siege mentality prevails.

channels constrict, and only good news is passed upward. The emergence of organized, vocal, special-interest groups increases the levels of conflict among organization members, and morale plummets. A "mean mood" overtakes the organization. Slack resources (such as contingency accounts, reserves, or new project funds) are eliminated, and with them go flexibility and adaptability to future changes. Centralized decision making escalates where top managers increase their control over a decreasing resource pool, and mistakes become both more visible and less affordable. Lower level employees become increasingly fearful of making important (risky) decisions. This leads to scapegoating of top leaders as the frustrations and anxieties of organization members mount. The credibility of the top leaders suffers because of their implied failure to avoid or turn around decline, and trust in the organization erodes. A short-term orientation predominates so that long-term planning is curtailed, and innovation— inherently costly and risky—is abandoned.

Because the "dirty dozen" are so prevalent in organizations experiencing an unintentional reduction in size, an important question is whether the same dynamics occur in organizations that are intentionally reducing their size. That is, do these negative organizational attributes also occur in firms that are downsizing?

A related issue refers to the relationship between downsizing and organizational effectiveness. Whereas the popular literature is full of prescriptions and projections about what managers ought to do when downsizing, almost no empirical studies have empirically investigated the effectiveness of these prescriptions. The question of whether organizational downsizing inhibits or enhances organizational performance has largely remained unaddressed, as has the more precise question of which particular downsizing processes are helpful and which are hurtful.

Tomasko (1987) briefly reviewed a consulting study by A. T. Kearney, Inc. comparing the sales, earnings, and market value growth of 26 name-brand firms with their industry averages. These firms—including Allied, Coca-Cola, Dana, Digital Equipment, General Electric, Hewlett-Packard, IBM, Johnson & Johnson, Merck, 3M, Schlumbreger, and Xerox—had fewer hierarchical levels among their salaried ranks (an average of 7.2 levels compared to an industry average of 10.8), and larger spans of control than the industry average (4.8 direct reports versus 2.6 for the industry). The sales growth of these 26 firms more than doubled the industry average, earnings growth was eight times higher than the industry average, and market value growth was nine times higher than the industry average. Not all these firms had downsized, and it is impossible to argue that downsizing was the explanation for their dramatic success compared to industry averages. But the Kearney data clearly raise a question about the association between downsizing and organizational effectiveness. This study attempts to address this question through both qualitative and quantitative analyses.

The third research question guiding this investigation was: *What are the "best practices" in downsizing; or, how do the most effective firms differ from the least effective firms in their approach to downsizing?* This question is motivated primarily by a desire to identify practical guidelines that can be used to help direct future downsizing activities. Of course, every organization's circumstance may be somewhat unique, and no universal prescriptions are applicable across the board. On the other hand, identifying downsizing strategies and processes that characterize highly effective firms, contrasted to those that characterize the least effective firms, provide some hints that can lead to prescriptive principles. The popular press regularly reports opinions and advice of "experts" on downsizing, yet little systematic, multiorganizational research has been done. It is useful, therefore, to identify aspects of downsizing that are grounded in more than a single case study or a personal downsizing experience. To that end, this investigation was partly guided by a desire to uncover and highlight the best downsizing practices.

NATURE OF THE STUDY

Organizations Studied

Firms in the American auto industry were selected because of the extensive downsizing that has occurred in that industry over the past decade and because of its size and importance in the American economy. Almost 40 percent of this nation's gross national product is accounted for by the automotive industry. Well over a million people work for the American auto companies alone (General Motors, Ford, and Chrysler), not to mention the myriad of related organizations and industries that serve as suppliers to and customers of the automobile companies. One in ten Americans has a family member with the benefits package of General Motors. Hence, actions that affect employment in these firms carry practical importance to a great many people. Moreover, in the 1980s more than a half million jobs were eliminated by downsizing activities in these firms as numerous and repeated downsizing initiatives were announced.

Thirty organizations were selected for inclusion in the study. They were chosen in order to maximize heterogeneity on several organizational dimensions—organization type, size, product mix, and downsizing history. Assembly plants, fabricating plants, supplier businesses, and corporate marketing and staff units were included. Some organizations were affiliated with a large parent organization; some were independent. In each case, however, firms were autonomous, strategic business units able to determine their own downsizing strategy. Each of the 30 organizations in the study had engaged in downsizing. Some downsized in years prior to the study (pre-1987); all but one downsized during the years of the study; and many were planning to downsize in future years as well. The smallest of these organizations employed approximately 100 employees at the outset of the study; the largest employed over 6,000.

Key Informants

Between 1987 and 1990, interviews were conducted every six to nine months with the head of each organization. The titles of these key informants ranged from chief executive officer to plant manager. This top manager was treated as the main source of ongoing information about how downsizing and organizational redesign activities were being implemented. In addition to the interviews, 2,001 questionnaires were collected from a sample of white-collar employees in these 30 organizations to assess their perceptions of strategies, corporate culture, leadership, and the outcomes of downsizing. In organizations with less than 300 white-collar employees, all received a questionnaire. When more than 300 white-collar employees existed, a cross-sectional sample was selected in the firm representing all functions and levels in the hierarchy.

Data-Gathering Procedures

Top managers were interviewed five times over the four-year period with each inter-view lasting from one and a half to two hours. This helped produce a chronology of the organizational changes taking place over the four years of the study, and it helped uncover ongoing strategies that were being implemented in connection with downsiz-ing. Both the decision-making rationale and the visible activities of top managers were assessed through these interviews.

Two questionnaires designed to obtain organizational descriptions of the firm were completed by the top manager, once at the beginning of the study and once near the end of the study. A third questionnaire obtained personal demographic data from each of these top managers. A fourth questionnaire, unique to this investigation of down-sizing, was distributed to 3,908 white-collar employees across the 30 firms, and 2,001 were returned, for a response rate of 51 percent. This questionnaire was completed during the third year of the study and contained questions on downsizing strategies, organizational characteristics, organizational changes, approaches to quality, organi-zational culture, communication patterns, and organizational effectiveness. (The interview instruments, questionnaires, and descriptive statistics for all variables are available from this chapter's first author. The quantitative and qualitative methods used to analyze questionnaire and interview data are described in Cameron and Mishra, 1991.)

HOW IS DOWNSIZING IMPLEMENTED?

Two major findings emerged regarding implementation processes. First, three types of implementation strategies were identified, and organizations were found to differ in the extent to which they engaged in these strategies. Second, two archetypal approaches to downsizing emerged, and organizations tended to adopt only one of them.

Three Implementation Strategies

Table 2.2 summarizes the three major downsizing strategies identified in the investi-gation. The first, labeled *workforce reduction strategy,* focuses mainly on eliminating headcount or reducing the number of employees in the workforce. It consists of activ-ities such as offering early retirements, transfers and outplacement, buyout packages, golden parachutes, attrition, job banks, and, in the extreme, layoffs and firings. These activities can be implemented immediately simply by handing down a directive. They are almost always implemented across the board, and they are designed to reduce headcount numbers quickly.

This strategy is similar to throwing a grenade into a crowded room, closing the door, and expecting the explosion to eliminate a certain percentage of the workforce. It is difficult to predict exactly who will be eliminated and who will remain. It is difficult to predict in advance, for example, which employees will take advantage of an early retirement offer or buyout package. It is also difficult to determine what knowledge, what institutional memory, and what critical skills will be lost to the organization.

Table 2.2. Three Types of Downsizing Strategies

| | Downsizing Strategy | | |
	Workforce Reduction	Organization Redesign	Systemic
Focus:	Workers	Jobs and units	Culture
Eliminates:	People	Work	Status quo processes
Implementation time:	Quick	Moderate	Extended
Temporal target:	Short-term payoff	Moderate-term payoff	Long-term payoff
Inhibits:	Long-term adaptability	Quick payback	Short-term cost savings
Examples:	Attrition	Eliminate functions	Involve everyone
	Layoffs	Merge units	Simplify everything
	Early retirement	Redesign jobs	Change responsibility
	Buyout packages	Eliminate layers	Continuously improve
Sample question on the survey:	To what extent have you used layoffs in reducing the number of salaried employees in your organization?	What has been eliminated or transferred out as part of the downsizing effort in this organization: functions, management levels, . . . [etc.]?	(Agree-Disagree) In our downsizing activities, we have closely coordinated with suppliers, customers, and the outside community.
No. of firms that implemented the strategy at least some time during the study period (*N* = 30)	29	15	12

Besides providing an immediate size reduction, the main purposes of this strategy are to wake up the organization to the serious condition that exists, to motivate cost savings in day-to-day work, and to unfreeze the organization for further change. Across-the-board cuts get attention. On the other hand, the harm caused by a workforce reduction strategy may offset the positive effects of unfreezing the organization. A dramatic example occurred in one of our organizations in which a 30-year employee in the purchasing department was the primary agent for ordering steel. Over the years, modifications in the types of steel and alloys being ordered had been made, but changes in the written specifications had not kept pace. Shortly after this purchasing agent accepted an early retirement option, an order was placed unknowingly for the wrong kind of steel. This produced a $2 million loss for the organization in downtime, rework, and repair. The organizational memory, as well as the expertise needed to do the work, left with the purchasing agent without any chance of replacement or retraining because of the nonprioritized method used in downsizing. Of the 30 organizations that were studied, 29 employed a workforce reduction strategy between 1987 and 1990 (Table 2.2). Yet, when implemented in the absence of other strategies, "grenade-type" approaches to downsizing are rarely positive and generally negative in their consequences. Evidence for this conclusion is provided later.

The second type of downsizing strategy is an *organization redesign strategy*. The primary focus of this strategy is to cut out work rather than workers. It often consists of activities such as eliminating functions, hierarchical levels, groups or divisions, and products. Other examples are redesigning tasks, consolidating and merging units, and reducing work hours. Because the redesign strategy is difficult to implement quickly, it is, by and large, a medium-term strategy. It requires some advanced analysis of the areas to be consolidated or redesigned, followed by an elimination or a repositioning of subunits within the organization to reduce required tasks.

Instead of piling more work on fewer employees and thereby risking overload and burnout, this work redesign strategy helps assure that changes are targeted at work processes and organizational arrangements. The downsized organization can achieve a greater degree of efficiency because of its simplified structure. Fifteen of the 30 organizations investigated implemented a redesign strategy at least once during the study, half as many as implemented a workforce reduction strategy (Table 2.2).

The third type of downsizing strategy is labeled *systemic strategy*. It is fundamentally different from the other two strategies in that it focuses on changing the organization's culture and the attitudes and values of employees. It involves redefining downsizing as a way of life, as an ongoing process, rather than as a program or a target. Downsizing is equated with simplification of all aspects of the organization—the entire system—including suppliers, inventories, design processes, production methods, customer relations, marketing and sales support, and so on. Costs all along the customer chain, especially invisible and unmeasured costs, are the main targets. Examples of downsizing targets include reducing wait time, response time, rework, paper, incompatibilities in data and information systems, number of suppliers, and rules and regulations. Instead of being the first target for elimination, employees are defined as resources to help generate and implement downsizing ideas. Every employee is held accountable for reducing costs and for finding improvements. A continuous improvement ethic is applied to the task of downsizing, and cost savings throughout the entire system of interorganization relationships are pursued.

Because this strategy takes a long-term perspective, it may not generate the immediate improvement in bottom-line numbers that a workforce reduction strategy will generate. Along with the redesign strategy, it may even require some initial investment in employee training, system diagnosis, and team formation. On the other hand, it avoids the need to continually implement additional headcount reductions each time cost savings are needed. One major U.S. auto company, for example, has announced 16 major downsizing efforts since the firm was founded—each time a workforce reduction strategy. During the 1987–1990 study period, 25 percent of the white-collar staff were eliminated in each of two cutbacks. To date, little attention seems to have been paid to implementing a systemic downsizing strategy in this firm. The culture and processes remain largely unchanged, and the same work is just being done by fewer people. Implementing a workforce reduction strategy may be necessary as a severe economic hardship is encountered, but the short-term payoffs may be negated by long-term costs. The objective of a systemic strategy, on the other hand, is to help avoid, over the long term, the need to implement continual, repetitive workforce reduction strategies. As noted in Table 2.2, only 12 organizations implemented systemic strategies in their downsizing efforts.

These three downsizing strategies are not mutually exclusive. In fact, all of the firms that implemented a systemic strategy also implemented a workforce reduction strategy. The latter strategy was used to get immediate results, while the former was used to position the organization for the future. Most organizations, however, implemented only one of the strategies—workforce reduction. They did not rely on multiple approaches.

Table 2.3 points out that organizations can be categorized on the basis of the depth and breadth of the downsizing strategies they employ. Firms that implement a greater number of actions of the same type (for example, layoffs, buyouts, and early retirements are all workforce reduction strategies) have more *depth* in their strategy. Firms that implement a greater variety of strategy types (for example, workforce reduction, organization redesign, and systemic strategies) have more *breadth* in their strategy. In this study, organizations were more likely to have depth than breadth in their downsizing strategies. The impact of this depth and breadth on organizational effectiveness is discussed in a later section.

Two Archetypal Approaches

The second major finding from our investigation of the processes used to implement downsizing was the emergence of two archetypal approaches to downsizing—reinforcement versus reorientation. [These archetypes were developed and tested in the doctoral dissertation of Freeman (1992), where they are labeled "convergence" and "reorientation."] Organizations tended to adopt one or the other of these archetypes in their downsizing efforts. By archetypal approach we mean the manner in which top managers defined downsizing and their orientation toward change. An extended discussion of these two archetypes is contained in Freeman and Cameron (in press), so we highlight only the central findings here.

These two archetypal approaches are similar to the models of change proposed by Meyer, Goes, and Brooks (Chapter 3 in this volume), and by Pettigrew (1985), Tushman and Romanelli (1985), Miller and Friesen (1980), and Golembiewski, Billingsley, and Yeager (1976). Each of these models articulates a distinction between two generic types of change—a revolutionary, metamorphic, or discontinuous change on the one

Table 2.3. Categorizing Organizations by Depth and Breadth of Downsizing Strategy

	Increasing Breadth (employing greater variety) --------------▶ Downsizing Strategy		
	Workforce Reduction	Organization Redesign	Systemic
Increasing Depth (employing a greater number) ⋮ ▼	Attrition Layoffs Early retirements Buyout packages Etc.	Layer elimination Unit combination Product removal Process rearrangement Etc.	System analysis Culture change Bottom design Coordination with outsiders Etc.

hand, and an evolutionary, incremental, or gradual change on the other. In this study, some organizations approached downsizing as an incremental change, where less severe changes were implemented, whereas others approached downsizing as a discontinuous change taking more revolutionary actions. In the first archetype, labeled *reinforcement,* managers set as their target for downsizing the maintenance and perpetuation of the current mission, strategy, and systems and focused on adapting to current environmental circumstances. In the second archetype, labeled *reorientation,* managers attempted to change the organization's mission, strategy, and systems and to discontinue previous activities.

Organizations that adopted different archetypes also tended to differ in other aspects of their organization: (1) structural change, (2) white-collar reduction strategy, (3) precedence for workforce reduction versus redesign, (4) amount and type of communication, (5) interorganizational relationships, and (6) effectiveness versus efficiency orientation. A particular approach to structural redesign, for example, is associated with a particular white-collar reduction strategy, a type of communication, interorganizational relationships, a culture type, and so on. The two main archetypal approaches are summarized in Table 2.4 and explained briefly below. Freeman (1992) contains the detailed statistical analyses.

Structural Change

Katz and Kahn (1978) proposed a hierarchy of structural changes in organizations as they grow, each change requiring progressively more organizational change:

1. Increasing the size of units without structural change.
2. Increasing the number of parallel units, as in adding new units.
3. Increasing the amount of differentiation within and between units.
4. Merger.

Table 2.4.   Two Archetypal Approaches to Downsizing

Reinforcement Approach	Reorientation Approach
Incremental downsizing and redesign	Discontinuous downsizing and redesign
Emphasis on lower-level, less radical downsizing approaches	Emphasis on higher-level, more radical downsizing approaches
Stability in top management team, technology, and systems	Change in top management team, technology, and systems
Changes in work instead of structure	Changes in structure instead of work
Reinforces mission and strategy	Redefines mission and strategy
Downsizing precedes redesign	Redesign precedes downsizing
Less extensive communication required	More extensive communication required
Less use of interorganizational relationships	More use of interorganizational relationships
Internal constituency orientation	External constituency orientation
Emphasis on efficiency criteria	Emphasis on effectiveness criteria
Focus on doing things better	Focus on doing different things
No. of firms that exhibited each pure approach: ($N = 30$)	
7	9

The converse of each of these changes implies four targets of organizational downsizing:

1. Decreasing the size of units without structural change (e.g., eliminating individuals or tasks).
2. Decreasing the number of parallel units (e.g., closing branches or product lines).
3. Decreasing differentiation (e.g., restructuring or clustering work units).
4. Divestiture or dissolution (e.g., eliminating entire businesses).

When organizations adopted a reinforcement approach to downsizing, they implemented less radical changes in downsizing requiring less redesign—for example, decreasing size without restructuring work. When organizations adopted a reorientation approach, they implemented more radical changes requiring a greater amount of redesign—for example, merging departments.

White-Collar Reduction Strategy

One form of white-collar downsizing relates to the portion of the job that is changed. For example, changes in *work* (e.g., eliminating tasks, reducing the number of people doing the same work, or increasing spans of control) require less change than changes in *technology* (e.g., automating work, changing materials management procedures, or reducing the number of employees needed through team formation). In turn, changes in technology require less change than changes in *structure* (e.g., reorganizing the top management team, eliminating hierarchical levels, or merging departments). When organizations adopted a reinforcement archetype, they implemented less change (i.e., they relied mainly on changes in work and much less on changes in technology and structure), than when they adopted a reorientation archetype. In the latter case, organizations implemented more changes in structure and technology rather than in just work.

Precedence of Workforce Reduction Versus Work Redesign

Whereas workforce reduction and work redesign are sometimes linked, organizations were found to differ in the extent to which one strategy took precedence over the other. Only half the organizations employed both workforce reduction and work redesign strategies, but they differed in which strategy was pursued as the most important target of downsizing. Some organizations focused, first and foremost, on making the organization *smaller*. Other organizations focused primarily on making the organization *different*. Whereas both downsizing and redesign occurred in organizations that adopted a reinforcement archetype and that adopted a reorientation archetype, one of these changes tended to take precedence over the other. Specifically, when organizations adopted a reinforcement archetype, downsizing (getting smaller) tended to be the primary target of the change. When organizations adopted a reorientation archetype, redesigning work (becoming different) tended to be the primary target of the change.

Amount and Type of Communication

Adopting a reorientation archetype requires that both larger amounts and more types of communication be used in order for this kind of change to be successful (see Daft,

Bettenhausen, and Tyler, Chapter 4 in this volume). This is because reorientations entail not only a new way of doing old things, but also doing completely new things. The break with old, established routines is more abrupt. Among the organizations in this study, greater amounts and more types of information were communicated in organizations that adopted a reorientation archetype than in those that adopted a reinforcement archetype.

Interorganizational Relationships

Because all organizations exist in a system of relationships with other organizations—for instance, customers, suppliers, and unions—downsizing does not occur in isolation. Other organizations are affected by downsizing activities, and they may affect or be a part of a firm's downsizing activities. Earlier it was stated that relatively few organizations adopted a systemic strategy in downsizing—that is, few included the broader system of interorganizational relationships in downsizing activities. The firms that did so, however, tended to be those that adopted a reorientation archetype as opposed to a reinforcement archetype. An alteration of the organization's mission, strategy, and structure (i.e., reorientation) was more closely associated with an altered relationship with outside organizations than was an incremental, reinforcement approach to downsizing.

Effectiveness Versus Efficiency Orientation

Whereas the distinction is not absolutely clear between effectiveness and efficiency, the two constructs have been treated differently in the literature. Effectiveness was characterized by Cameron and Whetten (1983) as "doing the right things," whereas efficiency was characterized as "doing things right." Organizations are usually judged to be effective if they at least minimally satisfy their strategic constituencies (see Cameron, 1987), with an emphasis on external constituencies. On the other hand, organizations are judged to be efficient if they run with precision and with little waste. Internal processes and practices take precedence in assessments of efficiency. When organizations downsize, the relative emphasis on effectiveness versus efficiency criteria might be expected to vary since a reinforcement archetype emphasizes doing the same things right (efficiency), whereas a reorientation archetype emphasizes doing different things (effectiveness). In this study, organizations that adopted a reinforcement archetype tended to emphasize efficiency criteria more than effectiveness criteria, whereas the reverse was true among organizations that adopted a reorientation archetype.

In sum, two archetypal approaches to downsizing seemed to be pursued by these organizations—a reinforcement archetype and a reorientation archetype. Sixteen firms were found to consistently reflect the patterns of activities described above: seven adopted a purely reinforcement archetype, and nine adopted a purely reorientation archetype. The remainder of the organizations shifted over the four-year period of the study: seven went from reinforcement to reorientation, and seven went from reorientation to reinforcement. More discussion of these mixed types is contained in Freeman and Cameron (in press). The most important finding here is that a framework of archetypes in downsizing was identified and consistencies in organizational strategies were uncovered.

These patterns lead to the second question in the research: "What impact do these downsizing strategies have on the organization itself? Under what circumstances does downsizing hinder or enhance organizational performance?"

WHAT ARE THE ORGANIZATIONAL EFFECTS OF DOWNSIZING?

In assessing the impact of downsizing on the organization, four different variable sets were used to indicate performance. Data on three were obtained from the questionnaire mentioned earlier, so they are perceptual in nature. The fourth came from secondary sources indicating productivity ratios in each firm (e.g., Harbour and Associates, 1990). We were surprised to discover that hardly any firms were willing to provide us with objective performance data. In the intensely competitive auto industry, such data are treated as highly confidential, and only a few managers were willing to share this information with us (some in a clandestine way). Hence, we obtained objective productivity data for only nine of the organizations in the study. Analyses of those nine firms confirm the findings from the questionnaire analyses described below and from the interview coding. However, because nine firms represent only a small, potentially biased subset of the organizations studied, because complete data is not available for all the nine organizations, and because of space limitations for the chapter, these objective data analyses and results are reported elsewhere (Cameron and Mishra, 1991) and are available from the first author.

In the sections that follow, we first report findings related to *overall improvement* in performance as a result of downsizing. Respondents were asked to rate on a five-point scale the extent to which organizational performance had improved as a result of downsizing. The factors that are significantly associated with improvement are reported. (Questionnaire items and descriptive statistics for all items and dimensions are available in Cameron and Mishra, 1991.) Second, ratings were obtained of the *overall effectiveness* of the organizations (1) relative to their past two years' performance, (2) relative to their best domestic and best global competitors, and (3) relative to their own corporate goals and to customers' expectations. These comparison standards (e.g., past performance, competitors, goals, and customers) against which respondents rated their own organization's performance were determined in the interviews to be the most important standards used by these firms. They were included as comparison standards in the questionnaire in order to improve the quality of the effectiveness ratings. Third, the factors most closely associated with the presence of the "dirty dozen," or *negative attributes,* are reported. Because these dysfunctional attributes are associated with most organizations that experience undesired decreases in size as a result of decline (see Cameron, Kim, and Whetten, 1987), the question was "Do these negative attributes also occur in organizations that *want* to reduce in size?" More specifically, "Are certain downsizing activities associated with organizations characterized by the negative attributes?"

Predictors of Organizational Improvement Ratings

Table 2.A in the appendix to this chapter lists the factors that were analyzed in association with organizational improvement. These factors were initially derived from the interviews conducted with the top manager in each of the 30 firms in the study. That is, the questionnaire was developed after two rounds of interviews had been conducted, and one important outcome of those interviews was the identification of factors that appeared to have an association with successful (and unsuccessful) organizational performance. Several questions in those first two rounds of interviews focused on aspects of the downsizing process with which a broad sample of respondents had been involved and on which they could provide information. A few items also were included in the questionnaire that had been proposed as important predictors in previous literature on downsizing, especially Applebaum, Simpson, and Shapiro (1987), Saporito, (1987), Tomasko (1987), Henkoff (1990), and Richardson (1988).

As mentioned above, the most powerful factors associated with improvement were identified, via preliminary regression analyses, then entered into a final multiple regression analysis. Table 2.5 shows the factors that are significantly associated with organizational improvement (or deterioration) as a result of downsizing.

These results highlight the negative effects of the downsizing approaches used by most organizations. In this study, in only six of the firms did respondents indicate that the firm implemented downsizing gradually and incrementally. This is consistent with McCune et al.'s (1988) survey of 100 downsizing firms in which 94 percent took less than two months to plan and implement downsizing. However, the firms that improved their performance in this study were those in which respondents indicated that preparation for downsizing occurred in advance. These organizations invested time and resources in systematically analyzing tasks, personnel skills, resource needs, time use, process redundancies, and so forth. This permitted firms to target downsizing activities—that is, to surgically eliminate unneeded work, processes, and positions—rather than to use an across-the-board approach in reducing the size of the firm. This is consistent with the second most powerful predictor of improvement—gradual, incremental implementation. A majority of managers in our interviews suggested that a rapid, quick-hit approach to downsizing was their method of choice. They reasoned that this approach didn't drag out the unpleasant process, it minimized employee fear

Table 2.5. Significant Predictors of Organizational Improvement (or Deterioration) During Downsizing

Factor (nature of the relationship)[a]	Beta
Systematic analysis of tasks and personnel in advance (+)	.234***
Gradual, incremental implementation (+)	.200***
Increased communication and participation (+)	.178***
Increased employee effort (+)	.099***
Downsizing via attrition (−)	−.229***
More work required for employees (−)	−.115***
Reward and appraisal system changed (−)	−.109***
No improvement in quality (−)	−.093***

Overall Equation

R^2	.430***
Adjusted R^2	.420***

[a]See Appendix Table 2.A, for all factors analyzed.
***$p < .001$

and anxiety associated with not knowing whose job might be eliminated next, and it administered the pain all at once. However, the opposite strategy was actually associated with organizational improvement: gradual reductions were consistently associated with performance increases. The uncertainty assumed to be associated with incremental downsizing was mitigated by a thoughtful, orderly implementation strategy. This result may be explained by the fact that the amount of uncertainty experienced at any one moment is smaller and more manageable when an incremental approach is used as opposed to a rapid, one-time downsizing action. (We are grateful to Karl Weick for this explanation.) Hence, the intuitive assumptions of most managers about speed of implementation did not foster improvement.

A third major predictor also helped reduce uncertainty—namely, increased communication and participation of employees in the downsizing process. When employees were involved in the downsizing decisions, when suggestions were sought and discretion was given to participants, performance improvements were present. This also explains why rapid downsizing does not foster improvement. Broad participation and idea sharing cannot occur if downsizing is implemented in a rapid-fire fashion. Consistent with this line of reasoning, performance improvements were also associated with more effort put forth by employees in the organization. Increased participation and communication by employees have been found in past research to produce increased effort (e.g., Vroom, 1964), and, by implication, improvement in organizational performance. That pattern of increased participation coupled with increased effort leading to improved performance seemed to be indicated by these results.

On the other hand, Table 2.5 also reports the factors that respondents identified as being associated with deteriorating organizational performance over time. These are not just the opposite of the factors associated with improvement; rather, they are a different set of factors associated with deterioration. The most powerful factor is downsizing via attrition—that is, imposing hiring freezes or not replacing individuals who leave the organization. This is a very common across-the-board downsizing approach, but it may leave the organization without crucial skills and human resources. In addition, downsizing that simply piles more work on remaining employees—the second major predictor of performance deterioration—also short-circuits improvement. Reducing numbers of positions or employees without a commensurate reduction in work has a negative influence on performance, partly because the remaining employees become overloaded or are required to do tasks for which they may not be trained. The third major predictor, changes in the reward and appraisal system, was indicated in this study by mandates such as eliminations of standard cost-of-living increases, mandated salary freezes, and forced rankings of all employees in performance appraisals. The across-the-board, top-down nature of such actions appeared to impede rather than enhance improvement. Finally, when respondents reported that their organizations had not improved the quality of their products and services during the past two years, overall firm performance deteriorated.

This last predictor relating to quality requires some explanation since quality emerged as a significant predictor in most of the statistical analyses. Moreover, it was a very significant factor associated with the 'best downsizing practices' in the interviews. Before reporting the results of other statistical analyses, therefore, a brief side trip is necessary in order to explain the quality factors being used to predict improvement, effectiveness, and the "dirty dozen."

Quality Culture As a Predictor of Organizational Performance

Cameron (1991) developed a model of quality culture in which three different approaches to quality assurance were described. These approaches are generalized orientations toward quality, and they constitute ways that organizations think about and define quality. That is, an organization's quality culture refers to its values and interpretations of quality as well as to the manner in which it pursues quality. It is not merely the presence of quality tools or techniques such as statistical process control, quality function deployment, continuous improvement cycles, design of experiments, and so forth. Differences in organizational profiles across quality cultures have been found to exist in a variety of manufacturing and service organizations (Cameron, 1991). The quality culture model identifies values, processes, and approaches that organizations implement in trying to achieve high levels of quality in products and services. Table 2.6 summarizes the attributes of each of the three types of cultures. No organization is characterized by only one approach to quality, but almost all have a dominant emphasis.

Up until the 1970s, most U.S. manufacturing and service organizations were characterized by an *error detection* culture. For example, in manufacturing products, firms emphasized inspecting and detecting errors. The goal was to avoid poor quality, to reduce waste, and to find and fix mistakes. Quality control departments and auditors inspected products and services after they had been produced. Products that didn't work were reworked or repaired. In providing staff support and customer service, the focus was on avoiding annoying people. Trying to protect against creating dissatisfac-

Table 2.6. A Model of Quality Cultures

Regarding Products	Regarding Customers
Error Detection	
Inspect and detect errors	Avoid annoying customers
Reduce waste, cost of failure, and rework	Respond to complaints quickly and accurately
Correct mistakes	Reduce dissatisfaction
Focus on the *output*	Focus on customer *needs* and requirements
Error Prevention	
Prevent errors	Satisfy customer expectations
Expect zero defects	Help customers avoid future problems
Design it right the first time	Obtain customer preferences in advance, and
Focus on the *process* and root causes	follow-up
	Focus on customer *preferences*
Creative Quality and Continuous Improvement	
Improve on current standards of performance	Surprise and delight customers
Create new alternatives	Engage in extra-mile restitution
Concentrate on things-gone-right	Anticipate customer expectations
Focus on managing *suppliers* and *customers*	*Create* customer preferences
as well as *processes*	

Source: Adapted from Cameron (1991).

tion led firms to develop systems that responded to customer needs and complaints accurately and on time. Firms focused on meeting expectations, specifications, and providing what customers required.

The 1980s saw a transformation in approach to quality, however, mainly because foreign competition's quality was so superior to most domestic companies. Plus, the offshore firms were operating with a different quality culture. In response to this challenge, many, although by no means most, domestic organizations shifted their quality focus. Their new quality culture focused on *error prevention,* or avoiding making mistakes in the first place. In producing products, the goal was to have zero defects by doing the work right the first time. The emphasis was on finding root causes of problems, adjusting the processes that produce the outcomes, and holding all workers accountable for quality, not just end-of-the-line inspectors. In providing customer service and staff support, the focus shifted to satisfying people (not just avoiding making them angry). The goal was to give service that made people want to come back and do business with the firm again. Obtaining customer preferences in advance and monitoring customer satisfaction after service delivery were crucial aspects of this approach. A shift occurred from focusing on customer requirements to focusing on customer preferences and from meeting expectations to exceeding expectations.

The third quality culture can be labeled *creative quality and continuous improvement.* This approach is typical of some of the very best firms in the 1990s. It couples continuous improvement, or Imai's (1986) "kaizen," with innovation, so that current standards of performance are always changing and improving. Small, incremental, continuous improvements are coupled with major leaps forward in which dramatic, one-time changes are created. These two processes spawn an emphasis on reaching levels of quality never before attained. In producing products, the focus is on designing and producing "things-gone-right" as well as avoiding "things-gone-wrong." The input, process, and output phases of production are merged so that managing suppliers and managing customers are as important as improving the firm's own work processes. Quality improvement is applied to all aspects of the firm's network of relationships. In providing customer service and staff support, the focus is on creating (not just exceeding) expectations and delivering services that surprise and delight customers. These firms emphasize continuously improving current levels of performance and being creative in delivering more than customers even hope for.

In assessing the quality culture that characterizes an organization, two kinds of measures were taken. One was an assessment of the extent to which firms were excellent or accomplished in each approach to quality; the second was the relative emphasis given to each generalized approach to quality. Figure 2.1 provides an example of a typical firm's profile of relative emphasis in these three quality cultures. Each point on the graph represents an empirically determined amount of emphasis given to each type of quality culture. Thus, both the achievement level in error detection, error prevention, and continuous improvement, as well as the relative emphases given to each of the different cultures were obtained. In questionnaire items and in interviews, employees had very little difficulty pinpointing the dominant quality culture that typified their firms. Every organization in this study gave at least some emphasis to each of the different cultures, but in every case one of the quality cultures dominated the others. When the organization gave the greatest relative emphasis to an error detection cul-

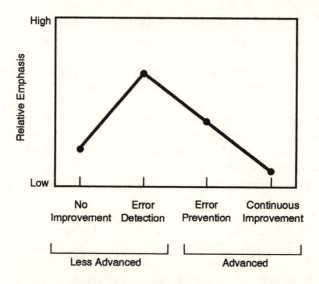

Note: The vertical axis on the graph shows the relative amount of emphasis given to each of the different quality cultures. These points were determined empirically by asking respondents to divide 100 points among descriptions of the different quality cultures. The most points were given to the quality culture that was most similar to the respondent's organization; fewer points were given to cultures that were less similar.

Figure 2.1.   A typical quality culture profile.

ture, it was labeled a "less advanced level of quality culture." When organizations gave the greatest relative emphasis to a culture of error prevention or to continuous improvement and creativity, it was labeled an "advanced level of quality culture."

Predictors of Organizational Effectiveness

Returning now to the question of what impact downsizing has on the organization, Table 2.7 reports the major predictors of effectiveness relative to three different standards: (1) the firm's own past performance, (2) its best competitors' performance, and (3) the firm's goals and expectations of customers. To avoid a complex and lengthy explanation of these three different statistical analyses, only a summary of the reoccurring and most powerful predictors is provided here.

The two factors that respondents identified as significant predictors in all three analyses of organizational effectiveness are (1) a gradual, incremental implementation of downsizing and (2) conducting a systematic analysis in advance of downsizing. Again, these two factors make clear the importance of avoiding quick-hit, grenade-type strategies and, instead, of investing the necessary time and resources in adequately preparing for well-planned, precise implementation. Involving employees through participation and increasing communication was an important factor in two of the analyses, as was establishing a set of downsizing strategies independent of outside mandate or encroachment. In both of these factors, key elements seem to be the enhance-

Table 2.7. Significant Predictors of Organizational Effectiveness (or Ineffectiveness) During Downsizing

Factor (nature of the relationship)[a]			Beta
Effectiveness Relative to Past Two Years' Performance			
Increased employee effort (+)			.094***
Downsizing via retirements (+)			.090***
Systematic analysis of tasks and personnel in advance (+)			.091**
Gradual, incremental implementation (+)			.068**
Advanced level of quality culture (+)			.112*
Excellence in creative quality (+)			.060*
Downsizing via layoffs (−)			−.100***
No improvement in quality (−)			−.133***
Multiple R	.403	Degrees of freedom	19,1231
R^2	.150	F	12.59
		Significance	.000
Effectiveness Relative to Best Competitors			
Established own downsizing strategies (+)			.074**
Excellence in error detection quality (+)			.095**
Gradual, incremental implementation (+)			.063*
Systematic analysis of tasks and personnel in advance (+)			.079*
Involved customers and suppliers in downsizing (+)			.073*
Less advanced level of quality culture (−)			−.099***
Multiple R	.337	Degrees of freedom	19,1228
R^2	.100	F	8.29
		Significance	.000
Effectiveness Relative to Firm Goals and Customer Expectations			
Involved customers and suppliers in downsizing (+)			.164***
Systematic analysis of tasks and personnel in advance (+)			.140***
Excellence in creative quality (+)			.081***
Increased communication and participation (+)			.083***
Established own downsizing strategies (+)			.063**
Gradual, incremental implementation (+)			.062**
Excellence in error detection quality (+)			.083**
Excellence in error prevention quality (+)			.066*
Downsizing via attrition (−)			−.128***
No improvement in quality (−)			−.118***
Downsizing by outsourcing (−)			−.059*
R	.570	Degrees of freedom	21,1183
R^2	.312	F	27.06
		Significance	.000

[a]See Appendix Table 2.A for all factors analyzed.

*$p < .05$

**$p < .01$

***$p < .001$

ment of discretion, involvement, and shared information within the firm. Taken together, these four major factors paint a picture of effective downsizing firms being characterized by planning, up-front investment in analysis, participation, and information exchange.

The other important recurring predictors relate to the quality culture of the firms. Respondents that rated their organizations as having a high level of excellence in creative quality as well as in error detection quality were more likely to be effective than those organizations that were not as accomplished in these aspects of quality achievement. However, in terms of relative emphasis, an advanced level of quality culture (i.e., dominated by an error prevention emphasis or a continuous improvement and creativity emphasis) was predictive of organizational effectiveness, whereas a less advanced level of quality culture (i.e., dominated by an error detection emphasis) was predictive of organizational ineffectiveness. Having no improvement in quality was a recurring predictor of ineffectiveness in two of the analyses. The other factors associated with ineffectiveness in the firms were examples of grenade-type downsizing strategies—downsizing via attrition, layoffs, and outsourcing.

In sum, analyses of organizational effectiveness suggest that planned, systematic downsizing where participation and involvement of employees occurs and where the firm has an advanced and improving quality culture are rated by respondents as the most effective firms. Ineffectiveness is associated with stagnant quality and downsizing via workforce reduction strategies.

Predictors of Negative Organizational Attributes

A third set of statistical analyses addressed the question of the impact of downsizing on the "dirty dozen" characteristics (see Table 2.1). Because these 12 negative attributes occur frequently in organizations that are experiencing decline, a central question was whether the same negative attributes arise when organizations purposefully reduce their size, as opposed to reducing size because of an unwanted decline.

Multiple regression analyses were conducted for each of the 12 negative attributes, using as predictors the factors listed in the Appendix. Table 2.8 summarizes the factors that were significantly associated with these 12 dirty dozen attributes. Rather than review in detail the regression equation for each attribute, however, Table 2.8 identifies the factors that had significant relationships with any of the dirty dozen. The number of significant relationships (of the 12 possible) is listed on the right in Table 2.8.

The most pervasive factors in mitigating against the 12 negative attributes are similar to those that predicted organizational improvement and organizational effectiveness. The factors associated with at least four (33 percent) of the negative attributes are predominantly human relations factors. For example, increased communication with and participation by organization members (10 significant relationships), increased employee effort (7), and increased teamwork (4) all are typical of organizations with low scores on the dirty dozen. Similarly, conducting a systematic analysis of tasks and personnel in advance of downsizing (9) and coordinating with outside organizations such as suppliers and customers in the downsizing process (6) characterize organizations that prepare for downsizing and do not simply use grenade-type approaches to workforce reduction. Of somewhat less importance were gradual, incremental imple-

Table 2.8. Summary of Major Predictors of the Dirty Dozen
During Downsizing ($p < .05$)

Factors	No. of Significant Relationships with the Dirty Dozen (nature of the relationship)[a]
Downsizing via attrition	9 (+)
Mandated downsizing motivated changes	8 (+)
More work required for employees	7 (+)
No improvement in quality	5 (+)
Less advanced level of quality culture	4 (+)
Downsizing via layoffs	4 (+)
Downsizing by outsourcing	4 (+)
Reward and appraisal system changed	4 (+)
Focus on process more than product quality	4 (+)
Downsizing via retirements	4 (+)
Downsizing by eliminating functions and/or management levels	1 (+)
Downsizing by eliminating products and/or suppliers	1 (+)
Established own downsizing strategies	1 (+)
Downsizing by transferring employees	1 (+)
Increased communication and participation	10 (−)
Systematic analysis of task and personnel in advance	9 (−)
Increased employee effort	7 (−)
Coordination with outside organizations in downsizing	6 (−)
Increased hourly and salaried teamwork	4 (−)
Gradual, incremental implementation	2 (−)
Advanced level of quality culture	2 (−)
Excellence in error detection quality	2 (−)
Excellence in creative quality	2 (−)
Excellence in error prevention quality	1 (−)
Downsizing by transferring employees	1 (−)

[a]See Appendix Table 2.A for all factors analyzed.

mentation and several of the quality culture factors. These latter two factors were of more central importance in predicting organization-level effectiveness, suggesting that the impact of gradual implementation and coordination with outsiders effects individual organization members less than it does overall organization performance.

The factors most powerfully associated with the presence of the negative attributes in organizations include several common workforce reduction downsizing strategies and a less advanced quality culture. That is, of the factors associated with at least four of the dirty dozen attributes, four are common workforce reduction strategies: downsizing via attrition (9 significant relationships), downsizing via layoffs (4), downsizing by outsourcing (4), and downsizing via retirements (4). Other factors include downsizing because of a mandated change from outside the firm (8), piling more work on remaining employees because jobs were reduced but not the work itself (7), and changes in the reward and appraisal system that made them seem inequitable or punishing (4). Making no progress in improving the quality of products and services (5) a less advanced quality culture (4) are also associated with the dirty dozen attributes.

Taken in total, these results suggest that downsizing that is implemented without preparation, that relies on workforce reduction (across-the-board) approaches, that restricts participation and teamwork, that increases the work required of remaining employees, and that does not help improve the quality of products and services is significantly associated with negative attributes in organizations. Whereas workforce reduction strategies were implemented by all organizations in this study, those organizations not characterized by the "dirty dozen" attributes supplemented those strategies with employee participation, teamwork, discretion, and a systematic analyses of the organization in advance.

Summary

In answer to the question "What are the organizational effects of downsizing?," these analyses suggest that the most commonly implemented form of downsizing—across-the-board, grenade-type approaches—are associated with organizational dysfunction. Organizational ineffectiveness, lack of improvement, and high scores on the dirty dozen attributes all are present when workforce reduction strategies such as layoffs, attrition, and buyout packages are used alone. Moreover, the lack of development of an advanced quality culture coupled with stagnant quality improvement are associated with these negative organizational performance indicators. On the other hand, firms whose performance was improving, effective, and absent the negative attributes are those that prepared for downsizing by conducting systematic analyses, involved employees, increased communication, and implemented strategies incrementally. An advanced quality culture was also an important characteristic of these firms.

Helping to facilitate the development of an advanced quality culture was an important role of managers in these organizations. In fact, in our interviews over the four-year period, this recurred as one of the most crucial ongoing responsibilities of the top managers in the most effective firms. It is to this top management responsibility, and to the characteristics of the best firms, that we now turn. The next section identifies the best downsizing practices by differentiating attributes of the highest performing firms from the others in this study.

WHAT ARE THE "BEST PRACTICES" IN ORGANIZATIONAL DOWNSIZING?

Two different procedures were used to identify the best downsizing practices in these firms. The first was a statistical analysis in which the very best firms—those with the highest scores on all the effectiveness indicators—were compared to the other firms in the study using discriminant analysis. This analysis identified the factors that were most typical of the very best firms in the study but not typical of the others. A richer set of data was obtained on the best practices, however, by means of the interview analyses. Stories, incidents, and mini case studies emerging from these interviews highlighted some of the most interesting processes used in downsizing that were not captured in the questionnaire. The statistical results are explained first, followed by the interview analyses.

Discriminating Highly Effective Firms from Others

The discriminant analysis results reported here differentiated the five most highly effective and improving firms in this study from the firms not performing as well. For illustrative purposes, Figure 2.2 provides a graph of the differences that exist between two firms that improved as a result of downsizing compared to three others that deteriorated. We wanted to find out, simply, how the most effective and improving firms downsized and what unique characteristics they possessed. Table 2.9 summarizes the organizational attributes and downsizing processes typical of the best five firms.

Similar to the regression analyses described above, a stepwise discriminant procedure was used to identify the most powerful factors. Results were consistent with those reported above, with a few notable additions. The best organizations were strongly characterized by involvement of all employees in improvement and participation in downsizing. Downsizing was viewed as an opportunity rather than a threat, and individuals were defined as resources to foster organizational improvement rather than costs that dragged down bottom-line financial performance. An advanced quality culture characterized the best firms, particularly excellence in error prevention quality. Organizations that did not perform well were stagnant in quality improvement and possessed a less advanced quality culture.

What was especially notable in the most effective organizations that did not emerge in earlier analyses was the role of the leader. The most effective organizations had dynamic, competent, knowledgeable leaders who articulated a clear, motivating vision of the future. In addition to the activities and strategies employed in the organization, the personal behavior of the top manager—that is, the extent to which he or she (1)

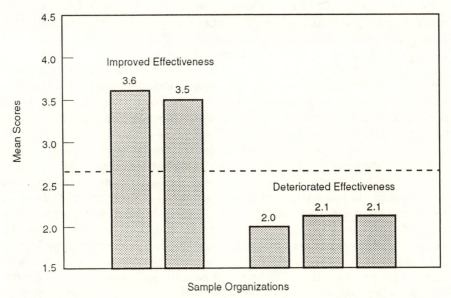

Figure 2.2. Improving versus deteriorating organizational effectiveness.

Table 2.9. Discriminating the Five Most Effective and Improving Firms from the Less Effective Firms

Factor	Coefficient[a]
All employees are involved in improvement activities.	.789***
Employees are involved in determining and designing changes.	.578***
Readiness to downsizing is created by opportunity, not threat.	.530***
Excellence in error prevention quality is present.	.469**
A new, exciting vision is articulated by top management.	.460***
Teams of salaried and of hourly employees are formed.	.460***
Coordination with outside organizations occur during downsizing.	.460***
A dynamic, competent, and knowledgeable leader exists in the firm.	.454**
An advanced quality culture exists, with emphasis on error prevention or creative quality and continuous improvement.	.410***
A systematic analysis of the organization occurred in advance of downsizing.	.307**
Quality of products and services is not improving.	−.527***
A less advanced quality culture exists, with emphasis on error detection.	−.416***
Advanced planning is neglected in implementing downsizing.	−.393**
Average significance of disciminant functions:	$p < .01$
Percentage of firms correctly classified based on their scores on these factors:	100%

[a]Correlation with the canonical correlation in the discriminant function.
**$p < .01$
***$p < .001$

excited and motivated employees, (2) praised them, (3) used symbolic means to provide a vision of future possibilities for them, and (4) remained accessible and visible to them—was a significant characteristic of the most effective and improving organizations. Finally, preparation for downsizing occurred in the highest performing organizations through systematic analysis of the organization and coordination with outside customer and supplier organizations. Organizations that performed poorly neglected planning and preparation and instead adopted a short-term strategy.

These results are not surprising nor are they counterintuitive. Rather, the factors that characterize the very best downsizing organizations just represent good management practices even under normal circumstances. What makes them unusual in downsizing situations, however, is that managers experience enormous pressure to abandon these management principles and attend only to the bottom line (see, for example, Ginzberg, 1985). Immediate headcount reductions make the financial ledger look good in the short run; quick-hit or across-the-board strategies are easier to implement and can help temporarily ameliorate infighting; and preparation and advanced analysis require time and resources that are hard to find when pressures to downsize are intense. Moreover, scapegoating of leaders and a politicized environment make it easy for top managers to distance themselves from employees to avoid criticism and antagonism. Rather than increasing visibility and participation, a natural tendency of top managers is to do the reverse. It is easy to understand, therefore, why most organizations are not characterized by these best practices. Only a small portion of organizations actually operate in harmony with the factors that typify the most highly effective and improving downsizing firms.

Uncovering Highly Effective Dualistic Processes

To elaborate the findings from these statistical analyses, and to gain a more thorough understanding of the strategies used by the most effective downsizing organizations, examples of successful downsizing processes were obtained from the interviews conducted with each top manager over the four-year period. These interviews uncovered examples of certain downsizing processes that were reported to produce outstanding results in organizations. These examples were not limited just to the five best firms; rather, several of these highly effective processes were implemented in more firms than those five during the four-year period of the study. In each case, the top managers reported that the downsizing process had a strong positive effect on their organizations. Objective evidence was not collected to corroborate these self-reported assessments by the managers, but almost universal agreement was found among the key informants that these processes contribute to high and improving organizational effectiveness over time.

Analysis of the stories and incidents related by these top managers suggested that sets of apparently contradictory or conflicting processes were associated with the best downsizing organizations. That is, downsizing processes that produced the most effective outcomes were those that required augmentation of one major downsizing activity with another that was often perceived as contradictory by the managers being interviewed. The contradictions are not inherent in these processes; they only existed in the minds of many of the managers interviewed in the study. That is, when implementing one downsizing process, most managers tended to ignore, even argue against, employing a seemingly conflicting process simultaneously. But, when managers implemented both of the apparently contradictory processes, the most positive (manager-reported) results occurred (see Cameron, et al., 1991). Six of the dualistic processes reported by managers to facilitate effective organizational downsizing are described below.

1. Downsizing was Implemented from the Top Down, but it was also Initiated from the Bottom Up

As mentioned above, strong, visible leaders who aggressively pursued a downsizing strategy and who clearly articulated a vision of the organization's future were associated with positive organizational performance when downsizing. Effective downsizing was managed and monitored by top managers; it required hands-on involvement and control that originated at the top of the organization. On the other hand, effective downsizing strategies were also recommended and designed by lower level employees. In effective downsizing, employees themselves analyzed job-by-job and task-by-task the operations of the firm. This sometimes happened in cross-functional teams, sometimes in blue-ribbon committees, sometimes in self-designed task forces. Members identified redundant jobs and partial tasks, found ways to eliminate organizational fat and improve efficiency, and planned ways in which the changes could be implemented.

In one particularly noteworthy organization, employees were told that if their jobs were eliminated, they would still receive full pay for a year. If they required retraining in order to find a new job (either inside the firm or outside the firm) it was arranged for, but the employees had to justify the expenditure in a proposal. Employees were encouraged to find ways to improve current products and processes within the firm, that is, to add to the firm's revenue stream. Some employees used the time to find jobs outside the firm; others found ways to try out ideas that improved both bottom-line (cost control) and top-line (innovative product ideas) results. A surprisingly large number of employees voluntarily recommended the elimination of their own jobs in order to take advantage of opportunities to do something creative that helped the firm. In a year's time, productivity increased over 50 percent and quality improved almost 30 percent. Downsizing targets were also exceeded. In this case, employees were treated as resources for organizational improvement, not liabilities to the bottom line.

Downsizing from the top down provided consistency, vision, and clear direction as well as visible, hands-on involvement. Downsizing from the bottom up helped foster innovation and improvements that would not have been possible if top management had simply mandated headcount reductions.

2. Universalistic, Across-the-Board Downsizing Processes Were Used, as Well as Selective, Particularistic Downsizing Processes.

Implementing across-the-board cutbacks was an effective way to temporarily capture employees' attention, mobilize the energy of all the organization's members, and overcome resistance to change by highlighting the seriousness of conditions faced by the firm. The announcement of an extensive retrenchment made it clear to everyone that the status quo was no longer acceptable. On the other hand, this universalistic approach produced liabilities (described earlier) that could be overcome only by a particularistic strategy. The most successful downsizing was characterized, therefore, both by universalism and by particularism. One particularistic strategy was a "value analysis" of all tasks in the organization, in advance of any downsizing. The question being addressed was "What *value* does this task have to the final product or service for which we are in business?" Conducted by the employees themselves, this analysis resulted in identifying the most valuable individuals, tasks, and jobs that were not only to be protected but strengthened. Investment increased in some areas at the same time that individuals and jobs in areas adding less value were reassigned, redesigned, or removed.

In concert with an across-the-board early retirement program, for example, one firm offered certain individuals incentives to remain with the firm while others were given incentives to retire early. At the same time, the quality control and work area maintenance functions were eliminated, and work was redesigned so all remaining employees were responsible for incorporating these tasks into their work. Training was made available to all employees focused on preparing them for the changes that were to take place. Discussions were held to change the work week from five 8-hour days to four 10-hour days to generate savings in maintenance, security, and energy costs.

3. Successful Downsizing Involved Managing the Transition for Employees Who Lost Their Jobs, as Well as the Transition for Survivors

The most effective organizations provided outplacement services, personal and family counseling, relocation expenses, and active sponsoring of employees whose positions were eliminated. Several successful top managers in this study proudly announced that none of their "downsized" white-collar employees was without a position someplace else. A wide variety of options was generated for these employees, including severance pay, benefit packages, retraining, and employment opportunities. Temporary consulting arrangements were even made available to some terminated employees. In short, the highly effective firms took responsibility for the transitions created by loss of employment.

On the other hand, white-collar employees who remained with the firm were likely to experience what Brockner (1988) labeled "survivor guilt," characterized by increased anxiety about loss of job, decreased loyalty to the firm, and guilt feelings about co-workers. Survivor guilt occurred when the remaining employees felt guilty about working overtime, for example, or receiving a paycheck when their friends and former co-workers were not working at all. In addition, many survivors felt that the traditionally valued attributes of good employees—loyalty, hard work, and personal competence—no longer counted in the firm. Individuals who displayed those traits still lost their jobs.

In addition to this deterioration in morale, practical work problems resulting in "survivor envy" were even more noteworthy. A common complaint among top managers was that downsizing created job demands that most of their managers were not qualified to fulfill. Survivors were often required to manage a larger number of employees, to maintain accountability for multiple (often new) functions, and to coordinate among more subunits than before downsizing. Many were simply not prepared to handle the increased work demands or the additional knowledge required. Management burnout was a common complaint. While outplacement support and attractive incentive packages were provided to those leaving the organization, survivors received disincentives, such as more work, smaller or no raises, loss of cost-of-living allowances, the same or a reduced title, demands to learn new tasks and to broaden areas of responsibility, and, sometimes, an escalation in the "dirty dozen" dynamics (e.g., loss of morale and teamwork, increased conflict and rigidity).

The most successful downsizing firms paid special attention to the transition experienced by employees who remained with the organization as well as those who exited. For example, one company held regular "forums" where information was shared on the company's and on major competitors' performance, and where Q&A sessions occurred with blue- and white-collar workers. Data that might have been confidential before was posted in several locations throughout the company so that organization members were included in downsizing planning and implementation. Special events were held to signal the end of the degeneration phase and the beginning of the regeneration phase of the company's life cycle (e.g., "launch lunches," a new company logo, new signs, paint, and colors in the production area). Survivors were involved in helping redesign and rationalize the firm's new work processes, and teams of employees were given input on the front end of major decisions and planning exercises. In short, survivors were made to feel trusted, valued, responsible, and involved.

A second way the transition faced by survivors was effectively managed was through changes in the human resource management (HRM) system. These HRM changes *preceded* as well as followed the implementation of downsizing strategies. For example, in one organization human resource training and development activities began months before the downsizing was implemented. White-collar and blue-collar employees attended a 40-hour training workshop on the implementation and implications of downsizing. The appraisal and compensation systems were also redesigned so that rewards were attached to the amount learned and the additional skills acquired by employees in their redesigned jobs. Incentives were thus put in place to motivate and reward survivors who faced new demands in a downsized organization.

In sum, the most effective firms paid attention both to the employees leaving the organization and to those remaining with the firm. Both groups maintained dignity and self-esteem, and highly effective firm performance reflected this investment.

4. Successful Downsizing Targeted Elements Inside the Organization, as Well as the System of Relationships Outside the Organization

The most effective processes involved an attack on any procedures that obstructed internal efficiency. Redundancies, excess costs, and surpluses, for example, were targeted directly. Internal data gathering and data monitoring became more systematic and precise so that previously unmeasured aspects of the business became monitored and regulated. Aspects of the work that were normally invisible—such as size of containers, distance indexes, number of parts per work station, number of pieces of paper involved, frequency of redundant communications, and so forth—were examined carefully to find areas in which costs could be reduced. The "tight ship" or "lean and mean" metaphors were typical of managers' descriptions.

On the other hand, the best downsizing practices also included the entire system of suppliers, customers, and distributors in planning and implementing downsizing. All outside units with whom the firm dealt were simultaneously targets of and partners in downsizing. For example, several firms reduced multiple, redundant single-item suppliers to a single-source supplier of systems of parts. Instead of 28 separate suppliers of an electrical component system, for example, one organization reduced that number to one supplier who provided the entire system. This in turn reduced the number of staff coordinators needed to administer supplier relations, including purchasing, inspection, negotiation, and accounts payable. That supplier was involved in many aspects of design, production, marketing, and service of the final product.

Similarly, reducing distribution points helped several firms improve on-time delivery and eliminate much of the overhead necessary to schedule, transport, and warehouse products for customers when multiple outlets were being maintained. Identifying targeted customer groups helped pare down marketing and sales activities so that efficiencies could be improved in advertising, sales, and customer follow-up. In general, effective downsizing was both internal and external in focus. In addition to targeted internal downsizing, the most effective downsizing was approached as a system concept. Multiple elements within the firm and in its outside environment were included in the downsizing processes.

5. Successful Downsizing Created Small, Semiautonomous Organizations, as Well as Large Integrated Organizations

Theoretically, small organizations tend to run more efficiently than large organizations because they are less encumbered by multiple layers of management, multiple staff functions, multiple sign-offs, and extended implementation time. On the other hand, large organizations can call upon economies of scale and integration to reap efficiencies not available to small organizations. Slack resources lead to flexibility, responsiveness, and multiple (innovative) perspectives not available in small organizations. The most effective downsizing was associated with the advantages of both small and large organizations.

The most effective downsizing strategies produced autonomous or semiautonomous units within the larger organization as well as strong, centralized functions. In the most successful downsizing efforts, unit leaders were given the responsibility to manage functions previously centralized at headquarters, or they were given profit-center responsibility and could decide for themselves which functions to eliminate, which to purchase from corporate headquarters, and which to contract out. For example, one large organization divided itself into three semiautonomous units that competed with one another on productivity and quality criteria. Within each of these units, area heads and team leaders were given control over virtually all the resources they needed to produce products in the most efficient way. Some decided that certain functions were not needed at the subunit level and could be purchased from a central staff unit at the parent company's headquarters (for example, finance and personnel). They were not required to match headquarters staff functions at the subunit level as they had been required to do before. The key was that in effective downsizing, unit managers had the necessary discretion and control over resources to improve efficiency and to contain costs at their small organization level.

At the same time, effective downsizing also produced efficiencies by centralizing functions and creating large organizations. The information-processing function was taken away from geographically dispersed subunits in one organization, for example, to form a large centralized system. Annual savings were estimated in the millions of dollars by eliminating redundancies. The merger and consolidation of several related subunits into a single larger entity made it possible for another organization to eliminate two management layers and about half the staff employees. Geographic or product reorganizations often produced larger, more centralized units within a (decentralized) parent company.

6. The Best Downsizing Practices Emphasized Downsizing as a Means to an End, as Well as the End in Itself

Downsizing was interpreted in some organizations as an admission of failure or weakness. More commonly it was considered to be a temporary, protective mechanism that would help the firm weather out the storm until a more normal growth orientation could be resumed. This negative interpretation generally resulted from downsizing being defined as a reactive strategy rather than a proactive strategy.

Most of the organizations in the study implemented downsizing primarily as a reaction to loss of market share or profitability, entrance of a lower-cost competitor, or a parent company mandate. In these cases, downsizing took on a defensive form. It tended to be associated with exclusive use of workforce reduction strategies (as opposed to organizational redesign and systemic strategies) and mechanistic shifts in organization structure (e.g., rigidity, restricted communication flows, and lower levels of employee involvement). On the other hand, a few firms seemed to interpret downsizing as an opportunity for improvement or as an aggressive strategy leading to enhanced competitiveness. A characteristic top manager comment was: "We're not getting smaller, we're getting better. It just happens that fewer employees is a way to accomplish it." In these firms downsizing was defined as a means to a more desirable end, and opportunities to expand as well as contract were sought.

In this study, the most successful downsizing involved both. That is, in the face of an unequivocal need to retrench, the most effective downsizing organizations, on the one hand, targeted downsizing as a central, critical outcome. "Taking out headcount" and "trimming the fat" were clear and consensual objectives. On the other hand, these organizations also expanded their alternatives beyond a single conventional strategy in order to achieve effectiveness. "Improving productivity" and "enhancing competitiveness" were labels that helped position downsizing as just one in a portfolio of strategies that could improve firm performance.

In the midst of a severe headcount reduction period, for example, one organization instituted a "Build with Pride Week" in the initial phases of downsizing in which family members were invited to the firm on one day, customers on another, suppliers on another, local government officials on another, and so on. Special events, special refreshments, and special decorations were used throughout the week to signal the beginning of a new era in the firm. Nonmanagement employees served as hosts and guides, and outsiders were permitted to question and observe workers as they performed their jobs. Dramatic improvements in productivity, product quality, and a sense of collective teamwork were reported outcomes of this event. Other firms made label changes, such as renaming the quality control department the customer satisfaction department, or generating names and slogans for subunit teams (e.g., one product design team became Delta Force—"seek and destroy errors before customers catch them"). The intent was not just to be cute, but to help create a different mindset among employees about the downsizing and redesign efforts, to define downsizing as an opportunity as well as a threat.

Summary

Of course, the unique circumstances of certain organizations may make these six "best practices" unworkable or impractical. It is possible that these six dualisms may not be universalistic principles that apply to all downsizing situations and all organizational units. On the other hand, a virtual consensus existed among key informants in the most effective firms in this study that these practices produce effective results. In particular, they agreed that the dualistic nature of these practices was a key to their success. Most managers adopted a unitary perspective by approaching downsizing with only one side of the strategy implemented. Effective managers implemented strategies that others labeled as contradictory.

PRESCRIPTIONS FOR MANAGERS AND QUESTIONS FOR ORGANIZATIONAL SCIENTISTS

We began this chapter arguing that organizational downsizing is likely to be a ubiquitous phenomenon in the foreseeable future. Consequently, understanding what downsizing processes are available to organizations, what their effects are on organizations' performance, and what are the best downsizing practices are important matters for investigation. These three questions have been the focus of this four-year study of downsizing: How do firms downsize? What is the effect on the organization? And what are the prescriptions for how to best accomplish downsizing? Taken together, the answers to these questions paint a mosaic of how the most successful firms approach downsizing.

Whereas it is obviously presumptuous to extrapolate from this limited sample of firms in the auto industry to other kinds of organizations, there do appear to be some principles that have general applicability. Table 2.10 presents some general conclusions that contrast "best practices" with "common practices" in downsizing. These conclusions are extrapolated from the analyses of the interview and questionnaire data, and their enumeration serves two purposes: (1) they can provide guidelines for managers who face the need to downsize their firms, and (2) they may serve as hypotheses for empirical investigation in future research on organizational downsizing.

By "best practices" we mean that these approaches or activities have a high probability of leading to organizational effectiveness and performance improvements. On the other hand, the "common practices" are typical of most firms' approaches to downsizing, yet they are likely to lead to ineffective performance and the "dirty dozen" attributes. This explains why most organizations that downsize do not accomplish their stated objectives and report negative consequences from the process (Bennett, 1991). We would argue that best practices represent a "right way" to downsize,

Table 2.10. Downsizing: Best Practices Versus Common Practices

Best Practices	Common Practices
General Orientations Toward Downsizing	
Downsizing is a way of life.	Downsizing is a program or target.
Downsizing is every employee's responsibility.	Downsizing is the responsibility of top management.
Downsizing is motivated by improvement.	Downsizing is motivated by impending crisis.
Downsizing is approached proactively as an opportunity.	Downsizing is approached reactively as a threat.
Downsizing reflects innovation coupled with continuous improvement.	Downsizing reflects conservatism and hunkering down.
A broad view of costs is taken.	Headcount is the first cost considered.
Human resources are defined as the most valuable resource.	Human resources are managed the same as inventories.
Effectively managing human resources is a priority.	Effectively managing financial ratios is a priority.
Specific Activities in Downsizing	
Preparation and extensive analysis	Immediate response (ready, fire, aim)
Free choice	Force choice
Employee involvement and participation	Top-down mandate of means and ends
Information about costs widely shared	Cost information kept secret at the top
Improvements in measurements and data bases	Status quo data collection
Multiple downsizing strategies	"Grenade-type" approaches
Consistency with organizational culture and vision	Viewed as a one-time activity
Active, aggressive, accessible leadership	Paranoid, defensive leadership
Pursuing an advanced quality culture	Stuck in a less advanced quality culture
Focusing on process improvements	Focusing only on product improvements
Focusing on "things-gone-right"	Focusing on "things-gone-wrong"
Humility leads to benchmarking	Not-invented-here syndrome
Advanced training of all employees	On-the-job training for those affected
Simplification (of structure, processes, products, technology)	Continued complexity

whereas the listed common practices represent a "wrong way." The guidelines in Table 2.10 are divided into two sections: general orientations toward downsizing, and specific activities in downsizing. Each is discussed briefly by way of conclusion.

General Orientations Toward Downsizing

Adopting a prescriptive and, therefore, oversimplistic stance, we would argue that the best way to downsize is to treat it as a way of life, not as a program or a target. This means that downsizing becomes every employee's responsibility, not just the responsibility of top management. Downsizing should be seen as an opportunity for continuously improving the organization, instead of just as a reaction to impending crisis. Anticipation and proactivity should characterize an organization's orientation toward cost containment as it integrates a continuous downsizing philosophy into its strategies and procedures, rather than treating downsizing as a threat to which the organization must simply react. Innovation and continuous improvement should be applied to downsizing as much as to growth and expansion activities, instead of adopting a conservative stance where hunkering down is designed merely to hold on until the status quo can be reestablished. Instead of viewing headcount (personnel) as the first cost to be cut, a broad view of costs should be taken in the firm so that human resources are defined as assets, not liabilities, and that they are empowered to find ways to contain costs or increase revenues. That is, instead of managing financial ratios as the highest priority, precedence should be given to managing the human resources. Regardless of the environmental circumstances of the firm, therefore, making downsizing a way of life suggests that employees must always be looking for ways to do more with less, to better utilize resources, and to continuously improve the organization in its pursuit of efficiency as well as effectiveness.

Specific Activities in Downsizing

More specifically, advanced preparation is required before downsizing activities can be effectively implemented, primarily through systematic analyses of skills, jobs, time use, and value-added activities. This contrasts to a more frequent "ready, fire, aim" approach in downsizing organizations. Top managers provide "free choice" to organization members to help identify targets for downsizing instead of more typical "forced choice" alternatives prescribed from above about how the organization will cope with its circumstances. Assuring employee involvement in designing and implementing downsizing strategies, rather than relying on top-down mandates of both means and ends, is necessary to avoid the negative organizational attributes typical of declining firms. Information on the state of the organization, therefore, should be widely shared with members so that they are aware of the current conditions and can help generate creative downsizing alternatives as well as improve standard efficiencies. Keeping cost information secret at the top of the organization engenders suspicion and eliminates a valuable source of ideas. This suggests, often, that improvements in data-gathering techniques should occur rather than relying on traditional databases. Competitor cost and performance information and internal cost data (e.g., per employee, per unit of output, per hour) are examples of requisite databases to be shared.

Downsizing should be accomplished through the use of multiple strategies (i.e., both redesign and systemic strategies) rather than relying solely on workforce reduction approaches. The approaches used should be in harmony with and incorporated into the organization's culture and be consistent with the leader's vision of the future, however, instead of treating downsizing as a one-time activity. The organization's leader, therefore, should be active, aggressive, and accessible to members and should be clear about the vision toward which the organization should be moving. The tendency for leaders to become paranoid and defensive in response to inevitable criticism is antithetical to effective downsizing. An important role of the leader is to foster a mature quality culture—to focus on error prevention and creative quality more than on mere error detection—so that the organization can focus on and celebrate good news more than bad news. That is, an emphasis on "things-gone-right" should take priority over an emphasis on "things-gone-wrong." Ideas for things-gone-right can come from benchmarking activities, which means studying systematically other organizations that have successfully downsized and borrowing ideas that can be used or improved back home. This often requires advanced training of employees in the implications and requirements of downsizing, rather than assuming that surviving employees will acquire the needed experience and knowledge on the job. Finally, successful downsizing should focus on simplifying routines, processes, work, products, customer relationships, and so on. Rather than maintaining continued structural, technological, and process complexity, and then eliminating headcount in an attempt to save money, the best downsizing practices create parsimony in the firm. Headcount reductions may or may not be involved.

Research Questions

Some of the research questions implied by these "right way" and "wrong way" conclusions include the following.

1. What differences exist between firms reflecting a "downsizing-as-a-way-of-life" philosophy and other firms?
2. What importance weighting should be given to the prescriptions for downsizing suggested above if an organization is to improve its effectiveness?
3. What are the main reasons these principles of good management get ignored or contradicted in firms that downsize?
4. Are organizations that downsize effectively fundamentally different in culture, structure, life cycle stage, or industry structure from organizations that do not?
5. Are these prescriptions applicable to all sizes of firms, all sectors of firms, and all declining or growing firms?
6. Under what environmental conditions might an across-the-board approach be the only (or best) alternative?
7. Are certain patterns or combinations of these downsizing prescriptions likely to produce more effective results than others?
8. When definitions of desired outcomes change—say, from improving performance to high performance, or from productivity to quality—do these prescriptions still hold?
9. What effect does the type of key informant have on the type of stories told, the type of prescriptions advocated, and the type of processes described?

10. What differences occur in best practices when a firm has downsized several times in the recent past compared to a firm that is downsizing for the first time?

Other questions could also be specified, of course, and these may not include the most important ones. Regardless of the research questions asked, scholars must begin to more thoroughly investigate this important organizational phenomenon. So little systematic research has been done to date on organizational downsizing, and so much need exists among management practitioners to understand and implement downsizing effectively, that to ignore this discrepancy is tragic. Certainly, organizational researchers should not downsize downsizing research!

NOTE

1. We would like to give special recognition and thanks to the 30 CEOs who graciously provided information to us on a regular basis over the four-year period of time that this study was conducted. Several thousand additional managers also deserve special thanks for completing questionnaires during that period. George Huber and Bill Glick have not only provided helpful comments and insights as this chapter has been revised, but they have done a masterful job coordinating the diverse projects that comprise this effort to understand the dynamics of organizational change. Financial support for this project was provided by the Army Research Institute. ARI's support has been invaluable in this endeavor. Of course, the findings and interpretations contained in this chapter are the responsibility of the authors and do not necessarily reflect the perspectives of ARI.

REFERENCES

Applebaum, S. H., Simpson R., and Shapiro, B. T. 1987. The tough test of downsizing. *Organizational Dynamics*, 68–79.

Ashby, W. R. 1956. *An introduction to cybernetics.* New York: Wiley.

Behn, R. 1980. How to terminate public policy: a dozen hints for the would-be terminator. In Levine, Charles (Ed.), *Managing fiscal stress* (pp. 310–322). Chatham, NJ: Chatham House.

Bennett, A. 1991. Downsizing doesn't necessarily bring an upswing in corporate profitability. *Wall Street Journal,* June 6, p. B1.

Benson, J. K. 1975. The interorganizational network as political economy. *Administrative Science Quarterly,* 20: 229–249.

Blau, P. M. 1970. A formal theory of differentiation in organizations. *American Sociological Review,* 35: 210–218.

Brockner, J. 1988. The effects of work layoff on survivors: research, theory, and practice. In Staw, Barry M., and Cummings, Larry L. (Eds.), *Research on organizational behavior,* Vol 10 (pp. 00–00). Greenwich, CT: JAI Press.

Cameron, K. S. 1987. A study of organizational effectiveness. *Management Science,* 32: 87–112.

Cameron, K. S. 1991. Quality and continuous improvement: a second-generation approach to organizational effectiveness. Paper presented at the Academy of Management Meetings, Miami.

Cameron, K. S., Freeman, S. R., and Mishra, A. K., 1991. Best practices in white-collar downsizing: Managing contradictions. *Academy of Management Executive,* 5: 57–73.

Cameron, K. S., Kim, M. U., and Whetten, D. A. 1987. Organizational effects of decline and turbulence. *Administrative Science Quarterly,* 32: 222–240.

Cameron, K. S., and Mishra, A. K. 1991. *Measuring organizational downsizing processes.* Technical Report. Ann Arbor: University of Michigan, School of Business Administration.

Cameron, K. S., Sutton, R. I., and Whetten, D. A. 1988. *Organizational decline.* Cambridge, MA: Ballinger.

Cameron, K. S., and Whetten, D. A. 1981. Perceptions of effectiveness over organizational life cycles. *Administrative Science Quarterly,* 26: 525–544.

Cameron, K. S., and Whetten, D. A. 1983. *Organizational effectiveness: a comparison of multiple models.* New York: Academic Press.

Cameron, K. S., Whetten, D. A., and Kim, M. U. 1987. Organizational dysfunctions of decline. *Academy of Management Journal,* 30: 126–138.

Carroll, G. R., and Delacroix, J. 1982. Organizational mortality in the newspaper industries of Argentina and Ireland: an ecological approach. *Administrative Science Quarterly,* 27: 169–198.

D'Aunno, T., and Sutton, R. I. 1987. Changes in organizational size: untangling the effects of people and money. Working Paper. Ann Arbor: University of Michigan, School of Public Health.

Ford, J. 1980. The administrative component in growing and declining organizations: a longitudinal analysis. *Academy of Management Journal,* 23: 615–630.

Freeman, J., and Hannan, M. 1975. Growth and decline processes in organizations. *American Sociological Review,* 40: 215–228.

Freeman, S. 1992. Organizational downsizing and redesign: a case of appropriated interpretation. Unpublished doctoral dissertation. Ann Arbor: University of Michigan, School of Business.

Freeman, S. R., and Cameron, K. S. 19XX. Organizational downsizing: a convergence and reorientation perspective. *Organizational Science,* (in press).

Galbraith, J. R. 1977. *Organizational design.* Reading, MA: Addison-Wesley.

Gilmore, T., and Hirschorn, L. 1983. Management challenges under conditions of retrenchment. *Human Resource Management,* 22: 341–357.

Ginzberg, E. 1985. *Resizing for organizational effectiveness: a report of a workshop.* New York: Columbia University, Career Center.

Golembiewski, R., Billingsley, K., and Yeager, S. 1976. Measuring change and persistence in human affairs: types of change generated by OD strategies. *Journal of Business Strategy,* 12: 133–154.

Greenhalgh, L. 1983. Organizational decline. In Bacharach, S. B. (Ed.), *Research in the sociology of organizations,* Vol. 2 (pp. 231–276). Greenwich, CT: JAI Press.

Greenhalgh, L., Lawrence, A. T., and Sutton, R. I. 1988. Determinants of workforce reduction strategies in declining organizations. *Academy of Management Review,* 13: 241–254.

Greiner, L. 1972. Evolution and revolution as organizations grow. *Harvard Business Review,* 49: 37–46.

Hall, R. 1976. A system pathology of an organization: the rise and fall of the old *Saturday Evening Post. Administrative Science Quarterly,* 21: 185–211.

Hambrick, D. C., and Schecter, S. M. 1983. Turnaround strategies for mature industrial product business units. *Academy of Management Journal,* 26: 231–248.

Hannan, M. T., and Freeman, J. 1984. Structural inertia and organizational change. *American Sociological Review,* 49: 149–164.

Harbour and Associates. 1990. *A decade later: competitive assessment of the North American automotive industry 1979–1989.* Troy, MI: Harbour and Associates.

Harrigan, K. R. 1982. Exit decisions in mature industries. *Academy of Management Journal,* 25: 707–732.

Heenan, D. A. 1990. The downside of downsizing. *Across the Board,* May, pp. 17–19.

Henkoff, R. 1990. Cost cutting: how to do it right. *Fortune,* 27: pp. 40–47.

Hirschman, A. O. 1970. *Exit, voice, and loyalty.* Cambridge, MA: Harvard University Press.

Hirschorn, L., and Associates. 1983. *Cutting back: retrenchment and redevelopment in human and community services.* San Francisco: Jossey-Bass.

Huber, G. P. 1984. The nature and design of post-industrial organizations. *Management Science,* 30(8): 928–951.

Imai, M. 1986. *Kaizen: the key to Japan's competitive success.* New York: Random House.

Ishihara X., and Morita, A. 1990. *The Japan that can say no.* Translated copy from the U.S. government.

Katz, D., and Kahn R. L. 1978. *The social psychology of organizations,* 2nd ed. New York: Wiley.

Kolarska, L., and Aldrich, H. 1980. Exit, voice, and silence: consumers' and managers' responses to organizational decline. *Organizational Studies,* 1: 41–58.

Krantz, J. 1985. Group processes under conditions of organizational decline. *Journal of Applied Behavioral Science,* 21: 1–17.

Lawrence, P. R., and Lorsch, J. W. 1967. *Organization and environment: managing differentiation and integration.* Boston: Harvard University, Graduate School of Business Administration.

Levine, C. H. 1985. Police management in the 1980s: from decerementalism to strategic thinking. *Management and Organization,* 45: 691–699.

McCune, J. T., Beatty, R. W., and Montagno, R. V. 1988. Downsizing: practices in manufacturing firms. *Human Resource Management Journal,* 27: 145–161.

McKinley, W. 1987. Complexity and administrative intensity: the case of declining organizations. *Administrative Science Quarterly,* 32: 87–105.

McLaughlin, D. J. 1988. Managing the downsizing. *Condensation and Benefits Management,* 4: 2–8.

Miles, R. H., and Cameron, K. S. 1982. *Coffin nails and corporate strategies.* Englewood Cliffs, NJ: Prentice-Hall.

Miller, D., and Friesen, P. H. 1980. Momentum and revolution in organizational adaptation. *Academy of Management Journal,* 23(4): 591–614.

Mintzberg, H., and McHugh, A. H. 1985. Strategy formulation in an adhocracy, *Administrative Science Quarterly,* 30: 160–197.

Montanari, J. R., and Adelman, P. J. 1987. The administrative component of organizations and the ratchet effect: a critique of cross-sectional studies. *Journal of Management Studies,* 24: 113–123.

Perry, L. T. 1986. Least-cost alternatives to layoffs in declining industries. *Organizational Dynamics,* Spring: p 48–61.

Pettigrew, A. M. 1985. *The awakening giant: continuity and change at ICI.* Oxford: Basil Blackwell.

Pfeffer, J., and Salancik, G. R. 1978. *The external control of organizations.* New York: Harper and Row.

Porter, M. E. 1980. *Competitive advantage: techniques for analyzing industries and competitors.* New York: Free Press.

Quinn, Robert E. & Cameron, Kim S. 1983. Organizational life cycles and shifting criteria of effectiveness. *Management Science,* 29: 33–51.

Richardson, P. R. 1988. *Cost containment: the ultimate advantage.* New York: Free Press.

Robertson, J. M. 1987. Downsizing to meet strategic objectives. *National Productivity Review,* Autumn: 324–330.

Rosenblatt, Z., and Mannheim, B. 1988. A model of workforce reduction strategies in high-tech organizations: a pilot study. Working Paper.

Saporito, B. 1987. Cutting costs without cutting people. *Fortune,* May 25, pp. 26–32.

Sutton, R. I. 1983. Managing organizational death. *Human Resource Management,* 22: 391–412.

Sutton, R. I. 1987. The process of organizational death: disbanding and reconnecting. *Administrative Science Quarterly,* 32: 542–569.

Sutton, R. I., and D'Aunno, T. 1989. Decreasing organizational size: untangling the effects of money and people. *Academy of Management Review,* 14: 194–212.

Thompson, J. D. 1967. *Organizations in action: social science bases of administrative theory.* New York: McGraw-Hill.

Thurow, L. C. 1986. White-collar overhead. *Across the Board,* 23: 234–242.

Tomasko, R. M. 1987. *Downsizing: reshaping the corporation for the future.* New York: AMACOM.

Tushman, M. L., and Romanelli, E. 1985. Organizational evolution: a metamorphosis model of convergence and reorientation. In Cummings, L. L., and Staw, B. M. (Eds.), *Research in organizational behavior,* Vol. 7 (pp. 171–222). Greenwich, CT: JAI Press.

Vroom, V. H. 1964. *Work and Motivation.* New York: Wiley.

Weitzel, W., and Jonsson, E. 1989. Decline in organizations: a literature integration and extension. *Administrative Science Quarterly,* 34: 91–109.

Whetten D. A. 1980. Sources, responses, and effects of organizational decline. In Kimberly, J. R., and Miles, R. H. (Eds.), *The organizational life cycle.* San Francisco: Jossey-Bass.

Womack, J., Jones, D., and Roos, D. *The machine that changed the world.* New York: Rawson Assoc.

Woodward, J. 1965. *Industrial organization: theory and practice.* New York: Oxford University Press.

APPENDIX: ANALYSIS OF THE DATA

Interviews were recorded and transcribed for each of the five rounds. Two separate researchers read the transcripts and independently identified the themes, issues, and strategies that characterized each organization. A specific coding scheme was developed, which helped interviewers identify and rate certain attributes. Agreement among the readers was very high in coding the interviews for the specific themes, issues, and strategies (i.e., reliability coefficient = .90).

The statistical analyses reported here focused on the downsizing questionnaire (as opposed to the instruments used in common by the five researchers in the ARI-sponsored study. Certain questionnaire items were combined to form "factors" that measured important concepts, particularly, the dimensions of downsizing strategies, organizational attributes, and effectiveness. Table 2.A summarizes the major factor categories that emerged from these procedures, along with their internal consistency reliabilities. Because there were too many factors to be included in one single statistical analysis, a stepwise procedure was used, by which the most important (statistically significant) factors were identified in two separate analyses. That is, one category of factors (e.g., downsizing processes) was included in one analysis, then a second category of factors (e.g., organizational attributes) was used in another analysis. The most important factors from each of these analyses were combined into a final analysis. It must be kept in mind that, whereas this procedure is legitimate, it restricts variance and tends to artificially elevate the amount of variance accounted for by the factors (see Cameron, 1987).

To address the first research question, simple correlations and tabular comparisons among variables helped identify patterns of downsizing strategies implemented in these organizations. The second question was addressed using multiple regression procedures, where the major factors associated with organizational improvement, with effectiveness, and with the presence of the "dirty dozen" were identified using the stepwise procedure above. The third question was investigated with discriminant analyses, where highly effective firms were compared to less effective firms, and the "best practices" of the effective firms were highlighted. (Again, the stepwise procedure was used.) Analyses of the interviews were also used to address this third question. For all three questions, qualitative analysis of the interviews supplemented and enriched the statistical analyses. In fact, several conclusions that were not obvious from the questionnaire data became clear because of the interview data.

Table 2.A. Factors Used in the Analysis of Organizational Improvement, Organizational Effectiveness, and Negative Attributes

Factor	No. of Items	Reliability
Desirable Outcomes		
Improvement resulting from downsizing	5	.78
Effectiveness relative to two past years' performance	2	.87
Effectiveness relative to best competitors	2	.84
Effectiveness relative to firm goals and customer expectations	2	.85

Table 2.A. (*Continued*)

Factor	No. of Items	Reliability
Dirty Dozen		
Centralized decision making	2	.50
Neglected long-term planning	2	.66
Abandoning innovation	2	.68
Resistance to change	1	
Decreasing morale	2	.62
Political pressure through special interest groups	2	.77
Nonprioritized cuts	2	.68
Lack of trust	2	.76
Increasing conflict and complaints	3	.78
Restricted communication channels	2	.61
No teamwork	1	
Poor leadership	3	.84
Downsizing Processes		
Downsizing via retirements	4	.67
Downsizing via attrition	3	.50
Downsizing via layoffs	5	.60
Downsizing by eliminating functions and/or management levels	3	.54
Downsizing by eliminating products and/or suppliers	2	.57
Downsizing by transferring employees	2	.57
Downsizing by outsourcing	3	.60
Involved customers and suppliers in downsizing	4	.59
Systematic analysis of tasks and personnel in advance	6	.71
Increased communication and participation	4	.60
Reward and appraisal system changed	2	.85
Increased hourly and salaried teamwork	3	.68
More work required for employees	2	.33
Gradual, incremental implementation	1	
Established own downsizing strategies	1	
Increased employee effort	1	
Mandated downsizing motivated changes	1	
New, exciting vision articulated	4	.77
Employees involved in improvement	4	.73
Downsizing motivated by opportunity	4	.61
Downsizing motivated by threat	5	.85
Quality Culture		
Excellence in error detection quality	1	
Excellence in error prevention quality	1	
Excellence in creative quality	1	
No improvement in quality	1	
Focus on process more than product quality	1	
Advanced level of quality culture	2	.75
Less advanced level of quality culture	4	.75

3

Organizations Reacting to Hyperturbulence

ALAN D. MEYER, JAMES B. GOES, and GEOFFREY R. BROOKS

> Order is heav'n's first law.
>
> Alexander Pope
>
> Toto, something tells me we're not in Kansas anymore.
>
> Dorothy in *The Wizard of Oz* by L. Frank Baum

EDITORS' SUMMARY

In this chapter, Meyer, Goes, and Brooks provide two new and extraordinarily important insights. The first has to do with the nature of change in a hyperturbulent environment. Few researchers have encountered hyperturbulent environments; fewer still recognized hyperturbulence when they saw it; and no one else has made as much sense out of the nature of organizational change in hyperturbulent environment as have these authors. Hyperturbulent situations are unusual. These researchers were lucky. But "luck" is preparation meeting opportunity. It is hard to imagine how any researchers could have exploited their opportunity more fully than did Meyer and associates.

The second extraordinarily important insight is that certain prescribed ways of thinking and acting (ways that are so much a part of the organizational science culture that deviations from them are akin to heresy) must be discarded when studying organizational change under hyperturbulent conditions. This insight, well argued and supported with unsettling examples, will cause considerable consternation in the research community. The authors state that "as our study progressed, one research design parameter after another slipped the shackles of experimental control and started behaving like a variable." For example, they had to change "the operationalization of the [dependent] variable 'organizational performance' as industry restructuring altered the meaning of high performance." Executive-level managers, although not necessarily interested in the nature or process of organizational science, will recognize in this chapter that the problems that hyperturbulent environments pose for researchers are also problems that managers face when attempting to understand, to plan for, or to control organizational change under hyperturbulent conditions.

The industry studied was the hospital industry during the 1980s. Fortunately, Meyer and associates recognized that what they learned about managing change in hyperturbulent conditions is not limited to this industry—indeed, the authors' conclusions do not and need not mention any particular industry. Of course, this simply highlights the fact that one of the important contributions of this chapter will be to stimulate research on hyperturbulent environments and research on radical change in other industries. Examples of observations that merit investigation in other contexts are the following: (1) "while discontinuous changes were overturning the existing industry order, there was no equilibrium to be sought,"; (2) strategic reorientations were most frequently associated with major environmental changes; (3) "hospitals were more likely to reorient their strategies in response to low performance relative to their competitors . . . reorientations were less likely to follow decline over time in their own performance"; and (4) hyperturbulence led to changes at three levels of analysis—the organization, the industry, and the interorganizational network.

Managing in changing conditions is qualitatively different from managing under steady-state conditions. Two important messages for managers in this chapter are that (1) hyperturbulence, which is likely to occur with increasing frequency, demands that organizations adopt radically new strategies in order to survive and that (2) hyperturbulence *is* survivable and presents unique opportunities for top managers who are prepared to reinvent their organizations. ■

Organizations change continuously and discontinuously, and so do their environments. Demographic, economic, and social trends prompt routine organizational adjustments (March, 1981). Geopolitical revolutions, technological breakthroughs, and stock market crashes jolt organizations into periodic reactions (Meyer, 1982). Quantum changes occasionally sweep through industries, altering competitive structures, redefining viable niches, relocating industry boundaries, and triggering metamorphic changes in organizational form (Meyer, Brooks, and Goes, 1990).

Based on a longitudinal field study in the health care industry, this chapter builds a general framework classifying these varieties of change within organizations and industries. It investigates causal processes operating over time and across levels of analysis. It describes environmental conditions ranging from steady state to hyperturbulence, the situation in which "environmental demands finally exceed the collective adaptive capacities of members sharing an environment" (McCann and Selsky, 1984: 460). Such conditions are not unique to the health care industry. Telecommunications, computers, airlines, electric utilities, and financial services are other industries in the throes of revolutionary change. Events that alter the trajectories of entire industries can overwhelm the adaptive capacities of resilient organizations and surpass the understanding of seasoned managers. However, our observations also suggest that hyperturbulence is survivable and may offer unique opportunities for collective action.

This chapter challenges some prescribed ways of thinking and acting when researching organizational change under hyperturbulent conditions. It chronicles an attempt to rigorously research organizational change that was confounded by the very changes the researchers were trying to understand. Selecting "change" as a research problem and adopting a longitudinal data collection strategy forced us to reconceptualize the study on the fly, led us into methodological mine fields, and produced results that continue to surprise us.

Thus, discontinuous change is the central theme of the chapter. We offer concepts, data, and interpretations germane to the causes of discontinuous change, to its effect on industries and on organizations, and to its impact on the social scientists who research it. The chapter's first section provides a retrospective overview of the study. The second section presents a chronological report of the research project, which unfolded in four phases. The third section takes stock of the processes and products of the research and suggests some conceptual, methodological, and practical implications.

PROLOGUE: A RETROSPECTIVE OVERVIEW

Social science research is usually partitioned into five sequential stages: conceptualizing, designing, observing, analyzing, and reporting. We began this study by moving through these stages in the prescribed sequence. But upon reaching the "observing" stage, discontinuous changes occurred in the research setting that threatened to invalidate our conceptual model and research design. As the study proceeded, we were obliged to cycle back, rethink our concepts, change our research methods, and update our findings. As the change processes we were studying grew more chaotic, the focus of the research expanded to include industry-level as well as organization-level change, discontinuous as well as incremental change, and historical as well as contemporary change. Figure 3.1 reconstructs the research process. Over the four-year course of the longitudinal study, the research team's focus oscillated among conceptualizing, designing, and observing.[1]

PHASE 1: ORGANIZATIONS ADAPTING TOWARD EQUILIBRIUM

Model 1: Organizational Adaptation

In January 1987, we set out to learn about the processes that keep organizations in synch with their environments. We decided to limit the study to a single industry. One reason was theoretical: since organizations' environments consist largely of other organizations, changes often reverberate through a group of competitors, and only a single-industry study could assess the extent to which changes observed in a given organization had been induced by prior changes in its competitors. A second reason was methodological: a single-industry study would let us compare organizations' responses to a uniform set of exogenous changes and estimate effects on performance. These considerations, coupled with experience gained in prior research in hospitals, led us to select as our study population the 55 medical-surgical hospitals located in four counties contiguous to the San Francisco Bay. Background interviews and journalistic

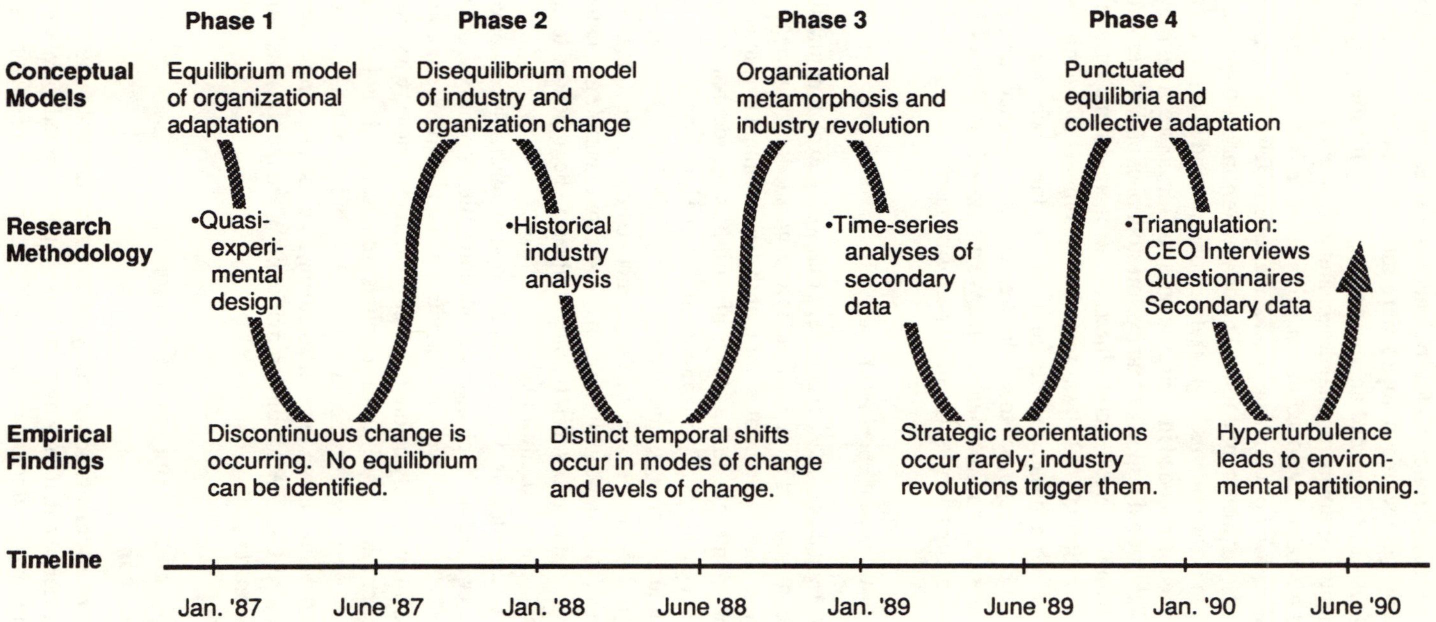

Figure 3.1. Phases in the hospital study.

Conceptual Models

Phase 1: Equilibrium model of organizational adaptation

Phase 2: Disequilibrium model of industry and organization change

Phase 3: Organizational metamorphosis and industry revolution

Phase 4: Punctuated equilibria and collective adaptation

Research Methodology

•Quasi-experimental design

•Historical industry analysis

•Time-series analyses of secondary data

•Triangulation: CEO Interviews Questionnaires Secondary data

Empirical Findings

Discontinuous change is occurring. No equilibrium can be identified.

Distinct temporal shifts occur in modes of change and levels of change.

Strategic reorientations occur rarely; industry revolutions trigger them.

Hyperturbulence leads to environmental partitioning.

Timeline

Jan. '87   June '87   Jan. '88   June '88   Jan. '89   June '89   Jan. '90   June '90

69

reports indicated that environmental turbulence was increasing in the hospital industry. Costs were rising, new technologies were diffusing, and significant regulatory
changes were afoot. So this seemed an appropriate setting for studying environmentally induced changes in organizational design and effectiveness.

We adopted a model developed in our prior research in this setting. This study
(Meyer, 1982) conceived of organizations as adaptive systems and reported on hospitals' responses to environmental jolts. The adaptation model theorized that when
jolts emanate from environments, organizations observe and interpret events according to theories of action encoded in their strategies and ideologies. After interpretation,
events elicit organizational responses that exploit stockpiles of slack resources, as constrained by behavioral repertoires crystallized in the organizations' structures.

Our intention in January 1987 was to extend this model of organizational adaptation by applying it to a broader spectrum of environmental changes. We expected,
for instance, to observe responses to secular trends and step-function shifts as well as
adaptations to transitory environmental jolts. We developed hypotheses linking adaptive responses to organizations' subsequent performances.

Methodology 1: A Quasi-Experiment

The study was designed as a quasi-experiment that would exploit naturally occurring
environmental changes (see Figure 3A.1 in the appendix to this chapter). Our plan was
to observe hospitals' antecedent states, wait for the environment to change, watch hospitals adapt, and then evaluate the effects of various antecedent-adaptation combinations on subsequent levels of performance and on the hospitals' final configurations
of strategy, structure, ideology, and slack. During July 1987, two members of the
research team spent three weeks in the San Francisco area conducting the first of four
scheduled waves of interviews with CEOs in a 30-hospital sample and gathering baseline questionnaire data on organizational variables. (The appendix to this chapter
describes data collection procedures.)

This method was designed to capitalize opportunistically on environmental
change. Although we hoped for change, we failed to anticipate the type or the intensity
of environmental change that we would encounter. Signs of trouble first surfaced during the six weeks immediately before our first wave of interviews, when two of the 30
hospitals in the sample merged, three hospitals were acquired, and six CEO successions occurred. As we hastily rescheduled interviews and recruited new informants, it
became clear that we had taken to the field during a period of quantum change in the
hospital industry. As Oscar Wilde once remarked: "When the gods wish to punish us,
they answer our prayers."

Findings 1: Discontinuity and Disequilibrium
Discontinuous Change

Organizations' environments occasionally undergo cataclysmic upheavals—changes
so sudden and extensive that they overwhelm organizations' adaptive capacities and
transcend top managers' understanding. In 1987, changes of this magnitude were
sweeping through the California hospital industry. Our CEO informants agreed that

the character of competition was undergoing rapid change, but they attributed changes to different causes and foresaw different outcomes. Most CEOs recognized that the industry's boundaries were shifting, but they expected future boundaries to stabilize in different locations. A number of hospitals, physicians, and insurers were experimenting with new organizational forms that intruded into each other's traditional domains, and many CEOs were forging linkages with competing hospitals and with firms in related industries.

In sum, data collected in our first wave of interviews indicated that organizational change was rampant, but the data displayed no systematic pattern. Some changes produced increases in interorganizational cooperation, while others produced increases in competition. Some hospitals were expanding their domains of activity, while others were consolidating. The exact causes of changes were unclear. CEOs found all this confusing and disorienting, as did the researchers.

Conceptual Disorientation.

The assumption that social systems exist in a state of equilibrium—or at least gravitate toward quasi-stationary equilibria—permeates both theories of organizations and the research methods routinely used to test the theories. Building on this implicit assumption, our Phase 1 conceptual framework treated adaptations as equilibrium-seeking responses by organizations. But it became apparent early in the first wave of CEO interviews that this adaptation framework could neither encompass the discontinuous environmental changes in progress nor account for the disparate organizational responses we were observing. The study's quasi-experimental research design, which also implicitly assumed equilibrium seeking, was invalidated as well. Simply stated, while discontinuous changes were overturning the existing industry order, there was no equilibrium to be sought.

PHASE 2: INDUSTRIES IN DISEQUILIBRIUM[2]

Model 2: Modes and Levels of Change

Both of the above "findings" suggested that the most pressing need was to develop a broader framework for thinking about organizational change. In the study's second phase, a review of the literature suggested classifying theories of change according to the *mode* of change (continuous or discontinuous) and the *level* at which it occurs (organization or industry).

The physical, biological, and social sciences portray the world changing in two fundamentally different modes. Continuous, or first-order, change occurs within a stable system that itself remains unchanged (Watzlawick, Weakland, and Fisch, 1974). Indeed, system stability often *requires* ongoing first-order change, such as the myriad of small compensatory steering movements that permit a bicyclist to maintain his or her equilibrium. Discontinuous, or second-order, change transforms fundamental properties or states of the system.

The level at which change occurs provides a second dimension for classifying theories about organizational change (Astley and Van de Ven, 1983). Traditionally, theorists have taken the organization as the relevant unit of analysis and focused on actions designed to alter organizational attributes to match environmental conditions. Recently, theories fashioned at the level of industries, populations, or groups of competing organizations have been imported from biology (Hannan and Freeman, 1977), human ecology (Hawley, 1950), and sociology (Scott, 1987), helping focus organizational researchers' attention on industry-level change processes.[3]

Figure 3.2 combines these two dimensions to classify theories about how organizations create and maintain alignments with their environments. It organizes the literature according to implicit and explicit assumptions about the nature and level of change. Four types of change are distinguished; of these, the one called revolution in the figure has been neglected by organization theory and research.

	First-Order Change	Second-Order Change
Firm Level	**Adaptation** Focus: Incremental change within organizations Mechanisms: •Strategic choice •Resource dependence Authors: Child (1972) Lindblom (1959) Miles & Snow (1978) Pfeffer & Salancik (1978) Weick (1979)	**Metamorphosis** Focus: Frame-breaking change within organizations Mechanisms: •Life cycles •Strategic reorientations Authors: Greenwood & Hinings (1988) Kimberly & Miles (1980) Miller & Friesen (1984) Tushman & Romanelli (1985) Greiner (1972)
Industry Level	**Evolution** Focus: Incremental change within established industries Mechanisms: •Natural selection •Institutional isomorphism Authors: Hannan & Freeman (1977) McKelvey & Aldrich (1983) Meyer & Rowan (1977) Scott (1987) Zucker (1987)	**Revolution** Focus: Emergence, transformation, and decline of industries Mechanisms: •Quantum speciation •Environmental partitioning Authors: Astley (1985) Barney (1986) Gould & Eldredge (1977) McCann & Selsky (1984) Schumpeter (1950)

Figure 3.2. Models of change within organizations and industries. *Source:* Adapted from "Environmental Jolts and Industry Revolutions: Organizational Responses to Discontinuous Change" by Alan D. Meyer, Geoffrey R. Brooks, and James B. Goes. *Strategic Management Journal,* 11 (Summer): 93–110. Copyright © 1990 John Wiley & Sons, Ltd. Reprinted by permission.

Adaptation

The figure's top left quadrant corresponds to theories of first-order change constructed at the organization level of analysis. These are termed *adaptation* theories, and they maintain that organizations track their environments more or less continuously and adjust to them purposely. Two mechanisms of adjustment have been proposed. Theorists espousing a "strategic choice" approach maintain that managers experiment with new products, structures, and processes. Successful variations are retained in organizations' structural designs and product-market domains. An alternate mechanism of organizational adaptation is proposed by the "resource dependence" perspective, in which managers are relegated to a lesser role since organizational changes are viewed as responses dictated by external dependencies. Nevertheless, the organization remains the principal unit within which change is seen as occurring, and first-order change is the principal mode emphasized in resource dependence theory. But whichever of these approaches is taken, the domain of theoretical explanation is limited to incremental changes within firms. Other events are exogenous to adaptation models. Adaptation models posit organization-level processes that construct idiosyncratic product-market domains, and thus increase interorganizational diversity over time.

Evolution

In the figure's lower left quadrant are models addressing how industries, or populations of competing organizations, undergo first-order change. We refer to these as *evolution* models because they maintain that although individual organizations are relatively inert, various forces propel populations of organizations toward alignment with prevailing external conditions. Two streams of evolutionary theory are differentiated by the dominant change mechanisms they posit. Population ecologists (e.g., Hannan and Freeman, 1977, 1984; McKelvey and Aldrich, 1983) emphasize blind variation, selection, and retention. They maintain that differential rates in the entry and exit of organizations cause populations to gradually evolve to fit the technical and economic constraints of environmental niches. Alternatively, institutional theorists (e.g., Meyer and Rowan, 1977; Scott, 1987) argue that organizations experience pressure to conform to the normative expectations of their institutional environments. Achieving "isomorphism" with such expectations allows organizations to gain legitimacy, garner resources, and increase their chances of surviving. Whereas population ecology theory assumes that competition for resources shapes populations by affecting entry and exit rates, institutional theory emphasizes competition for legitimacy and entertains the possibility of change within existing organizations. But although they emphasize different causal mechanisms, both the ecological and institutional approaches to evolution postulate population-level processes that increase the homogeneity of organizations over time.

Metamorphosis.

The top right quadrant of Figure 3.2 contains organization-level theories focusing on second-order changes. These are termed *metamorphosis* theories, because they maintain that organizations adopt stable configurations and possess inertia, but periodically undergo rapid, organization-wide transformations. Theorists have proposed various causal mechanisms that might drive metamorphic changes. These include progression through life cycle stages (Kimberly and Miles, 1980), shifts between strategic types (Miles and Snow, 1978), changes in structural gestalts (Miller and Friesen, 1984), and technological breakthroughs (Tushman and Romanelli, 1985). In any case, metamorphosis theories focus on frame-breaking changes confined within the boundaries of single organizations.

Revolution

The figure's lower right quadrant is reserved for theories focusing on second-order change in industries. Following Schumpeter (1950), we label these *revolution* models, because they propose that industries are restructured and reconstituted during brief periods of quantum change that punctuate long periods of stability. "Quantum speciation," a biological notion, has been proposed as a mechanism through which new organizational forms might emerge during such periods (Astley, 1985), and "environmental partitioning" has been suggested as a likely collective response of organizations already present in the industry (McCann and Selsky, 1984).

Organization theorists have rarely ventured into this quadrant. Metamorphosis theorists argue that progression between developmental stages (Kimberly and Miles, 1980) or radical innovations in technology (Anderson and Tushman, 1990) lead to second-order changes *within* organizations—but they have not addressed the issue of why or how second-order changes in the structure of an industry *itself* unfold. Van de Ven and Garud (1987) explain the emergence of new industries, but their framework is less germane to second-order changes that restructure existing industries. Barney (1986) discusses industry-wide Schumpeterian shocks, but he does not delineate their dynamics. Population ecologists describe how sets of competing organizations evolve, yet, as noted by Astley (1985) and Carroll (1984), they have little to say about how exogenous second-order changes redefine viable niches or trigger the emergence of new organizational forms.[4] Institutional theorists argue that coercive, mimetic, and normative forces bring organizations into alignment with each other and with the institutions upon which they depend (DiMaggio and Powell, 1983), but, as Barley and Tolbert (1988) note, processes through which institutions form and re-form have not been considered.

Methodology 2: Historical Industry Analysis

At this point in the study, the most pressing questions concerned the antecedents and dynamics of the surprising barrage of changes observed during the first wave of interviews. We believed that the model shown in Figure 3.2 could help isolate and interpret the cross-level processes connecting changes in industry structures with changes in organizations. A historical approach seemed necessary to delineate the industry's longitudinal cycle of contextual change, organizational response, and new context formation. Consequently, we shifted the unit of analysis from the organization to the industry and changed the time frame from real-time observation to retrospective data collection.

The analysis presented below draws on a data set assembled using a variety of methods: structured interviews with industry experts and hospital CEOs, naturalistic observations, responses to mailed surveys, inspection of organizational documents, and analysis of secondary data. Details are provided in the appendix to this chapter. In the discussion that follows, key conclusions of the analysis are presented as propositions.

Findings 2: Three Decades in the California Hospital Industry

During Phase 1 fieldwork, we developed a generic "environmental map" to help each CEO chart his or her hospital's position within the evolving industry (as described in the appendix). Depicted in the map were three distinct but interdependent sectors of health care: (1) the provider sector in which hospitals actually deliver acute care; (2) the insurance sector that insures and pays for such care; and (3) the pre/post acute-care sector that funnels patients into hospitals and provides care after their discharge. Our Phase 2 analysis of the industry's history focused on these sectors and examined their changing relationships over time. Figure 3.3 depicts the position of "General Hospital," a typical provider in the industry,[5] during each of three decades.

The 1960s: Evolution Through Isomorphism

For hospitals in the San Francisco area, the 1960s was a period when institutional forces produced a high level of interorganizational homogeneity. Perrow (1965) argues that medical professionals dominated hospital power structures during this period, imposing what institutional theorists term "normative isomorphism" (DiMaggio and Powell, 1983). In addition, governmental largesse funded by the Hill-Burton Act imposed pressures for "coercive isomorphism."

Many hospital administrators of this era equated strategic planning with writing a mission statement and commissioning an architect to draw up blueprints for expansion. Serious attempts by hospitals to differentiate their services or segment their markets were virtually nonexistent. The absence of strong competition for resources rendered such efforts unnecessary, and intense institutional pressures for conformity rendered them ill-advised. Any gains in market share won through adaptive change were likely to be offset by losses in legitimacy. Accordingly, hospitals' goals, structures, and missions closely resembled those of their competitors. CEOs perceived their environments as relatively tranquil and munificent. Metamorphic changes were rare, as hospitals grew incrementally by adding services in a well-established sequence. Conditions were predictable and competition was orderly. As Figure 3.3 suggests, interorganizational linkages to other hospitals were largely unnecessary. Links up to the insurance sector and down to the pre/post acute-care sector were straightforward.

Proposition 1. *Over time, an industry's evolutionary changes tend to increase the homogeneity of organizations within the industry.*

In economists' terminology, during the 1960s, hospitals resembled regulated, homogeneous oligopolists. Industry boundaries were distinct, entry barriers were high, and competition was negligible. In terms of the conceptual model in Figure 3.2, this was an era of evolution: industry-level first-order change was the primary change process operating; the most potent mechanisms of change were institutional ones; and the result was homogenization of the industry.

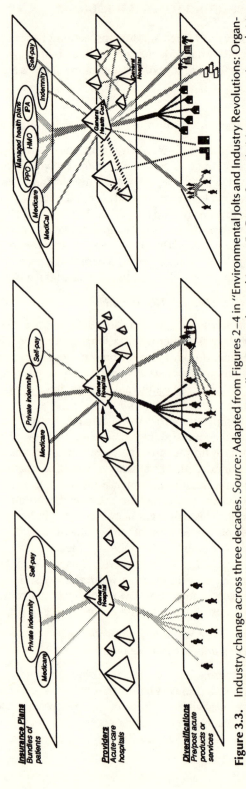

Figure 3.3. Industry change across three decades. *Source:* Adapted from Figures 2–4 in "Environmental Jolts and Industry Revolutions: Organizational Responses to Discontinuous Change" by Alan D. Meyer, Geoffrey R. Brooks, and James B. Goes. *Strategic Management Journal*, 11 (Summer): 93–110. Copyright © 1990 John Wiley & Sons, Ltd. Reprinted by permission.

The 1970s: Organizational Adaptation

In the decade that followed, adaptation replaced evolution as the dominant form of change, strategic and structural differentiation occurred, and diversity within the industry increased. As new technologies like CT scanners, kidney dialysis, and intensive care units came on line, hospital costs rose, resource scarcities emerged, and regulatory actions were triggered. Competition for patients increased, and newly imposed regulatory reviews of facility expansions and equipment purchases fomented political skirmishing. Hospitals grew to appreciate the concept of competitive strategy, and some hired consultants to help them develop one. By the mid-1970s, industry experts could readily classify many San Francisco area hospitals according to Miles and Snow's (1978) generic strategy types, as prospectors, defenders, analyzers, or reactors. Emerging competition, however, turned on non-price factors, since roughly 80 percent of all reimbursements were made on a cost-plus basis. The pre/post acute-care sector at the bottom of Figure 3.3 shows that fee-for-service medicine was fragmenting as specialties multiplied and group practices proliferated. Thus, both normative and coercive forces for isomorphism among providers were dwindling.

Proposition 2.   *Over time, adaptive changes undertaken by individual organizations increase the collective diversity of organizations within the industry.*

In fact, adaptive changes undertaken by individual organizations very likely had the collective effect of constraining industry-level change. Strategic differentiation partitioned patients into diagnostic subgroups, channeling certain subgroups to particular hospitals. This began to produce domain consensus (Thompson, 1967) that reduced uncertainty and limited rivalry. Hospitals' service differentiation and physicians' specialty referral networks developed in tandem, setting up predictable resource flows that both complicated and solidified the industry's collective structure. As Aldrich and Whetten (1981) have argued, dependence relations can stabilize interorganizational networks and hold environmental selection pressures in check.

Proposition 3.   *Over time, adaptive changes undertaken by individual organizations inhibit evolutionary changes within their industry.*

In the language of our framework, the 1970s was primarily a decade of adaptation. First-order change at the organization level became the predominant mode of change, driven both by resource dependence and by purposive incremental change. Executives luxuriated in a sense of professional progress and mastery of the environment. Hospital management was emerging as a bona fide profession with established educational institutions and recognized credentialing mechanisms. The industry environment was changing, but in ways that seemed comprehensible. Interorganizational diversity was increasing as many hospitals settled into distinctive strategic configurations. However, unseen stresses were accumulating, and the industry was drifting toward a period of rapid restructuring.

The 1980s: Industry Revolution

Second-order changes swept through the hospital industry during the 1980s (Shortell, Morrison, and Friedman, 1990). An early by-product of this industry revolution was a burst of metamorphic change within organizations. During the first half of the decade, most freestanding hospitals in the Bay Area underwent a corporate reorganization. The chief impetus for their metamorphoses was resource scarcity, and the chief objective was to expedite diversification strategies. For instance, as shown in Figure 3.3, General Hospital metamorphosed into General Health Corporation, a regional holding company that owned one hospital outright and was formally affiliated with four others. Then, General diversified into a number of pre and post acute-care products and services. Some, including a string of five urgent-care centers and several upscale residential nursing homes, probably qualify as vertical diversifications. Other projects are best viewed as related diversifications, like a joint venture with another hospital to acquire a wheelchair manufacturer. Still other diversifications—like the purchase of a local trucking business—are clearly unrelated.

Although the aforementioned changes were substantial, other changes occurring in the insurance sector overshadowed them. As shown in Figure 3.3, the health insurance market fragmented, largely due to explosive growth in "managed health plans." Initially, hospitals were so reluctant to turn away business that some contracted simultaneously with as many as 90 different plans, often at discounts exceeding 30 percent. These contract negotiations took place without sound actuarial data about the incidence of different diagnoses within the populations served, and without reliable internal data on the cost to the hospital of providing services. As the contract share of volume increased, hospitals rapidly found themselves holding considerable risk.

The 1980s was a decade of revolution in health care. Discontinuous changes restructured the industry. Long-established barriers partitioning health care into the medical-surgical sector, the insurance sector, and the pre/post acute-care sector were breached. Hospitals were thrust into the insurance business as insurance carriers built and bought medical clinics. In their offices, doctors began competing directly with the hospitals with which they were affiliated to perform outpatient procedures, to control diagnostic imaging, and to provide other lucrative ancillary services. Revolution in the industry cascaded down to the organization level, inducing organizational metamorphoses and spurring CEOs' efforts to adapt.

Proposition 4. *Revolutionary changes within an industry are associated with metamorphic changes within organizations.*

In sum, changes occurring within the hospital industry during these three decades may be characterized as evolution of a population of firms, giving way to adaptation within individual firms, followed by industry-wide revolution. Our historical analysis shows that the changes confronting organizations vary dramatically over time, as shifts occur in the predominant mode of change and the level at which it unfolds. However, the analysis also suggests that adaptation, metamorphosis, evolution, and revolution are not independent and mutually exclusive forms of change. That is, change processes associated with all four quadrants in Figure 3.2 may occur simultaneously, and the incidence or intensity of change in one quadrant may influence the incidence or intensity of change in another. A group of competing hospitals, each seeking to adapt within the same domain by cultivating distinctive competencies (first-order organization-level change), may simultaneously experience institutional pressure to display identical structural features (first-order industry-level change). The interplay of adaptive and evolutionary change will, over time, determine whether this particular set of organizations becomes more heterogeneous or more homogeneous.

After repacking our theoretical bags to include these new ideas, adding new questions to the interview schedules to address industry-wide issues, and recruiting new informants who occupied industry-level vantage points, we returned to the field for the second wave of data collection. This time CEO interviews were easier to conduct, since we had achieved some rapport during the first wave. The observations during Wave 2 strengthened and clarified our conviction that discontinuous changes at the industry level were under way and that these changes were linked to metamorphoses at the organization level.

PHASE 3: METAMORPHOSIS THROUGH STRATEGIC REORIENTATION

The historical industry analysis discussed in the last section generated four propositions about the relationships between industry and organizational change. Using Proposition 4 as a starting point, we next conducted a more systematic and quantitative investigation of the role metamorphic organizational change plays in aligning organizations and environments. Our goal was to test hypotheses on the relationships between revolutionary environmental changes, metamorphic organizational changes, and performance outcomes over time in a large sample of organizations. We developed and evaluated two models: (1) an organization-level model positing a reciprocal relationship between organizational performance and metamorphic changes in organizations and (2) a cross-level model predicting that metamorphic changes in organizations are influenced by revolutionary changes in organizations' industry environments.

Our focus was on metamorphic changes in organizational configurations of strategy and structure, termed "strategic reorientations" (Tushman and Romanelli, 1985). For our purposes, strategic reorientations were conceptualized as discretionary moves by top managers to improve competitive position. Unlike incremental or "fine-tuning" changes in strategy or structure, reorientations are radical shifts in strategic position and management perspective (Ginsberg, 1988). Reorientations "take organizations outside their familiar domains and alter bases of power" (Starbuck, 1983: 99); they involve simultaneous changes in a host of variables; and they shift organizations from one strategic type, configuration, or generic strategy to another (Greenwood and Hinings, 1988).

Model 3: Reorientations and Revolutions

Our organization-level model of strategic reorientation is shown in Figure 3.4. The model posits that strategic reorientations within organizations are related to their prior performances, and that reorientations can have positive or negative effects on subsequent performances, depending on performance levels prior to the reorientations. These relationships are formalized in the first three hypotheses below.

Pressures for strategic reorientation can originate within or outside organizations (Ginsberg, 1988). Even when no environmental imperative for change exists, top management may feel a need to develop a fundamentally new competitive posture. Such changes are often undertaken to improve organizational performance or competitive position. Indeed, unexpected environmental events such as exogenous technological

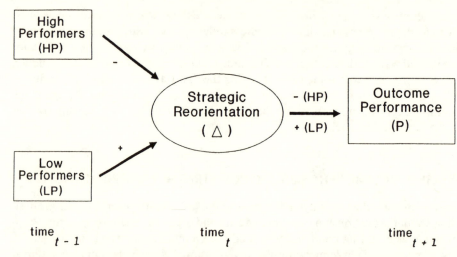

Figure 3.4.   An organization-level model of strategic reorientation processes.

breakthroughs or regulatory changes can act to trigger or enable strategic reorientations that have long been contemplated by management (Meyer, 1982). In general,
therefore, reorientations may occur within both low-performing and high-performing
organizations.

However, discontinuous changes are risky and costly, since they propel organizations into new domains and impose new demands on their structures and members
(Miller and Friesen, 1984). These may include developing new competences, products, or markets that require expenditures of time, money, and human capital. The
potential gains from a reorientation must be sufficient to offset the risks and costs
incurred in the attempt. Since low-performing organizations have less to lose and
more to gain if a reorientation succeeds, we expect low-performing organizations to
undertake strategic reorientations more often than high-performing organizations.

Hypothesis 1.   Organizations with low performance in one period $(t-1)$ are more
likely to undergo strategic reorientations in a subsequent period (t) than are organizations with high performance.

As rational decision makers, strategic managers are believed to recognize the
threats implicit in chronic low performance and to react by formulating appropriate
strategic changes. Assuming that the reasons for low performance were correctly diag-
nosed, and that a new strategy is successfully implemented, achievement of strategic
reorientation should have a positive impact on subsequent performance.

Hypothesis 2.   Among organizations with low performance in prior periods (LP_{t-1}),
those that undergo strategic reorientations (Δ_t) will achieve higher performance in later
periods (P_{t+1}) than will those that display strategic persistence.

For organizations that are performing poorly, an imperative for strategic change
seems obvious. However, strategic reorientations are sometimes seen as a means for
already successful organizations to maintain or improve their competitive positions.
Strategic managers are said to recognize opportunities for change, to accept the risks

implicit in change, and to manage the process to successfully achieve reorientation (Chandler, 1990). However, as we noted, reorientation is time-consuming, expensive, and risky, leading Peters and Waterman (1982) to advise managers that "if it ain't broke, don't fix it." Therefore, we propose that when successful organizations reorient their strategies, they place their record of superior performance in jeopardy.

Hypothesis 3. Among organizations with high performance in prior periods (HP_{t-1}), those that undergo strategic reorientations (Δ_t) will have lower performance in later periods (P_{t+1}) than will those that display strategic persistence.

Figure 3.5 shows our cross-level model, which depicts the relationship between revolutionary environmental change and metamorphic organizational change. As Meyer and Starbuck (1993) have noted, strategic reorientations almost always encounter resistance. They entail discontinuous changes that would redefine organizations' domains in fundamental respects. People lack experience outside their domains, so proposed reorientations evoke confusion and uncertainty. Reorientations invariably alter existing power distributions, and they often impugn current top managers' wisdom. Thus, managers may oppose reorientations to avoid uncertainty, maintain power, and protect their reputations. As a result, we propose that strategic reorientations will be infrequent events.

Hypothesis 4. Over a number of time periods ($t_1 \ldots n$), the number of organizations in a population that exhibit strategic reorientations ($\Sigma\Delta_t$) will be less than the number of organizations that do not exhibit strategic reorientations ($\Sigma\Delta_t$).

Since individual organizations generally resist change due to strategic or structural inertia (Hannan and Freeman, 1984), they can collectively act as a "brake" that slows

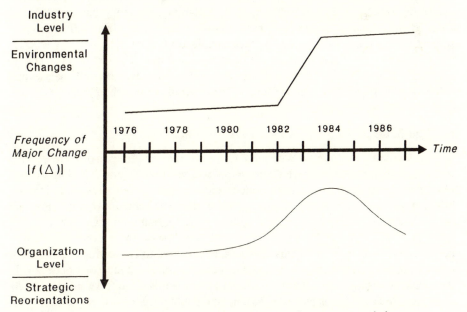

Figure 3.5. A cross-level model of industry and organizational change.

down industry change processes.[6] Large organizations in particular can resist change by expending slack resources, coopting environmental constituencies, or driving out marginal competitors. Meyer (1982) found that San Francisco hospitals reacted to a short-term environmental jolt (a doctor's strike) by absorbing slack and making temporary adjustments in their strategies and structures. When the strike ended, most hospitals returned to their prior forms and strategies. The jolt was insufficient in magnitude and duration to compel the hospitals to fundamentally reorient their strategies.

The enduring changes wrought by an industry revolution, however, demand more than temporary changes in organizations. Bedeian and Zammuto (1991) argue that major environmental changes produce discontinuities in the size or shape of environmental niches and thereby spur strategic changes in organizations. In fact, since organizations are usually so resistant to change, industry revolutions may sometimes be *necessary* to trigger reorientations. Both our historical analysis and our field interviews suggested that revolutions in the health care industry were likely to trigger reorientations in hospitals. Thus, as illustrated in Figure 3.5, we predicted that:

Hypothesis 5. Strategic reorientations will be more prevalent during periods of industry revolution than during periods of industry evolution [$f(\Delta_t|$ revolution$) > f(\Delta_t|$ evolution$)$].

Methodology 3: Multivariate Time-Series Analyses

Strategic reorientations and organizational performance were tracked in approximately 450 California acute-care hospitals over a period of 11 years. Hospital strategies were measured along three dimensions: product/market domain, competitive methods, and organizational resources. Performance was conceptualized in two ways: cross-sectionally relative to competitors and longitudinally within the organization over time. Three elements of performance (profitability, efficiency, and growth) were assessed. Strategy and performance measures were constructed from a time series of secondary data collected annually by the state. Factor and cluster analyses were used to generate a taxonomy of strategic configurations and track changes between configurations (i.e., reorientations). Hypotheses were tested using discriminant analyses and ANOVA. (Further details can be found in the appendix to this chapter.)

Findings 3: Organization-Level and Cross-Level Effects

We proposed that organizations undertake strategic reorientations in order to increase their performance and improve their competitive position (Figure 3.4). Three longitudinal relationships between performance and strategic reorientations were hypothesized at the organization level. Considerable support was found for Hypothesis 1, that low prior performance was associated with strategic reorientations (Goes, 1989). The strength of the relationship, however, varied depending on the conceptualization of performance used. Low performance measured relative to competing organizations proved a much better predictor of strategic reorientations than measures of decline in performance within the focal organization. In other words, hospitals were more likely to reorient their strategies based on weaknesses in relative competitive position. Reorientations in a particular hospital were less affected by its own track record of performance over time.

Mixed and limited support was found for Hypothesis 2, which predicted that low-performing organizations that reoriented strategies would subsequently outperform those that did not. Again, the strength of the relationship varied considerably by performance measure. Reorientations had stronger effects on profitability and growth than on efficiency. Reorientations also seemed more likely to lead to higher future performance measured within the focal organization over time than to higher future performance measured relative to competitors. Reorientations by low performers rarely resulted in an improved competitive position.

Finally, strong support was found for Hypothesis 3, which predicted that reorientations in high-performing organizations would have negative effects on performance. Strategic reorientations in high performers were generally found to be followed by substantial declines in profitability, efficiency, and growth. This finding implies that reorientations carry serious performance risks for organizations that are already succeeding with current strategies.

Overall, these results square with the image of organizations aligning and periodically realigning with their environments by undergoing strategic reorientations. Although the importance of particular performance measures as predictors or outcomes of reorientation varied, the hypotheses were generally supported. Prior performance emerges as a key variable in driving metamorphic changes in organizational strategy. In addition, future performance outcomes were influenced by strategic reorientations. Metamorphic change seems to play an important role in realigning organizations with changing environments.

However, as stated in Hypothesis 4, we expected strategic reorientations to be relatively rare events given the cost, time, and effort necessary to achieve them. This expectation was largely supported by the data. Table 3.1 presents the distribution of strategic reorientations observed in our sample over time. No more than about 10 percent of the hospitals made a reorientation in any given year. Across all years of the study, about 6 percent of the opportunities for reorientations resulted in actual changes between configurations. Indeed, only 142 hospitals in the sample (31 percent) underwent a strategic reorientation at any time during the eight years. Only 61 hospitals (14 percent) experienced more than one reorientation during this time span. In other words, almost 70 percent of the sample hospitals never made a strategic reorientation. This is an important finding, since it is at odds with another study finding that change in hospitals' "generic strategies" is common (Zajac and Shortell, 1989). While this contradiction may result from the different methodologies used in measuring strategic change, our findings nonetheless imply that formidable inertial forces within organizations resist reorientations.

However, significant variation in the pattern of strategic reorientations over time was also evident. The results in Table 3.1 indicate that strategic reorientations were positively associated with revolutionary changes in the structure of the industry, as we predicted in Hypothesis 5.

It has been argued that quantum changes in the California hospital industry peaked between the years 1981 and 1983 (Meyer et al., 1990; Shortell et al., 1990). Our secondary data analyses suggest that this discontinuous industry-level change may

Table 3.1. Cross Tabulation of Strategic Reorientations over Time

Year	Total Number of Hospitals	Total Number of Reorientation Opportunities[a]	Strategic Reorientations			No Strategic Reorientations	
			Number of Hospitals	% of Hospitals	% of Total Reorientations (1979–1986)	Number of Hospitals	% of Hospitals
1979	453	453	13	2.9	6.4	440	97.1
1980	449	436	39	8.9	19.2	397	91.1
1981	451	412	14	3.4	6.9	398	96.6
1982	457	443	40	9.0	19.7	403	91.0
1983	451	411	42	10.2	20.7	369	89.8
1984	459	417	17	4.1	8.4	400	95.9
1985	448	431	18	4.2	8.9	413	95.8
1986	443	425	20	4.7	9.9	405	95.3
TOTAL	—	3,428	203	5.9	100.0	3,225	94.1

[a]Given our coding scheme, strategic reorientations could only occur in years 1979–1986, and only hospitals that had *not* reoriented in the previous year could undergo a strategic reorientation.

have triggered discontinuous organization-level changes: more than 40 percent of all metamorphoses we observed over an eight-year period (1979–1986) occurred during the latter two years (1982–1983) of the industry revolution. Indeed, the number of strategic reorientations was significantly greater during this two-year period than during other periods of the study.

Additional support for this cross-level relationship comes from examining time-dependent changes in the emphasis hospitals placed on several strategic dimensions that we elicited with factor analysis. Figure 3.6 plots over time the average factor scores observed for two of these strategic dimensions: "low margin defense" and "service differentiation."[7] Major discontinuities in both curves coincided with the industry revolution (1981–1983), and the curves' individual trajectories appear congruent with the particular character of the health care revolution.

In other words, the preferred mix of strategy variables changed considerably as the structure of the industry underwent major changes. Consistent with increased regulatory emphasis on cost containment, the factor we label low margin defense received sharply higher emphasis throughout the industry. Key variables in the low margin defense strategy were innovation in service delivery and an emphasis on efficiency. Regulatory disincentives for inpatient hospitalization were invoked in 1982, followed almost immediately by incentives for increased delivery of outpatient services. Consistent with these regulatory changes, the factor we label service differentiation fell sharply and then rebounded. Hospitals rapidly abandoned marginal inpatient services, yet moved just as quickly into a variety of new outpatient delivery programs.

In sum, our findings suggest that organization-level strategic reorientations in the California acute-care hospital industry were strongly associated with performance, were relatively uncommon over time, and seemed to correspond to major structural changes under way in the industry. Proposition 4, which contended that revolutionary changes within industries trigger metamorphic changes within organizations, was generally supported in our longitudinal, quantitative analyses of secondary hospital data.

PHASE 4: COLLECTIVE RESPONSES TO INDUSTRY REVOLUTION

Methodology 4: Building Grounded Theory

Based on the Phase 2 historical analyses and Phase 3 time-series analyses, we reinterpreted Phase 1 reports of widespread CEO successions, restructuring, and strategic reorientations as organization-level responses to discontinuous industry-level change. However, as the fieldwork progressed, the growing significance of *inter*organizational responses became apparent. Hospitals were entering into operating agreements, asset-sharing arrangements, long-term contracts, and joint ventures with insurers, groups of doctors, employers, and other hospitals.

These collective responses to discontinuous change became the focus of the fourth phase of the study. Our goal at this point was to build theory by triangulating among data from observations, interviews, questionnaires, and archives. The process was largely inductive, and, as Eisenhardt (1989) recommends, it involved continuous comparison of data and theory. The methods are described in the appendix to this chapter, and the key findings are stated as propositions.

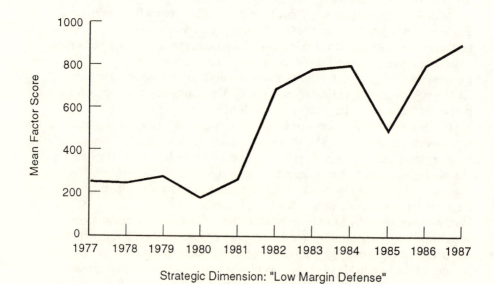

Strategic Dimension: "Low Margin Defense"

Calendar Year

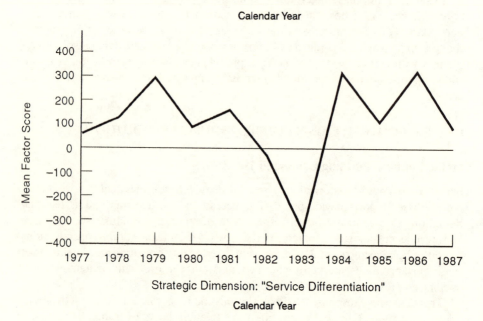

Strategic Dimension: "Service Differentiation"

Calendar Year

Figure 3.6a and b. Time-dependent changes in strategic emphasis.

Findings 4: Responses to Hyperturbulence

Table 3.2 summarizes in tabular form the trends ascertained through content analyses of data gathered at six-month intervals. In hospital executive suites, we noticed profound shifts over time in CEOs' activities, in their emotional states, and in the issues commanding their attention. The collective mood swung from optimism, though despair, to resignation; foci of attention shifted from primarily external to primarily internal; and pivotal activities moved from strategy formulation, to implementation, to retrenchment.

In the insurance sector, traditional indemnity insurance almost disappeared during this period, while executives' attitudes toward managed care ricocheted from optimism, to disenchantment, to determination to build equity positions in managed care plans. The financial naivete and "promiscuous contracting" that characterized the beginning of the period were replaced by tougher negotiation and a clearer understanding of hospital cost structures.

Early-1980s diversification into pre/post acute-care products and services gave way first to divestment and then to disaggregation. Nearly all hospitals that invested in primary care clinics or acquired unrelated businesses absorbed losses. Fierce competition for diagnostic imaging, laboratory, and other profitable ancillary services arose from physicians and external entrepreneurs. Frequently, to avoid ceding services outright to unaffiliated investors, hospitals spun them off in joint ventures with physicians from their own medical staffs. The result, in either case, was a hollowing out of the hospital.

The most intriguing change we observed over the two-year period was a pronounced shift away from competition between freestanding hospitals toward affiliation into overlapping regional networks. Network formation was in its early stages when we began our fieldwork, and it continued throughout the study. The processes generating networks, however, did not operate in a stable or consistent fashion over time. As shown in the collective action row of Table 3.2, we observed systematic longitudinal differences in (1) CEOs' self-reported motives for affiliating with networks, (2) the nature of linkages connecting networked organizations, and (3) the function, or role, that networks played in the industry. In the process of reconceptualizing networks, a set of concepts from the organizational literature was pressed into service.

Punctuated Equilibrium

Gersick (1991) describes recent shifts in theorizing about the development of human individuals, groups, and organizations, linking them to concurrent theoretical developments in evolutionary biology, physical science, and the philosophy of science. At issue in all these fields is the best way to conceptualize change. The older, better established *gradualist* position maintains that change unfolds in a piecemeal fashion through the incremental accumulation of many infinitesimal changes. The newer *punctuated equilibrium* view maintains that short bursts of quantum change are interspersed between long periods of stability. Gould and Eldredge (1977) characterize punctuated equilibria as changes that occur in large leaps. These changes follow a gradual accumulation of stress, which a system resists until it reaches its breaking point, or until a triggering event precipitates discontinuous change. Van de Ven (Chapter 8 in this volume) reports that organizational innovation involves similar dynamics.

Table 3.2. Time-Dependent Changes in Hospitals' Responses to Discontinuous Industry Change

	Wave 1, July 1987	Wave 2, January 1988	Wave 3, July 1988	Wave 4, January 1989
Medical-Surgical Acute-Care Sector	Great emphasis placed on formulating competitive strategies; less on implementation. Little change in organization structure. Performance: financial indicators and volume generally good. Mood is decidedly upbeat.	Strategy implementation now under way. Many structural reorganizations are in progress. Performance: generally high occupancy, but dwindling medicare reimbursement is troubling. Mood grows increasingly somber.	Many CEO successions, downsizing top management teams, adopting internal focus. Skim and differentiation strategies abandoned. Performance: mounting financial losses. Mood is to cut losses and weather storm. Gloom and doom abound.	Retrenching to core businesses. Downsizing continues at top and middle management levels. Performance: losses in competitive markets, profits in protected markets. Mood of realization that industry changes are irreversible, permanent.
Risk/ Reimbursement Sector	General optimism about managed care, coupled with fear of turning away business. Tempered by concerns about magnitude of discounting and ignorance about costs of providing services.	Disenchantment with managed care and renegotiation of contracts. More awareness of costs of providing services and overhead costs of low-volume contracts. Curtailment of "promiscuous contracting."	HMOs experience heavy losses, levy sizable premium increases. Indemnity insurance vanishing. Hospitals are growing more experienced and selective in negotiating with managed care contractors.	Competition increasingly revolves around managed care. New products being developed and marketed. Many hospital CEOs seek to supplement arms-length contracting with equity in HMOs to retain control.

Pre/post Acute-Care Sector	Diversification into pre-and post-acute care continues, but a retreat from primary care clinics is apparent. Concerted efforts are under way to foster a bottom-line orientation among M.D.s via education and indoctrination.	Back to basics sentiment surfaces. Divestiture of unrelated and many related businesses is now well under way. Hospital executives are devoting more attention to romancing and recruiting physicians to boost patient occupancy.	Divestment continues. Conviction grows that diversification does not make sense for hospitals. More vigorous physician recruitment by offering equity in joint ventures and subsidized medical office space as inducements.	Divestment gives way to disaggregation as core technologies are siphoned off or spun off. Joint ventures lead to hollowing out of the hospital. Joint ventures now essential for physician retention as well as recruitment.
Collective Action	Strong enthusiasm for affiliation: 70 percent of unaffiliated hospitals are actively courting network partners. Main benefit anticipated is area-wide contracting for managed care.	Marked decline in enthusiasm for affiliation. Many CEOs opt for either full merger or freestanding posture; avoid intermediate positions. Main benefit perceived now is better access to financing.	An unprecedented number of acquisitions, affiliations, and mergers have just been completed or are under way. Most link hospitals to HMOs or other "managed care" plans. Key motive now is survival.	No major new affiliations since July, but many deals hang in abeyance. Air of expectation: extensive and durable groupings may jell at any time. Sitting in limbo.

Source: Adapted from "Environmental Jolts and Industry Revolutions: Organizational Responses to Discontinuous Change" by Alan D. Meyer, Geoffrey R. Brooks, and James B. Goes. *Strategic Management Journal* 11 (Summer): 93–110. Copyright © 1990 John Wiley & Sons, Ltd. Reprinted by permission.

The notion of punctuated equilibria corresponded closely to events affecting our sample. As hospitals entered the 1980s, three stresses had been accumulating for some time. The first resulted from spectacular growth in "managed care," a term referring to health maintenance organizations (HMOs), preferred provider organizations (PPOs), and other new vehicles for financing and delivering health services. Second, a hospital building boom fueled by federal largesse during the 1960s and 1970s had saddled the industry with substantial excess capacity. Third, entry and mobility barriers had been weakened by competence-destroying innovations in medical technologies and services.[8] Characteristically, industry participants resisted change, and the stresses continued to build.

However, during 1982 and 1983, state and federal governments launched a fusillade of regulatory actions in an attempt to contain health costs by increasing competition. The most important actions were (1) initiating sealed-bid contracting for state-subsidized low-income patients, thereby creating incentives for operating efficiently and requiring hospitals to assume risk; (2) sunsetting the Certificate of Need review process, thereby removing a regulatory barrier to entry and mobility within the industry; and (3) basing the medicare payment system on diagnostic related groups (DRGs), thereby reimbursing services according to predetermined rates. In comparison to the demographic, technological, and epidemological changes then buffeting hospitals, these regulatory actions appeared relatively innocuous. But small causes can have large effects—the outcome was discontinuous change that surged through the California hospital industry.

Proposition 5. *Weak forces can trigger revolutionary change by releasing the accumulated pressure of prior technological, social, and political changes.*

Quantum Speciation and Dynamic Networks

In the biological process termed quantum speciation, new species arise when a small segment of an ancestral population is isolated at the periphery of its ecological domain. Here, because peripheries mark the edge of ecological tolerance for the form, conditions are harsh and selection pressures are intense. In these settings, favorable mutations spread quickly. If unsaturated ecological space exists, mutations proliferate. They occasionally displace the ancestral form and thus punctuate the evolutionary equilibrium.

Quantum speciation was a promising notion for conceptualizing the rapid formation of regional hospital networks. The networks themselves had properties akin to the organizational form that Miles and Snow term the "dynamic network." Miles and Snow (1986: 62) say this form is appearing "especially in service and high technology industries, as both a cause and a result of today's competitive environment." Dynamic networks connect selected components of formerly independent organizations. They are assembled for finite time periods to produce specific products or achieve specific objectives.

The 55 hospitals clustered around the shores of San Francisco Bay inhabit an ecological niche that is isolated from other hospital organizations in geographic, demographic, and regulatory terms. As competition and resource scarcities intensified in the early 1980s, several regional networks (like the one depicted in Figure 3.3 for General Hospital) appeared in this organizational population. These new interorganizational structures did not evolve in any gradual fashion. They did not, for instance, arise from the formalization of emergent social networks, the accretion of historical exchange patterns, or the crystallization of dependency relationships. Rather, our interviews indicated that these networks were analogous to biological mutations. They were brokered purposively by entrepreneurs to create new competitive vehicles for financing and delivering health care. They linked hospitals by superimposing governance structures ranging from markets to hierarchies. These linkages formed multiple layers of informal alliances, year-to-year contracts, joint ventures, and interlocking equity holdings. Hospitals connected by collaborative linkages for specified undertakings often competed vigorously in other areas. This cooperative overlay seems to fit Emery and Trist's (1965) assertion that, in turbulent environments, individual organizations, however large, cannot cope successfully in isolation but must establish cooperative relationships.

Proposition 6. *Revolutionary change within an industry stimulates the formation of transorganizational networks.*

During the study's second interviewing wave, we expanded the research design to obtain additional data from network brokers and affiliated executives. Brokers, we found, usually took the lead in connecting organizations. In some cases they linked participants by establishing an entirely new hierarchical entity. In others they acted as intermediaries who negotiated and contracted with participants individually. In still other cases brokers merely established and maintained various formal relationships, leaving the affiliated organizations as equal partners in an evolving network. As industry boundaries became permeable, many brokers formed linkages that spanned industries—acting at once as respondents to and as agents of industry revolution.

Brokers maintained that they added value by reconfiguring components of hospitals and connecting them to insurance providers and physician organizations. When asked to spell out how value was added, brokers' responses fell into three categories: efficiency, power, and synergy. The efficiency argument emphasized economies of scale and scope. Pointing to the network's ability to deliver health services at geographically dispersed locations under a single contractual relationship, brokers said they provided access to superior executive talent, contracting expertise, and management information systems. The power argument maintained that coalescing amassed bargaining power vis-à-vis large public and private customers, and that it facilitated lobbying and other collective strategies. The synergy argument turned on linking separate components with unique competencies, each pursing its core mission single-mindedly after diversionary activities had been stripped away and superfluous enterprises had been spun off. But whatever rationales brokers offered for affiliation, the networks they assembled forged brand new linkages between hospitals, physicians, and insurers.

Proposition 7. *Revolutionary change within an industry precipitates affiliations spanning industry boundaries.*

A less optimistic appraisal, however, came from our later interviews with hospital executives, the principal actors that the brokers were trying to connect. The enthusiasm voiced by executives for networks during Wave 1 had dwindled sharply by Wave 2, when several remarked that the benefits ascribed to networks had been exaggerated and were unobtainable without legally merging the affiliated institutions. As indicated by entries in the bottom row of Table 3.2, the rate at which network affiliations were being consummated and the benefits ascribed to affiliation proved highly unstable over the period of our study. One trend, however, was unmistakable: as time passed, CEOs' anticipation of benefits from synergy, efficiency, or power gave way to an over-powering desire to mitigate the uncertainties and scarcities arising from revolutionary change in the industry.

Partitioning the Environment

McCann and Selsky (1984) propose that when the collective adaptive capacity of a population of organizations is exceeded by environmental demands, a condition that they call *hyperturbulence* ensues. This, they contend, can lead to a partitioning of the environment. Organizations that are relatively resource-rich come together to form *social enclaves* within which resources are sequestered and turbulence is reduced. Selective membership criteria restrict admission to social enclaves. Prospective orga-nizational members must demonstrate their control of slack resources available for contribution to the enclave, and they must hold values and goals compatible with those of existing members. In a process of *social triage,* resource-poor organizations are left to fend for themselves in hyperturbulent *social vortices,* wherein "attempts at collaboration either will be highly fragile, episodic, and prone to setbacks or will be impossible" (McCann and Selsky, 1984: 466).

Events observed during and subsequent to Wave 4 suggested that environmental partitioning was under way in California's hospital industry. Faced with declining financial performance, disaggregation, downsizing, and the realization that their industry had undergone a quantum change, many executives were actively preparing their organizations for affiliation. The involution of embryonic dynamic networks toward social enclaves over the two-year period of our field interviews was evident in the increasing disparity in size and wealth of affiliated and unaffiliated hospitals and in the failure and abandonment of one network formed to link less affluent hospitals. Other evidence for the shift from dynamic networks to social enclaves comes from the case of a provisional alliance of several prominent hospitals. Legal affiliation was held in abeyance for over a year because one potential member was losing money. In inter-views with the alliance broker and CEOs of the hospitals involved, it was stated that the flow of red ink would have to be staunched before the arrangement could become permanent. When the beleaguered alliance member failed to return to profitability, the other hospitals severed their tentative links with it and formed a smaller enclave among themselves.

Proposition 8. *Revolutionary change in conjunction with resource scarcity fosters partitioning of industry environments and formation of social enclaves.*

According to McCann and Selsky's view of partitioning, when certain organiza-tions amalgamate to form relatively affluent enclaves, others which are isolated tend to be drawn into social vortices in which uncertainty is higher and resources are scarcer. The collaboration of some organizations actively worsens the conditions that confront others. These processes became increasingly evident in our sample. County-owned hospitals in particular seemed to be spiraling into vortices of extreme resource scarcity. They were obliged to treat medicaid patients, and expected to treat indigents. As the AIDS and crack cocaine epidemics advanced, private hospitals erected barricades diverting these patients to public hospitals. Because emergency rooms create portals affording entry to unwanted classes of patients, some private hospitals were led to cut emergency staffing levels or to discontinue emergency services altogether. (The proportion of all emergency services delivered by networked—as opposed to free-standing—hospitals in the San Francisco metropolitan area declined from about 35 percent to 20 percent just during the two years of our study.) Allegations were made of "patient dumping," where uninsured patients were transferred, or dumped, from private emergency rooms into public emergency facilities before they had been medically stabilized.

By 1990, emergency services had contracted to the point that periodic episodes of excess demand were occurring. Occasionally, the entire region's emergency care system crashed. Such an episode would typically begin when an overloaded county hospital placed its emergency room on "diversion" because no vacant critical-care beds were available. The result was to divert or reroute ambulances to other emergency facilities, inundating them with patients, absorbing their critical-care capacity, and leading them to go on diversion as well. These events then touched off a chain reaction that could throw an entire city into critical-care diversion, leaving emergency patients literally circling the city in ambulances. These events graphically illustrate how organizations coalescing into social enclaves can inadvertently isolate other organizations, plunging them into the vortex of hyperturbulence. In this grim example, social triage among organizations has cascaded down to produce medical triage among patients.

Proposition 9. *The amalgamation of certain organizations into social enclaves fuels social vortices that threaten the survival of unaffiliated organizations.*

In Phase 4 of our study, qualitative analyses probed the origins, functions, and transformations of regional health care provider networks. These collective structures appeared to represent a new organizational form emerging at a level between the organization and the industry. Our analyses suggest that, initially, the key functions of networks were pooling information and pursuing opportunities. However, as resource scarcities mounted, threats displaced opportunities, and the networks began to function as enclaves. Indeed, some of our CEO informants expected these new collective forms to drive their organizational ancestors into extinction. One predicted that in the year 2000 no freestanding hospitals will be left in the Bay Area. Other executives, determined to preserve their hospitals' autonomy, resolved to continue adapting existing strategies and structures incrementally. The relative effectiveness of changes unfolding at these two levels of analysis may well determine the structure of the industry during the 1990s.

EPILOGUE: TAKING STOCK OF RESEARCH PROCESSES AND PRODUCTS

This chapter has chronicled our study of organizations in a hyperturbulent industry. Selecting "change" as a research problem and adopting a longitudinal data-collection strategy led to unforeseen conceptual and methodological difficulties. Like the study, our account here has been more complex and fragmented than we intended initially. Therefore, in summing up we will try to synthesize our findings and speculations around three themes. First, the nature of change in and around organizations is considered. Second, some lessons about designing and conducting social science research are extracted from our experiences. Third, implications of the work for executive-level managers are suggested.

Implications for Theory: The Nature of Organizational Change

While tracking a homogeneous set of organizations over a brief span of time we observed a broad spectrum of changes. These changes varied both cross-sectionally and longitudinally in terms of rates, modes, and levels of analysis. Back in the library, however, it was a different story. Here, we were struck by how little attention organization theorists had devoted to differentiating change processes and specifying when, how, and why organizations in context undergo different types of change. Of particular note was the field's affinity for first-order change—adaptation models outnumbered metamorphosis models at the organization level; evolution models overshadowed revolution models at the population level. Perhaps this favoritism arises from tacit theories of change subsumed in paradigmatic constellations of assumptions, values, and taken-for-granted understandings.

Paradigms of Change

The first-order change paradigm summarized in Table 3.3 underpins most organization theory and research. Researchers usually assume quasi-stationary equilibrium conditions and focus primarily on incremental changes within organizations. Changes at all levels of analysis are seen as generally slow, steady, gradual, and continuous. Environments, however, are thought to change more slowly than organizations; organizations are thought to change more slowly than individual members; and the whole system is expected to change more slowly than an organization researcher's capacity for comprehending it. Organizations typically are viewed as loosely coupled aggregates whose separate components may be fine-tuned incrementally once weak constraints have been overcome. New forms of organizations are thought to evolve incrementally in response to new environmental conditions. Environmental discontinuities, according to some disciples of the first-order paradigm, are mere figments of observers' imaginations. Lenz and Engledow (1986: 343), for instance, argue that environments actually change continuously, but observers' cognitive limits lead them to *experience* the

Table 3.3. First- and Second-Order Change Paradigms

Assumptions	First-Order Paradigm	Second-Order Paradigm
Equilibrium	Quasi-stationary equilibrium	Punctuated equilibrium
Primary mode of change	Incremental change	Quantum change
Temporal distribution of change	Continuous progression	Episodic bursts
Rates of change across levels	Slower at higher levels of analysis	Faster at level of punctuation
Social system cohesion and constraint	Amalgam of weakly constrained components	Configuration of strongly constrained components
Origin of new organizational forms	Adaptation and/or selection	Speciation

changes as discontinuities. They speculate that "what executives reference as new competitive realities are probably new meanings assigned to continuous adjustments."

These first-order notions reinforce each other in subtle but powerful ways, and they fit Beyer's (1981: 166) definition of an ideology—"relatively coherent sets of beliefs that bind some people together and explain their worlds to them in terms of cause and effect relations." Granted, organizational researchers do acknowledge cases where first-order change assumptions are violated. But researchers typically discount such cases, portraying them as unrepresentative settings, outlying organizations, or noisy data containing unexplained variance. The ideological status of the first-order paradigm may explain the ease with which exceptions to first-order change have been brushed aside.

The second-order paradigm in the right-hand column of Table 3.3 represents a different set of assumptions, ones that have entered the organization literature more recently. Those who embrace it expect alternation between disequilibrium and equilibrium, with quantum change punctuating periods of stability. Change is seen as highly episodic, largely because organizations are viewed as configurations of tightly coupled components. These linkages are pliable up to a point, but if stretched beyond that point, they actively prevent change. Adherents to the second-order paradigm expect substantially more organizational change to occur through rapid transformations between comparatively stable states than through incremental transitions within those states. One result is that major transformations in organizational structure are expected to occur rapidly without a smooth series of intermediate stages. Another is that new organizational forms will emerge in rapid, episodic speciation events. The second-order paradigm ascribes no stable hierarchical ordering to rates of change. Since quantum changes can occur at multiple levels in social systems (Gersick, 1991), changes unfolding within a particular individual, department, organization, or industry may temporarily outstrip rates of change at all other levels. As we discovered in our study, quantum changes in industry structure can outrun organization researchers' efforts to understand them.

Within the second-order paradigm, organizational metamorphoses and industry revolutions are not regarded as mental events, outliers, or aberrations. Rather, they become natural by-products of routine processes. Stresses accumulate covertly during stable periods of first-order change, and they overturn the existing order when punctuated by second-order change. Extended periods of disequilibrium are likely to follow, sharply limiting the value of static analysis.

Multilevel Change

Our research underscores the multilevel nature of change processes. The study's initial design took the organization as its principal unit of analysis, but discontinuous changes led us to add two more inclusive units—the industry and the interorganizational network. At each of these levels, we observed discrete structures changing according to their own dynamics. At the organization level, top management teams formulated strategies intended to align hospitals with industry conditions. At the industry level, boundaries shifted and were breached as rivalry intensified. At the interorganizational level, "competitors" were drawn into networks of symbiotic relations that overlaid competitive relationships with collaborative and collusive ones.

Although change processes at these different levels were distinct, our historical analysis (Phase 2), our time-series analysis (Phase 3), and our qualitative analyses (Phase 4) all suggest that events on one level strongly influenced events on other levels.

An implication is that industries' structures cannot be adequately described by aggregating attributes of individual organizations, and that organizations' actions cannot be inferred or understood solely through analyses of industry-level data. However, the temporally lagged and idiosyncratic character of these cross-level relationships makes them hard to discern unless longitudinal research designs are adopted. Our experience highlights the limitations of studying environmental change and organizational adaptation using survey methods in multi-industry samples. However, studying change at multiple levels over time may require a second-order change in organizational research methods, which Pettigrew (1987: 655) describes as "ahistorical, aprocessual, and acontextual in character."

Most theories of change assume implicitly that organizational boundaries are distinct and remain intact throughout change processes. In times of revolutionary change, however, boundaries between organizations and their environments may become porous. In Kaufman's (1975) terms, organizational surfaces etherealize, permitting fluid exchange between organizations' interiors and their environments. In the aftermath of revolution, boundaries congeal, reducing exchange and increasing organizations' insularity. Moving up one level of analysis, our observations suggest that boundaries separating industries or populations of organizations also become permeable and mobile during periods of revolutionary change.

Our analyses indicate that organizations do not respond to their environments as independent, isolated actors. The hospitals we studied took collective action, and in so doing they shaped their future environments. Their collective interpretations and actions in a confusing milieu created the conditions they subsequently encountered. Intraindustry linkages superimposed cooperative relationships on competitive relationships and ushered in entirely new strategic options. Interindustry linkages joined diverse organizations in symbiotic relationships that helped lower and relocate industry boundaries. As resources grew scarcer, networks turned into social enclaves, and the collective action of members depleted resources available for nonmembers. Organizations are entangled in an ecology in which one competitor's actions help construct another competitor's environment. But since organizations are able to influence the context that influences them, they can play an active role in their own development.

Time-Dependent Change

Our research directs attention to the temporal ebb and flow of change processes across levels of analysis. The competitive and institutional pressures that environments impose vary over time, defining and altering niches for organizational populations. Our findings suggest that these pressures do not impinge on organizations continuously or shape them gradually. Tushman and Romanelli (1985) have argued that leaders have their most profound effects on organizations during major reorientations. Our study extends this line of argument to other potential influences on organizations at other levels of analysis. Technological and social change, for instance, appeared to affect hospitals' functioning most intensely during periods of discontinuous change, but these changes impacted organizations indirectly, having their greatest influence at the industry level rather than at the organization level. If this observation generalizes, it may explain the inability of past research to demonstrate strong effects of technology, societal culture, and other exogenous conditions on organizational structure. We may have been searching for effects at the wrong level of analysis.

Implications for Research: Turning Parameters into Variables

As mentioned in the chapter's prologue, the research enterprise is traditionally partitioned into sequential stages: conceptualizing, designing, observing, analyzing, and reporting. During the conceptual and design stages, investigators are enjoined to make choices that remain in effect throughout the inquiry. They are directed, for instance, to spell out assumptions, identify theoretical models, select appropriate units and levels of analysis, specify independent and dependent variables, choose sampling frames, and so forth. During the subsequent stages of observation, analysis, and reporting, these choices become parameters. To change them on the fly could contaminate data or even be interpreted as scientific fraud. Stigma attached to "post hoc theorizing," "data mining," and "dust-bowl empiricism" are handed down across generations of researchers. In short, researchers are indoctrinated to think first, then act.

But as our study progressed, one research design parameter after another slipped the shackles of experimental control and started behaving like a variable. Efforts to keep the sample of organizations intact, for example, were beleaguered by mergers, acquisitions, exits, and CEO turnovers. Sample attrition would have resulted not only in lost data, but also in nonresponse bias if organizations or informants who dropped out differed in analytically important ways. Consequently, we worked hard at maintaining friendly relations with CEOs; and, when successions occurred, we worked doubly hard to "re-enter" by building rapport with the new CEO (who had no stake in the research and suspected, no doubt, that our study might be part of the mess he or she had been hired to clean up). Despite considerable effort, the study's organizations and informants varied over time in ways that introduced unknown biases. The lesson is that samples in longitudinal research always present a moving target. One implication is that researchers should treat organizations' beginnings, endings, alliances, amalgamations, and boundaries as variables rather than as parameters.

Other research principles were violated in our study as well. Using different theories to explain the same phenomenon occurring at different times was one transgression. In a sense, theoretical models took on the role of dependent variables in our study: "Are the relationships observed between Variable X and Variable Y during Wave 1 best explained by Theory A, Theory B, or Theory C? Which theory offers the best explanation during Waves 2, 3, and 4?" Another infraction arose from our practice of occasionally changing the operationalization of the variable "organizational performance" as industry restructuring altered the meaning of high performance. In effect, the question "What's your dependent variable?" became an *empirical* question, not a theoretical one. Moreover, we conceptualized the same fundamental processes at different levels of analysis over the course of the study. The principal locus of strategy formation, for instance, shifted between Wave 1 and Wave 4 from individual organizations, to expanding interorganizational networks, and finally up to the industry level, as discontinuous change made organization-level strategic planning pointless.

Much like our CEO informants, we found that the burst of changes punctuating the industry equilibrium created paradoxes and violated assumptions of the schemata we used to frame and interpret our worlds as social scientists. Like our informants, we were forced to act first and think later as we tried to discover the implications of our actions and the meaning of the data they had elicited. Researchers typically justify code-of-conduct violations such as these by labeling the enterprise as "exploratory" and attempting to "build grounded theory." Yet even this avenue was closed to us, since, as Karl Weick remarked in his role as consultant to this research project, "you can't build grounded theory while the ground is moving."

In sum, in the setting we studied, conventional research design parameters turned out to be among the most important empirical variables. It is a truism that you can only get answers to the questions you are asking. Perhaps questions about social systems in disequilibrium are not being asked simply because they violate current conceptions about rigorous methodology. Industries in flux make unappealing research settings. Like earthquake victims, researchers are inclined to run for cover, wait for the dust to settle, and then return cautiously to sift through the debris. But analyses of data collected at a single point in time can only lead to an account of stable structures.

It is conceivable that conventional research designs have camouflaged the fact that the most significant variation in organizations occurs over time rather than across organizations, and it stems from discontinuous changes that simultaneously affect entire populations or industries. If this conjecture is correct, and if the recent upsurge in discontinuous industry-level change persists, then organizational research could become increasingly irrelevant to organizational practice.

Implications for Managerial Practice: Change Isn't What It Used to Be

What are the practical implications of viewing change as a discontinuous, multilevel, time-dependent process? In certain respects, our study leads to clear managerial prescriptions.

Inculcate Shared Values

Shared values are intangible aspects of organizations that often escape notice. Members take them for granted, and outsiders seldom observe them. Yet members of the high-performing hospitals we studied share sets of explicit values about what their organizations are doing and why. Because shared values inspire commitment and elicit cooperation, they can take the place of elaborate organizational structures and formal control systems. During periods of first-order change, shared values function as internal gyroscopes to ensure self-control by members. During periods of second-order change, they supply reservoirs of good will that countenance unorthodox manoeuvres. Our research on hospitals' responses to a disruptive doctors' strike (Meyer, 1982) showed that those faring best had value systems that endorsed dispersed influence in decision making, frequent strategic changes, and responsiveness to environmental events. Such hospitals both anticipated the strike and used it as a stimulus for long-run improvement. But although values favoring responsiveness may help organizations adapt to transitory environmental jolts, adjusting to major discontinuities is likely to demand more vigorous action.

The Best Defense Is a Strong Offense

Performing effectively during tranquil periods of first-order change probably remains the best preparation for discontinuous periods of second-order change. Most industries will concurrently support different competitive strategies, so top managers have considerable latitude in conceiving a strategic configuration for their organization. Among the hospitals we studied, those having unique strategies mated with internally consistent organizational structures appeared not only to perform best while their environments were changing gradually but also to adjust to discontinuities with somewhat more aplomb. This advantage accrued both to consistently aligned defenders pursuing a low-cost strategy, and consistently aligned prospectors pursuing a differentiation strategy. It arose not from executing ingrained action programs, but from tapping accumulated stockpiles of slack resources. The lesson is that top managers should articulate clear strategies for their organizations, develop structures that support those strategies, inculcate harmonious values, and invest slack resources wisely.

But Don't Rest on Your Laurels

When industry-wide revolutions come, shared values, slack resources, and lucid strategies merely buy time for organizations. These characteristics produced past successes, but in the face of changed environments they promote rigidity and complacency. Hard-won gains create resistance to change, and coherent values make abandoning ingrained responses difficult. Indeed, these are sensible organizational responses in normal circumstances, for as our time-series analyses of strategic reorientations suggest, high-performing organizations undertake such changes at considerable risk. However, discontinuities are abnormal circumstances, and managers encountering them must invent ways to slip the bonds of tradition, precedence, and past practice. This is not to say that executives experiencing industry revolutions should always initiate strategic reorientations. The considerable costs and risks attendant to organizational metamorphoses are magnified by industry revolutions. Executives should first consider updating existing strategies to fit new demands of postrevolutionary environments. In some cases this may be accomplished through unilateral organizational adaptation, but, as suggested below, it more often will involve multilateral collective action.

Prepare for Paradoxical Pressures

The discontinuous industry-level change we studied placed paradoxical demands on organizations. When the dust settled, the restructured health care industry contained much stronger incentives for cost-effective delivery of health services. This aspect of the change clearly favored habitually efficient, cost-conscious defender hospitals. Unfortunately, many defenders lacked the prowess in environmental scanning and interpretation needed to envision a new strategy for cutting costs in the radically changed industry, as well as the capacity for restructuring swiftly to implement an up-to-date defender strategy. As a result, defenders' responses often were too little, too late. Ironically, many defenders languished, locked into obsolete approaches in pursuit of an increasingly valued objective.

On the other hand, the velocity and extent of the discontinuity called for rapid and bold responses. This aspect of the industry revolution clearly favored habitually innovative prospector hospitals. But although prospectors' extensive environmental surveillance mechanisms forewarned them and their entrepreneurial values encouraged bold responses, prospectors' lack of experience in efficient operations left them ill-equipped to implement cost-control policies. As a result, prospectors' responses often were well conceived and comprehensive, but lacking experience, skills, or values promoting cost effectiveness, their responses were unsuccessful. Prospectors rarely store slack in financial form, preferring to invest it in human resources and state-of-the-art technologies (Meyer, 1982). Consequently, although some prospectors progressed rapidly down the efficiency learning curve, their financial reserves were consumed faster.

Due to paradoxical demands of this sort, we believe that the most promising responses to discontinuous changes are those that combine disaggregation and collective action.

Disaggregate and Affiliate

Fixed costs reduce organizational flexibility. As resource scarcities mounted in the hospital industry, many executives in our sample retrenched to their core businesses by stripping away nonessential activities and divesting unrelated ventures. Although these actions were motivated by financial exigencies, in many cases they yielded unexpected gains in flexibility and human resources. The flexibility came from cutting fixed costs and contracting or venturing for services previously offered in-house. The human resources became available when divestment released what often turned out to be a hospital's highest caliber managers from their preoccupation with unrelated ventures.

However, realizing the full potential of divestiture and disaggregation seemed to require coupling these activities with collective action. As we have noted, this involved a variety of cooperative linkages with suppliers, insurers, entrepreneurs, and competitors. The most appropriate pattern of collective action seemed to depend on a hospital's prior competitive strategy. Prospector hospitals, for example, often took the lead in brokering regional networks. Their networks were usually built around the concept of a "continuum of care," defined as a system linking primary, acute, and post-acute health services with some financing mechanism. Defender hospitals, on the other hand, were more likely to serve as low-cost producer nodes in a network, with executive talent, contracting expertise, information systems, and other services supplied from elsewhere in the system.

Industries undergoing revolutionary change pose dilemmas for managers. Revolutions create entrepreneurial opportunities by redefining potential niches and opening ecological space for new strategies and structural forms. Nevertheless, discontinuous change is enigmatic and paradoxical for managers. How can one prepare for conditions that are by definition unforeseeable? The events triggering discontinuous changes can appear so inconsequential, and the onset can be so sudden, that managers are forced to act before they understand the consequences of acting. But even in the throes of revolutionary change, astute managers can recognize and seize the opportunity to revitalize their organizations and reshape their environments. In the final analysis, we cannot predict the future—we can only invent it.

NOTES

The CEOs of 30 hospitals each participated in four field interviews and completed three lengthy questionnaires for this study. We thank them for their cordiality, patience, and invaluable assistance. We also are indebted to Raymond Miles for his advice in research design; to Arie Lewin, Peter Monge, John Slocum, Andrew Van de Ven, and Karl Weick for consultation throughout the project; and to William Glick, George Huber, Reuben McDaniel, Steve Shortell, and Ray Zammuto for their constructive comments on earlier drafts.

1. As with any retrospective reconstruction, there is a risk that logic, order, and rationality will be attributed post hoc to haphazard events. To guard against such biasing, we used the database approach described in the appendix to this chapter to identify and verify the phases and activities shown in Figure 3.1.

2. This section draws on Alan D. Meyer, Geoffrey R. Brooks, and James B. Goes, "Environmental Jolts and Industry Revolutions: Organizational Responses to Discontinuous Change," *Strategic Management Journal,* 11 (Summer): 93–110. © 1990 by John Wiley & Sons, Ltd.

3. McKelvey (1982) notes that the locus of an organizational population's boundaries depends on both conceptual and empirical issues (e.g., the specific research question being addressed and the particular organizations under investigation). For the purposes of our general discussion, the terms *population* and *industry* are used interchangeably to refer to a relevant set of competing organizations.

4. Although the population-level analyses conducted by Hannan and Freeman have attracted the largest share of attention, it should be noted that the population is one of several possible levels in the ecological analysis of organizations. Carroll (1984) terms this larger domain *organizational ecology* and argues that it includes analyses conducted at a lower level focusing on developmental changes within individual organizations *(organizational demography),* as well as analyses conducted at a higher level focusing on interactions between multiple populations *(community ecology).*

5. "General Hospital" is a fictitious name given to one of the hospitals in our research sample. Certain characteristics have been disguised to protect informants' anonymity.

6. We thank Reuben McDaniel for suggesting this notion.

7. The characteristics of these two dimensions are briefly summarized in the appendix to this chapter. For a complete discussion of the characteristics and interpretations of the four strategic dimensions, see Goes (1989).

8. For example, advances in outpatient surgery lower barriers between acute care, primary care, and group medical practice; ultra-expensive diagnostic and treatment technologies, such as magnetic resonance imaging or mobile lithotripsy, encourage nonmedical entrepreneurs to enter medical services markets.

References

Aldrich H., and Whetten, D. A. 1981. Organization-sets, action-sets, and networks: making the most of simplicity. In Nystrom P., and Starbuck, W. H. (Eds.), *Handbook of organizational design* (pp. 385–408). New York: Oxford University Press.

Anderson, P., and Tushman, M. L. 1990. Technological discontinuities and dominant designs: a cyclical model of technological change. *Administrative Science Quarterly,* 35: 604–633.

Astley, W. G. 1985. The two ecologies: population and community perspectives on organizational evolution. *Administrative Science Quarterly,* 30: 224–241.

Astley, W. G., and Van de Ven, A. 1983. Central perspectives and debates in organization theory. *Administrative Science Quarterly,* 28: 245–273.

Barley, S. R., and Tolbert, P. S. 1988. Institutionalization as structuration: methods and analytic strategies for studying links between action and structure. Paper presented at the Conference on Longitudinal Field Research Methods for Studying Organizational Processes, Austin, TX.

Barney, J. B. 1986. Types of competition and the theory of strategy: toward an integrative framework. *Academy of Management Review,* 11: 791–800.

Bedeian, A. G., and Zammuto, R. F. 1991. *Organizations: theory and design.* Chicago: Dryden Press.

Beyer, J. M. 1981. Ideologies, values and decision making in organizations. In Nystrom, P. C., and Starbuck, W. H. (Eds.), *Handbook of organizational design* (pp. 166–202). New York: Oxford University Press.

Carroll, G. R. 1984. Organizational ecology. *American Review of Sociology,* 10: 71–93.

Chandler, A. D. 1990. *Scale and scope: the dynamics of industrial capitalism.* Cambridge, MA: Belknap Press.

Child, J. 1972. Organizational structure, environment, and performance: the role of strategic choice. *Sociology,* 6: 2–22.

Dess, G., and Davis, P. 1984. Porter's (1980) generic strategies as determinants of strategic group membership and organizational performance. *Academy of Management Journal,* 27: 467–488.

DiMaggio, P. J., and Powell, W. W. 1983. The iron cage revisited: institutional isomorphism and collective rationality in organizational fields. *American Sociological Review,* 48: 147–160.

Eisenhardt, K. M. 1989. Building theories from case study research. *Academy of Management Review,* 14: 532–550.

Emery, F. E., and Trist, E. L. 1965. The causal texture of organizational environments. *Human Relations,* 18: 21–32.

Galbraith, C., and Schendel, D. 1983. An empirical analysis of strategy types. *Strategic Management Journal,* 4: 153–173.

Gersick, C. 1991. Revolutionary change theories: a multilevel exploration of the punctuated equilibrium paradigm. *Academy of Management Review,* 16: 10–36.

Ginsberg, A. 1988. Measuring and modeling changes in strategy: theoretical foundations and empirical directions. *Strategic Management Journal,* 9: 559–575.

Goes, J. B. 1989. Strategic change and organizational performance: a longitudinal study of California hospitals. Ph. D. dissertation. Eugene: University of Oregon.

Gould, S. J., and Eldredge, N. 1977. Punctuated equilibria: the tempo and mode of evolution reconsidered. *Paleobiology,* 3: 115–151.

Greenwood, R., and Hinings, C. R. 1988. Organizational design types, tracks, and the dynamics of strategic change. *Organization Studies,* 9: 293–316.

Greiner, L. E. 1972. Evolution and revolution as organizations grow. *Harvard Business Review,* 50 (4): 37–46.

Hannan, M. T., and Freeman, J. 1977. The population ecology of organizations. *American Journal of Sociology,* 83: 929–964.

Hannan, M. T., and Freeman, J. 1984. Structural inertia and organizational change. *American Sociological Review,* 49: 149–164.

Hartigan, J. A. 1975. *Clustering algorithms.* New York: Wiley.

Hawley, A. 1950. *Human ecology: a theory of community structure.* New York: Ronald Press.

Kaufman, H. 1975. The natural history of organizations. *Administration and Society,* 7: 131–149.

Kimberly, J. R., and Miles, R. H. 1980. *The organization life cycle.* San Francisco: Jossey-Bass.

Lenz, R. T., and Engledow, J. L. 1986. Environmental analysis: the applicability of current theory. *Strategic Management Journal,* 7: 329–346.

Lindblom, C. E. 1959. The 'science' of muddling through. *Public Administration Review,* 19: 79–88.

March, J. G. 1981. Footnotes to organizational change. *Administrative Science Quarterly,* 26: 563–577.

McCann, J. E., and Selsky, J. 1984. Hyperturbulence and the emergence of type 5 environments. *Academy of Management Review,* 9: 460–470.

McKelvey, W. 1982. *Organizational systematics: taxonomy, evolution and classification.* Berkeley: University of California Press.

McKelvey W., and Aldrich, H. 1983. Populations, natural selection and applied organizational science. *Administrative Science Quarterly,* 28: 101–128.

Meyer, A. D. 1982. Adapting to environmental jolts. *Administrative Science Quarterly,* 27: 515–537.

Meyer, A. D. 1991. Visual data in organizational research. *Organization Science,* 2: 218–236.

Meyer, A. D., Brooks, G. R., and Goes, J. B. 1990. Environmental jolts and industry revolutions: organizational responses to discontinuous change. *Strategic Management Journal,* 11 (Summer): 93–110.

Meyer, A. D., and Starbuck, W. H. 1993. Interactions between politics and ideology in strategy formation. In Roberts, K. (Ed.), *New challenges to understanding organizations: high reliability organizations* (pp. 99–116). Beverly Hills, CA: McMillan.

Meyer, J. W., and Rowan, B. 1977. Institutionalized organizations: formal structure as myth and ceremony. *American Journal of Sociology,* 83: 340–363.

Miles, R. E., and Snow, C. C. 1978. *Organizational strategy, structure and process.* New York: McGraw-Hill.

Miles, R. E., and Snow, C. C. 1986. Organizations: new concepts for new forms. *California Management Review,* 28(3): 62–73.

Miller, D., and Friesen, P. H. 1984. *Organizations: a quantum view.* Englewood Cliffs, NJ: Prentice-Hall.

Perrow, C. 1965. Hospitals: technology, goals and structure. In March, J. (Ed.), *Handbook of organizations* (pp. 910–971). Chicago: Rand McNally.

Peters, T. J., and Waterman, R. H. 1982. *In search of excellence: lessons from America's best-run companies.* New York: Harper and Row.

Pettigrew, A. M. 1987. Context and action in the transformation of the firm. *Journal of Management Studies,* 24: 649–670.

Pfeffer J. and Salancik G. R. 1978. *The external control of organizations.* New York: Harper and Row.

Schumpeter, J. A. 1950. *Capitalism, socialism and democracy.* New York: Harper and Row.

Scott, W. R. 1987. *Organizations: rational, natural and open systems,* 2nd ed. Englewood Cliffs, NJ: Prentice-Hall.

Shortell, S. M., Morrison, E. M., and Friedman, B. 1990. *Strategic choices for America's hospitals.* San Francisco: Jossey-Bass.

Smith, K. G., and Grimm, C. M. 1987. Environmental variation, strategic change and firm performance. *Strategic Management Journal,* 8: 363–376.

Starbuck, W. H. 1983. Organizations as action generators. *American Sociological Review,* 48: 91–102.

Thompson, J. D. 1967. *Organizations in action: social science bases of administrative theory.* New York: McGraw-Hill.

Tushman, M. L., and Romanelli, E. 1985. Organizational evolution: a metamorphosis model of convergence and reorientation. In Cummings, L. L., and Staw, B. M. (Eds.), *Research in organizational behavior,* Vol. 7 (pp. 171–222). Greenwich, CT: JAI Press.

Van de Ven, A., and Garud, R. 1987. A framework for understanding the emergence of new industries. In Rosenbloom, R., and Burgelman, R. (Eds.), *Research on technological innovation, management and policy,* Vol. 4 (pp. 195–225). Greenwich, CT: JAI Press.

Venkatraman, N., and Ramanujam, V. 1986. Measurement of business performance in strategy research: a comparison of approaches. *Academy of Management Review,* 11: 801–814.

Watzlawick, P., Weakland J. H., and Fisch, R. 1974. *Change: principles of problem formation and problem resolution.* New York: Norton.

Weick, K. E. 1979. *The social psychology of organizing.* Reading, MA: Addison-Wesley.

Zajac, E. J., and Shortell S. M. 1989. Changing generic strategies: likelihood, direction, and performance implications. *Strategic Management Journal,* 10: 413–430.

Zucker, L. G. 1987. Institutional theories of organizations. *Annual Review of Sociology,* 13: 443–464.

APPENDIX: DATA COLLECTION AND ANALYSIS METHODS

Retrospective Overview: Using Historical Methods

A data-based approach was used to reconstruct the research chronology and reduce self-serving biases. First, all available artifacts produced by the research were assembled. These included proposals, progress reports to the funding agency, pages from research notebooks, agenda of research team meetings, memos and letters exchanged by team members, electronic mail messages, methodological notes, raw data from interviews, handwritten field notes, hundreds of newspaper articles provided by a clipping service, working papers, and journal submissions. These documents were sorted into three categories—conceptual frameworks, research methods, and empirical findings. Documents were arranged in chronological order. Content analyses of these data were used in constructing the timeline in Figure 3.1 and in writing up the study's four phases.

Phase 1: Adapting Toward Equilibrium

Quasi-Experimental Research Design

Of the 55 medical-surgical hospitals in the four counties contiguous to San Francisco Bay, 40 were selected randomly and their CEOs' participation was solicited; 30 agreed to participate. Health care experts were impaneled to identify important environmental changes as these occurred over the course of the study.

Data were collected using multiple methods, with observations scheduled as shown in Figure 3A.1. During Wave 1, data on organizational antecedents (strategy, structure, ideology, and slack) were collected, as were measures of past performance and control variables. In Wave 2, hospitals' responses to subsequent environmental changes (the experimental treatments identified by the expert panel) were to be measured and performance was to be assessed. In Waves 3 and 4, responses and performances would again be measured. Organizational strategy, structure, ideology, and

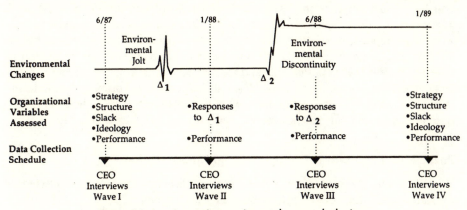

Figure 3A.1. A quasi-experimental research design.

105

slack were to be measured in Wave 4. However, when discontinuous industry-wide change invalidated this research design, it was abandoned.

Field Interview Methods

Interview procedures were as follows. During each three-week data-collection wave, structured interviews were conducted with CEOs about changes in organization design, strategy, environment, and performance. Most interviews were face-to-face in the CEOs' offices (55 percent); others were conducted via telephone conference calls (45 percent). Two researchers were present at each interview. Interviews were transcribed as near verbatim as possible, and transcripts were cross-checked. Over 1,500 pages of transcripts were produced.

Mapping Evolving Environments

Techniques for collecting "visual data" were developed to tap CEOs' capacities for making sense of discontinuous changes. This technique is useful when informants possess more complex cognitive maps than they can verbalize (Meyer, 1991). A generic diagram of the industry environment was constructed to show both the traditional domain of medical-surgical hospitals and adjacent domains offering new sources of competitive threats and opportunities. Three sectors were represented: (1) *providers,* the set of hospitals competing to supply acute care in the local market, (2) *insurance plans,* the set of patient groups amalgamated by some form of insurance plan, and (3) *diversifications,* the set of pre and post acute-care products and services into which hospitals potentially could diversify. Figure 3A.2 shows the visual instrument used to allow CEOs to map their hospitals' positions in the industry. The three sectors were depicted as planes floating in three-dimensional space, with different icons representing elements within each sector. Part (a) of the figure shows the generic map as presented to all CEOs; parts (b) and (c) show how this generic map was revised to show the unique positions described by two CEOs during Wave 1 interviews. Shifts in each hospital's position in the industry over time were charted by asking CEOs to update their latest map during Waves 2, 3, and 4.

Phase 2: Industries in Disequilibrium

Our historical analysis of the California hospital industry in the 1960s, 1970s, and 1980s drew on three types of data: (1) archival data from published sources, such as journalistic reports, newsletters of industry trade associations, and reports compiled by state and local governments; (2) time-series data obtained from the California Office of Statewide Health Planning and Development, the American Hospital Association, and the Northern California Hospital Council; (3) two primary data sets containing transcripts of structured interviews with industry experts and hospital CEOs, questionnaires, and naturalistic observations (Meyer, 1982; Meyer et al., 1990).

Phase 3: Metamorphosis Through Strategic Reorientation

We obtained highly detailed time series data on medical-surgical hospitals collected by the state of California. Covering a period of 11 years (calendar years 1976–1987), these data were uniquely suited to our Phase 3 objectives.

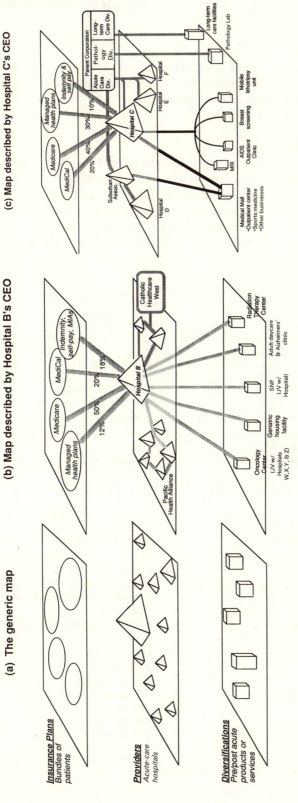

Figure 3A.2. Computer-generated maps of industry environments. *Source:* From "Visual Data in Organizational Research" by Alan D. Meyer. *Organization Science*, Vol. 2, Number 2, May 1991. Copyright © 1991 The Institute of Management Sciences, 290 Westminster Street, Providence, RI 02903. Reprinted by permission.

107

Sample

The sample consisted of all acute-care general surgical hospitals in the state of California, excluding those administered by the Kaiser Foundation. Kaiser hospitals were omitted due to incomplete data at the organization level. The sample size ranged from 443 to 457 hospitals over the study period.

Variables

Table 3A.1 lists variables used to tap three dimensions of organizational strategy: product/market domain, competitive methods, and organizational resources. Variables were selected based on widespread use in the industry and prior research, and for their demonstrated ability to discriminate among strategic configurations. Performance was conceptualized in two ways. The first reflected a hospital's performance relative to peer organizations (cross-sectionally), and the second reflected changes in

Table 3A.1. Strategy and Performance Variables

Dimension	Variable	Operational Definition
Product/market domain	Service diversity (SERVDIFF)	Scope of medical services provided
	Service concentration (SERVCON)	Average depth of medical services
	Service volume (VOLUME)	Gross patient revenues/bed
	Market demographics (MCARINT/MCALINT)	Ratio of medicare/mediCal patient revenues to gross patient revenues
Competitive methods	Advertising/promotion (ADSALES)	Advertising/gross patient revenues
	Marketing innovation (OUTPMIX)	Outpatient revenues/gross patient revenues
	Efficiency focus (EFFIC)	General services expenditures/gross patient revenues
	Research/development (RESEARCH)	Research expenditures/gross patient revenues
	Service innovation (NEWSERV)	Annual development of new services
Organizational resources	Size (LOGBEDS)	Log of acute care beds
	Staff diversity (STAFFDIV)	Number of different medical specialties
	Education/training (EDUCATE)	Education expenditures/gross patient revenues
	Administrative ratio (ADMRATIO)	Administrative payroll/total payroll
Performance	Profitability	Operating margin
		Profit margin
		Return on assets
	Efficiency	Average daily occupancy
		Fixed assets per patient day
		Average length of stay
	Growth	Annual growth in licensed beds
		Annual growth in patient days
		Annual growth in net revenues

performance within the focal organization over time (longitudinally). Based on prior research (Dess and Davis, 1984; Venkatraman and Ramanujam, 1986; Smith and Grimm, 1987), we used three operationalizations: profitability, efficiency, and growth. Table 3A.1 lists the different performance indicators used: relative profitability, relative efficiency, and relative growth, along with change in profitability, change in efficiency, and change in growth. Three lags were computed for each performance indicator.

Measuring Strategic Reorientations

We used a two-step method for identifying strategic configurations and tracking changes between them. First, strategy measures were factor-analyzed following Galbraith and Schendel (1983) and Dess and Davis (1984). Eleven common factor analyses (one for each data year) were conducted, and a four-factor solution was determined to be superior across all 11 years. This yielded a set of four strategic dimensions (factors) that explained the greatest variance among hospitals in the sample. Factor selection and identification were based on prior theoretical expectations, overall interpretability, and various diagnostic statistics (see Table 3A.2 for a count of strategy variables loading on factors over time).

The second step used cluster analysis to generate strategic configurations. Organizations were clustered into groups on the basis of their relative emphasis on the four strategic dimensions, as indicated by factor scores. A series of k-means iterative cluster analyses (Hartigan, 1975) were conducted over the 11-year period, and a five-cluster solution was selected based on prior theoretical expectations, interpretability, and diagnostic statistics. Each organization was thereby classified into a single configuration (cluster) for each year. Miles and Snow's and Porter's strategy typologies were used as general templates for identifying and labeling strategic configurations. For a complete discussion of factor and cluster characteristics, interpretations, and procedures, see Goes (1989).

By definition, a move from one cluster to another over time represented a strategic reorientation. However, underlying strategies are unlikely to change on an annual basis (Miller and Friesen, 1984; Greenwood and Hinings, 1988). Consequently, a conservative approach was adopted: if a hospital was classified into one cluster for two or more years, and subsequently classified into a different cluster for two or more years, a strategic reorientation was coded for the year of transition between clusters. This mitigated the problem of an organization falling near the boundary separating two clusters and cycling back and forth. As a result of this coding scheme, no strategic changes could occur in data years 1, 2, or 11.

The unit of analysis was a strategic reorientation or, more precisely, an "opportunity" for a strategic reorientation. In any given data year each hospital had an opportunity to change or not change its strategic configuration. Over the entire study, therefore, the sum of potential strategic reorientations (i.e., the sum of opportunities) equalled the sum of opportunities in each year pooled across eight years of potential change.

Hypothesis Testing

Hypothesis 1 was tested using discriminant analyses to assess the extent to which prior performance (lagged 0, 1, 2, and 3 years) predicted hospitals' membership in reorien-

Table 3A.2. Count of Variables Loading on Four Strategy Dimensions over Time

No.	Factor Title	Variables Loading at $\geq .4$	Years[a]
1	"Integrated defense"	Service concentration	11
		Service volume	11
		Size	11
		Staff diversity	11
		Education/training	11
		Administrative ratio	(−) 11
		Research and development	7
		Service differentiation	3
		Marketing innovation	(−) 2
2	"Low margin defense"	Market demographics	(−) 11
		Marketing innovation	11
		Education/training	10
		Efficiency focus	5
		Service differentiation	1
3	"Service promotion"	Advertising/promotion	11
		Efficiency focus	7
		Research and development	5
		Service concentration	(−) 1
		Staff diversity	1
		Administrative ratio	1
4	"Service Differentiation"	Service innovation	10
		Service differentiation	9
		Service concentration	(−) 2
		Research and development	2
		Efficiency focus	1
		Staff diversity	1
		Education/training	1

[a]Number of years in which the variable exhibited a substantial loading ($\geq .4$) on the factor. Minus signs (−) signify negative loadings.

tation and nonreorientation groups. Hypotheses 2 and 3 were tested using single-factor ANOVA to assess performance differences (lagged 0–4 years out) between low and high performers that did or did not reorient their strategies. Hypotheses 4 and 5 were tested using frequency analyses, cross-tabulation analyses, and ANOVA.

Phase 4: Responding Collectively to Industry Revolution
Assessing Collective Action

In Wave 2, we expanded the research design to obtain data from regional network brokers and CEOs of affiliated hospitals. Open-ended interviews were conducted with representatives of seven networks during Waves 2–4. Questions about collective actions and their consequences were added to interviews with hospital CEOs. Data from questionnaires, archives, and documents were also obtained.

Identifying Temporal Changes

Upon leaving the field after each wave, we reviewed our notes, identified changes in CEOs' environmental "maps," met to discuss key issues and concerns voiced by informants, and created tabular displays showing common themes characterizing the sample at that time. Each display suggested an interpretation of the industry that differed from previous interpretations. To elaborate and verify these temporal differences, interview transcripts were content-analyzed according to the four analytical categories shown in Table 3.2.

4

Implications of Top Managers' Communication Choices for Strategic Decisions

RICHARD L. DAFT, KENNETH R. BETTENHAUSEN, and
BEVERLY B. TYLER

> A business man's judgment is no better than his information.
> Robert P. Lamont

> I attribute the little I know to my not having been ashamed to ask for
> information.   John Locke

EDITORS' SUMMARY

Organizations are, in many respects, information-processing systems. Organizations are also instruments that top managers use to carry out strategies that the managers believe will put their organizations at a competitive advantage. Managers and organizational scientists know these things, so it is surprising to find that their respective literatures contain no studies of the relationships between organizational strategies and organizational information systems.

Daft, Bettenhausen, and Tyler investigated these relationships in a multiyear, multiorganizational study. In this chapter they describe how they addressed, and answered, four key questions: (1) How do top managers in organizations learn about the external environment? (2) How do they combine this information with information from internal sources to formulate business strategy? (3) How do they disseminate information about new strategies to relevant parts of the organization? (4) Do these processes differ depending on whether the strategy was intended to establish cost leadership or to differentiate the company's products and/or services?

A key concept in the study was the nature of the communication media that the CEOs used to acquire information in order to formulate strategy and that they used to disseminate information in order to implement strategy. Among their results were the development of a detailed profile of the information-gathering media used in strategy formulation and of a similar profile concerning the media used in strategy implementation. Another interesting result was their finding that both of these media-use profiles were greatly affected by whether the organization's strategy was that of a cost leader or of a differentiator.

The authors of this chapter have a rich history in the study of both organizational communications and organizational strategy. Here, for the first time, they bring these two fields together and thereby generate some new and interesting insights. For example, based on their prior knowledge and on the specific findings reported in the chapter, they set forth clear lines of reasoning to argue that the richness of the media used to obtain information during strategy formulation actually influences the subsequent decision processes (and presumably the subsequent strategic decisions). Similarly, they convincingly argue that the richness of the media used to disseminate information during implementation affects key factors such as the actual content of the implementation-focused communications, how the organization's structure is altered to facilitate implementation, and the CEO's expectation for compliance.

The managerial implication of the fact that the organization's strategy is related to the nature of the information-acquiring media that top managers use to develop the strategy is that administrators and information system designers should account for an organization's strategy as they make system design choices. The implication of this chapter for organizational scientists is especially interesting. Many studies have indicated that those aspects of an organization's design that are related to production and distribution must vary according to the organization's strategy. The research reported here suggests strongly that organizational scientists should also investigate the broad range of possible relationships between those design aspects related to, on the one hand, information acquisition and communication media and, on the other, corporate strategy. ■

Item: The Limited, the largest fashion retail chain in the United States, transmits a color representation of a new runway fashion to Hong Kong within 60 minutes of a store order. Within 41 days, 10,000 dresses will be designed, produced, and delivered to store racks, long before the original runway designs are available. Next for The Limited is high-definition television, which will provide instantaneous three-dimensional images from which U.S. store managers will order dresses and Asian factories will produce them (Hochswender, 1990).

Item: Many corporations, including Federal Express, General Mills, Chaparral Steel, 3M, Johnsonville Foods, Exxon, and Aetna Life and Casualty Company, are implementing self-managed teams. These teams break down communication barriers between departments and between the organization and its customers. These teams represent a dramatic increase in the simplest form of communication: talk. A team of Rubbermaid designers, marketers, and engineers, for example, talked face-to-face about and thereby developed a portable car office. Exxon has hourly workers participate in teams that talk face-to-face with customers. At Johnsonville Foods, the CEO turned over to employees the decision of whether to accept a request to manufacture sausage under a private label. Organized in teams of five to 20, employees discussed whether they could accept the higher workload and determined how to do it profitably (Dumaine, 1990).

Item: Corporate managers are experiencing new efficiencies by adding electronic communications to traditional face-to-face communications. One day the CEO of Duracell browsed through his new executive information system. Drilling down for data he discovered a discrepancy between the performance of U.S. and overseas work forces. Calling up more data he discovered that too many salespeople in Germany were wasting time calling on small stores. The German sales staff was cut, thereby improving performance efficiency (Main, 1989).

Item: Military decision makers coordinating thousands of aircraft sorties daily over the Persian Gulf relied on banks of computers and unimaginable amounts of data. High above the ground each AWACS radar plane kept track of nearly 1,000 aircraft—most were friendly, some were hostile, some unknown. A battery of computers in each AWACS plane produced Nintendo-like visual images that the crew used to guide an allied fighter plane to attack an enemy target. The scale of the air campaign was the largest in history, and without the technology boost for communication and coordination, operations would have been chaotic (Rebello, 1991).

Item: Companies such as Digital Equipment and Hewlett-Packard are increasing their use of communication technology and face-to-face communications at the same time. Digital brings together employees for one or two weeks to get to know one another at the start of a new project. Then team members are disbursed to their locations around the world, connecting and communicating by electronic mail. Hewlett-Packard uses videoconferencing to connect worldwide employees electronically and face-to-face at the same time.

These events in organizations illustrate two trends with respect to communications in organizations. The first trend is that *an increasing volume of data is being processed within organizations,* in large part due to the greater use of fast, efficient communication technology. Thus more data are provided to decision makers for use in scanning, operational decision making, and strategic choices. The second trend is toward *more face-to-face discussion and employee participation.* More people are involved in organizational decisions and are connecting face-to-face with one another (Rose, 1990). In one sense these two trends seem contradictory, because using communication technology could mean less face-to-face communication, but the trends toward what might be called high-tech and high-touch communications are occurring simultaneously.

The purpose of this chapter is to discuss how organizations are designed and how managers communicate to make sense of an increasingly complex and dynamic world. As Huber and Glick described in Chapter 1 of this volume, organizations are being hit from all sides with change. This chapter specifically examines how managers interpret environmental changes and how they communicate about new strategic initiatives, and then how these communication requirements affect organizational design. Porter (1991), who has written widely on competitive strategy, believes that two frequent and major management mistakes are not formulating an explicit strategy and not communicating the strategy to employees. Poor communication about strategy deprives the organization of the fundamental unity of belief and action among employees. Poor data collection may result in the absence of timely strategy, and poor communication to employees about a strategy deprives them of a clear sense of the organization's aims and objectives.

Our discussion in this chapter unfolds in the following manner. In the first section we provide an overview of organizational communications, including recent findings about communication requirements and about manager selection of communication media. Then we report a specific study of top executives in 29 businesses in three Texas industries and how they gathered and disseminated information about 130 changes in their competitive business strategy. The findings from the study are then used to propose a model about how organizations can be designed to fit environmental uncertainty. The final section moves beyond the data to propose ideas about how the selection of communication media influences strategy formulation and strategy implementation.

OVERVIEW OF ORGANIZATIONAL AND MANAGERIAL COMMUNICATION

The organizational use of larger and larger volumes of information has historically been associated with changes in communication technology and organization design (Yates, 1989). The introduction of the telegraph put the pony express out of business, but it also enabled the geographical coordination (and hence the growth) of large railroads, the first giant commercial organizations in the United States. The invention of vertical files to replace pigeonhole files changed data storage and retrieval, also enabling organizations to grow larger and to adopt a functional form of structure. The telephone enabled the separation of headquarters and field divisions, laying the foundation for multidivisional structures. The telephone's communication capacity also enabled the design of skyscrapers within which to house large organizations. Computers have more recently enabled organizations to structure themselves into nationwide and worldwide branches, franchises, or subsidiaries. Now, something over 100 years later, the pony express is back in business, thanks to Frederick Smith and Federal Express. Overnight mail allows companies such as New York Life and Cigna to go where the people are, hiring people in Ireland to analyze medical claims from people in the United States, for instance. Management guru Tom Peters uses a fax machine and telephone to run his $8 million a year consulting business on the West Coast from his remote farm on the East Coast (Warfield, 1990). This network structure finds the best people worldwide to do a job, connecting them via satellite communications, fiber optics, and overnight mail.

Yet along with the development of communication innovations we see an increased emphasis on face-to-face communications. As described in the previous section, many companies are redesigning themselves into autonomous teams within which employees with different specialties may talk face-to-face. Senior managers are walking around to communicate individually with employees and are speaking directly with customers. These old-fashioned communications reinforce a trend toward participative corporate cultures, the empowerment of employees, and greater closeness between employer and employee and between supplier and customer. When a key strategic decision was addressed, such as whether and when to launch a ground attack in the Persian Gulf war, President George Bush bypassed formal technical reports. He talked on the telephone repeatedly with other heads of government and sent Secretary of Defense Richard Cheney and Chairman of the Joint Chiefs of Staff Colin Powell for a firsthand look and face-to-face talks with Gulf Commander Norman Schwarzkopf and others on the scene. Bush's decision to attack the Iraqi army in Kuwait was based on personal conversations and personal reports to him.

Both top manager and organizational communications are related to organization design and the external environment. We know from Mintzberg's (1973) research that managers spend 80 percent of their time communicating. Other research indicates that organizational design—such as hierarchy of authority, division of labor, and coordination mechanisms—reflects organizational needs for information from the environment (Galbraith, 1973; Daft and Lengel, 1984). Organizational designs for the future are expected to be even more heavily influenced by information requirements from the environment. Huber (1984) proposed that postindustrial society will be characterized by more and increasing amounts of available knowledge, more and increasing complexity, and more and increasing turbulence for organizations. To cope with the greater need for information, new computer-based technologies, such as microcomputers, word processors, teleconferencing, electronic mail, and manager-friendly software, will be utilized and will themselves affect key organization design variables (Huber, 1990).

Amount and Ambiguity of Information About the Environment

Organizations facing greater external turbulence and complexity face two problems with respect to internal information processing. The first problem is the greater volume of data that must be processed; the second problem is the ambiguity of information. Volume and ambiguity are two features of an organization's "information environment" (Huber and Daft, 1987) with which organizations cope through their internal structure, communication media—such as meetings, telephone, and memos—and communication technology.

High information volume is a consequence of large organizational size; a fast-changing environment; a complex, diverse environmental domain; and a large knowledge base. There is more for the organization and its managers to know, more information to integrate into decisions. The organization must stay informed on the activities of customers, competitors, the government, and technological developments. How do organizations solve the demands of increasing information volume? Huber (1984) proposed several solutions. The organization may design specialized sensor units and boundary spanning departments. The handling of external information can become a formalized part of the organization. The top management team can specialize their monitoring activities and make decisions based on the integration of joint information. Computing and communication technologies can be acquired, such as the Workbench system used at Domino's Pizza headquarters to access external databases (Warfield, 1990), the electronic mail and videoconferencing systems used at Hewlett-Packard, or the executive information system used at Duracell.

Information ambiguity is a different kind of problem. The notion of ambiguity grows from the work on equivocality by Weick (1979; Daft and Weick, 1984). Ambiguity means that information has multiple meanings. Organizational environments that are unpredictable and rapidly changing often provide managers a messy, unclear field of view. People or groups can reach very different, yet equally defensible conclusions after observing the same "objective" cues. Ambiguity cannot be resolved by gathering additional data because managers are not sure what questions to ask or what data to gather, or how to interpret either current or forthcoming data. Indeed, new data may be confusing and may even increase uncertainty. In a study of 25 organizational decisions, Mintzberg, Raisinghani, and Théorêt (1976) found that many managers operated under what we call ambiguity because almost no information was given or easily obtained. Managers had to grope around to define and figure things out for themselves.

Recent research suggests that the solution to ambiguity is almost the opposite of the organizational specialization and communication technology used to solve the problem of information volume. Ambiguity is resolved via debate, clarification, and discussion through which managers shape a reality on which they agree. Research suggests that in ill-defined situations, managers must first create a common understanding before they make decisions others will comprehend and accept (Trevino, Daft, and Lengel, 1990; White, 1986; Daft and Lengel, 1986). Managers may talk things over to create a common idea, interpretation, or framework that provides a meaning for the ambiguous situation. An example of this approach is the communication required to bring about a new business strategy. Since multiple interpretations of the competitive environment are available, debate and feedback among managers enable them to agree about the meaning of information so that a strategic direction can be established.

In ambiguous situations managers typically use media characterized as low technology and high touch—they hash things out face-to-face, building up a shared understanding based on previously shared assumptions and experiences. Precise data typically do not clarify ambiguity. For example, the recent research on the success of homogeneous top management teams (Hambrick, 1987) suggests they form a common frame of reference. The decisions by companies such as Exxon, Federal Express, and Johnsonville Foods to use self-managed teams for making decisions about everything from strategy to production illustrate how a common understanding is reached through face-to-face communication. As we will discuss later, face-to-face communication often is more valuable for handling ambiguity than are the hard data provided by information systems.

Model of Organizational Information Requirements

The dual demands of information amount and ambiguity are illustrated in Figure 4.1. Volume and ambiguity together influence the information requirements or load experienced by an organization. *Information load* is defined as the amount of time and resources allocated to processing information to interpret the environment.

Cell 1 represents a low-moderate load, because ambiguity is high but required information volume is low. This could be a small organization in a changing environment, such as a Missouri shoe manufacturer during the recent period of decreasing tariff protection and increasing international competition. The company may have reliable suppliers and retail outlets, but the impact of new competition is difficult to define. Managers rely on personal discussions with outsiders and with each other, and use their judgment and experience to interpret events. Decision processes that encour-

Volume of Information About Environment

	Low	High
High	**1.** <u>Low-Moderate Information Load</u> Occasional ambiguous events; managers develop common grammar, gather opinions, define questions and actions.	**2.** <u>High Information Load</u> Rapid changes and ambiguous events; constant manager communications to gather opinions and analyze data to establish common grammer and answer explicit questions.
Low	**3.** <u>Low Information Load</u> Relatively clear situation; managers gather routine objective data, analyze data, answer objective questions.	**4.** <u>High-Moderate Information Load</u> Rapid changes, extensive data gathering and analysis; managers use scanning systems, and high technology to answer explicit questions.

Ambiguity of Information About Environment

Figure 4.1. Relationships between environmental characteristics and organizational information processing requirements.

age the exchange of opinions—such as devil's advocacy, dialectical inquiry, and the Nominal Group Technique—would all be suitable ways to formalize information exchange that would define a response to the environment (Schweiger, Sandberg, and Rechner, 1989). Or consider a company like ATI Medical Inc., which subjected its 305 employees to a "no-memo" policy, thereby facilitating continuous discussion and creativity for adapting to abrupt and ill-defined changes in the medical environment ("Enforcing a No-Memo Policy," 1988).

Cell 4 represents a high-moderate information load. An organization in this cell experiences a demand for high information volume, but the information is relatively clear. The organization can define those sectors and elements about which data are needed and can establish sensor units and communication technology to provide the necessary data. Managers know what questions to ask and the source of external data. For example, if the question pertains to the reaction of customers to certain product colors or package labels, a special study by a marketing firm may provide the answer. If inventory outages cause customer alienation, data about customer ordering patterns may provide an algorithm for inventory management. The cell 4 environment is where organizations can make the best use of computing and communications technologies. A large organization, for example, may be located in several countries, and sophisticated technology would enable it to process the enormous volume of data needed to keep abreast of key events in each locale.

Cell 2 represents the highest information load. Both ambiguity and volume of data are high. Personal discussion is needed to interpret fuzzy events and to resolve differences among managers. Other issues are amenable to the gathering of new data to answer specific questions. Information processing thus is a combination of both personal discussion and data from formal, technological channels. Special sensor units may be established to scan databases, but senior managers may be involved in an endless series of meetings and personal visits with customers or events in the environment. The cell 2 situation would be characterized by rapid change and unpredictable shocks, such as would occur during times of rapid technological development within emerging industries or during the launching of new products. Cell 2 was epitomized by companies affected by the Persian Gulf war, such as airlines (fuel costs) and military supply firms. Industries experiencing major change during the 1980s include hospitals, savings and loan institutions, and computer firms.

Cell 3 represents low information load because ambiguity and volume both are low. New problems do not arise often. Issues are clear enough that intense discussion is not needed to resolve different interpretations. Routine schedules, reports, and information systems provide the information base needed by managers. In today's world, organizations probably do not experience this kind of calm for very long. At one time rural banks, manufacturing plants, and retail stores fitted in this quadrant because they essentially used a routine technology in a stable environment.

Figure 4.1 illustrates that organizations must interpret their environments and that environments place different information demands on organizations. Depending on its environment, an organization may need to reduce ambiguity via face-to-face discussions or process a large amount of precise data, or both. In order to keep an organization in touch with the environment, it must be designed to ensure that decision makers receive information in an amount and form that facilitates effective interpretation and decision making.

Now let's turn to our final conceptual building block, media richness, and discuss how rich and lean communication media vary in their capacity to reduce ambiguity and to provide data to managers. These ideas form a basis for our study of how top managers gather information to formulate strategic initiatives, and of how managers communicate a new strategy to audiences both inside and outside their company.

Role of Media Richness

Recent research on information processing internal to organizations (Daft and Lengel, 1984, 1986; Daft, Lengel, and Trevino, 1987) distinguished between data and information and between media that convey information high or low in richness. *Information* is that which alters understanding. *Data* are symbols; they are the words, letters, and numbers that are sent or received. But data do not become information unless people use them to improve their understanding. Consider the following line of data printed in a recent *Wall Street Journal:*

38.5 25 McDonalds MCD .34 1.2 14 6200 32 29.5 29.5 -2

For many people this mishmash of numbers and letters is just data; it conveys no information, alters no understanding. Stockbrokers, however, recognize at a glance that it was a bad day for the McDonald's Corporation as well as for McDonald's stockholders.

Information richness pertains to the information-carrying capacity of data. Some data, like numbers and specialized jargon, have very precise meaning. Before these data can become information, both the sender and the receiver of the data must have learned or established common definitions. Other data, like a picture, a wink, or a shrug, are less precise but very meaningful. With a single glance a picture can convey more information than the proverbial thousand words.

Communication media differ in the richness of the information they deliver. A *communication medium* is the channel through which data are transmitted. Daft and Lengel (1984) and Daft and Huber (1987; Huber and Daft, 1987) propose that various media used in organizations can be organized into a richness hierarchy based on four features: (1) the opportunity for timely feedback; (2) the ability to convey multiple cues; (3) the ability to tailor messages to personal circumstances; and (4) the power to convey ambiguous or subjective material, which can be called language variety. Traditional information media—like face-to-face conversations, telephone calls, letters and statistical reports—and newer, computer-mediated electronic media—like teleconferencing and electronic mail—may be high on some features and low on others.

Based on previous research, communication media can be roughly organized into a richness continuum according to the number of features each processes (Daft and Lengel, 1986). Traditionally, face-to-face discussion is considered the richest medium because it enables immediate feedback and conveys cues associated with sociability, warmth, sensitivity, body language, and facial expression. At the other extreme, a written, unaddressed document such as a standard report or computer printout would be a lean medium, because there is no feedback and because cues are limited to numbers or words on paper. Media such as telephone, voice mail, and letters would rank in between these two extremes on the richness scale.

With respect to our earlier discussion of information load in organizations, *rich media* are characterized by high touch and qualitative data, and they are best for resolving ambiguity. *Lean media* are amenable to technology-based, high-volume data exchanges and are best for conveying quantitative data with precision and accuracy to large audiences.

The value of the richness continuum is that it brings together a diverse set of concepts about how managers process information (Fulk and Boyd, 1991). For example, considerable research has examined which media decision makers use to obtain information. Keegan (1974) examined human versus documentary sources; Aguilar (1967) focused on personal versus impersonal sources; O'Reilly (1982) looked at such things as when decision makers used files, formal reports, or group discussions. Short, Williams, and Christie (1976) evaluated media with respect to the extent to which users experience others as being psychologically present in the communication. The richness concept provides a theoretical basis for these distinctions and links them in a way that prescribes their differential use depending on the amount of data required or the ambiguity present in a situation.

Contextual and Symbolic Influences on Media Choice

Media communication choices are shaped by more than richness. The general pattern of research findings supports the idea that media are chosen according to how their information-carrying capacity fits the richness of the message (Rice and Shook, 1990). Perhaps more important, new research has shown that factors other than medium capacity influence selection among communication media. For example, Steinfield and Fulk (1986) found that geographical distance and time pressure significantly influenced media choice. Managers under time pressure were more likely to use the telephone regardless of message ambiguity. In addition, managers geographically distant tended to use electronic mail, again despite message ambiguity. With respect to new communication technologies, Thorn and Connolly (1987) proposed that access to the technology is important. Steinfield (1986) noted that without ready access to an electronic mail system, a manager's ability to use the system is out of the question. Moreover, a critical mass of users has to be established for an interactive medium like electronic mail to be chosen. Something as simple as office location can also affect media choice. Trevino, Lengel, and Daft (1987) found that managers sometimes chose face-to-face communication when the intended receiver was close by, such as in the next office, because a memo signaled too much formality and impersonality.

The medium of communication may also be selected for symbolic meaning that transcends the explicit message. In this way the medium itself becomes a message (Trevino et al., 1987). Consider how putting a message in writing may signal commitment to an idea, or how putting a sanction in writing signals officialness and legitimacy. A savvy manager may choose to meet face-to-face with an employee simply to show openness to a subordinate's ideas or to signal that the subordinate is part of the team. Feldman and March (1981) argued that managerial communication behavior represents ritualistic responses to the need to appear competent, intelligent, legitimate, and rational. And symbolic value of a medium may depend on organizational culture. One manager who congratulates a subordinate on 25 years of service with an electronic mail message may signal coldness and lack of concern. But in a computer user network, choosing to send a personal message via computer may signal that one is a member of the particular group (Fulk, Steinfeld, Schmitz, and Power, 1987). Thus symbolic reasons for using media are socially defined and may be independent of the information-carrying capacity of the medium.

The choice of a communication medium by senior executives to formulate or implement strategy thus may be the result of several factors. To explore the relationship between media choice and corporate strategy, top managers in several companies were interviewed to begin to define the strategy making/communication media relationship.

STUDY OF COMMUNICATION MEDIA USED FOR STRATEGIC DECISIONS

Nowhere is the issue of communication media choices potentially more important to the function of management than in the development of competitive business-level strategy. In developing strategy, executives must constantly scan not only their external business environment but also internal activities of the firm to identify potential threats or opportunities. Central to this formulation of strategy is the generation of a shared understanding of what the facts are and what they mean. Moreover, once a strategy is selected, top managers must communicate it internally so employees know the direction they are headed and why. The previous discussion of media richness theory provides a framework for understanding the amount and kind of information needed to formulate and implement competitive business strategy.

Our study is about how top manager communications are associated with strategic initiatives. Competitive strategy includes the actions a business takes to compete in the marketplace and position itself among its competitors. Porter's (1980, 1985) typology of competitive strategies seems particularly useful for classifying firms' strategic initiatives in a way that may correspond to the use of communication media. Two generic strategies identified by Porter are cost leadership and differentiation. *Cost leadership* emphasizes producing a standardized product at a very low per-unit cost for price-sensitive buyers. *Differentiation,* as a competitive strategy, refers to creating something that is unique for buyers who are relatively price-insensitive. Cost leadership and differentiation strategies are conceptually distinct, but White (1986) and Calori and Ardisson (1988) found that strategies were difficult to classify as "exclusively" cost leadership or differentiation. Rather, as Hill (1988) and Jones and Butler (1988) argued, differences between strategies are a matter of degree. Still, it is useful to consider the implications of cost leadership and differentiation as "pure types" while recognizing that these distinctions might blur when real strategic initiatives are considered.

Porter (1980) suggested that the cost-competitive strategy is usually implemented and tends to be most appropriate in industries that are relatively stable and predictable. Because competition based on price is common and familiar to firms attempting to implement a cost-leadership strategy, top management is likely to develop a systematic, preplanned response to actions taken by suppliers or competitors. With an adequate grasp of the situation, executives can formulate questions and seek objective answers or apply decision rules derived from past experience. Information gathering in this relatively stable environment is likely to answer specific strategic questions rather than to resolve persistent ambiguity. Information sources low in richness—such as standard operating reports, industry-wide databases, and quantitative studies—can quickly and efficiently provide information for formulating strategies that are intended primarily to establish or maintain cost-leadership positions.

On the other hand, a differentiation strategy is usually implemented and is deemed more appropriate in industries characterized by rapid technological change and instability. These environmental conditions generate ambiguity for top managers which, as we noted earlier, is reduced using media that allow debate, exchange of views, clarification, and creation of a shared interpretation. Rich media such as face-to-face discussions and meetings and telephone conversations allow executives to create meaning and converge on a common understanding. While information also may be obtained through lean media, the chances are it will not resolve the ambiguity inherent in rapidly changing environments.

To build on the ideas discussed so far in this chapter, let us now turn to the actual study of how top managers used communication media to send and receive internal and external information for strategy formulation and strategy implementation.

The Study

To learn how managers used information media to formulate and implement competitive strategy decisions, we conducted structured interviews at six-month intervals with top executives who were responsible for strategy in 29 Texas firms. Each executive identified the most important strategic initiatives they had implemented between January 1986 and June 1989. Presidents of eight Texas banks reported 42 initiatives; head administrators of six Texas hospitals presented 29 initiatives; and policy making executives of 15 Texas-based manufacturers described 59 initiatives. Executives were asked to indicate on a five-point scale the extent that each identified strategic initiative was (1) intended to reduce the firm's production/operating costs or capital costs and (2) intended to make the product/service different from competitors. These two scales indicated the extent to which the initiative was intended to be a low cost-leadership strategy (shortened throughout to "low cost strategy") or a differentiation strategy.

During the interview, the executives also indicated the extent to which they used each of 18 information-acquisition media in developing and choosing the strategic initiative. They were also asked about 22 common information-sending media for communicating the strategy to others for implementation. Both the information-acquiring and -sending media included internal and external channels as well as those high and low in media richness.

Table 4.1 shows examples of cost-leadership and differentiation strategic initiatives adopted by firms in the sample. A textile mill decided to cut costs and increase capacity by replacing existing weaving equipment with new automated technology. Two or three workers then could oversee an entire floor of machines. This strategy was intended strictly to lower cost and improve efficiency rather than to produce a differentiated product. A manufacturer of building products, windows, and storm doors made the decision to close a manufacturing plant in Denver and to close two company-owned warehouses. The manufacturing plant had not been profitable, hence its closure would reduce costs. Independent distributors were willing to maintain sufficient inventory to make the company's warehouse unnecessary.

Two differentiation strategies reported in urban hospitals were the adoption of a

Table 4.1. Examples of Strategies

Industry	
Cost leadership	
Manufacturer	Improve automation
	Close plant
	Close warehouses
	Store inventory with distributors
Bank A	Consolidate operations
	Reduce staff
	Merge with another bank
Differentiation	
Urban hospital	Use a tactical helicopter unit
	Add the "fine hotel" concept
Bank B	Add commercial services
	Offer a credit card

tactical helicopter unit and a "fine hotel" concept. The helicopter unit would bring serious cases to the hospital from 30 satellite hospitals, thereby providing fast service for acute-care patients, differentiating this hospital from others. The "fine hotel" concept meant that patients were met at the door by staff dressed like hotel doormen. Valet parking was available. Waiting rooms and recovery rooms were remodeled to resemble the plush lobbies and guest rooms of a fine hotel. This strategic initiative differentiated the hospital from its counterparts because elective surgery would more closely resemble a vacation or comfortable retreat than an unpleasant stay in an antiseptic hospital.

Two strategies used by banks in the sample to lower costs were to consolidate their own branch operations and to merge with another bank. One bank consolidated its own operations into fewer units, enabling cost savings by eliminating duplicate staff. The same tasks could be performed by fewer people. The decision by one bank to merge with another bank was similar in intent, enabling a reduction in cost while increasing market share. By contrast, a strategic initiative to add commercial services—such as keeping bank tellers available on Saturday and until 10:00 p.m. on weeknights—was solely for the purpose of differentiating its hours of service from competitors. The same was true of offering a credit card, which meant customers could have credit card service locally rather than through larger regional banks.

The communication media used by executives to formulate and implement these strategic initiatives were expected to differ substantially based on whether the purpose of the strategy was cost reduction or product differentiation. The patterns of media use were analyzed in our study of 29 Texas firms. Let us turn now to the results of the study.

Information-Acquiring Media for Strategy Formulation

Table 4.2 shows the 18 information-acquiring media used to develop new strategic initiatives. It indicates the average media use across all 29 Texas firms and 130 strategic

Table 4.2. Reported Average Use of Information-Acquiring Media for Strategy Formulation

Medium Number	Medium	Extent of Use[a]
1	Conversations with top management teams	3.94
3	Formal meetings with management teams	3.67
2	Conversations with salespeople and staff	2.93
7	Personal contacts with suppliers and customers	2.69
10	Accounting (P&L) reports	2.52
9	Computer/MIS reports	2.45
13	Analyses of computer databases	2.36
18	Consulting or information services	1.88
14	Newspapers and magazines	1.79
12	Memos and letters from employees	1.74
17	Commercial databases (government, industry)	1.62
8	Personal contacts with associates in other firms	2.29
6	Letters and calls from outsiders	1.79
5	Attendance at conferences and trade shows	1.76
15	Government notices or publication	1.52
Not Clustered:		
11	Special studies and staff reports	3.26
16	Market surveys	2.64
4	Formal meetings with other employees	2.41

[a]Means based on a five-point scale where 1 = low and 5 = high ($N = 130$).

initiatives. Based on cluster analysis techniques, the acquiring media are grouped to reflect how the information sources tended to be used together in organizations. Every source was used in at least one organization. The most extensively used media sources for developing strategy were informal conversations with members of the executive's top management team (3.94), defined as the CEO's immediate peers and subordinates, and formal meetings (3.67). These are relatively rich media, and they were used extensively in formulating over 60 percent of the reported strategic initiatives. The second most frequent cluster included conversations with salesman and staff (2.93) and personal contacts with suppliers and customers (2.69). Again, these are rich media that provide personal insights about external events. The third most frequent cluster included accounting reports (2.52), computer/MIS reports (2.45), and analyses of computer data bases (2.36). These media are lower in richness and provide data about how the firm is doing internally. Individual media frequently used but not clustered include special studies and staff reports (3.26), market surveys (2.64), which respondents said were used extensively in about one-third of the reported initiatives, and formal meetings with other employees (2.41). The remaining two clusters of media in Table 4.2 were used less frequently across organizations; extensive use was reported only for about 10–15 percent of the reported strategy changes.

Table 4.3 shows the partial correlations for the relationship between information-acquiring media and the extent to which strategy is low cost or differentiation. These data are based on the complete sample of 130 strategic initiatives. Table 4.3 also indicates our classification of whether information-acquiring media are high or low in rich-

Table 4.3. Partial Correlations Between Information-Acquiring Media and Low Cost or Differentiation Strategies[a]

		Location of Information Source	
		Internal	External

Richness of Information-Acquiring Media	High	*Low Cost*
		
		Differentiation
		Conversations with (.20*)
		  salespeople and
		  staff
			Low Cost
			  Letters and calls from outsiders (−.16[+])
			
			Differentiation
			  Attendance at conferences and (.26**)
			    trade shows
			
			  Personal contacts with (.18*)
			    suppliers and customers
			  Personal contacts with (.39**)
			    associates in other firms

	Low	*Low Cost*
		  Computer/MIS (.17[+])
		    reports
		  Accounting (P&L) (.28**)
		    reports
		  Special studies and (.20*)
		    staff reports
		  Memos and letters (.17[+])
		    from employees
		
		Differentiation
			Low Cost
			
			Differentiation
			  Market surveys (.20*)
			  Commercial databases (.16[+])
			  Consulting or information (.40**)
			    services

[a]Numerical entries are partial correlations controlling for the extent that the medium's use was also correlated with the other strategy.

$^{+}p < .10$
$^{*}p < .05$
$^{**}p < .01$

ness and whether the information source is internal or external to the organization. The partial correlations in Table 4.3 indicate the relationship between strategy and acquiring media use, after controlling for the extent to which the medium was associated with the other strategy. Partial correlation is used because there is a negative correlation ($r = -.5$) between low cost and differentiation strategies, and because partial correlation is a way to control for that part of the relationship that can be explained by the other strategy.

One clear finding shown in Table 4.3 is that those strategic initiatives designed for low cost leadership were associated with the use of lean, internal information-acquiring media such as computer/MIS reports, accounting reports, special studies and staff reports, and memos and letters from employees. Only one medium considered rich and external—letters and calls from outsiders—was significantly correlated with the low cost strategy, and this correlation was negative. The pattern in Table 4.3 suggests that external sources and rich media are not likely to be used to acquire information when a strategic decision pertains to low-cost issues.

Table 4.3 also contains partial correlations for the relationship among the information-acquiring media and the extent to which strategic initiatives differentiated products and services from those of competitors. The analysis here reveals a very different pattern of media usage. Executives relied heavily on acquiring information through external media, both rich and lean. Rich, external sources include attendance at conferences and trade shows, personal contacts with suppliers and customers, and personal contacts with associates in other firms. The external sources considered lower in richness include market surveys, commercial databases, and consulting or information services. Only one internal medium was associated with differentiation strategy, and that was conversations with salespeople and staff, a rich source of information. The heavy reliance on external sources presumably occurs because the differentiation strategy was formulated based on its potential fit with needs in the external environment. It is also interesting to note that the internal sources used so extensively for low cost strategies—computer/MIS reports, accounting reports, and special studies and staff reports—were not correlated with differentiation strategies, suggesting that these internal reports are of little value for assessing differentiation opportunities but are of great value for assessing the need or opportunity for lowering costs.

In quick summary, the initial data in Tables 4.3 indicate that executives used internal media of low richness more frequently for acquiring information relevant to cost-leadership initiatives. Differentiation strategies, perhaps because of their novelty and complexity, were associated with the frequent use of a larger number and variety of information-acquiring media, including internal and external media, to learn about the external environment. Now let's turn from media used to acquire information for strategy formulation to media used to send information about its implementation.

Information-Sending Media for Strategy Implementation

The second area in which media selection is important to strategic initiatives is for sending information to relevant audiences both inside and outside the firm. After adopting a strategic initiative, information about it must be communicated within the organization to gain compliance, and also to suppliers, regulators, customers, and other stakeholders so they understand the changes that are coming.

Table 4.4 shows the extent to which each of 22 communication information-sending media were used for strategic initiatives based on our interviews with executives of the 29 Texas firms. These 22 media represent typical communication channels used by executives, and the groupings in Table 4.4 are the results of a cluster analysis. They indicate how media were used together by CEOs to communicate strategy implementation. Six external and seven internal channels were characterized as high in richness, and six external and three internal channels were considered low in richness.

The medium used most extensively for strategy implementation was supervisory or department head meetings (4.42). Executives in the sample reported extensive use of this medium for 84 percent of the strategy initiatives reported. The top cluster of activities represents internal communications, of a fairly rich nature, including briefing sessions (3.59), memos and formal directives (3.06), orientation sessions (3.04),

Table 4.4. Reported Average Use of Information-Sending Media for Strategy Implementation

Medium Number	Medium	Extent of Use[a]
16	Briefing sessions	3.59
20	Memos and formal directives	3.06
19	Orientation sessions	3.04
22	Speeches by senior managers to employees	2.86
14	Committee or task force charged with dissemination	2.94
15	Training program or manual	2.70
3	Public relations and press releases	2.44
2	Advertising	2.26
11	Mass mailings	2.13
9	Television, radio and newspaper interviews	2.10
17	Informal champion persuading others	2.39
18	Grapevine	2.38
21	Pay inserts, house organs, or bulletin boards	2.10
7	Representative talks to buyers and suppliers	1.98
1	Speeches	1.78
8	Trade publications, articles	1.68
4	Conventions and conference presentations	1.54
6	Annual reports	1.50
10	Stockholders' meetings	1.45
12	10-K reports	1.06
Not clustered:		
13	Supervisory or department head meetings	4.42
5	Presentations for targeted external groups	2.53

[a]Means based on a five-point scale where 1 = low and 5 = high ($N = 130$).

and speeches by senior managers to employees (2.86). The next cluster, committee or task forces charged with dissemination (2.94) and training programs or manuals (2.70), also represents internal, rich media. The third cluster represents external communications, including public relations and press releases (2.44), advertising (2.26), mass mailings (2.13), and television, radio, and newspaper interviews (2.10), which were used with moderate frequency. The fourth cluster includes the idea champions persuading others (2.39), the informal grapevine (2.38), and pay inserts, house organs or bulletin boards (2.10), and includes both rich and lean ways of communicating strategy internally. Media in the final cluster were not used as extensively, with mean use scores below 2.00, and frequent use was reported for only about 10 percent of the strategic initiatives. 10-K reports were used extensively only once.

The partial correlation analyses for communication media used to send information about strategy implementation are reported in Table 4.5. Low cost strategy is expected to be correlated with lean media such as memos and formal directives because cost-containment data are well defined. The correlation analysis in Table 4.5 shows only two positive relationships for sending information about cost-leadership initiatives—representative talks to buyers and suppliers, and annual reports. All other partial correlations in this area are negative, indicating a tendency not to use those media to communicate about implementation of low cost strategies. Thus external communications such as advertising, public relations, TV, radio, and newspaper inter-

Table 4.5. Partial Correlations Between Information-Sending Media and Low Cost or Differentiation Strategies[a]

		Location of Information Receiver		
		Internal		External
Richness of Information-Sending Media	**High**	*Low Cost*		*Low Cost*	
		Committee or task force charged with dissemination	(−.18*)	Representative talks to buyers and supplier	(.39**)
				TV, radio, and newspaper interviews	(−.20*)
		Orientation sessions	(−.14+)	Stockholders' meetings	(−.26*)
		Differentiation		*Differentiation*	
		Briefing sessions	(.24**)	Speeches	(.33**)
		Informal champion persuading others	(.33**)	Presentations for targeted external groups	(.33**)
		Speeches by senior managers to employees	(.38**)	Representative talks to buyers and suppliers	(.28**)
	Low	*Low Cost*		*Low Cost*	
		Training program or manual	(−.17*)	Advertising	(−.21*)
		Memos and formal directives	(−.20*)	Public relations and press releases	(−.23*)
				Annual reports	(.22*)
				Mass mailings	(−.19+)
		Differentiation		*Differentiation*	
		Pay inserts, house organs, or bulletin boards	(.23**)	Advertising	(−.16+)
				Public relations and press releases	(−.17+)
				Annual reports	(.24**)
				Trade publications and articles	(.36**)

[a]Numerical entries are partial correlations controlling for the extent that the medium's use was also correlated with the other strategy.
+$p < .10$
*$p < .05$
**$p < .01$

views, stockholders' meetings, and mass mailings are simply not favored for low cost changes. Cost containment is an internal matter that will be recognized in the marketplace in the form of competitive prices. Moreover, internal communications of high richness, such as task forces, training programs, briefing sessions, idea champions, and orientation sessions, are also not positively correlated with low cost initiatives. Communications tailored to low cost strategies thus tend to be simple and direct, communicating the facts of the change.

Table 4.5 also shows the communication media relationships associated with implementation of strategic initiatives for product or service differentiation. These initiatives are likely to have little precedent and therefore are more ambiguous. Employees and outside customers can be expected to have many questions regarding unique product changes. Communicating about this strategy, therefore, is expected to be sent through rich media both internally and externally to create shared understandings. The findings in Table 4.5 show, first, that several partial correlation coefficients are positive, indicating several communication media are used. The large change associated with use of a differentiation strategy apparently requires a high volume of communications through multiple channels. Moreover, these communications are directed both externally and internally, and they include both rich and lean media. The partial correlations show positive relationships for five external and four internal channels. Three of the four internal channels are considered rich, including briefing sessions, idea champions, and speeches by senior managers. External communications are both rich and lean, including speeches, presentations, annual reports, representative talks to buyers and suppliers, and trade publications. The external and internal communication of differentiation strategy is handled by trumpeting the strategy in many directions through many channels.

Generally speaking, the findings in Table 4.5 support the theory, but the findings also go beyond the theory in an unexpected way. Our theory said that when strategic initiatives were intended to lower costs, communications would be internal and would use channels of lower richness. When the strategy was intended to differentiate the product or service, communications would be external as well as internal and would tend to be through rich channels. These relationships did appear, but the additional finding is that low cost strategies tended to have relatively few media correlations for strategy implementation, while differentiation strategies were communicated through lean as well as rich channels, both internally and externally. We explore the implication of these findings in more detail after examining industry differences.

Industry Differences

As we mentioned earlier, our sample consisted of organizations from three industries—banking, hospitals, and manufacturing. Some interesting variations in the extent of use of the various media appeared across industries that may indicate important differences in firm environments. Table 4.6 shows the average use of each medium both for receiving information for strategy formulation and for sending information about strategy implementation. The letters in Table 4.6 indicate whether media use is statistically different across industries.

A few overall patterns are identifiable in Table 4.6. First, on average, hospital senior executives used media somewhat less for gathering information than did executives in the other two industries. Second, the most frequently used sources are about the same for each industry, including conversations with top management teams (no. 1) and formal meetings with management teams (no. 3) and with other employees (no. 4). But beyond those media, differences emerge. Third, computer/MIS reports (no. 9) accounting reports (no. 10), and analysis of computer databases (no. 13), are used significantly more in banks, perhaps because of the financial nature of bank operations. Fourth, manufacturing firms seem better connected to receiving information from the outside world, including conversations with salespeople and staff (no. 2), attendance at trade shows (no. 5), letters and calls from outsiders (no. 6), and personal contacts with suppliers and customers (no. 7). Bank and manufacturing executives seem to use

Table 4.6. Average Use of Information-Acquiring and -Sending Media for Strategic Initiatives Within Each Industry

Description	Banks	Hospitals	Manufacturers
Information-Acquiring Media		*Extent of Use[1]*	
1 Conversations with top management teams	3.83[a]	3.70[a]	4.15[a]
2 Conversations with salespeople and staff	2.40[a]	2.48[a]	3.56[b]
3 Formal meetings with management teams	3.58[a]	3.59[a]	3.78[a]
4 Formal meetings with other employees	2.55[a]	2.22[a]	2.39[a]
5 Attendance at conferences and trade shows	1.40[a]	1.74[a,b]	2.03[a,b]
6 Letters and calls from outsiders	1.70[a,b]	1.37[a]	2.06[b]
7 Personal contacts with suppliers and customers	2.70[b]	1.93[a]	3.06[b]
8 Personal contacts with associates in other firms	2.15[a]	2.19[a]	2.44[a]
9 Computer/MIS reports	2.85[b]	1.70[a]	2.52[b]
10 Accounting (P&L) reports	3.05[b]	1.67[a]	2.56[b]
11 Special studies and staff reports	3.48[a,b]	2.63[a]	3.41[b]
12 Memos and letters from employees	1.63[a]	1.74[a]	1.83[a]
13 Analysis of computer databases	2.78[b]	1.81[a]	2.31[a,b]
14 Newspapers and magazines	1.60[a]	1.59[a]	2.02[a]
15 Governemnt notices or publication	1.38[a]	1.41[a]	1.69[a]
16 Market surveys	2.83[a]	2.30[a]	2.69[a]
17 Commercial databases (government, industry)	1.45[a]	1.44[a]	1.83[a]
18 Consulting or information services	1.70[a]	1.96[a]	1.96[a]
Information-Sending Media			
1 Speeches	1.22[a]	2.21[b]	1.98[b]
2 Advertising	3.10[b]	1.57[a]	2.00[a]
3 Public relations and press releases	2.24[a]	3.39[b]	2.11[a]
4 Conventions and conference presentations	1.20[a]	1.50[a,b]	1.82[b]
5 Presentations for targeted external groups	2.00[a]	2.75[a]	2.80[b]
6 Annual reports	1.15[a]	1.67[b]	1.68[b]
7 Representative talks to buyers and suppliers	1.59[a]	1.57[a]	2.46[b]
8 Trade publications and articles	1.51[a]	1.50[a]	1.89[a]
9 Television, radio, and newspaper interviews	2.41[b]	3.11[c]	1.36[a]
10 Stockholders' meetings	1.61[a]	1.00[a]	1.38[a,b]
11 Mass mailings	2.68[b]	1.71[a]	1.93[a]
12 10-K reports	1.00[a]	1.00[a]	1.14[a]
13 Supervisory or department-head meetings	4.63[a]	4.43[a]	4.25[a]
14 Committee or task force charged with dissemination	3.37[b]	3.11[a,b]	2.54[a]
15 Training program or manual	2.98[a]	2.39[a]	2.64[a]
16 Briefing sessions	3.56[a]	3.64[a]	3.59[a]
17 Informal champion persuading others	2.39[a]	2.61[a]	2.29[a]
18 Grapevine	2.27[a]	2.29[a]	2.50[a]
19 Orientation sessions	3.00[a]	3.00[a]	3.09[a]
20 Memos and formal directives	2.70[a]	3.39[a]	3.14[a]
21 Pay inserts, house organs, or bulletin boards	1.41[a]	2.89[c]	2.21[b]
22 Speeches by senior managers to employees	2.93[a]	2.71[a]	2.89[a]

[1]Entries are means based on a five-point scale where 1 = low and 5 = high. Means that *do not* share a common letter (a,b) in each row are significantly different ($p < .05$).

more information than hospitals, with bank sources tilted slightly more toward internal financial workings and manufacturing sources tilted more toward external information about specific customer groups as sources for strategic changes.

With respect to communication channels for implementing a strategy change, interesting differences again emerge. As shown in the bottom half of Table 4.6, hospitals, as public organizations, make greater efforts to manage impressions through public media channels. Hospitals scored significantly higher on the use of speeches (no. 1), public relations and press releases (no. 3), presentations for targeted external groups (no. 5), annual reports (no. 6), and television, radio, and newspaper interviews (no. 9). The hospitals seemed to make great effort to let the general public know about their strategic changes, probably because the entire public is the client base for these organizations. Internally, hospitals make greater use of lean media such as memos (no. 20) and pay inserts, house organs, or bulletin boards (no. 21), perhaps because hospitals in the sample are very large organizations.

Banks reported greater use of advertising (no. 2), mass mailings (no. 11), and task forces charged with dissemination (no. 14). Manufacturers, by contrast, made more frequent efforts to communicate through conventions and conference presentations (no. 4), presentations for targeted external groups (no. 5), annual reports (no. 6), and talks to buyers and suppliers (no. 7). Manufacturers seem to be more directed toward specific external groups, but they were not different from other industries with respect to internal communication channels for strategy implementation.

The industry differences revealed in Table 4.6 can be illustrated with a few examples. The hospital's strategic initiatives of a tactical helicopter unit and a "fine hotel" concept were adopted based on recommendations during informal meetings with members of top management teams and face-to-face conversations with medical staff. Like other organizations, rich media were used by hospital administrators for developing an awareness of the need and potential for these strategic initiatives. Once the decision was made to establish the helicopter unit, brochures were developed and distributed in conjunction with task force meetings, meetings with internal medical staff, and meetings with medical staff of the associated hospitals. For the helicopter unit, press releases were written and publicity was sought by radio and television interviews. Inside the hospital, memos and formal directives reinforced the messages sent through rich media. The fine hotel concept was implemented internally through department head meetings, memos, the in-house newspaper, and bulletin boards. More importantly, a major effort was made to get the word out externally, including a flurry of interviews and free publicity, culminating in ABC's Sunday night news featuring the hospital's new concept on network television. Publicity was a defining characteristic of strategy implementation.

The bank strategic initiatives, such as providing additional services and consolidating operations, began through extensive use of lean sources such as analyses of computer databases and accounting and MIS reports. In addition, bank executives reported that they held formal meetings to seek input from both the top management team and other employees, sources also used in other firms. Because layoffs were important to employees, employees were involved in disseminating information such as through department head meetings, orientation sessions, and a task force. The distinctive characteristic of banks was heavy reliance on computer analysis, MIS reports, and profit and loss reports for data acquisition, followed by efforts to communicate the change both internally and externally. External communication was by advertising and mass mailings to keep customers and potential customers informed.

The manufacturing firm that decided to close the manufacturing plant and to warehouse inventory with independent distributors illustrated the typical manufacturing pattern. Information was obtained through informal contact with independent distributors, individual salespeople, and members of the top management team. Special studies and analyses were also undertaken. Effort was made to target external groups that were affected by the change by presentations at trade shows. Internally, efforts were made to inform employees through department head meetings and briefing sessions.

To some extent the different information sources and implementation channels used by hospitals, banks, and manufacturers represent differences in industry environments. The hospital environment was more diffuse and hence somewhat more ambiguous. The environments of banks and manufacturers changed rapidly, but they were somewhat more defined and analyzable. Hence, a subset of media seemed to distinguish these firms from hospitals. The diffuse environment of hospitals meant a multimedia approach to the environment, including extensive publicity. Manufacturers communicated with specific external groups through conventions and direct talks with buyers and suppliers, while banks relied more on advertising, mass mailings, and task forces.

IMPLICATIONS OF THE RESEARCH FINDINGS FOR STRATEGIC MANAGEMENT AND ORGANIZATION DESIGN

In this chapter we described a number of ideas concerning organizational information processing and reported findings from a study of communication media associated with strategic initiatives. Now we will draw out the implications of these ideas and findings for managerial behavior and organization design. First, we review and summarize the implications of the specific empirical findings about low cost and differentiation strategies. Second, we discuss the relationship of the environment to information processing and organization design. This part of the discussion is somewhat conceptual and based on the research literature because the data did not test these ideas specifically. Third, we make suggestions about how managers' media use may influence their interpretation of the environment and the context within which strategy is implemented. These ideas go beyond the data but provide possibilities for managerial reflection and future research. Thus each subsequent part of this final section will be somewhat more removed from the data, but it is still based on the theme of the information media research.

Strategic Decisions and Information Processing

The basic relationships found from the research are summarized in Figure 4.2. The two types of strategic decisions, cost leadership and differentiation, were associated with different patterns of media use. For the most part, cost leadership was associated with less frequent media use and the use of media lower in richness. Information-acquiring media for the cost-leadership strategic decisions (cell 1) emphasized internal

Information Processing

	Acquiring Information (Formulation)	Sending Information (Implementation)
Cost Leadership	1. Use selective media to monitor internal operations: management information systems for statistical and accounting data, memos, and staff reports.	2. Use selective media to convey information directly to external groups affected by the change such as buyers, suppliers, and stockholders.
Differentiation	3. Use a range of media to gather large amount of information from external sources, emphasizing both rich and lean sources such as personal contacts, meetings, trade shows, surveys, and consulting reports.	4. Use rich media to convey internally such as briefings, task forces, and champions. Convey changes externally via multiple media, both rich and lean: speeches, presentations, direct talks, annual reports, and public press.

Strategic Initiatives

Figure 4.2. Summary of observed relationships between strategic decisions and information processing.

operations and systems, including statistical and accounting data, and special studies and staff reports. Written memos and letters to top management from employees also were about cost reduction. These media were effective for faithfully communicating data concerning the relatively well understood financial and cost-based processes within organizations.

The sending of information for implementing cost-leadership strategies conveyed the changes only to external groups affected by the changes (cell 2). Thus information about cost changes were communicated to buyers, suppliers, and stockholders.

Strategic decisions to differentiate products or services were associated with quite different communication tactics. Acquiring information was apparently a more time-consuming task because information was obtained from several external sources, much of it from rich, personal media but some also from lean media (cell 3). Thus managers formulating differentiation strategies used media such as personal contacts both inside and outside the firm, meetings, market surveys, and consulting services to learn about strategic needs. A differentiation strategy probably meant a larger change than a low cost strategy, and hence more information sources were used to evaluate its potential application.

Communication media used for sending information to implement differentiation strategies revealed efforts to send a large volume of information to make sure that relevant groups were informed about this substantial change. This apparently requires information to be sent both internally and externally through both rich and lean media (cell 4). The changes were communicated to employees through rich media such as briefings, task forces, and informal champions. Information was conveyed externally via many media, both rich and lean, such as speeches, presentations to targeted groups, talks with buyers and suppliers, annual reports, and press releases. Differentiation strategies typically involve a new way of doing business compared to low cost strategies, and hence rich media were used both to obtain and send information about the strategic decision both internally and externally. Moreover, because of the number of constituencies and the nature of the change, media lower in richness were also used for both obtaining and sending information. Organizations employing differentiation strategies appeared to allocate a large amount of resources to communication.

The Environment and Organization Design

Earlier in this chapter we discussed theoretical relationships between environmental characteristics and the information load within organizations, and summarized these in Figure 4.1. Although we did not test these ideas directly, our findings, as well as other research literature, provide a basis for proposing specific information designs within that theoretical framework.

During the period of time these data were collected, all 29 Texas organizations were caught in a rather turbulent environment. Oil prices had dropped sharply, and a recession had hit all three industries. Demand for manufactured products was down. Banks were experiencing financial difficulty because of large investments in real estate, deregulation, and the consolidation trend toward large, regional banks. Hospitals in Texas were also feeling the recession, although it affected health care less than it did manufacturing and banking. Hospitals were also experiencing the turbulence and uncertainty associated with massive changes in the health care industry, as documented in Chapter 3 in this volume. All of the CEOs reported major change and unpredictability in the environment, so our sample did not include what might be called a placid or stable external environment for any of the firms in the study.

Figure 4.3 revisits the two environmental dimensions of ambiguity and volume of information. In our sample, hospitals appeared to have a diffuse, ambiguous environment that changed simultaneously on a number of dimensions, which is representative of cell 2 in Figure 4.3. Both banks and manufacturers were experiencing frequent change, but the problems were often definable so that acquisition of specific data helped top managers reach strategic decisions. Thus banks and manufacturing firms in Texas during the time of the study tended to be representative of quadrant 4, where a large volume of data had to be processed, much of which could answer specific questions about the environment. Indeed, given the enormous changes taking place in the world today as discussed in Chapter 1 in this volume), most organizations probably experience changes typical of quadrants 2 and 4.

Recall that high ambiguity in information was expected to be associated with media high in richness, and high information volume with the more frequent use of lean media. Figure 4.3 reports a more detailed set of relationships based on our new understanding of how the environment is related to information processing. Compared to our earlier conjectures about information processing, two major new insights emerged from Figure 4.3:

1. Communication by strategic managers after the strategic decision, both internally and externally, is as big a part of a strategic initiative as is gathering information prior to the strategic decision. The research literature seems to pay more attention to strategy formulation and the scanning and interpretation of information leading up to the strategic choice. Our findings indicate that sending communications to employees and the external world is important for strategy implementation because the CEOs in our sample of organizations used multiple media for this task.

2. In ill-defined, ambiguous, changing environments, managers tend to use a range of media, both rich and lean, to gain a full perspective on the environment and the strategies needed. This means that a simple association of ambiguous environments with the use of rich media does not hold, because lean media also provide useful data to assist in interpreting these environments. This finding is consistent with research reported by Daft, Sormunen and Parks, (1988) for 50 manufacturers, which found that CEOs in high-performing firms in turbulent environments used multiple media to obtain information.

Consistent with the first insight about the importance of communicating after strategic decisions, Higgins and Diffenbach (1989) reported that many companies make a conscious effort to let both employees and external stakeholders know about their strategies, even though these procedures also inform competitors. Their survey of 500 chief executive officers found that companies utilized annual reports, face-to-face presentations, press releases, newspaper advertising, and in-house publications to send strategic messages to stockholders, bankers, security analysts, consumers, and employees. Indeed, the organizations that adopted policies of communicating corporate strategy found improved relations with the financial community, stockholders, and government agencies. They also found that morale of company employees was increased,

Volume of Information About Environment

	Low	High
High	**1. Low-Moderate Information Load** Strategy: Focused differentiation Acquire Info: Moderate amount from external sources, emphasize rich media, also use lean media Send Info: Rich media internally and externally, some lean Org. Design: Participative, decentralized, teams, "no memo" policy OK, low technology collegial	**2. High Information Load** Strategy: Differentiation Acquire Info: Large amount from external sources, both rich and lean Send Info: Signal changes widely internally and externally, with rich media, some lean Org. Design: Decentralize, informate, use high tech and high touch processes, teams, GDSS's
Low	**3. Low Information Load** Strategy: Drift, react Acquire Info: Lean media, internal and external, supplement with rich media Send Info: Lean media internally and to affected external groups Org. Design: Traditional bureaucratic form, centralized, vertical hierarchy emphasized, low tech and low touch	**4. High-Moderate Information Load** Strategy: Cost leadership Acquire Info: Lean media targeted to needed internal/external information, also some rich media Send Info: Signal changes to affected groups using rich and lean media Org. Design: Decentralize within high-technology systems, informate, data-bases, network organization, vertical structure and systems

Ambiguity of Information About Environment

Figure 4.3. Relationships among environment, strategy, information processing, and organization design.

that relations with both consumers and suppliers were improved, and that share value of the corporation increased. These benefits made abundant communication worthwhile, despite the potential for having information used against the company by competitors or unions.

Consistent with the second insight, managers' use of both rich and lean media may represent complementary communications. For example, Huber (1990) proposed that new technologies can actually enhance social communication by enabling people separated by time or distance to more frequently and reliably communicate with one another, and by increasing team effectiveness by facilitating intelligence development and decision making. Thus lean media may in some ways provide data and enhance social processes beyond what we previously expected.

Based on our findings and other research, we propose that organization design for information processing should resemble the relationships in Figure 4.3 Cell 1 characterizes a small to medium-size firm operating in an ambiguous, diffuse environment that changes moderately. A firm in this quadrant should adopt a focused differentiation strategy, which means that it focuses on a small, defined market, such as a specific geographical area or industry, and would attempt to differentiate its products from competitors rather than be a cost leader. This type of organization should try to acquire a reasonable amount of information from the external environment, using rich media supplemented with lean media. There would be face-to-face contact with customers and suppliers when possible, but the organization could also use surveys and accounting data as needed. Moreover, when a strategic decision is made, the organization should communicate outward, again with both rich and lean media, to let employees and relevant external consistencies know about the change. Multiple media are needed to explain the change to the external world. This type of organization is more likely to adopt an organization structure that uses a team approach, to adopt "no memo" type policies, and, in general, to stress face-to-face communication, although written and technology-based communications would be valuable supplements.

Cell 2 represents the largest need for information processing and the highest information load. An organization in this cell would tend to adopt a differentiation strategy because the external world is ill defined, so it needs to be known as different from other organizations. Acquiring information for strategic decisions should be in large amounts, from both internal and external sources, using a range of rich and lean media. Senior executives talk with the top management team, employees, and associates in other organizations; attend trade shows; and rely on databases, special studies, and accounting and MIS reports. When a strategic decision is made, top managers should then send information widely. The strategic decision helps define the organization, and it can be communicated outwardly through advertising, public relations, and annual reports and inwardly through briefings, speeches, and meetings with managers and employees. The organization design should stress a high capacity for information processing, both rich and lean. This type of organization could adopt a self-managed team structure, including cross-functional teams and participative decision making. Moreover, it could also adopt computer-based technology to facilitate team discussions and provide additional speed for acquiring and sending information. A great deal of time and energy will go into communicating because of the need to detect subtle changes in the environment and to inform stakeholders through outward communication.

Cell 3 probably is not typical of many organizations today. This represents a well-defined and slowly changing environment. Strategy here might be one of drift, or reacting only to infrequent external changes that simply can't be ignored. Relatively small amounts of information would be acquired from the external environment, with the majority of it coming through lean media, conveying facts and statistics about external events. When strategic decisions are made, they would be communicated internally through both rich and lean media, and communicated to some extent externally as well. Information acquisition would largely be through internal information systems. Organization design resembles the traditional bureaucracy, with a vertical chain of command and vertical information and control systems. This quadrant is something of an anachronism in today's turbulent world.

Cell 4 seems representative of the banks and manufacturing firms in our sample. Organizations experience rapid change but there is some understanding of what is happening in the environment ("a recession," "a drop in orders") and what data are needed, as well as who the relevant stakeholders are. Strategies in quadrant 4 would tend to be low cost because activities are sufficiently well defined that the organization can make moves to be a cost leader. Information should be acquired through lean media, which can be technology-based, and it can be supplemented with rich, face-to-face discussions with the management team, employees, and external individuals and groups. These organizations should provide statistics, accounting, and special reports from within the organizations for analysis prior to a new strategic decision. Information about a new decision will be targeted toward key external groups such as buyers and suppliers, as well as toward employees.

The organization in cell 4 should be designed to permit a high volume of information processing, especially through internal systems and external analyses. Technology could be a boon to strategic decision making in this quadrant, because of the additional data and social linkages it can provide (Huber, 1990). An organization would tend to have a vertical structure, complemented by computer-based information technology. Moreover, the technology could be used to "informate" employees (Zuboff, 1988), which means using the technology to decentralize decision making and provide information to employees who need it, thereby enabling the organization to respond quickly to external changes. Moreover, an organization in this environment has the potential to be designed as a network organization (Miles and Snow, 1984), with departments, divisions, or groups connected electronically for coordination and information sharing.

Quadrants 2 and 4 are probably most representative of the environments of companies today. The military coordination of aircraft sorties during the Persian Gulf war and organizations such as The Limited and Duracell illustrate the kinds of organization design that might be employed in quadrant 4. These designs use technology for speedy analysis of internal and external events, in a quantitative, precise way. This information can be complemented with rich information where needed. Organizations in quadrant 2 should be designed as decentralized, participative, team-based structures, such as those used by Federal Express, General Mills, 3M, and Johnsonville Foods. These organizations use rich, face-to-face communications, and at the same time they have technology-based information systems to provide a more complete picture of their external and internal worlds.

The ideas in Figure 4.3 are far from proven. They provide guidelines managers can use to think about when designing organizations to facilitate adequate information processing. Firms in rapidly changing, turbulent, hard-to-define environments must be prepared for a high volume of information processing, both before and after strategic decisions. Information processing must be both internal and external and may require more time and energy than expected, especially if an organization is moving from stable into turbulent times.

IMPACT OF COMMUNICATION MEDIA ON MANAGEMENT

In this final section we explore at a deeper level why managers select particular media to gain a perception of the world, and the impact of using specific media for strategy implementation. One of the intriguing findings from our study of top managers was that in high information-processing situations, multiple communication media were used, both to form perceptions about the environment and to communicate strategic decisions. Managers may select media based on their beliefs about their competitive environment. For example, if they feel the need for a low cost strategy they may select media that provide information relevant to that strategy. On the other hand, certain types of information processing may provide selective views of the world to managers. Each medium provides unique data about events that may yield an insight different from the data provided by an alternative medium. In that sense each medium is incomplete, which may explain why managers in our sample used multiple media of varying richness when strategic needs were difficult to diagnose. Although we proposed that rich media are better in ambiguous situations and lean media in well-defined situations, both may be needed in order to provide a more complete and accurate picture of a complex world to senior managers.

Thus to stimulate future research, to explain why information media may be related to strategy formulation, and to explain why multiple media seem to be used in key situations, we propose that rich versus lean information media shape certain perceptions of the world. Moreover, when a strategic decision is implemented, communicating it via rich versus lean media may have different impacts on information receivers in the organization and the external environment.

Strategy Formulation

We propose that the richness of media used to obtain information during strategy formulation may influence the decision process in five ways: how strategic managers think, how they plan, the judgment processes they use, the type of information they accept as legitimate, and where the strategic initiative is focused. These effects of information richness on strategy formulation are summarized in Table 4.7.

Communication media of low richness, because of their narrow capacity to convey cues, are hypothesized to induce strategic managers to think quantitatively and rationally about strategic initiatives. Communication media of higher richness carry a different and wider variety of information cues that encourage strategic managers to develop their thoughts in a more subjective and intuitive manner. Top managers who obtain extensive reports and detailed analyses for every decision when operating in a highly ambiguous, ill-defined environment run a risk of causing paperwork paralysis

Table 4.7. Relationship of Communication Media to Aspects of Strategy Formulation

Communication Media of Low Richness Induce Strategic Managers During Strategy Formulation	Communication Media of High Richness Induce Strategic Managers During Strategy Formulation
To think quantitatively and rationally	To think subjectively and intuitively
To plan in terms of financial results and performance	To plan in terms of the events and processes that cause performance
To use statistical judgment and computation in making strategic decisions	To use clinical judgment and experience in making strategic decisions
To accept formal data as a legitimate and authoritative representation of the strategic situation	To engage in a dialectic and take responsibility for the accuracy and validity of interpretation about the strategic situation
To focus on internal costs as the basis for strategic changes	To focus on external competitive events as the basis for strategic changes

and indecision. Technology-based communications can facilitate the speed of information, but they may encourage quantitative and rational decision making more than subjective and intuitive decision making.

Communication media of low richness, both written and technology-based, with their hard numbers orientation, may also induce strategic managers to plan in terms of financial results and bottom-line performance. The "softer" orientation of systems high in richness would allow managers to plan in terms of the events and processes that actually cause performance. Moreover, statistical analyses and computation would be the primary factors shaping strategic decisions when lean media are used. Media higher in richness allow strategic decisions when lean media are used. Media higher in richness allow strategic managers to use clinical judgment and past experience to a greater degree when evaluating strategic information.

Earlier we briefly discussed the idea that communication media convey symbolic cues. Media low in richness, including memos, databases, and special reports, symbolize to managers that formal data are a legitimate and authoritative representation of the organization's true situation. These media are considered credible in our culture. However, information obtained from media high in richness would enable strategic managers to understand strategic events in depth. By engaging in a dialectical process, managers may take personal responsibility for the adequacy and validity of the strategic initiative. Managers will be more personally involved when rich media are used and will be less likely to make arms-length impersonal decisions about strategy.

Finally, information from internal media low in richness will tend to lead managers to focus on internal costs as the basis for strategic decisions. Richer information media, on the other hand, enable managers to learn more about external competitive events as the basis for new strategic initiatives. By focusing on external competitive events, managers may obtain an information advantage in environments of high ambiguity, learning about opportunities or problems that other organizations miss. Organizations in stable, well-defined environments may find that internal costs are a sufficient basis for strategic decisions.

The proposed relationships in Table 4.7 help explain why managers use multiple media for adopting differentiation strategies in ambiguous environments. Such media provide unique perspectives and are associated with distinct mental pictures, planning, and judgment. Multiple media provide managers with an array of data and more complete insight, yielding whatever view is needed for the specific strategic initiative. Using one kind of media without others may limit managers' strategic perspective.

Strategy Implementation

Once strategic plans have been formulated, the richness level of information media may continue to play an important role by shaping how strategic decisions are implemented. We propose that communication media used for sending information will influence strategy implementation along the four categories summarized in Table 4.8: how strategic initiatives are communicated to the organization's members, how the organization's structure is altered, the level of the strategic manager's personal involvement, and expectations for compliance with the implementation of strategy.

Using communication media of low richness is expected to induce strategic managers to convey facts, hard data, and rational expectations about the proposed strategic decision. Information media of high richness allow strategic managers to convey their concerns, feelings, emotions, and values about the proposed strategic change. For major new strategies, such as differentiation strategies, the deeper concerns, emotions, and values are probably important for full implementation. For minor strategy decisions, especially those that are technical and related to cost reduction, the change can probably be communicated effectively with lean media. The same relationships would tend to be true of communications sent to the external environment, with rich media such as personal speeches conveying more depth and insight than mass mailings or annual reports.

An organization's structure may also be shaped by communications. Descriptions of structure typically focus on some aspect of patterned roles and relationships within

Table 4.8.   Relationship of Communication Media to Aspects of Strategy Implementation

Communication Media of Low Richness Induce Strategic Managers During Strategy Implementation	Communication Media of High Richness Induce Strategic Managers During Strategy Implementation
To convey facts, hard data measurements, and rational expectations to organization members	To convey feelings, concern, emotions, and values to organization members
To implement strategy by altering the organization's "framework" and formal systems	To rely on alterations in the organization's "processes" and meaning systems
To not be involved in personal networks and to be removed from the human side of strategic change	To be involved in personal networks and to rely on personal relationships for influencing strategic change
To expect compliance based on resource allocation, authority, legitimacy, and symbolic priority	To expect compliance based on shared understanding of the organization's strategy

organizations. The formalized configuration of roles, procedures, and information and control systems within an organization can be defined as its "framework" structure (Ranson, Hinings, and Greenwood, 1980). The patterned regularities of interaction among individuals within the organization create the organization's "processes." We hypothesize that using communication media of low richness will mean that strategy implementation relies on alternations in the organization's framework and formal systems. Individuals can be laid off and departments merged or reorganized as a way to reduce costs, and these precise changes can be communicated with letters and directives. Sending information through rich media enables strategic managers to alter the organization's processes and meaning systems. Thus rich media are hypothesized to allow managers to impact an organization "processes," while lean media will tend to impact the more well-defined "framework."

Information conveyed through lean media such as memos allow strategic managers to avoid involvement and development of personal networks and to be removed from the human side of changes following a strategic decision (Schmitz and Fulk, 1991). Rich media enable strategic managers to become involved in personal networks and to rely on personal relationships created by these networks to influence the implementation process.

Once strategic changes are chosen, the richness of communications may play an important role in top managers' expectations of compliance by organization members. Information of low richness will be associated with employee compliance based on levels of resource allocation, authority, legitimacy, and symbolic priority—the symbolic signals communicated with media of low richness. Information of high richness, however, induce top managers to expect employee compliance based on a shared understanding of the organization's strategic direction. For external stakeholders the same pattern is expected. Accounting and financial information and annual reports will tend to be seen as legitimate and trustworthy. Stakeholders will tend to accept simple, incremental new strategies on that basis. However, for more complex, difficult-to-understand strategies, richer media, such as stockholder meetings, personal visits, or trade shows, will convey a fuller understanding of the strategic change.

To briefly summarize, the ideas in Tables 4.7 and 4.8 suggest new relationships for study between communication media and patterns of strategy formulation and implementation. These relationships are hypothetical and need to be tested in future research. However, the reported use of multiple media by top managers in our sample is consistent with the notion that media play different information roles and provide managers with unique world views. The proposed relationships provide a starting point for understanding these relationships more fully.

CONCLUSION

This chapter has presented material pertaining to the communications surrounding strategic decision making in organizations. Communication is an important aspect of strategic management and organization design. Organizations can be thought of as information-processing systems. The use of communication media can be the result of organization design decisions and, hence, can shape how organizations adapt to the environment, make sense of external changes, and implement strategic initiatives. The frameworks provided in this chapter suggest ideas and patterns that define relationships between type of strategy and communication media, how communication is sent and received both internally and externally, and how organizations and managers process information to cope with increasingly turbulent and unpredictable environments.

NOTE

The authors would like to thank Bill Glick and especially George Huber for their helpful comments on earlier versions of this chapter. We also thank John Delery, K. Michelle Kacmor, Tommy Lasseigne, and Robert Pappas for their assistance in collecting media choice data. This study was initiated and the data were collected while it was supported by a research grant from the U.S. Army Institute for the Behavioral and Social Sciences.

REFERENCES

Aguilar, F. J. 1967. *Scanning the business environment.* New York: Macmillan.

Bennett, A. 1990. *The death of the organization man.* New York: Morrow.

Calori, R., and Ardisson, J. M. 1988. Differentiation strategies in stalemate industries. *Strategic Management Journal,* 9: 255–269.

Daft, R. L., and Huber, G. P. 1987. How organizations learn: a communication framework. In Bacharach S., and Tomasso, N. (Eds.), *Research in the sociology of organizations,* Vol. 5 (pp. 1–36). Greenwich, CT: JAI Press.

Daft, R. L., and Lengel, R. H. 1984. Information richness: a new approach to managerial behavior and organization design. In Staw, B. M., and Cummings, L. L. (Eds.), *Research in organizational behavior,* Vol. 6 (pp. 191–233). Greenwich CT: JAI Press.

Daft, R. L., and Lengel, R. H. 1986. Organizational information requirements, media richness, and structural design. *Management Science,* 32: 554–571.

Daft, R. L., Lengel, R. H., and Trevino, L. K. 1987. Message equivocality, media selection, and manager performance: Implication for information systems. *Management Information Systems Quarterly,* 11: 355–366.

Daft, R. L., Sormunen, J., and Parks, D. 1988. Chief executive scanning, environmental characteristics, and company performance: an empirical study, *Strategic Management Journal,* 9: 123–139.

Daft, R. L., and Weick, K. E. 1984. Toward a model of organizations as interpretation systems. *Academy of Management Review,* 9(2): 284–295.

Dumaine, B. 1990. Who needs a boss? *Fortune,* May 7, pp. 52–60.

Enforcing a no-memo policy. 1988. *Small Business Report,* July, pp. 26–27.

Feldman, M. S., and March, J. G. 1981. Information in organizations as signal and symbol. *Administrative Science Quarterly,* 26: 171–186.

Fulk, J., and Boyd, B. 1991. Emerging theories of communication in organizations. *Journal of Management,* 17: 407–446.

Fulk, J., Steinfield, C. W., Schmitz, J., and Power, J. J. 1987. A social information processing model of media use in organizations. *Communication Research,* 14: 529–552.

Galbraith, J. R. 1973. *Designing complex organizations.* Reading, MA: Addison-Wesley.

Hambrick, D. C. 1987. The top management team: key to strategic success. *California Management Review,* 30: 1–20.

Higgins, R. B., and Diffenbach, J. 1989. Communicating corporate strategy—the payoffs and the risks. *Long Range Planning,* 22(3): 133–139.

Hill, C. W. L. 1988. Differentiation versus low cost or differentiation and low cost. *Academy of Management Review,* 13: 401–428.

Hochswender, W. 1990. How fashion spreads around the world at the speed of light. *New York Times,* May 13, p. E5.

Huber, G. P. 1984. The nature and design of post-industrial organizations. *Management Science,* 30: 928–951.

Huber, G. P. 1990. A theory of the effects of advanced information technologies on organizational design, intelligence, and decision making. *Academy of Management Review,* 15: 47–71.

Huber, G. P., and Daft, R. L. 1987. The information environments of organizations. In Jablin, F., Putnam, I., Roberts, K., and Porter, L. (Eds.), *Handbook of organizational communication* (pp. 130–164). Beverly Hills, CA: Sage.

Huber, G. P., and Glick, W. H. 1993. Sources and forms of organizational change. In Huber, G. P., and Glick, W. H. (Eds.), *Organizational change and redesign: ideas and insights for improving performance.* New York: Oxford University Press.

Jones, G. R., and Butler, J. E. 1988. Costs, revenue, and business-level strategy. *Academy of Management Review,* 13: 202–213.

Keegan, J. W. 1974. Multinational scanning: a study of the information sources utilized by headquarters' executives in multinational companies. *Administrative Science Quarterly,* 19: 411–421.

Main, J. 1989. At last, software CEOs can use. *Fortune,* March 13, pp. 77–83.

Miles, R. E., and Snow, C. C. 1984. Fit, failure and the hall of fame. *California Management Review,* 26: 10–28.

Mintzberg, H. 1973. *The nature of managerial work.* New York: Harper and Row.

Mintzberg, H., Raisinghani, D., and Théorêt, A. 1976. The structure of "unstructured" decision processes. *Administrative Science Quarterly,* 21: 246–275.

O'Reilly, C. A. 1982. Variations in decision makers' use of information sources: the impact of quality and accessibility of information. *Academy of Management Journal,* 25: 756–771.

Porter, M. E. 1980. *Competitive Strategy: techniques for analyzing industries and competitors.* New York: Free Press.

Porter, M. E. 1985. *Competitive Advantage: creating and sustaining superior performance.* New York: Free Press.

Porter, M. E. 1991. Know your place. *INC.,* September, pp. 90–95.

Ranson, S., Hinings, B., and Greenwood, R. 1980. The structuring of organizational structures. *Administrative Science Quarterly,* 25: 1–17.

Rebello, K. 1991. Battles fought behind keyboards. *USA Today,* February 1, p. 5B.

Rice, R., and Shook, D. E. 1990. Relations of job categories and organizational levels to use of communication channels, including electronic mail: meta analysis and extension. *Journal of Management Studies,* 27: 195–229.

Rose, F. 1990. A new age for business? *Fortune,* October 8, pp. 156–164.

Schmitz, J., and Fulk, J. 1991. Organizational colleagues, media richness, and electronic mail: a test of the social influence model of technology use. *Communication Research,* 18: 487–523.

Schweiger, D. M., Sandberg, W. R., and Rechner, P. L. 1989. Experiential effects of dialectic inquiry, devil advocacy and consensus approaches to strategic decision making. *Academy of Management Journal,* 32: 745–772.

Short, J., Williams, E., and Baker, C. 1976. *The social psychology of telecommunications.* London: Wiley.

Steinfield, C. W. 1986. Computer-media aided communication in an organizational setting: explaining task-related and socioemotional uses. In McLaughlin, M. (Ed.), *Communication yearbook nine* (pp. 777–804). Beverly Hills, CA: Sage.

Steinfield, C. W., and Fulk, J. 1986. Task demands and managers' use of communication media: an information processing view. Paper presented at the annual meeting of the Academy of Management, Organization Communication Division, Chicago, IL.

Thorn, B. K., and Connolly, T. 1987. Discretionary data bases: a theory and some experimental findings. *Communication Research,* 14: 512–528.

Trevino, L. K., Daft, R. L., and Lengel, R. H. 1990. Understanding managers' media choices: a symbolic interactionist perspective. *Organizations and Communication Technology.* In press.

Trevino, L. K., Lengel, R. H., and Daft, R. L. 1987. Media symbolism, media richness, and media choice in organizations: a symbolic interactionist perspective. *Communication Research,* 14: 553–574.

Warfield, A. L. 1990. The team member workbench: a case study of an innovative information system at Domino's Pizza Distribution. Ph.D. Dissertation. Ann Arbor: University of Michigan.

Weick, K. E. 1979. *The social psychology of organizing,* 2nd ed. Reading, MA: Addison-Wesley.

White, R. E. 1986. Generic business strategies, organizational context and performance: an empirical investigation. *Strategic Management Journal,* 7: 217–231.

Yates, JoAnne. 1989. *Control through communication: the rise of system in American management.* Baltimore: Johns Hopkins University Press.

Zuboff, Shoshana. 1988. *In the age of the smart machine: the future of work and power.* New York: Basic Books.

5

Effects of Executive Team Demography on Organizational Change

CHARLES A. O'REILLY III, RICHARD C. SNYDER, and
JOAN N. BOOTHE

> We must all hang together, or assuredly we shall all hang separately.
>
> Benjamin Franklin

> The greatest ability in business is to get along with others and influence their actions.
>
> John Hancock

> Because top managers are often products of their company's administrative heritage, they also become its captive. In the face of changing environmental demands and new competitive realities, the bias in senior executives' experience can constrain an organization's ability to perceive its problems and overcome a strategic misfit.
>
> Bartlett and Ghoshal,
> *Managing Across Borders*, 1989: 143

EDITORS' SUMMARY

Why are executive teams important? Why should we focus on the demographic homogeneity of these teams, rather than on the average skills and abilities of the team members? How does demographic homogeneity affect organizational change through the dynamics of the executive team?

In this chapter, O'Reilly, Snyder, and Boothe effectively address these three questions. The answers they provide are interesting to both academics and practicing managers because the authors cogently summarize and interpret a stream of research and case examples in rich, theoretical explanations with obvious practical implications. The chapter is enhanced by O'Reilly's substantial research experience on team demography and his familiarity with many of the key firms and players in the electronics industry that the team studied.

Although academics and the business press tend to glorify individual leaders, quite often the true heroes of industry are the teams. In fact, recent research has found that the executive team has greater effects than the top executive does on organizational functioning. In this chapter, these authors argue that executive teams have their greatest effects through three main functions: (1) strategic leadership; (2) integration both internally and with critical outside constituencies; and (3) stimulating and supporting organizational learning.

A central theme in this chapter is the importance of the demographic homogeneity of the executive team, especially homogeneity in the tenure of its members. This orientation shifts our focus from skills and abilities of team members to the composition of the group itself. Substantial previous research, as well as the authors' current study, lend support to the argument that the demographic composition of the team is a very important determinant of the team's functioning.

The most unique and rewarding contributions of this chapter concern the explication of the processes by which executive team demography affects organizational change. Countering some popular arguments for "value in diversity," these authors argue that homogeneity in terms of length of service leads to positive team dynamics. This argument is supported by evidence from a series of interviews with top executives from 24 electronics firms. Homogeneity fosters cooperation, mutual trust, and an effective blend of personalities. Several cases are described to explicate these processes. Positive team dynamics are also shown to be important, because both executive team homogeneity and positive team dynamics contribute to increased adaptive change, reduced turnover among team members, and decreased frequency of political changes. These conclusions are supported by case descriptions and (in most cases) by longitudinal, quantitative analyses.

The managerial implications from this chapter are important. Rather than restricting staffing decisions to issues of individual abilities and job descriptions, executives should be more concerned with the composition of the top management team. Within this group of electronics firms, greater homogeneity in terms of tenure on the executive team is associated with more positive outcomes. Further, this chapter demonstrates the importance of positive team dynamics in contributing to increased adaptive changes and reduced political changes. These are important extensions of both the academic research literature and the prescriptions found in the business press. ■

Anyone who is even a casual reader of the business press in the United States over the past few years cannot help but be struck by the litany of bad news: recessions, downsizing, loss of competitiveness, and the downward spiral of many formerly great organizations. Gone are firms like Pan Am, Singer, Fairchild Semiconductor, Schlitz, American Motors, and others. Former leaders such as Columbia Pictures, Firestone, and Memorex now report to new owners. Still others such as International Harvester, Greyhound, and Atari survive but under very different and diminished circumstances. While the causes for these vary widely, there are a number of common themes that provide a rhythm for this unhappy song: increased competition, changing technology, and the greater complexity and uncertainty facing managers and organizations. The cliché that the pace of change is increasing is, unfortunately, true and almost impossible to ignore. The challenge facing the leaders of U.S. companies is how to adapt to these changes—to find ways to survive and prosper in the face of the turbulence.

Against this background of bad news, the business press provides an occasional counterpoint of success: firms that have adapted. Whether it is Total Quality Management (TQM) at Xerox, Ford, and Motorola; continual innovation and improvement at 3M and DuPont; or the sheer competitiveness and cost cutting at General Electric and Cypress Semiconductor—there are examples of firms that have adjusted, often painfully, and are prospering.

What are the differences in these firms compared to those that are less successful? While there are undoubtedly many reasons, a common theme seems to be that the survivors have learned how to adapt. They have changed to meet the new competitive circumstances. Sometimes this is driven by the threat of failure, sometimes by top managers correctly anticipating new technologies and markets. In an era of rapid and continual change, survival means change. As Jack Welch noted: "In the nineties the heroes, the winners, will be entire companies that have developed cultures that instead of fearing the pace of change, relish it" (Welch, 1990: 31).

To use Huber and Glick's apt phrase (see Chapter 1 in this volume), this "tiresomely fashionable" story could be easily dismissed if it weren't so obviously true. At its most abstract level, the moral is simple: a critical issue for top management in today's firms is the ability to deal with change. At a deeper level, the answer is anything but obvious. Should firms rely on new strategies, for instance those that emphasize core competencies? Or is the answer in new structural forms, such as network organizations, or in firm-wide culture change efforts relying on TQM? Regardless of where the answer is to be found, successful organizational change must almost always involve the CEO and the top executive team. It is this group, sometimes referred to as the top management team (TMT), that ultimately makes important decisions and resource allocations that help or hinder a firm in adjusting to changing conditions. It is here, in what Hambrick (1989) refers to as "strategic leadership," that the overall responsibility for the organization lies. Tushman, Newman, and Romanelli (1986: 15) capture the critical role of the top team's impact when they note:

> The data are consistent across diverse industries and companies, an executive team's ability to proactively initiate and implement frame-breaking change *and* to manage convergent change seem to be important factors which discriminate between organizational renewal and greatness versus complacency and eventual decline.

A growing body of empirical evidence points out that the top management team may be a more important determinant of an organization's ability to change and adapt than the chief executive officer alone (e.g., Finkelstein and Hambrick, 1990; Virany, Tushman, and Romanelli, 1991). These and other authors have noted that it is the TMT through which critical information is filtered and by which strategic decisions are made (Hambrick and Mason, 1984; Hurst, Rush, and White, 1989).

This leads to a deceptively simple question: "What makes a top management team effective or ineffective in fostering organizational change?" While the answer to this question is not fully known, the purpose of this chapter is to address one facet of TMT functioning. Specifically, we examine the relationships among TMT demography, team dynamics, and organizational change. To do this, we have organized the chapter into two sections. The first addresses the general topic of executive teams: Why are they important? Who are they? What do they do? And how can they facilitate or impede change? The emphasis here is on understanding, at a general level, how the composition of a TMT can affect team dynamics and the ability to adapt. The second section reports an empirical investigation of executive teams and organizational change based on a study of 24 electronics firms over a period of two years. Using interviews with CEOs at six-month intervals, we examine how the composition of the top group in terms of their experience working together affects their ability to function as a team, and how this affects the ability of the firm to adapt.

ROLE OF THE TOP MANAGEMENT TEAM

Why the TMT Is Important

Several prominent early writers about management and organizations recognized that effective leadership required the involvement of the entire executive group (e.g. Cyert and March, 1963; Thompson, 1967). However, as Hambrick (1989) observes, during the 1970s and 1980s this theme was essentially lost as researchers focused primarily on the role of the single leader, most often the CEO. Recently, attention has returned to considering the impact of the entire top management group on organizational performance. The evidence is promising. There is clear support for the conclusion that the top team, rather than the top person, has the greatest effects on organizational functioning (e.g., Ancona, 1990; Hage and Dewar, 1973; Hambrick and D'Aveni, 1992; Norburn and Birley, 1988). Recognition of the importance of the top management team should not be a surprise since the ability of an organization to anticipate and respond to changes in the environment rests on the decisions not just of the CEO, but of the entire executive group. As Barnard (1938: 215) suggested: "Executive work is not that of the organization, but the specialized work of *maintaining* the organization in operation." This requires the efforts of the entire team, not a single person, what Hambrick (1989: 6) refers to as "the study of strategic *leadership* [which] focuses on the people who have overall responsibility for an organization—the characteristics of those people, what they do, and how they do it."

While the TMT may serve many functions, three seem particularly critical for the success of the firm: strategic leadership, integration, and organizational learning. First, the executive group is centrally responsible for determining the strategic direction of the organization (cf. Frederickson and Iaquinto, 1989). Issues such as which industries to compete in and what technologies to pursue, and the basic question of how to achieve a sustainable competitive advantage, are typically resolved by the CEO and the senior team. Gupta (1988), for instance, suggests that a stronger relationship will be found if the top management team rather than the CEO is the unit of analysis. Eisenhardt and Schoonhoven (1990) report that TMTs were a major factor in the success or failure of semiconductor firms. Hambrick and D'Aveni (1992) show that deterioration of the top management team was a central element in the downward spiral of the 57 large corporate failures they studied. Thus, it is the TMT that provides strategic leadership and allocates strategic resources.

A second critical function provided by the TMT is that of boundary spanning and integration. In one sense, executive teams stand at a critical nexus within their organizations. On one side, they are often a focal point for linking the organization to outside constituencies. On the other, they bear ultimate responsibility for providing the integration across functional domains and ensuring the fit among strategy, structure, and process (Miller, 1991). When top management fails to provide this integration, the performance of the firm suffers (Doz, Angelmar, and Prahalad, 1985).

A third role the TMT serves is to foster organizational learning and to ensure that the firm adapts to changing circumstances. As shifts occur in environmental conditions or strategies, new competencies are often required. If executive teams persist in old modes of conduct in fundamentally altered contexts, failure is likely (Keck and Tushman, 1991). To survive, teams must engage in what Tushman and Keck (1989) refer to as both first-order and second-order learning. In the former case, during stable periods teams must be able to continually and incrementally improve by getting better and better at those things that offer them a competitive advantage. In the latter case, teams must recognize when to reorient themselves and shift the required competencies and processes within the team. Hambrick (1987: 2) addresses the issue of team competence and learning directly, suggesting that "the amounts of open-mindedness, perseverance, communication skills, vision, and other key characteristics that exist within the team clearly set the limits for how well the team—and, in turn, the firm—can operate." Thus, the team itself may be an important determinant of the ability of the organization to adapt.

Composition and Functioning of Executive Teams

Until now, we have considered the top management team in an abstract way. While the evidence is strong that the TMT can be a critical factor in the success or failure of an organization, we have not been concrete in defining who is on the team, what makes one more effective than another, or how they can facilitate change.

Who actually constitutes the top management team? Although the TMT is often referred to theoretically as the strategic apex (Mintzberg, 1979) or the upper echelon (Hambrick and Mason, 1984) of the organization, there is no generally accepted definition of who formally constitutes the TMT. Clearly, the most likely candidates include the chief executive officer (CEO) and his or her direct reports. Depending on the industry, the size of the firm, and the organizational structure, this group might vary considerably in team size and titles. In large firms the team might consist of the CEO, the chief operating officer (COO), presidents of subsidiaries, and/or a variety of executive or senior vice presidents. Some of these may be on the board of directors; others may not. In some cases, this group may function as an executive or operating committee. Different researchers, however, have not always adopted the same definition. For example, Wagner, Pfeffer, and O'Reilly (1984) use all vice presidents listed in the corporate directory. While this convention has been adopted by some (e.g., Hambrick and D'Aveni, 1992; Keck, 1991; Michel and Hambrick, 1992; Tushman and Keck, 1989), others have relied on variations of this approach. Critics, for instance, have observed that not all vice presidents are necessarily part of the inner circle and may not be actively involved in critical decisions. Therefore, others have sometimes defined the team differently. Finkelstein and Hambrick (1990) use those executives who are also on the board of directors. Wiersema and Bantel (1992) use only the top two levels of the organization. Bantel and Jackson (1989) asked the CEO to indicate who was on the team. In an investigation of the effects of TMT demography on firm innovation, Flatt (1993) analyzed both the most senior vice presidents (those with titles of executive vice president and senior vice president) and the more inclusive group of all vice presidents. She found dramatically different effects for the two groups, suggesting that who is identified as being on the team may help determine the findings.

Recognizing that definitions of who constitutes the executive team may depend on the nature of the research question posed, two aspects of the team seem important. First, the role of the TMT is almost always very different from most other organizational teams on several dimensions. The members of the TMT are themselves more visible. They serve as important symbols and a source of institutional leadership. Even inconsequential interactions may become major events. The members are also more likely to be accomplished, having risen through achievement within the firm or function. The tasks required are also likely to be more complex than those of other teams, frequently requiring a combination of internal and external balancing. Finally, the fact that the TMT is the focus of power within the organization means that the presence of politics is likely to be more pronounced. The nature of the task, the participants, and the use of power make top management teams far more salient and consequential than most other teams.

Second, while almost always complex, what makes a TMT function effectively may vary depending on the strategic context. Firms in one industry or those pursuing a particular strategy may require different competencies and different ways of functioning than those in another (e.g., Dess and Beard, 1984; Eisenhardt, 1990; Hambrick, 1987). However, while the specific competencies required may vary, effective teams must be able to focus their time and attention on the appropriate core processes, given the strategic context. That is, they must be effective at accurately perceiving and responding to external conditions and internally function well as a team. A failure on either account can put the organization at risk (Ancona, 1990).

Executive Team Demography

One key element that affects TMT functioning is its composition. Hambrick (1987) argues that the performance of an organization is ultimately a reflection of its top managers, and that, in addition, what happens to the organization is affected by the cognitive processing abilities, skills, experience, aptitudes, interpersonal dynamics, and other human factors of the TMT. While a number of studies have concentrated on these dimensions (e.g., Bower and Hout, 1988; Eisenhardt, 1990; Greiner and Bhambri, 1989), the focus here is on the demographic composition of the top management team, especially with regard to the distribution of length of service. The fundamental argument explored is that the integration and functioning of the TMT is at least partly affected by the demographic composition of the team.

Substantial previous research exists to support this argument. Pfeffer (1983) has noted that organizations are, at heart, relational entities defined by the interaction among the members. The ability of people to interact can be importantly affected by how similar are their values, attitudes, language, and common experience. A substantial literature from social psychology attests to the importance of demographic attributes as determinants of group and interpersonal interactions (e.g., Jackson et al., 1991; Shaw, 1981, Tsui and O'Reilly, 1989).

O'Reilly, Caldwell, and Barnett (1989), for example, demonstrate that homogeneity in tenure increases social integration and reduces turnover. Bantel and Jackson

(1989) show how increased functional heterogeneity among TMT members can enhance firm innovation. These and other studies speculate that the demographic composition of the executive group can affect critical aspects of group functioning such as trust, communication, conflict, supportiveness, and the ability to reach a consensus (Ancona, 1990). Hambrick and Mason (1984) offer a series of important propositions linking the demography of the senior team to organizational outcomes. For instance, they propose that homogeneous top teams will make strategic decisions more quickly than heterogeneous teams.

While there is an impressive and growing body of evidence demonstrating the importance of group demography in determining organizational outcomes such as strategic choice and firm performance (e.g., Keck, 1991; Wiersema and Bantel, 1992), a number of important questions remain unresolved. Two are relevant here. First, while it is intuitively reasonable, little research has examined the effects of TMT demography on group functioning. While social psychological research often postulates such associations, only a few studies have actually investigated these in organizational settings (e.g., O'Reilly et al., 1989; Tsui, Egan, and O'Reilly, 1992; Zenger and Lawrence, 1989). Whether or not these effects will hold at the executive team level is unknown.

A second unresolved issue concerns the importance of homogeneous or heterogeneous teams. Convincing arguments and evidence have been presented on both sides. For instance, Michel and Hambrick (1992) make the case that homogeneity in length of service within a group may result in more similar values and outlook, lead to less conflict arising from these differences, and result in higher levels of social cohesion (e.g., Bower and Hout, 1988; Katz, 1982; Murray, 1989). In making a similar point, Hambrick and Brandon (1988) cite Barnard (1938: 225), who argued that the compatability of executives is an important factor in organizational success unless it is taken to an extreme.

The opposite argument can also be made: too much homogeneity can lead to conformity and groupthink (Dess, 1987). TMTs may require heterogeneity in order to succeed. Virany et al. (1991) argue that executive teams with high stability and homogeneity may also succumb to inertia and be less likely to initiate organizational change. Dutton and Duncan (1987) posit that heterogeneity in beliefs will lead to a greater search for information and more momentum for change. Certainly there is evidence of group heterogeneity being associated with higher levels of creativity and innovation (Bantel and Jackson, 1989).

In an attempt to resolve this contradiction, Priem (1990) argues for a curvilinear relationship between team composition and performance. In his view, performance is likely to suffer with extreme levels of homogeneity or heterogeneity. The appropriate degree of homogeneity/heterogeneity is contingent on how much variation exists in the firm's environment. In stable environments, more consensus is productive, whereas in dynamic conditions, more heterogeneity may be required. Contrary to this position, O'Reilly and Flatt (1989) argue that homogeneity in the executive team may be a critical way to achieve the high levels of interdependence necessary for organizational innovation. Homogeneity based on length of service can promote identification with the larger goals of the organization and reduce resistance to change by diminishing misunderstandings and political dynamics within the team. They find TMT homogeneity to be positively associated with organizational innovation.

AN EMPIRICAL STUDY

Given the paucity of research and the complexity of the problem, it is easy to understand why findings might conflict. Nevertheless, the preponderance of evidence suggests that variations in the demographic composition of the executive group and how well this group interacts can affect organizational adaptation. In this chapter we investigate the relationships among TMT demography, team dynamics, and organizational change. Figure 5.1 provides a simplified general model outlining the expected associations. The general expectation underlying this study was that increased homogeneity of tenure in the TMT should be associated with more positive team dynamics; that is, more homogeneous teams should show higher levels of cooperation and less conflict. Homogeneity should also be associated with lower levels of turnover from the team and greater levels of adaptive organizational change. In addition, independent of TMT demography, we also expected positive team dynamics to be associated with lower levels of executive turnover and more adaptive change.

Assessing Organizational Adaptation and Change

Conceptually, it is straightforward to argue that organizations must change if they are to survive (e.g., Tushman et al., 1986). Even the organizational ecologists have noted that while organizational change initially increases the likelihood of failure, over time the probability of failing is likely to fall below the rate that exists with no change (Freeman and Hannan, 1991); that is, organizations that do not change may, in the long term, be more likely to fail than those that do attempt to adapt. However, while the conceptual point is easy to make, the measurement of change is much more complicated than it seems on the surface.

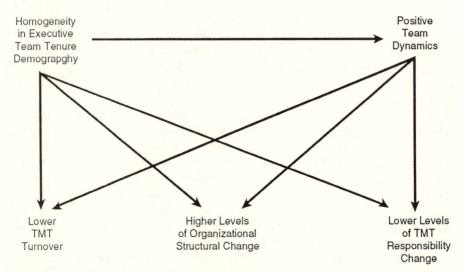

Figure 5.1. General model of associations between top management team (TMT) demography, team dynamics, and organizational change.

For instance, Downs and Mohr (1976) note that researchers have measured innovation in ways that may make findings difficult to compare. Thus, if innovation or change is assessed as the date of adoption of a given process or technology, the results may be different from those using a measure of the depth of adoption. Knowing when the first subunit of a firm adopted a new approach may be quite different from knowing when the final unit adopted it. Depending on the power of the microscope being used, one may see comparatively few or many changes. When investigating organizational change, the difficulty is how to know whether one is measuring something important or something trivial, something that is imposed or proactive, or something that is unique to the organization or industry or common across all firms and industries. This measurement problem is made more problematic since change may be continual such that a snapshot runs the risk of mistaking cause for effect (cf. Glick, Huber, Miller, Doty, and Sutcliffe, 1990). Making comparisons across organizations complicates the picture even more.

For instance, how does one evaluate an organization involved in a merger as compared to one engaged in an initial public stock offering? Is each a single change, or does one count the innumerable details involved in such transactions? What happens if one respondent notes that we "went public," a second highlights the major activities in the process leading up to the public offering, and a third recounts in great detail the steps involved? Obviously, in a time-constrained interview, the more time spent describing one change means that less time will be spent describing other changes. The problem is even more difficult when attempting to compare an event of some magnitude in one industry to the responses of another informant in a firm in another environment. A well-meaning respondent, trying to be accommodating to the interviewer and believing his or her firm to be engaged in important work, will fill whatever time is allotted for the interview with descriptions of changes that have occurred. The interview time allotted, coupled with the nature of the changes, dictate the level of detail described. The difficulty is making sense of these changes. A failure to acknowledge or deal with this problem may lead researchers to analyze and compare data in ways that obscure any real meaning. The danger, of course, is that the results of statistical analyses will be taken as meaningful and interpreted according to the researcher's categories, but perhaps not the informant's.

Three approaches to minimize this danger seem useful. First, in order to compare changes across organizations, very careful statistical controls need to be introduced for industry, size of the firm, age of the organization, and performance. A number of researchers have noted that a failure to control for these effects can lead to spurious interpretations of any findings (e.g., Dess and Beard, 1984; Hambrick, 1989). Hambrick and Mason (1984: 226) note that "because of the effect of industry characteristics all the propositions . . . should be thought to carry the important phrase 'within an industry.'" The concern is that uncontrolled variations in economic conditions, the nature of technology, or competition can easily affect the nature of changes faced by the TMT (Eisenhardt, 1990; Norburn and Birley, 1988). Similar variations in the size of the firm, its age, or its performance may also affect the rate and pace of changes (e.g., Miller, 1991; Wiersema and Bantel, 1992).

Beyond these controls, there is also a concern about misinterpreting the nature of the changes reported by the respondent. Researcher-imposed interpretations (e.g., strategic versus tactical, and reactive versus proactive) may be useful theoretical abstractions but miss the phenomenological meaning given by the informant. Thus, the use of actual counts of changes may provide a more grounded perspective than abstract aggregations or indices.

Finally, in this spirit, qualitative data should be used to illuminate the nature of the changes reported. Nomothetic approaches may not capture the meanings and reasons for the changes supplied by the respondent. Idiographic approaches, in combination with nomothetic analyses, offer the best chance of providing veridical insight into the change process. For this reason, qualitative descriptions of the changes provide a critical counterpoint to statistical analyses. Overall, these considerations suggest that in order to adequately investigate the relationships among executive team demography, team dynamics, and organizational change, the analysis should (1) focus on objective changes reported by the respondent rather than interpretations of these, (2) concentrate on intraindustry analyses with suitable controls for firm age, size, and performance, and (3) attempt to understand any quantitative findings in light of the qualitative descriptions offered by the informant.

Data

All data were obtained via structured one-hour interviews with the chief executive officer or, in the case of divisions of a larger corporation, the president or head operating executive. A description of the interview protocol is contained in Glick et al. (1990), which is reprinted as the appendix to this volume. This interview required the respondent to systematically provide an extensive accounting of all design and nondesign changes that had occurred during the previous six-month period. After responding to these questions, the CEO also provided data on his or her top management team, including responses to seven questions descriptive of the nature of the interactions within the group of his or her direct reports (the top management team). Four interviews were conducted over a consecutive 18-month period, with each interview approximately six months apart.

Sample

The original data collection involved interviews with CEOs from 35 electronics firms, all members of the American Electronics Association. This sample consisted of 23 firms still in operation and 12 executives from firms that had recently failed. Firms were participants in the Electronics Association Presidents' Forum. The intent was to offer a comparative perspective on top management teams of successful and failed ventures (e.g., Bruno, Leidecker, and Harder, 1986). This interview covered a broad range of topics, including company history, strategy, board of directors, background data on the founders and TMT, as well as the Glick et al. (1990) structured protocol. Unfortunately, the time requirements for the structured interview (minimum of 60 minutes) were too lengthy for some participants. As a result, the principal investigator of the study ruled the first data collection as unpermissible and all data were discarded. Goodstein and O'Reilly (1988) reported the results of this initial study. This necessitated a new start with a substantially different sample since the same data could not be collected from the same respondents for a second time.

Table 5.1 provides a listing of the 24 firms that became the basis for the study

Table 5.1. Firms in the Study

Firm	Product Line	Size (No. of Employees)	Company Age (Years)	Average TMT Size[a]
1	Battery manufacturer	950	12	5.0
2	Computer software	135	5	7.0
3	Electronic components	39	26	4.25
4	Computer equipment	102	7	4.0
5	Telecommunications	267	4	7.0
6	Computer software	74	10	10.25
7	Consumer electronics	92	18	7.75
8	Communication equipment	16	6	4.5
9	Computer software	20	21	4.0
10	Electronic equipment	130	18	5.0
11	Photo chemical equipment	26	10	5.25
12	Microwave components	83	10	7.25
13	Computer software	229	10	7.25
14	Digital recording equipment	120	18	7.0
15	Computer equipment	800	15	7.0
16	Electronic systems	788	16	9.75
17	Electronic equipment	405	40	6.25
18	Computer equipment	134	4	6.25
19	Computer software	310	8	7.67
20	Computer software	12	4	4.33
21	Computer software	272	6	9.25
22	Hazardous waste disposal	102	16	4.0
23	Electronic manufacturing	60	26	3.5
24	Electronic equipment	28	22	6.0

[a]TMT = direct reports, as reported by the CEO.

reported here. All firms were involved in the electronics industry, in either hardware, software, manufacturing, or service. Firms ranged in size from 12 to 950 employees, with an average of 212 employees. No firm in the sample was a new start-up in terms of founding date, although several firms were just in the process of bringing products to market. Firms ranged in age from four years to 40, with an average of 13.6 years. Each CEO listed his or her direct reports (the TMT). These varied from three to 11 across firms over the 24 months of the study and averaged 6.25.

Due to changes in CEOs, mergers and acquisitions, and firm failure, some attrition occurred during the time of the study. Sample size over time was: period 1 = 24; period 2 = 22; period 3 = 20; period 4 = 16.

Measures
TMT Demography

As indicated, during each interview, the CEO provided a current listing of his or her top management team and their dates of entry into the team. The team, defined by the CEO, generally consisted of all direct reports. Demographic homogeneity or heterogeneity for age and tenure was assessed using the coefficient of variation (CV), which is the standard deviation divided by the mean. A number of approaches have been taken to the measurement of demography in organizations (e.g., McCain, O'Reilly, and Pfeffer, 1983; Pfeffer and O'Reilly, 1987; Tsui and O'Reilly, 1989; Wagner et al., 1984), and a large number of measures are available (e.g., Blau, 1977; Teachman, 1980). Allison (1978) provides the most thorough review of these and observes that the coefficient of variation provides the most direct method for obtaining a scale invariant measure of dispersion. He notes: "For variables like age, where utility is neither strictly increasing nor especially relevant, the flat sensitivity of the coefficient of variation makes it the appropriate choice" (1978: 877). With the coefficient of variation, a higher value means greater variation (in age or tenure). Low values indicate comparative homogeneity. It is important to note that relative homogeneity is essentially independent of length of tenure; that is, it is possible to have a homogeneous team that has been together for a comparatively long, or short, period of time. The measure is not of length of service but how similar or dissimilar the TMT is without regard to mean age or tenure.

TMT Dynamics

TMT dynamics refers to the pattern of interaction and influence among the executive group (Greiner and Bhambri, 1989). To assess the functioning of the top management team, during each interview the CEO was asked to respond, using a seven-point scale ranging from not at all descriptive to very highly descriptive, to the seven questions shown in Table 5.2. Responses were summed to form an index of TMT dynamics. This index was scored so that a high value indicated positive team dynamics and a low score represented poor team interaction. The mean score across firms and time periods was 5.44 with a standard deviation of 0.69. In addition to responses to these questions, CEOs were also probed about how the team itself functioned. These qualitative responses were used to help interpret the quantitative analyses.

Turnover

Turnover was assessed across the four time periods by noting any additions or deletions to the TMT. A total of 70 additions and 63 deletions occurred during the study. Average turnover was 13 percent. Whenever a change in the TMT was noted, the CEO was asked to explain the circumstances and reasons for the change. These qualitative data were used to gain insight into the statistical findings.

Organizational Change

As indicated earlier, on the surface, organizational change is relatively easy to measure; that is, one simply asks the respondent, "What changes have occurred?" At a deeper

Table 5.2.   Items Used in the Assessment of Top Management Team Dynamics[a]

1. There is an effective and balanced allocation of responsibilities and expertise.
2. Team members willingly cooperate with each other.
3. There is an effective blend of personalities.
4. Conflict is dealt with openly and effectively.
5. There is a high level of mutual trust among team members.
6. There is a great deal of consensus about the overall strategic direction of the firm.
7. Interaction among team members is characterized by a high degree of political activity (reverse scored).

[a]CEO responded on a seven-point scale ranging from "not at all descriptive" to "very highly descriptive."

level, however, such measures may be flawed in that the nature and number of changes may reflect a number of important but unobserved influences that can render comparisons across respondents problematic. Four such concerns seem particularly relevant to interpreting any observed results: (1) performance of the firm; (2) nature of the industry; (3) size or scope of responsibility of the respondent; and (4) engagement of the CEO in the interview. The first three factors, if not explicitly controlled for in the analyses, will lead to noncomparable outcomes being treated as equivalent. For instance, changes reported by a respondent of a poorly performing firm in a highly competitive environment are certain to be different from those reported by a CEO of a company without competition (Hambrick and D'Aveni, 1992). Firms in different industries can face radically different environmental conditions, including different technologies, as well as variations in the pace of change and munificence of the resource base (Dess and Beard, 1984; Eisenhardt and Schoonhoven, 1990). The CEO of a large firm may have a very different scope of responsibility, which can easily affect his or her definition of what constitutes a "change" (Chandler, 1990). Finally, respondents' notions of what has changed and whether these changes are significant will obviously reflect a set of unmeasured characteristics such as memory, how focused or distracted the respondent is, whether the interview format is engaging, and so on.

Because of the potential biases introduced by these concerns, we developed a coding scheme that (1) concentrated on using objectively reported changes (e.g., specific reports of actual changes) rather than interpretation of the meaning of changes (e.g., strategic versus tactical, design versus nondesign, and important versus unimportant) and (2) were reflective of top management actions rather than reports of changes occurring in the organization that did not emanate from TMT causes. That is, we did not investigate changes that occurred when conditions were beyond the control of the CEO, such as changes in inputs or the external environment.

This coding scheme was developed by first generating a complete list of all changes reported by each CEO for each firm over the four time periods. This resulted in over 1,050 changes. Next, these changes were sorted by content into eight major substantive categories. Table 5.3 provides a brief description of these categories. For example, the first category is defined by changes in the composition of the top management team,

Table 5.3. Content Categories for Organizational Change[a]

1. *Changes in TMT composition* include the hiring, promotion, transfer, or departure of members of the TMT.
2. *Non-TMT personnel changes* include the hiring, promotion, transfer, or turnover of non-TMT members.
3. *Changes in organizational structure* include the creation or elimination of senior management positions, the reorganization of units, and the opening or closing of plants or other structurally autonomous divisions.
4. *Changes in strategy* include changes in pricing, products, markets, and modes of competing.
5. *Changes in manufacturing* include modifications to equipment or methods of production.
6. *Changes in control systems* include changes in budgets, incentives, planning systems, and culture.
7. *Changes in external environment* include financing, strategic alliances, and mergers.
8. *Changes in inputs* include regulatory or competitive changes, suppliers, and labor.

[a]Categories obtained from responses by CEOs in 24 firms in the electronics industry over a two-year period. Total number of changes = 1,050.

Category three changes were the focus of this study.

including reports of hiring, promotion, and departures of members of the team. The third category contains all reported changes in the structure of the firm, including the creation or elimination of positions, unit reorganizations, or the opening or closing of offices or divisions. Other categories encompass non-TMT personnel changes; changes in strategy, manufacturing, and control systems; and reports of changes in inputs such as supplies or in external environmental events such as financial terms, competitors, and mergers.

While the number and scope of reported structural changes from category three is large, only two specific subcategories are relevant for this study: (1) structural changes adopted by the TMT in order to adapt to external opportunities and threats and (2) changes internal to the TMT, such as responsibility and reporting relationships, thought to reflect potential political realignments within the team. Both measures are based on the counts of reported changes in that subcategory. For instance, structural changes include counts of the creation or elimination of a position (e.g., "create a director of training position"), reorganizations (e.g., "reorganized and flattened the organization," "created a new department"), or the opening or closing of an office or plant. TMT responsibility changes included items such as changed reporting relationships (e.g., "chief operating officer now reports to the board"), shifts in responsibility (e.g., "VP for product development is now VP engineering"), changes in titles (e.g., VP development and operations is now VP operations"), and modifications in relationships (e.g., "MIS reporting shifted from the CEO to the comptroller").

Performance

The overall rating of how well the firm was doing during the period each interview covered is called performance. We rated performance on a five-point scale (very poor to excellent) based primarily on profit and sales growth as reported by the CEO, as well as the overall sense the CEO conveyed as to how the company was doing. For most firms there was some variation over the four periods, with two-point swings common. Only two companies were at one extreme or the other during all four periods.

Control Variables

These included company age, firm size, and TMT size (see Table 5.1). Average company age was 13.6. Since several of the firms were in the early stages of product introduction, size of the firm was assessed by the number of employees rather than sales or revenues. The CEO of each firm indicated the names of those on the executive team. Average TMT size was 6.25.

Analysis

Given the four waves of data, a variety of analyses was used, depending on the questions addressed. These included cross-sectional or contemporaneous regressions for each period; cross-sectional regressions with lagged or aggregated dependent variables used to examine the temporal ordering among the variables; and pooled time series/cross-sectional (TSCS) analysis. The latter is methodologically the most difficult since many of the model assumptions for cross-sectional analysis are violated (e.g., Kmenta, 1986). For purposes of this report, the full complexity of these analyses is not covered. Only summary results are reported.

Findings

The model shown in Figure 5.1 summarizes the general hypotheses investigated here. In general, the expectation was that TMTs that were more similar or homogeneous with regard to tenure would display more positive team dynamics. This, in turn, would facilitate adaptive structural change, whether taking advantage of opportunities (e.g., growing and expanding) or responding to threats (e.g., retrenching or downsizing). Positive team dynamics were also expected to reduce TMT responsibility changes often motivated by organizational politics (Pfeffer, 1992). Finally, positive TMT dynamics were expected to lead to lower turnover among executives of the firm.

Table 5.4 presents the means, standard deviations, and correlations among variables. Several patterns are worth noting. First, a large coefficient of variation, which indicates increased heterogeneity within the team, is negatively associated with team dynamics, suggesting that increased heterogeneity is associated with less positive team interactions. Heterogeneity is also positively correlated with higher turnover within the TMT and less adaptive structural change. TMT dynamics is inversely related to turnover, suggesting that more positive team interactions are associated with lower rates of turnover. Better TMT dynamics are also positively associated with company age. Higher levels of structural change are related to larger firm size, confirming the need to control for this. Overall, these bivariate relationships are consistent with the proposed model but are silent with respect to causality and do not control for many of the confounding factors discussed previously. Therefore, a series of cross-sectional and pooled analyses were conducted. Contemporaneous and lagged dependent variables were examined, and controls were used for company size, age, and performance, as well as TMT size. Since all firms were from the same industry, no industry controls were used. Results of these quantitative analyses are largely summarized by the time series cross-sectional regressions reported in Table 5.5. These results are discussed using both quantitative and qualitative data.

TMT Demography and Team Dynamics

The first question to be investigated proposed that more homogeneous executive teams would also be characterized by better team dynamics. The quantitative results for this are very strong. Model 1 in Table 5.5 shows a statistically significant negative association between the CV for tenure (hereafter called *demography*) and TMT dynamics. This indicates that increasing levels of heterogeneity are independently related to reports of poor team dynamics after controlling for firm performance, company size, and team size. (Although the data are not reported in Table 5.5, all analyses were also conducted controlling for company age. This variable had no significant effects on the results and was dropped for reporting purposes in this chapter.) To determine the causal ordering, a series of additional analyses were run to examine the effect of TMT demography on subsequent team dynamics, as well as the reverse, to examine the team dynamics that affect subsequent demography. Results of these showed that demography affects dynamics, but not the opposite.

While of interest, the quantitative results supporting the first hypothesis are not illustrative of the complete picture. The qualitative results reveal a far richer picture of this relationship, with clear indications that heterogeneous top teams are often char-

Table 5.4. Correlations Among Variables ($N = 24$)

Variable	X	SD	1	2	3	4	5	6	7	8	9
1. CV tenure	74.1	27.5	—								
2. TMT dynamics	5.44	0.69	-.50**	—							
3. TMT turnover	0.13	0.15	.62**	-.49**	—						
4. Adaptive change	1.77	1.24	-.51**	-.02	-.05	—					
5. Responsibility change	1.41	0.94	-.05	-.32	.20	.15	—				
6. Company age	13.6	8.9	.01	.44**	-.27	-.25	-.13	—			
7. Company size (employees)	212	261	.04	.03	.12	.43**	.02	.09	—		
8. TMT size	6.25	2.24	-.02	-.17	.20	.34	.14	-.22	.43**	—	
9. Company performance	3.79	0.98	-.06	.12	-.08	.10	-.05	-.11	.17	.10	—

*$p < .05$
**$p < .01$ (one-tailed test)

Table 5.5. Pooled Cross-Section Time Series Regressions (Standardized Coefficients)

					Dependent Variables					
	TMT Dynamics	TMT Turnover			Adaptive Change			Responsibility Change		
Independent Variables	(1)	(2)	(3)	(4)	(5)	(6)	(7)	(8)	(9)	(10)
1. Company size	−.02	−.02	−.04	−.02	.25*	.26*	.25*	−.09	−.10	−.09
2. Company performance	.21+	.02	−.05	.02	.08	.15	.11	−.11	−.06	−.05
3. TMT size	−.16	.20+	.18	−.19+	.20+	.17	.17	.15	.10	.10
4. Period 2	.13	−.10	−.02	−.10	.04	.03	.07	.07	.12	.11
5. Period 3	.16	−.07	−.03	−.07	−.01	.00	.02	.16	.20	.20
6. Period 4	.18	−.05	−.01	−.05	.02	.03	.05	.34**	.38*	.37**
7. CV tenure	−.22**	.53**	—	.53**	−.21*	—	−.24*	.11	—	.06
8. TMT dynamics	—	—	−.11	−.01	—	−.13	−.17	—	−.27*	−.26*
Adjusted R^2	.05	.23	.00	.22	.15	.12	.17	.08	.22	.14
F ratio	1.63	4.39**	0.55	3.79**	3.01**	2.57*	3.00**	2.02+	2.86**	2.52*

+ $p < .10$
* $p < .05$
** $p < .01$ (two-tailed tests)

acterized by dissension. Interestingly, the dynamic aspects of this process become most visible with the entrance of a new TMT member, sometimes followed by a deterioration in team interaction. On occasion, this occurred even though there were high initial expectations that the new member would fit in and solve critical problems.

For instance, one company that was 17 years old at the start of the study had an executive team core made up of founders and people who had joined the company early on. About a year before the study began, two new TMT members were brought in from outside, one of whom was intended to take over as chief operating officer, relieving the CEO and founder of day-to-day responsibilities. While all went well at first, strains began to develop as it became apparent that the newcomers did not have the same vision for the future of the company as the old TMT did. When financial difficulties developed over problems with a new product introduction, rather than pull together the TMT split into factions, one led by long-term members who had been through this sort of thing before, and one by the newly appointed COO. Team dynamics deteriorated rapidly, and organizational politics became the order of the day.

In another case, a relatively young company developed problems when a new senior vice president was hired to replace a founding TMT member who had been terminated for performance reasons. The new senior vice president was welcomed with great expectations for his valuable expertise. Very quickly, however, personality clashes occurred. These were ascribed to the fact that "he simply does not understand this company." Dissension developed quickly, not only because of the newcomer but also as a general by-product of the conflict among TMT members about how to proceed. In other firms, similar events occurred as differences in common experience led to disputes in the allocation of responsibilities, diminished levels of trust and collaboration, and increased time spent on internal politics.

In contrast to these cases, there were companies with comparatively homogeneous teams and good dynamics. The oldest firm in the study, for example, has had a very stable TMT with carefully controlled turnover. Members of the team knew each other well. The level of trust and cooperation was very high. In several instances, companies in the study were family firms. Dynamics in these cases were generally quite good, and perhaps best when the family members were actually on the TMT rather than in subordinate positions. In one instance, for example, TMT dynamics and overall company morale improved when a son was promoted to a TMT position. The CEO's explanation was that prior to the promotion, the son's position had been ambiguous. This led to confusion and conflict.

Overall, the results reported here are consistent with previous research on group demography (O'Reilly et al., 1989). The evidence, quantitative and qualitative, is strong in showing how heterogeneity in the TMT can result in less effective patterns of interaction. It is important to note that these results do not suggest that homogeneous teams are less innovative or have less conflict. Homogeneous teams, however, were usually better able to deal with conflict and to build a consensus around important issues. It is also worth noting that homogeneity does not imply a long-tenured group. As Katz (1982) and Keck and Tushman (1991) have shown, it is often the case that new teams are necessary for change. What is relevant here is that teams be comparatively similar in their experience, be it long or short. Teams with widely varying amounts of experience appear more likely to suffer problems of communication and conflict.

TMT Demography, Dynamics, and Turnover

The second question explored suggested that both increased TMT homogeneity and positive team dynamics would independently be associated with lower levels of executive turnover. Models 2–4 in Table 5.5 report the quantitative tests of this hypothesis and show demography (CV tenure), but not team dynamics, to be associated with turnover. Increased heterogeneity of the team with regard to tenure is significantly linked to increased executive turnover.

Although the data are not shown in Table 5.5, additional analyses strongly support this finding. Each of the four cross-sectional regressions confirms the demography-turnover link and shows no relationship between TMT dynamics and turnover. Further, when the turnover is lagged, the results show that variation in demography in an earlier period is related to subsequent turnover. This is evidence in support of a temporal ordering among the variables. No evidence supporting the reverse, turnover affecting demography, was found. Further, there is evidence in both these data and other studies that the more distant members of the group are most likely to leave (O'Reilly et al., 1989; Wagner et al., 1984). It bears repeating that the measure of TMT demography (CV tenure) does not imply that longer serving teams are necessarily more homogeneous.

While the results for demographic effects on turnover are quite strong, no significant relationship between team dynamics and turnover is evident. This lack of any finding is somewhat puzzling. When cross-sectional models are reestimated without the demography measure, a significant negative association between TMT dynamics and turnover emerges. This suggests that the better the TMT functions, the lower the turnover within the team. Two potential interpretations are possible. First, it may be that the lack of a significant finding in the full model stems from weaknesses in the measure of team dynamics. Recall that the CEO was the only informant. A broader based measure using multiple respondents could be more accurate. Better still would be observational data on the functioning of the team. Alternatively, in spite of the intuitive sense the association between dynamics and turnover makes, it is possible that demographic dissimilarity may lead to a lack of social integration, as suggested by O'Reilly et al. (1989), which affects turnover independent of group dynamics.

Fortunately, the qualitative data shed light on this puzzle and suggest a direct relationship between dynamics and turnover even though the quantitative results do not. Recall the two organizations described previously in which new TMT members (heterogeneity) caused difficulties in the functioning of the team. In the first instance, the recently hired COO attempted to take over the board and have himself confirmed as the CEO. Negative team dynamics made it difficult for the executive group to concentrate on operating problems. Ultimately, the core members of the TMT prevailed and the COO was fired along with several of his supporters. This process, however, took several years to unfold, suggesting that the linkage between dynamics and turnover may take longer to work out than the 24-month time frame that bounded this study. As a footnote, it is interesting that, as of the final interview, the fired COO had been replaced by a person who, while new to the team, had a long working acquaintance with the founder/CEO.

In the second case, the new senior vice president was creating problems for the entire team. Other members strongly urged the CEO to get rid of the new person specifically because of the dissension he was creating and his lack of understanding of the company. While this drama was occurring, the quantitative data would show heterogeneity in the team to be related to poor TMT dynamics, but not to turnover. Ultimately, the CEO did fire the senior vice president and eliminated his position, reassigning his responsibilities among the remaining TMT members. As the CEO described it, after the departure the TMT coalesced and there was a "new dawn" with much more effective communications within the group. Again, however, this process took substantial time to work itself out. Firing a senior executive, especially one brought in with high expectations and needed expertise, is not something that is likely to happen quickly.

Not all the cases of demography, dynamics, and turnover involve the company attempting to solve its problems by letting disruptive elements go. In some cases TMT members departed because of their own unhappiness at being in a TMT with poor morale or negative dynamics, or because they themselves felt out of place demographically. One of the most dramatic examples in our group of companies involved a merger. About midway through the four interviews, a study company merged with another firm of about twice its size. The merger was friendly and all TMT members were retained, in many cases as TMT members of the newly formed company. They were, however, generally regarded as the newcomers on the team. Morale among these people fell and team dynamics generally deteriorated. People simply did not cooperate as well, nor did they retain the same company and interpersonal loyalties they had had previously. As of the fourth interview, a number of them had either departed or were expected to leave.

Overall, the results offer unequivocal support for the association between TMT demography and turnover. Heterogeneity within the team is related to turnover. This should not be interpreted as saying that only homogeneous teams have low turnover or that heterogeneous teams must necessarily have turnover. Rather, when coupled with qualitative evidence, the story seems more understandable. At the executive level, comparatively new members may bring with them different expectations and operating styles. They will also not have the shared understandings and perspectives that other members do. The result, in this study, is a less effective team, sometimes characterized by infighting and reduced attention to the problems of the business. One outcome may be subsequent turnover, although this may take considerable time to occur. It should be noted that it may well be that the newcomers' perspectives are those most needed by the firm. As Tushman et al. (1986) have shown, organizations may be highly inertial, changing only periodically and then only with the wholesale replacement of the top team. The results reported here are consistent with that view, suggesting that heterogeneous teams are less functional and may eject those most different, but perhaps most critical, for the firm's future.

TMT Demography, Dynamics, and Organizational Change

As we proposed, both demography and team dynamics were hypothesized to affect the types of organizational changes made. A homogeneous executive team and one with better team dynamics was expected to be more likely to make positive changes and less likely to engage in changes that might reflect political shifts. In the specific case, it was expected that the positive changes would be seen in structural alterations taken to capitalize on opportunities or to deal with threats. These structural changes include actions such as altering the functional organization, consolidating units, reorganizing subunits, and adding or deleting positions. TMT responsibility changes, on the other hand, were seen as more likely to reflect dysfunctional team dynamics as changes were made to accommodate political conflicts. These changes included actions such as creating or eliminating titles, shifts in executive team responsibilities, and changes in reporting relationships. Models 5–7 in Table 5.5 report the test of the impact of demography and dynamics on adaptive or structural change. Models 8–10 report results for responsibility shifts or political change. Recall that the general hypotheses were that homogeneity and dynamics would be independently associated with increased adaptive change and decreased political change. Figure 5.2 summarizes the overall empirical findings. Solid lines represent statistically significant relationships revealed in the quantitative analyses. Dotted lines represent associations strongly supported by the qualitative data but not quantitatively significant.

Adaptive Change

As seen in Models 5–7 in Table 5.5, adaptive structural change, or those changes made by the TMT to adapt to opportunities and threats, is negatively related to TMT demography. Heterogeneity within the executive team is significantly linked to less structural change, whereas homogeneity is positively associated with change. Although the data are not reported here, analyses using an aggregated dependent measure (e.g., TMT

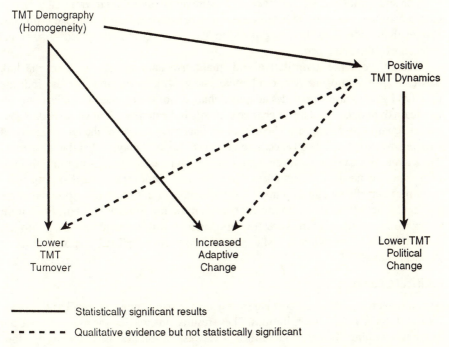

Figure 5.2.   Final model of organizational change as affected by TMT demography.

demography at time 1 predicting changes at subsequent times) strongly and significantly confirm the results presented in Table 5.5. Teams that are more similar with respect to length of service appear to engage in more adaptive changes.

Although it was expected that positive team dynamics would also facilitate adaptive structural change, the results shown in Table 5.5 do not support this. However, the qualitative data illustrate the linkages between a well-functioning team and constructive organizational change. For instance, the fastest growing organization over the 24 months of the study had a very homogeneous team, strong positive team dynamics, and the highest average number of structural changes. The CEO was very aggressive with strong interests in the effects of structure. He had a team, including some co-founder members, that supported him and was willing to go along with trying things out. In general, the changes were positive and oriented to expansion.

In another case, a smaller company with a homogeneous team also had been quite active organizationally. They opened an office in another city, not only because they saw opportunities for expansion, but also because certain TMT members personally wanted it. And, although the data are not reported here, it is worth noting that this company has also been quite creative with regard to marketing and product introduction.

It was not always the young, fast-growing companies with a homogeneous TMT that made changes. The oldest company in the study, which is relatively stable in size, had one of the more homogeneous teams. It was also one of the more active companies with regard to organizational change. The CEO had his eye very much open for opportunity and had his team behind him so that he could move to take advantage of them.

The less homogeneous teams generally were not as active organizationally. In one case, a company with a quite heterogeneous team had been facing financial problems. Rather than addressing them organizationally, the CEO has attempted to solve his problems by replacing people.

Overall, both the quantitative and qualitative data strongly support the link between TMT homogeneity and adaptive change. Additional analyses also indicate that TMT demography precedes adaptive change, not the reverse. The effect of positive team dynamics on adaptive change is clearly indicated by the qualitative data, but not the quantitative analysis. These findings may reflect some of the issues discussed with regard to dynamics and executive turnover. Again, it may be that the measure of TMT dynamics is not accurate enough. A more robust assessment using multiple indicators may be needed. Nevertheless, the qualitative findings suggest that poor team dynamics may distract the executive team from concentrating on operational matters and act to focus their attention inward toward resolving conflicts and tensions within the executive group. This interpretation is consistent with the results shown in Models 8–10 of Table 5.5, which link TMT dynamics to changes in TMT responsibilities or political change.

Political Change

As can be seen in Table 5.5, there is a strong inverse association between TMT dynamics and shifts in TMT responsibilities. These results indicate that the more positive the group functioning, the fewer the shifts in TMT responsibilities and reporting relationships. Teams with poor dynamics have far more of these changes. Interestingly, in this instance TMT demography is not related to organizational change; only team dynamics are related to political shifts within the executive group. Additional analyses using a lagged measure of change confirm that TMT dynamics precede changes in the team. Thus, reverse causality with change in the top team leading to less favorable team interaction does not seem likely.

The qualitative data are useful in understanding these results. There is a flavor coming through in many of the interviews that many changes in TMT responsibilities reflect attempts to deal with poor dynamics and are the direct result of political jockeying for privilege and position. For instance, when a senior executive leaves the company, that person's responsibilities are often reassigned to other TMT members. When a team is characterized by poor dynamics, the resulting interactions can divert the team's attention away from constructive change. In the example cited earlier where the chief operating officer mounted an attempt to oust the CEO, changes in TMT responsibilities were clearly related to the poor dynamics. The various senior members of the team shifted their own responsibilities to improve their power positions and, to the extent they had control, adjusted responsibilities of their supporters. After the new COO left, a further massive reshuffling took place in an attempt to repair the damage to the team dynamics that had taken place.

For the company with the senior vice president who created TMT dissension, TMT responsibility shifts took place largely as he was leaving, in an attempt to find combinations of people who could work together after he left. It is particular interesting that his position was eliminated and his responsibilities reallocated to other TMT members. The CEO conveyed the sense that this reflected an attempt to purge the company of the departed manager's influence as quickly as possible.

Although several companies in the group had strong CEOs, one CEO in particular stood out as critical and activist. His team dynamics were typically lower than average. He reported a number of TMT responsibility changes, apparently motivated by attempts to get people to work together better. In another case, a company in financial trouble had negative and deteriorating dynamics over the study. While the CEO's shifts in responsibilities were, in part, related to attempts to find the combination that could best deal with the financial problems, he also made it clear that some of the responsibility shifts were directed at attempts to shore up morale and address adverse team dynamics.

The case of the family company in which the son was added to the TMT is another illustration of how dynamics relate to TMT responsibility change. Here the CEO perceived a problem in how the team was functioning. Adding the son to the team changed not only his responsibilities but also those of other team members. This change clarified what had been some misunderstandings and subsequently improved the functioning of the team.

In general the companies with positive dynamics reported low levels of responsibility change or related these changes to other events in the organization. For example, the company with the second highest average number of TMT responsibility changes over the four interviews also happened to have quite positive dynamics. This is a company with an activist CEO who, during the study, was clearly responding to new opportunities as they developed. On closer inspection, it turns out that many of the responsibility changes reflect adjustments necessary to accommodate the company's growth.

Overall, both the quantitative and qualitative data show how poor team dynamics can result in political infighting within the executive team. With adaptive change, both demography and team dynamics were factors. With TMT responsibility changes, team dynamics appear to be the primary determinant. TMT demography, while clearly affecting team dynamics (Hypothesis 1), seems to have less of a direct effect.

Additional Analyses

Although they are not reported in Table 5.5, two additional sets of analyses were run. First, the coefficient of variation was decomposed into the mean and the standard deviation. This was done to examine the separate effects of length of service and its variance and to examine explicitly the effects of mean tenure and variation in the composition of the executive team. There were no effects on political change, consistent with the results shown in Table 5.5. Increased variation in team tenure had a significant negative effect on structural change and a positive effect on executive turnover; that is, independent of the mean tenure of the TMT, increasing variation was associated with less adaptive organizational change and higher rates of turnover. These analyses confirm Hypotheses 2 and 3 and show that it is diversity in the team, not length of service, that leads to these effects.

Although not the focus of this study, analyses equivalent to those reported in Table 5.5 were also run using age rather than tenure as the demographic variable. Previous studies have typically found age to be a less important factor than tenure in affecting organizational performance (e.g., O'Reilly and Flatt, 1989). Results here showed very few effects for TMT age, either using the coefficient of variation or its disaggregated components. There were marginal effects ($p < .10$) on structural change and turnover. Older executive teams showed less structural change and lower levels of turnover. These effects, however, were weak, especially when compared to TMT tenure. Age of the executive group does not appear to be an important determinant of organizational change.

CONCLUSIONS AND IMPLICATIONS

During the two-year period of this study, the top management teams of the companies investigated were confronted with a wide variety of changes. Four of the firms faced major threats to their existence and survived these crises. Several firms failed and went out of existence. Three firms were involved with mergers or acquisitions. Three others had CEO changes. Four other firms had a comparatively uneventful time during the two years. Three of the companies were highly innovative and successful and were featured in a number of business press accounts for their accomplishments. Although all firms were in the same industry, a number of them were in declining or intensely competitive segments and were required to play a largely defensive game. Others were more fortunate and were in an expansionary mode. In terms of strategic intent, firms in the sample ranged from innovators or first movers who relied on being first to the market, to fast seconds who preferred to wait for others to introduce a product or technology, to low-cost producers and niche players. Thus, although the number of firms studied is not large, the sample does seem to be representative of the smaller firms often found in the electronics industry. The range of threats and opportunities faced by the top management teams also seems broadly representative of the sorts of crises faced by these organizations.

Overall, a reasonably clear picture emerges from the qualitative and quantitative data. As shown in Figure 5.2, the composition of the top management team appears to be an important factor that affects how well the team functions, as well as its ability to make adaptive organizational changes and the likelihood of executive turnover. Teams that are comparatively similar in terms of tenure are characterized by better team dynamics, higher levels of adaptive organizational change, and lower levels of turnover from the team. Relatively heterogeneous teams have less positive team functioning, less adaptive change, and more shifting of responsibilities within the team. The evidence also suggests that team demography affects changes in group dynamics and organizational change, not the reverse.

This study has deliberately focused on the relative homogeneity/heterogenity of the TMT with regard to length of service. We did not report the impact of long or short tenured teams or the effect of other demographic characteristics such as age or functional backgrounds. Other studies have investigated these effects. For instance, Keck (1991) notes that as a group ages it tends to become less flexible and open to alternative ways of doing things. In the cement industry, for example, she finds increased variation in age to be associated with lower financial performance. Miller (1991) and Finkelstein and Hambrick (1990) also show increasing tenure to be linked to increased risk aversion and diminished information processing. These and other studies (e.g., Norburn and Birley, 1988; Murray, 1989) suggest that the average tenure of a top management team may have positive or negative effects depending on the strategic context in which the firm operates.

In our sample of electronics firms, teams must deal with rapid changes. Fast cycle times are important. As Bower and Hout (1988) note, firms in this environment need fast learning. This comes from management teams characterized by positive team dynamics, including quick communication and mutual trust. To achieve this, people need some stability in working procedures and social patterns. As Rod Canion, the former CEO of Compaq Computer, pointed out, the idea is not to burn up energy in conflict and internal political disputes: "You can't have continuity unless you retain people" (Webber, 1990: 116). In our view, it is the homogeneity of teams that provides this stability and enhances team dynamics. This is also consistent with research that has shown that TMTs with previous experience working together are more successful than those who have not worked together before (Goodstein and O'Reilly, 1988; Wiersema and Bantel, 1992).

What are the practical implications for management? Two general points seem worth noting. First, there is a growing body of evidence documenting the effects of team demography on important organizational outcomes such as innovation, team functioning, and turnover (e.g., Flatt, 1993; Wagner et al., 1984). Managers should not ignore the potential negative effects from having a highly heterogeneous top team. This suggests paying attention not only to the succession of individual managers but also to entire teams. As Priem (1990) suggests, there may be situations in which too much or too little heterogeneity can be dysfunctional. Hambrick (1987) and Tushman et al. (1986) show how critical a new team can be when firms adopt new strategies or face dramatically changed environments. A second practical consideration is to be sensitive to the importance of effective group functioning. Teams do not automatically function well. Indeed, executive teams are often composed of strong individuals who are used to being in charge. Efforts need to be considered to help the group function as a unit as well as to accomplish its tasks. Failure to do this may diminish the ability of the organization to adapt and to increase nonproductive political activities.

The conclusions we have drawn about the importance of tenure homogeneity do not imply that heterogeneity is always dysfunctional. As Priem (1990) argues, it may be that extreme homogeneity can lead to a diminished capability for change. Tushman and colleagues have offered vivid illustrations of this danger (e.g., Tushman and Keck, 1989; Tushman et al., 1986). Similarly, heterogeneity in functional background among team members may have beneficial effects (e.g., Bantel and Jackson, 1989; Hambrick, 1987; Keck, 1991). The point to be emphasized here is that when an executive team operates in a turbulent context, there may be an important premium on their ability to function effectively as a group and to avoid conflicts and misunderstandings that can slow them down and deflect their attention. In the study reported here, comparatively homogeneous groups were better able to implement adaptive changes and to avoid political shifts.

These findings corroborate and extend previous research on the effects of organizational demography in two important ways. First, the results clearly link team demography to group dynamics. Very little previous research has explored this association, and then only with lower level groups (O'Reilly et al., 1989; Zenger and Lawrence, 1989). Second, the results presented here also link TMT demography directly to organizational structural change. Earlier research has shown team demography to be related to strategic changes (e.g., Finkelstein and Hambrick, 1990; Wiersema and Bantel, 1992) and to innovation (e.g., Bantel and Jackson, 1989; Flatt, 1993; O'Reilly and Flatt, 1989), but not directly to short-term structural change. This is important in that it provides more convincing evidence for the impact of TMT demography on the short-term performance of the organization. It also demonstrates the important but often nonobvious role of demography in organizations (Pfeffer, 1983).

REFERENCES

Allison, P. 1978. Measures of inequality. *American Sociological Review,* 43: 865–880.

Ancona, D. 1990. Top management teams: preparing for the revolution. In Carroll, J. (Ed.), *Applied social psychology and organizational settings* (pp. 99–128). Hillsdale, NJ: Erlbaum.

Bantel, K., and Jackson, S. 1989. Top management and innovations in banking: does the composition of the top team make a difference? *Strategic Management Journal,* 10: 107–124.

Barnard, C. 1938. *The functions of the executive.* Cambridge, MA: Harvard University Press.

Bartlett, C. and Ghoshal, S. 1989. *Managing across borders: The transnational solution.* Boston, MA: Harvard Business School Press.

Blau, P. M. 1977. *Inequality and heterogeneity.* New York: Free Press.

Bower, J., and Hout, T. 1988. Fast-cycle capability for competitive power. *Harvard Business Review,* Nov.–Dec., pp. 110–118.

Bruno, A., Leidecker, J., and Harder, J. 1986. Why firms fail: patterns of discontinuance among Silicon Valley high technology firms. Working Paper. Stanford, CA: Stanford University, Graduate School of Business.

Chandler, A. D. 1990. *Scale and scope: the dynamics of industrial capitalism.* Cambridge, MA: Belknap Press.

Cyert, R. M. and March, J. G. 1963. *A behavioral theory of the firm.* Englewood Cliffs, NJ: Prentice-Hall.

Dess, G. G. 1987. Consensus on strategy formulation and organizational performance: competitors in a fragmented industry. *Strategic Management Journal,* 8: 259–277.

Dess, G. G., and Beard, D. W. 1984. Dimensions of organizational task environments. *Administrative Science Quarterly,* 29: 52–73.

Downs, G., and Mohr, L. 1986. Conceptual issues in the study of innovation. *Administrative Science Quarterly,* 21: 700–714.

Doz, R., Angelmar, D., and Prahalad, K. 1985. Technological innovation and interdependence: a challenge for the large complex firm. *Technology in Society,* 7: 105–125.

Dutton, J., and Duncan, R. 1987. The creation of momentum for change through strategic issue diagnosis. *Strategic Management Journal,* 8: 279–296.

Eisenhardt, K. 1990. Speed and strategic choice: how managers accelerate decision making. *California Management Review,* 32: 1–16.

Eisenhardt, K., and Schoonhoven, C. 1990. Organizational growth: linking founding team, strategy, environment, and growth among U.S. semiconductor ventures, 1978–1988. *Administrative Science Quarterly,* 35: 504–529.

Finkelstein, S., and Hambrick, D. C. 1990. Top management team tenure and organizational outcomes: the moderating role of managerial discretion. *Administrative Science Quarterly,* 35: 484–503.

Flatt, S. 1993. A longitudinal study in organizational innovativeness: how top management team demography influences organizational innovation. Ph.D. Dissertation. Berkeley: University of California.

Frederickson, J. W., and Iaquinto, A. L. 1989. Inertia and creeping rationality in strategic decisions. *Academy of Management Journal,* 32: 516–542.

Freeman, J., and Hannan, M. 1991. Technical change, inertia, and organizational failure. Working Paper. Ithaca, NY: Cornell University, Graduate School of Management.

Glick, W. H., Huber, G. P., Miller, C. C., Doty, D. H., and Sutcliffe, K. M. 1990. Studying changes in organizational design and effectiveness: retrospective event histories and periodic assessments. *Organization Science,* 1(3): 293–312.

Goodstein, J., and O'Reilly, C. 1988. It's what's up top that counts: the role of executive team demography and team dynamics in determining firm success and failure. Working Paper. Berkeley: University of California, School of Business.

Greiner, L., and Bhambri, A. 1989. New CEO intervention and the dynamics of deliberate strategic change. *Strategic Management Journal,* 10: 65–86.

Gupta, A. K. 1988. Contingency perspectives on strategic leadership: current knowledge and future research directions. In Hambrick, D. C. (Ed.), *The executive effect: concepts and methods of studying top managers* (pp. 147–178). Greenwich, CT: JAI Press.

Hage, J., and Dewar R. 1973. Elite values versus organizational structure in predicting innovations. *Administrative Science Quarterly,* 18: 279–290.

Hambrick, D. 1987. The top management team: key to strategic success. *California Management Review,* 30: 1–20.

Hambrick, D. 1989. Guest editor's introduction: putting top managers back in the strategy picture. *Strategic Management Journal,* 10: 5–15.

Hambrick, D. C., and Brandon, G. L. 1988. Executive values. In Hambrick, D. C., (Ed.), *The executive effect: concepts and methods for studying top managers* (pp. 3–34). Greenwich, CT: JAI Press.

Hambrick, D. C., and D'Aveni, R. 1992. Top team deterioration as part of the downward spiral of large corporate bankruptcies. *Management Science,* 38: 1445–1446.

Hambrick, D. C., and Mason, P. A. 1984. Upper echelons: the organization as a reflection of its top managers. *Academy of Management Review,* 9: 193–206.

Hurst, D. K., Rush, J. C., and White, R. E. 1989. Top management teams and organizational renewal. *Strategic Management Journal,* 10: 87–105.

Jackson, S., Brett, J., Sessa, V., Cooper, D., Julin, J., and Peyronnin, K. 1991. Some differences make a difference: individual dissimilarity and group heterogeneity as correlates of recruitment, promotion and turnover. *Journal of Applied Psychology,* 76: 675–689.

Katz, R. 1982. The effects of group longevity on communication and performance. *Administrative Science Quarterly,* 27: 81–104.

Keck, S. 1991. Top executive team structure: its implications for organizational performance. Working Paper no. 0A90-041. Texas A&M University. College Station.

Keck, S., and Tushman, M. 1991. Environmental and organization context and executive team characteristics. Working Paper. New York: Columbia University, Graduate School of Business.

Kmenta, J. 1986. *Elements of econometrics.* New York: Macmillan.

McCain, B. E., O'Reilly, C. A., and Pfeffer, J. 1983. The effects of departmental demography on turnover: the case of a university. *Academy of Management Journal,* 26: 626–641.

Michel, J., and Hambrick, D. 1992. Diversification posture and the characteristics of the top management team. *Academy of Management Journal,* 35: 9–37.

Miller, D. 1991. Stale in the saddle: CEO tenure and the match between organization and environment. *Management Science,* 37(1): 34–52.

Mintzberg, H. 1979. *The structuring of organizations: the synthesis of the research.* Englewood Cliffs, NJ: Prentice-Hall.

Murray, A. 1989. Top management group heterogeneity and firm performance. *Strategic Management Journal,* 10: 125–141.

Norburn, D., and Birley, S. 1988. The top management team and corporate performance. *Strategic Management Journal,* 9: 225–237.

O'Reilly, C. A., Caldwell, D. F., and Barnett, W. P. 1989. Work group demography, social integration, and turnover. *Administrative Science Quarterly,* 34: 21–37.

O'Reilly, C., and Flatt, S. 1989. Executive team demography, organizational innovation, and firm performance. Paper presented at the 51st Meetings of the Academy of Management, San Francisco.

Pfeffer, J. 1983. Organizational demography. In Staw, B. M., and Cummings, L. (Eds.) *Research in organizational behavior,* Vol. 5 (pp. 299–357). Greenwich, CT: JAI Press.

Pfeffer, J. 1992. *Managing with power.* Cambridge, MA: Harvard Business School Press.

Pfeffer, J., and O'Reilly, C. 1987. Hospital demography and turnover among nurses. *Industrial Relations,* 26: 158–172.

Priem, R. 1990. Top management team group factors, consensus, and firm performance. *Strategic Management Journal,* 11: 469–478.

Shaw, M. 1981. *Group dynamics: the psychology of small group behavior.* New York: McGraw-Hill.

Teachman, J. 1980. Analysis of population diversity. *Sociological Methods and Research,* 8: 341–362.

Thompson, J. D. 1967. *Organizations in action: social science bases of administrative theory.* New York: McGraw-Hill.

Tsui, A., Egan, T., and O'Reilly, C. 1992. Being different: relational demography and organizational attachment. *Administrative Science Quarterly,* 37: 549–579.

Tsui, A., and O'Reilly, C. 1989. Beyond simple demographic effects: the importance of relational demography in superior-subordinate dyads. *Academy of Management Journal,* 32: 402–423.

Tushman, M., and Keck, S. 1989. Environmental and organization context and executive team characteristics: an organization learning approach. Working Paper. New York: Columbia University, Graduate School of Business.

Tushman, M., Newman, W., and Romanelli, E. 1986. Convergence and upheaval: managing the unsteady pace of organizational evolution. *California Management Review,* 29: 1–20.

Virany, B., Tushman, M., and Romanelli, E. 1992. Executive succession and organizational outcomes in turbulent environments: an organization learning approach. *Organization Science,* 3: 72–91.

Wagner, G. W., Pfeffer, J., and O'Reilly, C. A. 1984. Organizational demography and turnover in top management groups. *Administrative Science Quarterly,* 29: 74–92.

Webber, A. 1990. Consensus, continuity, and common sense: an interview with COMPAQ's Rod Canion. *Harvard Business Review,* July–Aug. pp. 115–123.

Welch, J. F. 1990. Today's leaders look to tomorrow. *Fortune,* March 26, p. 30.

Wiersema, M., and Bantel, K. 1992. Top management demography and corporate strategic change. *Academy of Management Journal,* 35: 91–121.

Zenger, T., and Lawrence, B. 1989. Organizational demography: the differential effects of age and tenure distributions on technical communication. *Academy of Management Journal,* 32: 353–376.

6

The Impact of Upper-Echelon Diversity on Organizational Performance

WILLIAM H. GLICK, C. CHET MILLER,
and GEORGE P. HUBER

> A corporation is held together as much by shared management beliefs as by
> formal authority.   Alvin Toffler, *The Adaptive Corporation*, 1985: 18

> Honest differences of views and honest debate are not disunity. They are the
> vital process of policy-making among free men.   Herbert Hoover

EDITORS' SUMMARY

The makeup of an organization's upper echelon is a critical determinant of the
organization's performance. Indeed, when thinking about designing an organization, it is difficult to argue that any component is worthy of more attention
and concern than the upper-echelon team.

In this chapter, Glick, Miller, and Huber look at the influence of upper-echelon diversity on organizational performance. Based on previous research and
on interviews with over 120 chief executives, they build a process model of the
effects of demographic, structural, and cognitive diversity of upper-echelon
management teams. They then test and improve the model with data from 79
strategic business units.

Despite considerable theorizing, there is relatively little consensus about
the effects of upper-echelon management diversity. One line of reasoning is
that diversity stimulates creativity, change, and innovation, and that these factors increase organizational performance, particularly in fast-changing environments. A second line of reasoning is that team diversity stimulates comprehensive decision making which, in turn, contributes to organizational performance.
A third line of reasoning focuses on the beneficial stabilizing influence of homogeneity. When the upper echelon is homogeneous, it is more likely to have a
stronger culture with shared values, terminology, and belief structures. These
factors facilitate communication, problem solving, fast decision making, and
high levels of organizational performance. Stated in negative terms, this line of
reasoning suggests that diversity leads to conflict, a lack of cohesion, misun-

derstanding between diverse groups, parochialism, negative political activity, and poor organizational performance. The implication of this third line of reasoning is that organizations should select, attract, promote, and retain individuals who are similar to the executives on the upper echelon.

Glick and his associates found that the validity of these lines of reasoning varied with the dimension on which the team was diverse. For preference diversity, they found more evidence for the negative effects of diversity suggested by the third line of reasoning. Preference diversity concerning human resource goals had the most negative effects on comprehensiveness and cohesion. In terms of belief diversity, however, they found support for the second line of reasoning. Belief diversity in terms of the efficacy of advertising stimulated comprehensiveness in decision making in the upper-echelon team.

An interesting and controversial finding that follows from their research is that comprehensiveness of decision making is positively related to profitability in turbulent environments, but slightly negatively related in very low turbulence environments. This challenges conventional thinking concerning rapid decision making in more turbulent environments. Although turbulence may put a premium on rapid decision making, the current research and recent case studies indicate that upper-echelon decision making can be simultaneously comprehensive and fast. The theoretical and methodological improvements in this chapter are sensible and lend credibility to both the implications for upper-echelon research and the recommendations for upper-echelon executives. ■

The possible effects of upper-echelon diversity are both diverse and contradictory. Diversity may stimulate change or it may instill stability through a delicate but sacred balance of power. When team members have more diverse backgrounds, responsibilities, beliefs, or values, there may be more conflict, confusion, creativity, innovation, political activity, parochialism, competition, risk reduction, and comprehensive decision making. Diversity may either increase or decrease organizational performance. Diversity may be coupled with better environmental scanning and more informed decision making. Members in diverse teams, however, are more likely to disagree with each other and find faults with the status quo. Diversity may inhibit the development of a strong culture, standardization of procedures, good communication, and cohesion. Adding diversity to a relatively homogeneous group may increase confusion and excitement as new ideas are introduced to the group.

Because these possible effects are vitally important to organizational leaders and members, managing diversity has been the focus of many publications in the managerial (Cox and Blake, 1991; Stewart, 1991; "Welcome to the Woman-Friendly Company," 1990) and academic press (Bartlett and Ghoshal, 1989; Cosier and Schwenk, 1990; Lawrence and Lorsch, 1967; McCann and Galbraith, 1981; Mintzberg, 1979).

This chapter integrates many of the disparate and conflicting arguments about the effects of diversity to present a more comprehensive model of diversity. Diversity is defined in terms of demographic, structural, and cognitive characteristics of the upper echelon of an organization. The integrative model of diversity is based on previously published research on diversity and information provided by over 120 chief executives in a series of interviews (described in Glick, Huber, Miller, Doty, and Sutcliffe, 1990, reprinted as the appendix of this volume; see also Chapter 7 in this volume). During these interviews about the recent changes in their organizations, many of the chief executives mentioned diversity or homogeneity in terms of their organization's structure or the composition of their upper-echelon team. Their comments are used to develop and illustrate the arguments in our comprehensive model. We empirically tested this model using data from a second data set that involved a combined telephone interview procedure and mailed survey completed by most of the upper-echelon managers in 79 organizations. The chapter concludes with an improved model of the effects of diversity and implications for future research and for managing diversity more effectively.

EFFECTS OF UPPER-ECHELON DIVERSITY IN ORGANIZATIONS

Diversity may have a wide variety of outcomes, as suggested by the opening paragraph. We focus our theory building on open systems effectiveness and profitability, along with three intervening process variables: comprehensiveness of decision making, communication, and cohesion. Open systems effectiveness is the ability to acquire resources, which is more formally defined as "the ability of the organization to exploit its environment in the acquisition of scarce and valued resources" (Yuchtman and Seashore, 1967: 898).

Three Perspectives on Diversity

One reason that organizational researchers and management practitioners have discussed so many possible consequences of upper-echelon diversity is that diversity has been portrayed in terms of three major sets of characteristics in an organizational context: demographic, structural, and cognitive. These three sets of characteristics correspond to major theoretical streams that pervade organizational science and sociology. Each is described briefly.

Demographic Diversity

Demographic diversity refers to differences in relatively objective characteristics of members of the organization, such as age, gender, tenure, and functional background. To the extent that all of the upper-echelon members joined the organization at the same time, they are less diverse in terms of organizational tenure. Demographic diversity of the upper echelon also may be characterized in terms of tenure on the upper-echelon team rather than tenure in the organization. Low diversity in tenure on the upper-echelon team occurs most frequently when a group of founders dominates the organization or when the upper echelon is replaced en masse by the shareholders or by a new CEO.

Given differences in responsibilities, career paths, training, and reward structures, managers with different functional backgrounds are often expected to think and behave differently. In many organizations, however, there are very small differences in the functional backgrounds of upper-echelon team members. Two processes may lead to low upper-echelon diversity in terms of functional backgrounds. In some organizations the only way to the top is through the dominant functional unit (e.g., marketing at Procter and Gamble, finance at General Motors, or engineering at Hewlett Packard). In other organizations, the road to the top winds through all functional and geographic units to ensure that each executive is capable of taking a broad perspective of the business (e.g., International Business Machines is also known as "I've Been Moved"). Low diversity of the upper echelon can be disrupted by the introduction of a maverick with a different career history, such as the legendary promotion of the production-oriented John Reed at Citibank.

Research concerning the consequences of demographic diversity in organizational contexts began in the late 1970s. Example works include those by Blau (1977), Pfeffer (1983), Pfeffer and Moore (1980), and Stewman and Konda, (1983). This research and theory development drew heavily on sociological theories of conflict (Turner, 1986). The underlying rationale in conflict theories is that differences among people, classes of people, organizations, and so on are expected to lead to change.

Structural Diversity

Diversity in organizational structures can be characterized in many ways, including the form and degree of departmentation (Duncan, 1979; McCann and Galbraith, 1981; Price, 1968; Seiler, 1963; Walker and Lorsch, 1968); the form and degree of diversification (Chandler, 1962; Daniels, Pitts, and Tretter, 1985; Williamson, 1975); the degree of specialization of work responsibilities; stratification in communication patterns; and the degree of differentiation into distinct, identifiable units (Lawrence and Lorsch, 1967). We focus on structural diversity between units that are led by upper-echelon managers. Structural diversity between upper-echelon units is usually coupled with homogeneity *within* organizational units, homogeneity that may be identified by function, by customer, by geographical location, or by other criteria. Homogeneity within units typically facilitates internal communication and coordination; coordination *across* units, however, is hampered to the degree that the units are very distinct and separated from each other.

Research and theory development on structural diversity has a long history that is based on sociological theories of equilibrium. The assumptions about equilibrium in structural diversity are most apparent in the open systems perspectives of Lawrence and Lorsch (1967) and Katz and Kahn (1978). They argue that effective organizations differentiate internally so as to maximize their responsiveness to different elements in their environment. Separate organizational subunits are often more flexible and responsive because each type of customer, supplier, regulator, or other constituency is served by a single department or group in the organization. To the extent that each subunit can customize its responses to the environment autonomously from the rest of the organization, each segment of the environment is likely to be better served. Thus, based on these arguments, structural diversity should match the diversity of the environment. As the mix of customers, suppliers, and other environmental elements changes over time, however, the process of matching structural and environmental diversity shifts from a simple equilibrium process to a process of dynamic equilibrium with built-in time lags between unanticipated changes in the environment and changes in organizational design.

More recent theory development on structural diversity has been based on conflict theories. In contrast with Lawrence and Lorsch's assertion that highly differentiated organizations need to use more elaborate (and expensive) forms of coordination to integrate their disparate subunits, Weick (1982) argues for high differentiation and low integration of the subunits to maximize adaptability of the organization. This argument is more consistent with an assumption of constant flux and change in the organization's environment. In complex, rapidly changing environments, organizations need to differentiate themselves in order to be as complex, dynamic, and diverse as their environments. Because the different parts of an organization's environment make inconsistent demands on the organizational subunits, highly differentiated subunits will inevitably be in conflict with each other. Thus, rather than forcing the subunits to coordinate with each other, Weick (1982) suggests that organizations will be more adaptable and effective if they allow the differentiated subunits to operate autonomously from each other. A similar argument is provided by Simon (1973), who argues that subunit autonomy is necessary for avoiding information overload in an information-laden world. This autonomy, however, also has several limitations, such as reduced organizational learning among the autonomous subunits (Huber, 1991) and the costs of redundant labor and equipment.

In this chapter we examine the consequences of structural diversity predicted by both equilibrium and conflict theories. We narrow our focus, however, by considering only one form of structural diversity, departmentation—that is, the degree to which subunits of the firm are specialized in terms of geography, market segment, or function.

Cognitive Diversity

Cognitive diversity of the upper echelon can be characterized in terms of differences in preferences and beliefs among the members of the upper echelon. Broadly speaking, cognitive diversity refers to variation in beliefs about cause-effect relationships and variation in preferences about different goals for the organization (Miller, 1990). More specifically, we conceptualize preference diversity in terms of operative goals. Following Perrow (1961: 854), we assume that operative rather than official goals are "most relevant to understanding organizational behavior." Operative goals (e.g., to maximize sales growth) "designate the ends sought through the actual operating procedures of the organization" (Daft, 1986: 96). Official goals (e.g., to maximize shareholder wealth) reflect basic missions and are often too abstract and unassailable to be useful.

We conceptualize belief diversity in terms of cause maps concerning the efficacy of different strategies. Cause maps contain concepts (i.e., variables) joined together by arrows that indicate the existence of cause-effect relationships (Hall, 1984). Beliefs concerning cause-effect relationships are among the most important beliefs in organizations (Beyer, 1981; Sproull, 1981; Thompson and Tuden, 1959; Weick and Bougon, 1985), and disagreements surrounding such beliefs are often the most difficult to reconcile (Beyer, 1981). One of the most important functions of an upper-echelon team is to handle disagreements about the efficacy of pursuing alternative strategies to accomplish organizational goals. Rarely will all members of an upper-echelon team agree entirely about the consequences of pursuing different strategies.

Although members of an upper-echelon team may agree that one strategy may lead to ruin, and that some operative goals are desirable for the organization, they also may disagree on other strategies or goals. Thus, it is possible for an upper-echelon team to be diverse in terms of some, but not necessarily all, beliefs and preferences.

Cognitive diversity is one of the newer areas of organizational research. Although cognitive diversity can be interesting in its own right, characteristics of cognitive diversity have appeared most commonly as unmeasured intervening variables for explaining the processes that link demographic and structural diversity to their consequences (for examples, see O'Reilly, Caldwell, and Barnett, 1989; Pfeffer, 1983; Wagner, Pfeffer, and O'Reilly, 1984; and Zenger and Lawrence, 1989). The following section examines the effects of demographic diversity and departmentation on cognitive diversity. In conjunction with the subsequent sections on the effects of diversity on organizational processes, the theoretical arguments position cognitive diversity as an intervening process linking demographic diversity and departmentation with organizational processes and performance. Figure 6.1 summarizes these direct and indirect effects of demographic and structural diversity.

Effects of Demographic Diversity and Departmentation on Cognitive Diversity

Although the three perspectives on diversity are conceptually distinct, they are likely to be related to each other. Many causal arguments that link demographic diversity and departmentation to organizational outcomes either implicitly or explicitly posit cognitive diversity as an important intervening process. The dominant opinion is that demographic diversity leads to cognitive diversity, which then harms organizational performance (McCain, O'Reilly, and Pfeffer, 1983; Pfeffer, 1983; Wagner et al., 1984; Zenger and Lawrence, 1989). A common argument is that demographic similarity leads to shared values and beliefs, which then lead to greater social similarity, integration, communication, and other organizational processes. Studies by McCain et al. (1983), Wagner et al. (1984), and Zenger and Lawrence (1989), showed empirical support for the links between demographic diversity and organizational processes, but the mediating effects of cognitive diversity have been left unexamined. Anecdotal evidence from our interviews (described in the appendix of this volume), however, supports the importance of cognitive diversity as an intervening factor linking demographic diversity and organizational processes. In one organization a new CEO was brought in from the outside while the rest of the upper-echelon team was left intact. Within four months the CEO was forced out because he viewed things differently. In another organization warring factions developed when several newcomers formed a

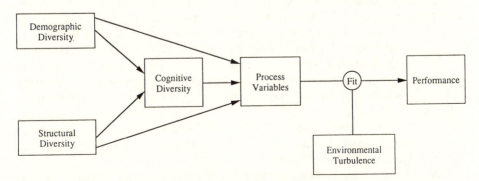

Figure 6.1. General model of the effects of upper-echelon diversity.

coalition against the entrenched majority. The new group resisted the norms and beliefs of the longer term employees, leading to dysfunctional organizational outcomes.

Although most researchers have argued that demographic diversity positively influences cognitive diversity, a partially dissenting opinion is voiced by Kanter (1977), who argues that preference and belief *homogeneity* actually may be enhanced by demographic diversity in terms of tenure with the organization and tenure in the upper echelon. Rather than hiring or promoting a large cohort at the same time, Kanter recommends staggering new recruits so that the processes of attraction, selection, and attrition (Schneider and Reichers, 1983) can have maximum impact on the socialization of each new member. Although this increases demographic diversity in terms of tenure on the upper-echelon team, Kanter argues that slowing these processes leads to "homosocial reproduction" and perpetuates a dominant set of beliefs and preferences in an organization. Similar arguments are found in discussions of clan control (Ouchi, 1981) as a characteristic of Japanese (and some U. S.) organizations that encourage lifetime employment coupled with slow promotions. Both of these dissenting opinions, however, are focused primarily on the negative effects of tenure diversity on cognitive diversity. Both Kanter (1977) and Ouchi (1981) seem to agree with the dominant opinion that diversity in terms of age and functional background are likely to lead to cognitive diversity.

Organizational scholars also are divided in their predictions of the effects of structural diversity on cognitive diversity. One line of argument is that greater functional departmentation leads to more dissimilar reward structures across departments, larger differences in interaction patterns, and stronger parochialism (Duncan, 1979; Lawrence and Lorsch, 1967; McCann and Galbraith, 1981). Theoretically, these effects can lead to differences in preferences and beliefs that then affect organizational processes.

Similarly, more geographically based departmentation is associated with lower proximity between units. This reduces communication across departmental boundaries and encourages responsiveness to local conditions (Duncan, 1979; McCann and Galbraith, 1981). These processes lead to belief diversity when isolated geographic groups independently develop different beliefs about the causal efficacy of different organizational strategies. For example, one of the CEOs interviewed in our initial study (see the appendix in this volume) reported that he had moved to consolidate all operations in one central location to reduce geographical departmentation and misunderstandings among the departments. In another organization, the CEO attempted to consolidate his rapidly expanding operations from several buildings into one large building in order to develop a shared identity and strategic vision for the organization.

The effects of strong market departmentation are expected to be very similar to those of geographic departmentation, with even greater effects on preference diversity. One of the interviewed CEOs explained a shift away from strict market departmentation as an effort to reduce conflict due to differences in preferences and strategies employed by the different market units. Each of the market units had developed an overly parochial view of its market and often argued over transfer prices rather than working together for common goals.

A partially contradictory argument is that the form and degree of departmentation is unrelated to cognitive diversity because most managers are very capable of adopting a generalist perspective despite their functional, geographic, or market-oriented responsibilities. Common wisdom and early experimental research by Dearborn and Simon (1958) suggested that managers in production, marketing, and finance each adopt different perspectives. A recent replication and extension of this research by Walsh (1988), however, found that managers adopted a generalist perspective in an experimental exercise. Thus, there is mixed evidence for expecting departmentation to be related to cognitive diversity.

Effects of Diversity on Organizational Processes

To really understand and manage the effects of demographic, structural, and cognitive diversity on organizational outcomes, it is important to examine their intervening effects on organizational processes (see Figure 6.1). The intervening influences of three critical process variables are examined in this research: comprehensiveness of decision making, amount of rich communication, and cohesion. Each of these three organizational process variables has been cited as an important antecedent of organizational performance in several previous studies.

Comprehensiveness of Decision Making

Comprehensiveness of decision making is one of the most frequently cited intervening variables in process explanations linking diversity with organizational performance. The current research, however, is the only empirical test of the link between diversity and comprehensiveness (see Miller, 1990, for a more in-depth report of the portions of this research that are related to comprehensiveness). Comprehensiveness is defined as the extent to which an upper-echelon team "attempts to be exhaustive or inclusive" in making strategic decisions (Fredrickson and Mitchell, 1984: 402). Behaviors that indicate the level of comprehensiveness include the extent to which "brainstorming" sessions occur, the number of alternative solutions that are considered, and the extent to which quantitative analyses are conducted.

Preference and belief diversity are expected to positively influence comprehensiveness because differences in preferences and beliefs often surface in the context of specific strategic decisions. One specific argument that suggests positive effects of diversity on comprehensiveness concerns costs. Because higher levels of comprehensiveness are expensive financially and temporally (Fredrickson and Mitchell, 1984), they are more likely to occur under conditions of high disagreement than under conditions of low disagreement. When there are many disagreements surrounding a strategic decision, upper-echelon managers are more likely to be motivated to engage in more discussions and to commission more analyses. Lower levels of comprehensiveness are more likely to be associated with lower levels of disagreement.

A second argument suggesting positive effects concerns curiosity. Specifically, disagreements generated by preference and belief diversity are likely to influence managers' curiosity, which in turn affects comprehensiveness (cf. Nemeth, 1986). That is, for many managers, being exposed to disagreements likely results in curiosity concerning the value of various positions. The curiosity, in turn, leads the managers to carefully consider some or all of the positions and/or to commission analyses designed to determine the soundness of some or all of the positions.

A final argument suggesting positive effects is somewhat more complex than the preceding two arguments. As suggested earlier, preference and belief diversity are expected to negatively affect upper-echelon cohesion. Cohesion, in turn, is expected to negatively affect comprehensiveness. Thus, cohesion is expected to mediate partially the effects of preference and belief diversity on comprehensiveness.

The principal reason for expecting a negative relationship between cohesion and comprehensiveness relates to a desire for amicable relations. Specifically, cohesive management teams are expected to want to maintain amicable relations by avoiding disagreements that surface during comprehensive decision processes. If this expectation is true, managers in cohesive teams would be less likely to play devil's advocate and less likely to insist on consulting outsiders to confirm or disconfirm beliefs held by other team members. Ideas put on the table early would go relatively unchallenged and uninvestigated. In contrast, managers in teams that are not cohesive would be quite willing to challenge opinions put forth by their colleagues. These managers would be more likely to encourage debate and initiate investigations designed to uncover flaws in their colleagues' reasoning. Even if the managers exhibit low levels of preference and belief diversity, attempts at discrediting colleagues may occur if cohesion is very low (i.e., if team members disliked each other very much).

Relatedly, Janis (1972: 9) has argued that extremely high levels of cohesion can lead to groupthink—"a deterioration of mental efficiency, reality testing, and moral judgment that results from in-group pressures." Group members are thought to value group membership to the point where fear of ostracism and fear of membership loss result in conformity and unquestioned acceptance of ideas from an early decision contributor or from a group leader. Particularly problematic is the fact that the group as a whole often refuses to seek or accept input from outsiders.

In summary, many arguments support the prediction of a positive effect of cognitive diversity on comprehensiveness of decision making. This prediciton is very clearly imbedded in several techniques employed by the movement for Total Quality Management, or TQM (Imai, 1986; Juran, 1989; Malcolm Baldrige National Quality Award Consortium, 1990; Ozeki and Asaka, 1990), including the following: structuring quality circles to represent diverse perspectives; management by fact; root cause analysis; extensive documentation and analysis of processes and outcomes; seven why's; world class benchmarking; and comprehensive definitions of the cost of quality. Each of these techniques is designed to stimulate more comprehensive decision making by forcing organizational members to confront the diversity of perspectives in their organization.

Although this is the dominant perspective, there are three arguments that predict a negative, rather than a positive, effect of cognitive diversity on comprehensiveness. First, cognitive diversity often implies that different people will use their own specialized language, images, and stories to communicate with each other. To the extent that this leads to communication failures, people are likely to want to avoid the frustrating, lengthy discussion processes required for comprehensive decision making. Second, preference diversity often implies disagreement over strongly held preferences that will not be compromised. Thus, comprehensive decision making may lead to head butting rather than to issue resolution. Both of these arguments suggest that cognitive diversity may lead to an emphasis on individualistic rather than consensual decision making. This occurred most prominently in one of the interviewed organizations, where the vice president of manufacturing was ultimately dismissed after repeatedly ignoring inputs from others. It is also reflected in a common practice that was reported by one CEO where group facilitators encouraged diverse group members to be more empathetic with each other and to engage in cross training to facilitate group discussions.

The third argument for doubting the positive effects of cognitive diversity on comprehensiveness is more complex and very debatable. The core of this argument is that higher diversity may stimulate more comprehensiveness at first, but, over time, the process of engaging in lengthy discussions and resolving many disagreements through a comprehensive decision process leads, ultimately, to a decrease in cognitive diversity. This countervailing process emphasizes the learning that occurs during the making of strategic decisions and suggests that teams consistently engaging in more comprehensive processes will not maintain their cognitive diversity over time.

This last reason for doubting the positive effects of cognitive diversity may be plausible, but it must be challenged on the grounds that preferences and beliefs may be difficult to alter in the context of comprehensive strategic decision making. One reason is that strategic issues by their very nature are unstructured and ambiguous: "almost nothing is given or easily determined" (Mintzberg, Raisinghani, and Théorêt, 1976). Given the high level of ambiguity, discussions and analyses are often inconclusive and therefore are unlikely to alter the schemas (i.e., cognitive structures) underlying managers' preferences and beliefs (which explains the frequent need for negotiation, compromise, and autocratic CEO intervention). Schemas that are altered probably will be those that are specific to a particular decision (e.g., schemas underlying preferences concerning concrete alternatives for a particular strategic decision rather than the more enduring schemas underlying preferences concerning somewhat more abstract organizational goals). Further, because strategic decisions involve nonroutine, novel issues (Mintzberg et al., 1976), many schemas that are altered will be irrelevant for the next strategic decision.

A second reason the schemas may be difficult to alter is that organizational and personal factors driving these schemas tend to be fairly stable. An upper-echelon manager's functional background, for example, likely has a major impact on preferences and beliefs and tends to be stable from one decision to the next. Managers with different functional backgrounds appear to "come to a problem with different experience, cognitive elements, goals, values, and priorities" (Daft and Lengel, 1986: 564). For example, managers with backgrounds primarily in output functions (i.e., marketing and sales) often favor growth as an organizational goal, whereas managers with backgrounds primarily in production often favor efficiency (Hambrick and Mason, 1984). Daft and Lengel (1986: 564) note that a "person trained as a scientist may have a difficult time understanding the point of view of a lawyer. A common perspective does not exist. Coding schemes are dissimilar."

A third reason schemas are difficult to alter is that people are naturally resistant to inconsistent information (O'Sullivan and Durso, 1984), especially when ambiguity is high.

Despite the counterarguments, we initially decided to adopt the dominant perspective and hypothesized that *preference and belief diversity positively influence the comprehensiveness of decision making.*

Demographic diversity might also affect comprehensiveness of decision making through several processes. Because of the indirect effects through cognitive diversity, a positive effect of demographic diversity on comprehensiveness might be expected.

Independent of these indirect effects, however, demographic diversity may have negative effects because of a lowered tolerance for and understanding of others. Recent recruits to the upper-echelon team are likely to see the old-timers as part of the problems that they need to correct. The old-timers, however, are likely to be convinced that the young upstarts just don't understand the nature of their business and quickly get tired of hearing how things are done by the former employer or teacher of the new recruits. These misunderstandings are created by the superficial perception of dissimilarity and may be unrelated to actual dissimilarity in beliefs and preferences. In the context of demographic diversity, all parties are likely to avoid long exhaustive debates on the root causes of a problem; conflict avoidance behaviors are often seen as more acceptable when people come from different backgrounds and have limited expectations about their abilities to resolve conflicts constructively.

Although the indirect effects of demographic diversity on comprehensiveness mediated by cognitive diversity may be positive, the direct effects that are independent of cognitive diversity are likely to be negative. Thus, we tentatively hypothesized that *demographic diversity negatively influences the comprehensiveness of decision making.*

Structural diversity is also likely to affect comprehensiveness of decision making both directly and indirectly. In the case of market departmentation, both the direct effects and the indirect effects mediated by cognitive diversity are likely to be positive. When upper-echelon managers are given responsibility for different market segments through market departmentation, they are given incentives to argue strongly for their market areas. Although these incentives may become internalized as differences in beliefs and values, in the short run, the incentives intensify argumentation by each manager for his or her department's interests. In some organizations, this may take on overtones of political maneuvering where extensive analyses and the use of large quantities of information may symbolically legitimate one manager's position (Feldman and March, 1981; Pfeffer, 1981a,b). When managers are very focused on their own market segment, rather than taking a corporate perspective, each manager will be motivated to develop his or her own analyses and evaluations. As a group, this results in multiple, competing analyses and a thorough evaluation of many alternative solutions. To the extent that the chief executive considers these analyses and evaluations, the final decision making process will be very comprehensive.

Geographic departmentation may also effect comprehensiveness of decision making; however, the independent, direct effect is likely to be negative rather than positive. That is, to the extent that upper-echelon team members are each responsible for geographically dispersed units, they are less likely to be able to come together in a central location to engage in comprehensive decision making. The logistical costs of frequent interaction will directly reduce the comprehensiveness of decision making by upper-echelon managers with geographically dispersed responsibilities. Thus, we hypothesized that *greater market departmentation and lower geographic departmentation positively influence the comprehensiveness of decision making.*

Amount of Rich Communication

Preference and belief diversity were expected to negatively influence the amount of rich communication among upper-echelon managers. Rich communication is defined as communication involving face-to-face conversations and phone conversations, as opposed to communication involving memos and impersonal letters (Daft and Lengel, 1986; see also Chapter 4 of this volume). The rationales for this expectation are that (1) managers who like one another (see the following section on cohesion) are more likely to talk to one another; (2) managers with similar beliefs and values tend to share the same experiences, images, and specialized language that makes communication easier and less frustrating; (3) managers with similar values can be more empathetic with each other; and (4) managers are less likely to get into disagreements about fundamental issues. These arguments are supported in several empirical studies (see, for example, Lincoln and Miller, 1979). They are also supported by anecdotal evidence from our interviews with CEOs. One reported that his organization was dropping out of a joint venture with another organization, led by people with very different beliefs and values, due to aggravation over broken communication. He felt that cognitive diversity had contributed directly to several blunders, including pricing goods below cost. A second CEO was using a goal clarification process, including several workshops and retreats, in order to decrease preference diversity and thereby improve communication. She was clearly aware of the importance of developing a shared vision in order to improve communications and organizational performance. Thus, we hypothesized that *preference and belief diversity negatively influence the amount of rich communication.*

Demographic diversity is also likely to affect communication patterns for a number of reasons (Zenger and Lawrence, 1989). It indirectly affects communication through cognitive diversity and through cohesion, as described below. Further, demographic diversity tends to decrease trust and conflict resolution abilities, leading to an increased probability of mutual frustration and avoidance. One of the CEOs explicitly recognized the importance of communication problems created by demographic diversity and set up a task force on managing diversity to combat the problem. Thus, we hypothesized that *demographic diversity negatively influences the amount of rich communication.*

Although structural diversity is expected to affect communication indirectly through cognitive diversity, we are not aware of any strong arguments for independent, direct effects of structural diversity in terms of function or market. Thus, we did not explicitly hypothesize any effects for these two variables. We did, however, hypothesize that *structural diversity in terms of geography negatively influences the amount of rich communication.*

Upper-Echelon Cohesion

Preference and belief diversity were expected to negatively influence upper-echelon cohesion, defined as the extent to which upper-echelon managers like one another and stick up for each other (cf. O'Reilly et al., 1989). This expectation was based on social psychological arguments about interpersonal attraction and inferred evaluations (cf. Condon and Crano, 1988). The idea of inferred evaluation suggests that individuals assume that a person who agrees with them also likes them. This argument, combined with the frequent observation that individuals tend to like those who like them (Aronson and Worchel, 1966; Condon and Crano, 1988), yields the expectation of a negative relationship between cognitive diversity and upper-echelon cohesion.

Similarly, cognitive diversity may also negatively affect cohesion due to a lack of trust and freedom to fail (Kanter, 1983). To the extent that someone has the same values and beliefs, managers tend to be predisposed to be more trusting and forgiving. People with similar beliefs and preferences are expected to make similar decisions given the same information. If and when one of their projects fails, it can be interpreted as an honest mistake rather than as a stupid, ill-conceived project.

A negative association between cognitive diversity and interpersonal attraction has been frequently observed in the context of pairs of individuals. Condon and Crano (1988: 789) note that "the ubiquity of this result, and the wide range of research settings in which it has been found, render the similarity-attraction link one of social psychology's most dependable research findings." Based on our interviews of CEOs, this interpersonal effect appears to apply also to cohesion of upper-echelon teams. One organization introduced a major restructuring of rewards to decrease preference diversity and eliminate frequent managerial bickering. The CEO was trying to get everyone focused on the customer and overall profits rather than their own individual compensation. In another organization, the CEO described his attempts to reduce grievances by using several participative mechanisms to clarify beliefs, reduce belief diversity, and develop common goals. Thus, we hypothesized that *preference and belief diversity negatively influence upper-echelon cohesion.*

Demographic diversity is also expected to negatively affect upper-echelon cohesion (Murray, 1989; Tsui and O'Reilly, 1989). Part of this effect is due to the mediating influences of cognitive diversity: demographic diversity contributes to cognitive diversity, which negatively effects cohesion. Another part of the overall effect of demographic diversity, however, is independent of cognitive diversity. First, demographic diversity leads to less frequent interactions among the upper-echelon team members. When demographic diversity is low, the teams are more likely to have spent time together and developed more trust from experience. Second, when demographic diversity is low, team members are more likely to perceive each other as being similar. Thus, they are more likely to be attracted to and trust each other.

A counterargument is that demographic diversity in terms of tenure may lead to more cohesion due to an intensification of the socialization processes leading to homosocial reproduction (Kanter, 1977). Despite this one counterargument, however, we hypothesized that *demographic diversity negatively influences upper-echelon cohesion.*

Structural diversity is also expected to have direct and indirect effects on upper-echelon cohesion. The effects of greater functional departmentation are most likely to be mediated by cognitive diversity, as functional departmentation fosters parochial views and cognitive diversity. Geographic and market departmentation, however, are also likely to have direct, negative effects on cohesion due to less frequent and more stratified interactions among upper-echelon team members. Interactions are less frequent and more stratified because upper-echelon managers tend to be more autonomous and usually need to interact less when both geographic and market departmentation are high. In one of the interviewed organizations, the CEO introduced a major restructuring to centralize the marketing function for several product lines to increase cohesion throughout the organization. In another organization, geographically dispersed units were moved to a central location to increase cohesion and eliminate foot-dragging in the implementation of new strategies. Thus, we hypothesized that *greater market departmentation and greater geographic departmentation negatively influence upper-echelon cohesion.*

Effects of Diversity on Organizational Performance

Although upper-echelon comprehensiveness of decision making, communication, and cohesion are important and useful processes to monitor in organizations, we are also interested in understanding the consequences of diversity on open systems effectiveness (the ability to acquire resources) and profitability. Demographic, structural, and cognitive diversity are unlikely to have direct effects on organizational performance, but they are likely to have indirect effects mediated by upper-echelon cohesion, communication, and comprehensiveness of decision making. The effects of each of these intervening process variables are examined below.

Comprehensiveness of Decision Making

Most strategy and organizational scholars agree that comprehensiveness is positively related to organizational performance in relatively placid (slow-changing and predictable) environments (e.g., Andrews, 1971; Fredrickson, 1984; Fredrickson and Mitchell, 1984; Nutt, 1976). The principal argument is that placid environments do not require management teams to respond frequently or quickly to opportunities or problems. This, in turn, allows rich discussions to take place and large amounts of information to be collected and processed thoroughly. Extensive analyses, dialectical inquires, and so forth can all be completed and used in determining organizational actions. Such analyses and inquires increase the probability that important decision variables are identified and accurately assessed, that functional beliefs are adopted regarding how these decision variables relate to each other and to the organization, and that functional outcome preferences are adopted (Fredrickson, 1984).

There is less agreement, however, concerning how comprehensiveness relates to performance in relatively turbulent (fast-changing and unpredictable) environments. Many scholars believe that the level of comprehensiveness should fit the level of turbulence faced by the organization. Specifically, many scholars believe that more comprehensiveness leads to greater performance in less turbulent environments, but that less comprehensiveness leads to increased performance in more turbulent industries (e.g., Fredrickson, 1984; Fredrickson and Mitchell, 1984; Nutt, 1976). The principal argument is that turbulent environments require management teams to act frequently and quickly and that this requires rapid collection and processing of information. Because comprehensive decision making is thought to be very time consuming, it is argued that organizational actions should be selected not through highly comprehensive decision processes, but through intuition, heuristics, or imitation in more turbulent contexts.

A contrasting argument supports the view that comprehensiveness has a positive effect in both placid and turbulent environments. The argument is that turbulent environments require management teams to determine if the conditions underlying opportunities and threats are highly transient and this, in turn, requires the collection and thorough analysis of a great amount of information. If management teams adapt their organizations to transient conditions, the environment soon will not support them (Aldrich, 1979). If they fail to adapt to nontransient conditions, the environment will also not support them. In relatively fast-changing, unpredictable environments, higher levels of comprehensiveness may be needed to distinguish transient from nontransient conditions.

The argument suggesting a negative effect in relatively turbulent environments is provocative but may not be more valid than the argument suggesting a positive effect. Fortunately, Fredrickson and Mitchell (1984) and Fredrickson and Iaquinto (1989) have provided relevant empirical data. They studied comprehensiveness and performance in the forest products industry, an industry previously identified by Dess (1980; Dess and Beard, 1984) as one of the more dynamic industries in the United States. Their empirical results clearly suggest a negative effect (cf. Fredrickson and Mitchell, 1984; Fredrickson and Iaquinto, 1989). Further, consistent with conventional wisdom, Fredrickson and his colleagues found comprehensiveness to be positively related to performance in an industry previously identified by Dess and his colleagues as one of the more stable industries in the United States, the paint and coatings industry. The only counterevidence was provided by Bourgeois and Eisenhardt (1988; Eisenhardt, 1989) based on a clinical study of a total of 12 firms. They found that comprehensiveness was positively related to performance despite the extremely high turbulence faced by these firms, largely because the more successful firms were able to make comprehensive decisions rapidly. Despite this counterevidence, on balance, it seemed reasonable to hypothesize that *a stronger fit between the comprehensiveness of decision making and environmental turbulence leads to greater open systems effectiveness and greater profitability.*

In short, to the extent that the comprehensiveness of their decision making is higher in less turbulent environments (i.e., to the extent that the fit is stronger), organizations will be higher performers.

Amount of Rich Communication

The amount of rich communication is expected to have positive effects on organizational performance because communication leads to better coordination and integration of the organization, and because rich communication leads to better quality decisions. Open, frequent communications among the upper-echelon team members facilitate the exchange of information that is critical to the effective functioning of an organization. This obvious relationship is underscored by the plethora of communication training sessions targeted to all levels of organizations, from the boardroom to the shop floor. It is also supported by the extensive use of teams and task forces in several of the organizations whose CEOs we interviewed. Task forces were explicitly designed and encouraged as communication vehicles for soliciting ideas from diverse parts of the organization and to send clear messages back to all relevant parties regarding any changes in procedures or strategy. Thus, we hypothesized that *increasing the amount of rich communication among the upper-echelon team members leads to greater open systems effectiveness and greater profitability.*

Upper-Echelon Cohesion

The cohesion of the upper-echelon team is also expected to have strong, positive effects on organizational performance. Cohesion is associated with better coordination and integration of the organizational subunits, trust, and freedom to fail on innovative projects. In one of the interviewed organizations, the CEO complained that a lack of cohesion had contributed directly to late shipments and a loss of control over operations. In another organization, disagreements between managers led to critical work stoppages. Subsequent changes introduced by the CEO included changes in authority and responsibilities to reduce the divisive bickering. From all accounts, these changes appeared to be responsible for clear improvements in organizational performance that were reported in later interviews. Given these unequivocal arguments for improving cohesion, we hypothesized that *greater cohesion among the upper-echelon team members leads to greater open systems effectiveness and greater profitability.*

A Model of the Effects of Upper-Echelon Diversity

The series of hypotheses presented above are summarized in Figure 6.2. The general argument is that demographic and structural diversity lead to both components of cognitive diversity (preference and belief diversity). Cognitive diversity, demographic diversity, and structural diversity, then, have direct effects on the organizational process variables (upper-echelon comprehensiveness of decision making, amount of rich communication, and cohesion). (The direct effects of demographic and structural diversity on organizational process variables are omitted from the figure for simplification.) Finally, these process variables have direct effects on organizational performance. As reflected in the arguments, references, and examples above, this model is based on previously published research on organizational processes and information collected during a series of semiannual interviews with more than 120 CEOs from a variety of organizations.

In the second phase of our study, we empirically tested the model shown in Figure 6.2 on a second set of organizations that were randomly sampled from a broader variety of industries than those included in the initial interviews. In this phase of the research we hoped to validate all or parts of the theoretical model in order to better understand the effects of upper-echelon diversity.

STUDY DESIGN FOR TESTING THE MODEL

Industries and Organizations Studied

Because we were interested in developing and testing theory that is generalizable across a broad variety of contexts, and because we believed that environmental characteristics are important contextual factors, the current sample was drawn in two steps. First, we selected a heterogeneous set of industries that was highly diverse in terms of three critical environmental characteristics: stability, munificence, and predictability. Stability and predictability were considered important because they are the two main sub-dimensions of turbulence. Munificence was included as a potentially important control variable in the analyses with performance. In munificent industries, most everyone's performance tends to be good.

Second, we randomly sampled up to 20 strategic business units in each of these industries (note that many strategic business units are independent firms). In initial telephone interviews, these strategic business units were screened to include only those units with at least two levels of management and at least 15 employees. (A more detailed description of the sample and sampling procedure is contained in the appendix to this chapter).

The chief administrators (e.g., presidents, general managers, and division vice

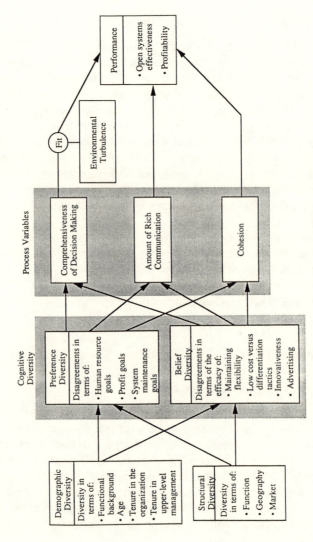

Figure 6.2. Expected effects of upper-echelon diversity.

presidents) of the 396 sampled business units were contacted and asked to participate in the study with their upper-echelon teams, as described below. Seventy-nine agreed to participate. The participation rate of 20 percent of the sampled business units is consistent with prior work done by organizational researchers. After the chief administrator had committed to participating in the study, participation by individual members of the upper-echelon team was exceptionally high, with 82 percent of the mailed surveys being completed and returned.

Procedures

Chief administrators of eligible business units were mailed an introductory letter, an information sheet describing the overall research project, a form for listing the members of their upper-echelon team, a fax cover sheet, and a return envelope. The upper-echelon team was defined for the chief administrator as including the chief operating officer (if the position existed) and all other individuals who reported directly to himself or herself and to the chief operating officer. Ten to 20 days later, the administrator was called so that any questions could be answered and so that he or she could be asked to participate in the study. If the administrator agreed to participate, he or she was asked to return the listing of the upper-echelon team. After gaining the administrator's commitment to the project, we mailed one of three versions of the questionnaire to each member of the upper-echelon team, including the chief administrator. (The average upper-echelon team included 4.4 members.) A follow-up letter and an additional copy of the appropriate questionnaire were sent to each manager who had not returned his or her questionnaire three weeks after he or she should have received it. If one or more members of a given business unit had returned a completed questionnaire, then a second follow-up letter and another copy of the appropriate questionnaire were sent to managers from the unit who had not responded to the first follow-up letter.

Measures of the Variables

Two types of questions were asked of each member of the upper-echelon team. First, questions about cognitions and demographic characteristics were focused on attributes of the individual respondents (i.e., the individual executives). We aggregated these responses using variance or Euclidean distance statistics to measure upper-echelon team diversity. The second set of questions was worded to elicit descriptions of business unit and team characteristics, thereby treating the respondents as key informants (Seidler, 1974), rather than as subjects. (The questionnaires are available from the authors as CODE Technical Report 12.) Recall that the focus of this study is on characteristics of the business unit and the upper-echelon team.

Diversity

Demographic diversity was assessed in terms of dissimilarity of the upper-echelon team members in functional background, age, tenure in the organization, and tenure on the upper-echelon team. Specifically, with the exception of functional background, each of these dimensions was assessed with a direct question to each respondent and then summarized with a coefficient of variation to assess the demographic diversity of the team. Functional background of each respondent was assessed in terms of the number of years that the individual had worked in each of eight different functional areas. The diversity measure was then constructed with the Euclidean distances among the upper-echelon team members, averaged to the level of the team.[1]

Structural diversity was assessed in terms of the degree to which the business was departmentalized by market segment, geographic location, and functional area. In each business unit, the upper-echelon managers reported on these three dimensions of structural diversity using nine questionnaire items.

Preference diversity was measured by asking each respondent to rate the importance of 17 operative goals taken from a competing values model of effectiveness (Dess, 1987; Quinn and Rohrbaugh, 1983). For each business unit in the sample, coefficients of variation were calculated for each of the 17 items. Each coefficient indicates the extent to which upper-echelon managers within a business unit disagree over the importance of a given goal. Following factor analysis and other scale development methods, these 17 measures were summarized into preference diversity concerning (1) human resource goals, (2) profit goals, and (3) system maintenance goals.

Belief diversity was conceptualized in terms of upper-echelon managers' beliefs about the existence of cause-effect relationships (i.e., their cause maps). More specifically, we focused on the perceived efficacy of 22 business tactics that might affect the long-term profitability of the organization. The list of business tactics was based on the work of Porter (1980) and Robinson and Pearce (1988). Respondents were asked how positively or negatively each of the business tactics would influence long-term profitability in their organization. Similar to the preference diversity measure, coefficients of variation were calculated for each business unit and summarized into a smaller set of dimensions. The final dimensions of belief diversity reflected disagreements concerning the efficacy of (1) maintaining flexibility, (2) low cost versus differentiation tactics, (3) innovativeness, and (4) advertising.

Organizational Processes

Comprehensiveness of decision making was assessed with eight questionnaire items developed by ogilvie and Glick (1990) based on Fredrickson's work (cf. Fredrickson, 1984; Fredrickson and Mitchell, 1984; Fredrickson and Iaquinto, 1989). The *amount of rich communication* was assessed with two questionnaire items which were based on Daft and Lengel's (1986) work. Three items adapted from O'Reilly et al. (1989) were used to measure *upper-echelon cohesion.*

Organizational Performance

Open systems effectiveness was assessed with two questionnaire items developed by Glick, Huber, Miller, Doty, and Sutcliffe (1990) based on the work of Quinn and Rohrbaugh (1983), Scott (1987), and Yuchtman and Seashore (1967). Profitability is a relatively concrete outcome variable that was assessed with a single questionnaire item.

Environmental Characteristics

The predictability, stability, and munificence of each industry were assessed archivally through the Compustat II industry-segment data file (Standard and Poor's Compustat Services, 1986) following the operational definitions of Dess and Beard (1984) and Wholey and Brittain (1989) (for further details, see Glick, ogilvie, and Miller, 1990).

Turbulence was defined as the reverse-scored combination of stability and predictability and was used to construct the fit term in the model, as described in the analysis section. *Munificence* was not included in the original theoretical model, but was included as a control variable in all equations predicting organizational performance. Each industry's scores on turbulence and munificence were assigned to each strategic business unit in that industry.

Analyses

The first set of analyses explored the reliability and validity of the measures. Specifically: factor analyses were used to assess the extent to which multiple items for a given variable appeared to measure the same underlying construct; interitem reliability analyses were applied to all measures based on multi-item scales; and interrater reliability analyses (Glick, 1985; Shrout and Fleiss, 1979) were conducted for all measures where multiple raters had rated a common target (i.e., a common organizational or team characteristic).

The second set of analyses explored the validity of the diversity-performance model in Figure 6.2. The empirical evaluation of the model was complicated by the existence of a fit term that precluded simultaneous parameter estimation using model fitting programs such as LISREL (Joreskog and Sorbom, 1984). Thus, the model was evaluated in several stages using multiple regression.

The fit term between environmental turbulence and comprehensiveness of decision making was estimated following the residual fit analysis procedures suggested by Drazin and Van de Ven (1985). The fit analysis captures the argument that business units will perform better if the upper-echelon managers engage in a level of comprehensiveness that is appropriate for (i.e., fits) the level of turbulence faced by the business unit. In our arguments about fit, we implicitly assumed that turbulence and comprehensiveness of decision making would be negatively related in high-performing business units. If this assumption is correct, then fit is defined as the inverse of the absolute value of the deviation of the business unit from the regression line formed by regressing comprehensiveness on turbulence in a subsample of high-performing business units.

RESULTS AND DISCUSSION

Correlations, means, standard deviations, and reliabilities are presented in Table 6.1. The ICC (1,k) interrater reliabilities (Glick, 1985; Shrout and Fleiss, 1979) have a mean of .57. The Cronbach alpha interitem reliabilities have a mean of .75. These interitem reliabilities are generally acceptable, but the interrater reliabilities are low in several cases. Low reliabilities are likely to result in weaker results than we would otherwise expect in our main tests of the theoretical model, presented below.

Effects on Cognitive Diversity
Results

To test the effects of demographic and structural diversity on cognitive diversity, each of the three dimensions of preference diversity (diversity concerning human resource

Table 6.1. Correlations, Means, Standard Deviations, Interitem Reliabilities, and Interrater Reliabilities

	Variables[a]									
	Demographic Diversity				Structural Diversity			Preference Diversity		
Variables	(1)	(2)	(3)	(4)	(5)	(6)	(7)	(8)	(9)	(10)
Demographic diversity in terms of:										
(1) Functional background										
(2) Age	.15									
(3) Tenure on the upper-echelon team	.12	.30*								
(4) Tenure with the organization	.15	.26*	.64***							
Structural diversity in terms of:										
(5) Function	.39***	.10	.04	.07						
(6) Geography	.00	−.19	−.07	−.09	−.45***					
(7) Market	−.07	−.03	−.10	−.06	.25*	.18				
Preference diversity in terms of:										
(8) Human resource goals	−.15	.10	.01	−.03	.06	−.11	−.08			
(9) System maintenance goals	.13	.04	−.15	−.10	.16	.10	.34**	.05		
(10) Profitability goals	−.08	−.09	.02	−.03	.13	−.02	.20	−.12	.05	
Belief diversity in terms of:										
(11) Maintaining flexibility	−.11	.21	−.10	−.14	−.01	.00	−.04	.21	.18	.20
(12) Low cost vs. differentiation tactics	.17	.01	.05	.21	.14	−.11	.03	−.19	.10	.03
(13) Innovativeness	.13	.03	−.17	−.09	.13	−.11	.05	.20	.22	.02
(14) Advertising	.39**	.14	.02	.08	.17	.13	.34**	.00	.43***	.02

196

Variable										
Process variables:										
(15) Comprehensiveness	.28*	.08	−.21	−.16	.17	.05	.14	−.31**	.02	−.12
(16) Amount of rich communication	.28*	.11	.14	.09	−.11	.05	−.15	−.11	.04	−.24*
(17) Cohesion	.02	.03	.16	.27*	−.08	.14	−.04	−.35**	−.22	−.07
Environmental variables:										
(18) Turbulence	−.24*	.01	−.05	−.11	−.12	.01	−.16	.17	.00	−.12
(19) Munificence	.17	.14	.23	.27*	−.06	.09	−.14	.00	.16	−.15
Performance variables:										
(20) Open systems effectiveness	.00	.25*	.21	.03	−.19	.20	.11	.02	.04	.01
(21) Profitability	.15	−.01	.17	−.04	−.06	.18	.09	−.14	−.01	−.17
N	72	70	70	70	81	81	81	70	70	70
Means	22.00	15.08	77.06	71.11	11.69	8.67	8.04	105.42	67.58	29.64
Standard deviations	9.89	5.25	34.15	32.33	3.43	3.23	2.84	45.58	27.78	14.40
Interitem reliabilities[b]				.86	.86	.86	.70	.86	.71	.61
Interrater reliabilities[c]				.53	.53	.68	.55			

[a]Numbers correspond to the variable numbers in the first column on the left.

[b]Interitem reliability estimates are alphas, except as noted below.

[c]Interrater reliability estimates are intraclass correlations [ICC (1,k)—1 c.f., Shrout and Fleiss, 1979].

[d]Interitem reliability estimates are standardized item alphas. Corresponding scales are based on standardized items.

*p < .05
**p < .01
***p < .001

continued

Table 6.1. (Continued) Correlations, Means, Standard Deviations, Interitem Reliabilities, and Interrater Reliabilities

| | Variables[a] | | | | | | | | | | |
| | Belief diversity | | | | Process variables | | | Environmental variables | | Performance variables | |
Variables	(11)	(12)	(13)	(14)	(15)	(16)	(17)	(18)	(19)	(20)	(21)
Belief diversity in terms of:											
(11) Maintaining flexibility											
(12) Low cost vs. differentiation tactics	.10										
(13) Innovativeness	.10	.11									
(14) Advertising	.10	.13	.26*								
Process variables:											
(15) Comprehensiveness	−.18	.06	.00	.25*							
(16) Amount of rich communication	−.06	.09	.04	.20	.13						
(17) Cohesion	−.21	.20	−.14	.07	.26*	.31**					
Environmental variables:											
(18) Turbulence	.09	−.11	.04	−.08	−.32**	.03	−.08				
(19) Munificence	.03	−.05	−.05	−.13	−.03	.04	−.05	−.19			
Performance variables:											
(20) Open systems effectiveness	.06	−.13	−.15	.06	−.10	.11	.02	.06	.16		
(21) Profitability	−.10	−.12	−.19	.17	.17	.04	.14	−.03	.23*	.40***	
N	70	70	70	70	85	85	84	81	81	85	85
Means	.00	121.83	54.16	.00	.07	10.72	14.89	.00	.11	8.58	3.63
Standard deviations	2.33	35.75	19.75	1.73	4.08	1.46	2.54	1.76	.18	2.92	1.39
Interitem reliabilities[b]	.67[d]	.61	.64	.66[d]	.91	.83	.88	.71		.79	.77
Interrater reliabilities[c]					.46	.32	.47			.77	.77

goals, profit goals, and system maintenance goals) and each of the four dimensions of belief diversity (diversity concerning the efficacy of maintaining flexibility, low cost versus differentiation tactics, innovativeness, and advertising) were regressed on demographic and structural diversity. These results are presented in Tables 6.2 and 6.3.

Despite expectations for strong effects from both the academic and managerial press, demographic and structural diversity only had three clearly significant effects on cognitive diversity out of a possible 49 effects. None of the overall equations predicting preference diversity were statistically significant and only belief diversity concerning the efficacy of advertising was predicted significantly by demographic and structural diversity. Teams that were more diverse in terms of functional backgrounds and in business units with stronger market departmentation were predictably more diverse in their beliefs about the efficacy of spending additional money on advertising. The strength of this latter effect is indicated by the adjusted R^2 of .18 reported in the last column of Table 6.3. This means that 18 percent of the variation in belief diversity in terms of the efficacy of advertising was predicted by demographic and structural diversity.

Implications

An encouraging implication of these results is that CEOs do not need to worry about demographic and structural factors producing cognitive diversity except, possibly, belief diversity about the efficacy of advertising. Demographic and structural diversity do not doom an organization to perpetual disagreements over preferences about operative goals for the organization, or to perpetual disagreements over beliefs about the efficacy of most business tactics.

In the context, however, of decisions concerning the allocation of resources to advertising, disagreements are fairly predictable. In these decisions, disagreements

Table 6.2. Preference Diversity Regressed onto Demographic and Structural Diversity[a]

	Preference Diversity in Terms of		
	Human Resource Goals	System Maintenance Goals	Profitability Goals
Demographic diversity in terms of:			
Functional background	−.19	.06	−.13
Age	.12	.10	−.10
Tenure on the upper-echelon team	.02	−.15	.11
Tenure with the organization	−.06	−.02	−.05
Structural diversity in terms of:			
Function	.12	.15	.12
Geography	−.02	.15	−.01
Market	−.09	.26+	.19
Adjusted R^2	.00	.07	.00

[a]Table entries are standardized regression coefficients ($N = 68$).
+$p < .10$
*$p < .05$

Table 6.3. Belief Diversity Regressed onto Demographic and Structural Diversity[a]

	Belief Diversity in Terms of Efficacy of:			
	Maintaining Flexibility	Low Cost vs. Differentiation Tactics	Innovativeness	Advertising
Demographic diversity in terms of:				
Functional background	−.13	.13	.13	.31*
Age	.30*	−.06	.05	.12
Tenure on the upper-echelon team	−.08	−.13	−.22	−.05
Tenure with the organization	−.15	.28+	.01	.06
Structural diversity in terms of:				
Function	.07	.04	.05	.08
Geography	.08	−.09	−.09	.16
Market	−.07	.02	.02	.25*
Adjusted R^2	.01	.00	.00	.18**

[a]Table entries are standardized regression coefficients ($N = 68$).
+$p < .10$
*$p < .05$
**$p < .01$

should be anticipated when there is diversity in terms of functional backgrounds and strong market departmentation. Specific issues that will stimulate disagreements include the efficacy of building name recognition for the firm, the importance of prestige and recognition for innovativeness, and the efficacy of spending more on advertising than most other firms in the industry.

Effects on Organizational Processes

As discussed earlier and as shown in both Figures 6.1 and 6.2, demographic, structural, and cognitive diversity are expected to affect organizational performance through their effects on three process variables: comprehensiveness of decision making, amount of rich communication, and cohesion. The effects of diversity on these processes are described below.

Effects of Preference Diversity

Results. Cognitive diversity had clear effects on both upper-echelon comprehensiveness of decision making and on cohesion, with 12 percent and 16 percent of the variance predicted, respectively, as shown in Table 6.4. The significant effects of preference diversity were uniformly negative. This is consistent with our hypothesis about cohesion, but it runs counter to the more controversial hypothesis concerning the comprehensiveness of decision making. Disagreements over the importance of human resource goals had negative effects on both comprehensiveness and cohesion. Disagreements over the importance of system maintenance goals had a negative effect on cohesion.

Although we had tentatively accepted the dominant arguments in favor of a positive effect of preference diversity on comprehensiveness of decision making, the

Table 6.4 Comprehensiveness, Amount of Rich Communication, and Cohesion Regressed onto Cognitive Diversity[a]

	Comprehensiveness	Amount of Rich Communication	Cohesion
Preference diversity in terms of:			
Human resource goals	−.32*	−.13	−.27*
System maintenance goals	−.08	−.04	−.26*
Profitability goals	−.15	−.26*	−.07
Belief diversity in terms of the efficacy of:			
Maintaining flexibility	−.10	.00	−.12
Low cost vs. differentiation tactics	−.02	.05	.17
Innovativeness	.01	.02	−.09
Advertising	.30*	.22	.20
Adjusted R^2	.12*	.03	.16*

[a]Table entries are standardized regression coefficients ($N = 69$).
*$p < .05$

results seem to support the counterarguments presented earlier. Specifically, the results are most consistent with the arguments that preference diversity leads to frustration due to a lack of shared values and lower perceived similarity. This contributes to both lower cohesion and lower comprehensiveness of decision making. As managers become frustrated and distrustful of their peers, they are more likely to emphasize more ad hoc, less comprehensive decision making. Thus, disagreements concerning preferences are much more likely to lead to fragmentation and truncated decision processes than to stimulating curiosity or a compulsion to resolve disagreements through analysis and discussion.

Implications. From a managerial perspective, the implications are rather clear. If managers want to increase comprehensiveness of decision making and upper-echelon cohesion, then efforts should be made to increase value congruence in the upper-echelon team. Value similarity can be strengthened by managing the processes of selection, attraction, and attrition of upper-echelon managers, by value and goal clarification exercises, and by conscious articulation of the values and goals of the organization by the chief administrator in conjunction with the upper-echelon team.

Effects of Belief Diversity

Results. In contrast to the effects of preference diversity, the one significant effect of belief diversity on the process variables was positive (see Table 6.4). Comprehensiveness of decision making was enhanced by diversity in terms of beliefs about the efficacy of advertising. This supports the dominant arguments that are reflected in our initial tentative hypothesis. Differences in these beliefs appear to support minority influence and an avoidance of groupthink in upper-echelon teams. The diversity of opinions on the efficacy of advertising helps the upper-echelon teams to avoid selective perception and to consider a broader array of issues and alternatives; the teams in this study with greater belief diversity in terms of advertising did not shy away from the confrontations that often occur in comprehensive decision making.

Implications. Overall, the effects of preference and belief diversity suggest that the most cohesive, communicative, and comprehensive upper-echelon teams agree on values, but exhibit significant disagreement on tactics and strategies. Legitimate disagreements over tactics can lead to mutual respect, but disagreements over goals can fragment the team. One implication of these findings is that efforts to develop a strong culture should be focused on developing shared values and a respect for the individual's beliefs.

Effects of Demographic and Structural Diversity

Results. As shown in Table 6.5, the significant demographic and structural effects are positive. Market departmentation positively affects the comprehensiveness of decision making and functional background diversity positively affects the amount of rich communication. Upper-echelon managers with responsibilities for distinct market units apparently devote more attention to making comprehensive decisions. As argued earlier, when each of the upper-echelon team members is responsible for a very distinct market segment, he or she probably has to be more comprehensive in order to justify additional resources for his or her unit. Further, upper-echelon managers exhibiting functional background diversity apparently communicate more, rather than less. Counter to our earlier argument, it appears that background diversity leads to heightened communication as a method of briding differences.

Implications. In comparison with the moderately strong effects due to cognitive diversity presented in Table 6.4 (with adjusted R^2's of .12, .03, and .16), the slightly weaker effects of demographic and structural diversity (with adjusted R^2's of .11, .07, and .04) suggest that academics and practitioners should devote more attention to cognitive diversity rather than focusing exclusively on demographic or structural diversity. This recommendation should be particularly appealing to managers because cognitive diversity is often much more manageable than is demographic or structural diversity.

Table 6.5. Comprehensiveness, Amount of Rich Communication, and Cohesion Regressed onto Demographic and Structural Diversity[a]

	Comprehensiveness	Amount of Rich Communication	Cohesion
Demographic diversity in terms of:			
Functional background	.08	.29*	.17
Age	.17	.08	−.04
Tenure on the upper-echelon team	−.20	.10	−.01
Tenure with the organization	−.06	−.02	.27+
Structural diversity in terms of:			
Geography	.08	.23+	.15
Market	.30*	−.15	−.08
Adjusted R^2	.11*	.07+	.04

[a]Table entries are standardized regression coefficients ($N = 68$).
+$p < .10$
*$p < .05$

Effects of Diversity on Organizational Performance
Results

Table 6.6 shows the effects of the process variables on open systems effectiveness and profitability, using the hypothesized fit model and controlling for environmental munificence. Surprisingly, none of the predicted effects was supported.

We were particularly surprised to find that neither comprehensiveness of decision making nor the fit between comprehensiveness and turbulence was related to performance. Previous research has linked these variables in a variety of contexts (Bourgeois and Eisenhardt, 1988; Eisenhardt, 1989; Frederickson, 1984; Frederickson and Iaquinto, 1989; Frederickson and Mitchell, 1984). One possible explanation for these nonsignificant results is the formulation of the arguments in terms of a fit between comprehensiveness and turbulence. We defined fit as conformance to the linear relationship between comprehensiveness and turbulence in a subsample of high-performing business units. This is the definition preferred on the basis of conceptual arguments by recent authors such as Drazin and Van de Ven (1985; Van de Ven and Drazin, 1985). An alternative definition of fit treats fit as a multiplicative interaction of the standardized scores of comprehensiveness and turbulence (Van de Ven and Drazin, 1985; Zedeck, 1971). Although the conformance formulation of fit is conceptually distinct from a multiplicative interaction (particularly for business units that have extreme values on either comprehensiveness or turbulence), both interpretations are consistent with the previous empirical research in this area. Previous research has only examined the comprehensiveness-performance relationship in a limited number of contexts that represent selected values of turbulence rather than a continuous range of turbulence. Thus, for example, Frederickson (1984; Frederickson and Iaquinto, 1989; Frederickson and Mitchell, 1984) found a positive effect of comprehensiveness in moderately low turbulent environments and a negative effect in more turbulent environments. These findings are easily explained by either fit or interaction effects.

A test of the interaction hypothesis is presented in Table 6.7 as an alternate to the fit hypothesis. The results for profitability are supportive of a contingency argument. Contrary to some of the previous research (Frederickson, 1984; Frederickson and

Table 6.6. Performance Variables Regressed onto Comprehensiveness, Amount of Rich Communication, Cohesion, Turbulence, and Munificence: Residual Fit Model[a]

	Open Systems Effectiveness	Profitability
Comprehensiveness	−.06	.17
Amount of rich communication	.11	.01
Cohesion	.05	.14
Turbulance	.06	.07
Comprehensiveness-turbulence residual fit	.08	.05
Environmental munificence	.18	.27*
Adjusted R^2	.00	.03

[a]Table entries are standardized regression coefficients ($N = 79$).

*$p < .05$

Table 6.7. Performance Variables Regressed onto Comprehensiveness, Amount of Rich Communication, Cohesion, Turbulence, and Munificence: Interaction Model[a]

	Open Systems Effectiveness	Profitability
Comprehensiveness	−.07	.15
Amount of rich communication	.11	.01
Cohesion	.00	.07
Turbulence	.06	.06
Comprehensiveness-turbulance interaction	.10	.24[+]
Environmental munificence	.17	.25[*]
Adjusted R^2	.00	.09[+]

[a]Table entries are standardized regression coefficients ($N = 79$).
[+]$p < .10$
[*]$p < .05$
[**]$p < .01$
[***]$p < .001$

Iaquinto, 1989; Frederickson and Mitchell, 1984), however, the positive interaction term implies that in more turbulent environments, comprehensive decision making improves, rather than hurts, profitability. More comprehensive teams apparently are more effective in determining which changes in their environments should be ignored as transient changes and which changes should be addressed. This interpretation was confirmed by examining the correlations between comprehensiveness and profitability in high versus low turbulent subsamples. Among the most turbulent third of our sample, the correlation between comprehensiveness and profitability was .63 ($p <$ .001), while this correlation was .03 (nonsignificant) in the least turbulent third of our sample. Point estimates from the regression equation provide an even more extreme view for business units in very low turbulent industries (such as hobby shops, dry dairy producers, and manufacturers of refuse systems). In these very low turbulent industries, increasing comprehensiveness actually reduces profitability.

To further investigate the idea that comprehensiveness has a positive effect in turbulent industries but a negative effect in very placid industries, a comprehensiveness-turbulence deviation term was entered in additional regression analyses. This deviation term reflects the extent to which a business unit's comprehensiveness does not match its level of turbulence. The deviation approach to fit is often used instead of the conformance and interaction methods reported above (Drazin and Van de Ven, 1985).

The results of regressing performance on the comprehensiveness-turbulence deviation are presented in Table 6.8. Eleven percent of the variance in profitability is predicted by the fit between comprehensiveness and turbulence and by environmental munificence. This is clear support for the positive influence of comprehensiveness in more turbulent industries and a negative influence in very placid industries.

Our results from a diverse set of business units directly contradict the earlier findings of Frederickson (1984; Frederickson and Iaquinto, 1989; Frederickson and Mitchell, 1984) that were based on two unique industries. These results are consistent, however, with the positive effects of comprehensiveness in extremely turbulent environments reported by Eisenhardt (1989; Bourgeois and Eisenhardt, 1988). We believe

Table 6.8. Performance Variables Regressed onto Comprehensiveness, Amount of Rich Communication, Cohesion, Turbulence, and Munificence: Deviation Fit Model[a]

	Open Systems Effectiveness	Profitability
Comprehensiveness	−.07	.16
Amount of rich communication	.12	.02
Cohesion	.00	.02
Turbulance	.09	.16
Comprehensiveness-turbulence deviation	−.09	−.30*
Environmental munificence	.17	.26*
Adjusted R^2	.00	.11*

[a]Table entries are standardized regression coefficients ($N = 79$).
*$p < .05$

that the results reported here are more valid than Frederickson's earlier research because of (1) improvements in the measurement of turbulence that capture turbulence due to zero-sum competition (for details, see Glick, Ogilvie, and Miller, 1990), (2) refinements in Frederickson's measure of comprehensiveness that were partially validated by Ogilvie and Glick (1990), (3) a slight increase in sample size, and (4) the greatly increased diversity of our sample. The most important of these improvements is undoubtedly the increased diversity of our sample. Because Frederickson (1984; Frederickson and Iaquinto, 1989: Frederickson and Mitchell, 1984) examined only two industries, it is very possible that some unique characteristics of those industries confounded the effects that were interpreted as turbulence effects. This possibility is particularly likely because the differences in turbulence between his two industries are not as large as we had believed during the theory construction phase of our study. As we started data collection, Glick, Ogilvie, and Miller (1990) ranked 583 industries. In this new ranking, Frederickson's (1984) forest products industry (SIC 2421) ranked 196th highest in turbulence, while Frederickson and Mitchell's (1984; Frederickson and Iaquinto, 1989) paint and coatings industry (SIC 2851) ranked 112th. The industries in the current study ranked from 3rd to 583rd in terms of turbulence, with a standard deviation of 196.

Implications

Although we clearly believe that the current results are more valid and generalizable than those from previous research in this area, we must caution readers that these results concerning comprehensiveness and turbulence are controversial. Attempts to replicate our results should be high on the research agenda of several academics.

In the meantime, however, given the best available information, we encourage executives in more turbulent environments to be more comprehensive in their decision making processes, while executives in less turbulent environments should conserve their resources and be somewhat less comprehensive. Executives in turbulent environments should be particularly sensitive to the possibility of overreacting to changes in their environment. More comprehensive analyses of the situation may lead to the conclusion that it is cheaper and more profitable to ride out the storm and stick to a coherent strategy than it is to make a series of disjointed, short-term tactical moves. Executives in less turbulent environments should seriously evaluate the amount of time and resources that they spend on making comprehensive decisions. In less turbulent environments, incremental decision making (Lindblom, 1959; Quinn, 1989), a strategy of pursuing small wins (Weick, 1984), experimentation (Campbell, 1969; Staw, 1982), and test marketing can be inexpensive and profitable methods of innovation that do not require elatorate and expensive analyses.

CONCLUSIONS AND ADDITIONAL IMPLICATIONS

In this chapter, we developed an integrative process model of the effects of upper-echelon diversity on performance in organizations. We posited a series of effects of demographic and structural diversity mediated through cognitive diversity and the functioning of the upper-echelon team and ultimately affecting open systems effectiveness and profitability of the business unit (see Figure 6.1). Three different explanations were considered in developing this model:

1. Diversity stimulates creativity, change, and innovation, which enhance organizational performance, particularly in turbulent environments.
2. Diversity stimulates comprehensive decision making which in turn influences organizational performance.
3. Diversity reduces cohesion and communication, and leads to conflict avoidance and superficial, noncomprehensive decision making, both of which contribute to poor organizational performance.

The theoretical model summarized in the hypotheses and in Figure 6.2 was based on our examination of published research and interviews that we had with top managers in a variety of organizations. It was the first attempt to explicate and integrate the explanations that link demographic, structural, and cognitive diversity with organizational performance. This initial theoretical model was then tested and improved by analyzing data from upper-echelon managers in a diverse sample of 79 organizations.

The most controversial finding of this research is that comprehensive decision making was very positively associated with profitability in turbulent environments, but negatively associated in extremely stable environments. This runs counter to Frederickson's (1984; Frederickson and Iaquinto, 1989; Frederickson and Mitchell, 1984) conclusions, but it is consistent with research in extremely turbulent environments by Eisenhardt (1989; Bourgeois and Eisenhardt, 1988). Given the strengths of the current research that are noted above, we believe that these new results should help managers improve profitability if they adopt the appropriate level of comprehensiveness of decision making.

Other major conclusions and implications of this study are the following:

- *Demographic and structural diversity* affect cognitive diversity and the process variables (comprehensiveness, communication, and cohesion), but these effects are not as pervasive as suggested by the managerial and academic literatures.
  - Executives do not need to be overly concerned about the effects of demographic and structural diversity on cognitive diversity.

- Thus, executives should focus on other means of managing preference and belief diversity.
- Researchers looking at the effects of demographic and structural diversity should not assume that cognitive diversity mediates these effects.

- *Preference diversity* in terms of human resource goals negatively affects comprehensiveness of decision making and cohesion. Preference diversity in terms of system maintenance goals negatively affects cohesion.

   - Business units that want to increase comprehensiveness and cohesion can expect positive results from efforts to develop consensus on human resource goals through values clarification exercises, and by selection, attraction, and attrition of upper-echelon managers.
   - Explanations of the effects of preference diversity should emphasize the potential for frustration and avoidance of unresolvable conflicts that may develop as a result of preference diversity in terms of human resource goals and preference diversity in terms of system maintenance goals.
   - Preference diversity is not a single variable. Researchers must think more specifically about preference diversity in terms of types of values, such as preference diversity in terms of human resource goals.

- *Belief diversity* in terms of the efficacy of advertising has positive effects on comprehensiveness.

   - Managers can stimulate comprehensiveness by emphasizing belief diversity in terms of the efficacy of advertising.
   - Researchers should articulate more clearly their ideas concerning possible positive and negative effects of belief diversity in terms of specific types of beliefs and in terms of specific process variables and performance outcomes.

- *Open systems effectiveness* (i.e., the ability to acquire resources) apparently is unaffected by the process variables that we examined.

   - Managers need not be overly concerned about deficient team processes harming open systems effectiveness.
   - Researchers should devote more attention to developing process explanations of open systems effectiveness. Further, direct effects of the diversity variables on open systems effectiveness should be examined.

- *Profitability* is directly enhanced by munificence and greater comprehensiveness in turbulent environments but less comprehensiveness in very stable environments. Further, when the industrial context is turbulent or moderately turbulent, consensus concerning human resource goals and diversity concerning the efficacy of advertising indirectly enhance profitability through their effects on comprehensiveness.

   - The managerial implications for enhancing profitability are straightforward. Managers should encourage more comprehensive decision styles in most environments. In very stable environments, however, less comprehensive decision making will be more profitable.
   - Researchers should attempt to replicate the results concerning comprehensiveness. They should also investigate the direct effects of diversity that are not mediated by the three process variables examined in the current study.

These implications should be interpreted somewhat cautiously given the limited amount of research in this area, low interrater reliabilities for some of our measures, the moderate but not large sample size, and the cross-sectional nature of our data collection which prohibits any unequivocal statements about causality from this study. Despite these limitations, these implications should contribute significantly to both managerial practice and the improvement of research and theory in this area.

NOTE

1. We gratefully acknowledge Harold Doty for his expertise on these analyses.

REFERENCES

Aldrich, H. E. 1979. *Organizations and environments.* Englewood Cliffs, NJ: Prentice-Hall.

Andrews, K. R. 1971. *The concept of corporate strategy.* Homewood, IL: Dow Jones-Irvin.

Aronson, E., and Worchel, S. 1966. Similarity versus liking as determinants of interpersonal attractiveness. *Psychonomic Science,* 5: 157–158.

Bartlett, C. A., and Ghoshal, S. 1989. *Managing across borders: the transnational solution.* Boston: Harvard Business School Press.

Beyer, J. M. 1981. Ideologies, values, and decision making in organizations. In Nystrom, P. C., and Starbuck, W. H. (Eds.), *Handbook of organizational design* (pp. 166–202). New York: Oxford University Press.

Blau, P. M. 1977. *Inequality and heterogeneity.* New York: Free Press.

Bourgeois, L. J., and Eisenhardt, K. M. 1988. Strategic decision processes in high velocity environments: Four cases in the microcomputer industry. *Management Science,* 34: 816–835.

Campbell, D. T. 1969. Reforms as experiments. *American Psychologist,* 24: 409–429.

Chandler, A. D. 1962. *Strategy and structure: chapters in the history of the American industrial enterprise.* Cambridge, MA: MIT Press.

Condon, J. W., and Crano, W. D. 1988. Inferred evaluation and the relation between attitude similarity and interpersonal attraction. *Journal of Personality and Social Psychology,* 5: 789–797.

Cosier, R. A., and Schwenk, C. R. 1990. Agreement and thinking alike: ingredients for poor decisions. *Academy of Management Executive,* 4(1): 69–74.

Cox, T. H., and Blake, S. 1991. Managing cultural diversity: implications for organizational competitiveness. *Academy of Management Executive,* 5(3): 45–55.

Daft, R. L. 1986. *Organization theory and design,* 2nd ed. St. Paul, MN: West Publishing.

Daft, R. L., and Lengel, R. H. 1986. Organizational information requirements, media richness, and structural design. *Management Science,* 32: 554–571.

Daniels, J. D., Pitts, R. A., and Tretter, M. J. 1985. Organizing for dual strategies of product diversity and international expansion. *Strategic Management Journal,* 6: 223–237.

Dearborn, D. C., and Simon, H. A. 1958. Selective perception: a note on the departmental identifications of executives. *Sociometry,* 21: 140–144.

Dess, G. G. 1980. The relationship between objective and subjective measures of manufacturers' competitive environments: implications for firm economic performance. Ph.D. Dissertation. Seattle: University of Washington, Graduate School of Business.

Dess, G. G. 1987. Consensus on strategy formulation and organizational performance: competitors in a fragmented industry. *Strategic Management Journal,* 8: 259–277.

Dess, G. G., and Beard, D. W. 1984. Dimensions of organizational task environments. *Administrative Science Quarterly,* 29: 52–73.

Drazin, R., and Van de Ven, A. H. 1985. Alternative forms of fit in contingency theory. *Administrative Science Quarterly,* 30: 514–539.

Duncan, O. D. 1975. *Introduction to structural equation models.* New York: Academic Press.

Duncan, R. 1979. What is the right organization structure? Decision tree analysis provides the answer. *Organizational Dynamics,* 7: 59–80.

Eisenhardt, K. M. 1989. Making fast strategic decisions in high-velocity environments. *Academy of Management Journal,* 32: 543–576.

Feldman, M., S. and March, J. G. 1981. Information in organizations as signal and symbol. *Administrative Science Quarterly,* 26: 171–186.

Financial Accounting Standards Board. 1987. Financial reporting for segments of a business enterprise. *Statement of financial accounting standards no. 14.* Stanford, CT: Financial Accounting Standards Board.

Fredrickson, J. W. 1984. The comprehensiveness of strategic decision processes: extension, observations, and future directions. *Academy of Management Journal,* 27: 445–466.

Fredrickson, J. W., and Iaquinto, A. L. 1989. Inertia and creeping rationality in strategic decisions. *Academy of Management Journal,* 32: 516–542.

Fredrickson, J. W., and Mitchell, T. R. 1984. Strategic decision processes: Comprehensiveness and performance in an industry with an unstable environment. *Academy of Management Journal,* 27: 399–423.

Glick, W. H. 1985. Pitfalls of organization climate research. *Academy of Management Review,* 10: 296–311.

Glick, W. H., Huber, G. P., Miller, C. C., Doty, D. H., and Sutcliffe, K. M. 1990. Studying changes in organizational design and effectiveness: retrospective event histories and periodic assessments. *Organization Science,* 1(3): 293–312.

Glick, W. H., ogilvie, d., and Miller, C. C. 1990. Assessing dimensions of task environments: intra-industry and aggregate industry measures. Paper presented at the Annual Meeting of the Academy of Management, San Francisco.

Hall, R. I. 1984. The natural logic of management policy making: its implications for the survival of an organization. *Management Science,* 30: 905–927.

Hambrick, D. C., and Mason, P. A. 1984. Upper echelons: the organization as a reflection of its top managers. *Academy of Management Review,* 9: 193–206.

Heise, D. R. 1969. Problems in path analysis and causal inference. In Bogata, E. F., and Bohrnstedt, G. W. (Eds.), *Sociological methodology* (pp. 38-73). San Francisco: Jossey-Bass.

Huber, G. P. 1991. Organizational learning: an examination of the contributing processes and a review of the literatures. *Organization Science,* 2(1): 88–115.

Imai, M. 1986. *Kaizen: the key to Japan's competitive success.* New York: Random House.

Janis, I. L. 1972. *Victims of groupthink: psychological studies of foreign policy decisions and fiascoes.* Boston: Houghton Mifflin.

Jöreskog, K. G., and Sörbom, D. 1984. *LISREL VI: user's guide,* 3rd ed. Mooresville, IN: Scientific Software.

Juran, J. M. 1989. *On leadership for quality: an executive handbook.* New York: Free Press.

Kanter, R. M. 1977. *Men and women of the corporation.* New York: Basic Books.

Kanter, R. M. 1983. *The change masters: innovation for productivity in the American corporation.* New York: Simon and Schuster.

Katz, D., and Kahn, R. L. 1978. *The social psychology of organizations,* 2nd ed. New York: Wiley.

Lawrence, P. R., and Lorsch, J. W. 1967. *Organization and environment: managing differentiation and integration.* Boston: Harvard University, Graduate School of Business Administration.

Lincoln, J. R., and Miller, J. 1979. Work and friendship ties in organizations: a comparative analysis of networks. *Academy of Management Journal,* 24: 181–199.

Lindblom, C. E. 1959. The science of "muddling through." *Public Administrative Review,* 19: 79–88.

Malcolm Baldrige National Quality Award Consortium. 1990. *1990 application guidelines.* Gaithersburg, MD: United States Department of Commerce, National Institute of Standards and Technology.

McCain, B. E., O'Reilly, C., and Pfeffer, J. 1983. The effects of departmental demography on turnover: the case of a university. *Academy of Management Journal,* 26: 626–641.

McCann, J., and Galbraith, J. R. 1981. Interdepartmental relations. In Nystrom, P. C., and Starbuck, W. H. (Eds.), *Handbook of organizational design: remodeling organizations and their environments,* Vol. 2 (pp. 60–84). New York: Oxford University Press.

Miller, C. C. 1990. Cognitive diversity within management teams: Implications for strategic decision processes and organizational performance. Ph.D. Dissertation. Austin: University of Texas, Graduate School of Business.

Mintzberg, H. 1979. *The structuring of organizations: the synthesis of the research.* Englewood Cliffs, NJ: Prentice-Hall.

Mintzberg, H., Raisinghani, D., and Théorêt, A. 1976. The structure of "unstructured" decision processes. *Administrative Science Quarterly,* 21: 246–275.

Murray, A. I. 1989. Top management group heterogeneity and firm performance. *Strategic Management Journal,* 10: 125–141.

Nemeth, C. J. 1986. Differential contributions of majority and minority influence. *Psychological Review,* 93: 23–32.

Nutt, P. C. 1976. Models for decision-making in organizations and some contextual variables which stipulate optimal use. *Academy of Management Review,* 1: 147–158.

ogilvie, d., and Glick, W. H. 1990. A study of strategic planning processes and how information systems are used in strategic planning. Working Paper. Austin: University of Texas, Department of Management.

O'Reilly, C. A., Caldwell, D. F., and Barnett, W. P. 1989. Work group demography, social integration, and turnover. *Administrative Science Quarterly,* 34: 21–37.

O'Sullivan, C. S., and Durso, F. T. 1984. Effect of schema-incongruent information on memory for stereotypical attributes. *Journal of Personality and Social Psychology,* 47: 55–70.

Ouchi, W. G. 1981. *Theory Z.* Reading, MA: Addison-Wesley.

Ozeki, K., and Asaka, T. 1990. *Handbook of quality tools: the Japanese approach.* Cambridge, MA: Productivity Press.

Perrow, C. 1961. The analysis of goals in complex organizations. *American Sociology Review,* 26: 854–866.

Pfeffer, J. 1981a. Management as symbolic action: the creation and maintenance of organizational paradigms. In Cummings, L. L., and Staw, B. M. (Eds.), *Research in organization behavior,* Vol. 3 (pp. 1–52). Greenwich, CT: JAI Press.

Pfeffer, J. 1981b. *Power in organizations.* Marshfield, MA: Pitman Publishing.

Pfeffer, J. 1983. Organizational demography. In Cummings, L. L., and Staw, B. M. (Eds.), *Research in organizational behavior,* Vol. 3 (pp. 299–357). Greenwich, CT: JAI Press.

Pfeffer, J., and Moore, W. L. 1980. Average tenure of academic department heads: the effects of paradigm, size, and departmental demography. *Administrative Science Quarterly,* 25: 387–406.

Porter, M. E. 1980. *Competitive strategy: techniques for analyzing industries and competitors.* New York: Free Press.

Price, J. L. 1968. The impact of departmentalization on interoccupational cooperation. *Human Organization,* 27: 362–368.

Quinn, J. B. 1989. Strategic change: logical incrementalism. *Sloan Management Review,* 30(4): 45–60.

Quinn, R. E., and Rohrbaugh, J. 1983. A spatial model of effectiveness criteria: towards a competing values approach to organizational analysis. *Management Science,* 29: 363–377.

Robinson, R. B., and Pearce, J. A. 1988. Planned patterns of strategic behavior and their relationship to business-unit performance. *Strategic Management Journal,* 9: 43–60.

Schneider, B., and Reichers, A. E. 1983. On the etiology of climates. *Personnel Psychology,* 36: 19–39.

Scott, W. R. 1987. *Organizations: rational, natural, and open systems,* 2nd ed. Englewood Cliffs, NJ: Prentice-Hall.

Seidler, J. 1974. On using informants: a technique for collecting quantitative data and controlling measurement error in organization analysis. *American Sociological Review,* 39: 816–831.

Seiler, J. A. 1963. Diagnosing interdepartmental conflict. *Harvard Business Review,* Sept.-Oct., pp. 121–132.

Shrout, P. E., and Fleiss, J. L. 1979. Interclass correlations: uses in assessing rater reliability. *Psychological Bulletin,* 86: 420–428.

Simon, H. A. 1973. Applying information technology to organization design. *Public Administration Review,* 33: 268–278.

Sproull, L. S. 1981. Beliefs in organizations. In Nystrom, P. C., and Starbuck, W. H. (Eds.), *Handbook of organizational design: remodeling organizations and their environments,* Vol. II (pp. 203–224). London: Oxford University Press.

Standard and Poor's Compustat Services. 1986. *COMPUSTAT II.* New York: Standard and Poor's Compustat Services.

Staw, B. M. 1982. Counterforces to change. In Goodman, P. S., and Assoc. (Eds.), *Change in organizations* (pp. 87–121). San Francisco: Jossey-Bass.

Stewart, T. E. 1991. GE keeps those ideas coming. *Fortune,* August 12, pp. 41–49.

Stewman, S., and Konda, S. L. 1983. Careers and organizational labor markets: demographic models of organizational behavior. *American Journal of Sociology,* 88: 637–685.

Thompson, J. D., and Tuden, A. 1959. Strategies, structures, and processes of organizational decision. In Thompson, J. D., Hammond, P. B., Hawkes, R. W., Junker, B. H., and Tuden, A. (Eds.), *Comparative studies in administration,* (pp. 195–216). Pittsburgh: University of Pittsburgh.

Tsui, A., and O'Reilly, C. 1989. Beyond simple demographic effects: the importance of relational demography in superior-subordinate dyads. *Academy of Management Journal,* 32: 402–423.

Turner, J. H. 1986. *The structure of sociological theory.* Chicago: Dorsey Press.

Van de Ven, A. H., and Drazin, R. 1985. The concept of fit in contingency theory. In Cummings, L. L., and Staw, B. M. (Eds.), *Research in organization behavior,* Vol. 7 (pp. 333–365). Greenwich, CT: JAI Press.

Wagner, G. W., Pfeffer, J., and O'Reilly, C. A. 1984. Organizational demography and turnover in top-management groups. *Administrative Science Quarterly,* 29: 74–92.

Walker, A. H., and Lorsch, J. W. 1968. Organization choice: product vs. function. *Harvard Business Review,* Nov.-Dec., pp. 265–278.

Walsh, J. P. 1988. Selectivity and selective perception: an investigation of managers' belief structures and information processing. *Academy of Management Journal,* 31: 873–895.

Weick, K. E. 1982. Management of organizational change among loosely coupled elements. In Goodman, P. S., and Assoc. (Eds.), *Change in organizations* (pp. 375–408). San Francisco: Jossey-Bass.

Weick, K. E. 1984. Redefining the scale of social problems. *American Psychologist,* 39: 40–49.

Weick, K. E., and Bougon, M. G. 1985. Organizations as cognitive maps. Working Paper. Austin: University of Texas, Graduate School of Business.

Welcome to the woman-friendly company—where talent is valued and rewarded. 1990. *Business Week,* August 6, pp. 48–55.

Wholey, D. R., and Brittain, J. 1989. Characterizing environmental variation. *Academy of Management Journal,* 32: 867–882.

Williamson, O. E. 1975. *Markets and hierarchies: analysis and antitrust implications.* New York: Free Press.

Yuchtman, E., and Seashore, S. E. 1967. A system resource approach to organizational effectiveness. *American Sociological Review,* 32: 891–903.

Zedeck, S. 1971. Problems with the use of "moderator" variables. *Psychological Bulletin,* 76: 295–310.

Zenger, T. R., and Lawrence, B. S. 1989. Organizational demography: the differential effects of age and tenure distributions on technical communication. *Academy of Management Journal,* 32: 353–376.

APPENDIX: DATA COLLECTION AND ANALYSIS METHODS

To draw the sample for testing our initial theoretical model, we identified a set of industries on the basis of a study of 583 industries reported by Glick, ogilvie, and Miller (1990), who used data from the Compustat II industry-segment data file (Standard and Poor's Compustat Services, 1986) which includes financial information that is required by the Financial Accounting Standards Board (1987: 7–8) for

> each business segment from all firms that are publicly traded. The data set includes information about these subunits for all firms traded on the New York Stock Exchange and the American Stock Exchange, and the major NASDAQ companies traded over the counter. Accountants for each firm identify their reportable business segments based on the Financial Accounting Standards Board definition of a business segment as a group of businesses that are related in terms of the nature of their products, production process, markets, and/ or marketing methods. Annual financial reports are required for business segments that account for ten percent or more of the firm's consolidated revenues, profits, or assets. This data set is very representative of moderate to large publicly traded firms. It does not include information from privately held firms, or firms that are traded in local or restricted markets. . . . The major advantages of this data set are the ability to disaggregate the data below both the industry and firm level. Thus, the data can be used to capture within-industry shifts in resources and the data are much more specific to a single industry than organization level data.

The *a priori* analyses used to assess the industry characteristics were initially based on 14,382 business segments drawn from 7,055 firms in 963 industries. However, business segments from 380 industries were deleted because fewer than five business segments were available for each of the 380 industries. Estimates of industry characteristics based on fewer than five business segments are probably unreliable.

The *a priori* analyses provided measures of predictability, stability, and munificence for each of the 583 industries (cf. Glick, ogilvie, and Miller, 1990). Based on these measures, industries were selected for the current study using the following guidelines. Industries were selected such that a minimum of 16 business segments would be available for each of 27 cells in a 3 × 3 × 3 table formed by cross-classifying the three environmental variables (low, moderate, and high classifications were used for each variable). A few industries were then added to selected cells in order to ensure positive correlations between predictability and the other environmental variables [positive correlations had been observed in the larger population of industries and business segments (for additional details, see Miller, 1990)]. This procedure led to the final selection of 71 industries.

Within each industry, we then randomly sampled up to 20 business segments to be contacted. It should be noted that some of the business segments found in the Compustat II file do not correspond to independent firms, autonomous subsidiaries, or autonomous divisions (i.e., not all segments correspond to strategic business units). In many instances, a business segment corresponds to activities occurring in multiple units of a firm that operates in several different industries. These segments are unusable for our purposes because the Compustat data cannot be linked to a single business unit with a single structure or administrator. Such segments were identified and screened out by contacting a public relations person in each relevant firm and asking if the firm still had operations in that business segment and if that segment corre-sponded to an independent firm, autonomous subsidiary, or autonomous division. Seventy-eight of 535 segments were screened out by this criterion. Further, 31 seg-ments that were identifiable strategic business units were screened out because they had fewer than two levels of management or fewer than 15 employees, as in the inter-view portion of this study (Glick et al., 1990, reprinted as the appendix to this volume). Thirty additional segments were dropped at this stage due to our inability to locate appropriate contact people after at least five attempts.

7

Understanding and Predicting Organizational Change

GEORGE P. HUBER, KATHLEEN M. SUTCLIFFE,
C. CHET MILLER, and WILLIAM H. GLICK

> Prediction is hard, especially about the future.   Neils Bohr

> The executive of the future will be rated by his ability to anticipate his
> problems rather than to meet them as they come.   Howard Coonley

EDITORS' SUMMARY

In this chapter, Huber, Sutcliffe, Miller, and Glick provide us with an encompassing analysis of the determinants of organizational change. This is an important contribution because organizational changes are of great and increasing importance. They affect organizational performance. They create new work tasks and new social relationships in the workplace. They create high workloads and stress levels for managers. The study reported here makes clear that the frequencies of different types of organizational changes are predictable, and it indicates which factors predict the frequencies of which types of change. Armed with this knowledge, managers can better prepare themselves, their employees, and their organizations for the consequences of change, to the benefit of all concerned.

In contrast with individual prior studies, in this study the authors considered a variety of factors that might reasonably be thought to cause or constrain organizational change. They identified 24 such factors and were able to group them into five categories (which they called constructs): (1) characteristics of the organization's environment, (2) characteristics of the organization's performance, (3) characteristics of the organization's top manager, (4) characteristics of the organization's strategy, and (5) characteristics of the organization's structure. After discussing how each factor might affect organizational change, the authors report the results of their longitudinal study of change in 119 diverse organizations.

Drawing on survey data concerning the nature of the organizations environment, performance, strategy, and structure, and on data from interviews with the top managers of the organizations, interviews focused on determining the number and nature of recent changes, the authors build and use statistical models to determine the extent to which the factors are predictive of (1) externally focused changes, (2) internally focused changes, (3) changes in organizational form, and (4) total organizational changes. The results of these analyses, along with their prior examinations of the literature and their theorizing, lead the authors to six conclusions:

1. The frequencies of different types of organizational changes (externally focused changes, internally focused changes, and changes in organizational form) are predictable from information known beforehand.
2. Factors from all five categories (organizational environments, organizational performance, top manager characteristics, organizational strategies, and organization structure) are predictors of organizational change.
3. Different factors predict different types of change.
4. The frequency of different types of organizational change can generally be predicted more accurately if factors from more than one construct are used.
5. An elaborate theory of the determinants of organizational change is theoretically and empirically justifiable.
6. An understanding of organizational change requires consideration of many factors, but prediction requires consideration of just a few. The trick is knowing which few.

This chapter concludes with a discussion of the implications, four for managers and three for organizational scientists, that follow from the more specific, detailed findings of the study. ■

Organizational change—that is, change in how an organization functions, who its members and leaders are, what form it takes, or how it allocates it resources—pervades and continuously reshapes both our personal world of work and the larger world of organizations that surround us. Organizational change frequently demands our participation as individuals and certainly deserves our attention as professionals attempting to understand the world of organizations.

Two facts in particular motivate the study of organizational change. The first is that organizational change is important. It is very important. It is important to all employees, as it directly affects work environments and social relationships. It is especially important to managers, as it so strongly impacts their workloads and stress levels. And it is important to organizational scientists, as organizational change is a phenomenon that has effects at all levels of analysis from individuals to industries.

The second fact motivating the study of organizational change is that the subject, as a whole, is not well understood, at least not in the sense that there is a general model for understanding and predicting the phenomenon. The literature on organizational development, one of the two largest bodies of writings related to organizational change, is normative and narrow. It strongly emphasizes improving the quality of working life of organizational members, and it focuses greatly on process interventions. It takes little explicit account of the wider set of factors that determine organizational change, as is clear in the review by Faucheux, Amado, and Laurent (1982), and, consequently, it is not a suitable basis for arriving at a more eclectic understanding of the organizational change phenomenon. The literature on organizational innovation, the other large body of work related to organizational change, considers only the subset of changes that are "new to the organization" and tends to consider only changes that are uniform in their nature across organizations.

Thus, while it is not necessarily to their discredit, the two largest bodies of writings related to organizational change inform us very little about other forms of organizational change that often have major impacts on the organization's members and on its performance. Among these are changes in the existence, location, or nature of organizational subunits; changes in the membership or in the distribution of authority of the top management team; changes in the priorities given to achieving different organizational goals; and changes in the organization's means or tactics for maintaining and improving relationships with key constituencies or resource controllers. The organizational science literature contains very little organized knowledge about the factors that determine such changes. Organizational change, on the whole, is not well understood.

This chapter is about organizational change. In it we develop a comprehensive model for understanding organizational change and also report the results of a two-year study in which the model was verified as an accurate predictor of change in a wide variety of organizations.

To identify the factors associated with organizational change, we conducted several literature reviews (cf., Huber, 1991; Huber and Daft, 1987; Huber, Miller, and Glick, 1990; Miller, 1990; Miller, Glick, Wang, and Huber, 1991). We found that at least two dozen factors might reasonably be thought to prompt or retard change. Because they are so many in number, it is helpful to group them. One grouping, compatible with the managerial and organizational literatures, is the following: (1) characteristics of the organization's environment, (2) characteristics of the organization's performance, (3) characteristics of the organization's top manager, (4) characteristics of the organization's strategy, and (5) characteristics of the organization's structure. From now on we refer to these five groups of factors as *constructs*.[1]

In the remainder of this introductory section, we overview the constructs and factors that our reviews and general knowledge of the field indicate are possible determinants of organizational change and also describe the general nature of what we found in our study to be the validity of these constructs and factors as predictors of different types of organizational change.

Organizational Environments

Common managerial wisdom and a number of organization science theories (e.g., open systems theory, institutional theory, and resource-dependence theory) inform us that organizations must attain and maintain a satisfactory fit with their environments. Often, this means that they must adapt to environmental changes. Turbulence, competitiveness, and complexity are environmental characteristics that have often been suggested as determinants of organizational changes (cf., Aldrich, 1979; Hrebiniak and Joyce, 1985; Huber, 1984; Mohrman and Mohrman, 1989), and were used in the study reported here as predictors of organizational change. We verified that organizational environments do determine organizational change; after controlling for organizational size, we found that the frequencies of organizational change estimated using information about the antecedent environments of the organizations in our study predicted quite well the actual frequencies of change in these organizations. ($r = .41$, $p < .01$).

Organizational Performance

Nothing captures the attention of managers so quickly as significant and unexpected decreases in organizational performance. While it may be true that managers scan their organization's environment for threats and opportunities, they also—and perhaps more systematically—monitor their organization's performance. When gaps are observed between actual performance and desired performance, searches for "fixes" are initiated (cf., Cyert and March, 1963: Ch. 4; Mintzberg, Raisinghani, and Théorêt, 1976), and often result in organizational changes. There are also reasons to believe that increases in organizational performance could lead to organizational change, and that even antecedent levels of organizational performance can affect the frequency of organizational change. In the organizations we studied, the frequencies of changes estimated using prior performance-related information and controlling for the effect of size were significantly correlated with actual frequencies of changes ($r = .36, p < .01$). Performance seems to affect the frequency of change but, as we will show, the relationships are fairly complex.

Top Manager Characteristics

Everyday observation shows that managers deliberately create some changes in organizations and retard others, and that these propensities vary across managers. For example, it appears that managers are more sensitive to information related to their current or previous work responsibilities, and that this biases their predispositions to recognize or not recognize the need for changes in different functional areas of the organization. It is also thought that demographic attributes, such as age and education, influence managers' reactions to change-inducing events, and some scientific evidence seems to support this belief (cf., Kimberly and Evanisko, 1981; MacCrimmon and Wehrung, 1990). Finally, it is commonly believed that the tendency to encourage or discourage change is related to certain personality variables, such as the manager's need for achievement or belief in the controllability of events. As will be seen, we found that the ability of different types of top manager characteristics to predict organizational changes varied greatly. When used collectively, information about top manager characteristics resulted in estimated frequencies of changes that were correlated moderately with actual frequencies, after accounting for size ($r = .36, p < .01$). It seems that the characteristics of top managers are determinants of the activity levels that occur in organizations.

Organizational Strategy

It seems likely that an organization's strategy affects the frequency of change in the organization. For example, an organization having a strategy of frequently introducing new products or entering new markets would have a high frequency of organizational change, since such changes generally require changes in organizational processes, personnel, resource allocations, and forms in order to be implemented. In contrast to this prospector strategy, an organization maintaining a defender strategy by operating as a low cost producer might initiate organizational changes only infrequently, since the implementation of change inevitably consumes costly resources. With the effects of size accounted for, the correlation between the frequencies of changes estimated with information about strategies and the frequencies actually encountered was modest but statistically significant ($r = .33, p < .01$). Thus strategies were predictive, but not strongly predictive.

Organizational Structure

A number of structural characteristics might serve to facilitate or constrain organization change. For example, some research indicates that centralized decision making is positively associated with the frequency of administrative changes and is negatively associated with the frequency of technological changes (Kimberly and Evanisko, 1981). As another example, if the work processes of an organization are highly standardized, they are generally more difficult to change than if they are more varied and less formalized. Structural specialization and interdependence are also factors that can easily be hypothesized to affect the frequency of organizational change. As with organizational strategy, after controlling for size, organizational structure was just modestly predictive ($r = .31, p < .01$).

The above paragraphs indicate that organizational changes are determined by factors associated with five quite different constructs. This idea, captured in Figure 7.1, seems commonsensical. But it is also interesting, because relative to the models or speculations concerning organizational change that are implicit or explicit in most writings, the model shown in Figure 7.1 is much more encompassing of the phenomenon.[2]

The factors indicated in Figure 7.1 are variables that we believed might determine organizational change, by either prompting it or retarding it. Most readers can easily recall or imagine specific instances where one or more of these factors might affect, or was thought to have affected, an organizational change. On the other hand, the generalizability of specific instances is always open to question. Unfortunately, except for the literature on technological innovation, systematically acquired and evaluated evidence concerning the determinants of organizational change is in short supply. In an attempt to overcome some of these problems and to investigate the determinants of organizational change more systematically and more comprehensively, we conducted a two-year study of organizational change in 119 organizations. In the next section of the chapter we briefly describe the nature of the study. (Details and elaborating notes about the methodology are contained in Appendix 7A.)

The five correlations noted in the above paragraphs suggest that the factors shown in Figure 7.1 might collectively predict quite accurately the level of change occurring in a given organization. But they do not begin to tell us all that we would like to know. They provoke, but do not answer the following questions:

1. Which factors are good predictors, and which are not?
2. What types of organizational changes are predicted by which factors?

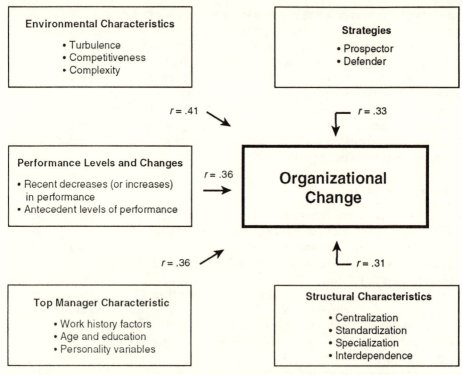

Figure 7.1.   Constructs and factors associated with organizational change.

3. What is the collective predictive capability of the factors?
4. Why are the predictive factors predictive and the nonpredictive factors not predictive?

After describing the nature of the study,[3] in the main section of the chapter we use
the literature, the results from our study, and our own judgment to answer these four
questions. At the end of the chapter we set forth our thoughts and speculations concerning the implications of the research results for managers and for organizational
scientists. But first let us describe how we learned what we learned.

NATURE OF THE STUDY

A matter that strongly influenced our study was that of causality. We were interested
in identifying the determinants of organizational change. Because a longitudinal study
is much more useful for assessing the causal directionality of an association between
variables than is a cross-sectional study, we conducted a longitudinal study. Although
longitudinal studies cannot prove that antecedent conditions or events caused subsequent events, except in highly unusual cases they can rule out the converse. As a consequence, when there is a theoretical basis for believing that the antecedents are causal
to the subsequent events, observed correlations are generally regarded as evidence of

causality. In this study, except for the top manager's personality variables, all factors interpreted as causal were observed before the organizational changes took place.

Organizations Studied

Nothing in the previous discussion, or in the forthcoming discussion of possible determinants of change, is specific to organizations of any particular region, industry, or size. Consequently, it was appropriate to examine change in a wide variety of organizations. Data were obtained from a heterogeneous set of 119 organizations geographically dispersed with clusters of organizations in California, Michigan, Ohio, Illinois, Texas, and Virginia. The industrial composition was 23 percent heavy manufacturing, 26 percent light manufacturing, 26 percent health care, 7 percent financial institutions, 10 percent educational institutions, and 8 percent all other services. The organizations ranged in size from 16 to 6,000 full-time employees. The mean number of employees was 1,121; the median was 397. Heterogeneity was constrained by the requirements that each organization must (1) serve an external constituency, (2) have primary responsibility for its strategy and design, and (3) include at least two managerial levels. Seventy percent of the organizations were divisions of other organizations.

Data Collection: Interviews and Mailed Questionnaires

For each organization, we collected information about the important changes through a series of three interviews with the top manager (72 percent of the cases) or with another member of the top management team identified by the top manager as qualified to provide this information (most often the chief operating officer). All interviewers either possessed or were obtaining Ph.D. degrees in organizational science. The interviews were spaced approximately six months apart and concerned the changes that occurred during the previous six months. With respect to the information used in this study, all interviews were procedurally identical. (The interview procedures and instruments are available from the authors as CODE Technical Reports 01 and 05.) Within approximately a month after the first interview, a mailed questionnaire was used to obtain from these top manager informants information about their organization's environment, strategy, performance, structure, processes, and technology. (This 122-question instrument is hereafter called the Organizational Profile Questionnaire and is available from the authors as CODE Technical Report 06.) Finally, approximately six months after the third interview, a mailed questionnaire was used to obtain from the top manager of each organization information about various of his or her personal and professional characteristics. (This 43-question instrument is hereafter called the Top Manager Profile Questionnaire and is also available from the authors as CODE Technical Report 09.)

Assessing the Changes and Their Possible Determinants

The nature and frequency of changes initiated or encountered by each organization were obtained using semistructured interviews in which the organization's top manager or other key informant was asked to take a total of about 20 minutes to very briefly describe to the interviewer each of "the important changes that occurred over the last six months." The informants were told that they would be able to elaborate on their descriptions of the changes after all were briefly described (and this was true). The limit of 20 minutes was an attempt to reduce the effect of variations in talkativeness on the number of reported changes.

Although we and others have previously recommended the use of multiple key informants when studying organizational processes (Huber and Power, 1985), several reasons caused us to choose the organization's top manager as the single key informant in this study. These are discussed at length in Glick, Huber, Miller, Doty, and Sutcliffe (1990), reprinted as the appendix of this volume. One deserves brief mention here. It is that the organization's top manager is most often the most veridical informant about important organizational changes. Managers not at the very top of the organization, because of their more limited responsibilities, are sometimes not well informed about particular changes. In addition, functional managers are likely to be systematically biased in their assessment of which changes are important. To use their listings of important changes would be to use less valid data.

Of course top managers have biases as well. While using only one informant does allow the informant's idiosyncratic biases to affect the data for that informant's organization, we believe that these idiosyncratic biases enter our models either in the form of the top manager characteristics that we assessed or as random error, rather than as systematic error affecting other factors of interest. Biases that characterize top managers as a class, in their role as key informants, enter our models as a constant.[4]

Some of the changes reported were changes in the organization's environment or in its performance. Most of the changes reported were organizational changes— changes in the organization's processes, personnel, allocation of resources, or form. After the interview, the interviewer coded each change into one of 12 predefined coding categories. One category was for environmental changes, and another was for performance changes. The ten remaining categories were the organizational changes. We grouped these ten into (1) changes primarily directed at targets outside the organization (such as customers or regulatory agencies); (2) changes primarily directed at internal processes (such as changing manufacturing methods) or conditions (such as employee motivation); and (3) changes in organizational form (such as separating Sales from Marketing) (see Table 7.1). The four dependent variables of the study are the frequencies of each of these three types of organizational change (i.e., externally focused changes, internally focused changes, and changes in form) and the total frequency of organizational changes that occurred in each organization during the six-month period previous to the third interview. In total, 1,001 organizational changes were reported during the third round of interviews. The number of reported changes occurring during the previous six months ranged from 0 to 24 across the 119 organizations. The mean was 8.4.

Discussions of the reliability of the codings of the changes, and also of an analysis directed at the issue of using weighted frequencies of change as our dependent variable, where the weights would indicate the relative importance of the change, are included in Appendix 7A of the chapter. The methods used to assess the 25 factors examined in this study are described in detail in Appendix 7A.

Table 7.1.   Ten Predefined Categories of Organizational Changes Grouped into Three
Types of Organizational Changes

Externally Focused Changes

- Important changes in the organization's externally focused strategy (e.g., changes in products, markets, emphases).
- Important changes in the way the organization interacts with its customers, clients, or parent organization (e.g., introducing electronic funds transfer or the solicitation of orders by phone).

Internally Focused Changes

- Important changes in the organization's internally focused goals, philosophy, or culture (e.g., decisions to focus on human resource development, cost control, or employee participation).
- Important changes in the way the product or service is produced (e.g., changes in equipment, techniques, or sequencing of activities).
- Important changes in administrative procedures (e.g., changing control or incentive systems).
- Important changes in internal coordination or communication procedures (e.g., introducing electronic mail weekly meetings).
- Important changes in specific personnel or in staffing levels (e.g., additions, deletions, transfers, reassignments) that are not changes in organizational form.

Changes in Organizational Form

- Important changes in the responsibility or resources of top management team members (i.e., of the CEO or of any manager who reports to either the CEO or the chief operating officer).
- Important changes in responsibility or resources at the other levels in the organization.
- Important additions or eliminations of a major organizational unit.

The Analyses

The model shown in Figure 7.1 and its elaboration on the succeeding pages may be more explanatory than other theories of organizational change because more factors are considered as possible determinants. Its completeness, however, disallows its testing with a simple, one-shot analysis. There are too many predictors relative to the number of organizations. Consequently, we conducted the analyses in three stages. The stages were the same for all five constructs (i.e., for environment, performance, top managers, strategies, and structure).

For each construct, in stage 1 we regressed each of the four dependent variables (i.e., the frequencies of externally focused changes, internally focused changes, changes in organizational form, and all changes together) on the collectivity of size, the several factors grouped under the construct, and the interactions of these factors with size. The benefit of these stage-1 analyses is that, repeated across the five constructs, they enabled us to test all of the hypotheses implied in Figure 7.1.[5] This stage was theory-driven, or at least argument-driven.

In stage 2 we developed "trimmed models" for each construct. Each of these more parsimonious models was composed of the subset of all hypothesized predictors that individually explained a significant ($p < .10$) increment of the variance in the frequency of the respective type of change.[6] This approach resulted in simpler models that explained, on average, about the same amount of variance as did the more elaborate initial models developed in stage 1. The benefits of the stage-2 analyses are that they enabled us (1) to learn if additional predictive power beyond that attained in stage 1 could be achieved by including only statistically significant predictors and (2) to obtain sharper insight into the determinants of organizational change by screening out those hypothesized determinants that could not be empirically validated. To enhance the chapter's readability, we discuss and present in the body of the chapter the results of the stage-2 analyses only. The results of the stage-1 analyses are presented in Appendices 7C through 7G.

Stage 3 of the analysis, to be described later, involved development and testing of change-predicting models that included factors from more than one construct. Minor departures from this general approach occurred and are noted where applicable. Details concerning the sample sizes used in the analyses appear in Appendix 7A of the chapter. The mean values and intercorrelations for all variables are shown in Appendix 7B.

With this brief description of how we conducted the study out of the way, let us turn to the crux of the chapter. In the next section we discuss why each of the factors shown in Figure 7.1 might cause or constrain organizational change, and we report the results of our attempts to confirm or refute our reasoning.

DETERMINANTS OF ORGANIZATIONAL CHANGE

This section is organized around the five constructs shown in Figure 7.1: organizational environments, organizational performance, top manager characteristics, organizational strategy, and organizational structure. In each subsection, we consider in some detail the possible effects on organizational change of each of the several factors associated with one of these constructs. Specifically, we discuss the frequency of changes, but the general line of reasoning seems to apply to the importance or magnitude of changes as well. In these discussions we do not distinguish among different types of changes (although we do in the analyses presented later). As we reviewed the literatures concerning the factors that might affect organizational change, we generally found little basis for concluding that a particular factor would influence some particular type of organizational change, but would influence no other. And we did little speculating on the matter ourselves. Consequently, our hypotheses are probably somewhat biased in the direction of being general. But, given our interest in developing a more general explanation of the phenomenon than is currently available, it seems more appropriate to err in this direction than in the reverse.

As will be seen in the analyses, we statistically controlled for the direct effects of organizational size on organizational change. This seems necessary because size could influence organizational change in a variety of ways. For example, larger organizations might have more internally generated and internally focused changes per unit of time than smaller organizations, as there are both more sources and more targets of change. We also consider the idea that various factors might affect the frequency of organizational changes differently in small organizations than in large organizations. That is, we consider the effects on organizational change of the interaction of organizational size with each of the other possible determinants of organizational change. Because there are so many of these factors, for each of the five constructs we discuss the possible interaction effect of organizational size and just one of the factors from the construct. However, since there seem to be few, if any, such interactions that cannot reasonably be considered as possibly having an effect on organizational change, we test each of them for their usefulness as a predictor.

We also considered controlling for the organization's age, as more mature organizations might be less likely to change. We felt, however, that after some threshold is reached, age would be only a weak measure of maturity, as across time organizational rejuvenations or other organizational metamorphoses and transformations would seem to interrupt whatever underlying relationship might exist between age and maturity. In addition, only 5 percent of the organizations were less than five years old, so the sample consists largely of mature organizations; 85 percent were ten or more years old. Consequently, we did not control for organizational age.

Let us turn now to discussing the effects of the factors noted in Figure 7.1. We begin with those associated with organizational environments.

Organizational Environments

Changes in organizational performance, particularly sudden, downward performance changes, lead to organizational changes. However, in order to avoid performance downturns, or to create upturns, managers initiate some organizational changes in response to early warnings of environmentally based threats or opportunities. In at least this way, then, organizational environments are determinants of organizational change.

The variety of specific events, trends, and states of organizational environments that might lead to organizational changes is enormous, and in many instances these sources of change are quite idiosyncratic in terms of their effects on a particular organization. Listing them, then, does not contribute to developing a general theory for predicting or understanding organizational change. Instead, we consider more general characteristics of organizational environments. Environmental turbulence, competitiveness, and complexity seem to have been studied or discussed more than any others as environmental characteristics logically related to organizational change.

Turbulent Environments

Environments in which events occur frequently and unpredictably are turbulent. When these events have clear and important implications for future performance, managers set in motion actions to exploit them (if they are opportunities) or guard against them (if they are threats). Thus it seems reasonable to conclude that *organizational changes are more frequent in more turbulent environments.*

Competitive Environments

Environments in which needed resources are limited and where actions by other organizations affect the proportion of these resources that any organization can acquire are competitive. How the competitiveness of an environment might influence organizational change would seem to vary across organizations. For example, if an organization competes by initiating new products or services or entering new markets, more competition would force more innovation—that is, more change. On the other hand, if the organization defends its current market position by producing and selling at a low cost, more competition might inhibit change, at least in the short run, because introducing change usually involves increases in cost or decreases in productivity.

Thus, defender manufacturers often attempt to use current equipment and buildings as long as possible. Of course, a defender manufacturer might instead introduce new technologies quite frequently, if these result in cost savings. As another example of how the effect of competitiveness might vary across organizations, top managers who see themselves as having high levels of discretion might be stimulated to change their organizations more frequently in a highly competitive environment. In contrast, threat-rigidity theory (Staw, Sandelands, and Dutton, 1981) suggests that under intense competition top managers who see themselves as having little discretion would choose to "hunker down" and would consequently change their organizations infrequently. So, it seems that across a population of organizations with a mix of strategies, of top managers, and possibly of other interacting characteristics, *there is no overall, main effect of environmental competitiveness on organizational change.*

Complex Environments

Environments that tend to contain many components, to contain diverse components, and to have diverse components that are interconnected are complex. Living systems theory reminds us that these features tend to be related: "As a system's components become more numerous, they become specialized, with resulting increased interdependence" (Miller, 1978: 109). Of course, the more numerous and diverse are the components of an environment, where each component can prompt an organizational change, the more turbulent is the environment and the more frequent are the adaptive changes. Thus, all else equal, the greater the environmental complexity, the greater the environmental turbulence and, consequently, the greater the frequency of organizational change.

$$\begin{array}{ccc} \text{Environmental} & \Rightarrow & \text{Environmental} & \Rightarrow & \text{Organizational} \\ \text{Complexity} & & \text{Turbulence} & & \text{Change} \end{array}$$

Another way that environmental complexity could be positively related to organizational change is through its impact on organizational specialization. Ashby's Law of Requisite Variety (Ashby, 1968, 1969) captures the idea that degree of specialization within an organization's structure must be congruent with the variety of key components in the environments with which the organization interacts. We will explain later, and merely assert here, the idea that more specialized organizational structures tend to generate more organizational changes. Thus, all else equal, the greater the environmental complexity, the greater the degree of organizational specialization and, consequently, the greater the frequency of organizational change.

$$\begin{array}{ccc} \text{Environmental} & \Rightarrow & \text{Specialization} & \Rightarrow & \text{Organizational} \\ \text{Complexity} & & \text{of Structure} & & \text{Change} \end{array}$$

Individually and together, these two lines of reasoning suggest that *organizational changes are more frequent in complex environments.* They also suggest that, if the variation in change attributable to environmental turbulence and structural specialization is accounted for, *there is no overall main effect of environmental complexity on organizational change.* (We are indebted to Alison Davis-Blake for this insight.)

Interactions of Environment with Size

In order to survive, small organizations, generally having less control over their environment and generally having lower levels of reserve resources, might be forced to make more adaptive changes in the face of high levels of competition than would large organizations. On the other hand, large organizations generally have more options and resources for responding to external pressures and generally have more control over their environment. Thus, although managers in both small and large organizations might desire to make changes in the face of competitive environments, it is more likely that managers in large organizations will be able to do so. We conclude, then, that the interactive effect of environmental competitiveness with size is positive. These conflicting lines of reasoning make empirical investigation especially attractive. Similar discussions could be developed concerning the interactions of turbulence and complexity with size.

Results from the Study

In the stage-1 analysis, the organization's size; the turbulence, competitiveness, and complexity of its environment; and the interactions of these three environmental factors with size were tested simultaneously as predictors of organizational change. (Results are shown in Appendix 7C.) In stage 2 we developed the more parsimonious trimmed models that contain only those environment-related factors and interactions that reliably predicted the frequency of organizational change. These models, developed using the procedure described earlier, are shown in Table 7.2.[7]

We had hypothesized that environmental turbulence leads to organizational change. As can be seen in Table 7.2, this was validated for all types of change—for internally focused change, externally focused change, changes in form, and total changes.

Table 7.2. Environmental Characteristics As Determinants of Organizational Changes: Trimmed Regression Models[a]

Determinants	Externally Focused Changes	Internally Focused Changes	Changes in Form	Total Changes
Turbulence	.24**	.30**	.24**	.34**
Competitiveness	—	—	—	—
Complexity	—	—	—	—
Size	—	.23**	—	.19*
Turbulance × size	—	.13	—	—
Competitiveness × size	—	.10	.24**	.23**
Complexity × size	—	—	—	—
Adjusted R^2	.05*	.22**	.11**	.25**
Adjusted R^2 after controlling for size	.05*	.11**	.11**	.17**

[a]Based on data from 119 organizations. Entries are standardized regression coefficients and indicate the relative influence of the determinants on the frequency of change.

$^+p < .10$

$*p < .05$

$**p < .01$

It is not surprising that competitiveness was not predictive of change, given our earlier reflections on the ambiguous effects of the conflicting forces. It may be, if the effects of contingencies (such as strategy and top manager characteristics) on the competitiveness-change relationship are taken into account, that competitiveness would be found to relate to the frequency of changes. We had also argued that the effects of complexity on change is only indirect, operating through environmental turbulence and through specialization of organizational structure. Thus, since turbulence was included in the models, it is also not surprising that complexity did not have a significant effect. The positive effect of the interaction of competitiveness with size might be because large organizations generally have greater control over their environment and more, and more varied, options and resources with which to make changes in organizational form in response to competitive environments.

The overall conclusion to be drawn from these results is that *environmental turbulence and the interaction of environmental competitiveness with size are highly significant predictors of different types of organizational change.* It is also clear that organizational size and various interactions of environmental factors with size have different effects on different types of organizational change.

Environments can affect organizational change because they contain threats and opportunities that managers react to by making organizational changes. Sometimes, however, managers fail to notice environmental changes, or fail to act on them. Sometimes the changes give no warning. Such conditions can lead to downturns in organizational performance that, in turn, lead to organizational changes. For example, as shown in Chapter 2 in this volume, environmental decline (an environmental change) can lead to lower sales revenues (a performance change), which, in turn, can lead to organizational downsizing (an organizational change). Let us turn now to examining the possible effects of organizational performance on organizational change.

Organizational Performance

The top managers of poorly performing organizations are almost invariably under pressure from one or more stakeholder groups to increase organizational performance on some dimension or other. Investors press for increased profits or market share. Workers press for higher incomes. Customers press for better quality and lower prices. To increase organizational performance often requires organizational change, so we might expect organizational changes to be more frequent in low-performing organizations. On the other hand, low-performing organizations tend to have fewer opportunities and resources for undertaking changes, and therefore management might be less inclined to generate changes. We believe that this latter condition would be temporary, as unhappy stakeholders would eventually force change by withholding resources regardless of management's inclinations. Finally, looking at the same issues somewhat differently, we note that the managers of high-performing organizations might be more complacent and thus initiate fewer changes. So, on balance, we believe that *organizational changes are negatively related to organizational performance.*[8]

The above discussions concerned whether the steady-state level of performance is associated with organizational change. In contrast, let us now consider whether changes in performance lead to organizational change. It seems clear that major downturns in performance lead to major changes in organizations (cf., Miller and Friesen,

1980; Tushman and Romanelli, 1985), and everyday observations demonstrate that even modest downturns in organizational performance can lead to organizational changes such as cutting costs, increasing advertising, and replacing managers who "aren't getting the job done." It seems inevitable, then, that *organizational changes are more frequent when organizational performance decreases than when it remains constant.*

Increases in organizational performance might also result in organizational changes. For example, increases in performance can lead to increases in organizational slack that is eventually allocated to create or facilitate organizational changes. Moreover, increases in performance might reduce the perceived riskiness of actions that, while apparently desirable, were previously held in abeyance until the level of performance had increased. Although performance increases could lead to inaction as a result of complacency, we believe that this condition would be temporary, either because of management's increased aspirations or the increased aspirations of those stakeholders concerned with that particular dimension of organizational performance. Consequently, we hypothesize that, in general, *organizational changes are more frequent when organizational performance increases than when it remains constant.*

Interactions of Performance with Organizational Size

Because small organizations generally have fewer options and resources and less control over their environment, it seems likely that decreases in performance would be more threatening and would be responded to more frequently with organizational changes. It also might be that, because smaller organizations are more controllable by their top managers or because they are generally less burdened with the inertia that sometimes retards change in larger organizations, increases in performance might lead more frequently to organizational changes in smaller organizations. Similar arguments concerning the effects of interactions with size could be offered for each of the other factors included in the performance construct.

Results from the Study

As discussed earlier, we believed that antecedent levels of performance as well as changes in performance are both determinants of organizational change. In the stage-1 analysis, we first analyzed the effects of antecedent performance levels on subsequent organizational changes. We examined the simultaneous effects of size, the levels of growth performance and efficiency performance, and the interactions of these two performance level factors with size. Overall, the antecedent levels of performance were not very determining of organizational change. (These results are shown in Appendix 7D.1.)

Turning from antecedent levels of performance to changes in performance, we analyzed the simultaneous effects of size, the changes in growth performance and efficiency performance, and the interactions of these two types of performance change with size. The performance changes were more predictive of organizational changes than were performance levels. A note of caution is in order, however, when making this comparison, as the levels of performance and changes in performance were assessed with different instruments and at different times. (Appendix 7D.2 contains the results of the analyses.)

In the stage-2 analysis, all performance-related factors and their interactions with size were analyzed as predictors of organizational change, using the procedure described earlier. The resulting trimmed models, one for each type of change, include all terms that individually explain a significant ($p < .10$) increment of the variance in the frequency of that type of change. Table 7.3 contains these models.

Let us first consider the effects of antecedent levels of performance. We had hypothesized that organizational change is negatively related to organizational performance. Table 7.3 shows that both growth performance and efficiency performance, were negatively related to externally focused changes and that efficiency performance was also negatively related to internally focused changes. These three findings support the idea that high levels of performance reduce the felt need to make changes.

Let us now turn from examining the effects of levels of performance to examining the effects of changes in performance. As hypothesized, performance changes led to organizational changes. The fact that downturns in growth were strongly and positively related to externally focused changes and to changes in organizational form makes sense in view of the reasoning presented earlier, and the effect on changes in organizational form in particular confirms the findings of Miller and Friesen (1980) and the conclusions of Tushman and Romanelli (1985) that major structural changes tend to occur when organizational performance declines. Upturns in growth were positively related to externally focused changes. This finding supports our earlier idea that desirable but risky changes might be held in abeyance until performance improves. Upturns in efficiency performance were negatively related to internally focused

Table 7.3. Performance Levels and Changes As Determinants of Organizational Changes: Trimmed Models[a]

Determinants	Externally Focused Changes	Internally Focused Changes	Changes in Form	Total Changes
Growth performance	$-.18^+$	—	—	—
Efficiency performance	$-.17^+$	$-.17^+$	—	$-.18^*$
Downturns in growth	$.19^*$	$.18^+$	$.26^{**}$	$.26^{**}$
Upturns in growth	$.35^{**}$	—	—	$.28^{**}$
Downturns in efficiency	—	—	—	—
Upturns in efficiency	—	$-.17^+$	—	—
Size	—	$.28^{**}$	—	$.26^{**}$
Growth × size	—	—	—	—
Efficiency × size	—	—	—	—
Downturns in growth × size	—	—	—	—
Upturns in growth × size	—	—	—	—
Downturns in efficiency × size	$.17^+$	—	$-.18^*$	$-.17^+$
Upturns in efficiency × size	$.18^+$	$.24^*$	—	$.22^*$
Adjusted R^2	$.19^{**}$	$.14^{**}$	$.09^{**}$	$.21^{**}$
Adjusted R^2 after controlling for size	na	.02	na	$.13^{**}$

[a]Based on data from 100 organizations. Entries are standardized regression coefficients and indicate the relative influence of the determinants on the frequency of change.
$^+p < .10$
$^*p < .05$
$^{**}p < .01$

changes, and the interaction with size was positively related to both externally focused and internally focused changes. This suggests that upturns in efficiency reduce the frequency of changes in large organizations more than in small organizations.

The overall results show that *externally focused changes are significantly affected by antecedent performance levels and by performance changes.* The results also indicate that levels and changes of organizational performance have much more effect on externally focused changes (adjusted R^2 for model without size adjustment $= .19$) than they do on internally focused changes (adjusted R^2 after statistically controlling for size $= .02$).

Characteristics of the Organization's Top Manager

> There is a growing knowledge base about large-scale organization change. This literature is quite consistent on at least one aspect of effective system-wide change—namely, executive leadership matters. The executive is a critical actor in the drama of organization change. Nadler and Tushman, 1990: 77

Nadler and Tushman's clear articulation of this idea not only sharpens in our minds what we already believe, but causes us to consider which top manager characteristics are related to organizational change.

Managers vary in the extent to which they initiate changes overall, as well as changes of different kinds. Organizational scientists have offered three explanations. One is that differences in managers' current or previous job responsibilities affect the number of changes they direct at different components of the environment or toward different functional areas in the organization. A second is that demographic attributes, such as age and education, increase or decrease managers' overall inclination to initiate change. The third is that certain personality variables determine managerial proactiveness. Each of these explanations deserves elaboration. We begin with discussions of the effects of the top manager's work history. We then turn to discussing the effects of demographic attributes. Finally, we discuss the effects of various personality variables.

Work History

Experience with Throughput and Output Functions. Top managers having more experience with throughput functions (e.g., production) or output functions (e.g., marketing) probably initiate more changes in that functional area then they do in the other. This follows from the reasoning of Gupta (1988) and Hambrick and Mason (1984) that managers may think more about the familiar domain, and thus would probably think of more changes for that domain, and the finding of Gabarro (1987) that top managers new in their job tended to initiate a wave of changes, primarily in the functional areas where they had the most experience. In addition, with respect to adopting innovations proposed by someone else, top managers are more likely to understand the positive attributes of a proposed change related to a more familiar domain. Consequently, we hypothesize that (1) *the frequency of externally focused changes is positively related to the top manager's level of experience with output functions* and (2) *the frequency of internally focused changes is positively related to the top manager's level of experience with throughput functions.*

Tenure in the Organization. Top managers with longer tenure in their organization are more likely to have been socialized into accepting the organization as it is, to accepting "the way we do things here." The literature reviewed by Finkelstein and Hambrick (1990) supports this idea, as does their finding that the mean tenure in the firm of the top management team members was negatively related to changes in firm strategy. Thus, it seems reasonable to conclude that *organizational changes are less frequent when top managers have longer tenure in the organization.*

Tenure in the Position. Let us first consider the effect of tenure on the inclination to initiate change. In this regard it seems likely that top managers new to their position would make more changes because they bring a fresh perspective to their task or because superordinates or boards of directors have mandated change. Over time the effects of these conditions would wane and the top manager would become more inclined to accept the organization as it has become and would consequently initiate fewer changes. Research by Gabarro (1987) and Miller (1991) support this reasoning.

Let us turn now to considering the effects of tenure on the ability to implement change, rather than on the inclination to initiate it. Top managers with longer tenure in their position usually have built up more legitimacy and therefore would tend to be allowed by stakeholders or superordinates to make more changes than short-service managers. In addition, top managers with long tenure in their position probably have emplaced more loyal subordinates and learned how to deal with the local environmental and organizational realities, and therefore they can obtain desired changes. Kimberly and Evanisko (1981) found a weak positive association between tenure of top managers and technological innovation (but no association between tenure and administrative innovation). Of course, legitimacy and power can be used to avoid or thwart change as well, so their effect on the frequency of change though the control of change is not clear.

Thus we have two lines of reasoning. Considering the ability to implement change, it seems that tenure in the position would be positively related to change. Considering the inclination to initiate change, it seems that tenure would be negatively related to change. Hambrick and Fukutomi (1991) consider both these lines of reasoning and some closely related arguments, and imply that change would be curvilinearly related to tenure—that is, it would be greatest at intermediate lengths of tenure, after the ability to implement change has increased but before the inclination to initiate change has appreciably declined. It seemed to us, too, that *organizational changes are most frequent when top managers are at intermediate durations of tenure in their position.*

Demographic Attributes

Educational Level. It is conventional wisdom that higher levels of education result in more complex approaches to problem solving and decision making, approaches in which more factors and more interrelationships among the factors are considered. As a consequence, more highly educated top managers are thought to be more likely to be receptive to change and more likely to detect the need for change. Consistent with this reasoning, Becker (1970), Kimberly and Evanisko (1981), and Rogers and Shoemaker (1971) found that highly educated top managers are more likely to have their organizations try new administrative procedures. Thus we hypothesize that *organizational changes are more frequent when the top manager is more highly educated.*

Age. Age might be negatively related to risk-taking propensity because older managers may have more to lose and less opportunity to recover. This suggests that older managers initiate fewer changes, since at least some changes entail risk. The empirical support for this reasoning has not surfaced, however (cf. MacCrimmon and Wehrung, 1990). In addition, older managers might initiate some changes in order to reduce risk. It seems likely, especially after other top manager characteristics are accounted for, that *top manager age is not a determinant of organizational change.*

Personality Variables.

Let us now consider the effects of personality variables, since "it is now widely accepted that the differences among chief executive officers (CEO's)—including general managers of strategic business units (SBU's) within the corporation—are at least as profound as the similarities among them" (Gupta, 1988: 147).

Internal Locus of Control. The extent to which people believe that they have control over important events is called internal locus of control. Top managers lower on internal locus of control would seem less likely to initiate change because, believing that forces beyond their control determine important organizational outcomes, they see little point in being proactive. Consistent with this reasoning, Miller, Kets de Vries, and Toulouse (1982), and Miller and Toulouse (1986) found that chief executives of firms pursuing strategies that involve product innovation tended to be higher in internal locus of control than chief executives of firms pursuing strategies that involve little innovation. An interesting counterargument to this reasoning is that, in circumstances where other forces are prompting change, managers who are high on internal locus of control may resist change in the belief that they can effectively manage the situation with the structures, personnel, and resource allocations currently in place, while those low on this personality dimension may not resist such forces. The resulting correlation, then, between internal locus of control and organizational change would be negative. While this is an interesting line of reasoning, we suspect that the circumstances where it would apply are less common. Thus, in keeping with the thinking of Hambrick and Mason (1984), we conclude that, overall, *organizational changes are more frequent when top managers are high on internal locus of control.*

Perceived Discretion. While conceptually similar to locus of control, perceived discretion refers more specifically to the latitude of managerial action. As Hambrick and Finkelstein (1987) argue, discretion is not absolute and resides in part within the manager; an executive's discretion is partly determined by his or her ability to envision and create multiple courses of action. The arguments concerning the possible relationships between organizational change and perceived discretion parallel those concerning organizational change and internal locus of control. On balance, it seems reasonable to believe that, across a variety of organizations and situations, *organizational changes are more frequent when top managers see themselves as having high levels of discretion.*

Need for Achievement. It seems likely that need for achievement is related to initiation of change, as people who are high on this personality variable are likely to be proactive in seeking ways to fulfill their desire to do better. While Miller and Toulouse (1986) were unsuccessful in one attempt to find an association between the top manager's need for achievement and of the firm's innovativeness, they were successful in a subsequent attempt (Miller, Droge, and Toulouse, 1988). On balance, it seems reasonable to believe that *organizational changes are more frequent when top managers have a higher need for achievement.*

Tolerance for Ambiguity. The extent to which a person is comfortable with uncertain situations, is called tolerance for ambiguity. Because creating an important organizational change generally involves uncertainty about the consequences, it seems likely that managers low on tolerance for ambiguity would initiate fewer changes than those who are more tolerant. On the other hand, it is easy to imagine changes made in order to reduce uncertainty or ambiguity—for example, lobbying government agencies, conducting market analyses, or training managers as backups to other managers. We suspect, however, that initiating changes such as these is actually more related to need for achievement than it is to intolerance for ambiguity. Thus, on balance, we conclude that *organizational changes are more frequent when top managers are high on tolerance for ambiguity.*

Interactions of Top Manager Characteristics with Organizational Size.

Whatever the effects that a top manager's characteristics may have on the frequency of organizational change, it seems that they would be greater in small organizations. For example, it is in small organizations that top managers can be most attuned to what is going on and can most directly control the implementation of decisions to change.

Hambrick and Finkelstein (1987) and Gupta (1988) have called attention to the fact that organizational inertia and constraints in the organization's environment are responsible for much of the variation in observed managerial proactiveness. In addition, most important decisions in organizations are influenced by several managers, not all of whom have the same propensities regarding change. Consequently, the effects of any one manager's personality on change is diluted by the effects of the personalities of the other managers involved. Thus, even though it is interesting to think about how individual differences in managerial characteristics relate to managerially initiated organizational changes, we must be cautious in our thinking about how much variation in the top manager's actual change-initiating or change-retarding behavior is accounted for by his or her work history, demographic attributes, and personality variables.

Results from the Study.

Because the total number of top manager characteristics was large relative to the sample size, the stage-1 analysis involved three analyses, conducted in parallel. That is, we separately used work histories, demographic attributes, and personality variables to predict the frequencies of the different types of change. In each of these analyses we included size as a control variable and also the interaction of the managerial characteristics with size.

In the stage-1 analyses, all work history factors or their interactions with size were predictive of either externally focused changes or internally focused changes, but for only internally focused and total changes did they collectively predict a significant proportion of the frequency of organizational change. None of the work history factors or their interactions were predictors of changes in organizational form. (Results are in Appendix 7E.1.)

When we analyzed the effects of the top managers' demographic attributes, neither age nor education nor their interactions with size were predictive of any types of change, either individually or collectively (data not shown). Any influence on organizational change resulting from these factors, if it exists, is overwhelmed by the influence of other factors.

The analysis of the personality variables subconstruct was straightforward. Size, each of the four variables (internal locus of control, perceived discretion, need for achievement, and tolerance for ambiguity), and the interactions of these variables with size were used to predict each of the various types of change. There were few significant relationships, but of course we must keep in mind that the factor reliabilities of these factors were marginal. (Results are in Appendix 7E.2.)

Because no terms from the top manager demographic attribute model even approached statistical significance, in the stage-2 analyses we developed the trimmed top manager characteristics model using only the terms from the work history and personality constructs. Table 7.4 shows the results.

Previous experience with output functions was negatively related to the frequency of externally focused change, contrary to our expectations. It may be that this experience, rather than leading to more sensitivity to this sector and, consequently, more actions, as we had hypothesized, may instead give top managers the confidence to stay on a fixed course of action or to reject various proposals for change that a less experienced manager might accept. Another possible explanation is that managers promoted from within, and previously head of an output function, might view the function as not in need of any changes.

We had hypothesized that the frequency of organizational change would be greatest at intermediate levels of the top manager's tenure in position. To test this idea, we

Table 7.4. Top Manager Characteristics As Predictors of Organizational Change: Trimmed Regression Models[a]

Determinants	Externally Focused Changes	Internally Focused Changes	Changes in Form	Total Changes
Experience with output functions	$-.27^{*}$	—	—	—
Tenure in position	$-.32^{**}$	$-.26^{**}$	—	$-.28^{**}$
Internal locus of control	—	—	$-.20^{+}$	—
Size	—	$.37^{**}$	$.39^{**}$	$.48^{**}$
Experience with output $\times$ size	$-.25^{+}$	—	—	—
Experience with throughput $\times$ size	—	$.25^{**}$	—	—
Perceived discretion $\times$ size	$.24^{*}$	—	$.20^{+}$	$.21^{*}$
Tolerance for ambiguity $\times$ size	$-.36^{**}$	—	—	—
Adjusted R^2	$.12^{**}$	$.28^{**}$	$.18^{**}$	$.30^{**}$
Adjusted R^2 after controlling for size	na	$.12^{**}$	$.05^{+}$	$.13^{**}$

[a]Based on data from 78 organizations. Entries are standardized regression coefficients and indicate the relative influence of the determinants on the frequency of change.

$^{+}p < .01$

$^{*}p < .05$

$^{**}p < .01$

first used a model that included size, years of experience in throughput, years of experience in output, years in current position, and the square of years in current position as predictors of organizational change. If years in current position were positively related to change and its square were negatively related, this concave-downward curve would validate the hypothesis. The results did not support our thinking. The squared term was not significant ($p > .10$). Years in current position was negatively related to organizational change for internally focused and externally focused changes, and it was not related to changes in organizational form. The combination of these findings implies that the tendency to initiate or support change begins to decline so strongly and so early in the top manager's tenure that the early rise associated with the possibly increased ability to implement change, if it exists, is not identifiable with data such as that used in this study. (The variable tenure in position ranged from 1 to 31 years, with a mean of 8.4 years and a median of 7 years.) A second implication of the negative relationship between tenure and change is that the tendency to initiate change is a stronger force affecting the frequency of change than is the ability to implement change.

Internal locus of control was not associated with the frequency of externally or internally focused changes, but it was negatively related to changes in organizational form. This finding supports the argument that top managers high on internal locus of control may be more prone to resist proposed changes in form, believing that they can effectively manage the situation with the structures, personnel, and resource allocations currently in place.

A number of interactions between top manager characteristics and organization size were significant. Each is explainable either with the argument that in small organizations top managers have more power to implement change (negative interaction effects), or that in large organizations top managers have more, and more varied, mechanisms or resources with which to implement change (positive interaction effects).

An overall conclusion to be drawn from the study is that *top manager characteristics influence organizational change, but their influence varies greatly depending on the type of change being considered,* being greatest for internally focused changes. A second overall conclusion is that *work history variables are more predictive of change-related behavior than are personality variables,* a finding congruent with the thinking of Hambrick and Mason (1984).[9]

Organizational Strategy

Authorities such as Miles and Snow (1978) and Porter (1980, 1985) generally hold that single-business organizations are more successful if they pursue just one business strategy. On the other hand, it is apparent that some organizations do pursue multiple strategies (Porter, 1985: 17). Sometimes they are in the process of changing strategies; sometimes they are managing and marketing different product lines; and sometimes they are indecisive. Our approach, then, is not to think in terms of where on a bipolar continuum an organization resides, but to consider the degree to which the organization is pursuing each distinguishable strategy.

Our reading of the literature indicated that the prospector and defender strategies of Miles and Snow (1978) were the most likely to be related to different types of organizational change. In particular, because in many situations its more successful products and services will be copied by its competitors, and thus will no longer be different, an organization pursuing a prospector strategy must often innovate. Attempts to innovate will result in organizational changes. Consequently, we believe that *organizational changes are more frequent when organizations pursue a prospector strategy.*

The case is not so clear for organizations pursuing a defender strategy. Since the implementation of change is costly, it is easy to imagine instances in which an organization defending its market by being a low cost producer would choose to retain its present equipment, facilities, or form as long as possible. On the other hand, if improvements in administration or production technology enable competitors to achieve lower costs, then an organization pursuing a defender strategy by maintaining low costs must introduce changes to match or surpass the performance levels achieved by its competitors. Thus, it seems at present we must conclude that *the effects on organizational change of pursuing a defender strategy are unclear.*

Interactions of Strategy with Size.

We just concluded that the effects of pursuing a defender strategy are unclear. It may be that examining the interactions of strategy with size will help clarify the effect of pursuing a defender strategy. That is, the argument that organizations pursuing a defender strategy would initiate few organizational changes in order to minimize the cost of replacing equipment or facilities seems more valid for small organizations, as they generally have smaller reserves of and more difficult access to capital. The competing argument, that organizations pursuing a defender strategy might introduce change in order to keep up with the cost-reducing innovations of competitors, might be more valid in the case of larger organization, as they generally have access to the resources required to implement such changes. Thus, it might be that organizational changes in organizations pursuing a defender strategy are less frequent in small organizations than in large organizations.

Results from the Study.

The stage-1 initial models included size, the two strategy factors, and the interactions of the strategies with size. (Results appear in Appendix 7F.) The stage-2 trimmed models are shown in Table 7.5.

We had hypothesized that a prospector strategy would be positively related to organizational change. The results in Table 7.5 show that this strategy was not related to either externally focused changes, changes in organizational form, or total changes, but it did appear to be weakly and negatively related to internally focused changes. This latter result is perplexing. It may be a spurious finding, but it also might follow from what we found when investigating the interaction. The negative effect on change of the interaction between a prospector strategy and size suggests that there is, in fact, a more positive relationship between change and pursuit of a prospector strategy in small organizations than there is in large organizations. A split-half analysis confirms this. For the 60 smallest organizations the relationship between change and pursuit of prospector strategy is more positive ($r = .15$) than it is for the 59 largest organizations ($r = -.27$); the difference is significant ($p < .01$). Perhaps the inertial forces commonly associated with size contribute to this result.

With respect to the effects on change of a defender strategy, we earlier noted the

Table 7.5. Organizational Strategies As Determinants of Organizational Change: Trimmed Regression Models[a]

Determinants	Externally Focused Changes	Internally Focused Changes	Changes in Form	Total Changes
Prospector strategy	—	−.15[+]	—	—
Defender strategy	—	—	—	—
Size	—	.30**	.22**	.29**
Prospector strategy × size	−.19*	−.22**	—	−.23**
Defender strategy × size	.20**	.23**	.15[+]	.27**
Adjusted R^2	.06*	.23**	.06**	.19**
Adjusted R^2 after controlling for size	.06*	.12**	.01	.11**

[a]Based on data from 119 organizations. Entries are standardized regression coefficients and indicate the relative influence of the determinants on the frequency of change.
[+]$p < .10$
*$p < .05$
**$p < .01$

possibility of conflicting forces. The lack of a significant main effect suggests that our reasoning was correct: the fact that there is a need in some situations to introduce change in pursuit of a defender strategy and a need in other situations to retard change in order to control costs may result in no net effect. This line of reasoning is further supported by the interaction analysis. The positive effect on all types of change of the interaction between the defender strategy and size suggests that, in pursuit of low cost defense, large organizations introduce new work processes or technologies and small organizations retard change. This makes sense, given the greater resources of large organizations. The interesting conclusion to be drawn from these analyses is that *the frequency of organizational change cannot, in general, be predicted from a knowledge of the organization's strategy, but it can be predicted from the interaction of strategy and size.*

Organizational Structure

Our examination of the literature indicated that the following four structural characteristics might determine the frequency of organizational change: centralization of decision making, standardization of procedures, specialization of function, and interdependence of production or distribution processes. In addition, each of these characteristics is an attractive component of a theory of organizational change in that each has been found to be an important component of other organizational theories (cf., Child, 1984; Mintzberg, 1979), and interconnectedness among theories is a desirable goal.

Centralization of decision making at the upper levels of an organization is generally thought to be negatively related to organizational change. One reason is that logistical delays and losses of information occur as proposals for change move upward through the hierarchy. Another reason is that in more centralized organizations the number of hierarchical levels between the decision-making level and the decision-implementing level is greater and, because resistance to change can occur at each of the multiple hierarchical levels, fewer changes would actually eventuate. Finally, in more decentralized organizations there are more decision makers having the authority to initiate change. This suggests that, all else equal, more changes would be initiated. Thus it seems reasonable to conclude that *organizational changes are less frequent in more centralized organizations.*

Standardization refers to homogeneity of organizational procedures. Standardization can be attained and maintained by means of strong professional or social norms or through formalization, where formalization refers to the extent that procedures are codified in written form rather than in human memories. Standardization generally develops because it is useful. For example, when procedures are standardized, behaviors and outcomes are more predictable and it is easier to coordinate and manage operations. Sometimes, too, standards take on a meaning of their own and become part of "the way we do things," independent of their original usefulness. Because standards are valued, and because organizational changes might lead to destandardization, change will more often be resisted in more standardized organizations. Consequently, it seems likely that *organizational changes are less frequent in organizations characterized by greater standardization.*

Specialization, as a characteristic of organizational structure, refers to the variety among the functions performed by different subunits or employees. Because different kinds of subunits tend to be linked to different components of the organizational environment, organizations characterized by higher levels of specialization are exposed to a wider variety of environments, each with its attendant threats and opportunities. More threats and opportunities, in turn, lead to more responses and more organizational changes. In addition, because specialized personnel are especially sensitive to threats and opportunities in their particular domains, they are more likely to initiate organizational changes. On the other hand, specialization could result in a diversity of beliefs and preferences that might lead to immobilizing conflict or to tortuous decision-making procedures, either of which could deter initiation of change. The frequently observed positive association between specialization and innovation (cf., the review by Damanpour, 1991) suggests to us that, on balance, *organizational changes are more frequent in organizations characterized by greater specialization.*

Interdependence among many organizational units is generally necessary for them to collectively contribute to the production of goods or services. Conflicting arguments are associated with interdependence as a determinant of change. On the one hand, when interdependence is high, a given change can create a cascade of other changes. And, of course, interdependence sometimes facilitates recognition of the need for change and thereby increases the frequency of change. On the other hand, interdependence can inhibit managers from initiating changes because of resistance from personnel or units who are not the targets of the change, but who might be negatively affected by the change. Thus, what is clear is that *the effect of interdependence on organizational change is unclear.*

Interactions of Structure with Size

As an example of how size might alter the effect of a structural characteristic on organizational change, consider the idea set forth just above—that a change in an organization with high interdependence might lead to a cascade of changes. If this were the dominant effect of interdependence, it might be greater in large organizations, as in larger organizations the strings of interconnected units or processes are likely to be longer. Thus, while overall the conflicting arguments concerning the effect of interdependence on change might make it difficult to draw conclusions, it seems likely that whatever is the net effect of interdependence on organizational change, it is of greater magnitude in larger organizations.

Analyses and Results

In stage 1, we used size and the four structural characteristics and their interactions with size simultaneously to predict each type of organizational change. (Results are contained in Appendix 7G.) In stage 2, we developed the trimmed models. These are shown in Table 7.6.

Contrary to our thinking, the results in Table 7.6 indicate that centralization was not negatively related to organizational change. It may be that situations favoring a positive relationship between centralization and change (i.e., where information and authority are concentrated and coincident), are sufficiently prevalent that they counterbalance the situations that we considered in our earlier discussion (i.e., situations favoring a negative relationship), with the result being no overall relationship, as found in this study. Standardization tended to curtail change, as hypothesized. Specialization was not related to change, contrary to our earlier reasoning. Perhaps this is because high levels of specialization cause changes associated with different units or functions to be local in their effects, and therefore not "important" in the view of our top manager informants. Or it may be that specialization was not well assessed with the single measure used. Organizational interdependence was positively related to internally focused changes for larger organizations. This finding supports our earlier idea that cascades of organizational changes initiated by just one or two changes might be longer in larger organizations.

Table 7.6. Structural Characteristics As Determinants of Organizational Changes: Trimmed Regression Models[a]

Determinants	Externally Focused Changes	Internally Focused Changes	Changes in Form	Total Changes
Centralization	—	—	—	—
Standardization	−.20*	−.22**	−.22*	−.29**
Specialization	—	—	—	—
Interdependence	—	—	—	—
Size	—	.39**	.29**	.37**
Centralization × size	—	—	—	—
Standardization × size	—	—	—	—
Specialization × size	—	—	—	—
Interdependence × size	—	.20*	—	.14
Adjusted R^2	.07*	.21**	.08**	.19**
Adjusted R^2 after controlling for size	.07*	.09**	.04**	.10**

[a]Based on data from 119 organizations. Entries are standardized regression coefficients and indicate the relative influence of the determinants on the frequency of change.

$^+p < .10$

$^*p < .05$

$^{**}p < .01$

The most general conclusion to be drawn from these analyses is that *standardization of organizational procedures retards all types of change.* This is hardly surprising in the cases of externally and internally directed changes, but is not intuitively obvious in the case of changes in organizational form (see the nature of this variable in Table 7.1).

Interim Summary

What have we learned, up to this point, from both developing the theoretical arguments and conducting the statistical analyses? Four summary conclusions seem appropriate.

1. The frequencies of all three types of organizational changes (externally focused changes, internally focused changes, changes in organizational form), and total organizational changes, are predictable from information known beforehand.
2. Factors from all five predictor constructs (organizational environments, organizational performance, top manager characteristics, organizational strategies, and organization structure) are predictors of organizational change.
3. Different factors predict different types of change.
4. An elaborate theory of the determinants of organizational change is theoretically and empirically justifiable.

This last conclusion must be qualified in two ways. First, our study does not prove causality; it demonstrates sequential association. Our belief that these particular predictors are in fact determinants follows from the reasoning presented earlier in the chapter. The second necessary qualification is to note that none of the analyses underlying the conclusion forced factors from different constructs to compete against one another as predictors (except for the universal inclusion of size as a predictor). We turn now to addressing this issue.

Integrative, Multiconstruct Models

Two interesting questions are prompted by the previous discussions and analyses:

1. To what extent is the predictability of organizational change increased when the best predictors drawn from different constructs are used in combination?
2. When the most predictive terms from all constructs compete against one another as predictors, which are sustained and which yield to others?

Our approach to answering these questions was twofold. First, for each type of organizational change, we created and tested an integrative, multiconstruct model that included all of the factors and interactions that had been identified in the five trimmed models (Tables 7.2 through 7.6) as strong predictors of that type of organizational change. We refer to these as initial models. Because we had complete data on all constructs from only 67 organizations, it was necessary to begin the stage-1 analyses with parsimonious models. We therefore chose to include in these initial models only those terms that in one or more of the trimmed models had been predictive at the .05 level of significance. The results of these analyses are shown in the first data columns of Tables 7.7 through 7.10.

Our second approach to answering the above two questions was to develop a trimmed model for each type of change, beginning with the same parsimonious set of potential predictors that was included in the initial model but, as before, seeking the model that included any and all predictor terms that individually explained a significant ($p < .10$) increment of the variance in the frequency of change. These trimmed models appear in the last data columns of Tables 7.7 through 7.10. The following discussions are based on the trimmed models.

Externally Focused Change

As shown in Table 7.7, upturns in growth performance were good predictors of externally focused changes. Apparently this type of performance change energizes organizations to capitalize on their gains or to take initiatives previously held in abeyance. The results also indicate that a large proportion of the variation in the frequency of externally focused changes is a consequence of the interactive effects of strategy and size. Recalling that we did not categorize organizations as pursuing either one or the other strategy, but rather assessed the organization's pursuit of each strategy, it is interesting to see that a prospector strategy tends to lead to externally directed changes in small organizations, but not in large organizations, while a defender strategy is associated with externally directed changes in large organizations, but not in small organizations. It seems worth noting that these three predictor terms, in aggregate, explain as much of the adjusted variance as much as does the ten-term initial model.

We earlier noted our interest in answering the question, "To what extent is predictability of externally focused changes increased by combining the best predictors from different constructs?" To obtain the answer, we compared the proportion of adjusted variance in externally focused changes explained by the multiconstruct model (.26) with the proportion explained by the best single-construct model (.19) (see

Table 7.7. Determinants of Externally Focused Change: Integrative, Multiconstruct Models[a]

Determinants[b]	Initial Model	Trimmed Model
Turbulence	.17	—
Downturns in growth	.12	—
Upturns in growth	.30**	.34**
Experience with output functions	−.04	—
Tenure in position	−.19	—
Standardization	.09	—
Perceived discretion × size	−.05	—
Tolerance for ambiguity × size	−.03	—
Prospector strategy × size	−.31**	−.34**
Defender strategy × size	.33**	.26*
Adjusted R^2	.26**	.26**
Adjusted R^2 after controlling for size	na	na

[a]Based on data from 67 organizations. Entries are standardized regression coefficients and indicate the relative influence of the determinants on the frequency of change.

[b]Predictor terms that were significant at the .05 level in Table 7.2 through 7.6.

$^+ p < .10$

$^* p < .05$

$^{**} p < .01$

Table 7.3). The increase is nearly 40 percent. While caution must be observed when drawing conclusions from comparisons of nonidentical data sets (the 67 organizations associated with Table 7.7 are an ecologically determined subset of the 100 organizations associated with Table 7.3), these values do suggest that there is advantage to be gained by drawing on multiple constructs.

Internally Focused Changes

Table 7.8 shows that the surviving terms in the trimmed model were environmental turbulence, the top manager's tenure in his or her position, organizational size, and the interaction of organizational interdependence with organizational size. All terms influence internally focused changes in the directions hypothesized earlier. After controlling for the effect of size, approximately one-fourth of the adjusted variance in the frequency of internally focused changes is explainable with these four predictors. It is interesting to observe that externally focused changes and internally changes are explained with very different sets of factors and interactions. In fact, there are no terms common to the two trimmed models!

Turning once more to the question, "To what extent is predictability of internally focused changes increased by combining the best predictors from different construct?," we see that, after controlling for size, the multiconstruct model explains .26 of the (adjusted) variance in the internally focused changes. The best single-construct model explains .12 (see Tables 7.4 and 7.5). The increase is over 100 percent. While the same caution applies as before, there certainly seems to be much to be gained in predictability by avoiding the use of single-construct models.

Changes in Organizational Form

It is apparently more difficult to predict changes in organizational form than it is to predict externally or internally focused changes. Perhaps this is because some changes

Table 7.8. Determinants of Internally Focused Changes: Integrative, Multiconstruct Models[a]

Determinants[b]	Initial Model	Trimmed Model
Turbulence	.24*	.29**
Tenure in Position	−.23*	−.30**
Standardization	−.05	—
Size	.29*	.27**
Prospector strategy × size	−.05	—
Defender strategy × size	−.03	—
Upturns in efficiency × size	.14	—
Experience with throughput × size	.16	—
Interdependence × size	.30*	.41**
Adjusted R^2	.40**	.39**
Adjusted R^2 after controlling for size	.26**	.26**

[a]Based on data from 67 organizations. Entries are standardized regression coefficients and indicate the relative influence of the determinants on the frequency of change.
[b]Predictor terms that were significant at the .05 level in Tables 7.2 through 7.6.
$^+p < .10$
$^*p < .05$
$^{**}p < .01$

in form occur as a result of internal power struggles. Our study did not capture data concerning this variable. Confirming our earlier theoretical arguments, environmental turbulence, downturns in growth performance, and the interaction of downturns in efficiency with size were factors that predicted changes in organizational form.

Examining the extent to which the predictability of changes in organizational form is increased by combining the best predictors from different constructs leads to the conclusion that the predictability of the most predictive single-construct model, the top manager characteristics model (see adjusted $R^2 = .18$ in Table 7.4) is essentially equal to that of the multiconstruct model (see adjusted $R^2 = .20$ in Table 7.9). Not surprisingly, the dominant predictors were the same in both models.

Total Changes

The impressive feature about the models to predict total changes is that they explain nearly one-half of all of the variance in the frequency of organizational change (see Table 7.4). This is an extraordinarily high proportion relative to the outcomes of most attempts to predict or explain organizational events.

Even after controlling for size, the proportion of (adjusted) variance in the frequency of total change explainable with the trimmed multiconstruct model is .30 (see Table 7.10). Since the proportion for the best single-construct model is .17 (see Table 7.2), the increase in predictability of total changes obtained by combining the best predictors from different constructs is over 70 percent.

Examination of these multiconstruct models leads to two observations. The first is that the frequency of different types of organizational change generally can be predicted more accurately if factors from more than one construct are used. The multiconstruct models were generally much more predictive than the average of the single-construct models. This reinforces our earlier observation that an elaborate theory of the determinants of organizational change is theoretically and empirically justifiable. The second observation contrasts with the first, but does not contradict it. It is that, while many factors affect or are correlated with the three types of organizational change (see the initial models in Tables 7.7, 7.8, and 7.9), a relatively high proportion

Table 7.9. Changes in Organizational Form: Integrative, Multiconstruct Models[a]

Determinants[b]	Initial Model	Trimmed Model
Turbulence	.26*	.32**
Downturns in growth	.21[+]	.23*
Standardization	.07	—
Size	.16	—
Competitiveness × size	.15	—
Downturns in efficiency × size	−.21[+]	−.30**
Adjusted R^2	.21**	.20**
Adjusted R^2 after controlling for size	.13**	na

[a]Based on data from 100 organizations. Entries are standardized regression coefficients and indicate the relative influence of the determinants on the frequency of change.

[b]Predictor terms that were significant at the .05 level in Tables 7.2 through 7.6

[+]$p < .10$

*$p < .05$

**$p < .01$

Table 7.10. Total Changes: Integrative, Multiconstruct Models[a]

Determinants[b]	Initial Model	Trimmed Model
Turbulence	.22*	.30**
Efficiency performance	−.01	—
Downturns in growth	.20+	.13
Upturns in growth	.20*	.16
Tenure in position	−.25**	−.31**
Standardization	.00	—
Size	.35*	.30**
Competitiveness × size	.11	—
Perceived discretion × size	.14	—
Prospector strategy × size	−.13	—
Defender strategy × size	.26*	.36**
Upturn in efficiency × size	.19	—
Adjusted R^2	.49**	.45**
Adjusted R^2 after controlling for size	.33**	.30**

[a]Based on data from 67 organizations. Entries are standardized regression coefficients and indicate the relative influence of the determinants on the frequency of change.
[b]Predictor terms that were significant at the .05 level in Tables 7.2 through 7.6.
+$p < .10$
*$p < .05$
**$p < .01$

of the variance in the frequency of organizational change can be predicted with relatively few factors or their interactions with size (see the corresponding trimmed models). This may be a consequence of correlations among competing predictors, although the correlation table in Appendix 7.B suggests that this is not generally the case. It may also be that there is a good deal of inherent random or idiosyncratic variation in the frequency of organizational change—that is, there may be a relatively low level of explainable variance. If this is so, and if only a few variables are necessary to explain nearly all of the explainable variance, it will be extremely difficult for additional variables to add significantly to the predictive power of a model already containing these few variables.

The two global conclusions to be drawn from these analysis of integrative, multiconstruct models are the following:

1. The frequency of different types of organizational change can generally be predicted more accurately if factors from more than one construct are used.
2. An understanding of organizational change requires consideration of many factors, but prediction requires consideration of just a few. The trick is knowing which few.

DISCUSSION AND SUMMARY

Implications for Top Managers

It has been said that the true test of managers occurs when they must manage change. Top managers, in particular, are involved in two change-related processes. One is creating change. The other is coping with change. Both processes increase top managers' workloads and stress levels.

Creating organizational change is one of top management's most critical and difficult tasks. The research reported here alerts us to two factors that seem to affect the creation of change and that are at least partially controllable by top managers. One is the top manager's tenure in his or her current position. This factor was strongly negatively related to internally focused organizational changes. This finding suggests that boards of directors or parent organizations desiring a faster rate of change should consider bringing new top managers into the organizations they oversee and should consider nonliberal limits on the tenure of the top managers of these organizations. The finding also suggests that top managers themselves must somehow continuously unshackle their mind-sets about what needs to be done and how it can best be accomplished as their tenure in their position lengthens. They need to repeatedly or continuously rejuvenate themselves. If they do not, it is likely that they will miss opportunities to initiate or facilitate worthwhile organizational changes.

A second factor found here to be related to organizational change is standardization of work processes and ways of operating. In the single-construct analysis (Table 7.6), this factor was found to be significantly and negatively related to the frequency of changes that management chose to implement and that were presumably desirable. Of course, even though standardization apparently retards some presumably desirable changes, it is often an attractive structural characteristic because it contributes to operating efficiency. Space considerations do not permit detailed development of approaches for reconciling this dilemma, but an example of such an approach is to standardize a large proportion of the subunits that perform similar functions in order to gain efficiency and to simultaneously encourage other subunits to deviate initially or to change over time. These latter units, by so testing nonstandard practices, will undoubtedly learn more, and this learning can then be codified and transferred into the standardized units. Huber, Ullman, and Leifer (1979) described an application of this approach. The unstandardized units are also better candidates for organizational experiments, as they are more flexible and familiar with change.

Let us turn now from creating change to coping with necessary change. The organization and its managers can better cope with the workload imposed by change if they have prepared, and they can be better prepared if they can predict when organizational changes will become more necessary and, hence, more frequent. The longitudinal nature of the research reported here makes clear that prediction is possible. There are action implications of this finding. For example, although organizational growth and increased interdependence of organizational subunits are themselves changes to be mastered, we found here that even after these processes are complete and the related change dynamics have come to a halt, the new organization thus created will continue to generate significantly more changes than did the previous organization. So, the managerial challenge is not only one of weathering the storm of growth and increased interdependence. It is also one of being prepared for a permanently heightened workload and stress level.

While predicting the level and general nature of organizational change is possible, as shown in this research, the accuracy and timeliness of such forecasts are likely to be enhanced if the organization creates active sensors and means of integrating and interpreting the observations acquired by these sensors. The article by Huber and

McDaniel (1986) contains guidelines and discussions about how this might be accomplished. One suggestion is to position procedures within the organization to ensure that *nonroutine* messages move quickly and reliably from the sender to the person who needs to know their contents. Creating such procedures would seem to result in large payoffs to organizations in dynamic, complex, and hostile environments. Too often, mechanisms for dealing with nonroutine messages are not designed and implemented because managers focus on systems for efficiently processing *routine* messages. While routine messages are more frequent, it is nonroutine messages that often give timely warnings of the need to change.

Another implication from the findings of this study is that, if environmental turbulence increases or if organizational performance either increases or decreases, organizational changes will tend to follow. This means increased workload and increased stress levels. These increases can be smoothed and their dysfunctional effects attenuated with some preparation. Example preparations include (1) "clearing the decks"— that is, delegating, postponing, or completing work at hand; (2) alerting people to the fact that increased workloads are forthcoming but that the organization is readying itself, and thus partially immunizing them against the threat of change; and (3) creating change-doing units, such as task forces or "collateral organizations." (A collateral organization coexists with the operating organization and has the same members, but it has missions and structures different from the operating organization. An example would be where the "regular organization" would shut down its operations every Friday at noon and all its members would turn for the rest of the day to their collective task of planning for a major change.)

Implications for Organizational Scientists

When a literature largely contains studies that examine either one specific technology or one type of organization, it is very difficult to integrate the reported findings into a generalizable theory. Unfortunately, the literature on within-organizational innovation is characterized by such studies, and this is the largest literature in the general area of organizational change. Of course, the study of organization change demands either archival or longitudinal field research, the latter having well-documented high costs. So, we were not surprised to find in our review of the literature that relatively little progress has been achieved toward development of a general theory of organizational change. The research results reported here comprise a first cut at such a theory.

As a start, the trimmed models in Tables 7.2 through 7.6 identify at least ten factors that influence organizational change. The models strongly suggest that the frequency of organizational change can be explained with factors from each of five constructs, and they demonstrate that organizational change can be predicted with information obtainable beforehand. The findings captured in Tables 7.2 through 7.10 are a start toward a theory of organizational change to be improved on and elaborated by other researchers. It seems appropriate to offer a few suggestions toward this end.

One implication of the study is that researchers should more frequently act on the fact that factors associated with a variety of constructs and subconstructs influence organizational change. Twenty-two factors or their interactions with size were predictive of at least one major type of change. All constructs surfaced in even the most conservative trimmed models (in Tables 7.7 through 7.10), where factors from the different constructs competed for inclusion. The proportion of variance explained by these elaborate multiconstruct models is high relative to that typically observed when studying organizational processes. The time has passed for using simple models to study organizational changes.

A second implication is that we should be precise in our thinking and statements about the determinants of organizational change. We should think more than we have in terms of specific factors and their causal relationships with specific types of change. It was found here that distinctly different sets of factors predict different kinds of changes.

A final implication of the study is that investigations of the consequences of organizational change on managerial workloads and stress levels now have the potential to be more useful. Studies of the nature and consequences of increased workload, such as that by Meier (1963) and those reported and reviewed in Riley and Zaccaro (1987), would be more useful if workload is predictable. And it seems to be so—this study showed that organizational change is predictable, and managerial and organizational workloads increase when organizational change increases. Assuming, then, that changes in managerial and organizational workloads can be predicted, studies of their nature and consequences have much greater practical value.

Strengths and Weakness of the Research and Recommendations for Researchers

Thorngate (1976: 126) and Weick (1979: 35–42) note that it is impossible for any theory to be simultaneously "general, accurate, and simple." As we noted earlier, our goal was to achieve a more comprehensive understanding and portrayal of organizational change. We turn now to discussing the generalizability, accuracy, and simplicity of our model in view of this goal, and we also consider how these three features of the model might be improved with methodological choices different from those we made.

Generalizability

We noted earlier that many studies of organizational change tend to be narrowly focused, examining just one type of change or just one or a few determining factors, and tend to be conducted in just one industry. Except under very unusual circumstances, it is extremely difficult to develop a general theory by combining the findings from such disjointed studies. Believing that generality of a theory is associated with the more comprehensive understanding that we sought, we chose to adopt a research methodology that gave us a good chance of reaching more generalizable conclusions than those typically obtained. For example, we examined over 1,000 changes that covered ten categories of change and that took place in 119 organizations differing in size, industry, location, and other respects. These features suggest strongly that our findings are more generalizable than those from most previous studies of organizational change.

While the organizations tended to be clustered near the investigators' universities, there seems to be no particular reason to believe that this common practice (cf., Miller et al., 1982 and Mintzberg et al., 1976), reduces the generalizability of the findings. In this respect, our sample mirrors that of Miller et al. (1982: 243) in which "factors such as ease of access, logistics, location, and the cooperativeness of executives decided whether or not a firm was studied. Though the sample is not strictly random, the broad representation of types and sizes of businesses, and the lack of dominance of any one type of firm or industry in the sample gives these findings a reasonably high degree of generality." Using nearby organizations as field sites also has important benefits. In our study, this choice was made in order to maximize the likelihood that top managers would participate through a long and time-consuming study because they would see themselves as helping researchers from a local university and because they would respond favorably to the personal attention of being interviewed face-to-face. We doubt that use of nearby organizations appreciably affected the results of the study except in the positive sense that it very likely reduced attrition.

Accuracy

To develop a generalizable theory and achieve a comprehensive understanding, we chose to include a large number of factors. This could have affected the accuracy of our results both negatively and positively. If we had used fewer factors, we could have asked more questions about each—we could have included more items in the Organizational Profile and Top Manager Profile description questionnaires. This would undoubtedly have increased the reliabilities of the scales used to assess these factors and would have reduced the chance that we would be unable to find significant relationships between the factors and the organizational changes. In particular, this choice probably adversely affected our ability to find the top manager personality variables to be predictive and thus may have reduced the accuracy of the models shown in Tables 7.4 and 7.7 through 7.10. (See the relatively marginal reliabilities of these variables in Appendix 7B.) And, of course, moreover, the fact that the accuracy of our assessments of the factors varied across factors (i.e., not all reliabilities were the same) indicates that caution is in order when comparing the relative predictive power of the factors.

The benefit of including many factors is apparent, however. In this study we were able to use the same data set to investigate the predictive validity of factors from five different constructs, and we were able to show that impending change is quite predictable. The approach enabled us ultimately to predict nearly a third of the variance in the frequency of a variety of organizational changes (see Table 7.10) and, if size is also included as a predictor, nearly half of the variance.

Elegance, Parsimony, and Simplicity

To develop a more complete understanding of the determinants of organizational change, we began with a more elaborate model (Figure 7.1) than have any other researchers. Pursuit of this same goal led to generating hypotheses not explicitly included in the model and to testing interactions between size and other factors as possible determinants of change. So it is clear that the overall model implied in our discussion and analyses is not simple. In comparison, the trimmed models shown in Tables 7.2 through 7.10 are relatively simple; they are as simple as they can be without deleting highly significant predictors and thus reducing our understanding of the determinants of the particular type of organizational change under consideration.

We could have reasonably theorized and tested an even more elaborate model. In the study we examined the effects of 25 factors that might affect the frequency of organizational change. We also investigated the possibility that the interactions of 24 of these factors with organizational size influenced organizational change. But there are

276 possible interactions among these 24 factors that we did not test. Some, perhaps many, of these interactions are determinanats of the frequency of organizational change. We leave investigation of these possible explanations of organizational change to other researchers and research efforts.

As a final recommendation for future studies, we note that a still more elaborate model would further enhance understanding and probably increase predictability. The specific nature of the elaboration would be to include in the model the causal linkages among the constructs or among the factors. Organizational science contains much theory concerning the causal associations between, for example, environment and structure, strategy and structure, or strategy and top manager characteristics. If this theory is incorporated into an elaborate model of organizational change, and then found to be valid in this role, both the theory and our understanding of organizational change would be greatly enriched.

Conclusions

Six conclusions seem to follow from the reasoning and analyses reported in this chapter.

1. The frequencies of different types of organizational changes (externally focused changes, internally focused changes, and changes in organizational form) are predictable from information known beforehand.
2. Factors from all five categories (organizational environments, organizational performance, top manager characteristics, organizational strategies, and organization structure) are predictors of organizational change.
3. Different factors predict different types of change.
4. The frequency of different types of organizational change can generally be predicted more accurately if factors from more than one construct are used.
5. An elaborate theory of the determinants of organizational change is theoretically and empirically justifiable.
6. An understanding of organizational change requires consideration of many factors, but prediction requires consideration of just a few. The trick is knowing which few.

Summary

Organizational changes are important. They affect organizational performance. They create new work tasks and new social relationships in the workplace. They create high workloads and stress levels for managers. Given these facts, and the fact that anticipated organizational changes can be implemented more effectively and efficiently, it seems important to learn about organizational change and how its occurrence can be predicted. The study reported here makes clear that the frequencies of different types of organizational changes are predictable, and it indicates which factors predict the frequencies of which types of change. Armed with this knowledge, managers can better prepare themselves, their employees, and their organizations for the consequences of change, to the benefit of all concerned.

Notes

This research was supported through a contract with the Basic Research Program of the Army Research Institute. The authors greatly appreciate the contributions of subcontractors Kenneth Bettenhausen, Kim Cameron, Richard Daft, Alan Meyer, and Charles O'Reilly, with the help of their doctoral students, collected and provided three-quarters of the data used in the study reported here. We also wish to thank Harold Doty, who set up the database and helped design the questionnaires, and Alison Davis-Blake, James Fredrickson, John Huber, and Andrew Van de Ven, who provided detailed, constructive comments on earlier versions of this chapter. Finally, we are enormously indebted to the many top managers who provided the information used in this study.

1. We believe that organizational culture also determines organizational change. We do not pursue this idea further because organizational culture varies with the organization's environment, strategy, structure, and leadership, constructs already in our model. We might also have studied the effects of managerial endeavors such as goal setting. We recognize that changes are more likely when encouraged by means of such behaviors or processes, but we see such activities as operational responses to the more fundamental factors discussed above.

2. The model shown in Figure 7.1 is both relatively complex and relatively simple. It is complex in that it contains many more factors than do most models of organizational change. It is simple in that it does not portray the many interrelationships that we believe exist. That is, it does not show that the effects of some factors on organizational change are mediated or moderated by other factors. If it portrayed all such plausible relationships, it would be exceedingly complex and the relationships would be so numerous that describing them would push this chapter and the reader beyond reasonable limits.

3. Technical details of the research methodology are contained in Appendix 7A of the chapter. The data used in the study were collected as part of the larger study of changes in organizational design and effectiveness described in Glick, Huber, Miller, Doty, and Sutcliffe (1990), reprinted as the appendix of this volume.

4. The use of the same informant to provide information about the organization (on the organizational profile questionnaire described earlier) and information about changes (in the interview) could have introduced a common-method bias. Because the nature of the two types of information elicited was very different, because the response mode was very different (closed-end, numerical, written responses on the organizational profile questionnaire versus open-end, oral response questions in the interview), and because the two types of information were gathered a year apart, it seems unlikely that common-method variance significantly affected our results.

5. Actually, prior to this first stage we used multivariate regression analyses to ascertain whether it was appropriate to carry out subsequent analyses. That is, for each construct, we regressed the three types of change simultaneously on the respective multiple regression model that contained all of the predictor terms. All of these analyses were significant ($p < .10$), except for the one using the top manager demographic characteristics of age and education as predictors.

6. The approach involved beginning with a model that included all terms included in the stage-1 analyses and then applying a backward elimination procedure to arrive at a model that included only the predictor terms that individually explain a significant ($p < .10$) increment of the variance.

7. Because the predictor terms are not perfectly orthogonal, when used simultaneously in a trimmed regression model (see Note 5), some of them may not be statistically significant components of the model.

8. We note in passing that the disinclination or inability of top managers to institute change may be a cause of low performance. If this is so, and if we assessed the level of organizational

change at some time before we assessed performance, then we might find that less frequent organizational change leads to lower organizational performance. Thus the algebraic sign of the hypothesized relationship between organizational performance and organizational change depends on whether we think of the performance level as antecedent to managerial initiatives or whether we think of initiatives as occurring prior to performance measurement. This highlights the fact that the algebraic sign of an observed relationship can be confidently interpreted only in the case of a longitudinal study.

9. A note of caution is in order here. The work history variables may have been more predictive because they may have been more accurately measured than the personality variables. Such a cautionary note applies elsewhere in this chapter as well (and should accompany many more of the research results reported in the organizational science literature than it does).

REFERENCES

Aldrich, H. E. 1979. *Organizations and environments.* Englewood Cliffs, NJ: Prentice-Hall.

Ashby, W. R. 1968. Variety, constraint, and the law of requisite variety. In Buckley, W. (Ed.), *Modern systems research for the behavioral scientist* (pp. 129–136). Chicago: Aldine.

Ashby, W. R. 1969. Self-regulation and requisite variety. In Emery, F. E. (Ed.), *Systems thinking* (pp. 105–124). Harmondsworth, Middlesex, England: Penguin Books.

Becker, M. H. 1970. Factors affecting diffusion of innovations among health professionals. *American Journal of Public Health,* 60: 294–304.

Child, J. 1984. *Organization: a guide to problems and practice.* London: Harper and Row.

Cyert, R. M., and March, J. G. 1963. *A behavioral theory of the firm.* Englewood Cliffs, NJ: Prentice-Hall.

Damanpour, F. 1991. Organizational innovation: a meta-analysis of determinants and moderators. *Academy of Management Journal,* 34: 555–590.

Dess, G. G., and Robinson, R. B. 1984. Measuring organizational performance in the absence of objective measures: the case of the privately-held firm and conglomerate business units. *Strategic Management Journal,* 5(3): 265–274.

Faucheux, C., Amado, G., and Laurent, A. 1982. Organizational development and change. *Annual Review of Psychology,* 33: 343–370.

Finkelstein, S., and Hambrick, D. C. 1990. Top management team tenure and organizational outcomes: the moderating role of managerial discretion. *Administrative Science Quarterly,* 35: 484–503.

Gabarro, J. J. 1987. *The dynamics of taking charge.* Boston: Harvard Business School Press.

Glick, W. H., Huber, G. P., Miller, C. C., Doty, D. H., and Sutcliffe, K. M. 1990. Studying changes in organizational design and effectiveness: retrospective event histories and periodic assessments. *Organizational Science,* 1(3): 293–312.

Gupta, A. K. 1988. Contingency perspectives on strategic leadership: current knowledge and future research directions. In Hambrick, D. C. (Ed.), *The executive effect: concepts and methods of studying top managers* (pp. 147–178). Greenwich, CT: JAI Press.

Hambrick, D. C., and Finkelstein, S. 1987. Managerial discretion: a bridge between polar views of organizational outcomes. *Research in Organizational Behavior,* 9: 369–406.

Hambrick, D. C., and Fukutomi, G. D. S. 1991. The seasons of a CEO's tenure. *Academy of Management Review,* 16(4): 719–742.

Hambrick, D. C., and Mason, P. A. 1984. Upper echelons: the organization as a reflection of its top managers. *Academy of Management Review,* 9(2): 193–206.

Hrebiniak, L. G., and Joyce, W. F. 1985. Organizational adaptation: strategic choice and environmental determinism. *Administrative Science Quarterly,* 30(3): 336–349.

Huber, G. P. 1984. The nature and design of post-industrial organizations. *Management Science*, 30(8): 928–951.

Huber, G. P. 1991. Organizational learning: an examination of the contributing processes and a review of the literatures. *Organization Science*, 2(1): 88–115.

Huber, G. P., and Daft, R. 1987. The information environments of organizations. In Jablin, F. M., Putman, L. L., Roberts, K. H., and Porter, L. W. (Eds.), *Handbook of organizational communication* (pp. 130–164). Beverly Hills, CA: Sage.

Huber, G. P., and McDaniel, R. R. 1986. The decision-making paradigm of organizational design. *Management Science*, 32(5): 572–589.

Huber, G. P., Miller, C. C., and Glick, W. H. 1990. Developing more encompassing theories about organizations: the centralization-effectiveness relationship as an example. *Organization Science*, 1: 11–39.

Huber, G. P., and Power, D. 1985. Retrospective reports of strategic-level managers: guidelines for increasing their accuracy. *Strategic Management Journal*, 6(2): 171–180.

Huber, G. P., Ullman, J., and Leifer, R. 1979. Optimum organization design. *Academy of Management Review*, 4(4): 567–578.

Kimberly, J. R., and Evanisko, M. J. 1981. Organizational innovation: the influence of individual, organizational, and contextual factors on hospital adoption of technological and administrative innovations. *Academy of Management Journal*, 24(4): 689–713.

MacCrimmon, K. R., and Wehrung, D. A. 1990. Characteristics of risk taking executives. *Management Science*, 36(4): 422–435.

Meier, R. E. 1963. Communications overload: proposals from the study of a university library. *Administrative Science Quarterly*, 17(1): 521–544.

Miles, R. E., and Snow, C. C. 1978. *Organizational strategy, structure, and process*. New York: McGraw-Hill.

Miller, C. C. 1990. Cognitive diversity within top management teams: implications for strategic decision processes and organizational performance. Ph.D. Dissertation. Austin: University of Texas: Graduate School of Business.

Miller, C., Glick, W., Wang, Y., and Huber, G. 1991. Understanding technology-structure relationships: theory development and meta-analytic theory testing. *Academy of Management Journal*, 34(2): 370–399.

Miller, D., 1991. Stale in the saddle: CEO tenure and the match between organization and environment. *Management Science*, 37(1): 34–52.

Miller, D., Droge, C., and Toulouse, J. M. 1988. Strategic process and content as mediators between organizational context and structure. *Academy of Management Journal*, 31(3): 544–569.

Miller, D., and Friesen, P. H. 1980. Momentum and revolution in organizational adaptation. *Academy of Management Journal*, 23(4): 591–614.

Miller, D., Kets de Vries, M. F., and Toulouse, J. M. 1982. Top executive locus of control and its relationship to strategy-making, structure, and environment. *Academy of Management Journal*, 25: 237–253.

Miller, D., and Toulouse, J. 1986. Chief executive personality and corporate strategy and structure in small firms. *Management Science*, 32(11): 1389–1409.

Miller, J. G. 1978. *Living systems*. New York: McGraw-Hill.

Mintzberg, H. 1979. *The structuring of organizations: the synthesis of the research*. Englewoods Cliff, NJ: Prentice-Hall.

Mintzberg, H., Raisinghani, D., and Théorêt, A. 1976. The structure of "unstructured" decision processes. *Administrative Science Quarterly*, 21: 246–275.

Mohrman, S. A., and Mohrman, A. M. 1989. The environment as an agent of change. In Mohrman, A. M., Mohrman, S. A., Ledford, G. E., Cummings, T. G., Lawler, E. E., and Associates, *Large-scale organizational change:* pp. 35–47. San Francisco, CA: Jossey-Bass.

Nadler, D. A., and Tushman, M. L. 1990. Beyond the charismatic leader: Leadership and organizational change. California Management Review, 32(2): 77–97.

Porter, M. E. 1980. *Competitive strategy: techniques for analyzing industries and competitors.* New York: Free Press.

Porter, M. E. 1985. *Competitive advantage: creating and sustaining superior performance.* New York: Free Press.

Riley, A., and Zaccaro, S. (Eds.) 1987. *Occupational stress and organizational effectiveness.* New York: Praeger.

Rogers, E., and Shoemaker, F. 1971. *Communication of innovation: a cross-cultural perspective.* New York: Free Press.

Staw, B., Sandelands, L., and Dutton, J. 1981. Threat-rigidity effects in organizational behavior: a multi-level analysis. *Administrative Science Quarterly,* 26: 501–524.

Thorngate, W. 1976. Possible limits on a science of social behavior. In Strickland, L. H., Aboud, F. E., and Gergen, K. J. (Eds.), *Social psychology in transition* (pp. 121–139). New York: Plenum Press.

Tushman, M. L., and Romanelli, E. 1985. Organizational evolution: a metamorphosis model of convergence and reorientation. In Cummings, L. L., and Staw, B. M. (Eds.), *Research in organizational behavior,* Vol. 7, (pp. 171–222). Greenwich, CT: JAI Press.

Venkatraman, N., and Ramanujam, V. 1987. Measurement of business economic performance: an examination of method convergence. *Journal of Management,* 13(1): 109–122.

Weick, K. E. 1979. *The social psychology of organizing,* 2nd ed. Reading, MA: Addison-Wesley.

APPENDIX 7A. DETAILS AND NOTES CONCERNING THE RESEARCH METHODOLOGY

Assessing the Changes

The interviewer codings of all interviewers were checked by a noninterviewer trained in the use of the coding scheme. There was an interrater reliability of 67 percent (Cohens' k) for these two independent coders. In cases of disagreement, the interviewer's code was used unless it was clear that the interviewer had made a mistake in applying the coding categories. This occurred in only 5 percent of the cases.

We also considered using as our measure of organizational change weighted frequencies, where the weights would indicate the relative importance of the change. (Of course, to an extent importance had already entered our measure, since the key informants were asked to list only "important" changes.) To explore the empirical consequences of using a measure that reflected finer graduations of importance, the two lead authors independently coded each organizational change according to its importance, using a 3, 2, 1 scale, where these values corresponded, respectively, to strategically important changes, important but not strategically important changes, and less important changes. Recognizing that the importance of changes depends on the context, we judged the importances after considering the respective organization's size and industry and also the key informant's elaborative comments about the change. These latter were obtained during the interview, but after the 20-minute listing of changes. Interrater reliability was .85. All differences were resolved through discussion. (Further details of this coding are available from the authors as CODE Technical Report 14.) One of these three values was used to weight each change from each interview.

The mean weights for externally focused changes, internally focused changes, changes in organizational form, and total changes were, respectively, 2.31, 1.73, 1.89, and 1.89. The correlations between the frequencies and the weighted frequencies were, respectively, .96, .96, .95, and .96. One explanation for these high correlations became apparent during the interviews themselves. It was obvious that the occurrence of a more important change tends to create a larger cascade of subordinate or consequent changes, thus increasing the number of changes and ensuring a high association between the frequency of more important changes and the frequency of total changes. Given these high correlations, and the general goal of building theories with simple and easily replicated variables, we decided to restrict our analyses to the study of unweighted frequencies.

ASSESSING THE FACTORS THOUGHT TO DETERMINE CHANGES

Organizational Size

We measured size as the number of full-time employees plus one-half of the number of part-time employees. These numbers were obtained using the Organizational Profile Questionnaire described earlier. Because the effects of differences in size are likely to diminish as size increases, the actual measure used in the analyses was the natural logarithm of the organization's size.

Environment

We collected information on the characteristics of each organization's environment approximately 12 months before we collected the information on organizational changes (i.e., 12 months prior to the third interview), using the mailed Organizational Profile Questionnaire described earlier. The informants responded on seven-point Likert scales. Factor analyses were used to validate a priori scales. After questionnaire items that did not appear to measure the respective environmental characteristic were deleted, the number of items that resulted were as follows: six were used to measure turbulence, two to measure competitiveness, and one to measure complexity. Interitem reliability analysis (Cronbach's alpha) was used to ascertain the internal consistency of the scales. Reliability of the turbulence scale is .77 and of the competitiveness scale is .75.

Antecedent Levels of Performance and Changes in Performance

Antecedent levels of performance were assessed by having the top managers answer questions concerning their organization's performance, on several dimensions, relative to the performance of other organizations in their industry, and, separately, answer questions concerning their organization's performance relative to their current goal, what they "would like it to be." Because objective measures of organizational performance must be adjusted for industry effect and for geographical effect (many of the sample's financial institutions were in Texas where, during the period of the study, most financial institutions did poorly relative to the industry as a whole), and because industry data were not available in the great majority of cases (many of the private sector organizations were subunits of other organizations, and 20 percent of the organizations were in the public or not-for-profit sector), we necessarily used managerial assessments of organizational performance. Previous research has shown managerial assessment to be significantly correlated with objective measures of performance (Dess and Robinson, 1984; Venkatraman and Ramanujam, 1987). Whatever systematic biases are inherent in the managers' performance assessments (e.g., a bias to see or report more positive performance), they did not affect our results, as they appear as a constant in the regression models rather than in the coefficient of the performance predictors. The antecedent level of performance data were obtained using the Organizational Profile Questionnaire described earlier.

As before, factor analyses were used to validate a priori scales and to delete questionnaire items that did not appear to measure relevant underlying factors. The outcome of this process was that two factors were validated. One was a two-item factor related to the extent to which the organization was able to obtain resources for growth, and the other was a two-item factor related to the ability of the organization to obtain high levels of output per employee. The Cronbach alpha reliability of the growth performance scale is .69 and of the efficiency performance scale is .79.

Performance changes were measured by counting either the number of performance downturns, or (separately) the number of performance upturns, reported in the second and third of the three interviews combined. (Because of an interview protocol violation in some of the first-round interviews, we did not include any performance change data reported in the first round.) Including the changes from multiple interviews increased the number of downturns or upturns used to predict, and this was useful as the number of performance changes reported per interview across all three rounds of interviews was only 1.44 for changes in growth and .84 for changes in efficiency. Including the changes from multiple interviews also combined the effects of performance changes that were responded to very quickly with those that were responded to after a longer period (up to 12 months), thus making the measure less sensitive to a particular lag effect. This overall approach resulted in four measures of performance change, i.e., two levels of valence (downturns or upturns) crossed with two types of performance (growth versus efficiency).

Top Manager Characteristics

Earlier we described three types of managerial characteristics that are likely to be causally related to the frequency of organizational change: (1) work history characteristics, such as tenure in the organization; (2) demographic attributes; and (3) personality variables, such as tolerance for ambiguity. Using the Top Manager Profile Questionnaire mailed approximately six months after the third interview, we obtained information about the top manager's years of employment with the organization, years in the current position, and years in each of several business functions, and we also obtained information about his or her college-level education and age. Education was coded as no academic degree, one academic degree, or more than one academic degree. Experience with output functions was the sum of years of experience in marketing and in sales. Experience with throughput functions was the sum of years of experience in basic line operations and in accounting. Note that the issue is experience with throughput operations, rather than experience in managing throughput operations. A great deal of what corporate accountants do is to examine and seek improvement in the efficiency of throughput operations. In this way they become intimately familiar with the throughput function.

In analyzing the effects of the work history variables, we did not include the tenure of the top managers in their organizations, but instead included only their tenure in their current positions. We took this approach in developing this prediction model for three reasons. First, the two variables were highly intercorrelated ($r = .52, p < .01$), and we were concerned about multicolinearity. Second, a top manager's inclination toward organizational change is more likely to be related causally to tenure in the position rather than to tenure in the organization because appointments to the top manager position are often accompanied by a mandate for change and a clear honeymoon period for introducing change (Hambrick and Fukutomi, 1991). Although the top manager may have been with the organization for many years, his or her promotion to the top position is often viewed as a transition through which the organization is no longer committed to past practices. Third, by eliminating the top manager's tenure in the organization, we decreased the number of predictors in an already crowded model. Thus our analyses only include the top manager's tenure in his or her current position and omits tenure variables that are likely to be correlated, but have less powerful causal effects.

Because we believed that the effects of experience, either with output or throughput processes or in a person's current position, increase at a decreasing rate with time, we tested as measures of experience not only the number of years but also the square root and natural log transformations of the number of years. Of these three alternatives, the square root of years was the most predictive, and so it was used in all analyses that involved experience in throughput and output functions and tenure in position.

Also using the Top Manager Profile Questionnaire, we assessed the personality variables of (1) internal locus of control, (2) perceived discretion, (3) need for achievement, and (4) tolerance for ambiguity. Responses were made on seven-point Likert scales. Factor analysis was used to validate a priori scales and to delete items that did not appear to measure the respective personality variable. The result was that each of the four factors was measured with a four-item scale. The reliabilities for these four factors are .64, .54, .68, and .58, respectively.

Strategy

Information assessing organizational strategy was obtained approximately a year prior to the third interview using the Organizational Profile Questionnaire. Factor analyses were used to validate a priori scales and to delete questionnaire items that did not appear to measure the prospector and defender strategy factors. The results were that four items used to measure each of these factors. Interitem reliability analysis was used to ascertain the internal consistency of the scales. Reliability of the prospector strategy scale is .75 and of the defender strategy scale is .63.

Structural Characteristics

The four structural characteristics discussed in the theory section (i.e., centralization, standardization, specialization, and interdependence) were also assessed using the Organizational Profile Questionnaire. Again, factor analysis was used to validate a priori scales. After questionnaire items that did not appear to measure the respective structural characteristics were delted, centralization was measured with seven items, standardization with five items, specialization with one item, and interdependence with two items. The Cronbach alpha's reliability for centralization is .77, for standardization .78, and for interdependence .65.

SAMPLE SIZES AND STATISTICAL POWER

The sample sizes used in these analyses range from 119 to 67 and vary primarily because many of the top managers did not complete the Top Manager Profile Questionnaire, either by choice or because at the end of the two-year data collection cycle their organizations were no longer participating in the study (organizations were merged or acquired, went bankrupt, or lost interest in participating in the research). The sample sizes vary secondarily (1) because the analyses examining the effects of top manager characteristics include only those organizations in which the same top manager informant provided all of the interview data and (2) because of incomplete or missing data from particular organizations. The statistical power of the regression analyses shown in Tables 7.2 through 7.10 range from .75 to .99.

Appendix 7.B. Descriptive Statistics, Pearson Correlations, and Reliabilities of the Variables[a]

Variable	N	Mean	Standard Deviation	Reliability	1	2	3	4	5	6	7	8	9	10	11
1. Externally focused changes	119	1.52	1.60	—	—	.34**	.24**	.59**	.24**	.04	.16	.01	-.03	.11	-.20*
2. Internally focused changes	119	4.04	3.36	—	—	—	.37**	.86**	.37**	.20*	.04	-.26**	.09	-.01	-.14
3. Changes in form	119	2.85	2.46	—	—	—	—	.73**	.26**	.12	.21*	.09	.07	.06	-.13
4. Total changes	119	8.41	5.61	.77	—	—	—	—	.41**	.19*	.16	-.11	.08	.06	-.20*
5. Turbulence	119	5.11	1.04	.75	—	—	—	—	—	.46**	.32**	.13	.42**	.04	.01
6. Competitiveness	119	6.16	1.19	—	—	—	—	—	—	—	.20*	.20*	.32**	.03	-.05
7. Complexity	119	5.66	1.35	—	—	—	—	—	—	—	—	.24**	.09	.08	.09
8. Prospector strategy	119	4.71	1.25	.75	—	—	—	—	—	—	—	—	.09	-.02	.01
9. Defender strategy	119	5.41	1.11	.63	—	—	—	—	—	—	—	—	—	.07	.43**
10. Centralization	119	4.03	.93	.77	—	—	—	—	—	—	—	—	—	—	-.02
11. Standardization	119	4.42	1.09	.78	—	—	—	—	—	—	—	—	—	—	—
12. Specialization	119	4.64	1.47	—	—	—	—	—	—	—	—	—	—	—	—
13. Interdependence	119	4.47	1.75	.65	—	—	—	—	—	—	—	—	—	—	—
14. Efficiency performance	119	4.70	1.14	.79	—	—	—	—	—	—	—	—	—	—	—
15. Growth performance	119	3.89	1.59	.69	—	—	—	—	—	—	—	—	—	—	—
16. Decreases in growth	100	1.13	2.24	—	—	—	—	—	—	—	—	—	—	—	—
17. Increases in growth	100	2.18	3.10	—	—	—	—	—	—	—	—	—	—	—	—
18. Decreases in efficiency	100	.56	1.20	—	—	—	—	—	—	—	—	—	—	—	—
19. Increases in efficiency	100	1.21	1.83	—	—	—	—	—	—	—	—	—	—	—	—
20. Tenure in position	79	8.38	5.52	—	—	—	—	—	—	—	—	—	—	—	—
21. Years in output functions	79	.67	1.41	—	—	—	—	—	—	—	—	—	—	—	—
22. Years in throughput functions	79	2.37	2.00	—	—	—	—	—	—	—	—	—	—	—	—
23. Age	79	2.16	7.43	—	—	—	—	—	—	—	—	—	—	—	—
24. Education	79	2.51	.62	—	—	—	—	—	—	—	—	—	—	—	—
25. Internal locus of control	79	4.92	1.03	.64	—	—	—	—	—	—	—	—	—	—	—
26. Perceived discretion	79	4.38	.88	.54	—	—	—	—	—	—	—	—	—	—	—
27. Need for achievement	79	5.18	.85	.68	—	—	—	—	—	—	—	—	—	—	—
28. Tolerance for ambiguity	79	4.21	1.05	.58	—	—	—	—	—	—	—	—	—	—	—
29. Size	119	5.97	1.59	—	—	—	—	—	—	—	—	—	—	—	—

[a]The number of observations used to compute the correlations is the smaller of the two numbers indicating the number of observations of the respective variables.

*p < .05

**p < .01

Appendix 7.B Descriptive Statistics, Pearson Correlations, and Reliabilities of the Variables[a] (Cont.)

	12	13	14	15	16	17	18	19	20	21	22	23	24	25	26	27	28	29
1. Externally focused changes	.04	.04	-.20*	-.15	.18	.30**	-.05	.16	-.22*	-.13	.11	-.15	.02	-.17	.06	-.10	.02	-.00
2. Internally focused changes	-.12	.13	-.13	-.04	.14	.11	.12	.15	-.27*	-.02	.21*	-.06	.10	.09	.04	.01	.03	.35**
3. Changes in form	-.07	-.05	.01	.10	.27**	.10	.00	-.05	-.16	-.10	-.05	.01	.12	-.20	.10	.02	.12	-.22**
4. Total changes	-.09	.07	-.13	-.02	.26**	.20	.06	.11	-.29*	-.09	.14	-.08	.12	-.07	.08	-.02	.07	.31**
5. Turbulence	-.04	.20*	.06	.09	.13	.09	.04	.06	-.11	-.06	.21	-.06	-.13	.01	.15	.09	-.07	.23**
6. Competitiveness	-.15	.21*	.10	.31**	.22*	.07	-.09	.02	.04	.13	.27**	-.19	-.16	-.08	.13	-.06	-.12	.01
7. Complexity	-.06	-.13	.06	-.07	.15	.02	.07	.01	-.08	-.21*	-.07	.16	.23*	-.21	-.03	.11	.06	.25**
8. Prospector strategy	.20*	-.05	.11	.08	.24*	.21*	-.03	-.00	.15	-.06	-.17	.02	.10	-.12	.15	-.06	.08	-.19*
9. Defender strategy	.05	-.50**	.23**	.35**	-.06	.06	-.21*	.17	.17	.09	.35**	-.14	-.29**	.01	.15	-.05	-.34**	.30**
10. Centralization	.03	.09	-.03	-.07	.17*	-.03	.11	.01	-.04	-.20	-.09	-.01	.17	.01	-.22*	-.04	-.03	.14
11. Standardization	.15	.24**	.15	-.05	-.23*	-.11	-.12	-.00	.16	-.15	-.05	-.11	.00	-.10	-.19	-.06	-.41**	.31**
12. Specialization	—	-.04	-.00	-.10	-.17*	.11	.04	-.03	.08	.25*	-.11	.29**	-.05	.04	.04	-.09	.02	-.07
13. Interdependence	—	—	.02	.08	-.09	.01	-.04	.06	-.03	.07	.35***	-.20	-.28**	.19	.01	-.00	-.30**	.12
14. Efficiency performance	—	—	—	.39**	-.04	.11	.04	-.06	.11	.13	-.08	-.19	.04	.15	-.12	-.06	-.02	.02
15. Growth performance	—	—	—	—	.12	.12	-.04	.05	.18	.12	.15	-.02	-.20	.13	.29**	.14	.03	.04
16. Decreases in growth	—	—	—	—	—	.12	.37**	.06	-.00	.04	.07	-.21	.04	-.11	.10	-.10	.04	.04

	17	18	19	20	21	22	23	24	25	26	27	28	29
17. Increases in growth	—												
18. Decreases in efficiency	.09	—											
19. Increases in efficiency	.33**	.11	—										
20. Tenure in position	-.07	.22	-.05	—									
21. Years in output functions	-.14	-.15	.12	-.08	—								
22. Years in throughput functions	.08	-.12	-.07	-.23*	.11	—							
23. Age	-.01	.09	.03	.28**	-.12	-.03	—						
24. Education	.11	.13	.06	-.15	-.21	-.27*	-.08	—					
25. Internal locus of control	.21	.15	-.09	.01	.18	.06	.17	-.03	—				
26. Perceived discretion	-.00	-.24*	-.06	-.12	-.07	.18	-.14	-.01	.13	—			
27. Need for achievement	-.01	.11	-.11	-.08	-.12	.07	-.03	.04	.11	.32**	—		
28. Tolerance for ambiguity	-.15	.15	-.05	-.18	-.12	-.08	-.07	.21	-.03	.32**	.29**	—	
29. Size	-.19	.08	.09	.06	-.36**	.00	.03	.17	-.08	-.02	.02	-.05	—

[a] The number of observations used to compute the correlations is the smaller of the two numbers indicating the number of observations of the respective variables.

*$p < .05$, **$p < .01$

Appendix 7C. Environmental Characteristics As Determinants of Organizational Changes: Initial Regression Models[a]

Determinants	Externally Focused Changes	Internally Focused Changes	Changes in Form	Total Changes
Turbulence	.27**	.32**	.20*	.35**
Competitiveness	−.15	.06	−.04	−.02
Complexity	.13	−.16+	.10	−.02
Size	−.11	.27**	.11	.18*
Turbulence × size	−.19	.12	.01	.05
Competitiveness × size	.17	.11	.20*	.20*
Complexity × size	.11	.00	.07	.06
Adjusted R^2	.06+	.23**	.10**	.23**
Adjusted R^2 after controlling for size	.08+	.09**	.06*	.14**

[a]Based on data from 119 organizations. Entries are standardized regression coefficients and indicate the relative influence of the determinants on the frequency of change.

+$p < .10$
*$p < .05$
**$p < .01$

Appendix 7D.1. Antecedent Performance Levels As Determinants of Organizational Changes: Initial Regression Models[a]

Determinants	Externally Focused Changes	Internally Focused Changes	Changes in Form	Total Changes
Growth performance	−.07	.01	.09	.03
Efficiency performance	−.18+	−.14	−.03	−.15
Size	.01	.35**	.22*	.31**
Growth performance × size	.13	−.00	−.04	.02
Efficiency performance × size	−.01	−.07	.01	−.04
Adjusted R^2	.02	.11**	.02	.08*
Adjusted R^2 after controlling for size	.03	.00	.00	.00

[a]Based on data from 119 organizations. Entries are standardized regression coefficients and indicate the relative influence of the determinants on the frequency of change.

+$p < .10$
*$p < .05$
**$p < .01$

Appendix 7D.2. Performance Changes As Determinants of Organizational Changes: Initial Regression Models[a]

Determinants	Externally Focused Changes	Internally Focused Changes	Changes in Form	Total Changes
Downturns in growth	.23*	.14	.29**	.28**
Upturns in growth	.23+	.07	.20	.20+
Downturns in efficiency	−.11	.09	−.11	−.03
Upturns in efficiency	.09	.12	−.17	.02
Size	.03	.26*	.17	.23*
Downturns in growth × size	−.08	−.14	−.05	−.17
Upturns in growth × size	−.10	−.10	.04	−.07
Downturns in efficiency × size	−.06	.04	−.18+	−.08
Upturns in efficiency × size	.21*	.27**	.04	.24*
Adjusted R^2	.11*	.11*	.11*	.16**
Adjusted R^2 after controlling for size	.12**	.05+	.08*	.13*

[a]Based on data from 100 organizations. Entries are standardized regression coefficients and indicate the relative influence of the determinants on the frequency of change.
+$p < .10$
*$p < .05$
**$p < .01$

Appendix 7E.1. Top Manager Work History Factors As Predictors of Organizational Changes: Initial Regression Models[a]

Determinants	Externally Focused Changes	Internally Focused Changes	Changes in Form	Total Changes
Experience with output functions	−.29*	.02	−.01	−.08
Experience with throughput functions	.09	.13	−.08	.08
Tenure in position	−.27*	−.23*	−.18	−.29**
Size	−.00	.39**	.37**	.39*
Experience with output functions × size	−.15	−.09	−.03	−.11
Experience with throughput functions × size	.17	.21*	.07	.21*
Tenure in position × size	.06	−.17+	−.04	−.10
Adjusted R^2	.06^{ns}	.31**	.11*	.30**
Adjusted R^2 after controlling for size	.06	.13**	.00	.11**

[a]Based on data from 78 organizations. Entries are standardized regression coefficients and indicate the relative influence of the determinants on the frequency of change.
+$p < .10$
*$p < .05$
**$p < .01$

Appendix 7E.2. Top Manager Personality Variables As Determinants of Organizational Changes: Initial Regression Models[a]

Determinants	Externally Focused Changes	Internally Focused Changes	Changes in Form	Total Changes
Internal locus of control	−.15	.10	−.22*	−.07
Perceived discretion	.13	.04	.12	.11
Need for achievement	−.10	−.04	−.04	−.06
Tolerance for ambiguity	.04	.06	.11	.09
Size	.12	.45**	.39**	.47**
Internal locus of control × size	−.08	.01	.04	−.00
Perceived discretion × size	.25+	.19	.18	.26+
Need for achievement × size	.01	.03	.06	.05
Tolerance for ambiguity × size	−.22+	.01	−.01	−.06
Adjusted R^2	.02^{ns}	.14*	.15**	.20**
Adjusted R^2 after controlling for size	.01	.00	.00	.00

[a]Based on data from 78 organizations. Entries are standardized regression coefficients and indicate the relative influence of the determinants on the frequency of change.
+$p < .10$
*$p < .05$
**$p < .01$

Appendix 7F. Organizational Strategies As Determinants of Organizational Change: Initial Regression Models[a]

Determinants	Externally Focused Changes	Internally Focused Changes	Changes in Form	Total Changes
Differentiation strategy	.06	−.16*	.17+	−.01
Low cost strategy	−.02	.06	.02	.04
Size	−.02	.28**	.25**	.27**
Differentiation strategy × size	−.19*	−.21*	−.09	−.21**
Low cost strategy × size	.22*	.23**	.18+	.28**
Adjusted R^2	.04+	.21**	.07*	.17**
Adjusted R^2 after controlling for size	.05+	.10**	.03	.08**

[a]Based on data from 119 organizations. Entries are standardized regression coefficients and indicate the relative influence of the determinants on the frequency of change.
+$p < .10$
*$p < .05$
**$p < .01$

Appendix 7G. Structural Characteristics As Determinants of Organizational Changes: Initial Regression Models[a]

Determinants	Externally Focused Changes	Internally Focused Changes	Changes in Form	Total Changes
Centralization	.10	−.08	.02	−.01
Standardization	−.20*	−.27**	−.22**	−.31**
Specialization	.11	.01	−.03	.02
Interdependence	.10	.14	−.03	.10
Size	.01	.39**	.30**	.37**
Centralization × size	.05	.05	−.00	.04
Standardization × size	.13	−.08	.06	.02
Specialization × size	.00	.03	−.05	−.00
Interdependence × size	.13	.22*	−.08	.13
Adjusted R^2	.03	.20*	.03	.15**
Adjusted R^2 after controlling for size	.05	.08*	.00	.07*

[a]Based on data from 119 organizations. Entries are standardized regression coefficients and indicate the relative influence of the determinants on the frequency of change.

[+]$p < .10$
[*]$p < .05$
[**]$p < .01$

II

REDESIGNING ORGANIZATIONS

8

Managing the Process of Organizational Innovation

ANDREW H. VAN DE VEN

> No thing is created suddenly, any more than a bunch of grapes or a fig. If you tell me you desire a fig, I answer you that there must be time. Let it first blossom, then bear fruit, then ripen.
> Epictetus

> Great discoveries and improvements invariably involve the cooperation of many minds.
> Alexander Graham Bell

EDITORS' SUMMARY

In this chapter, Van de Ven develops a process model of organizational innovation that can be used by innovation managers to guide their actions and by organizational scientists both as a basis for further research on innovation processes and as an aid in developing theories of organizational change in general. He begins by examining the classic innovation model developed by Everett Rogers, highlighting the fact that it pertains particularly to the development and marketing of innovations by organizations and the adoption of these innovations by individuals. He then introduces the multi-investigator, multiorganization, multiyear Minnesota Innovation Research Program (MIRP) and describes six "complexities" that he and his associates in the MIRP studies found to commonly occur in the intraorganizational development and adoption of innovations (as contrasted with development by organization and subsequent adoption by individuals). The capstone to these two efforts is a model of organization innovation formed by superimposing the MIRP complexities on Rogers's classic model.

Along the way, Van de Ven draws on the MIRP studies and his extensive knowledge about innovation to share some fresh insights. The first of these, of course, is his explicit articulation of the features that differentiate innovation adoptions by individuals and organizations. The second is his highlighting of the differences between organizational innovations that have their origin inside the organization and those that have their origin outside. One particularly interesting section concerns the detrimental consequences of restricting innovation-related activities to those that are central to the core novel idea. Another insight concerns the benefits of implementing an innovation broadly and simultaneously across organizational levels and divisions, rather than sequentially. Also interesting are the observations that "innovation success more often represents a socially constructed reality than an objective reality" and that those who are "least ready or willing to adopt the innovations may be those who need it most." These insights will undoubtedly stimulate discussion, and perhaps rebuttal, and eventually more empirical research. In this role they constitute an important contribution to organizational science.

The contribution of Van de Ven's chapter to managerial practice includes the several recommendations it contains for managing the process of organizational innovation. Some of these are explicit and some implicit. They cannot be given a fair hearing in this summary, but it seems worthwhile to note some of the issues addressed: (1) the use of intermediate deadlines; (2) the changing of evaluation criteria over time; and (3) the need to complete innovations quickly and keep them simple while at the same time allowing for modification and "reinvention." Managers are having to deal with innovation more than ever before. In this chapter Van de Ven's portrayal of the organization processes is informative, succinct, and as firmly based in strong theory and empirical observation as any to be found. ■

Change is both a routine and novel fact of organizational life. To stay in business, most organizations have developed effective and efficient routines to manage a wide variety of recurring changes, such as adapting to business cycles, yearly product revisions and introductions, and personnel turnover and executive succession. These commonplace changes are typically managed by standardized procedures previously established. Occasionally, these routine organizational changes are punctuated by novel changes for which no established procedures exist. As Chapters 2, 3, and 7 in this volume demonstrate, these unprecedented changes are often triggered by serious deteriorations in an organization's performance, discontinuous shifts in an organization's environment or industry, or frame-breaking technological innovations that render an organization's design and capabilities obsolete. Managing these novel changes is far more complex and unpredictable than managing routine changes because the former require developing and implementing new change procedures, while the latter entail implementing tried-and-tested procedures. In other words, novel changes are organizational innovations, whereas routine changes are not.

This chapter proposes a set of principles for managing novel changes based on knowledge gained from studies of organizational innovation. Part one reviews Rogers's (1962, 1983) model of innovation adoption and diffusion, which is perhaps the most widely shared view of the innovation process by scholars and practitioners alike. While this model is robust in explaining innovation adoption by individuals, it does not adequately address the developmental process often observed when the organization is the locus of innovation. In an attempt to remedy this situation, Part two of this chapter describes the process patterns during innovation development that were commonly observed in a wide variety of organizational innovations studied by the

Minnesota Innovation Research Program (MIRP). The elements of these developmental patterns deal with the organizational preconditions that enable and motivate innovation, the proliferation of activities and setbacks that occur as the process of innovation development and adoption unfolds, and how the novelty, size, and temporal duration of an innovation influence its likelihood of success or failure.

We revise and extend Rogers's model of innovation so that it can better address these characteristics of innovation development in organizations. In so doing, our goal is to provide an enriched model of innovation that builds on the strong conceptual and empirical foundation that Rogers's model provides. This goal is *not* achieved by replacing Rogers's model with yet another model, particularly since the literature is already populated with many alternative innovation process models that are conceptually weak and have little if any empirical support—a conclusion drawn by Schroeder, Van de Ven, Scudder, and Polley (1986) after a review of 16 different process models in the literature. Our goal is also *not* achieved if the reader concludes that Rogers's model of innovation by individuals is incompatible with a model of organizational innovation. Individual and organizational processes represent micro- and macroforces of the same dynamics—that is, the actions of people, working individually and collectively, to invent, develop, resist, and transform innovative ideas into implemented realities. Our goal *is* achieved if this chapter offers an enriched model from which one can derive practical suggestions for managing the process of innovation and change from both the microindividual and the macroorganizational perspectives.

ROGERS'S BASIC INNOVATION ADOPTION/DIFFUSION MODEL

Our point of departure is the classic model of innovation development and adoption by individuals illustrated in Figure 8.1, which was developed by Everett Rogers and is perhaps the most widely shared view of the innovation process. The model represents a culmination of Rogers's own research (encompassing three decades) and a synthesis of over 3,100 published innovation studies (see Rogers, 1962; 1983; Rogers and Shoemaker, 1971). This model portrays the process of innovation over time as a linear sequence of three basic stages, beginning with the invention of an idea (which comes from a recognition of needs or problems and basic or applied research), through its development, production, and testing into a concrete device or program, and culminating in its diffusion to and adoption by users.

Depending on the innovations being examined, various authors have expanded or modified activities within these three basic stages, and, as a result, specialized fields of study and research have emerged for each innovation stage. For the idea invention stage, an extensive literature has developed on individual and group creativity primarily by psychologists (e.g., Cummings, 1965; Amabile, 1983; Angle, 1989) and on "technology push" versus "demand pull" by economists (e.g., Rosenberg, 1982; Thirtle and Ruttan, 1987). Although less extensively studied than the other stages, the development stage is gaining more research attention by management scholars (e.g., Burgelman, 1983; Kanter, 1983; Tushman and Romanelli, 1985; Van de Ven, Angle, and Poole, 1989). Finally, Rogers (1983) notes that no area in the social sciences has perhaps received as much study as the innovation diffusion and adoption stage.

Most of the research related to this third stage has focused on diffusion, which is

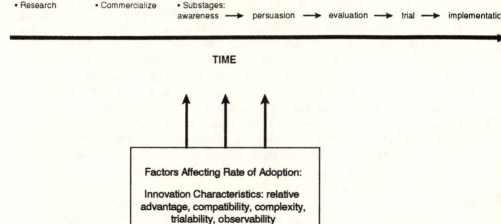

Figure 8.1. Rogers's basic model of the process stages in innovation: invention, development, and diffusion/adoption. *Note:* This illustration combines Rogers's basic stages of the innovation process with the basic factors that predict the rate of innovation adoption. *Source:* Adapted from Everett M. Rogers, 1983, *Diffusion of Innovations,* 3rd Ed. New York: Macmillan: pp. 165, 233.

largely concerned with the marketing, dissemination, and transfer of an innovation to individual end users. Far less has dealt with adoption, or the process by which recipient users select and implement an innovation. Of this smaller subset of adoption studies, most have focused on statistically examining relationships between various "input" factors (characteristics of user individuals, organizations, and the innovation) and "output" factors (rates of innovation adoption), leaving the adoption *process* itself least understood. It is well established that functionally similar organizations respond and perform differently in adopting similar innovations (Barley, 1986). The sequence of events in the development and adoption of an innovation makes a difference in determining whether the innovation will be an eventual success or failure.

As Figure 8.1 illustrates, Rogers's model focuses principally on five substages in the process of innovation diffusion and adoption. First, the innovation unit starts by marketing and creating awareness of its innovation through a variety of communication channels such as the print media (newsletters, journals, advertisements, and leaflets), which is often followed by personal contacts and informal influence of opinion leaders. Once the awareness of an alternative is established, the next subphase involves the arousal of interest by a potential user of the innovation. Various preconditions, such as felt need, organizational innovativeness, norms, resources, and communication behavior influence the arousal of interest by a potential adopter. Rogers's model assumes that the potential adopter engages in a mental evaluation of the innovation, and that the likelihood of an adoption decision increases when the innovation promises to have a strong relative advantage over alternatives, when the innovation is highly compatible with existing practices and is not too complex, when the innovation can be tried out, and when the results of the innovation can be observed. According to the model, an adoption decision typically leads to an actual trial implementation of the innovation. Positive outcomes from the trial will lead to continued use and institutionalization of the innovation by the adopting organization; negative outcomes will lead to rejection.

Rice and Rogers (1980) report that although extensive empirical support for this adoption process model has been established for individual adopters (such as farmers adopting the best practices as promoted by the U.S. Agricultural Extension Agency), mixed results have been obtained when the organization is the locus of innovation adoption. Organizations are complex political systems consisting of many functional specialties and administrative hierarchies that often compete for influence and resources in the adoption and implementation of project priorities. As a consequence, innovation development and adoption decisions often tend to be used for partisan purposes: heralded by some, attacked and sabotaged by others, and apathetically ignored by the majority who are preoccupied with other organizational priorities (Dahl and Lindblom, 1976).

For example, Clark (1987) reports on a study of a hospital-design team initially consisting of the senior administrative staff and a small group of professional nurses working with the British Department of Health and Social Security. They decided to adopt a standard design package developed in the department which had been devised to produce cost-effective decisions by placing all medical treatment activities in a central location. During the early stages of design, the medical staff of the design team made no serious interventions or contributions even though the proposed designs had considerable implications for the medical hierarchy and for the allocation of space and resources. Then, at a very late stage, when it became apparent to them that the new hospital, if built as designed, would require considerable alterations in their working conditions and in their professional control of activities, they became much more active, thereby necessitating architectural alterations during the commissioning of the new hospital.

PROCESS PATTERNS IN ORGANIZATIONAL INNOVATION FROM MIRP STUDIES

As this case exemplifies, the process of innovation development and adoption by organizations is considerably more complex than by individuals. Building on this idea, this part of the chapter describes the developmental pattern commonly observed in a wide variety of organizational innovations studied by the Minnesota Innovation Research Program (MIRP). It provides the basis for suggesting how Rogers's model of innovation development and adoption for individuals can be extended for organizations.

As Van de Ven, Angle, and Poole (1989) discuss in greater detail, MIRP was launched in 1983 to develop a grounded theory of the process of innovation development. MIRP involved more than 30 researchers who organized themselves into 14 interdisciplinary study teams to track the innovations listed in Figure 8.2. MIRP researchers adopted a common framework and methodology to compare findings across the innovations studied. This framework defines the process of innovation development with five core concepts which were used to observe how innovative *ideas* are developed and implemented by *people*, who engage in *transactions* (or relationships) with others and make the adaptations needed to achieve desired *outcomes* within changing institutional and organizational *contexts*. Beginning with historical baseline data, these concepts were repeatedly measured using interviews, surveys, onsite observations, and archival records as the innovations developed over time in their natural field settings. Whenever a change was observed in terms of any one of these five concepts it was defined as an event. A systematic recording of events as innovations developed over time was the central task for all the MIRP studies. Van de Ven and Poole (1990) describe these research procedures. As of July 1992, all but one had come to a natural conclusion (whether implemented or terminated).

Elements of the Innovation Process Identified in the MIRP Studies

Schroeder, Van de Ven, Scudder, and Polley (1986, 1989) examined the processes of development in seven technical and administrative innovations studied by MIRP. By systematically comparing longitudinal case histories on the development of the innovations, they found that none of the innovations developed in a simple linear sequence

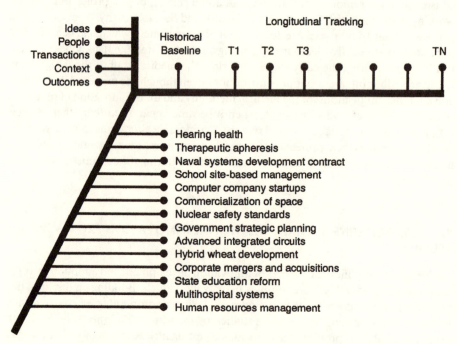

Figure 8.2.   The Minnesota Innovation Research Program.

of stages or phases of activities over time, as Rogers's model in Figure 8.1 proposes. Instead, in each of the innovations, they observed a much messier and more complex progression of events over time. However, patterns of regularity were found in these messy and complex developmental progressions. Specifically, six elements or characteristics were commonly found in the process of development of all the innovations. These six common elements are the following.

1. The innovation process consists of an accretion of numerous events performed by many different people over an extended period of time. The process does not conform to the Western cultural practice of attributing innovation to the discrete acts of a single entrepreneur on a particular date and at a particular place. In each innovation studied by MIRP, the innovation process began with an extended gestation period that lasted several years, during which a variety of coincidental events occurred and set the stage for launching an organizational innovation or change process.

2. Concentrated actions to allocate resources and initiate innovation development are triggered by "shocks" (not mere persuasion) produced by direct personal confrontations with needs or problems. These shocks are sufficiently large to trigger the attention and action of organizational participants. When people reach a threshold of sufficient dissatisfaction with existing conditions, they initiate action to resolve their dissatisfaction.

3. Once innovation development work begins, the process does not unfold in a simple linear sequence of stages and substages. Instead, it proliferates into complex bundles of innovation ideas and divergent paths of activities by different organizational units. More specifically, after the onset of a simple unitary progression of activity to develop an innovative idea, the process diverges into multiple, parallel, and interdependent paths of activities.

4. Setbacks are frequently encountered during the innovation process, either because plans go awry or unanticipated environmental events occur which significantly alter the ground assumptions of the innovation. These setbacks either signal rejection of the innovation or opportunities for learning through reinvention.

5. Innovation receptiveness, learning, and adoption speed are facilitated when the innovation is initially developed within the user organization, and they are inhibited when end users are provided no opportunities to reinvent (or modify) innovations that were initially developed elsewhere. Organizational participants not involved in the development or reinvention of an innovation tend to view it as an external mandate. Regardless of whether an innovation is initially developed inside or outside the adopting organization, the adoption process is facilitated by modifying the innovations to fit the local situations, extensive top management involvement and commitment to the innovation, and the use of various techniques to maintain task completion and momentum throughout the developmental period.

6. Management cannot ensure innovation success, but can influence its odds. The odds of success increase with experience and learning from past trials at innovation, and they decrease with the novelty, size, and temporal duration of an

innovation venture. Thus, the odds of success are not only a function of the number of times an organization has undertaken the innovation journey in the past but also the complexity of the journey it has chosen to undertake next.

These six process elements are interrelated and provide a scenario of innovation development and adoption that is considerably different from Rogers's model. Whereas Rogers's model, illustrated in Figure 8.1, portrays the innovation process as unfolding in a simple linear sequence of stages or phases over time, the six process elements unfold in a partially cumulative progression of multiple paths of activities. This progression of innovation development activities tends to unfold in the following way.

In the beginning, a set of seemingly coincidental events occur in an organization, which set the stage for initiating an innovation. Some of these gestating events are sufficiently large to "shock" the action thresholds of organizational participants to undertake concerted efforts to launch the development or adoption of an innovation. As innovation development begins, the process soon proliferates from a simple unitary process into divergent, parallel, and convergent progressions of ideas and activities over time. Some of these activities in the multiple progression are conjunctive (related through a division of labor among functions and interdependent paths of activities), and many appear to be disjunctive (unrelated in any noticeable form of functional interdependence). Many component ideas and paths perceived as being interdependent and conjunctive at one time are often reframed or rationalized as being independent and disjunctive at another time when the innovation idea or circumstances change. Problems, mistakes, and setbacks frequently occur as these developmental paths are pursued, and they provide opportunities either for learning or for terminating the developmental efforts. Innovations stop when they are adopted and implemented by an organization, or when resources run out or political opposition prevails and further developmental efforts are terminated. Schroeder et al. (1986: 521) concludes: "It is clear that the messy and complex progression observed in the innovation cases cannot be reduced to a simple sequential progression model of stages or phases as the vast majority of process models in the literature suggest."

Modifications of Rogers's Model and Prescriptions for Managing the Innovation Process

We will now discuss each of the six process elements and indicate how modifications could be made in Rogers's model (Figure 8.1) to deal with them. We will also discuss the practical implications of modifying Rogers's model by making suggestions for managing the organizational change journey.

Temporal and Contextual Preconditions for Innovation

Organizational innovations are not initiated on the spur of the moment, nor by a single dramatic incident, nor by a single entrepreneur. In most of the innovations studied by MIRP, as Van de Ven, Venkataraman, Polley, and Garud (1989) report, an extended gestation period existed, often lasting three or more years, in which people engaged in a variety of activities that set the stage for innovation. Many initial events during the gestation period were not intentionally directed toward adopting an innovation. Some events triggered recognition of the need for change—for example, deteriorating organizational performance, such as Cameron et al. (Chapter 2 in this volume) describe, or changing environmental conditions, such as Huber et al. (Chapter 7 in this volume) and Meyer et al. (Chapter 3 in this volume) describe. Other events generated awareness of the technological feasibility of an innovation—for example, the discovery of cytoplasmic male sterilization that made hybrid wheat possible (Knudson and Ruttan, 1989). "Technology-push" and "demand-pull" events such as these often launched "intrapreneurs" (Pinchot, 1985) on courses of action that, by chance, intersected with independent actions of others. These intersections provided occasions for people to recognize and access new opportunities and potential resources. Where these occasions were exploited, people modified and adapted their independent courses of action into interdependent collective actions to undertake concerted efforts to initiate an innovation.

While the basic model in Figure 8.1 posits that an innovation adoption decision is a relatively straightforward result of knowledge and persuasion, these observations emphasize that chance plays a significant role in affecting the decision and subsequent course of innovation adoption. Increases in the number of initiatives undertaken by a large number of interacting people increases the probability of stimulating innovation. This proposition reinforces the bias-for-action principle of Peters and Waterman (1982). Perhaps Louis Pasteur's adage that "chance favors the prepared mind" best captures the process that sets the stage for innovation.

The important practical question then becomes: "What can organizations do to increase their preparedness to capitalize on the chance of innovation?" Angle (1989) proposes that managers structure the organization's context to *enable* and *motivate* innovative behavior. This context includes the legitimacy, resources, structure, and culture of the encompassing organization that innovation groups draw on to enable and constrain their innovative behaviors. Amabile (1988), Angle (1989), and Kanter (1988) summarize a large body of research indicating that innovation is facilitated in organizations that provide a context to both enable and motivate innovation; it does not occur where either enabling or motivating conditions are absent.

Three studies of successful organizational innovation in hospitals, reviewed by Van de Ven (1990), provide examples of the organizational culture and legitimacy that enable and motivate innovative behavior. Each of the hospitals was a highly respected, long-established, and very successful institution, located at the hub of its respective industry and community networks. During the periods of innovation adoption, these hospitals had moderately low personnel turnover rates, long-run strategic time horizons that connected diverse organizational activities to core institutional missions (providing quality care to meet changing patient needs), and high commitments of top management and medical staffs to their respective innovations, and they were making significant investments both in new technologies and their professional staffs. While the relative influence of any one of these elements on innovation is difficult to assess, when combined they exemplify the ingredients of an organizational context that enables innovation. Moreover, in each case, recognition and motivation of the need for innovation was triggered by many (not one or a few) events over an extended period of time (often several years) and involved many different people both within and outside the hospitals.

In the short term, pragmatically there is little that managers can do to directly change organizational culture and legitimacy, for they are the historical by-products of previous organizational activities and interactions with its environment. These innovation-enabling characteristics are long-term with macroconsequences produced by the accumulation of many microactions that preoccupy the short-term attention of organizational participants.

The immediate context for most innovations is the organization itself, and much can be done to modify the immediate context of an organization. Organizations are complex social systems that provide templates for playing out many distinctive roles important to innovation. The design of an organization's structure, systems, and practices influence the likelihood that innovation ideas will surface and that, once surfaced, they will be developed and nurtured toward realization. Furthermore, the organization is the most direct source of the resources needed to support innovation efforts.

With respect to structure, there are several features that will affect the gestation of innovative activities. The more complex and differentiated the organization, and the easier it is to cross boundaries, the greater the potential number of sources from which innovative ideas can spring. However, as Kanter (1983) discusses, with increasing organizational size and segmentation come complexity and bureaucratic procedures. These often constrain innovation unless special systems are put in place to motivate and enable innovative behavior. Key motivating factors include providing a balance of intrinsic and extrinsic rewards for innovative behaviors (Amabile, 1983). While people work for pay to make a living, incentive pay (i.e., monetary rewards contingent on performance and in addition to base salary) seems to be a relatively weak motivator for innovation; it more often serves as a proxy for recognition. Angle (1989) found that individualized rewards tend to increase idea generation and radical innovations, whereas group rewards tend to increase innovation implementation and incremental innovations.

However, the presence of motivating factors, by themselves, will not ensure innovative behavior. Angle (1989) emphasizes that enabling conditions are equally necessary, such as:

- Resources for innovation.
- Frequent communications across departmental lines, among people with dissimilar viewpoints.
- Moderate environmental uncertainty and mechanisms for focusing attention on changing conditions.
- Cohesive work groups with open conflict resolution mechanisms that integrate creative personalities into the mainstream.
- Structures that provide access to innovation role models and mentors.
- Moderately low personnel turnover.
- Psychological contracts that legitimate and solicit spontaneous innovative behavior.

Angle concludes that normal people have the capability and potential to be creative and innovative. The actualization of this potential depends on whether management structures an organizational context that not only motivates but also enables individuals to innovate.

Shocks: The Triggering Mechanism

While a conducive organizational climate sets the stage for innovation, concrete actions to undertake specific innovations appear to be triggered by "shocks," from sources either internal or external to the organization (Schroeder et al., 1989). For example, Chapter 3 in this volume, on the reform of health care organizations in the San Francisco Bay area, reviews a number of "shocks," including the introduction of the DRG payment reimbursement system, increasing competitiveness of the hospital industry, and radical new ideas about the alignment of health care institutions by organizational entrepreneurs.

The reason why shocks are needed to trigger innovation is based on a simple model of decision making embedded in Rogers's basic model: when people reach a threshold of dissatisfaction with existing conditions, they initiate action to resolve their dissatisfaction. The problem, however, is that many changes in organizations and environments do not trigger the action thresholds of organizational participants because human beings are unconsciously highly adaptable. Small and gradual changes over time provide insufficient stimulation to reach people's recognition thresholds for action (Helson, 1964). People adapt to gradually changing conditions, and often they fail to notice that conditions have signaled the appropriateness of a novel or significant change. As a consequence, unless the stimulus is of sufficient magnitude to exceed their action thresholds—that is, a "shock"—people do not move into action to correct their situation, which over time may become deplorable. Opportunities for innovation are either not recognized or not accepted as important enough to motivate innovative action.

Organizational designs to run efficiently and reliably often have the effect of programming people into cognitive routines or habits that desensitize them to novel events (Starbuck, 1983). This habit-bound perception is particularly prevalent in contexts where people perform repetitive tasks. As argued elsewhere (Van de Ven, 1986: 595), "what people do most is often what they think about least."

Once an individual's recognition threshold for change is reached, then the person's motivation to support or resist the change becomes relevant. Change is often threatening, because it offers the possibility that coping mechanisms once adequate under the old situation may no longer suffice. People who were "winners" may now be lucky to break even. Adding to the relatively passive blinders that people wear, because of habit or inattention, are the active blinders stemming from such defense mechanisms as denial and shifting risks from individuals to groups. So, for a variety of reasons, it may be difficult for people to notice change of the sort that should by all rights stimulate them to innovate. The management of attention is a central problem in managing the innovation journey (Van de Ven, 1986).

A variety of mechanisms can be put into place for redirecting and jostling the attention of organizational members so that subtle changes and needs will be noticed. For example, Normann (1985) observed that well-managed companies are not only close to their customers, as Peters and Waterman (1982) suggest, but they search out and focus on their most demanding customers. Empirically, von Hippel (1981) has shown that ideas for most new product innovations come from customers. So also, Utterback (1971) found that about 75 percent of the ideas used to develop product innovations came from outside the organization. Direct contacts with customers not only force organizational participants to acknowledge problems and needs, but by being outside the organizational unit, customers are not trapped by its bounded rationality. Outsiders can see ways to approach problems other than the ways organizational participants are used to taking for granted. Thus, we suggest that placing people in direct personal confrontations with the sources of organizational problems and opportunities is necessary to reach the threshold of concern and appreciation required to motivate most people to act (Van de Ven, 1980). Personal exposure increases the likelihood of triggering action thresholds that affect a person's awareness of changing technological, organizational, and environmental needs.

Complex Proliferation of Innovation Development Activities

In tracking the development of a wide variety of technical and organizational innovations studied by MIRP, Schroeder et al. (1986) found that shortly after a decision is made to undertake an innovation, the process becomes too complex to manage, as the initially simple innovation process proliferates into diverse pathways. More specifically, after the onset of an initial simple stream of activity to develop or adopt an innovative idea, the process quickly diverges into multiple and parallel paths of activities. Some of the proliferation is produced by dividing the labor among functions and organizational units (e.g., between R&D, manufacturing, and marketing functions, or between headquarters and district organization sites) required to develop a given innovation. These specialists, in turn, develop different conceptions of the innovation. Some of the proliferation is produced by the fact that a given organizational change typically entails a bundle of related innovations (e.g., a new technological procedure requires adopting new administrative procedures, new occupational roles, and new conceptions of suppliers and customers), and each involves a different development and adoption process. Finally, other organizational activities may appear unrelated to the innovation, but often compete for scarce resources thus thwarting the direction of the innovation adoption process. As a consequence, after a short initial period of simple unitary activities, the management of innovation soon proliferates into an effort of "trying to direct controlled chaos" (Quinn, 1980).

This proliferation of activities over time appears to be a pervasive but little understood characteristic of organizational change and innovation processes. The basic model in Figure 8.1 assumes that the innovation in concept and scope remains intact as it is adopted. The MIRP observations suggest a need to extend the model to address the continuous redefinitions of the innovation that are made by organizational participants into terms that they can understand and which are compatible with their organizational cultures.

Moreover, they show that it is not correct to depict users within the organization as developing or adopting only a single innovation. Many users are simultaneously choosing from diverse sets of innovations in many different areas, such as equipment, organizational structures, and new work practices (Clark, 1987). As one innovation manager reported, this proliferation creates the problem of "trying to plant an oak tree when there are inexorable pressures to grow a bramble bush."

Much of this complexity is the result of innovation managers striving to achieve too much too soon, thereby becoming embroiled in many activities that are not necessary or essential to develop an innovation (Van de Ven and Polley, 1990). For example, Van de Ven et al. (1989) observed organizational participants to exhibit an impatient quest to "leapfrog" into developing an overall program or business without evaluating the basic merits of the core innovation. This happened when an innovation unit undertook efforts to scale-up manufacturing facilities, develop marketing strategies, and launch R&D projects on future product generations without adequately evaluating and demonstrating that the root—new technology—was technically feasible and commercially viable. Ironically, this tendency often delays development of the core innovation idea because organizational participants become preoccupied with efforts that do not contribute directly to the immediate tasks needed to develop the basic idea. Instead, much effort is devoted to preengineering systems that may be necessary to adopt families or generations of the innovation. In the process of doing this, basic problems inherent to the core idea are often masked and go unquestioned until setbacks arise (as we will discuss).

Administrative reviews are periodically conducted to evaluate progress during innovation development. However, such reviews are often poor substitutes for the "acid test" of introducing the innovation to end users or to the market. Restricting and simplifying innovation activities to the core novel idea decreases cost and time to implementation. Moreover, it tends to decrease the costly mistakes of investments in innovations that do not meet the market test. Small mistakes are more tolerable and correctable than large mistakes.

Setbacks, Mistakes, and Learning Disabilities

A fourth process element commonly encountered during the development of organizational innovations is that mistakes and setbacks frequently arise, either because initial plans go awry or because unanticipated environmental events occur that significantly alter the ground assumptions and context of the innovation. Just as Mintzberg, Raisinghani, and Théorêt (1976) found in their studies of unstructured decisions, Van de Ven et al. (1989) reported in the MIRP studies that the typical initial response to setbacks was to adjust resources and schedules, which provided a "grace period" for innovation development. But with time, many of the problems encountered accumulate into vicious cycles because additional resources or slack time only masked more fundamental problems—namely, the difficulties in detecting, correcting, and learning from mistakes. Many of these setbacks and errors were not corrected because one or more of the following conditions created a learning disability: (1) it was difficult to discriminate substantive issues from "noise" in systems overloaded with a combination of positive, negative, and mixed signals about performance over time; (2) innovation champions escalated their commitments to a course of action by ignoring "naysayers" and proceeding "full scale ahead"; (3) some innovation participants called prematurely for changes in a course of action when minor or correctable problems were encountered; and (4) in-process criteria of innovation success often shifted over time as the initial euphoria with an innovation waned and as new, more exciting alternatives became apparent to organizational participants. Innovation units are often composed of heterogeneous people who view the same events differently. Thus, while many errors were detected, very few were corrected because information was not shared or similarly interpreted. Those uncorrected sometimes "snowballed" to crisis proportions before they were addressed. Many learning experiences could not be acted on because of the time lag required to change a course of action.

The classic study by Pressman and Wildavsky (1973) examined the implementation efforts by the federal Economic Development Administration of a new program that appeared to be destined for success in providing jobs for poor blacks by offering public works grants and loans to local enterprises. More than six years later, however, public works construction had not been finished and there were few new jobs for unemployed blacks. Initial agreements among federal, regional, and local officials slowly dissolved into a host of disagreements over the "details" of implementation. These details included changing actors, diverse perspectives, and multiple negotiations and clearances among decision makers, all leading to a geometric growth of interdependencies and delays over time. Delays came from (1) unplanned accidental occurrences, (2) blocked efforts by participants who wanted to stop the program, (3) alternative time priorities, and (4) delays caused by delay itself. Commitment and momentum to seeing a program through to completion wane with time when progress is slower or less successful than expected.

An immediate recommendation that emerges from these findings is the need to structure opportunities and slack resources to detect and correct mistakes when they occur, before they grow into vicious cycles. However, it is not clear that additional resources or slack time will necessarily facilitate trial-and-error learning in highly ambiguous situations. Trial-and-error learning may be far more difficult to achieve than has been assumed to be the case. With highly novel undertakings, one can seldom rely on past routines or plans to guide behavior. Moreover, the highly ambiguous information participants typically receive and the idiosyncratic experiences they encounter greatly circumscribe rational learning processes (March and Olsen, 1976). Instead, these conditions spawn "superstitious learning" (Levitt and March, 1988). Because information is often unreliable, ambiguous, or late, and because most innovation participants have not experienced other innovations from which to develop inferences, it becomes difficult to correctly identify cause-and-effect relationships. As a consequence, there is a blurring between "success" and "failure" as results become interpreted against varying personal perspectives and frames of reference (Dornblaser, Lin, and Van de Ven, 1989).

Perhaps the root problem for why little learning is observed as setbacks arise exists in the basic innovation process model itself, which many organizations have come to use to guide their action. The linear sequence of invention, development, and adoption stages in Figure 8.1 minimize opportunities for learning. As Pressman and Wildavsky (1973: 135) emphasize: "Learning fails because events are caused and consequences are felt by different organizations." Thus, just as "planners should not be separated from doers" (p. 135) and "implementation should not be divorced from policy" (p. 143), innovation adoption should not be separated from innovation invention and development.

Rice and Rogers (1980) develop a related idea by emphasizing that *reinvention facilitates adoption*. Reinvention is a process of recreating an innovation in a different context or from a different perspective. Reinvention is akin to reverse engineering a prototype in order to understand how it was initially created, and so that it can be recreated to fit a particular circumstance or setting. Reinvention is fundamentally a learning process that is triggered by the inevitable setbacks and mistakes people encounter as they attempt to implement an innovation. When invention and development activities are divorced from implementation and adoption, the learning process is short-circuited because different people experience these activities. As Pressman and Wildavsky (1973) conclude, implementation and adoption must not be conceived as processes that take place after innovation invention and development. Learning requires that these activities become fused in the innovation process and that interaction occurs among the people principally concerned with invention, development, and implementation. This interaction occurs more readily in "homegrown" innovations than in innovations developed elsewhere.

In the organizations where innovations are "homegrown," Schroeder et al. (1986) found that implementation and adoption activities often occur throughout the developmental period. For example, this was frequently observed when cross-functional committees and combined developer-user teams met repeatedly to review, advise, and apply experimental products and ideas that emerged during the innovation process. Concentrated efforts to link the "new" with the "old" throughout the developmental period provide organizational participants more opportunities to address problems in a new design and more time to modify it to fit applied situations than is possible when organizations adopt innovations developed elsewhere. Therefore, "homegrown" innovations normally require less time to implement and institutionalize than do externally induced innovations.

Linking and integrating the "new" with the "old" is generally a more viable adoption strategy than switching and replacing existing organizational arrangements with those of a new innovation. This is because, in a world of scarcity, organizations must make trade-offs between investing resources in existing or new programs. As a consequence, it is often not economically feasible for innovations to be mere additions to existing organizational programs; the "old" and the "new" must somehow be integrated to yield a coherent, cost-effective operation.

It is also not politically practical for many organizational innovations to replace existing organizational programs, because of the history of investments and commitments made to making these (yesterday's innovations) work. However, such a possibility is often perceived to exist by organizational participants not involved in the development of the innovation. Therefore, the innovation often represents a threat to the established order. Instead, if they are to be implemented and become institutionalized, innovations must overlap or integrate with existing organizational arrangements.

5. Adoption of Innovations

Organizations can take a number of steps to facilitate reinvention and learning as they adopt innovations initially developed elsewhere. These steps include (1) modifying and adapting the innovation to fit the organization's local situation, (2) active involvement of top management with the innovation, and (3) applying a number of techniques that facilitate coordination among diverse and distracted groups of people to meet key deadlines and maintain momentum for innovation adoption. Recommendations for undertaking each of these steps are as follows.

Conventional wisdom suggests that efforts to implement an innovation should begin on a small scale and then spread incrementally based on prior small success stories (Greiner, 1970). While this approach provides one way to deal with proliferating complexity (others will be suggested below), it may often not be a wise strategy to deal with organizational political life. For example, in one MIRP study, Lindquist and

Mauriel (1989) compared two common alternative strategies for adopting and implementing innovations: a *breadth* strategy in which the innovation is implemented across all organizational units simultaneously, and a *depth* strategy in which the innovation is implemented and "debugged" in a demonstration site before it is generalized to other organizational units. They found that the breadth strategy was more successful than the depth strategy in adopting and institutionalizing site-based management in two public school districts. Several explanations were provided for this surprising finding:

- Once the depth strategy is introduced and heralded by top management, the demonstration project loses visible attention, support, and institutional legitimacy from top-level managers as their agendas become preoccupied with other pressing management problems.
- With a breadth strategy, top management stays in control of the innovation implementation process, thereby increasing, rather than decreasing, its power. Moreover, slack resources within the control of top management can ensure success better than can limited budgets for innovation to a demonstration site.
- There is a trade-off between implementing a few components of an innovation in breadth versus implementing all components in depth in a particular demonstration site. Fewer hurdles and resistances to change are encountered when a few (and presumably the easy) components of an innovation are implemented across the board to a few (and presumably supportive) stakeholders, than when all (both easy and hard) components of a program are implemented in depth with all partisan stakeholders involved.
- With a depth strategy, it is easier for opposing forces in other parts of the organization to mobilize efforts to sabotage a "favored" demonstration site than it is to produce positive evidence of the merits and generalizability of an innovation.

In another MIRP study, Bryson and Roering (1989) examined the introduction of an administrative innovation (the adoption of new planning systems) in six local governmental agencies. They found that each attempt to adopt the innovation was prone to disintegration because:

- External events and crises frequently occurred, distracting participants' attention and priorities, and taking away any slack resources available to adopt the innovation.
- The adoption process itself was partially cumulative—what occurred before was sometimes remembered and had to be accounted for, even though past actions and decisions became inconsistent with, or contradictory to, subsequent turns of events.
- Participants became bogged down with information overload, conflicting priorities, and divergent issues that were outside of their decision jurisdictions or domains.

Bryson and Roering (1989) made three useful recommendations for enhancing innovation adoption that echo earlier suggestions made by Burgelman (1983). First, the involvement of a process facilitator committed to continuing with the adoption process is important, particularly when difficult hurdles and setbacks arise. Second, since disruptions and setbacks cause delays and interest wanes with time, the process should be structured into key junctures—deadlines, conferences, and peak events. These structured junctures in the adoption process establish key deadlines to perform planned intermediate tasks, force things to come together, and facilitate unplanned intersections of key ideas, people, transactions, and outcomes. Third, a willingness to be flexible is necessary, not only regarding criteria of acceptable innovation adoption but also regarding arguments geared to many different evaluation criteria. Dornblaser et al. (1989) found that the managers and resource controllers of the innovations studied by MIRP often changed their criteria of innovation success over time. They observed that innovation success more often represents a socially constructed reality than an objective reality.

Because organizations are complex hierarchical systems, contradictory part-whole relations are often produced when systemwide innovations are introduced. An organizationwide innovation or change developed by one organizational unit often represents an externally imposed mandate to adopt the innovation to other, often lower-level, organizational units. Thus, Angle and Van de Ven (1989) report that a top management or policy unit may express euphoria about the innovation it developed for the entire organization, while frustrations and oppositions to that same innovation are expressed by the affected organizational units. Such a situation often presents itself when a systemwide innovation is attempted by externally mandating that all organizational units adopt the innovation.

Such a situation was reported in another MIRP study by Marcus and Weber (1989) when they examined the organizational effectiveness implications of two different reactions taken by 28 American nuclear power companies in response to a new set of nuclear safety procedures mandated by the U. S. Nuclear Power Commission. They found that the nuclear power plants with relatively poor safety records tended to respond in a rule-bound manner that perpetuated their poor safety performance. On the other hand, those plants whose safety records were relatively strong tended to retain their autonomy by adapting the standards to their local situations, a response that reinforced their strong safety performance. Ironically, those least ready or willing to adopt the innovations may be those who need it most.

The Marcus and Weber study provides an important and generalizable principle for the adoption of externally imposed innovations. Be forewarned of the possible consequences of passive acceptance of external dictates by those who strictly follow the letter of the law; they may do so in "bad faith" that may not achieve the results intended. Some autonomy is necessary for an adopting unit to identify with and internalize an innovation. Mere formal compliance is insufficient. The disposition of innovation adopters is likely to be negatively affected if they are not granted a sufficient level of autonomy, and it is their disposition that is often critical in assuring successful adoption. The "not invented here" syndrome is well known in all sorts of organizations. Adopting agencies or organizations that have not developed any sense of commitment to those innovations may well behave bureaupathically and simply do what the letter of the law requires.

Contingencies in the Innovation Development Process

The one best way to manage organization innovation and change may never be found, notwithstanding the many process models in the literature (reviewed by Poole and Van de Ven, 1989) that propose a unitary sequence of stages and steps for organizational innovation and change. Instead, a sophisticated manager will try to identify those contingent factors and alternative processes that influence what works and what does not work. In particular, we believe that many of the innovation process complexities described in this chapter are more pronounced in innovations of greater novelty, size, and duration.

Radical Versus Incremental Innovations. Some innovations change the entire order of things, making the old ways obsolete and perhaps sending entire businesses the way of the slide rule or the buggy whip. Others simply build on what is already there, requiring only modest modification of the old world view. As Rogers's model proposes, innovations of different levels of novelty need to be managed differently. Five dimensions of innovation novelty are distinguished in Rogers's model: an innovation's relative advantage, compatibility, complexity, trialability, and observability. These dimensions of novelty are important, not only for predicting an innovation's rate of adoption and diffusion but also for evaluating an organization's capabilities to undertake the development process. Indeed, some organizations may be well suited to one type of innovation but not the other. For example, an organization that values and rewards individualism may have the advantage in radical innovation, while a more collectivist system may do better at an incremental one (Angle, 1989). Pelz (1985) found that the stages of the innovating process were more disorderly for technically complex innovations than for technically simple innovations.

Innovation Stage and Temporal Duration. Transitions from innovation invention to development to adoption activities often entail shifts from radical to incremental and from divergent to convergent thinking. As innovations approach the culminating institutionalization step, they become more highly structured and stabilized in their patterns and less differentiated from other organizational arrangements (Zaltman, Duncan, and Holbeck, 1973; Lindquist and Mauriel, 1989).

The developmental pattern and eventual success of an innovation is also influenced by its temporal duration. The initiation of an innovation represents an initial stock of assets that provides an innovation unit a "honeymoon" period to perform its work (Fichman and Levinthal, 1988). These assets reduce the risk of terminating the innovation during its honeymoon period when setbacks arise and when initial outcomes are judged unfavorable. The likelihood of replenishing these assets (by obtaining additional funding for innovation development) is highly influenced by how long it takes to complete the change process. Interest and commitment wane with time. Thus, after the honeymoon period, innovations terminate at disproportionately higher rates, in proportion to the time required for their implementation. As Pressman and Wildavsky (1973: 130) state "The advantages of being new are exactly that: being new. They dissipate quickly over time. The organization ages rapidly. Little by little the regulations that apply to everyone else also apply to it."

Size and Scope of the Innovation. It may be that small organizations have the advantage in starting up an innovation but that larger organizations with more slack resources have the advantage in keeping an innovation alive until it is completed. Van de Ven et al. (1989) found that venture capital was short term, more risky, and more difficult to obtain than was internal corporate venture funding. Larger organizations offer a more fertile ground for sustaining and nurturing spin-off innovations. Also, there may be more places to "hide" something in a larger organization, until such time as an innovation can stand on its own. Yet, large organizations seem to need bureaucratic systems in order to manage, and this is not particularly conducive to innovation. The message to managers is to keep finding ways to remain flexible, to permit sufficient power to concentrate on innovation, to build access to technical competence, and to listen attentively to the views of those directly responsible for implementation—factors that Burgelman (1983), Kanter (1983), and Nord and Tucker (1987) found were critical success factors for adopting innovations in large organizations.

CONCLUDING DISCUSSION

This chapter examined the process of organizational innovation over time from the initial organizational conditions that enable and motivate the launching of an innovation effort, to the process complexities that arise during innovation development, and through to the hurdles of innovation implementation and adoption by end users. We began with a review of Rogers's (1962, 1983) basic model of innovation development. After considering it in light of the findings from the Minnesota Innovation Research Program, we concluded that Rogers's model requires some extensions to adequately address the process complexities commonly encountered in organizational innovation.

In particular, the findings from the MIRP suggest that Rogers's model of organizational innovation can be enriched by viewing innovation stages and factors as activities, and by not assuming that these activities occur in any particular sequence over time. Thus, instead of viewing the innovation process as proceeding in a linear sequence of stages, it is both more accurate and flexible to view the process as a multiple progression of invention, development, and adoption activities over time, as Figure 8.3 illustrates. In addition to these technical innovation activities, a variety of administrative and contextual events occur during the process that alter the organizational and environmental settings of an innovation. Thus, instead of viewing these as unchanging starting factors affecting the rate of innovation adoption as in Figure 8.1, we propose in Figure 8.3 that events pertaining to changes in organizational administrative arrangements and environmental context be studied over time, in the same manner as invention, development, and adoption activities. In so doing, one can gain not only a richer appreciation of how these technical and institutional activities unfold over time, but also how they are related and thereby facilitate and constrain the overall process of innovation.

This multiple progression of the innovation process can be studied by recording the occurrence of innovation activities and events along each of the five activity tracks outlined in Figure 8.3. For example, the invention activities track would not only include the occurrence of the initial idea that triggered innovation development, it would also record whenever any changes occurred to further invent, develop, implement, and adopt the innovation idea. So also, the adoption/diffusion track would include all activities related to people "buying into" or rejecting the innovation at any time during its development—be it an idea, a prototype design, or a concrete organizational program. Clearly, events pertaining to innovation invention, development,

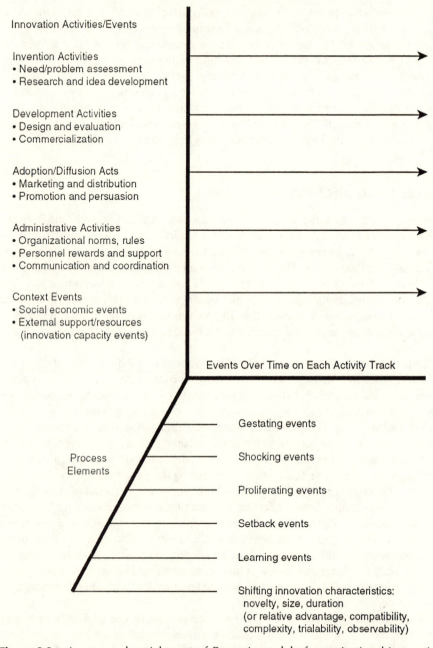

Innovation Activities/Events

Invention Activities
• Need/problem assessment
• Research and idea development

Development Activities
• Design and evaluation
• Commercialization

Adoption/Diffusion Acts
• Marketing and distribution
• Promotion and persuasion

Administrative Activities
• Organizational norms, rules
• Personnel rewards and support
• Communication and coordination

Context Events
• Social economic events
• External support/resources
  (innovation capacity events)

Events Over Time on Each Activity Track

Process
Elements

Gestating events

Shocking events

Proliferating events

Setback events

Learning events

Shifting innovation characteristics:
novelty, size, duration
(or relative advantage, compatibility,
complexity, trialability, observability)

Figure 8.3. A proposed enrichment of Rogers's model of organizational innovation.
Note: This model enriches Rogers's model in Figure 8.1 by (1) viewing innovation stages as activities or events that occur throughout the process over time, (2) viewing administrative and context factors not as constants, but as emerging and changing through events and activities over time, and (3) adding a third axis that tracks the occurrence of six process elements of organizational innovations that were identified in the Minnesota Innovation Research Program.

adoption, administration, and context activities listed in Figure 8.3 occur repeatedly, and often in no necessary temporal order. Recording these different types of activities along multiple tracks (rather than a single track as has been done in the past) greatly liberates one from the erroneous and confining assumption that the process of organizational innovation and change proceeds in a simple linear sequence of stages.

Viewing the developmental process as a progression of multiple activities facilitates creation of new ways to think about and manage organizational innovation and change. For example, three dimensions are useful for understanding the relationships among activities over time: conjunctiveness, cumulativeness, and intensity. Some activities in the multiple progression process may be *conjunctive* (i.e., related through a division of labor among functions and/or temporally lagged to reflect their logical or hierarchical connectedness), and many activities may be *disjunctive* (i.e., unrelated in a noticeable form of functional or temporal interdependence). Some activities in the multiple progression process may be *cumulative* (i.e., ideas or products of activities performed earlier carry over and become the inputs for subsequent activities), but many activities may only be *partially cumulative* or dropped over time (i.e., forgotten, not learned, discarded, or terminated). Finally, the *intensity* in which these activities are performed may vary at certain times, but all the activities may be occurring simultaneously over time. If it is empirically found that only invention activities occur in the first period, that developmental activities predominate in the second period, and that adoption activities dominate in the third period, then the multiple progression reduces to the special case of a simple linear sequence of stages, as shown in Figure 8.1. However, in all the innovations studied by MIRP, we reported that the developmental progression was considerably messier and more complex and thus could not be reduced to a linear sequence of stages or phases of activities.

In addition to shifting stages and factors from Rogers's model into progressions of multiple activities over time, Figure 8.3 contains a third axis dealing with the six process elements commonly observed during organizational innovation and change. As discussed before, many of these process elements occur repeatedly throughout the innovation process. They are represented as a third dimension in Figure 8.3, since there is no necessary temporal order or period in which they occur. However, as outlined below, when they do occur they often require different managerial strategies and skills.

1. Innovation and change are facilitated when organizations create a stage that enables and motivates innovation. It was found that stage-setting initially involves an extended gestation period lasting several years and involving many organizational participants (not on the spur of the moment, nor by a single dramatic incident, nor by a single entrepreneur). However, once the innovation process begins, repeated efforts at restructuring the organizational and environmental settings are necessary to transform innovative ideas into practical realities for adoption and diffusion.

2. "Shocks" (not mere persuasion), produced by exposing individuals to direct personal confrontations with needs or problems, are necessary to trigger attention and action for innovation. When people reach a threshold of sufficient dissatisfaction with existing conditions, they initiate action to resolve their dissat-

isfaction. Managing the attention of innovation participants is critical to initiate innovation development, and it is an ongoing challenge for linking technical possibilities with market or end-user needs throughout the innovation process.

3. Once innovation activities begin, the process does not unfold in a simple linear sequence of stages and substages; instead, it proliferates into complex bundles of innovation ideas and divergent paths of activities by different organizational units. Organizations that manage change successfully find ways to keep the innovation process relatively simple in the face of constant pressures to proliferate into related and unrelated paths to the core innovation idea.

4. Setbacks and mistakes are frequently encountered during the innovation process, either because plans go awry or because unanticipated organizational and environmental events occur which significantly alter the ground assumptions of the innovation. These setbacks signal either rejection of the innovation or opportunities for learning through reinvention. Learning fails when events are caused and consequences are felt by different individuals. Through reinvention, organizational participants learn by reconnecting the causes and consequences of innovation invention, development, and adoption activities to changing organizational and environmental circumstances.

5. Innovation adoption is facilitated by modifying the innovations to fit the local organizational situations, through extensive involvement and commitment by top management in the innovation, and by use of various techniques that maintain task completion and momentum throughout the adoption process.

6. Organizational change processes vary with the novelty, size, and temporal duration of the innovations being developed and adopted. The greater the novelty, size, and temporal duration of an innovation, the more the above process elements are prevalent and the more complex the innovation process. Changes in an innovation's novelty, size, and temporal duration reflect shifts in Rogers's characteristics of an innovation as it develops over time: its relative advantage, compatibility, complexity, trialability, and observability. The more an innovation venture achieves these characteristics over time, the more simple will be the subsequent development and adoption/diffusion processes.

No doubt organizations will experience other elements of the innovation process as they attempt to manage novel changes. We focused on these six process characteristics because they were empirically validated in the wide variety of innovations studied by MIRP. Some of the principles that emerged from the revision of Rogers's model were presented as prescriptive guidelines for maneuvering the innovation and change journey. Settings of organizational innovation different from those observed in MIRP may suggest different principles. Thus, further research in other settings is necessary to verify the principles offered. However, when substantiated, we believe the principles can substantially improve the odds of successfully managing organizational change and innovation.

It should be emphasized that the applied principles offered here will *not ensure* innovation success. The reason for this caveat rests with a concluding principle that underlies all the key processes along the innovation journey: *management cannot con-*

trol innovation success; only its odds. This principle implies that a fundamental change is needed in the control philosophy of conventional management practice.

Professor Bill McKelvey (1982: 447–448) at UCLA tells the story of the 1976 Winter Olympics, where Franz Klammer won the men's downhill skiing competition. When interviewed after the event and asked how he managed to turn in such an incredible performance, he said that he had chosen to "ski out of control." He knew that there were many other top-level skiers entered against him, several of whom might outpace him on any given day, if he were to ski his normal speed—that is, under control. He chose, instead, to ski so fast that he abandoned any sense of control over the course. While obviously this was not a sufficient condition for victory, he saw it as a necessary condition. Staying "in control" would virtually ensure a loss, while skiing "out of control" would make it at least possible to win.

Innovation and change managers may have an important lesson to learn from this vignette. By definition, an innovation is a leap into the unknown. If an innovation is to have a chance to succeed, traditional notions of managerial control may need to be relaxed somewhat. It is not that such letting go will ensure success, merely that it may be a necessary condition.

A number of practical consequences follow if innovation success is recognized to be a probabilistic process. First, innovation success or failure would more often be attributed to factors beyond the control of innovators. This, in turn, will decrease the likelihood that the careers of innovation managers will be stigmatized if their innovation fails and will increase the likelihood that they will be given another chance to manage future innovations. After all, one cannot become a master or professional at anything if only one trial is permitted. As we reported, relatively little trial-and-error learning occurred once the journey was initiated for a given innovation. Repeated trials over many innovations are essential for learning to occur and for applying these learning experiences to subsequent innovations. It is largely through repeated trials and the accumulation of learning experiences across these trials that an organization can build an inventory of competence and thereby progressively increase its odds of innovation success.

In order for this to happen, Connie Gersick suggested to me that we need to develop ways to let managers practice innovation skills in relatively safe environments. Management educators could act on this idea by developing training programs, possibly with simulation exercises and cases, for managers to take before they embark on the innovation journey. Furthermore, to continue our analogy, managers should have opportunities to hone their skills on "beginner slopes" by launching small and inexpensive innovations before they strike out "on the Alps" by directing major and expensive innovations that are central to the future viability of their organizations.

NOTES

I am grateful for very helpful comments and suggestions on an earlier draft of this chapter from Laura Cardinal, Connie Gersick, Bill Glick, George Huber, Everett Rogers, and Frederick Williams.

REFERENCES

Amabile, T. M. 1983. *The social psychology of creativity.* New York: Springer-Verlag.

Amabile, T. M. 1988. A model of creativity and innovation in organization. In Staw, B. and Cummings, L. (Eds.), *Research in organizational behavior,* Vol. 10 (pp. 123–169). Greenwich, CT: JAI Press.

Angle, H. A. 1989. Psychology and organizational innovation. In Van de Ven, A., Angle, H., and Poole, M. S. (Eds.), *Research on the management of innovation: the Minnesota studies* (pp. 135–170). New York: Ballinger/Harper and Row.

Angle, H. A., and Van de Ven, A. H. 1989. Suggestions for managing the innovation journey. In Van de Ven, A., Angle, H., and Poole, M. S. (Eds.), *Research on the management of innovation: the Minnesota studies* (pp. 663–697). New York: Ballinger/Harper and Row.

Barley, S. 1986. Technology as an occasion for structuring: evidence from observations of CT scanners and the social order of radiology departments. *Administrative Science Quarterly,* 31: 78–108.

Bryson, J., and Roering, W. 1989. Mobilizing innovation efforts: the case of government strategic planning. In Van de Ven, A., Angle, H., and Poole, M. S. (Eds.), *Research on the management of innovation: the Minnesota studies* (pp. 583–610). New York: Ballinger/Harper and Row.

Burgelman, R. 1983. Corporate entrepreneurship and strategic management: insights from a process study. *Management Science,* 29(12): 245–273.

Clark, P. 1987. *Anglo-American innovation.* Berlin: Walter de Gruyter.

Cummings, L. L. 1965. Organizational climates for creativity. *Academy of Management Journal,* 8: 220–227.

Dahl, R. A., and Lindblom, C. E. 1976. *Politics, economics, and welfare.* Chicago: University of Chicago Press.

Dornblaser, B. M., Lin, T., and Van de Ven, A. H. 1989. Innovation outcomes, learning, and action loops. In Van de Ven, A., Angle, H., and Poole, M. S. (eds.), *Research on the management of innovation: the Minnesota studies* (pp. 193–218). New York: Ballinger/Harper and Row.

Fichman, M., and Levinthal, D. A. 1988. Honeymoons and the liability of adolescence: a new perspective on duration dependence in social and organizational relationships. Unpublished Paper. Pittsburgh, PA: Carnegie Mellon University, Graduate School of Industrial Administration.

Greiner, L. E. 1970. Patterns of organizational change. In Dalton, G., Lawrence, P. R., and Greiner, L. E. (Eds.), *Organizational change and development* (pp. 213–229). Homewood, IL: Irwin-Dorsey Press.

Helson, H. 1964. Current trends and issues in adaptation-level theory. *American Psychologist,* 19: 23–68.

Kanter, R. M. 1983. *The change masters: innovations for productivity in the American corporation.* New York: Simon and Schuster.

Kanter, R. M. 1988. When a thousand flowers bloom: structural, collective and social conditions for innovation in organizations. In Staw, B. M., and Cummings, L. L. (Eds.), *Research in organizational behavior,* Vol. 10 Greenwich, CT: JAI Press.

Knudson, M. K., and Ruttan, V. W. 1989. The management of research and development of a biological innovation. In Van de Ven, A., Angle, H. L., and Poole, M. S. (Eds.), *Research on the management of innovation: the Minnesota studies* (pp. 465–488). New York: Ballinger/Harper and Row.

Levitt, B., and March, J. G. 1988. Organizational learning. In *Annual review of sociology,* 14. Greeneich, CT: JAI Press.

Lindquist, K., and Mauriel, J. 1989. Depth and breadth in innovation implementation: the case of school-based management. In Van de Ven, A., Angle, H., and Poole, M. S. (Eds.), *Research on the management of innovation: the Minnesota studies* (pp. 561–582). New York: Ballinger/Harper and Row.

March, J. G., and Olsen, J. P. 1976. *Ambiguity and choice in organizations.* Bergen, Norway: Universitetsforlaget.

Marcus, A., and Weber, M. 1989. Externally induced innovation. In Van de Ven, A., Angle, H., and Poole, M. S. (Eds.), *Research on the management of innovation: the Minnesota studies* (pp. 537–560). New York: Ballinger/Harper and Row.

McKelvey, B. 1982. *Organizational systematics: taxonomy, evolution, and classification.* Berkeley: University of California Press.

Mintzberg, H., Raisinghani, D., and Théorêt, A. 1976. The structure of "unstructured" decision processes. *Administrative Science Quarterly,* 21: 246–275.

Nord, W. R., and Tucker, S. 1987. *Implementing routine and radical innovations.* Lexington, MA: D. C. Heath.

Normann, R. 1985. Developing capabilities for organizational learning. In Pennings, J. and Associates, *Organizational strategy and change.* (pp. 217–248). San Francisco: Jossey-Bass.

Pelz, D. C. 1985. Innovation complexity and the sequence of innovating stages. *Knowledge: Creation, Diffusion, and Utilization,* 6(3): 261–291.

Peters, T. J., and Waterman, Jr., R. H. 1982. *In search of excellence: lessons from America's best-run companies.* New York: Harper and Row.

Pinchot, G. III. 1985. *Intrapreneuring.* New York: Harper and Row.

Poole, M. S., and Van de Ven, A. H. 1989. Toward a general theory of innovation processes. In Van de Ven, A. H., Angle, H. L., and Poole, M. S. (Eds.), *Research on the management of innovation: the Minnesota studies* (pp. 637–662). New York: Ballinger/Harper and Row.

Pressman J. L., and Wildavsky, A. B. 1973. *Implementation.* Berkeley: University of California Press.

Quinn, J. B. 1980. *Strategies for change: logical incrementalism.* Homewood, IL: Irwin-Dorsey Press.

Rice, R., and Rogers, E. 1980. Reinvention in the innovation process. *Knowledge: Creation, Diffusion, and Utilization,* 1(4): 499–514.

Rogers, E. 1962. *Diffusion of Innovation,* 1st Ed. New York: Free Press.

Rogers, E. 1983. *Diffusion of Innovations,* 3rd Ed. New York: Free Press.

Rogers, E., and Shoemaker, F. 1971. *Communication of innovation: a cross-cultural perspective.* New York: Free Press.

Rosenberg, N. 1982. *Inside the black box: technology and economics.* Cambridge: Cambridge University Press.

Schroeder, R. G., Van de Ven, A. H., Scudder, G. D., and Polley, D. 1986. Managing innovation and change processes: findings from the Minnesota Innovation Research Program. *Agribusiness Management,* 2(4): 501–523.

Schroeder, R. G., Van de Ven, A. H., Scudder, G. D., and Polley, D. 1989. The development of innovation ideas. In Van de Ven, A. H., angle H. L., and Poole, M. S. (Eds.), *Research on the management of innovation: the Minnesota studies* (pp. 107–134). New York: Ballinger/Harper and Row.

Starbuck, W. H. 1983. Organizations as action generators. *American sociological review,* 48: 91–102.

Thirtle, C. G., and Ruttan, V. W. 1987. *The role of demand and supply in the generation and diffusion of technical change.* New York: Harwood Academic Publishers.

Tushman, M. L., and Romanelli, E. 1985. Organizational evolution: a metamorphosis model of convergence and reorientation. In Cummings, L. L., and Staw, B. M. (Eds.), *Research in organizational behavior,* Vol. 7 (pp. 171–222). Greenwich, CT: JAI Press.

Utterback, J. 1971. The process of technological innovation within the firm. *Academy of Management Journal,* 14: 75–88.

Van de Ven, A. H. 1980. Problem solving, planning, and innovation: Part II. Speculations for theory and practice, *Human Relations,* 33(11): 757–779.

Van de Ven, A. H. 1986. Central problems in the management of innovations. *Management Science,* 32(5): 590–607.

Van de Ven, A. H. 1990. The process of adopting innovations in organizations: three cases of hospital innovations. In Guile, B., Laumann, E., and Nadler, G. (Eds.), *Designing for technological change* (pp. 00–00). Washington, D.C.: National Academy Press.

Van de Ven, A. H., Angle, H. A., and Poole, M. S. (eds.) 1989. *Research on the management of innovation: the Minnesota studies.* New York: Ballinger/Harper and Row.

Van de Ven, A. H., and Polley, D. 1990. Learning while innovating. Discussion Paper. Minneapolis: University of Minnesota, Strategic Management Research Center.

Van de Ven, A. H., and Poole, M. S. 1990. Methods for studying innovation development in the Minnesota Innovation Research Program. *Organization Science,* 1(3): 313–335.

Van de Ven, A. H., Venkataraman, S., Polley, D., and Garud, R. 1989. Processes of new business creation in different organizational settings. In Van de Ven, A., Angle, H., and Poole, M. S. (eds.), *Research on the management of innovation: the Minnesota studies* (pp. 221–298). New York: Ballinger/Harper and Row.

von Hippel, E. 1981. Users as innovators. In Rothberg, R. R. (Ed.), *Corporate strategy and product innovation* New York: Free Press.

Zaltman, G., Duncan, R., and Holbek, J. 1973. *Innovations and organizations.* New York: Wiley.

9

Designing Global Strategic Alliances: Integrating Cultural and Economic Factors

JOHN W. SLOCUM JR., and DAVID LEI

> Many business opportunities have been lost or joint ventures crippled because of failures in understanding or in managing cultural diversity; getting the economics right may be futile if you've got the culture wrong.
>
> James E. Austin
> *Managing in Developing Countries*, 1990: 345

> The cultures of U. S. corporations find visual and symbolic expression in logos, slogans, and rituals. But such concrete manifestations have little meaning for Korean employees, whose cultural tradition is introspective and not necessarily explicit.   Sang M. Lee, Sangjin Yoo, and Tosca M. Lee
> *Organizational Dynamics*, Spring 1991

EDITOR'S SUMMARY

The wide proliferation of alliances of varying degrees of sophistication between global firms makes it necessary for senior management to understand the critical success factors inherent in each type of alliance. Simple alliance designs, such as those involving licensing in manufacturing and service industries, depend primarily on economic factors for implementation. More complex alliance designs, such as joint ventures and consortia arrangements, require a more sophisticated understanding and tight meshing of cultural factors to ensure both fast organizational learning of new skills and smoothness of implementation. Because many U. S. firms have come to rely on global alliances to develop new products and to gain access to new markets, management practitioners and researchers need a conceptual framework to understand which alliance design is most suitable for particular purposes, as well as the underlying implementation issues associated with each.

In this chapter, Slocum and Lei explain how economic and cultural factors do, and should, affect the design of global strategic alliances. They also provide numerous examples in which alliances were effective or ineffective depending on whether these factors were adequately considered. Finally, they describe how five different types of global strategic alliances can be designed to enhance their effectiveness.

The chapter is characterized by its novelty and rigorous precision. While other authorities have asserted that cultural issues must be considered in the design of global alliances, Slocum and Lei articulate four specific cultural factors and describe their practical design implications for global strategic alliances. Further, they describe both the direct effects of these factors and the interactive effects, along with the four economic factors, on the design of the alliances. In addition, their differentiation of alliances into a five-category taxonomy heightens both the managerial usefulness of the predictions and the rationale for theory building.

Their contribution is leading edge and is solidly grounded in theory. Organizational scientists and well-read managers will recognize and appreciate the authors' demonstration of how global alliances vary on key design characteristics such as structure (four dimensions), information integration mechanisms (nine mechanisms), control strategies (market, bureaucratic, and clan), reward systems (performance-based versus hierarchy-based), and culture (market to clan). And although there is relatively little validated theory concerning culture, the authors' ideas about how a host country's culture is linked to various types of alliances are well reasoned.

The chapter contains two important messages for managers. The first is that, for global strategic alliances to be effective, their design must include a sophisticated interweaving of economic and cultural factors. Fortunately, the chapter gives some operational guidance on the nature of what this interweaving should be. The second important message is that alliances are opportunities for managers to learn not only about technologies and markets but also about alliance designs in general and about one specific focal alliance in particular. Certain facets of the design will help or hinder the transformation of this learning into a useful redesign of the alliance.

The principal implications of the chapter for organizational scientists are threefold. The first implication is that, when considering the role of organizational culture as a characteristic of organizational design, an institutional theory perspective should be adopted. That is, not only must the organization's culture be congruent with its other design features, such as its structure, but also it must be congruent with the culture of the nation in which it operates. This seems obvious once stated, but Slocum and Lei are among the first to put this point into the literature and to set out some examples of what these necessary congruencies are. The second implication for organizational scientists is that the transactions-cost perspective is a hopelessly narrow basis for the design of global strategic alliances. The third implication is that the strategic management perspective, which is already richly multidisciplinary and has recently recognized the role of alliances as vehicles for learning, can further enrich itself by incorporating cultural values as a variable to be considered in the development and implementation of policies and strategies. ■

During the past several years, much has been written about the need for strategic business alliances as a means for managing the complexities of worldwide organizations (cf., Hamel, Doz, and Prahalad, 1989; Osborn and Baughn, 1990; and Lei and Slocum,

1991). Popular business journals such as *Fortune* and the *Harvard Business Review,* as well as editorials in the *Wall Street Journal,* have urged top managers to form strategic alliances as one way of entering the global market. Global strategic alliances are increasingly being viewed as critical vehicles by which firms compete in the global marketplace. Although research interest in strategic alliances has grown steadily during the 1980s, advances in economics, strategic management, and organizational theory have only recently begun to develop new conceptual frameworks and models to examine and classify specific types of alliances and their supporting organization designs.

Global strategic alliances represent an important group of structural designs that enable firms to enhance and redesign their information-processing capabilities and their scope of organizational learning when competing in highly complex and diversified product markets (Rapoport, 1991). Alliances have become useful mechanisms in aiding managers' efforts to cope with accelerating rates of environmental change and to restructure their competitive activities. Alliances not only help firms manage high levels of environmental complexity and change but also serve as a basis for organizational learning (Huber, 1991). Learning involves organizational adjustment instigated by changes in the environment. Effective learning facilitates a firm's ability to cope with change and recapture its sources of competitive advantage. Learning enables firms to develop a strategy congruent with their environment. Top managers do not adapt or respond to an objective environment, but they define an environment with their firm's particular interests. Successful executives manage their environment in such a way as to facilitate their organization's survival and learning. One important form that this interaction can take is the creation of alliances that reflect the cultural values and economic perspectives of top management.

This chapter sets forth an organizing framework intended to help researchers and professional practitioners in diagnosing the various issues that arise when creating strategic business alliances. Our underlying premise is that economic forces and cultural values jointly impact the choice of a specific global business alliance. Top management's task in designing an alliance is to use both economic factors and cultural values to optimize efficiency, risk, and learning simultaneously in a worldwide business. Economic factors are usually the main consideration for a decision to form a strategic business alliance, but an understanding of cultural values is one of the keys to successful implementation of an alliance (Lorange and Roos, 1991; Schneider and Meyer, 1991)). Figure 9.1 displays how these two factors affect the choice of strategic business alliances and the implementation processes.

Viewing strategic global business alliances with our framework can be helpful to both managers and academics in several ways. First, studying economic factors can help in formulating, describing, and analyzing the design requirements for global alliances. Second, our framework can help managers in generating a checklist of issues that they must consider in reviewing different strategic global alliances. Such a checklist can serve as a basis for managers mapping their organization's overall strategy and those of their competitors. It will enable them to understand their comparative strengths and weaknesses. Third, our framework can highlight apparent discrepancies between design and implementation requirements that may impede necessary change.

This chapter is divided into three parts. First, we use several different theoretical perspectives to look at various economic factors that prompt firms to consider engaging in global strategic alliances. Conditions such as economies of scale, learning effects,

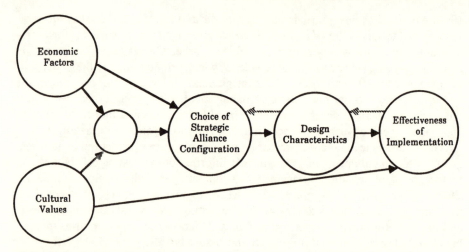

Figure 9.1. Relationship between economic factors and cultural values within a strategic business alliance configuration.

risk reduction, and opportunities to shape competitors' actions are considered. Second, we focus on the critical role of cultural values and how these are likely to influence the organization design mechanisms that enhance alliance implementation and stability. It is our contention that as alliance configurations become more complex, the degree to which cultural values are mutually understood and managed by both partners will determine the alliance's effectiveness and stability. Economic factors may prompt firms to consider certain alliance modes, but more complex alliances depend on managing and bridging cultural values to enhance learning and stability. Third and finally, we focus on three broad types of alliance configurations: licensing, joint ventures, and consortia (or chaebols).

FOUR ECONOMIC FACTORS THAT INFLUENCE STRATEGIC ALLIANCES

In the broadest sense, firms enter into strategic alliances to obtain benefits not available through arms-length market transactions, internal development, or outright merger (Porter and Fuller, 1986). The four most important economic factors contributing to the rapid growth of alliance activity are the need for creating economies of scale, learning new skills and technologies, shaping industry evolution, and reducing risk.

Creating Economies of Scale and Critical Mass

The need to achieve economies of scale in critical value-adding activities prompts the formation of many strategic alliances. Pooling resources increases the scale of activities that could not be achieved by either partner acting alone. As many high-technology industries face scarcer resources and higher risks of development, firms are entering into alliances across different functional activities (manufacturing and marketing, for instance) to build a critical mass or presence in an industry. For example, in joint ventures where partners are endowed with mutually complementary value-adding skills, pooling their efforts furthers the prospect of scale and specialization benefits across activities. An example is the joint venture of General Motors and Toyota in their Fremont, California, plant. Where partners are endowed with strengths in the same value-adding activities, a joint venture could provide a new mechanism that not only improves current projects but also enables future scale-intensive projects to be implemented faster. Economies of scale become especially important as globalization across industries tends to increase the minimum efficient scale needed for state-of-the-art plants.

Learning New Skills and Technologies

Strategic alliances assist firms in learning new skills, technologies and capabilities from their partners. Compared with internal development efforts, strategic alliances help firms gain a new perspective on problems by integrating different technologies and skills into projects that they previously could not envision. The scope for faster organizational learning is broadened significantly when firms are able to learn from multiple sources (Prahalad and Hamel, 1990). Hamel et al. (1989) note that many firms enter into joint ventures as a means of enhancing their own strategic vision, learning new competencies, or reducing the time needed for developing new projects. For example, Thomson's joint venture with JVC is intended to help the French electronics giant fine-tune its skills in manufacturing highly precise microelectronic components that are increasingly vital to products in a broad range of industries. This alliance also enables JVC to learn how to compete in the European market. Alliances become network mechanisms that transmit the flow of information between partners and enable both to accelerate learning and diffusion of competitive skills.

Shaping Industry Evolution

Firms in many industries engage in alliances to enhance the evolution of the industry itself. Strategic alliances designed to shape industry evolution exert themselves in at least three ways. First, licensing and joint venture activities diffuse certain technologies that require standardization early in the product's life cycle. These predetermine the path of industry activity. The software and computer chip industries are laden with strategic alliances designed to promote and standardize certain operating systems and processing techniques.

Second, firms in very dynamic industries engage in strategic alliances not only to help amortize development costs but also to position their firms to capitalize on idiosyncratic value-adding activities. For example, in the pharmaceutical and chemical industries, extensive cross-licensing agreements exist not only to specialize R&D activities across firms, but also to maintain a high level of industrywide innovativeness and dynamism.

Third, alliances can shape the path of competitor entry and evolution within industries as well. Alliances of this type may work both horizontally (across firms with similar value-chain configurations) and vertically (across firms that are in a supplier-manufacturer relationships). For example, Japanese firms engaged in *keiretsu* alliances (societies of businesses) seek both to shape the pace of industry growth and globalization and to control the type of skills and technologies that are likely to be developed among competitors.

Reducing Risk

All alliances are motivated, to some extent, by the need to reduce economic risk. Strategic alliances help global firms hedge financial risks that no organization alone could bear. In high-technology industries—such as aerospace, telecommunications, computers, and machine tools—the costs and risks of product development have risen exponentially during the past decade. Moreover, the extreme complexities of integrating many different technological bases into a single product class have substantially raised the fixed costs of entry and product development. The irony is that many once separate industries have become related by way of digital technologies and miniaturization (Ferguson, 1990). The proliferation in the number and type of skills needed for capitalizing new technologies is often beyond the scope of any one firm.

While the economic reasons for forming strategic global alliances are relatively clear, evidence regarding how economic reasons impact the implementation process is often unclear. For example, it has often been claimed that one source of the competitive advantage for Japanese firms is the low cost of capital in Japan. Recent studies (e.g., Ferguson, 1990; Ghoshal, 1987) indicate that often there are practically no differences in the cost of capital between U. S. and Japanese firms. When cost differences do exist, they arise from sourcing and specialization gained from membership in a keiretsu. Similarly, the low wage rate in Japan has also been posited as the primary reason for the success of Japanese organizations that market their goods in the United States. Once again, recent evidence indicates that the Honda and Nissan plants in the United States have been able to retain practically the same cost advantages over U. S. manufacturers as they had for their production in Japan. Therefore, comparative cost structures can provide organizations with strategic advantages, but the realization of how such economic benefits accrue to benefit an alliance is not clear. Consequently, we believe that a broader view should be taken.

One way of taking this broader perspective is to recognize the quality of a society's human and institutional resources. These soft societal factors can provide benefits as real to the global firm as the economic factors previously discussed, but they are often overlooked by organization designers. Consistent with this perspective, in the next section we will focus on how the values of a society subtly affect the behaviors of managers in organizations.

CULTURAL VALUES

During the past several years, increasing attention has been paid to how values of managers affect organizational design issues (e.g., Hambrick and Brandon, 1988; Rodriques, 1990). Robert Haas, chairman and CEO of Levi Strauss & Co., states that if companies are going to react quickly to changes in their marketplace, corporate control through values must increase, while control through bureaucratic rules must decrease. As designers delegate more authority to those managers who must implement the strategy, mechanistic structures will not facilitate the type(s) of learning that will bring out needed design changes in global firms. Values will provide a common theme for aligning a variety of organizational change approaches and for designing stable and efficient alliances.

Our goal for this section is not to review and synthesize the common approaches to cultural values, but to apply a schema for understanding value differences across cultures. This schema, developed by Hofstede (1980), is widely recognized as one of the most encompassing value systems in the literature (Jackofsky and Slocum, 1988). It can aid our understanding of the formation and effectiveness of various global strategic business alliances.

A *value* is a broad tendency to prefer a certain state of affairs over others (Hofstede, 1980: 19). The values that people hold about what is desirable and undesirable are embedded in a culture. *Culture* is not a characteristic of individuals, but a collection of individuals who share common values. The influence of national culture in shaping the values of executives has been extensively studied (Hofstede, 1980; Jackofsky, Slocum, and McQuaid, 1988; Hambrick and Brandon, 1988). In Hofstede's schema, there are four cultural values that have consequences for managers: power distance, uncertainty avoidance, individualism-collectivism, and masculinity-femininity. We shall briefly describe each of these dimensions and indicate how it affects managerial behavior. The effect of these values on the implementation of a business alliance strategy will be discussed more fully later.

Power Distance

The extent to which a culture accepts the inequality of the distribution of power between people is called *power distance*. Inequality can occur in a variety of areas, such as social status, prestige, wealth, and the like. The process by which these inequalities are manifested differs widely between societies. In societies with small power distances, such as those in Austria, Israel, Sweden, and the United States, status differences between managers and subordinates are downplayed. Under these conditions, subordinates prefer a consultative decision style that minimizes the power differences between superior and subordinates. Managers in these societies focus on empowering subordinates. The empowering process is predicated on trust and on the subordinate's ability for self-management. In cultures where there are large power differences, such as those in India, Mexico, the Philippines, and Venezuela, centralization of authority is more common and managers employ a more autocratic than democratic leadership style, believing that they are "entitled" to privileges.

Uncertainty Avoidance

Uncertainty avoidance refers to the extent to which people in a culture feel threatened by uncertain or ambiguous situations and try to avoid them. Hofstede contends that organizations use the same techniques as cultures in trying to reduce uncertainty. In primitive cultures, rites and rituals were prescribed by priests to ensure winning wars or reaping bountiful crops. In organizations, rites, rituals, and ceremonies perform similar functions (Trice and Beyer, 1991; Jermier, Slocum, Fry, and Gaines, 1991). Rituals promote positive social cohesion because they concur with the values of the people involved. On the other hand, uncertainty-avoiding organization rituals, such as writing memos and reports to document one's behaviors, may have little positive effect on the individual's performance.

In high uncertainty avoidance cultures, such as those in France, Italy, Japan, Peru, and Portugal, organizations rely on experts and outside consultants for specialized advice, adopt impersonal control and planning systems based on rules and regulations, are highly formalized, and are concerned with employment security and not taking risks. In lower uncertainty avoidance cultures, such as those in Ireland, the Netherlands, Sweden, and the United States, managers are more willing to take risks and to tolerate deviant behaviors of subordinates. In general, there are fewer rules, rituals, and formal standards of behavior.

Individualism-Collectivism

Individualism implies a loosely knit social structure in which people are supposed to take care of themselves and of their immediate family. *Collectivism* implies a tightly knit social structure in which people differentiate between in-groups and out-groups. People expect that in-groups, such as clans and organizations, will protect their members. Members feel that they should be extremely loyal to their in-group. Riesman, Glazer, and Denney (1953), in their seminal work, *The Lonely Crowd,* characterize the North American culture as strongly individualistic, whereas the majority of Asian cultures are characterized as highly collective. This broad characterization has not changed dramatically since 1953. Countries that Hofstede and others have labeled as collective include Brazil, Japan, Korea, Mexico, and Taiwan; countries rated as high in individualism include France, Italy, the Netherlands, Sweden and the former West Germany.

The level of individualism-collectivism has been found to affect members of organizations in a variety of manners. Managers operating in cultures that place a high value on individualism frequently move from company to company (cosmopolitans), believe that the company is not responsible for the welfare of its employees, and believe that higher quality decisions are made by individuals rather than by groups. In cultures that value collectivism, managers are attracted to larger, as opposed to smaller, organizations, attach more importance to one's position in the structure than to one's discretion in performing his or her job, and are morally and socially involved within their organizations.

Masculinity-Femininity

The fourth dimension along which cultures can vary is masculinity-femininity. *Masculinity* refers to the extent to which dominant values in a culture reflect assertiveness, acquisition of tangible things, advancement, and earnings. *Femininity* refers to values of cooperation, quality of life and environment, empathy, and service. In masculine cultures, such as those in Italy, Japan, Mexico, Switzerland, and the former West Germany, people believe that extrinsic organizational rewards (salaries and advancements) are symbols of the successful high achiever. Large-scale organizations are popular; economic growth is seen as a more important problem than conservation of the environment; people should try to excel at being the best; and people live to work. In more feminine cultures, such as those in the Netherlands, Spain, Sweden, and Taiwan, people place more emphasis on cooperation (as opposed to conflict), working conditions, employment security, conservation of the environment, and working to afford to live.

The consequences for organizations are severalfold. In masculine societies, managers believe that the company has the right to interfere in the personal lives of its employees if that is needed for the benefit of the organization. Earnings, individual recognition, advancement, and job challenge are important symbols of success. Traditions going back several centuries are honored ways of conducting business. In more feminine societies, managers practice Theory Y (as opposed to Theory X), praise people through social rewards, use group or team approaches to solve problems, and value the soft intuitive skills more than the hard analytical skills.

INTERACTION OF ECONOMICS AND CULTURAL VALUES

Our thesis is that economic factors and cultural values interact to determine both the choice of alliance configuration and the effectiveness of the implementation process. The requirements of managing the four previously discussed economic factors may prompt the selection of a particular alliance structure. The role of cultural values, however, has profound significance for enhancing the implementation and stability of alliance arrangements, especially the more complex ones. For example, licensing arrangements, which represent the simplest form of alliance activity, are often little more than a formalized arms' length market relationship designed to manage transaction costs across the partners. The national values of the partners' host countries are of little importance to the execution of licensing agreements. On the other hand, the success of chaebols in South Korea is embedded as much in the tightly woven and nurtured cultural values as in the economic factors that provide its solid foundation. (A *chaebol* is a South Korean business group, such as Samsung, Hyundai, Lucky-Goldstar, consisting of large, diversified companies that are owned and managed by family members or relatives that produce an array of products for the global marketplace.) We contend that cultural values are of far greater importance than economics for selecting and managing cross-firm relationships and activities in chaebols than in other types of strategic alliances.

We find that a significant factor in managing cross-border alliances is that of reconciling and harmonizing the different cultural values that both partners bring with them (Hamel et al., 1989). Many U. S. firms have entered into global strategic alliances with European and Japanese partners only to find that these alliances prove very difficult or unworkable because of cultural misunderstandings that were not previously considered. The numerous obstacles that General Electric encountered in its series of alliances with Fujitsu Fanuc in factory automation and with Samsung in microwave ovens were at least partly due to the great chasm in national values that GE faced in its relationships with these partners.

Table 9.1 presents the different elements of organization design that we use to understand the types of strategic alliances. We focus on the formal dimensions of structure, modes of integration, control mechanisms, reward systems, and corporate cultures that reinforce the alliance's design. The considerable research and literature

Table 9.1. Global Strategic Alliances and Their Design Characteristics

Type of Strategic Alliance	Top Manager's Assumptions about Environment	Characteristics of Alliance Designs				
		Structural Dimensions[a]	Integrating Mechanisms[a]	Control Strategies	Reward Systems	Culture Required to Support the Design
License Agreements			Hierarchy	Market	Performance-based	Market
Manufacturing industries	Simple/stable	Formalization	Rules	↓	↓	↓
Service industries	Simple/stable	Specialization	Plans	Bureaucratic		
Joint Ventures			Direct contact			
Functional specialization	Dynamic/stable	Standardization	Liaison roles	↓		
Product shared value-added	Dynamic/complex		Task forces			
			Permanent teams			
			Integrating roles			
Consortia	Dynamic/complex	Centralization	Integrating departments	Clan	Hierarchy-based	Clan

[a]Each alliance structure has a different configuration of structural dimensions and integrating mechanisms.

on environment-organization relationships reveal that top management's underlying assumptions of the environment are often as important as the actual environment itself in influencing organization design. What managers assume about their environment is a function of their cognitive beliefs and processes, as well as the economic forces confronting them. The environment is classified along dimensions of simple to complex and stable to dynamic in order to capture the notions of complexity and change.

ORGANIZATION DESIGN CHARACTERISTICS FOR GLOBAL STRATEGIC ALLIANCES

Structural Dimensions

We have chosen four structural dimensions (formalization, specialization, standardization, and centralization) to describe the internal characteristics of each alliance. These dimensions have proven their usefulness in the management literature and can provide a framework for describing and comparing alliance designs. *Formalization* pertains to the amount of written documentation in the organization. *Specialization* is the degree to which organizational tasks are subdivided into separate jobs. *Standardization* is the extent to which work activities are performed in a uniform manner. *Centralization* refers to the hierarchical level that has the authority to make a decision.

Integrating Mechanisms

There are a number of mechanisms that managers can use to achieve integration. These mechanisms vary on a continuum from the hierarchical chain of command to integrating departments. We have adopted Galbraith's (1973) ninefold classification framework of integration mechanisms. These are listed in order in Table 9.1 as representing an organization's mode of integration from inexpensive and simple to the more complicated and expensive mechanisms of coordination. Galbraith proposes that when managers confront high environmental uncertainty, they choose strategies that are characterized by high interdepartmental activity and high product diversity. To achieve integration, they select mechanisms further down the list than those selected by managers who are pursuing organizational strategies characterized by low uncertainty and diversity. We propose that the center of integration for each alliance moves from comparatively simple licensing arrangements to complex arrangements in chaebol alliance structures. The *center of integration* corresponds to the dominant coordination mode or means which the alliance will utilize to provide consistency of actions. It is analogous to the center of gravity concept that strategic management researchers employ when describing the dominant force that influences choice of strategy.

Control Strategies

Top managers can choose among a variety of strategies to maintain control. Ouchi (1980) identified three control strategies that managers could adopt: market control, bureaucratic control, and clan control. The use of *market control* requires that outputs are such that a price can be assigned based on competition in the marketplace. Without competition, price will not be an accurate reflection of an organization's internal efficiency. *Bureaucratic control* is the use of rules, policies, hierarchy of authority, written documentation, and other bureaucratic mechanisms to standardize behavior and assess performance. *Clan control* is the use of values, rites of passage, traditions, and shared beliefs to control behavior. Organizations that use clan control require trust among employees. Clan control is important when ambiguity and environmental uncertainty are high. Under these conditions, the organization cannot accurately assess the price it puts on its outputs, because rules and policies might not be able to specify appropriate behavior in advance.

Reward Systems

Kerr and Slocum (1987) illustrate that an organization's reward system represents a particularly powerful means for reinforcing an organization's culture. The reward system defines the relationship between the organization and the individual member by specifying the terms of exchange. That is, it specifies the contributions expected from members and the values and norms to which the members must conform. Kerr and Slocum distinguished two types of reward systems: hierarchy- and performance-based. *Hierarchy-based* reward systems use subjective indicators of performance, promote people from within the organization, stress the development of the manager by movement across functional and divisional boundaries, and use informal feedback systems to reward appropriate behaviors. *Performance-based* reward systems use quantitative measures of an employee's behavior, tie compensation directly to performance, and provide few mechanisms of integration between managers and divisions. Hierarchy-based reward systems generate clan cultures, whereas performance-based reward systems are closely aligned with market cultures.

We have alluded that each alliance is created to achieve a myriad of goals. The organizational designs that are appropriate for each alliance are now discussed. Each alliance is designed to cope with the complexity of its environment and to provide a mechanism for learning. The process of executing its design to realistically cope with the exigencies of its environment requires an understanding of the balance between economic factors and cultural values.

TYPES OF GLOBAL ALLIANCES

Licensing Arrangements—Manufacturing Industries

Licensing arrangements have become more prominent in recent years. Many licensing arrangements involve coproduction and supplier agreements in which another firm engages in developing the licensor's technologies or other innovations. On a global basis, licensing agreements represent a purchase of technology in exchange either for market entry into a new region or for help in further refinement of the innovation. Some of the most important economic factors prompting companies to consider licensing their technologies to other firms include the following:

- Inability to capitalize on the technology by itself.
- Desire to preempt the competition by setting industrywide standards early in a product's life cycle.
- Need to maintain industrywide discipline and high levels of innovation in fast-changing technologies.
- Prospect of lucrative sales and service contracts associated with proprietary technology and production processes.

Economic and competitive motives drive licensing arrangements between foreign and domestic alliance partners. Because licensing is an arms' length transaction formalized in a contract or other agreement, its implementation is executed solely through legal and other negotiated channels. The relative importance of cultural values in implementing licensing agreements is minor. They only impact the translation of the concepts and terms in the legal document. The alliance is based on matching partners' market strengths and economic interests. Table 9.2 portrays the dimensions of organization design found in manufacturing-based licensing arrangements.

The structural dimensions of formalization, specialization, standardization, and centralization rate high within this form of alliance. The terms of the arrangement are very specific. Licensors deal with each licensee using standardized performance criteria. This reflects high levels of pooled interdependence among licensees. Manufacturing-based licensing is usually organized along a geographic or a technological dimension. This allows for high levels of specialization across a number of different licensees so that the licensor can control the pace and diffusion of technological development. Authority is delegated through the terms of the agreement. Since licensors, in most cases, are able to erect high switching cost barriers with the licensee, bureaucratic control mechanisms are well defined. These are tightly enforced through performance-based reward criteria.

U. S. firms that have entered into licensing arrangements with foreign firms to develop technological innovations include Sun Microsystems and N.V. Philips. The Dutch giant has the production and distribution capabilities to market Sun's RISC chips in ways unavailable to the U. S. firm. Sun is hoping that its RISC chips, used primarily in workstations and computers, will eventually find their way into consumer products and other industrial products that Philips also manufactures.

Licensors can also disseminate the technology faster across the industry than they could going it alone. The desire to preempt competitors in setting industry standards is a powerful inducement to license new and even unproven technologies early on. Within the computer industry, for example, many firms are racing to license technol-

Table 9.2. Strategic Business Alliance: Licensing Agreements in Manufacturing Industries and Their Design Features

Structural Dimensions	Center of Integration	Control Strategies	Reward System	Culture
High formalization High specialization High standardization High centralization	Hierarchy	Market	Performance-based	Market

ogies to potential users in an attempt to set industrywide standards early on. MIPS Computer Systems licensed its newest microprocessor designs to Siemens of Germany to penetrate the market quickly. It has also signed licensing agreements with Digital Equipment Corp., Texas Instruments, Cypress Semiconductor, Bipolar Integrated Technology of the United States and with Fujitsu, NEC, and Kubota of Japan to produce its chips and market new computers based on its designs.

Cross-licensing is common in industries where R&D and other fixed costs are exorbitant, and where aggressive competition is necessary for maintaining industrywide discipline and innovation. The pharmaceutical and chemical industries are replete with cross-licensing arrangements between global firms to amortize R&D costs and to promote specialization of different research-based competencies.

Licensing arrangements in manufacturing industries are designed to help firms specialize their activities around fast-changing technologies. The need to preempt competitors' innovation efforts, as well as to set industrywide standards early in product life cycles, make licensing agreements viable platforms for managing and perhaps controlling the pace of industrywide change. Cross-licensing is particularly useful in those industries whose technologies move rapidly and in a discontinuous manner. Because technologies are evolving so quickly, very few firms can monitor and manage all of these changes by themselves. Licensing is the simplest way of redirecting a firm's efforts to participate and control the spectrum of new product development through delegation and explicit control mechanisms.

Licensing Arrangements—Service Industries

Service and franchise-based firms have long engaged in licensing arrangements with foreign partners. These range from Anheuser Busch in beverages, McDonald's in restaurants, and Avis Rent-A-Car in rental systems to numerous global hotel chains. Licensing arrangements in service-based industries are especially attractive for managers in mature domestic industries for two reasons: (1) they establish an early market penetration with little direct investment, and (2) they employ a fairly standardized marketing approach to create and control a global image.

As is the case with manufacturing industries, licensing in services reflects strong economic and competitive motives. Formalized by a well-defined legal contract, the role of cultural values in implementing service-based licensing agreements is small. Since licensees are expected to perform largely on an independent basis with local self-initiative, it is important for the licensor to socialize managers and other key personnel in the company's underlying basic values and philosophies. Thus, some degree of value reconciliation and mutual understanding of local practices and customs is important to smooth out the execution of the arrangement. Table 9.3 presents the basic organization design configurations found in the service-based licensing arrangement.

Desiring to enter new markets quickly and without substantial capital investment, U. S. firms have actively trained and worked with licensees to develop customized marketing programs in each region without compromising their overall global image. By building up a strong cadre of loyal licensees, U. S. firms have been able to build a substantial and sustainable global presence. This has helped to outflank domestic rivals at home with less international presence. Avis, for example, has franchisees

Table 9.3. Strategic Business Alliance: Licensing Agreements in Service Industries and Their Design Features

Structural Dimensions	Center of Integration	Control Strategies	Reward System	Culture
High formalization High specialization High standardization High centralization	Hierarchy	Market	Performance-based	Market

throughout the world that use the company's logo and specific corporate-developed procedures in exchange for royalty fees. In addition to a thorough training program, Avis maintains tight financial and marketing control over franchisees' activities to ensure high levels of performance, often measured along quantitative assessments of profitability and customer satisfaction.

As is the case with manufacturing industries, licensing in services is designed to help the parent firm develop a global presence through careful partner selection, delegation, and performance-based reward systems. Services-based licensing is especially useful in helping the parent firm learn of early changes and new trends that occur in different regional markets. Licensees monitor customer preferences, tastes, and requirements. Since successful licensing in services and franchises depends on a high level of loyalty and commitment, many firms have redesigned their training and development programs to ensure that licensees are thoroughly familiar with corporate philosophy, values, and procedures.

Joint Ventures—Functional Specialization

The vast number of global joint ventures consummated over the past few years heralds a recognition that more sophisticated alliances are needed to compete in many capital-intensive and fast-moving industries. Joint ventures that specialize functional activities across partners involve creating a new entity in which each partner brings and contributes a distinctive competence in particular value-adding activity (e.g., one produces and another markets). These ventures are closely associated with the "X-form" of alliance described by Porter and Fuller (1986). "X-form" describes ventures that represent attempts by partnering firms to compensate for one another's weakness by relying on the other's source of strength. The complementary strengths of both partners help reduce the amount of capital investment and risk that one partner would otherwise have to incur. Although specific configurations of functional specialization ventures will differ according to mission and industry, they share the following underlying economic and competitive motives: (1) the need for quasi-vertical integration with low levels of investment intensity; (2) the need for economies of scale and scope in value-adding activities; and (3) the need to learn a partner's core competence or skill or to gain market access.

While these economic and competitive motives may induce firms to consider specialization joint ventures, the understanding and harmonization of different cultural values become critical to smooth implementation and alliance stability. Even though switching costs for both partners is likely to be high because of complementary economic strengths, these alliances can face many rough obstacles to smooth implementation when different cultural values are meshed without careful planning.

Table 9.4 presents the structural and integrative dimensions of organization design for specialization joint ventures. These ventures reflect a high level of specialization according to their partners' complementary distinctive competencies. Where one partner manufactures while the other partner controls market access, a specialization venture is likely to ensue. This is particularly salient when both firms face resource scarcity and a high risk in translating innovations into new products. Levels of standardization and formalization will vary across specific ventures, but range in the middle. The need for partners to understand one another's different operating procedures, quality standards, planning processes, and reporting relationships must occur. These ventures are also likely to exhibit a medium degree of centralization, since day-to-day contact along functional lines requires sequential planning that is frequently adjusted to meet the vagaries of the situation. The center of integration will move more toward linking roles and away from rules and performance standards found in licensing arrangements. Authority is delegated to managers closest to the area of action. Integration depends not only on the formal structure but also on the cooperative efforts of key personnel (e.g., design engineers or manufacturing personnel) for effective implementation of the alliance. Many of these ventures are organized along crucial value-adding functions, such as marketing and distribution. Integration is particularly important when the joint venture involves organizations from two different national cultures. On the one hand, the economic imperatives of specialization ventures mandate high levels of functional coordination; on the other hand, managing flows of technology and skills across partners from different cultural backgrounds depends on managers that can understand and trust one another. This occurs only after long personal contact and socialization. Reward systems are likely to reflect the dual needs of balanced economic contributions from both partners, as well as the intricacies of learning and skill transfers.

Examples of how specialization ventures must reconcile both economic motives for creating the alliance and harmonizing different national values for smooth implementation include those of JVC-Thomson (Japan-France) and Ford-Mazda (U. S.-Japan). In both cases, each partner needed the others' value-adding capabilities, which it did not have. In the Thomson-JVC case, a French electronics and defense firm teamed up with a Japanese consumer electronics giant in order to learn the latter's skills in precision manufacturing of microelectronics. JVC desired to learn how to produce and market to an increasingly important European marketplace. As a national firm strongly influenced and once controlled by the French government, Thomson

Table 9.4. Strategic Business Alliance: Joint Ventures-Functional Specialization and Their Design Features

Structural Dimensions	Center of Integration	Control Strategies	Reward System	Culture
Medium formalization High specialization Medium standardization Medium centralization	Plans and liaison roles	Bureaucratic	Mixed hierarchy and performance-based	Mixed clan and market

embodied many of the macrocultural characteristics described by Hofstede (1980): high power distance, high uncertainty avoidance, medium to high individualism, and medium masculinity. JVC, a well-entrenched Japanese firm, exhibited many of the management practices embedded in the national culture of Japan: medium power distance, high uncertainty avoidance, medium individualism, and high masculinity. The meshing of these disparate cultural dimensions was reflected in the way both firms viewed their partnership. Thomson designed the alliance so that sufficiently high levels of organizational learning could occur (reflecting high uncertainty avoidance), while JVC attempted to control the flow of technology in a measured approach (also reflecting high uncertainty avoidance). Partners working with one another also evidenced high levels of corporate training and development practiced in each company (medium individualism). The strong direct interest in the venture's success demonstrated each society's high uncertainty avoidance.

The Ford-Mazda relationship exemplifies a specialization venture focusing on design and production value-adding activities. Ford believed it needed Mazda's highly sophisticated skills to design and produce a new generation of compact cars. Mazda needed Ford's access to the U. S. market, as well as Ford's production facilities to bypass possible quotas and to lower costs. Escort cars designed by Mazda and assembled by Ford in Michigan are the product of this specialization joint venture. The different national values that both partners brought to the venture were manifested in the alliance's implementation. The United States has a low to medium power distance, low to medium uncertainty avoidance, high individualism, and high masculinity. Japan rates medium on power distance, high on uncertainty avoidance, medium on individualism, and high on masculinity. The meshing of these different cultural bases implies that both partners may not view their participation in the venture with the same underlying assumptions. High uncertainty avoidance indicates that the Japanese find technology transfers to a foreign partner to be a risky proposition, since it may create a new competitor. On the other hand, low uncertainty avoidance for Ford managers means learning as much as possible from its foreign partner. An alliance blending differences on this dimension means that application of technology and learning may not occur equally in both partners. A difference in individualism scores posed problems in implementation, as well. Japanese management practices encouraged conformity and adherence to plans. In contrast, U. S. managers typically prefer to make changes in plans along the way.

Even before the car was made, there were implementation problems. Mazda engineers wanted to get the car designed and produced as quickly as possible. Their entire design and production was driven by tight deadlines. No one ever missed them (high uncertainty avoidance). When Ford engineers were even just a few days late, the Mazda engineers were absolutely furious at them. Many Ford engineers had to work 80 hours a week to make sure that future deadlines weren't passed. Ford engineers also found an absence of bureaucracy at Mazda. While Ford engineers spent time sending ideas up the hierarchy for review and getting approvals, their counterparts at Mazda did almost no paperwork. Once the design was approved by senior management, the cultural value of power distance ensured that there were no revisions made or offered by subordinates.

To the extent that partners show considerable differences along cultural dimensions, greater integrative efforts are needed to understand and reconcile them for alliance stability. The JVC-Thomson partnership reflects both organizations' high levels of uncertainty avoidance, particularly on matters of learning skills and technologies. The Ford-Mazda relationship reflects the mutual need by both partners for critical skills, but also the potential for asymmetric learning and other conflicting patterns of decision making that emanate from differences in individualism and other dimensions.

Specialized joint ventures help accelerate many firms' efforts to change and refocus their value-adding activities by renewing sources of competitive advantage. The JVC-Thomson and Mazda-Ford ventures expanded both firms' organizational learning potential in ways that neither firm could accomplish alone. In each case, partners were able to learn new skills and technological refinements from each other. This is critical in global industries, such as automobiles and consumer electronics, where manufacturing technologies are becoming more sophisticated. In addition, specialization ventures provide firms with a window on new technologies and production methods utilized by their partners. This form of external alliance-based learning greatly complements internal formal R&D efforts to develop and nurture critical core competences for competitive advantage. Unlike licensing agreements, which are implemented essentially through contracts, successful learning of new skills in specialization ventures requires both firms to recognize the potent differences in the partners' underlying national values and to design the alliance carefully around them.

Joint Ventures—Product Shared Value-Added

Another form of joint venture that has surfaced in recent years is one in which both partners participate and share in similar value-adding activities (e.g., they design, produce, and market jointly). Unlike the specialization ventures in which partners pool complementary strengths, shared value-added ventures involve partners with relatively equal competencies. These ventures are closely related to the Y-form of alliance described by Porter and Fuller (1986). The term *Y-form* is used to describe attempts by partnering firms to bring similar types of strengths to the venture; they are searching for greater critical mass in shared and similar value-adding activities. Shared value-added ventures are particularly useful for firms that face growing levels of risk and faster organizational learning when developing new products and technologies that approach global economies of scale, such as commercial aircraft and robotics. Some of the economic and competitive motives prompting shared value-added ventures include (1) fast upgrading and assimilation of different technologies and skills for a given product class by learning a partner's skills; (2) desire to shape the evolution of competitive activity in that industry; and (3) economics of scale that neither partner can generate alone.

Some of the most recently consummated shared value-added ventures include IBM and Siemens to design and produce the next generation of 64-megabit chips, Fuji-Xerox in photocopying and imaging, Corning Glass's numerous ventures with partners in glass and fiber optics, and Texas Instruments and Hitachi in computer chips. When compared with specialization ventures, shared value-added ventures depend even more on understanding and the harmonization of different cultural values for effective implementation. The switching costs, of course, are commensurately higher, but so are the risks for unintended technology loss and "de-skilling." Since these ventures involve constant day-to-day contact between managers in the same value-adding activities, the problems of high reciprocal interdependence are present. Table 9.5 presents the organization design characteristics of shared value-added ventures.

Shared value-added ventures are organized along product lines. Because partnering involves bringing together similar or related strengths and competencies, structural dimensions of formalization, specialization, standardization, and centralization are likely to be low. As risks in technology development grow, levels of differentiation will remain low to provide the possible benefits of faster learning and economies of scale. These would be greatly diminished in a highly differentiated venture. The center of integration is more complex and costlier than those of specialization ventures. It often involves a combination of linking roles, task forces, and committees to integrate across many different skill sets brought by both partners. Continuous everyday contact between managers requires integrative efforts that move steadily closer to a team-based approach and away from cumbersome hierarchical integrative mechanisms. Control strategies and mechanisms for managing shared value-added ventures reflect the need for both bureaucratic and clan approaches. Providing the context for building scale economies requires some degree of bureaucratic control, while learning and nurturing new skills demand a high level of managerial autonomy. In addition, reward systems are also likely to reflect a hierarchical pattern, because it is difficult to quantify specific measures of technological innovation, skill upgrading, and organizational learning by individual members.

An example of how global firms have dealt with the problem of reconciling different cultural values into shared value-added ventures is provided by Corning Glass Works and its numerous global partners. Corning's series of ventures represents a novel approach to understanding and managing disparate cultural values, whose maladjustment could easily compromise the alliance's stability and usefulness. Corning is currently involved in some 23 different global ventures. Its partners include Siemens for fiber optics, Ciba-Geigy in medical diagnostic equipment, Samsung in fiber optics and television tubes, Asahi glass in new optics fabrication technology, and several other ventures in China and elsewhere. Faced with a plethora of different cultures, Corning manages each of its ventures in the following way to ensure effective implementation. First, the company undertakes a long "prenuptial" courtship with each prospective alliance partner to assess its motives and the quality of its management. Only after top management is comfortable with the prospective partner do negotiations on alliance formation proceed. Second, Corning does not insist on complete dominance in each venture; instead, it does not hesitate to use the Corning name in a secondary role—for example: Ciba-Corning, Siecor, Samsung-Corning, and Dow-

Table 9.5. Strategic Business Alliance: Joint Ventures-Product Shared Value-Added and Their Design Features

Structural Dimensions	Center of Integration	Control Strategies	Reward System	Culture
Medium–low formalization	Liaison roles	Clan	Hierarchy-based	Clan
Low specialization	Task forces			
Low standardization				
Low centralization				

Corning. This helps downplay the need for imposing U. S. values on a disparate set of alliance partners. In effect, Corning tries to integrate itself with the values brought by the other parent firm to the joint venture. Third, Corning believes in giving each joint venture considerable autonomy and insists that its partner do the same. By providing real autonomy from corporate parents, managers from both organizations have the scope and discretion to engage in the kind of day-to-day compromising and personal negotiation that is necessary for stability and learning. This element is also consistent with U. S. managers' propensity for relatively low levels of power distance.

In another setting that highlights the critical role of values in implementing global alliances, AT&T has become adroit in formulating and implementing its series of strategic alliances across Europe. The U. S. telecommunications and computer giant has been anxious to expand its presence across the continent, but it stumbled in one of its earliest joint ventures with Olivetti of Italy. Unlike Corning Glass Works, in which the U. S. partner fully understood the need for harmonizing and smoothing out different cultural value differences, AT&T approached its venture with Olivetti without recognizing the salient differences between U. S. and Italian cultural values and operating styles. Originally conceived as a vehicle for sharing production and marketing of computers, the venture ran into serious implementation difficulties. Olivetti, an old-line Italian firm, embraced many of these cultural characteristics: medium power distance, relatively high uncertainty avoidance, medium-to-high individualism, and high masculinity. AT&T probably rates significantly lower in uncertainty avoidance and much higher in individualism. Some of the deep cultural differences that manifested themselves in day-to-day relationships included Olivetti's allegations of AT&T's insistence that the venture solve its own problems (resulting from differences in individualism), heavy-handedness in negotiations (an outcome of high individualism and power distance), and less emphasis on structuring venture activities (emanating from the U. S. firm's lower uncertainty avoidance). In addition, what complicated the venture's stability was a gradual but discernible divergence in the partner's original missions: telecommunications and computers did not technologically converge as quickly as either firm believed. Both sides had different opinions concerning a myriad of short- and long-term financial results.

The difficulties AT&T experienced with Olivetti may have actually helped AT&T learn more of the European marketplace, as well as understand different values and cultures between nations. In managing its series of alliances with other partners, such as Italtel of Italy, Telefónica of Spain, and N. V. Philips of the Netherlands, AT&T took an approach similar to that of Corning. For example, it maintained a low public profile to avoid a perception of dominance, relied more on local nationals to give an accurate picture of domestic political and economic conditions, and created a European, rather than an American, identity.

Finally, another venture in which the U. S. partner had to understand and manage deep cultural differences is that of General Electric's jet-engine venture with Snecma of France. Conceived originally as a means for both firms to participate in supplying aircraft built by Airbus Industrie, the GE-Snecma deal is now among the most successful ventures in Europe, with over $11 billion in commitments secured in 1989. Once a government-controlled concern, Snecma's managers illustrated many of France's distinctive cultural characteristics: relatively high power distance, very high uncertainty avoidance, medium individualism, and medium-to-low masculinity. On all four dimensions, the U. S. managers reflect different cultural values of the United States. In particular, values of lower uncertainty avoidance, higher masculinity, and lower power distance were noted. These differences manifested themselves in the way the French managers approached problems. According to executives in the venture, the French managers viewed problem solving through data accumulation, while U. S. managers were more intuitive (reflecting the differences in uncertainty avoidance). The French also preferred to bring in consultants from their armed forces and government, while GE preferred to use its own executives (power distance and masculinity differences). Nevertheless, the venture has worked well, not only because of its 50-50 structure but also because both sides have given their senior executives broad authority to manage the day-to-day operations. Although both firms share equally in the production and marketing of the commercial jet engines, some specific tasks have been divided among the partners to speed up production time: GE manages most of the system design and high-technology work, while Snecma builds the fans, boosters, and turbines.

Shared value-adding ventures enable firms to participate across a host of different technologies and skills contributed by both partners. The meshing of disparate cultural values from the parent firms into the venture entails significant changes in the reward systems to nurture close, day-to-day contact between managers. The examples of Corning Glass Works and AT&T show how firms must often change their venture policies every time a new partner from a different culture is brought in. Successful implementation of these ventures depends on both partners' recognition of the critical role values play in organization design and learning. As Corning found out, every venture is different and requires mutual adjustment because of the value differences found across the world.

Nevertheless, successful shared value-adding ventures require both partners to ensure that the venture has enough autonomy to chart its own path. This will allow the managers themselves to create and redesign the venture's unique reward systems and culture to encourage learning from one another.

Chaebols

According to Steers, Shin, and Ungson (1989) and Lee, Yoo, and Lee (1991), chaebols share some common organizational features that reflect deep-seated cultural values of Korean society. First, chaebols are controlled by families through stock ownership. This is important since the Korean cultural tradition places responsibility on the eldest son to inherit most of the family property and to assume decision-making responsibility. Family members hold both financial and top management positions.

Second, chaebols are managed by one strong paternalistic male figure. The CEO assumes personal responsibility for most decisions and makes many of the decisions. This is rooted in the Confucian tradition that requires decision makers to balance the needs of the organization and the harmony of the group. Decision making is centralized and the structure is highly formalized. For example, Chung Ju-Yung, founder and former chairman of the Hyundai Group, made all decisions. No one dared to challenge him (high power distance). Every morning between 6:00 and 6:30, he would receive telephone calls from Hyundai's foreign operations. This high degree of centralization of decision making is characteristic in most chaebols and reflects a value of high uncertainty avoidance. It is the subordinate's job to make his superior's decision work and not question it.

Third, there are centralized planning and coordination boards. The primary functions of these boards are to analyze data and present recommendations to the chairmen for decision making. The planning board often plays a major role in human resource decisions. This group is responsible for screening all candidates and assigning college graduates hired by the chaebol to member organizations. These actions ensure continuity and coordination of human resources across organizations. This group is also responsible for overseeing the overall salary and bonus system used within each chaebol.

Fourth, there are close personal ties between the South Korean government and the chaebols. The government uses its power through preferential loans and interest, licensing authorizations, and the inclusion or exclusion of companies in its five-year economic development plans. To assure continued success, the chaebols support the incumbent political party and make donations to the "right" causes. Failure to politically support the party has led to termination of financing and bankruptcy, as in the case of the Kukje Group.

Fifth and finally, educational credentials are critical to a manager's success. Attending a prestigious Korean college almost guarantees the student a job with one of the best chaebols. For example, at Lucky-Goldstar, of the 15 top executives, 73 percent graduated from Seoul National University; at Samsung, 55 percent graduated from Seoul National University; and in Sunkyong, 75 percent graduated from Seoul National University. School ties are important in a status-oriented society (high masculinity) and ensure that the newcomer has a value system embraced by the chaebol's elite management team.

These characteristics greatly affect the designs of chaebols, as shown in Table 9.6. South Korean managers place more emphasis on personal contacts and relationships than on written contracts. In licensing joint ventures, for example, personal relationships are often utilized to secure a business deal, but little time is spent on nurturing these. Economic factors most often dedicate the relationship of the parties. In chaebols, interpersonal networking across members' organizations in the chaebol is fostered by the movement of human resources across organizations and the active role of the planning group in influencing these practices. Most Korean managers spend considerable time in developing and nurturing personal relationships. These relationships govern decision making. When a manager submits his proposal for a new product to his peers, it serves to tell others of the new venture and quickly diffuses responsibility for implementing the decision after it had been made by the planning committee.

Table 9.6. Strategic Business Alliance: Consortia and Their Design Features

Structural Dimensions	Center of Integration	Control Strategies	Reward System	Culture
Low formalization	Task forces	Clan	Hierarchy-based	Clan
High specialization	Integrating roles			
Low standardization	Integrating departments			
Medium–high centralization				

Maintaining personal relationships and enhancing mutual gains are critical in such situations.

According to Steers et al. (1989), another aspect of maintaining personal relationships is the concept of *nunch'i*. *Nunch'i* roughly translates as "the look in someone's eyes." Korean managers pride themselves in their ability to read someone's face. In developing personal relationships, nonverbal behavior is critical. There is a Korean proverb that translates "one who does not have *nunch'i* cannot succeed." The ability to silently read the other manager's mind and to understand the problem from that manager's perspective is salient. Relationships and not legal contracts govern decisions.

IMPLICATIONS FOR ORGANIZATION SCIENTISTS

During the 1960s, most theoretical and empirical studies in strategic management focused on examining the economic behavior of single-business and vertically integrated firms in domestic, oligopolistic settings. With the advent of resource scarcity and inflation during the 1970s, strategic management and organizational theory researchers focused on diversification and resource dependency issues. The strategic business unit was the unit of analysis. The 1980s brought the full impact of global competition and economic restructuring home to U. S. firms. Researchers are now beginning to reflect this trend. As we enter the mid-1990s, organizational science needs to balance its efforts between studying domestic and hierarchically structured organizations and studying global networks and hybrid organizational arrangements. Additional theoretical development is especially needed concerning alliances and other hybrid organizational arrangements that involve managers from two or more different cultural value systems. This is fertile ground for multidisciplinary theory and research, and studies in this area will continue to grow.

From an economic transactions-cost perspective, Borys and Jemison (1989) note that strategic alliances may be thought of as hybrid organizational arrangements that lay somewhere between "markets and hierarchies" (Thorelli, 1986; Williamson, 1985). Viewed in this way, alliances represent alternative organization designs that transfer and distribute new benefits among the original partners—benefits that neither partner could have garnered on its own. Alliances are presumed to function in a fairly stable manner as long as economic conditions for optimizing efficiency exist (Jarillo, 1988). While a pure transactions-cost approach to examining alliances can provide some useful platforms for building theory, the major pitfall of this perspective is that it tends not to consider potential contingency influences (e.g., product life cycle or technological intensity) that could provide more insight into selecting the actual mode of alliance configuration. Moreover, a transactions-cost perspective assumes that the parties to the alliance share a common set of underlying economic assumptions, similar propensity for opportunism, and tolerance for ambiguity—factors that may not weigh equally across different cultures.

From a strategic management perspective, alliances are viewed increasingly as mechanisms to enhance organizational learning of new skills and capabilities to build sources of competitive advantage (Hamel et al., 1989; Ohmae, 1989). Unlike the pure transactions-cost approach, researchers in strategic management have developed numerous theories concerning the rise and purposes of alliances. The recent focus on strategic alliances as new research areas is a timely development, given the field's continued emphasis on building a multidisciplinary approach to theory development and inquiry. However, we have argued that research on the relative importance of cultural values in managing implementation issues needs to be undertaken (Milliman, Von Glinow, and Nathan, 1991).

Developing theories and studies that are able to simultaneously reconcile the need to understand economic and cultural values with a multicultural perspective is a challenging task. Economic and environmental changes may give rise to numerous opportunities for developing theories concerning strategy formulation, but an understanding of how different cultures are vital linchpins to strategy implementation is needed. This is particularly important in alliances, networks, and other hybrid arrangements.

As a starting point for testing our thesis that managers need to consider both economics and cultural values, we offer the following propositions:

> *Proposition 1:* Licensing arrangements are driven purely by economic and competitive factors. Cultural values of both partners are tangential to implementation.
>
> *Proposition 2:* In both specialization and shared value-added joint ventures, economic conditions of scale, learning, and risk reduction may induce alliance formation, but managing different cultural values becomes the driving element for effective implementation.
>
> *Proposition 3:* In chaebols, cultural values dominate the choice of alliance partner and implementation processes; economic conditions are largely tangential.

As alliances grow more complex, the following characteristics of an organization's design are likely to occur:

> *Proposition 4:* The center of integration is likely to move from hierarchy to integrating teams as the environment becomes more dynamic and the alliance configuration embodies the design characteristics of chaebols.
>
> *Proposition 5:* The control strategy will move from a market form to a clan form as the environment becomes more dynamic and the alliance configuration becomes more complex.
>
> *Proposition 6:* Market-based performance reward systems are likely to predominate in the more elementary alliance configurations; hierarchy-based reward systems will predominate in complex chaebols.

IMPLICATIONS FOR MANAGERS

The strategic alliances outlined in this chapter have themes that characterize their structure, information-processing capabilities, control strategies, and reward systems. These features create designs that facilitate organizational learning in each strategic alliance. At the same time, alliances resist change for several reasons. First, alliances are shaped by a coherent array of structural dimensions and control systems. These determine the standards of success, what information is attended to, and what behaviors the reward system reinforces. It also establishes parameters that create premises for learning. In fact, each alliance controls the amount and scope of learning. This makes it hard for managers to recognize fundamentally new problems that were never envisioned in designing the original alliance.

Second, managers resist change because they are inextricably embedded in the political interests of the alliance they helped design. Successful managers have learned, internalized, and honed a repertoire of strategic skills and resources.

Third, the design characteristics of each alliance's structure are mutually reinforcing. Trying to change one design characteristic in a manner that is inconsistent with other design characteristics will lead to instability of the alliance.

Matching Organizational Learning with Alliance Design

Matching alliance configuration with quality of learning requires managers to understand the inherent limitations of the information-processing capabilities of each type of alliance. For example, licensing arrangements accommodate themselves well to simple forms of static learning that require little continuous feedback to upgrade skills, technologies, or production processes. On the other extreme, shared value-added joint ventures and chaebols are designed to enhance continuous learning for all participants involved. However, highly sophisticated alliances may seriously underperform and actually denigrate learning potential when each partner limits itself to static learning. An alliance structure may become one-sided or highly unstable when a partner attempts to engage in continuous learning within a simple alliance framework. Table 9.7 highlights the potential fits between static and continuous learning with complexity of alliance design.

In cell 1 of Table 9.7, simple alliance configurations work well with static forms of learning. The primary rationale for the alliance is economic and performance-based. Partners within the alliance view the arrangement as enhancing economies of scale, filling out their product line(s), or increasing returns on an existing investment. The history of Avis, Hertz, McDonalds, and other aggressive licensors of patents and brand names is marked by one-shot transfers of knowledge and skills. Each franchisee's performance is subsequently evaluated by short-term, market-based criteria. Learning remains confined to operational efficiency and gradual upgrading of relatively routinized skills. Even manufacturing industries may exhibit some of the characteristics of

Table 9.7. Matching Organizational Learning with Alliance Design

| | | Alliance Configuration | |
		Simple	Complex
Organizational Learning	**Static**	Cell 1 Strategic fit Criteria: Economic	Cell 2 Strategic misfit
	Continuous	Cell 3 Strategic misfit	Cell 4 Strategic fit Criteria: Cultural values

static learning with alliance simplicity, such as the numerous cross-licensing and cross-marketing arrangements found in the chemical and pharmaceutical industries. The role of cultural values pales as the significance of return on investment and other economic criteria increases.

In cell 2 of Table 9.7, the combination of alliance complexity with static learning leads to a serious misfit between each partner's information-processing capability and the alliance's objectives. For example, the highly touted joint venture between DuPont and Philips viewed the alliance as a simple way to build size and scale. This alliance soon came under fierce attack from better financed and more aggressive continuous-learning competitors. Many joint ventures in cell 2 face the problem of a mismatch between partners' skills and capabilities with the intention of the alliance. When partners formulate a highly complex alliance with static learning goals, the usual result is that the temporarily enhanced economies of scale and efficiency contributed by both partners eventually decays over time because of superior technological advances made by other competitors. Although values are important to making the relationship work, a limited focus on building size and scale still makes this combination unworkable.

Cell 3 of Table 9.7 also represents a serious misfit between a simple alliance configuration and the potential for continuous learning. For example, when one partner in a licensing arrangement views the alliance as a basis for filling out his product line and the other partner engages in aggressive, proactive learning of the underlying technology, the end result is that the licensor eventually becomes dependent on the licensee over time. The licensing relationship between General Electric and Samsung in microwave ovens typifies the potential misfit between simple alliance forms and when a partner seeks to expand learning potential beyond the scope of the alliance's framework. Westinghouse may be facing a similar phenomenon in its relationship with ASEA Brown-Boveri, an aggressive European producer of power generation equipment. Westinghouse views its joint venture with ABB as a means to consolidate its mature, power-generation business, while ABB looks at the venture as a way to learn new skills and technologies that it has not yet mastered.

Cell 4 typifies a strategic fit between highly complex alliance designs with advanced, continuous learning. In this case, both partners have committed themselves to continuous learning within the context of an alliance mechanism that demands carefully managed cultural blending and mutual understanding of values. IBM and Siemens' series of shared value-added joint ventures concerning 16-M and 64-M computer chips matches the technological capabilities of the two giants, as well as the underlying corporate and national cultures. As further evidence that the two firms have potentially sidetracked any possible cultural obstacles, their joint work on 16-M chips will be undertaken in IBM's facility in a third country, France.

Thus, managers competing within a global environment need to understand the relative contribution of their alliance mechanism to building competitive advantage, along with the potential for different kinds of learning. A serious mismatch between alliance design with different forms of learning will lead to instability and to potential exit from the business itself. On the other hand, a close match between alliance design with learning potential enhances both partners' skills and encourages future forms of collaboration.

NOTES

Support for this research was given by the Halliburton Foundation in cooperation with the Center for Research, Cox School of Business, and the U. S. Army Research Institute for Behavioral and Social Sciences. The authors would like to acknowledge the constructive comments made by Joan Brett, Laura Cardinal, Gary Hamel, George Huber, Dileep Hurry, Ellen Jackofsky, Ray Miles, Richard Osborn, and Robin Pinkley.

REFERENCES

Borys, B., and Jemison, D. 1989. Hybrid arrangements as strategic alliances: theoretical issues in organizational combinations. *Academy of Management Review,* 14: 234–249.

Ferguson, C. H. 1990. Computers and the coming of the U. S. Keiretsu. *Harvard Business Review,* 68(4): 55–70.

Galbraith, J. R. 1973. *Designing complex organizations.* Reading, MA: Addison-Wesley.

Ghoshal, S. 1987. Global strategy: an organizing framework. *Strategic Management Journal,* 8: 425–440.

Hambrick, D. C., and Brandon, G. L. 1988. Executive values. In Hambrick, D. C. (Ed.), *The executive effect: concepts and methods for studying top managers* (pp. 3–34). Greenwich, CT: JAI Press.

Hamel, G., Doz, Y. L., and Prahalad, C. K. 1989. Collaborate with your competitors—and win. *Harvard Business Review,* 67(1): 133–139.

Hofstede, G. 1980. *Culture's consequences: individual differences in work-related values.* Beverly Hills, CA: Sage.

Huber, G. 1991. Organizational learning: an examination of the contributing processes and a review of the literatures. *Organization Science,* 2(1): 88–115.

Jackofsky, E. F., and Slocum, J. W., Jr. 1988. CEO roles across cultures. In Hambrick, D. C. (Ed.), *The executive effect: concepts and methods for studying top managers* (pp. 67–100). Greenwich, CT: JAI Press.

Jackofsky, E. F., Slocum, J. W., Jr., and McQuaid, S. 1988. Cultural values and the CEO: alluring companions? *Academy of Management Executive,* 2: 39–49.

Jarillo, J. C. 1988. On strategic networks. *Strategic Management Journal,* 9: 34–41.

Jermier, J., Slocum, J. W., Jr., Fry, L. W., and Gaines, J. 1991. Organizational subculture in a soft bureaucracy: resistance behind the myth and facade of an official culture. *Organization Science,* 2: 170–194.

Kerr, J., and Slocum, J. W., Jr. 1987. Managing corporate cultures through reward systems. *Academy of Management Executive,* 1: 99–108.

Lee, S. M., Yoo, S., and Lee, T. M. 1991. Korean chaebols: corporate values and strategies. *Organizational Dynamics,* 19(4): 36–50.

Lei, D., and Slocum, J. W., Jr. 1991. Global strategic alliances: payoffs and pitfalls. *Organizational Dynamics,* 19(3): 44–62.

Lorange, P., and Roos, S. 1991. Why some strategic alliances succeed and others fail. *Journal of Business Strategy.* Jan.-Feb., pp. 25–30.

Milliman, J., Von Glinow, M. A., and Nathan, M. 1991. Organizational life cycles and strategic international human resource management in multinational companies: implications for congruence theory. *Academy of Management Review,* 16: 318–339.

Ohmae, K. 1989. Companyism and do more better. *Harvard Business Review,* 67(1): 125–132.

Osborn, R. N. and Baughn, C. C. 1990. Forms of organizational governance for multinational alliances. *Academy of Management Journal,* 33: 503–519.

Ouchi, W. G. 1980. Markets, bureaucracies and clans. *Administrative Science Quarterly,* 25: 129–141.

Porter, M. E., and Fuller, M. 1986. Coalitions and global strategy. In Porter, M. E. (Ed.), *Competition in global industries* (pp. 315–344). Boston, MA: Harvard Business School Press.

Prahalad, C. K., and Hamel, G. 1990. The core competence of the corporation. *Harvard Business Review,* 68(3): 79–93.

Rapoport, C. 1991. Why Japan keeps on winning. *Fortune,* July 15, pp. 76–77; 80–81; 84–85.

Riesman, D., Glazer, N., and Denny, R. 1953. *The lonely crowd: a study of changing American character.* New York: Doubleday.

Rodriques, C. A. 1990. The situation and national culture as contingencies for leadership behavior: two conceptual models. In Nath, R. (Ed.), *Advances in international comparative management,* Vol. 5 (pp. 51–68). Greenwich, CT: JAI Press.

Schneider, S. C., and Meyer, A. 1991. Interpreting and responding to strategic issues: the impact of national culture. *Strategic Management Journal,* 12: 307–320.

Steers, R. M., Shin, Y. K., and Ungson, G. R. 1989. *The chaebol: Korea's new industrial might.* New York: Harper and Row.

Thorelli, H. B. 1986. Networks: between markets and hierarchies. *Strategic Management Journal,* 7: 37–51.

Trice, H. M., and Beyer, J. M. 1991. Cultural leadership in organizations. *Organization Science,* 2: 149–169.

Williamson, O. E. 1985. *The economic institutions of capitalism.* New York: Free Press.

10

(Re)Designing Dynamic Organizations

PETER R. MONGE

> He [sic] that will not apply new remedies must expect new evils.
>
> Sir Francis Bacon

> If you want to understand something, try to change it.
>
> Walter Fenno Dearborn

EDITORS' SUMMARY

Almost all prescriptive work on organization design is focused on achieving a good fit or match among an organization's components or among the organization's design and the determinants of its design. Although it may consider "turbulent environments" and "executive succession," rarely does it operationally deal with the dynamics of the relationships among these components or determinants. This chapter by Monge is unusual and commendable in that it examines the process of organizational design from a dynamic perspective and describes a set of techniques that an organization designer can use to analyze and deal with the dynamics of these relationships.

The first section of the chapter presents Alexander's error reduction perspective of design. The essence of this perspective centers on minimizing misfits for the organization outcome values that an organization design is intended to control. *Misfits* are defined as the difference between target values specified by the designer for organization outcome variables and the actual values created by the design. *Organization design* is viewed as an iterative process that attempts to improve organization effectiveness by successive approximation.

The second section presents a strategy for identifying dynamic design variables and for assessing the dynamic relation between alternative designs and organization effectiveness. The initial focus is on the relation between target values specified by managers and actual values generated by designs. These are combined to create the values for the misfit variables. Next, the relations between misfit and design variables are explored in terms of six components: magnitude, trend, continuity, rate of change, duration, and cyclicity. These components are applied to the relations between single design and outcome variables, as well as to relations between clusters of design and outcome variables. All relations are examined over time.

The third section examines a major research effort in the area of open office design. This example is reviewed because it followed a fairly precise design process that did not include the procedures described in this paper. That shortcoming provides a opportunity to illustrate the advantages of the dynamic error reduction perspective.

The fourth and final section concludes with implications for organization designers and organizational scientists and with step-by-step guidelines that direct implementation of the design strategy described and proposed. ■

> The process of design, even when it has become self-conscious, remains a process of error reduction. (Alexander, 1964: 120)

Starbuck and Nystrom (1981: xiii) assert that "all designers hope to improve organizations—to make organizations more efficient, more humane, more rational, more fun, more useful to societies, more profitable for owners, more satisfying to members, more submissive to top managers, more democratic, more stable, more flexible, or whatever." As the "or whatever" qualification indicates, this extensive list was not intended to be exhaustive. Nonetheless, the list amply demonstrates the large, diverse, and often conflicting objectives that face those who attempt to design organizations.

A logical question raised by the Starbuck and Nystrom list centers on how an organization designer can meet so many diverse objectives. The question is all the more difficult in light of Alexander's (1964: 59) apt observation that a designer's *"chances of success are small because the number of factors which must fall simultaneously into place is so enormous"* (italics in original).

Over the past two decades *organization design* has come to refer to the academic speciality that explores the relation of different configurations of structures, processes, and technologies to selected organizational outcomes, most typically organizational effectiveness (Lewin and Huber, 1986). This speciality adds the normative component to the descriptive and explanatory components of traditional organization science. It seeks to develop guidelines for establishing organizational forms to achieve organizational effectiveness.

Different configurations of structure, process, and subunit integration lead to different organizational forms. Naturally, there has been considerable interest in developing a comprehensive taxonomy of organizational forms. For example, McKelvey (1982) describes five organization forms in ancient Mesopotamia—hunters, temples, producers, palaces, and commercials—but says little about how this society created these particular forms at this particular juncture of human civilization or how they apply to the contemporary world. Miles and Snow (1978) describe four business strategies that are aligned with different configurations. Three of these, the defender, the analyzer, and the prospector forms, represent stable ways of moving through the organization's adaptive cycle with its environment. The fourth form, the reactor, is unstable. Burns and Stalker (1961) describe two organizational forms, the mechanistic and the organic. The former was viewed as rigid and inflexible, the latter as fluid and adaptable to environmental demands. Mintzberg (1979) presented a typology of five different structural configurations: the simple structure, machine bureaucracy, professional bureaucracy, divisionalized form, and adhocracy.

While each of these taxonomies is interesting, none has been widely accepted as the foundation for a continuing program of research (for an exception, see Shortell and Zajac, 1990). Unfortunately, organization scholars have yet to agree on what constitutes organizational form. Nor have they developed a widely accepted taxonomy for contemporary organizations. Until such a taxonomy is developed, there is little point in attempting to design an organization to follow a predetermined form. In the absence of known forms, how can people design organizations? If there are few templates or blueprints, what form should they attempt to design? If stakeholders pose multiple, often conflicting, organizational requirements, and if there are no known forms to match requirements, how should people go about the process of designing organizations?

Designs are often tied to functions. The well-known dictum "form follows function" (or, equivalently, structure follows strategy) suggests that there is a known relation between a design and what it is intended to accomplish or how it is intended to operate. Further, this dictum specifies that designers must first know what is to be accomplished before a design can be specified. Designers typically assume that not all designs will accomplish a given function. Designers also face the reality that some designs best serve one function while others best serve another. A design that must serve conflicting functions simultaneously requires compromise.

The organization design literature contains numerous interesting findings about relations among variables, as even a cursory examination of Nystrom and Starbuck's (1981) monumental *Handbook of Organizational Design* quickly reveals. Unfortunately, the organization design research literature contains three major shortcomings. First, many findings are based on single-point-in-time, cross-sectional, correlational research designs. The consequence of this is that very little knowledge exists about how the relations among organization design and effectiveness variables change over time in terms of trends, cycles, and lead/lag relations. Second, most of the research is based on scientific description of the relations among existing organizational forms. Thus, little is known about the process of introducing new forms into organizations and the resulting impact on performance variables. Third, as Van de Ven and Drazin (1985) argue, most studies examine single relations among pairs of variables; consequently, little is known about the more complex dynamic interactions that occur among clusters of variables that comprise design subsystems. Correction of these limitations constitutes an important agenda for the community of organization design research scholars.

This chapter is intended to help those interested in organizational design make some progress in overcoming these three limitations. To do so, it examines the process of organization design from a dynamic error reduction perspective, and then describes a set of analytic techniques that a designer can use during the design process. The chapter is organized into four sections. The first section presents Alexander's (1964) error reduction perspective of design. The second section presents a set of analytic techniques developed by Monge (1990). These techniques can be used with Alexander's design strategy for examining the relations among dynamic design and effectiveness variables and for monitoring the dynamic relations between alternative designs and organization effectiveness. The third section provides an example of the dynamic analysis of error reduction in the design of open offices. The final section explores several implications for managers that stem from the preceding work.

ON DESIGNING ORGANIZATIONS

Alexander (1964) provides a provocative perspective on the design process. Though the book was originally addressed to issues in architectural design, urban and regional planning, and commercial design, Van de Ven and Drazin (1985) argue that the framework sheds considerable light on the problem of organization design. This section presents the major aspects of Alexander's ideas.

Alexander begins his analysis at the simplest level by distinguishing form from context and specifying the relation between the two in terms of fit:

> Every design problem begins with an effort to achieve fitness between two entities: the form in question and its context. The form is the solution to the problem; the context defines the problem. In other words, when we speak of design, the real object of discussion is not the form alone, but the ensemble comprising the form and its context. Good fit is a desired property of this ensemble which relates to some particular division of the ensemble into form and context.   (Alexander, 1964: 15–16)

Of course, fit is also a key construct in the thinking of organization scientists. (See especially, Joyce, Slocum, and Von Glinow, 1982; Miles and Snow, 1978; Miller, 1987; Mintzberg, 1981; and Van de Ven and Drazin, 1985.)

The interesting question Alexander asks is: "What constitutes good fit?" The answer that most designers give to this question is to look for a harmonious match between context and form—that is, between requirements and design. This is not the correct strategy, he argues, because people generally do not perceive good fit. Rather, they perceive misfit, those areas where there are problems, incongruities, and discomfort. When applied to design this principle implies that "we should always expect to see the process of achieving good fit between two entities as a negative process of neutralizing the incongruities, or irritants, or forces, which cause misfit" (p. 24).

Alexander defines a misfit as the extent to which a design fails to fulfill a context requirement. Thus, a misfit is the discrepancy between a required value of a context variable and actual values of the same variable produced by the designer's design. Typically, the required value is specified by the designer, though specifications are also often produced by other stakeholders, such as sponsors or owners. Note that in organization terms, the context is often, though not always, the external environment. Both external environments and internal conditions can create contexts (see Joyce and Slocum, 1990). Requirements are generated by designers and other stakeholders in response to perceptions of needs or problems in specified contexts. Requirements are what designs are intended to accomplish to remove or diminish problems, present or anticipated. Whether the requirements are achieved, and whether achieved requirements resolve the problems, are issues to be discussed later.

Most designers tend to focus their attention on either the functional requirements *or* on the design—that is, on the context generating the requirements *or* on the form. This, Alexander says, is wrong, partially because it leads designers to focus on individual units of analysis, which are either the elements of the context or the elements of the form. Rather, the proper focus is the form-context ensemble, which is a relational unit of analysis. Each fit or misfit variable should be a relationship between context and form—that is, between the required values of context variables specified by the designer and the actual values of the same variables generated by the design of the designer.

Alexander distinguishes formal and functional definitions: "Every form can be described in two ways: from the point of view of what it is, and from the point of view of what it does. What it is is sometimes called the formal description. What it does, when put in contact with other things, is sometimes called the functional description" (p. 89).

The functional description contains those elements that describe how the form should operate to meet the requirements of the context—that is, how the design will solve the problem or accomplish the desired objective. In fact, most designers are accustomed to developing functional requirements and searching for designs to meet the requirements. But, Alexander asserts, such a list is essentially infinite and therefore, intractable. In support of this assertion he offers a page filled with 21 specifications for a teakettle that he says barely begins to capture the full set of requirements (see Table 10.1). What is needed is a way to narrow the infinite list to a manageable, finite size.

He offers two solutions to this problem. The first is to arrange the list into hierarchical levels of abstraction, as shown in Figure 10.1 for the case of the teakettle. Here, 11 of the 21 requirements are grouped into three categories of production, safety, and use. These are themselves included under a higher category called "function." The remaining ten are grouped into two categories of capital and maintenance, which are

Table 10.1. Twenty-one Requirements for a Teakettle

It must not be

    too small.
    easy to let go of by mistake.
    hard to store in the kitchen.
    hard to get the water out of.
    hard to pick up when it is hot.
    too expensive (the material it is made out of).
    too hard to clean on the outside.
    a shape which is too hard to machine wash.
    a shape which is unsuitable for whatever reasonably priced metal it is made out of.
    too hard to assemble.
    too difficult to keep free of scale.
    hard to fill with water.
    uneconomical to heat small quantities of water in, when it is not full.
    so tricky to hold that accidents occur when children or invalids try to use it.
    able to boil dry and burn without warning.
    unstable on the stove while it is boiling.

It must not

    let the water in it cool too quickly.
    corrode in steamy kitchens.
    appeal to such a minority that it cannot be manufactured in an appropriate way because of small
      demand.

It must

    pour cleanly.
    be able to withstand the temperature of boiling water.

Source: From Alexander (1964: 60).

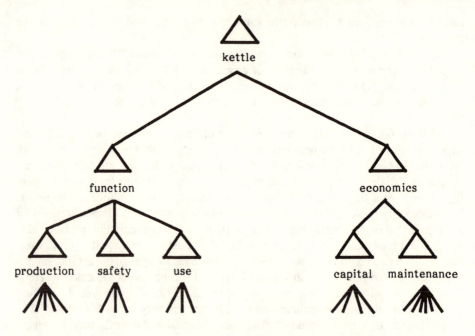

Figure 10.1. Hierarchical classification of 21 design requirements for a teakettle. *Source:* Alexander, 1964: 62.

included under the category of "economics." Organizing requirements into hierarchical levels of abstraction permits the designer to address the problem at various levels.

The second solution is to focus on misfits. Effective designs are the ones that deal best with the potential misfits. As he says:

> If we think of the requirements from a negative point of view, as potential misfits, there is a simple way of picking a finite set. This is because it is through misfit that the problem originally brings itself to our attention. We take just those relations between form and context which obtrude most strongly, that demand attention most clearly, which seem most likely to go wrong. We cannot do better than this.   (p. 26)

Were there only one or two misfit variables, unrelated to each other (or to other misfits), unchanging through time, developing a solution would be a relatively simple task. Unfortunately, three problems create major complications. First, in most practical situations a fairly large set of misfit variables exists rather than only one or two. Designs typically produce multiple misfits, complex results that fail to match the complete set of requirements to some degree. Second, multiple misfits rarely occur in isolation. Misfits tend to interact with each other in interconnected clusters. Finally, misfits change over time. The fact that most organization design problems consist of (1) multiple misfits, (2) that interact in clusters, and (3) change over time suggests that the development of organization form-context solutions to a set of misfit variables requires a complex, interactive, dynamic process.

The first two problems, the number of misfits and their interactions, are closely related. When multiple misfits exist, three conditions can occur. First, the variables may be unrelated. Though this rarely happens, when misfits do occur in isolation, each can be resolved independently. Second, all variables may be related to all other variables. In this situation, a change in one misfit variable produces a change in all variables. If this occurs, little can be done, since the level of complexity will typically exceed the capacity of the designer. As Hedberg, Nystrom, and Starbuck (1976: 42) suggest, this situation "requires greater analytic capability than designers, or any other people, possess." Finally, some misfit variables may be related to each other but others may not. Clusters of interrelated misfits comprise subsystems that are typically loosely coupled to each other (Orton and Weick, 1990). This condition is tractable since complex systems of relations can adapt if "the adaptation can proceed subsystem by subsystem, each subsystem relatively independent of the others" (p. 41). As Van de Ven and Drazin (1985: 346) argue, such a systems approach characterizes "the holistic patterns of interdependencies that are present in social systems."

The third problem created by the existence of multiple misfits is that they change over time. This problem can be viewed from two perspectives, the immediate and the long term. From the immediate view, we can

> picture the process of form-making as the action of a series of subsystems, all interlinked, yet sufficiently free of one another to adjust independently in a feasible amount of time. It works, because the cycles of correction and recorrection, which occur during adaptation, are restricted to one subsystem at a time. (Alexander, 1964: 43)

This suggests that the set of dynamic interactions among misfit variables is a crucial element of the solution. Consequently, it is important that the designer identify which misfit variables are interrelated within clusters as well as how clusters are related to each other. In organizational terminology, this implies that organizations should be designed as dynamic, loosely coupled, self-adjusting subsystems (Weick, 1976; Orton and Weick, 1990).

From the long-term perspective, the problem of changing misfits has different implications, for both context and form. Contexts change their requirements. Growth and decline of environments produce changing expectations and demands. When relevant requirements become obsolete, they need to be updated or discarded altogether. And forms change through a variety of transforming agents, such as age, deterioration, growth, and adaptation. Forms also need revision, modification, adaptation, and, in time, replacement. Some misfits improve with age; others decline.

Alexander's solution to the design problem centers on the analysis of misfit variables and their interrelations. He clusters those variables that are strongly connected to each other into hierarchical subsystems consisting of two to ten (or more) interrelated misfits in each subsystem. Subsystems are loosely connected to each other with one or two interlinkages. As Alexander says:

> Every aspect of a form, whether piecelike or patternlike, can be understood as a structure of components. Every object is a hierarchy of components, the larger ones specifying the pattern of distribution of the smaller ones, the small ones themselves, though at first sight more clearly piecelike, in fact again patterns specifying the arrangement and distribution of smaller components.

> Every component has this twofold nature: it is first a unit, and second a pattern, both a
> pattern and a unit. Its nature as a unit makes it an entity distinct from its surroundings. Its
> nature as a pattern specifies the arrangement of its own component units. (pp. 130–21)

Alexander's design strategy provides sets of misfit variables that are hierarchically clustered into loosely coupled semiautonomous subsystems, as shown in Figure 10.1. The result is a structure of relations that encompasses both the requirements for context variables and the actual values of variables; these actual values are generated by the form that was designed as a solution to meet those requirements.

Although this static representation has many attractive features, it also has one major shortcoming. Specifically, it fails to capture the dynamic relations between contexts and forms—that is, between requirements and designs. As such, any static design solution to context requirements is bound to become quickly obsolete. What is required to produce enduring forms is a flexible, dynamic process for creating forms and for continually adapting them to changing context requirements. The following section addresses this issue and develops a set of techniques for incorporating dynamics into the design process.

ADDING DYNAMICS TO MISFITS

Monge (1990) presents a dynamic analytic strategy for studying organization change that can be adapted to the design context. The technique focuses on studying the patterns of organizational variables plotted on time graphs to observe their history of change. The plots can be developed for any time frame and units that are relevant to the designer, whether days, weeks, months, years, or other periods. Plotting even a few points in time will show trends, cycles, and discontinuities. The resulting information is important because it provides a basis for determining how the selected variables have behaved in the past. History provides the backdrop for interpreting the present and for forecasting the future.

The strategy has two major components for studying dynamics. The first component consists of examining individual variables and assessing their temporal characteristics. The second consists of examining the temporal relations among variables. Since recent work on organization design has emphasized the importance of organizational effectiveness (Lewin and Minton, 1986), it is useful to apply both components of the strategy to two sets of variables, a context set and a design set. The resulting strategy consists of examining the temporal characteristics of the same variables in each set, context, and design, as well as examining the dynamic relations between variables in the two sets.

It is interesting to consider how Alexander's views regarding misfits can be applied to the notion of organization effectiveness. His approach shifts the focus from effectiveness to ineffectiveness. When *ineffectiveness* is viewed as a misfit variable, it is defined as the difference between the required value for an organizational variable specified by the designer and the actual value for this variable produced by the organization design. This definition of ineffectiveness will be used throughout the remainder of this chapter.

Studying Temporal Characteristics of Individual Variables

Studying individual design or ineffectiveness variables over time involves consideration of six characteristics: magnitude, trend, continuity, rate of change, duration, and cyclicity. These characteristics describe most (though not all) of the temporal change that any organizational variable can display. Figure 10.2 clarifies the nature of these characteristics. It is important to note that this type of graph shows the behavior of either the design or the ineffectiveness variable without reference to each other or to other variables. That is, this graph shows the temporal behavior of individual variables in isolation before examining temporal relations between variables.

To utilize this strategy, an organization designer selects and plots a variable of interest. Plotting a variable over time is a simple, straightforward matter. For example, Figure 10.3 is a graph of the level of slack resources in a firm. As of August 1992, the firm's level of slack resources had a magnitude of three on a ten-point scale. The graph shows a downward trend in this level over the past three years, with a rate of change of approximately 10 percent per year. The data also display a yearly cycle that has peaks during the summer and valleys during the winter holidays. Similar graphs can be created for other design and context variables.

Two types of variables that a designer might select are design variables and context variables. Typical design variables include level of slack resources and number of lateral relations (Galbraith, 1974), information-processing capacity (Galbraith, 1977), equivocality (Weick, 1978), environmental interdependence (Mackenzie, 1986), specialization (Huber and McDaniel, 1986), and information richness (Daft and Lengel, 1986). Typical context variables include growth, productivity, profit, morale (Campbell, 1977), and capacity to process information (Galbraith, 1974).

Graphing Misfits

Alexander's design strategy suggests that misfits should be studied along with individual context and form variables. Fortunately, misfits can be as easily graphed as either individual context or form variables.

Recall that a misfit is the discrepancy between the required values of a variable specified by a designer and the actual values produced by a design. Although both are interesting, it is not necessary to choose between graphing the required and the obtained values and graphing the misfit variables because all three types of data can be plotted on the same graph. If the units of the required and/or actual variables and the misfit variables are not the same, the data collected by designers or managers can be drawn on a graph with two vertical axes. Figure 10.4 provides an example of plotting the data values for the required variable, the actual variable, and the misfit variable on the same graph. By doing this, the changes in required and actual values that lead to defined changes in misfit can be identified. For example, Galbraith (1977: 36–37) defines uncertainty as *"the difference between the amount of information required to perform the task and the amount of information already possessed by the organization"* (italics in original). "Information required" is the value of the variable specified by the designer; "information acquired" is the actual value produced by the design; and the difference between the two, uncertainty, is the misfit or ineffectiveness variable. To

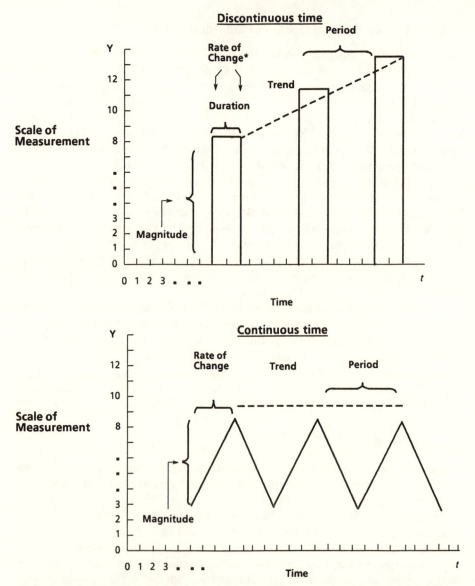

Figure 10.2. Five dimensions of dynamic analysis: continuity, magnitude, rate of change, trend, and cyclicity. Additionally it is useful to specify the duration of discontinuous variables. *Source:* Monge, 1990: 411. *Note:* The rate of change is instantaneous from 0 to 8 and from 8 back to 0 for this discontinuous example. In the continuous-time example, it is two units of change in Y per one unit of change in time.

graph these three variables, a designer or manager would need to collect data over time on the first two variables and compute the values for the third variable (uncertainty) by taking the difference between information required and information acquired.

In Figure 10.4, the amount of information is shown as two separate values on the vertical X axis. The first is the required information (X_1); the second is the acquired

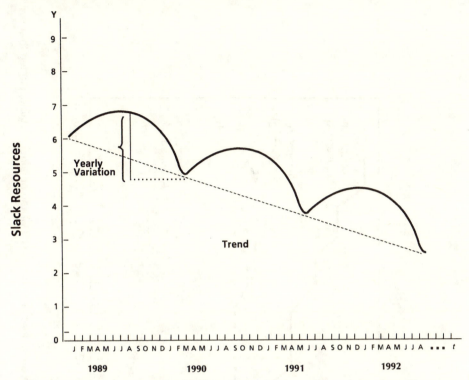

Figure 10.3.   Slack resources (Y) graphed over a three-year period showing a 10 percent per year decline in trend and an average of 20 percent variation in slack.

information (X_2). The difference between the two is graphed on the vertical Y axis as the misfit or ineffectiveness variable. Of course, all three values are plotted against the horizontal axis representing time, labeled t.

This graph vividly displays the fact that design misfits can change in three ways. First, the actual value produced by the design can change; second, the required value generated by the context can change; and third, both can change. In the example in Figure 10.4, the amount of information required changes over time, as does the information acquired. Depending on how both these values change, the misfit can be improved or worsened. Figure 10.4 illustrates two other interesting features. First, the amount of acquired information increases steadily over time. However, as more is discovered about the problem, more information is required by the designer or other stakeholder. Moreover, the required information increases at a faster rate than the obtained information. Consequently, the misfit graph shows uncertainty, the information required-acquired misfit variable, getting increasingly worse despite the fact that the amount of acquired information is steadily increasing! This example is like the one described by Galbraith (1977: 46) in the design of aircraft. He describes how aircraft design usually contains high uncertainty and high information needs. As a consequence, target goals are often missed. This typically leads to the recalibration of goals and to a redefinition of needed information.

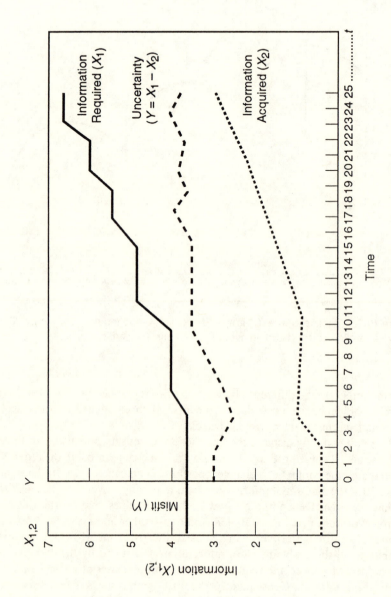

Figure 10.4. Information required (X_1), the specification variable, and information acquired (X_2), the obtained variable, plotted to show changes in uncertainty (Y) over time, the misfit.

Studying Relations Among Clusters of Misfits

The second component of the dynamic strategy is to examine the relations among variables over time. The example in the preceding section examined the temporal relation between values required by a designer, actual values of acquired information produced by a design, and the resultant misfit. While this information is useful, particularly the dynamic aspects, it fails to provide two other important pieces of information: (1) information about the values of the design variable itself and (2) the relation between the design variable and the ineffectiveness misfit. Remember that misfit variables were earlier defined as the discrepancies between required values of a context variable specified by the designer and actual values of the variable produced by designs. Since it is important to determine what causes misfits, it is important to study the relation between design variables and misfits—that is, between the values related to the design itself and the discrepancy between context requirements and the actual values of those variables generated by the design.

Five dimensions describe most of the important temporal relations among variables. As shown in Figure 10.5, these are history, magnitude of change, rate of change, lag, and permanence. These five dimensions apply to both variables plotted in the figure. Consider the values of the design variable, X, and the values of the misfit or ineffectiveness variable, Y, while examining the implications of the figure. In this example, the historical relation between the two variables is constant, with neither the design nor the ineffectiveness variable changing over a nine-month period. A designer makes an organization design change of one unit at the ninth month, which lasts for one month. Nothing happens to the ineffectiveness variable for three months, which represents a three-month lag relation. The ineffectiveness variable then begins to decline at the rate of a third of a unit per month for six months. The total magnitude of change is one unit in the design variable for a period of one month and two units in the ineffectiveness variable that are permanent.

Figure 10.5 presents the relation between a pair of variables, specifically, a design variable and a misfit variable (actually, a trio of variables, since a misfit is the difference between two values). While dyadic relations are informative, Alexander also suggests that clusters of variables that constitute subsystems should be examined together, particularly clusters of misfits. Because clusters of misfits constitute subsystems, examining them together enables a designer to assess their degree of interaction. This idea leads to Figure 10.6.

Figure 10.6 shows a time graph of a cluster of two design variables and an ineffectiveness variable to which they are related. The variables are an adaptation of Galbraith's (1974) design variations for information processing. The first design variable is investment in vertical information systems; the second is the number of lateral relations. The ineffectiveness variable is information-processing capacity: the discrepancy between the capacity required by the context and the capacity generated by the organization design. To simplify this example, assume that the context-generated information-processing requirement remains constant, while the information-processing values generated by the changes in design are free to vary, though this is not necessary in practice. The misfit is measured on a scale from zero to one, though the limits rarely occur. Zero means that the required processing capacity has been achieved; there is an absence of ineffectiveness—that is, no misfit. One means complete misfit or total inef-

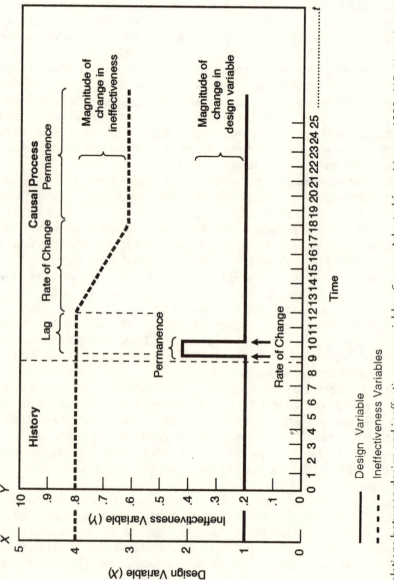

Figure 10.5. Relations between design and ineffectiveness variables. *Source:* Adapted from Monge, 1990: 415. *Note:* A one-unit change in a design variable leads to a two-unit decline in ineffectiveness.

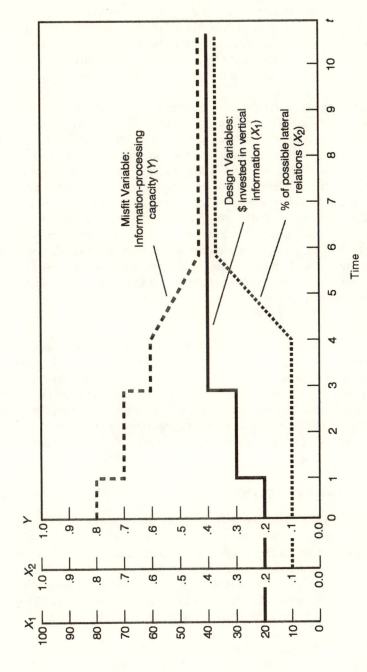

Figure 10.6. Impact of a cluster of two design variables—dollars invested in vertical information (X_1), and percentage of possible lateral relations (X_2)—on information processing capacity (Y), a misfit variable.

fectiveness. The investment variable is measured in dollars, and the number of lateral relations is measured as a percentage of possible lateral relations.

The figure illustrates that incremental increases in investment in vertical information systems leads to a decrease in the ineffectiveness of information-processing capacity. Similarly, increases in lateral relations produce decreases in ineffectiveness. Further, since they are additive across time, together they have a larger impact than either alone.

It can also be useful to represent the relation of a design variable to multiple ineffectiveness variables. For example, a study of noise in office environments, concluded that "people's experience of noise affects their environmental satisfaction, job satisfaction, and ease of communication, and does not differ across job types" (Brill, Margulis, Konar, and BOSTI, 1985: 191). These relations between a design variable and three ineffectiveness variables are shown in Figure 10.7. The ineffectiveness variables consist of the discrepancy between the designer-specified levels of environmental satisfaction, job satisfaction, and ease of communication and the actual levels generated by the design. As designers decrease the level of ambient noise over time, they can see just how the ineffectiveness of environmental satisfaction, job satisfaction, and ease of communication also decreases. In particular, designers can see where further reductions in noise level, such as additional changes in the design, do not alter the ineffectiveness variables.

This section has presented a set of analytic techniques that managers can use in designing dynamic organizations. As with most analytic techniques, the alternative presented here is quite general and can be used with a wide variety of organization contexts, requirements, and designs. Since nothing has been said about choosing specific design variables and which design variables would be cost effective, it will be helpful to illustrate the analytical procedures with a concrete example. The next section does this in the context of designing open office environments for organizations.

DESIGNING AN OPEN OFFICE

Every organization contains the residue of previous choices about organization design. Each redesign encapsulates remnants of earlier forms. The current organizational form is a cumulative manifestation of multiple past decisions about how the organization should operate. The commonplace, "this is how we do it around here," describes how people think their organizations function. Sometimes it is a template for collective views of how their organization, properly designed, should function. In other situations it is an unfortunate, dysfunctional consequence of organizational history.

Ironically, as Lewin and Minton (1986) observe, empirical studies of organizational design and effectiveness are relatively rare. Organization scientists typically study relations among variables in extant organizations to establish scientific laws. Rarely have they examined how people determine the functional requirements for their organizations, how they select particular forms to fulfill those requirements, and how they continuously assess and subsequently adjust their choices.

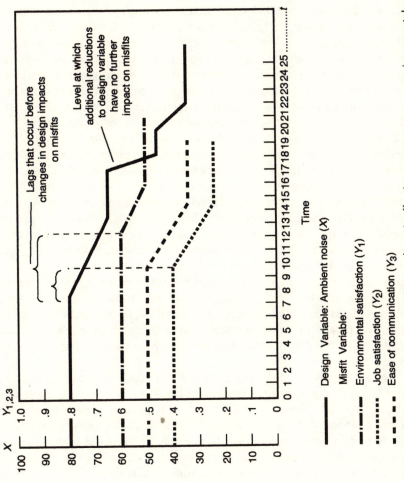

Figure 10.7. Impact of a design variable, ambient noise (X), on three *ineffectiveness* measures—environmental satisfaction (Y₁), job satisfaction (Y₂), and ease of communication (Y₃). *Note:* Reductions in ambient noise reduce three misfits, though with different time lags. Reduction of noise beyond a specific level has no further impact on ineffectiveness.

One interesting exception to this situation is the area of open office design. This section reviews a major effort by Brill et al. (1985) to (a) conduct research regarding relations among design variables and organization outcomes, (b) establish office design criteria (requirements), and (c) determine feasible alternative forms to meet the criteria (see also Ornstein, 1989). The section concludes with an examination of how Alexander's error reduction perspective and the analytic techniques described in this chapter could be usefully applied to the design of an open office.

Brill and colleagues studied the relation of office design variables to organization outcomes. They studied nearly 6,000 office workers in 70 firms over a five-year period. The primary organization outcomes of interest were job satisfaction, environmental satisfaction, ease of communication, and job performance. The observed predictors were 18 facets of office environments clustered into four categories: characteristics of the workspace (physical enclosure, windows, etc.), ambient conditions (temperature, light, and noise), psychophysical constructs (privacy, communication, comfort, etc.), and facilities design and management (participation, flexibility, etc.).

Their research led to numerous interesting conclusions. For example, in discussing the effect of noise above a given threshold on outcome measures, Brill et al. conclude that "people's experience of noise affects their environmental satisfaction, job satisfaction, and ease of communication, and does not differ across job types" (p. 191). Another example is provided in their conclusions about ease of communication and satisfaction. They say that "ease of communication affects both job and environmental satisfaction" (p. 224). Further, they state that "those who participate [in designing their work spaces] have higher job satisfaction and satisfaction with the environment than those who don't. Increased job satisfaction is a function of participation in and of itself while increased environmental satisfaction can be attributed to environmental improvements resulting from participation" (p. 66). In this latter example, smaller misfit constitutes greater participation; zero misfit implies maximum or total participation. As in the case of the ambient noise example, a threshold or boundary condition is likely beyond which smaller misfits are unlikely to occur or to have any impact if they do occur.

The conclusions of their research led to the creation of a set of criteria for office design. Separate criteria were created (a) for individual work spaces (for 11 different job types), (b) work groups, and (c) large areas. For example, since research showed that "the presence or absence of windows in an individual's workspace seems to have little effect on job performance or satisfaction," the criterion was established that window areas should be given "to everybody, by using it as main circulation, with access to a band of services and amenities across from the window wall" (p. 120). Similarly, since research "findings imply that job performance is no higher for those visually supervised than those not," the criterion was established to subdivide "large floor areas with panels above eye height" (p. 123).

Criteria, of course, are relatively useless unless they are used to develop designs. The Brill et al. open office project undertook this task. The design criteria were submitted to three well-known architectural firms. Each firm presented a set of "design interpretations," drawings of specific office plans intended to fulfill the design criteria (included in Brill et al., 1985). Although there are interesting similarities, the three organization designs are surprisingly different, at least to an untrained eye. Of course, these differences raise the question of which design is best—in terms of which best meets the design criteria. Unfortunately, Brill et al. do not address this question. Perhaps this omission is attributable to their failure to view this process from a dynamic error reduction perspective.

Application of Alexander's error reduction perspective and the dynamic analytic graphing techniques described earlier provide a very different orientation to this organization design problem. First, rather than focus on the design as a fulfillment of the requirements as the three architectural firms did in the design interpretations, the process should focus on the misfit variables, the values of the variables specified by the design requirements compared to the values attained by the actual design. For the previous ambient noise example (see Figure 10.7), the *designers* would focus on the misfit variables of environmental satisfaction, job satisfaction, and ease of communication. Since designs operate only in relation to their context, the unit of analysis should be the misfit relation between design and context rather than either alone. Designs are best judged by the degree of context misfit they generate. The process of organization design is the process of minimizing context misfit.

Second, organization designs are almost never permanent. Design solutions to design requirements should be seen as first approximations in the process of misfit or error reduction. As the nature and size of the misfit becomes known, considerable additional adjustment would be required, perhaps even continual adjustment. Further, changes are as likely to occur in the required values as in the actual values generated by the design. Thus, both components of the misfit variable should be carefully studied for the sources of misfit.

Third, a monitoring system should be created for tracking both the misfit variables and the design variables. This requires measurement of the two components of each misfit variable (required and actual) and the values of the design variables. Further, by graphing these over time it is possible to determine how changes in design affect misfits. Trends, cycles, and lead/lag relations are the primary focus of this process.

Had the Brill et al. (1985) research group employed this perspective, they would have seen their design project as the first step in an ongoing redesign effort. First, they would have treated the design criteria as the first half of the misfit equation. To complete the equation they would have taken measurements of the actual values achieved by the designs and computed the misfit values. By comparing the misfit values for the three separate designs, Brill et al. would have had a basis for an initial comparative evaluation among the designs.

Second, recognizing that designs are rarely permanent, Brill et al. would have asked the three architectural firms to indicate the changes they would recommend in their designs. These changes would be based on the information about the degree of misfit between the required values specified by Brill et al. and the actual values generated by the architect's design. Either or both sides of the misfit equation would be open for examination. The goal of this step would be to minimize the misfit.

Third, Brill et al. would establish an ongoing monitoring system. The monitoring system would include the values of the misfits and the values of the design variables, both plotted over time. The focus of the monitoring system would be on tracking the impact of design changes on the values of the misfits. Thus, the trends, cycles, and lead/lag relations would be crucial.

IMPLICATIONS

Designing Dynamic Organizations

One of the most frequent commonplaces in organization lore and contemporary society is that the only permanence is change. In many organizations the implementation of a major reorganization is barely complete before the next one is under consideration. Sometimes, one reorganization simply redoes what a previous one had already accomplished. Sometimes, ironically, a new reorganization undoes a past reorganization. Most often, it is difficult to determine just what each reorganization accomplished. And all too often reorganization is undertaken solely for the sake of change itself, as was well documented in Burrough and Helyar's (1990) painstaking analysis of the career of Ross Johnston, the recently deposed CEO of RJ Reynolds Industries. As Johnston seemed to believe, since the business of management is the business of changing the organization, management wasn't managing unless it was reorganizing. Clearly, most organization design efforts occur in already existing, previously designed organizations.

The ideas presented in this chapter have important implications for designing and redesigning dynamic organizations—either new organizations or already existing ones—in dynamic environments. This section briefly reviews the guidelines that have been presented and describes how they can be used to design, monitor, and redesign a dynamic organization.

1. *Select organization variables.* The organization design process begins with the selection of the organization variables that managers want to influence. These variables are the aspects of the organization and its environment which managers want to change with the organization design. These might include any of the effectiveness criteria established by Campbell (1977), Lewin and Minton (1986), or several others.

2. *Specify design requirements.* Once the organization variables are selected, managers should specify the desired values or range of values for these variables. These required values are the criteria against which the values generated by the design will be evaluated.

3. *Focus on misfits and error reduction.* Design requirements are relatively useless without information about the actual values of the required variables created by the designs. Thus, from the outset it is important that the design process conceptually focus on misfits. In this chapter misfits have been called organization ineffectiveness variables. Conceptually, it is these that the design seeks to minimize.

4. *Cluster large systems into subsystems of misfits.* Large systems are relatively intractable. Initially, managers may choose to focus on relatively small systems. If large systems are chosen, managers should cluster variables together that constitute subsystems of the larger system. Subsystems such as personnel, financial, and production will be easier to influence and manage if they are tightly coupled internally but loosely coupled with each other.

5. *Select design variables.* The existing research literature on organization

design is an important foundation for knowledge about design variables and about relations between organization design and organization outcomes. However, as stated earlier, much of this knowledge is correlational. Hence, managers should extrapolate about how these static relations behave over time. It is important to attempt to specify trends, cycles, lead/lag relations, and points where the changes no longer hold.

6. *Design and emplace the monitoring system.* The focus for the monitoring system is the misfit ineffectiveness variables and the design variables.

7. *Implement the design.*

8. *Implement the monitoring system.* Baselines are important as early reference points. Data should be gathered at frequent, regular intervals. Enough data points should be collected to detect trends and perhaps cycles in the misfit variables. If the design variables are also changing, data should be collected at sufficient points in time to see if there is any systematic relation between design changes and misfit changes (see Monge, 1990, and Monge, Farace, Eisenberg, Miller, and White, 1984, for additional details).

9. *Evaluate the design.* Managers should focus the evaluation process on minimizing error. Over time, good designs will show a trend toward the reduction of misfit, especially in relatively stable environments. Changes that occur in the design variables should lead to decreases in the ineffectiveness variable.

10. *Adjust the design or the specific design requirements.* Organizational design always takes time, and original conditions may have changed by the time the design is completed and implemented, making it less appropriate than originally anticipated. Managers can change the design on the basis of the evaluation process. Alternatively, managers may change the values of the requirements.

CONCLUSION

Organizations are highly complex entities. They are extremely difficult to understand and manage. As Weick (Chapter 11) and others in this volume amply demonstrate, the management process is further complicated by highly subjective and interpretive processes, by personal and political entities, and by seemingly counterintuitive and little-known organizational influences. The dynamic error reduction process of organization design described in this chapter is subject to all these complications. Yet, by focusing on minimizing error over time and by continuously examining temporal relations between design and misfit variables, this dynamic design process solves several problems of previous organization design strategies. At the very least it provides a complex, dynamic, error reduction strategy that recognizes that the management of organizations is a complex, dynamic, error reduction enterprise.

NOTES

My thanks go to several colleagues who provided very helpful comments on earlier drafts of this manuscript: Eric Eisenberg, Janet Fulk, Bill Glick, George Huber, Jennifer Monohan, Dru Pagliosotti, Deanna Schwarz, John Slocum, JoAnne Wyer, and Bob Zmud.

REFERENCES

Alexander, C. 1964. *Notes on the synthesis of form.* Cambridge, MA: Harvard University Press.
Brill, M., Margulis, S. T., and BOSTI. 1985. *Using office design to increase productivity,* Vols. 1–2. Buffalo, NY: Workplace Design and Productivity.
Burns, T., and Stalker, G. M. 1961. *The management of innovation.* London: Tavistock.
Burrough, B., and Helyar, J. 1990. *Barbarians at the gate: the fall of RJR Nabisco.* New York: Harper and Row.
Campbell, J. P. 1977. On the nature of organizational effectiveness. In Goodman, P. S., and Pennings, J. M. (Eds.), *New perspectives on organizational effectiveness* (pp. 13–55). San Francisco: Jossey-Bass.
Daft, R. L., and Lengel, R. H. 1986. Organizational information requirements, media richness and structural determinants. *Management Science, 32,* 554–571.
Galbraith, J. R. 1974. Organization design: an information processing view. *Interfaces,* 4: 23–26.
Galbraith, J. R. 1977. *Organization design.* Reading, MA: Addison-Wesley.
Hedberg, B. L. T., Nystrom, P. C., and Starbuck, W. H. 1976. Camping on seesaws: prescriptions for a self-designing organization. *Administrative Science Quarterly,* 21: 41–65.
Huber, G. P., and McDaniel, R. R. 1986. The decision-making paradigm of organizational design. *Management Science,* 32(5): 572–589.
Joyce, W. F., and Slocum, J. W. Jr. 1990. Strategic context and organizational climate. In Schneider, B. (Ed.), *Organizational climate and culture* (pp. 130–150). San Francisco: Jossey-Bass.
Joyce, W. F., Slocum, J. W. Jr., and Von Glinow, M. A. 1982. Competing models of fit. *Journal of Occupational Behavior,* 3: 265–280.
Lewin, A. Y., and Huber, G. P. 1986. Organization design: introduction to the focused issue. *Management Science,* 32: 513.
Lewin, A. Y., and Minton, J. W. 1986. Determining organizational effectiveness: another look and an agenda for research. *Management Science,* 32: 514–538.
Mackenzie, K. 1986. Virtual positions and power. *Management Science,* 32: 622–642.
McKelvey, W. 1982. *Organizational systematics: taxonomy, evolution, and classification.* Berkeley: University of California Press.
Miles, R. E., and Snow, C. C. 1978. *Organizational strategy, structure, and process.* New York: McGraw-Hill.
Miller, D. 1987. The genesis of configuration. *Academy of Management Review,* 12: 686–701.
Mintzberg, H. 1979. *The structuring of organizations: the synthesis of the research.* Englewood Cliffs, NJ: Prentice-Hall.
Mintzberg, H. 1981. Organization design: fashion or fit? *Harvard Business Review,* January–February, pp. 103–116.
Monge, P. R. 1990. Theoretical and analytical issues in longitudinal research. *Organization Science,* 1: 406–431.
Monge, P. R., Farace, R. V., Eisenberg, E. M., Miller, K. I., and White, L. L. 1984. The process of studying process in organizational communication. *Journal of Communication,* 34: 22–43.
Nystrom, P. C., and Starbuck, W. H. (Eds.). 1981. *Handbook of organizational design,* 2 vols. New York: Oxford University Press.
Ornstein, S. 1989. The hidden influence of office design. *Academy of Management Executive,* 2: 144–147.
Orton, J. D., and Weick, K. E. 1990. Loosely coupled systems: a reconceptualization. *Academy of Management Review,* 15: 203–223.

Shortell, S. M., and Zajac, E. J. 1990. Perceptual and archival measures of Miles and Snow's strategic types: a comprehensive assessment of reliability and validity. *Academy of Management Journal,* 33: 817–832.

Starbuck, W. H., and Nystrom, P. C. 1981. Designing and understanding organizations. In Nystrom, P. C. and Starbuck, W. H. (Eds.), *Handbook of organizational design,* Vol. 1 (pp. i–xiii). New York: Oxford University Press.

Van de Ven, A. H., and Drazin, R. 1985. The concept of fit in contingency theory. In Cummings, L. L., and Staw, B. M. (Eds.), *Research in organizational behavior,* Vol. 7 (pp. 333–365). Greenwich, CT: JAI Press.

Weick, K. E. 1976. Educational organizations as loosely coupled systems. *Administrative Science Quarterly,* 21: 1–19.

Weick, K. E. 1979. *The social psychology of organizing,* 2nd ed. Reading, MA: Addison-Wesley.

11

Organizational Redesign As Improvisation

KARL E. WEICK

A way of seeing is a way of not seeing.

G. Poggi. *The British Journal of Sociology,* December, 1965

Today is not yesterday—We ourselves change.—How then can our works and thoughts, if they are always to be the fittest, continue always the same.

Thomas Carlyle

One mistake the arts would never make is to presume that a part or role can be exactly specified independent of the performer, yet this is the idea that has dominated work organizations for most of the twentieth century.

Peter B. Vail, *Managing As a Performing Art,* 1989: 124

EDITORS' SUMMARY

In this chapter, Weick challenges, and greatly enriches, our understanding of organizational design. Highlighting the dynamic and fluid nature of organizations, he calls for a perspective that emphasizes design as a verb rather than design as a noun, a perspective that acknowledges unpredictability rather than one that seeks and portrays stability. He goes further and reminds us that an organization's design is what people believe it to be, that what people believe it to be reflects what they believe it was, that perceptions of what it was are therefore the basis for what people do, and that what people do in organizations is, in effect, the organization's design.

In creating and conveying his message that organizational design is more than what it is typically thought to be, Weick uses two vehicles simultaneously. One is an explication of the rationale for studying organizational design, a rationale that includes arguments that most scholars would accept at face value, such as "the design of an organization determines the distribution of resources, authority, and information, and thus affects the ability of managers to make and implement timely, sound, and acceptable decisions." Weick identifies the assumptions implicit in each of these five reasons, and then offers and justifies alternative assumptions that lead to a more dynamic and perceptually based view of organizational design. The other is the metaphor of organizational design as theatrical improvisation rather than as architecture. As developed here, the implications of the metaphor for organizational scientists are (1) to think of organizational design as a continuous activity, (2) to recognize that the initiation of redesign has widely varied origins, and (3) to act on the fact that at any given moment the organization's design is a complex interpretation, not a simple chart. The implications of the metaphor for managers include the three above plus two others: (4) choose and manage subordinates in accord with the idea that resourcefulness is more crucial than resources and (5) a little structure goes a long way. ∎

> I suspect that much organizational illness can be attributed to the contrived (though time honored) ways in which humans are differentiated, constrained, controlled and directed, rewarded and punished, and limited to tasks that others have decided are appropriate to a given job. The illusion is that there is no alternative. (McEachern, 1984: 81)

The activity of architectural design often serves as the metaphor for organizational design, as in Khandwalla's (1977: 260) statement that "the formed world is the only habitable one." In its earliest stages, the overarching study, called the CODE study, (see Appendix of this volume) that led to this book was itself described using imagery consistent with this metaphor.[1] Organizational design modeled along the lines of architectural design is viewed as a bounded activity that occurs at a fixed point in time. The activity is largely decision making, concentrated in a small group, which translates intentions into plans. The plans are based on assumptions of ideal conditions and envision structures rather than processes. The structures are assumed to be stable solutions to a set of current problems that will change only incrementally.

While the metaphor of architecture is a compelling model for organizational change, it is not the only one. I hope to demonstrate that an alternative metaphor, design as improvisational theater, corrects many of the blind spots induced by the metaphor of architecture. The idea of design as improvisation would suggest that Khandwalla's statement should be rewritten to read, "the forming world is the only habitable one." The revised assumptions that lie behind this rewrite include such ideas as redesign is a continuous activity, responsibility for the initiation of redesign is dispersed, interpretation is the essence of design, resourcefulness is more crucial than resources, the meaning of an action is usually known after the fact, and a little structure goes a long way.

In a group of improvisational players, there are always more possible meanings for their actions than the group can ever use, so their problem is to agree on a sufficient number of meanings to make coordinated action possible. But agreements are held to a minimum so that people retain the capability to make individual adjustments to local irregularities. In improvisational theater, coordination occurs not so much because people have identical views of "the" design, but because they have equivalent views of what is happening and what it means. Equivalence allows both coordination and individual expression to occur simultaneously. As a result, people are able to accomplish collectively what they could not do individually, but also to cope individually with unexpected problems by virtue of their diverse capabilities. The design that produces this complex mixture tends to be emergent and visible only after the fact. Thus, the design is a piece of history, not a piece of architecture.

The remainder of this chapter explicates the idea of organizational design as improvisation, by contrasting it with the idea of organizational design as architecture. The vehicle for this contrast is a statement, written in the early stages of the CODE study, which addressed the question, "Why study organizational design?" This statement implies several assumptions that are consistent with idea that design resembles architecture. Several of these implied assumptions are identified, and then they are rewritten to illustrate the idea that design resembles improvisation. The meaning of each rewritten assumption is then discussed in the adjacent text.

The complete text of the 16-line CODE statement is shown in Table 11.1 and in Fig. 2 of the Appendix of this volume. The specific portions of this text from which the implied assumptions are drawn, are identified throughout by the line number(s) where these portions are stated.

IMAGES OF IMPROVISED DESIGN

CODE PHRASE: "The design of an organization determines" (line 1).

Implied Assumptions

1. A design is a blueprint.
2. A design is constructed at a single point in time.
3. Designs produce order through intention.
4. Design creates planned change.

Alternative Assumptions

1.1 A design is a recipe.
2.1 Designing is continuously reconstructed.
3.1 Designs produce order through attention.
4.1 Design codifies unplanned change after the fact.

The phrase *organizational design* contains a trap. The trap is that the word design can be used as a noun as well as a verb. When people in organizations talk about the design of an organization, they tend to equate it with things like organization charts, written procedures, and job specifications. Features of organizations that are less thing-like and more continuous, fleeting, and emergent, are easily overlooked. As a result, organizational designs tend to focus on structures rather than processes and to contain few provisions for self-correction.

Improvisation is about process and about designs that are continuously reconstructed. Starbuck and Nystrom (1981: 14) captured this idea perfectly when they said, "a well-designed organization is not a stable solution to achieve, but a developmental process to keep active." Kilmann, Pondy, and Slevin (1976: 7) made essentially the same point when they argued that one-time design strategies make sense if the environment is basically placid, but continuous redesign is necessary when the environment becomes turbulent. If the architecture metaphor tempts people to introduce the

Table 11.1. Why Study Organizational Design?

- 1 To a great extent, the design of an organization determines the distribution of resources, authority, and information.
  2 As a consequence, it directly impacts the ability of individual managers to make and to implement
  3 timely, technically and economically sound, and organizationally acceptable decisions.
  4 The ability to make and implement such decisions, in turn, affects the effectiveness of the organization.

- 5 Related to the reason above, the design of an organization directly affects a manager's ability to
  6 coordinate and control the activities of subordinates in order to enhance organizational performance.
  7 Proper organizational design can therefore make the difference between having an effective, well-run organization
  8 and having one with recurrent crises and organizational inefficiencies.

- 9 Organizational environments are changing more rapidly than ever before. Because the effectiveness of
  10 an organizational design erodes over time as the environment changes, the organization must be designed
  11 to fit current and future environments, not the environment of the past.

- 12 Innovative technologies are continuously being introduced in modern organizations. The effectiveness of
  13 different organizational designs depends on the technology and how the work is done.

- 14 Modern communication and computing technologies facilitate the process of coordination and control
  15 and make new organizational designs feasible. New communication and computing technologies can also
  16 increase organizational effectiveness in current or previously abandoned organizational designs.

349

design process at only a few fixed points in time, then this should lead to lower performance as the rate of environmental change accelerates.

Designs As Recipes

One way to shift attention from the static to the dynamic in organizational design is to move from the assumption that a design is a blueprint to the assumption that a design is a recipe. Simon (1962) used the contrast between blueprints and recipes to illustrate two different ways to describe complex systems. Complex systems can be described using descriptions that resemble blueprints (e.g., a circle is the locus of all points equidistant from a given point) or by descriptions that resemble recipes (e.g., to construct a circle, rotate a compass with one end fixed until the other arm has returned to its starting point). Blueprints, organizational charts, musical scores, pictures, diagrams, and chemical formulae all capture the way we sense the work. These devices help us identify and label what we see. For example, an organizational chart helps us see who is at the center and who are at the periphery of information flows.

But what blueprints can't do is capture how that sensed world came into being. It takes a recipe to do that. Recipes, organizational values, expressive notations in music, self-actuated museum demonstrations, strip maps, and differential equations all describe actions that generate the objects specified in blueprints.

To many designers, a blueprint is the goal and the recipe is the means to get there. As Simon puts it, the basic problem in design is, given a blueprint, what is the corresponding recipe that will achieve it? That way of formulating the question is too narrow. It illustrates the limits of the architectural metaphor. Blueprints are assumed to exert control over more of the design process than is consistent with what we know about either organizations or people. Architects may treat blueprints as givens, but people who improvise treat them as emergents. The givens for people who improvise are the recipes and routines by which they generate actions that could become any one of several different blueprints.

A typical recipe for design sounds like this. Take a hierarchy and flatten it; take an executive committee and enlarge it; find an elite and join it; turn these five notes into a composition. In each case a starting point is specified—hierarchy, committee, elites, musical notes. And an action is also specified—flatten, enlarge, join, compose. But what is not specified in advance are the structures that will emerge as these actions and starting points are mixed together. Even when detailed blueprints supposedly drive the design process, this same open-ended quality is present. Events are set in motion, but the orderliness they will create remains to be discovered.

Design, viewed from the perspective of improvisation, is more emergent, more continuous, more filled with surprise, more difficult to control, more tied to the content of action, and more affected by what people pay attention to than are the designs implied by architecture. Even though improvisation may involve more uncertainty, it does not thereby become any less effective. Emergent, continuous designing is sensitive to small changes in local conditions, which means the design is continuously updated as people and conditions change.

If we view designing as improvisation and designs as recipes, then there are at least three additional implications that run counter to traditional views of organizational design.

Designs As Attention

The notion of improvisation implies that attention rather than intention drives the process of designing. As we saw earlier, blueprints portray the world we sense and recipes portray the way that world is enacted. Since the only things we can sense are enacted events that have already taken place, attention rather than intention becomes central to the design process. The importance of attention is often missed since, in organizations as in architecture, design is focused on the future (see lines 10 and 11 of the CODE statement) and blueprints are treated as tools of intention. In actuality, design is focused on the past and blueprints are tools of attention. Design is focused on extrapolations of the past since the past contains the only data we have to work with. And blueprints influence attention rather than intention because they contain categories and relationships that are imposed on elapsed actions to make them more sensible.

This complex mixture of attention, designs formed in retrospect, and sense-making that always occur "too late" is visible in Mintzberg and McHugh's (1985: 160) analysis of the Canadian Film Board between 1939 and 1975. They found that the periods that unfolded as if they were the result of intended designs actually consisted of patterns that emerged gradually, sometimes fortuitously, out of elapsed actions made sensible after the fact. The patterning of film board actions, and the designs in which those actions were imbedded, were the product of attention rather than intention. The key point is that designing often consists of a shifting pattern of attention and meaning imposed on an ongoing stream of social activity, rather than a stable pattern of intention imposed a priori on events initiated to achieve an outcome.

As a variation on this point, it is important to note that design often codifies previous unplanned change rather than creates future planned change. The assumption that design creates planned change is implicit in a question asked in much of the research reported in this book: "When was it definitely decided to make this change?" Respondents could have been asked, "When was it definitely decided that this change had been made?", a question that more closely taps the emergent, retrospective origin of many designs. The idea that design is a process of codification starts with the notion that events often simply unfold. When viewed retrospectively, with a specific framework in hand, elapsed events seem to cohere as if they had been designed. The coherence is partly an artifact of selective attention and partly the artifact of actions which themselves fall into habits, patterns, and routines. It is not that the coherence is undesigned. Rather, the source of the coherence in the design lies elsewhere than in intention. There was not a transition from imagination, through intention, into execution. Instead, there was an imaginative interpretation of execution that imputed sufficient coherence to the execution that it could easily be mistaken for an intention.

Designs As Bricolage

Design is clearly a process of sense-making that makes do with whatever materials are at hand. This is perhaps our sharpest point of departure from the architectural view, so it needs to be spelled out explicitly. From the perspective of improvisation, designing is synonymous with bricolage, and the designer acts like a bricoleur. The terms bricolage and bricoleur come from Levi-Strauss's (1966) research on the savage mind.

The French word *bricolage* (which has no precise equivalent in English) means to use whatever resources and repertoire one has to perform whatever task one faces. Invariably the resources are less well suited to the exact project than one would prefer, but they are all there is. The person who engages in bricolage is called a *bricoleur*, which means roughly a Jack-of-all-trades or someone who is a professional do-it-yourself person (Levi-Strauss, 1966: 17). A bricoleur should not be confused with an odd job man, because considerably more knowledge about materials is assumed in the case of the bricoleur.

The defining characteristic of a bricoleur is that this person makes do with whatever tools and materials are at hand. These resources are always heterogeneous because, unlike the materials available to the engineer, the bricoleur's materials have no relation to any particular project. Elements are collected and retained on the principle that they may come in handy (p. 18). Engineers take on only those projects for which they have the necessary raw materials and resources, whereas bricoleurs do not similarly restrict themselves. The bricoleur's materials are not project-specific, but, instead, they represent the contingent result of all of the previous uses to which those items have been put. The materials, in other words, mean whatever they have been used for in the past. The more diverse these uses, and the more fully the materials themselves are understood, the more innovative will the bricoleur be in improvising new designs from this stock of materials.

When the bricoleur begins to work on a project, "his first practical step is retrospective" (p. 18). He interrogates the existing set of materials to see what it contains. What it contains is defined in large part by the uses to which it has been put up to that point. It is these prior uses (what the object signifies) that are manipulated and recombined in an effort to advance the project. Through the use of generalization, analogies, and comparisons, the bricoleur assembles new arrangements of elements. Prior history can preconstrain the ways in which the materials are interpreted, but this limitation is not unique to bricoleurs.

Two recent discussions of the bricoleur each have added some nuances to our understanding of this improvisational mode of design. Harper (1987) found the embodiment of the bricoleur in a small backwoods garage in upstate New York, a man named Willie who improvised Saab automobile repairs, wood burning stoves, tractor parts, and solutions to whatever problems people brought him, using odds and ends that he had accumulated over the years. Willie's genius is apparent in photographs 67 and 68 (p. 109), which show his "tractor"—a vehicle made from a 1929 International truck rear axle and seat, a 15-horsepower motor from a hay baler, front wheels from a Chevrolet car, a steering box from a 1942 one and one-half ton truck, and a gas tank from an outboard motor. The tractor could pull enormous loads in superlow, yet travel up to 40 miles per hour. What Harper's analysis shows is that the bricoleur is a thinker who makes creative use of whatever builds up during the process of work.

Thayer's (1988) recent discussion of bricolage in the context of leadership provides a second extension of the basic concept. He argues that the main function of any leader is to draw organization out of the raw materials of life (p. 239) by using ingeniously whatever is at hand. Each instance that the leader faces is a unique combination of resources and beliefs. And other than the recipe to "make do," there is no fixed procedure that the leader can follow to convert that assortment of resources into a more meaningful organization. As Thayer puts it: "The leader's function is . . . fixing things on the spot through a creative vision of what is available and what might be done with it" (p. 239). The act of drawing organization out of whatever is at hand is not a random exercise. What makes for skilled bricolage is intimate knowledge of resources, careful observation, trust in one's intuitions, listening, and confidence that any enacted structure can be self-correcting if one's ego is not invested too heavily in it.

If there is a key to success as a bricoleur it is buried in Levi-Strauss's statement that objects "are not known as a result of their usefulness; they are deemed to be useful or interesting because they are first of all known" (p. 9). Willie does not know about hay baler motors because they are useful ways to power a tractor. It's the other way around. Because he knows these motors so well, he is able to see that the one he has in hand can help him solve the problem of finding power for his tractor. Exhaustive observation and systematic cataloging of relations and connections (Levi-Strauss, 1966: 10) are necessary for successful bricolage.

With this background in place, we can now return to the issue of organizational design. If we think of designers as people who improvise, then the materials they have available to work with are the residue of their past experience and the past experience of people in their design group, the meanings attached to this past experience, observational skills, and their own willingness to rely on imaginative recombination of these materials. These elements are focused more on the past than on the future. And they are affected more by the ways in which people have codified the past than on how they envision the future. From the perspective of the bricoleur, efforts to improve organizational design fail for at least five reasons: (1) people are too detached and do not see their present situation in sufficient detail; (2) past experience is either limited or unsystemized; (3) people are unwilling or unable to work with the resources they have at hand; (4) a preoccupation with decision rationality makes it impossible for people to accept the rationality of making do; and (5) designers strive for perfection and are unable to appreciate the aesthetics of imperfection (Gioia, 1988).

Willie's tractor had post hoc orderliness, which suggested that it must be the product of intentional design. Some intention clearly was involved since he did not assemble the pile of junk in his back lot into a piece of sculpture, a buzz saw, or a boat anchor. But the important point is that he did not collect his junk pile and then add to it to fit some preconceived plan of how to make a tractor. Instead, he essentially looked at the pile of junk, said to himself, "somewhere in that pile of junk is a tractor," and then proceeded to discover the tractor in the set of materials which, up to that point, had not been organized under this concept. By saying in essence, what I have here is enough for my purposes, Willie transformed himself from an engineer into a bricoleur. And, in doing this, Willie developed his tractor into properties which an engineer working with blueprints and imagined constraints, might well have said were impossible to attain in a vehicle of this size and weight. This is not to argue that bricolage is superior to engineering. Only that it is not demonstrably worse. The connotations of the word design have tempted many people to overlook that possibility.

There are more routes to orderliness than the one through intention, planning, and implementation. Orderliness can also result from improvisation based on intimate knowledge of resources. Intimate knowledge often suggests artful recombinations of seemingly miscellaneous materials, which can make a large difference. It is that theme to which we turn next.

MYTHS SURROUNDING THE DESIGN PROCESS

CODE PHRASE: "The design of an organization determines the distribution of resources, authority, and information" (line 1).

Implied Assumptions

  5. An organization has only a single design.
  6. The design determines the distribution of resources.
  7. Designs are large structures that are stabilized.

Alternative Assumptions

  5.1 An organization has multiple designs.
  6.1 The distribution of resources determines the design.
  7.1 Designs are small structures that are amplified.

If we take the position that design is often emergent, improvised, locally rational, and built from whatever resources are at hand, then design loses some of its force as a driving condition for organizational change. If design becomes fully formed, visible, and influential relatively late in the history of a group, then it should strongly reflect the effects of events that occurred earlier in its history. Very few of those events will be directed explicitly to issues of design. Instead, most of them will be related simply to doing the work.

If design is essentially an outcome of work, rather than an input to it, then several designs should exist in any one organization since several different kinds of work occur simultaneously. Furthermore, the distribution of resources to do the work will determine the designs, and small, early events will have a disproportionately large effect on the content of the eventual design. Each of these three mechanisms reflects a different assumption than is visible in the CODE statement. And each of these alternative assumptions is consistent with the idea that organizational design is an exercise in improvisation.

The Myth of Singular Design

An organizational design is not a monolithic entity. Any reference to "the" organizational design is misleading because it makes the "assumption of homogeneity" (Dornbusch and Scott, 1975: 77). This is the assumption that the technology of an organization is essentially the same across tasks and occupational groups and the social structure is the same across work units. Typically, however, multiple structures and designs are found within a single organization, which means it is more accurate to describe organizations as a group of groups, a set of shifting coalitions, or as a federation of subcultures. This means that designs usually characterize smaller groups of people doing more specific tasks than is usually implied when people describe an organizational design as if it fits the organization as a whole.

Any attempt to construct "the" design is doomed because there is no such thing. Instead, designers need to answer the question, "Design in whose view?" To answer that question, they need to know what stream of activities, produced by what people, in the service of what goals, over what time period, has had some design attributed to it retrospectively, and now needs to have that design respecified.

The Myth of Resource Dependence

The second assumption about monolithic design that we need to reexamine is the idea that designs determine the distribution of resources. Within organizational theory, one of the more influential theories concerning resources is the view that organizations can be understood if we know the pattern of their resource dependence. Pfeffer and Salancik (1978) argue that social actors become powerful when they control resources that are critical to the organization's survival, especially when these resources cannot be obtained elsewhere. Since organizational designs tend to form around coalitions that control scarce resources, there is reason to question the idea that design determines resource distribution.

Hall (1984), in his study of the demise of the *Saturday Evening Post,* found that between 1940 and 1947 the magazine faced critical problems of supplies and printing capacity due to wartime conditions. The production operations coalition rose to power during this period since they were able to reduce some of the uncertainty concerning the critical resources of paper, ink, and printing. Their ascendance was reflected in the emergent design. After the war, when supplies were no longer a problem, the critical uncertainty became declining circulation. The coalition concerned with circulation and promotion gained ascendance, operations people lost influence, and the design shifted once more. Thus, the idea of resource dependence suggests that the distribution of resources determines design, rather than the other way around.

But we can go one step further. The concept of bricolage implies that resources are not as scarce, nor are they distributed as unevenly, as Pfeffer and Salancik suggest. The discussion of bricolage sensitized us to the possibility that there are many more potential resources, in many more places in organizations, than we usually assume. The reason we miss this possibility is that we maintain narrow definitions of what constitutes a resource. And we assume that a resource has a fixed meaning and there is limited substitutability of one resource for another one.

If we adopt a view of resources that is more consistent with the idea of bricolage—resources are pragmatic and are defined by the conditions of their use—then the distribution of the skills of bricolage, rather than the distribution of resources, should affect how the organization functions. It is the ability to combine old resources in new ways to reduce new uncertainties that determines organizational effectiveness. Thus, designs don't determine resource distribution; it's the other way around. Further, it is not the resources per se that determine design, but the capability to create resources from the residue of past experience.

Whether we adopt the idea of resource dependence or the idea of resource improvisation, resources become influential in the determination of design. To redesign an organization means that people need to redefine the crucial uncertainty facing the organization, to specify the critical resources needed to address that newly identified uncertainty, and then to encourage people either to find or to improvise the resources required. Resort to bricolage as a means to resolve critical new uncertainties should be more apparent in organizations that favor generalists than in organizations that favor specialists.

The Myth of Large Causes

The third assumption about monolithic design that we need to reexamine concerns the size and stability of designs. A design modeled after architecture typically covers many units, is worked out in some detail, and represents a relatively stable large structure that is put in place intact. The picture of design that is implied by the combination of improvisation, retrospect, and emergent orderliness is somewhat different. The primary image in this alternative view is summarized in this recipe: a little structure goes a long way (Weick, 1989).

To grasp the sense in which small structures can generate large designs, consider a self-fulfilling prophecy. Self-fulfilling prophecies are just another way of saying that expectations make a difference. A self-fulfilling prophecy was defined by Robert Merton as "an unconditional prediction or expectation about a future situation such that, first, had it not been made, the future situation envisaged would not have occurred, but because it is made, alterations in behavior are produced which bring about that envisioned situation, or bring that envisioned situation to pass" (cited in Henshel, 1987: 2).

The key event in a self-fulfilling prophecy involves an expectation that causes an envisioned situation to materialize. Prophecies, therefore, become tools of design. They set forces in motion which produce determinant structures that weren't there before. New structures are created because the prophecy alters behaviors, and the altered behaviors are the means by which the prophecy is fulfilled.

To see how this works, consider a bandwagon effect in an election (Henshel and Johnston, 1987). A bandwagon effect occurs when the predicted winner in an election poll gains additional votes as a result of the publication of the poll. The poll is a prophecy, and it becomes a self-fulfilling prophecy when it leads people to alter their behavior in ways that lend validity to the prophecy. Henshel and Johnston (1987) found that poll forecasts do alter behavior, but not in the ways we thought. Poll forecasts that reach some level of credibility and accuracy lead key individuals to increase their financial contributions, volunteerism, and endorsements, and these three inputs modify campaigns. It is these altered campaigns that affect voters and lead them to alter their behaviors so the prophecies of the polls are fulfilled. Notice that there is nothing mysterious or nonrational about the way this mechanism works. Choices to increase one's support for a candidate based on polls is a rational choice made by people who stand to benefit if the candidate is elected.

The bandwagon effect is an even better example of emergent designs with small beginnings than may be apparent. So far, we have suggested that expectations make a difference. But they make even more of a difference when they recycle. Once an election poll gains credibility, it becomes more likely that the forecast will alter behavior even more quickly and even more strongly, which makes it even more accurate, which raises its credibility even more, and so on. If one expectation is a source of a design, then a self-confirming expectation that recycles and amplifies should produce a more stable design that organizes an increasingly large set of resources. Something that started small in the form of an expectation grows into a complex structure of interdependent people because a self-fulfilling prophecy became a *serial* self-fulfilling prophecy. Small initial increments in funds, people, and endorsements were amplified into more powerful variables that determined outcomes. The self-fulfilling prophecy and the events it triggered became the design, although no one intended this outcome. Furthermore, it would be hard to predict the size of the structure that eventually emerged, given the inconspicuous events with which it started.

The scenario we have described is not confined to election campaigns. It is the essence of emergent design. The things designers *expect* will happen may predict the designs they achieve better than will their statements about what they plan to have happen. Creating a bandwagon through serial self-fulfilling prophecies that amplify is not that much different from creating a social movement or becoming an idea champion. In both cases, the incipient design starts small but enlarges rapidly. The beginning creates the conditions for its own perpetuation and enlargement. While it is possible to design an expectation that amplifies, it is more likely that elements combine with less deliberation around smaller starting points that are more capricious. Again, the resulting design is no less orderly nor is it necessarily any less effective. What it is, however, is less bound by the limits of the designer's imagination, more subject to the vagaries of improvisation, and more likely to assume unexpected shapes.

MANAGERS AND IMPROVISED DESIGN

CODE PHRASE: Design "impacts the ability of individual managers" (line 2).

Implied Assumptions
   8. Design affects managerial ability.
   9. Managerial action is individual.

Alternative Assumptions
   8.1 Managerial ability affects design.
   9.1 Managerial action is social.

Organizational designs can have an impact on managerial ability, as the CODE statement suggests, in the sense that formalized relationships make it easier or harder to get things done, in the sense that designs provide more or less discretion to do what one is best able to do, and in the sense that designs carry provisions for more or less corrective feedback. But the idea of design as improvisation highlights the opposite direction of impact—namely, ability has an impact on design. It is important to understand this opposite relationship because it suggests determinants of design that people often overlook.

Managerial Ability and Design

The idea that ability affects design was implicit in the previous discussion of bricolage. People who have skills at bricolage often are able to transform a large number of miscellaneous resources into a small number of critical resources through imaginative recombination. These recombinations may remove critical uncertainties. If they do, this means that the people who built the critical resources acquire more power and a bigger say over what form the organization will take. The skilled bricoleur affects design because people defer to, seek out, comply with, and attribute power to those who are able to reduce critical uncertainties. These acts of deference can become stabilized into repetitive sequences that then become a new emergent structure.

The idea that ability affects design is also implicit in the choice to deal with technical complexity through greater complexity of the performer rather than greater complexity of the structure. Scott (1987: 236) has called this choice a watershed in organizational design. Rather than divide the work and parcel it out to differentiated groups, designers keep the work intact and assign it to complex, flexible performers called professionals. When the work is handled by professionals, organic structures tend to replace mechanistic structures (Weick and McDaniel, 1989), the locus of authority is task-specific, and interdependence is intermittent rather than constant. Regardless of what designs professionals enact, the point is that complex skills embodied in a single actor have an impact on organizational design.

But ability affects design in a still more basic sense. Ability affects perception: people see those things they can do something about (Jervis, 1976: 374–375). And ability affects goal setting: people feel they should do what they can do (Dornbusch and Scott, 1975: 86). People see the world as filled with projects that fit their capabilities, and they see these projects as the ones that need doing. If the content of design is affected by what people notice, and if people notice those things about which they can do something, then generalists—people such as a bricoleur who are able to do many different things—should notice more options and enact a greater variety of designs than specialists see and do. Improvements in design expertise should come not so much from direct schooling in blueprints for design as from development of a larger response repertoire.

Managerial Self-Efficacy and Design

While actual skill development is an important determinant of design, one's *perception* of that level of skill development may be equally influential in the determination of design, as is suggested by the work of Bandura and his associates (1986). The sense of self-efficacy experienced by designers should affect the designs they produce. The key ideas about efficacy include the following.

When people transform their knowledge and abilities into action, this transformation is mediated by thoughts about themselves and their capabilities. These thoughts concern such things as perceived capability to mobilize motivation, to control perturbing thoughts, to persevere, to bounce back from failure, and to exert some control over the environment. These beliefs affect how much of one's skills will actually be mustered to cope with the demands of a task. Thus, given the same level of skill, a person will perform poorly, adequately, or extraordinarily, depending on self-efficacy (Bandura and Wood, 1989). High self-efficacy is associated with a rapid recovery from failure and reverses (Bandura, 1990: 317), persistence in the face of obstacles, the effective control of intrusive thoughts that focus attention on the self rather than on the task, a perception of the environment as controllable, the likelihood of setting higher goals and remaining committed to them for longer periods, and the increased ability to visualize the future in terms of scenarios of success rather than scenarios of failure.

The relevance of efficacy to organizational design is the following. To construct designs in dynamic environments requires that information from diverse sources be integrated, that design options be identified, and that exploratory learning occur concurrently with management of the ongoing organization. There is a need for the creative and persistent use of complex sets of capabilities in order to exercise some control over the environment and the organization. Success in forming and enacting these complex capabilities is mediated by self-referential thought:

> Operative self-efficacy is a generative capability in which multiple subskills must be continuously *improvised* [italics added] to manage ever-changing circumstances. . . . (I)ndividuals who believe themselves to be inefficacious are likely to effect limited changes even in environments that provide many opportunities. Conversely, those who have a firm belief in their efficacy, through ingenuity and perseverance, figure out ways of exercising some measure of control in environments containing limited opportunities and many constraints. (Bandura and Wood, 1989: 805–806).

Beliefs about self-efficacy and the controllability of the environment trigger something akin to a self-fulfilling prophecy for design. People who believe the environment can be enacted and that they have the capabilities to do so, are motivated to make strong, persistent efforts to control it, which increases their chance for success. If they succeed, this validates their sense of efficacy and their perception of controllability. If they fail, the effects of the failure are transient and become the occasion for learning rather than self-doubt (Elliott and Dweck, 1988). People who doubt their efficacy and view environments as uncontrollable exert less effort for shorter periods, which thwarts successful control. Unfortunately, this confirms their prophecy that things are uncontrollable and that they don't have sufficient skills to change this reality (Bandura and Wood, 1989: 811).

If we assume that better design comes from focusing on the task than from focusing on the self, then high self-efficacy is an important antecedent of design because it encourages people to pay attention to the task. People with lower self-efficacy doubt their problem-solving capabilities, the controllability of the environment, and their likelihood of success, and these doubts become self-confirming through their debilitating effects on action. The doubts suggest that redesign is fruitless, and these doubts become intrusive thoughts, which make it that much harder to visualize and enact any design that is an improvement. The design process become impoverished, not because people lack the skills for design, but because they lack the beliefs that convert those skills into action.

Managerial Groups and Design

One outcome of the CODE assumption that design impacts the ability of individual managers is a blind spot regarding the ways in which ability rather than the environment shapes design. But another, more subtle, blind spot lurks in the phrase "individual manager" because it presumes that there is such a thing. In many ways, the idea of an individual manager is a fiction. Managing is a composite of partial contributions made by many individuals whose identity is defined by their social relations. Management work is profoundly social, which means that the dispersion and meaning of a design is not easily controlled. Designs don't create social systems; they are created by social systems. And design effectiveness is determined by the existing social relationships that are engaged by the design.

Organizational design is social rather than individual in the obvious sense that it is built of social entities such as the top management team (Hurst, Rush, and White,

1989), the interact (Weick, 1979), the vertical dyad linkage between superior and subordinate (Graen and Scandura, 1987), or the interaction order (Barley, 1986: 101). In all of these cases, the important point is that "decisions are made either in the presence of others or with the knowledge that they will have to be implemented, or understood, or approved by others" (Burns and Stalker, 1961: 118).

But organizational design is also social in the less obvious but more fundamental sense that the individual is not separable from the human whole: "'Society' and 'individuals' do not denote separable phenomena, but are simply collective and distributive aspects of the same thing, the relation between them being like that between other expressions, one of which denotes a group as a whole and the other the members of the group, such as army and the soldiers, the class and the students" (Cooley, 1964: 37). If a person goes off alone into the wilderness, that person goes with a mind formed in society, and communication continues through memory, imagination, and books (p. 49). The imagined presence of others is no less real than their actual presence. Individuals who retrospectively label some pattern as a design speak on behalf of their associates (Chatman, Bell, and Staw, 1986), speak through the language they were socialized into, speak from a place in a social structure complete with reputation and status and expectations, and speak to prove their entitlement to continue to be regarded as a member in good standing.

When Allport (1954: 5) crafted his influential definition of social psychology as "an attempt to understand and explain how the thought, feeling, and behavior of individuals are influenced by the actual, imagined, and implied presence of other human beings," he provided a framework that is useful also for the scholar of organizational design. The thought, feeling, and behavior that go into the construction of a design, and that are reciprocally shaped by that design, are never individual and solitary. Designs are shaped in the service of others who matter, just as those others who matter are themselves shaped by the designs they construct. Designs reflect social interests, and they also structure social interests. Any act by an "individual manager" is actually an act by a representative, whose stature and membership are on the line. Whether high stakes are involved depends on the availability of alternative social resources. The smaller the number of alternatives, the higher the need to enact designs that are acceptable in the eyes of those who matter. Even if this drama is played out in imagination, it is no less real. What is unreal is to regard it as the activity of just one person.

INTERPRETATION AND IMPROVISED DESIGN

CODE PHRASE: Designs affect "the ability to make and implement" "timely, . . . sound, and . . . acceptable decisions" (lines 2–3).

Implied Assumptions

    10. Decisions determine effectiveness.
    11. The purpose of design is to facilitate decision making.
    12. People decide and then they act.

Alternative Assumptions

    10.1 Interpretations determine effectiveness.
    11.1 The purpose of design is to facilitate interpretation.
    12.1 People act and then they interpret.

Improvisation is largely an act of interpretation rather than an act of decision making. People who improvise have to make sense of unexpected events that emerge, which means they are more concerned with interpreting what has happened than with deciding what will happen. They may decide to start some activity, such as implementing a design, and they may also try to control how the activity will unfold. Nevertheless, this control is never complete, and unintended consequences are commonplace. These unintended consequences force people to revise their sense of what is happening and what can be accomplished. And it is these revised interpretations, rather than the initial decisions, that guide action and constitute the actual design in use. That design in use is shaped more by action than by plans, and more by interpretations than by decisions. In this section, we look briefly at the role of interpretation in design.

Interpretation and Decision Making

To interpret means to encode external events into internal categories that are part of the group's culture and language system (Daft and Weick, 1984). The act of interpretation involves creating maps or representations that simplify some territory in order to facilitate action. A common simplification is the interpretation that events require some kind of decision to be made. It is this sense in which design becomes an issue of interpretation before it becomes an issue of decision making. As Brown (1978: 376) has shown, power in organizations is exercised by those who design the frameworks, which then determine what it means to "make decisions." Frameworks affect what we see and what we ignore, which then affect the scope and content of decision making.

The way in which interpretation takes precedence over decision making can be illustrated using the idea of decision strategies put forward by Thompson and Tuden (1959). They argued that decision makers need to use different strategies to make decisions, depending on whether their associates agree or disagree on their preferences for outcomes and whether these associates agree or disagree about the causal structure of the problem (i.e., which means leads to which outcomes). If people agree on both preferences and means-ends relations, then the appropriate design for decision making is one that allows for a programmed, routine response. If people agree on preferences but not on causal structure, a case that is common among professionals, then the appropriate design is one in which collegial interaction among equals results in a judgment. Disagreement on preferences with agreement on causal structure favors a design in which people can work out a compromise among the various representatives who favor different preferences. Complete disagreement requires a design that increases the probability that some inspiring vision will emerge on which people can agree.

Each of these four decision strategies—computation, judgment, compromise, and inspiration—favors a different design, but the prescribed design presumes that preferences and causal structure are fixed. To design for interpretation means that we back up one step. The designer now asks the question, "What design will enable people to achieve more agreement on preferences and causal structure so that they can make greater use of computation and routine to make decisions?" The design prescription implied here is that people and responsibilities should be distributed so that people find it easier to agree on preferences and/or causation.

If the environment is loosely coupled and indeterminant, then there may be no conceivable design that will improve agreements about causal structure. In that case, the designer who is sensitive to interpretation should encourage patterns of interaction that make it more likely that people will come to some agreement in their preferences for outcomes. The current push to change corporate culture (e.g., O'Reilly, 1989) can be understood as an effort to increase agreement on preferences in the face of an inability to get much agreement about what leads to what in a turbulent world. The push for more agreement on preferences is a push for conditions that favor collegial, professional interaction and a more thorough use of informed judgment to make tough decisions.

Notice that most organizations have preferred decision strategies already in place from earlier design exercises. For example, they may have a representative structure, such as in union-management negotiations, where they hammer out a compromise, given their dissimilar preferences and similar views of causal structure. But, as the pace of environmental change intensifies and as novel competitive pressures arise, old views of causal structure no longer work and dominant new views are hard to come by. As a result, the old pattern of agreements on causal structure that made compromise a plausible decision strategy now breaks down, even though the strategy of compromise is retained. The situation has changed into one in which inspiration is appropriate, yet the people involved continue to act as if compromise still makes sense.

What is needed in the face of this impasse is a design that does one of two things. Either it enables people to learn more about their environment and rebuild some agreements about causal structure—in which case they can continue to use compromise—or it enables them to generate truly novel solutions that are so compelling and so elegant that they inspire commitment from everyone. These two designs have points of overlap. In both cases, an openness to information and experimentation is beneficial. But the inspirational design requires more attention to persuasion, passion, and conversion, and thus it is more like a social movement than is the more incremental, more deliberate, more dispassionate, more cumulative design involved in rebuilding solid agreements about the nature of causation in a complex world.

In all of these scenarios, interpretation is a key to effectiveness, and the purpose of design is to facilitate interpretation. Once an interpretation is stabilized, then people can design for decision making. In the face of causal indeterminacy, many designs for interpretation help people adopt "the mantle of professionalism" and become more sensitive to issues of value (Ranson, Hinings, and Greenwood, 1980: 6). The design issue is not how to apply judgment to decision making. The design issue is how to construct a capability for judgment in the first place. That issue is an act of interpretation, because it necessitates an effort to get agreement on preferences. In order to construct such a framework, people have to encode events into a common set of values and implications. Once that commonality is achieved, then they can begin to act like professionals.

Organic organizational structures often turn out to be excellent generic designs, not so much because they are better suited to deal with high environmental uncertainty, but because they encourage the dense interactions that enable people to come to agreements about preferences and sometimes even causal structures (Weick and McDaniel, 1989). It is these agreements which then make it possible for people to use decision strategies that are better suited to deal with uncertainty. When interpretation is the issue, people need to design for agreement rather than for effectiveness. Effectiveness focuses too much attention on decision making and rationality and too little attention on what assumptions, frameworks, and resources people impose that give shape to that decision making.

Interpretation and Sense-Making

If organizational design is to generate unequivocal interpretations, as well as effective decisions, then it must provide a way to focus the interpretation process. Otherwise, people are flooded with plausible interpretations for what their elapsed actions mean. One way to focus interpretation is through the use of behavioral commitment. The idea is that if a design creates structural conditions in which a behavior is difficult to change, then interpretation will focus on those socially acceptable reasons that justify the irrevocable action. Organizational design incorporates a sensitivity to the interpretation process when it creates those conditions in which specific behaviors become the anchor around which expectations, beliefs, and attitudes form.

The background for this proposal lies in Salancik's (1977) discussion of behavioral commitment. The basic ideas are these. Normally, when people act, their reasons for doing things are either self-evident or uninteresting, especially when the actions themselves can be undone, minimized, or disowned. Actions that are neither visible nor permanent can be explained with casual, transient explanations. As those actions become more public and irrevocable, however, they become harder to undo; and, when those same actions are also volitional, they become harder to disown. When action is irrevocable, public, and volitional, the search for explanations becomes less casual because more is at stake. Explanations that are developed retrospectively to justify committed actions are often stronger than beliefs developed under other, less involving, conditions. A tenacious justification can produce selective attention, confident action, and self-confirmation. Tenacious justifications prefigure both perception and action, which means they are often self-confirming.

Commitment focuses sense making on three things: an action, a socially acceptable justification for that action, and the potential of subsequent activities to validate the justification. Thus commitment is a an outcome of improvised design that facilitates interpretation. Commitment ties together behaviors, explanations, social support, and expectations into a plausible causal sequence. This sequence can become a causal loop that either stabilizes or amplifies the pattern. It is these patterns which people come to label as sensible episodes. Different commitments lead to different patterns and a different sense of what is happening.

The importance of design in sense making can be illustrated using Smircich and Morgan's (1982: 258) description of the management of meaning; they propose that "leadership lies in large part in generating a point of reference, against which a feeling of organization and direction can emerge." An improvised design creates a point of reference around which meaning forms. To redesign is to respecify this generative point. Our proposal is that behavioral commitment is one way to create this point of reference. Thus, commitment is important because it sets sense making in motion and imposes some constraints on the form it will take.

Commitments can persevere, diffuse, and enlarge. And it is this capability which makes them important for design. Staw (1982: 116) has described this possibility in a way that unites several themes we have been developing: "When technology is ambiguous and products are value laden, commitment to goals and procedures, whatever they are, may be sufficient for proper adjustment to the environment. At the extreme, a 'school of thought' may be created (as in university life) where successful organizational leaders are those who can convince others that their own commitments are the standard to be achieved."

Several points are worth noting in Staw's description. First, commitment enables people to cope with turbulent environments. Second, commitment is a way to cope with unclear cause-effect relationships ("technology is ambiguous") and disagreement about preferences ("products are value laden"). Third, any old commitment can trigger the process of interpretation—all we need is something that animates people so they begin to generate actions, which can then become patterned. Fourth, although Staw says that commitment encourages "adjustment to" the environment, the phrase "creation of" could be substituted just as easily to allow for the possibility of enactment. Fifth, commitments to goals and procedures may stimulate justifications which turn into a "school of thought," a paradigm, or a system of interpretation. Sixth, leaders who try to persuade others to adopt the leader's commitment as a standard are managing interpretation. Seventh, commitment to goals and procedures represents a basic act of organizing, since consciously constructed procedures to reach goals are the defining property of organizations for many analysts.

Interpretation and Action

Commitment becomes a more plausible tool of design when we assume that people act their way into meaning. When people improvise and then look back over their actions to see what they might have meant, they often discover decisions that they apparently made, although they didn't realize it at the time (Garfinkel, 1967). Thus, action is decision-*interpreted,* not decision-driven. Actions are crucial because they constrain meaning and structure and organizational form. It is these constraints that people seem to lose sight of when they assume that decisions affect action.

Think back to the earlier example of bandwagon effects. Serial self-fulfilling prophecies create a trail of public, irrevocable, voluntary actions by pollsters, contributors, and candidates, which become justified into an "organized campaign." The organized campaign is an emergent design that forms out of irrevocable forecasting, contributing, and campaigning that become linked into causal sequences that amplify. As the linkages among these actions become tighter, expectations become stronger, action is shaped more fully by expectations, and actions become less variable—all of which represent an increase in social order.

Actions can be an important source of meaning and structure that hold a system together, but only when these actions become salient anchors for justification. When attention is focused on a handful of actions, the process of interpretation also becomes focused. Designs in the service of interpretation differ materially from designs in the service of decision making. Designs for interpretation presume that people are confused rather than ignorant, and that confusion is reduced by interaction, opportunities for consensual validation, self-organizing, collective memory, conversation, and narratives (Orr, 1990)—in short, by rich communication media. A growing number of organizational observers identify phenomena such as paradox (e.g. Quinn and Cameron, 1988), dilemmas (Aram, 1976), and dualities (Munch, 1982) as everyday accompaniments of decision making. The problem with environments is no longer solely one of uncertainty, with a corresponding need for increased quantities of information. Advanced information technologies (e.g., Huber, 1990) have lessened this problem. The problem now is more one of multiple meanings.

Designs that help people remove equivocality are needed to cope with multiple meanings. Those designs tend to be more social, more tolerant of improvisation, and more affected by action than is true for designs grounded in decision making.

FORMS OF CONTROL IN IMPROVISED DESIGN

CODE PHRASE: "Manager's ability to coordinate and control the activities of subordinates" (lines 5–6).

Implied Assumptions

13. Control is differentially distributed.
14. People impose controls.
15. Activities are the object of control.

Alternative Assumptions

13.1 Control is equally distributed.
14.1 Ideas impose controls.
15.1 Ideas are the object of control.

The model of control usually assumed by designers is that it is unilateral, top down, tied to positions, hierarchical, and formal. Some individuals exert control over other ones, and either the process or the outcome of activities is the object of control. When Perrow (1986: 129) discussed first-order controls, such as giving orders, direct surveillance, and imposition of rules, and second-order bureaucratic controls, such as specialization and standardization, he described the two forms of control that are usually associated with design.

If we adopt the idea of design as improvisation, then direct control becomes more difficult, partly because people do not have exact standards against which improvised performance can be measured. Instead, when people improvise they often discover the standards for performance simultaneous with the discovery of what the actions produce in the first place. Direct control of improvisation is also difficult because it is self-defeating to standardize performance. The advantage of improvisation is that it is responsive to ongoing change in the organization and the environment, and standardization removes this advantage. Since the essence of improvisation is that people use many different means to accomplish outcomes, behavior control (Ouchi, 1979) is meaningless. And since realized outcomes often differ from intended outcomes, outcome control may also be difficult.

Control by Premises

Given the many ways in which an improvised performance is ambiguous, any attempt to impose control over this performance using traditional forms of control is apt to fail. Surveillance of improvisation is difficult, and it is unclear what one is looking for even if surveillance is possible.

But improvisation is not without control. It is controlled by frames of reference (Shrivastava and Mitroff, 1984) that participants take for granted. Perrow (1986) calls these third-order controls. They are embodied in such things as the vocabulary of the organization, procedural and substantive routines, preferred communication channels, selection criteria, meeting agendas, and socialization practices. Control through premises is just as influential in shaping behavior as is control through rules or bureaucratic standardization. But premise control is also less obtrusive, more cognitive, more tied to language, and more volitional, since "the subordinate *voluntarily* restricts the range of stimuli that will be attended to ("Those sorts of things are irrelevant,' or 'What has that got to do with the matter?') and the range of alternatives that would be considered ('It would never occur to me to do that')" (Perrow, 1986: 129).

The ways in which third-order controls affect behavior are subtle and easily overlooked by the designer who finds it easier to see the material controls represented by tangible orders, rules, surveillance, standardization, specialization, and hierarchy. Third-order controls are more subtle but no less forceful because:

> They limit information content and flow, thus controlling the premises available for decisions; they set up expectations so as to highlight some aspects of the situation and play down others; they limit the search for alternatives when problems are confronted, thus ensuring more predictable and consistent solutions; they indicate the threshold levels as to when a danger signal is being emitted . . .; they achieve coordination of effort by selecting certain kinds of work techniques and schedules." (Perrow, 1986: 128).

We have already been introduced to third-order controls in the previous discussion of behavioral commitment. We saw that people act their way into meanings when they try to explain elapsed actions. If some of those important elapsed actions were done publicly and irrevocably and volitionally, they will be especially salient since they are clearly the responsibility of the people who did them. The reasons people invoke to justify these visible behaviors become potential third-order controls for other actions. Not only do these justifications explain the committed action, they also are often communicated to other personas as premises they can use to express themselves and to interpret the actions of other people. The justifications become a crucial part of the cognitive infrastructure that articulates and gives substance to the organization. The organization actually becomes defined in part by the recurrent justifications that people adopt to express and interpret organizational action. Justifications that deviate from these conventions can call into question the person's tacit claim that he or she is a member in good standing.

The importance of justification as a tool for design is suggested by Lucas's (1987: 147) statement that "organizations define and think themselves out through repertoires of patterned actions, a capacity to develop, implement, and maintain justifications for structures of existing repertoires, and through negotiating rules for changing these repertoires." Justifications are one of many forms by which organizations define and think themselves into existence. Justifications are socially acceptable reasons people give themselves for choosing to do something in public that is irrevocable. As these reasons accumulate into patterns of affirmation, restriction, and permission, they guide people and enable them to judge others and justify themselves to those others. Sets of justifications should form coherent and workable systems of interpretation that create a corporate culture. To describe the organization in this way is to suggest that control is widely rather than narrowly dispersed, that ideas rather than people impose controls, and that ideas rather than activities are the object of control.

If we argue that organizations *are* cultures, rather than *have* cultures, as does Meek (1988: 459), then everyone in the organization, including those at the top, is equally subject to third-order control: "Most anthropologists would find the idea that leaders create culture preposterous: leaders do not create culture. It emerges from the collective social interactions of groups and communities. . . . The chief is as much a part of a local culture as are his tribal or clan compatriots." The notion that control is differentially distributed tends to be associated with the view that organizations have cultures that can be changed from the top. Cultures are not that easy to change, nor are they the exclusive property of people at the top. As ideas diffuse through the organization, control also becomes diffused since people now adopt similar premises for their decisions.

While it is obvious that resources such as expertise and capital are differentially distributed, there are general capabilities such as bricolage and improvisation that enable people to reduce some of this differential. Because ideas can originate anywhere within the organization and diffuse to any other part, third-order controls are potentially available to a much larger number of participants than are the controls of rules and standardization. This means that redesign can be initiated in a wider variety of places, and that anyone with a compelling framework is a potential designer. As organizations come more and more to resemble networks (e.g., Miles and Snow, 1986), the notion of dispersed design becomes more plausible.

Control by Paradigms

If ideas rather than people impose control, then we must learn more about what form these compelling ideas take. A recurrent suggestion is that systems of ideas in organizations resemble paradigms in science (Shrivastava and Mitroff, 1984: 19; Brown, 1978; Bresser and Bishop, 1983: 598–592; Pfeffer, 1982). If we assume that paradigms contain organizational designs and guide action, then we have a vehicle by which ideas, interpretations, and justifications exert control.

Pfeffer (1982: 227–228) describes a paradigm as a "technology, including beliefs about cause-effect relations and standards of practice and behavior, as well as specific examples of these, that constitute how an organization goes about doing things." Since justifications often take the form of beliefs about cause-effect, standards, and examples, they are important elements in paradigms. Paradigms tend to be closed systems, closed in the sense that they are not just a view of the world, but also contain procedures for inquiring about the world and categories to collect the observations that are stimulated by these inquiries. Paradigms are powerful tools of interpretation.

Paradigms can create strong preconceptions that prefigure observation. This possibility suggests that paradigms could produce behavioral confirmation in ways similar to those reviewed earlier in the context of serial self-fulfilling prophecies. Justifications might do more than simply provide rationales for designs that are internally compelling. They might also shape actions in ways that validate the rationales.

The way in which specific justifications may generate an organizational design, preserved in a paradigm, is suggested by Ross and Staw's (1986) careful study of Expo 86. The explanations adopted to justify the investment of more resources into Expo

86 included such justifications the following: we will inject 15,000 man-years of jobs into the economy; this will show that Vancouver is the equal of Toronto and Montreal; British Columbia will be seen as the province that completes its projects; this shows what the Social Credit government can do; and Expo 86 will increase our chances to get a major league baseball team. These justifications gave meaning to the sponsor's decision to proceed with funding of Expo 86, but they also provided evocative images that defined the event for people who were unclear about what it was and what it meant.

These justifications for Expo 86 can be viewed evaluatively as biased statements that reflect an escalation of unrealistic expectations. But they can also be viewed descriptively as reasons held for a reason, which diffused and organized people who were originally both detached from and puzzled by the initial commitment. The justifications replaced disorganization with organization, and microcommitments with macroconsequences. Justifications of a few imposed an order, focus, and meaning on many. The justifications that accumulated around Expo 86 gradually became a set of third-order controls that shaped how people thought about the event and how they acted to validate these thoughts.

Control by Enacted Stability

When justifications become combined into paradigms, they often have effects similar to those of formal structure: "Since robust ideologies incorporating harmonious values elicit self-control and voluntary cooperation they can substitute for formal structures designed to achieve the same ends" (Meyer, 1982: 55).

Contingency theories (e.g., Lawrence and Lorsch, 1967) begin with some variation of the theme that mechanistic structures are best suited to stable environments, while organic structures are more appropriate for changing environments. Typically, environmental change is viewed as something largely outside the influence of organizations. The position we are developing suggests a different conclusion. Justifications, assembled into paradigms, can be enacted into a changing environment, thereby imposing some stability on it. Perception guided by a coherent paradigm can prefigure an environment. And confident action based on that prefiguring can actually move the environment in the direction of those paradigmatic preconceptions. That possibility is the important design point that is implicit in serial self-fulfilling prophecies.

But the key point is not that environments can be enacted so they become more consistent with preconceptions. The key point is more basic than this. Any environment that becomes more consistent with preconceptions also becomes more stable and more predictable. And as the environment becomes more stable and predictable, it becomes better suited to mechanistic organizational forms. The effect of paradigms on the environment may depend less on the content of the paradigm than on the fact that the paradigm represents a plausible map of the environment and helps stabilize the environment. If the paradigm stabilizes the environment and makes it more predictable, then mechanistic organizational forms become more appropriate.

In a way any old paradigm will do. As long as the paradigm improves prediction, allows a higher level of agreement on cause-effect relations and/or preferences, and encourages people to act as if their prophecies are valid, then the result will be more environmental stability, a more favorable setting for mechanistic structures, and a setting in which application of a rational model will be more appropriate. Recall that in the bandwagon example, decisions to increase financial contributions, work, and endorsements were rational responses to increases in polling accuracy produced by self-fulfilling prophecies.

Thus, we wind up in the same place as do many designers, with their highly specified designs and mechanistic structures animated by rational procedures. But we get there through a very different route. Essentially, we argue that people enact stability and rationality into the environment when they justify behavioral commitments, engage in subsequent activities that reaffirm earlier justifications, pool justifications into paradigms, and deploy these paradigms like serial self-fulfilling prophecies. Stability comes from tight coupling between action and cognition that is created by the necessity to explain behavioral commitments to oneself and to important peers. This tightened coupling represents a focused actor, engaged in focused action, that can change existing environments and enact new ones. Persistent action that is backed by a supportive paradigm can stabilize environments and make reasoning and formalization more successful.

Strong paradigms built from justifications impose perceptual as well as material stability on the changing environment, at least for short periods of time. These temporary stabilities allow the activation of short-term routines to deal with inputs. And these temporary stabilities tend to be the dominant forms of control in improvised designs.

SOURCES OF CHANGE IN IMPROVISED DESIGNS

CODE PHRASE: "Proper organizational design can therefore make the difference between having an effective, well-run organization and one having recurrent crises and organizational inefficiencies" (lines 7–8).

Implied Assumptions

    16. An effective organization has few crises and inefficiencies.
    17. Recurrent crises and inefficiencies reduce current effectiveness.
    18. Proper organizational design reduces current inefficiency.

Alternative Assumptions

    16.1 An effective organization has many crises and inefficiencies.
    17.1 Recurrent crises and inefficiencies increase future effectiveness.
    18.1 Proper organizational design exploits crises and inefficiencies.

One of the ironies of a successful organizational design is that its very effectiveness makes redesign and learning more difficult. If crises and inefficiencies are held to a minimum in the interest of order and high performance, then this creates the wrong context for learning and redesign. Redesign is stimulated by trial and error, experiments, failures, rough edges, and novel juxtapositions, *if* people aren't overwhelmed by anxiety when old designs fail and new ones are not yet obvious (Weick, 1985). Continued effectiveness in a changing environment requires continuous redesign. And continuous redesign requires both crises that suggest new ways of operating and resilient people who are able to spot these new ways of operating. A system in which crisis and efficiency are muted in the name of effective operation has lost some of its capability for adaptation, creativity, and learning (Weick, 1977). Crisis and inefficiency benefit redesign, but this possibility is often lost on designers who measure the quality of their design by how well things seem to be running right now.

Inefficiency As a Source of Change

To rethink the role of crisis and inefficiency in organizational design, we first need to reexamine the concept of effectiveness. Discussions of design tend to treat effectiveness criteria as fixed criteria of performance that reflect adaptation. An alternative way to view effectiveness criteria is as variable sources of sense-making that preserve adaptability. Adaptive organizations often change scorecards so that they measure what their current design makes possible. Thus, when confronted with ineffective performance, people are just as likely to change their criteria of effectiveness as they are to change their designs. They act, and then treat the consequences of their actions as their intentions. As a result, their existing organizational design is reaffirmed as an appropriate design.

Effectiveness, viewed in the context of improvisation, is simply one kind of explanation that is used to make sense of elapsed action. Effectiveness has little meaning a priori (Cummings, 1983: 193) because there is nothing for it to explain until action takes place. Once action occurs, then effectiveness is one of many categories that suggest what the action may have meant. But notice an interesting twist. All action is effective with respect to some criterion. The problem is simply to locate that criterion, to use it to interpret one meaning of the action, and then to convince other people that this is a plausible meaning for what occurred. The problem of interpretation involved in judgments of effectiveness is no different from the problem of interpretation involved with behavioral commitment. In both cases, the goal is to explain the elapsed action.

This line of argument has several implications for design. First, it suggests that there is nothing magical about "effectiveness," especially considering that Campbell (1977: 36–39) found 30 different indices of effectiveness that have been used by researchers and practitioners. With that much diversity in indicators, judgments of effectiveness are nothing but an exercise in interpretation. Second, crises and inefficiencies stimulate learning and reinterpretation. Actions that prove hard to justify often stimulate a wider, more vigorous search for explanations that may uncover novel rationales for design (Grandoori, 1987). Third, there can be value in inefficient actions. Starbuck and Nystrom (1983: 152–153), who have written extensively on this theme, reflect the flavor of these discussions when they note:

> Benefits can arise from accepting goal disagreements, shifting attention from one goal to another, using sophisticated forecasting techniques while distrusting their forecasts, questioning strategies and procedures that have clearly succeeded, altering constraints that define acceptable behavior, and lowering goals after failures or unsuccessful searches. Such actions sharpen perceptions, encourage experimentation, and foster improvements. Judgments about organizational effectiveness generally undervalue information, discovery, and learning. Effectiveness that falls below the best performance attainable is nevertheless desirable if it includes information about better criteria or better methods. Conversely, superficially optimal effectiveness is actually undesirable if it forecloses learning.

Consider the example of information overload. Among the responses to information overload are omission, greater tolerance for error, queueing, filtering, abstracting, use of multiple channels, escape, and chunking (Miller, 1978: 131–152). While each of these responses is an inefficient use of information input, each also may reveal that some of that input is actually dispensable, as well as that new ideas in the form of new priorities, new methods of coping, and different categories, make more sense in the context of current problems.

Collateral Organization As a Source of Change

In general, the willingness to cultivate inefficiency and crisis to improve design is motivated by doubts that any one design can anticipate change and stimulate ongoing innovation. Crises and inefficiencies expand repertoires and update understanding of the environment. But they also make ongoing functioning more difficult, which is why Huber (1984: 941) proposed the importance of the collateral organization. Two organizations, with the same members, operate side by side, one being the experimenting organization and the other being a set of more mechanistic roles and procedures to exploit the discoveries of the experimenting organization. The concept of simultaneous participation in more than one organization structure is a valuable means to preserve the divergence necessary for change and the convergence necessary for stability.

Collateral organizations, however, make sizeable demands on people, require clear switching rules, and can create nightmares of accountability (e.g., which system did you think you were in when you made that blunder?). At a minimum, design efforts should target inefficiencies as *both* a threat and an opportunity, and then inquire thoroughly which of those two possibilities best preserves the adaptability of the organization. Inefficiencies often preserve a diverse response that might prove beneficial in a different environment. If the environment is changing rapidly and might soon assume some quite different form, and if the inefficiencies can be isolated from the rest of the system, then they might well be protected from designers and accountants alike since they may comprise the core of the next generation of design.

DYNAMICS OF CHANGE IN IMPROVISED DESIGN

CODE PHRASE: "Organizational environments are changing . . . rapidly . . . [which] erodes [the effectiveness of an organizational design] over time" (lines 9–10).

Implied Assumptions

19. Environments change more rapidly than do organizations.
20. Designs construct organizations to fit environments.
21. Designs are relatively permanent.

Alternative Assumptions

19.1 Organizations change more rapidly than do environments.
20.1 Designs construct environments to fit organizations.
21.1 Designs are relatively transient.

Rapid environmental change is often the impetus for organizational redesign. Use of the word "erodes" in the CODE statement to describe the effect of this environmental change on the organization implies a gradual, almost imperceptible, loss of fit over a long period of time. The imagery of erosion also implies that periods of redesign are infrequent. There should be intermittent small changes in design intended to prop up those features that seem to be losing their value. The overall picture is one of permanency with minor variations in the same form rather than a change from one form to a very different form (Greenwood and Hinings, 1988). The implication is that it is hard to change an organization. And once it is changed, it's hard to change it again. Thus, the rapidly changing environment usually outruns the less rapidly changing organization.

But that difference in the speed of change makes sense only when designers draw a sharp boundary between organizations and environments. What they miss is the arbitrariness of the line separating organization from environment. They miss this because they neglect the ways in which people construct the environments that supposedly outrun them.

Change in Enacted Environments

Starbuck (1976: 1069) made the case that organizations construct their own environments: "Organizations' environments are largely invented by organizations themselves. Organizations select their environments from ranges of alternatives, then they subjectively perceive the environments they inhabit. The processes of both selection and perception are unreflective, disorderly, incremental, and strongly influenced by social norms and customs."

But the issue of the environment is not simply one of perception. It also involves action. As Starbuck shows later (p. 1081), organizations play an active role in shaping their environments—partly because they seek environments that are sparsely inhabited by competitors; partly because they define their products and outputs in ways that emphasize distinctions between themselves and their competitors; partly because they rely on their own experience to infer environmental possibilities; and partly because they need to impose simplicity on complex relationships. The key mechanism in all of this, a mechanism specified earlier, is that these perceptions and actions validate one another in ways that resemble self-fulfilling prophecies: "It is primarily in domains where an organization believes it exerts influence that the organization attributes change to its own influence, and in domains where an organization believes itself impotent, it tends to ignore influence opportunities and never to discover whether its influence is real. . . . Moreover, it is the beliefs and perceptions founded on social reality which are especially liable to self-confirmation" (p. 1081).

March and Olsen (1989: 46), writing about political institutions, observed that the actions of each participant often are part of the environment of others. This means that the environments of each person are partly self-determined as each reacts to the other. When environments are created, actions taken in "adapting to" an environment are partly responses to one's own previous actions reflected through the environment. A common result is that small signals are amplified into large ones.

If people enact their environments, then a loss of fit between the organization and the environment takes on a new meaning. A loss of fit means that the organization has developed capabilities, resources, and limitations that have not yet been acted into the environment. The environment continues to demand from the organization capabilities that it no longer possesses. But the origin of this mismatch lies inside the organization, not outside. The problem is not a turbulent environment. The problem is a turbulent organization. Since the organization is changing faster than the demands it faces, the remedy is a more forceful, more intense application of the organizational design now in place to modify that environment.

When an organization has developed more rapidly than has an environment, it may take some redesign to ensure that the organization has a more forceful impact on the environment and shapes it toward newly acquired competencies. The advanced organization confronting an outdated environment needs essentially to strengthen what it already has in place. It needs to strengthen its culture, become more proactive, act like a true believer, intensify action rationality, and reaffirm its commitments, all in an effort to change the beliefs and actions of those people who comprise the environment (Eccles and Crane, 1988).

Change in the Enactor of Environments

If we assume that the purpose of design is to construct environments to fit organizations, then the key question is not so much "What is out there?" as "What is in here?" What the organization has available affects what it sees out there, as we saw in assumption 8.1, "Managerial ability affects design." And what the organization has available is something that can only be known by action, not by thinking (Mintzberg, 1990). Designs that facilitate the construction of environments encourage bricolage, deutero-learning (Bateson, 1979), rich assessment of situations (Daft and Lengel, 1986), rotation among assignments to discover and create strengths, careful attention to the interpersonal linkages that comprise the environment (Eccles and Crane, 1988), efforts to raise confidence and self-efficacy (Weick, 1983), development of a culture that promotes enacting rather than reacting, and the accomplishment of small wins (Weick, 1984). Designs that fit environments to organizations encourage gerrymandering. The boundaries of environments are drawn in such a way as to benefit the organization's interests and current strengths. Once interests are acted into the environment, the organization becomes constrained by requirements that are tailored more closely to its strengths.

If redesign is driven more by changes that originate inside the organization than by changes that originate outside, then any one design should have a short life, since there are so many prods to internal change. With frequent internal changes, there is more demand for these frequent changes to be expressed. Any one design is relatively transient because competence, experience, insight, resilience, and aspirations change often. While routines may freeze an organization and erode only under constant pressure from the environment, there are many routines designed explicitly to keep an organization unfrozen (Weick, 1977). By definition, designs based on improvisation will reflect a continually changing set of competencies as resources are recombined in increasingly novel ways. As people are encouraged to grow and develop, the basis for new designs will also expand.

If designs originate in ideas, interaction, shifting competencies, and retrospect, then organizations should be characterized by a succession of short-lived designs that evaporate rather than erode. Designs disappear abruptly rather than fade because they are competence-specific. As competence changes, so too does design.

The possibility that designs are transient seems to lie just below the surface even in formulations dedicated to the discovery of optimal long-term designs. For example, Huber, Ullman, and Leifer (1979: 568) note that, "it may be that the closest we can come to an optimum design in a real organization is a *situation* where an organization designer's goals are maximized because *momentarily* and as far as anyone can determine, his constraints are satisfied" [italics added].

Transient designs are visible in the class of organizations that Lanzara (1983) labels as "ephemeral." He observed organizations that emerged immediately after a violent earthquake in southern Italy in 1980 and concluded that the most basic feature shared among them was that "they do not assume their own survival or permanence as a requirement for identity and effectiveness of performance. In other words, ephemeral organizations are there to disappear, after displaying a great deal of activity. They have no past and no future, they live in the present. They do not tell stories about themselves and do not project their own image into the future, but take the chance of the present" (p. 88). Contrasts between formal and emphemeral organizations are listed in Table 11.2.

Ephemeral organizations have only local intelligence that is short-sighted. Their level of intervention is the street level (p. 92). This implies action rationality, abrupt rather than gradual changes in effectiveness, sensitivity to local conditions, and insuf-

Table 11.2.   Contrast Between Formal and Ephemeral Organizations

Traits	Formal Organizations	Ephemeral Organizations
Boundaries	Clear	Fuzzy
Leadership	Central locus, relatively constant	Shifting, lacking
Membership and recruitment	Contractual	Permeable, fluid, noncontractural
Commitment	External; extrinsic reward	Internal; self-reinforcing intrinsic reward
Size	Large organisms	Small units
Organizational structure	Formal, unusually hierarchical, (tree-like)	Informal, heterarchical (network-like)
Division of work	Highly differentiated, bureaucratic	Rudimentary
Tasks	Specialized, high expertise required	Nonspecific, low expertise required
Roles	Prescribed by authority	Self-prescribed
Rules and procedures	Explicitly mapped out; only partially internalized	Implicit, not mapped, and varying; fully internalized
Activities	Institutionalized, routine, domain-induced	Ad hoc, informal, need-induced
Performance	Measured by "accounting" (economic efficiency)	Measured by "organizing" (practical effectiveness)
Memory	Long-ranged	Short-spanned
Intelligence	Global; central locus	Local; distributed; short-sighted
Information flows	Vertical	Horizontal

Source: Adapted from Lanzara, 1983; p 88.

ficient duration for anything like erosion to occur. While any one ephemeral organization has minimal adaptability since it is tailored to meet local needs and the needs of the creator for self-expression (pp. 79–80), the form itself has considerable adaptability. Following the earthquake disaster, official institutions and government relief agencies were slow to mobilize and inept once they did mobilize (p. 74). The unresponsiveness and vulnerability of large systems, structured strictly by formalized procedures, became visible immediately in extreme situations. Unless procedures are loosened, commitments to action are strengthened, and role identities are broadened, nothing gets done.

As Lanzara concludes: "In a world which has suddenly become turbulent, unreliable, unpredictable, and where the value of the 'precedent', once indisputable, is becoming of little help for present and future action, it would not be surprising if human societies and their members relied less and less on formal, longstanding institutions and procedures, and more and more on informal, ephemeral arrangements" (p. 92).

Improvised designs such as those made visible by ephemeral organizations start small, enlarge quickly, disappear abruptly, and reappear often. The fate of these designs is more dramatic and fitful than is suggested by the term "erosion." Furthermore, people rather than environments may be the impetus to that erosion. If designs are capacity-driven, then changes in experience, perception, and ability, rather than changes in the environment, should be the focus of attempts to diagnose declining effectiveness.

CONCLUSION

Vaill (1976: 77) expressed many of the same reservations about the metaphor of architecture that I expressed when he observed:

> Design behavior is, in fact, much more creative and unpredictable than our culture would have us believe. The term "engineering" derives from the same root as "ingenuity." What is it that the designer is really doing? Terms like "groping," "intuiting," "experimenting," come readily to mind. Perhaps the design of physical and/or mechanical entities is a quasi deductive process, but the designs of organizations in which human beings are going to live and work certainly is not. How is it, then, that we are unable to look at organization designs for what they are—highly imperfect and tentative representations of what the world should be like, with debatable values buried down inside them (sometimes deliberately disguised), representations whose principal defensible function is that they trigger off debate among real men about real problems? This is about the most that can be said of organization designs. Why do we experience such a strong compulsion to let these designs exert more influence than this? [italics removed from original].

I have tried to show that good designs are those designs that incorporate the intuiting, experimenting, and arguing that are prominent in improvisation. Designing occurs more often but is less conspicuous than the metaphor of architecture implies. To design is to notice sequences of action that are improvements, call attention to them, label them, repeat them, disseminate them, and legitimize them.

People who construct one-time intentional, deliberated designs, construct entities that are imposed on social settings that they neither control nor fully understand. In doing this, they overlook the improvisational character of organizational design. They overlook the emergent designs that bubble up when capability changes. They overlook the ways in which interdependent actors become self-organizing in the face of under-specified designs. They overlook the power of retrospect. And they overlook the ways in which action generates its own meaning.

In turbulent periods, orderliness is limited to short-lived transactions, intelligence is reduced to local expertise, and determinacy covers only those events close together in time and space. While no one questions that it would be desirable to have grand and stable designs in times of turbulence, the organization is not sufficiently homogeneous to support concerted action, nor is the environment sufficiently determinant to encourage accurate, long-term prediction. Instead, the way out of turbulence may lie in continuous improvisation in response to continuous change in local details. Designing replaces design.

NOTES

1. This study is hereafter referred to as the CODE study and is described in Glick, Huber, Miller, Doty, and Sutcliffe (1990), reprinted as the Appendix to this volume.

REFERENCES

Allport, G. W. 1954. The historical background of modern social psychology. In Lindzey, G. (Ed.), *Handbook of social psychology,* Vol. 1 (pp. 3–56). Reading, MA: Addison-Wesley.

Aram, J. D. 1976. *Dilemmas of administrative behavior.* Englewood Cliffs, NJ: Prentice-Hall.

Bandura, A. 1986. *Social foundations of thought and action: a social cognitive theory.* Englewood Cliffs, NJ: Prentice-Hall.

Bandura, A. 1990. Conclusion: reflection on nonability determinants of competence. In Sternberg, R. J., and Kolligian Jr., J. (Eds.), *Competence considered* (pp. 315–362). New Haven: Yale University.

Bandura, A., and Wood, R. E. 1989. Effect of perceived controllability and performance standards on self-regulation of complex decision-making. *Journal of Personality and Social Psychology,* 56: 805–814.

Barley, S. 1986. Technology as an occasion for structuring: evidence from observations of CAT scanners and the social order of radiology departments. *Administrative Science Quarterly,* 31: 78–108.

Bateson, G. 1979. *Mind and nature.* New York: Dutton.

Bresser, R. K., and Bishop, R. C. 1983. Dysfunctional effects of formal planning: two theoretical explorations. *Academy of Management Review,* 8: 588–599.

Brown, R. H. 1978. Bureaucracy as praxis: toward a political phenomenology of formal organizations. *Administrative Science Quarterly,* 23: 365–382.

Burns, T., and Stalker, G. M. 1961. *The management of innovation.* London: Tavistock.

Campbell, J. P. 1977. On the nature of organizational effectiveness. In Goodman, P. S., and Pennings, J. M. (Eds.), *New perspectives on organizational effectiveness* (pp. 13–55). San Francisco: Jossey-Bass.

Chatman, J. A., Bell, N. E., and Staw, B. M. 1986. The managed thought: the role of self-justification and impression management in organizational settings. In Sims Jr., H. P., and Gioia, D. A. (Eds.), *The thinking organization* (pp. 191–214). San Francisco: Jossey-Bass.

Cooley, C. H. 1964. *Human nature and the social order.* New York: Schocken.

Cummings, L. L. 1983. Organizational effectiveness and organizational behavior: a critical perspective. In Cameron, K. S., and Whetten, D. A. (Eds.), *Organizational effectiveness* (pp. 187–203). New York: Academic Press.

Daft, R. L., and Lengel, R. H. 1986. Organizational information requirements, media richness and structural design. *Management Science,* 32: 554–571.

Daft, R. L., and Weick, K. E. 1984. Toward a model of organizations as interpretation systems. *Academy of Management Review,* 9(2): 284–295.

Dornbusch, S. M., and Scott, W. R. 1975. *Evaluation and the exercise of authority.* San Francisco: Jossey-Bass.

Eccles, R. G., and Crane, D. B. 1988. *Doing deals.* Cambridge, MA: Harvard Business School.

Elliott, E. S., and Dweck, C. S. 1988. Goals: an approach to motivation and achievement. *Journal of Personality and Social Psychology,* 54: 5–12.

Garfinkel, H. 1967. *Studies in ethnomethodology.* Englewood Cliffs, NJ: Prentice-Hall.

Gioia, T. 1988. *The imperfect art.* New York: Oxford University Press.

Graen, G. B., and Scandura, T. A. 1987. Toward a psychology of dyadic organizing. In Cummings, L. L., and Staw, B. M. (Eds.), *Research in organizational behavior,* Vol. 9 (pp. 175–208). Greenwich, CT: JAI Press.

Grandoori, A. 1987. *Perspectives on organization theory.* Cambridge, MA: Ballinger.

Greenwood, R., and Hinings, C. R. 1988. Organizational design types, tracks, and the dynamics of strategic changes. *Organization Studies,* 9: 293–316.

Hall, R. I. 1984. The natural logic of management policy making: its implications for the survival of an organization. *Management Science,* 30: 905–927.

Harper, D. 1987. *Working knowledge.* Chicago: University of Chicago Press.

Henshel, R. L. 1987. Credibility and confidence feedback in social prediction. Paper presented at the Plenary Session of the VII International Congress of Cybernetics and Systems, University of London.

Henshel, R. L., and Johnston, W. 1987. The emergence of bandwagon effects: a theory. *Sociological Quarterly,* 28: 493–511.

Huber, G. P. 1984. The nature and design of post-industrial organizations. *Management Science,* 30(8): 928–951.

Huber, G. P. 1990. A theory of the effects of advanced information technologies on organizational design, intelligence, and decision making. *Academy of Management Review,* 15: 47–71.

Huber, G. P., Ullman, J., and Leifer, R. 1979. Optimum organization design: an analytic-adaptive approach. *Academy of Management Review,* 4: 567–578.

Hurst, D. K., Rush, J. C., and White, R. E. 1989. Top management teams and organizational renewal. *Strategic Management Journal,* 10: 87–105.

Jervis, R. 1976. *Perception and misperception in international politics.* Princeton, NJ: Princeton University Press.

Khandwalla, P. N. 1977. *The design of organizations.* New York: Harcourt, Brace, Jovanovich.

Kilmann, A. H., Pondy, L. R., and Slevin, D. P. 1976. Patterns and emerging themes in organization design. In Kilmann, R. H., Pondy, L. R., and Slevin, D. P. (Eds.), *The management of organization design,* Vol. 1, (pp. 1–15). New York: North-Holland.

Lanzara, G. F. 1983. Ephemeral organizations in extreme environments: Emergence, strategy, extinction. *Journal of Management Studies,* 20: 71–95.

Lawrence, P., and Lorsch, J. W. 1967. *Organization and environment.* Boston: Harvard University Business School.

Levi-Strauss, C. 1966. *The savage mind.* Chicago: University of Chicago Press.

Lucas, R. 1987. Political-cultural analysis of organizations. *Academy of Management Review,* 12: 144–156.

March, J. G., and Olsen, J. P. 1989. *Rediscovering institutions: the organizational basis of politics.* New York: Free Press.

McEachern, A. W. 1984. *Organizational illusions.* Redondo Beach, CA: Shale.

Meek, V. C. 1988. Organizational culture: origins and weaknesses. *Organization Studies,* 9: 453–473.

Meyer, A. D. 1982. How ideologies supplant formal structures and shape responses to environments. *Journal of Management Studies,* 29: 45–61.

Miles, R. E., and Snow, C. C. 1986. Organizations: new concepts for new forms. *Califronia Managemetn Review,* 28(3): 62–73.

Miller, J. G. 1978. *Living systems.* New York: McGraw-Hill.

Mintzberg, H. 1990. The design school: reconsidering the basic premises of strategic management. *Strategic Management Journal,* 11: 171–195.

Mintzberg, H., and McHugh, A. H. 1985. Strategy formation in an adhocracy. *Administrative Science Quarterly,* 30: 160–197.

Munch, R. 1982. Talcott Parsons and the theory of action: II. The continuity of the development. *American Journal of Sociology,* 87: 771–826.

O'Reilly, C. 1989. Corporations, culture, and commitment. *California Management Review,* 31(4): 9–25.

Orr, J. E. 1990. Sharing knowledge, celebrating identity: community memory in a service culture. In Middleton, D., and Edwards, D. (Eds.), *Collective remembering* (pp. 169–189). London: Sage.

Ouchi, W. G. 1979. A conceptual framework for the design of organizational control mechanisms. *Management Science,* 25: 833–848.

Perrow, C. 1986. *Complex organizations: a critical essay,* 3rd ed. New York: Random House.

Pfeffer, J. 1982. *Organizations and organization theory.* Boston: Pitman.

Pfeffer, J., and Salancik, G. R. 1978. *The external control of organizations.* New York: Harper and Row.

Quinn, R. E., and Cameron, K. S. 1988. *Paradox and transformation.* Cambridge, MA: Ballinger.

Ranson, S., Hinings, B., and Greenwood, R. 1980. The structuring of organizational structures. *Administrative Science Quarterly,* 25: 1–17.

Ross, J., and Staw, B. M. 1986. Expo 86: an escalation prototype. *Administrative Science Quarterly,* 31: 274–297.

Salancik, G. R. 1977. Commitment and the control of organizational behavior and belief. In Staw, B. M., and Salancik, G. R. (Eds.), *New directions in organizational behavior* (pp. 1–54). Chicago: St. Clair.

Scott, W. R. 1987. *Organizations: rational, natural, and open systems,* 2nd ed. Englewood Cliffs, NJ: Prentice-Hall.

Shrivastava, P., and Mitroff, I. I. 1984. Enhancing organizational research utilization: the role of decision makers' assumptions. *Academy of Management Review,* 9: 18–26.

Simon, H. A. 1962. The architecture of complexity. *Proceedings of the American Philosophical Society,* 106(6): 467–482.

Smircich, L., and Morgan, G. 1982. Leadership: the management of meaning. *Journal of Applied Behavioral Science,* 18: 257–273.

Starbuck, W. H. 1976. Organizations and their environments. In Dunnette, M. D. (Ed.), *Handbook of industrial and organizational psychology* (pp. 1069–1123). Chicago: Rand McNally.

Starbuck, W. H., and Nystrom, P. C. 1981. Why the world needs organizational design. *Journal of General Management,* 6: 3–17.

Starbuck, W. H., and Nystrom, P. C. 1983. Pursuing organizational effectiveness that is ambiguously specified. In Cameron, K. S., and Whetten, D. A. (Eds.), *Organizational effectiveness* (pp. 135–161). New York: Academic Press.

Staw, B. M. 1982. Counterforces to change. In Goodman, P. S. and Assoc. (Eds.), *Change in organizations* (pp. 87–121). San Francisco: Jossey-Bass.

Thayer, L. 1988. Leadership/communication: a critical review and modest proposal. In Goldhaber, G. M., and Barnett, G. A., (Eds.), *Handbook of organizational communication* (pp. 231–264). Norwood, NJ: Ablex.

Thompson, J. D., and Tuden, A. 1959. Strategies, structures, and processes of organizational decision. In Thompson, J. D., Hammond, P. B., Hawkes, R. W., Junker, B. H., and Tuden, A. (Eds.), *Comparative studies in administration* (pp. 195–216). Pittsburgh: University of Pittsburgh.

Vaill, P. B. 1976. The expository model of science in organization design. In Kilmann, R. H., Pondy, L. R., and Slevin, D. P. (Eds.), *The management of organization design,* Vol. 1, (pp. 73–88). New York: Holland.

Weick, K. E. 1977. Re-punctuating the problem. In Goodman, P. S., and Pennings, J. M. (Eds.), *New perspectives on organizational effectiveness* (pp. 193–225). San Francisco: Jossey-Bass.

Weick, K. E. 1979. *The social psychology of organizing,* 2nd ed. Reading, MA: Addison-Wesley.

Weick, K. E. 1983. Managerial thought in the context of action. In Srivastava, S. (Ed.), *The executive mind* (pp. 221–242). San Francisco: Jossey-Bass.

Weick, K. E. 1984. Small wins: redefining the scale of social problems. *American Psychologist,* 39: 40–49.

Weick, K. E. 1985. A stress analysis of future battlefields. In Hunt, J. G. (Ed.), *Leadership and future battlefields* (pp. 32–46). Washington: Pergamon-Brassey's.

Weick, K. E. 1989. Organized improvisation: 20 years of organizing. *Communication Studies,* 40: 241–248.

Weick, K. E., and McDaniel, R. R. Jr. 1989. How professional organizations work: implications for school organization and management. In Sergiovanni, T. J. and Moore, J. H. (Eds.), *Schooling for tomorrow* (pp. 330–355). Boston: Allyn and Bacon.

III
CONCLUSION

12

What Was Learned About Organization Change and Redesign

> Change is the only constant. — Source unknown
>
> It is the theory which decides what we can observe. — Albert Einstein
>
> It is a capital mistake to theorize before you have all of the evidence. — Sherlock Holmes, *A Study in Scarlet*

Change preoccupies managers. Managers are on the front lines reacting to new threats and opportunities, initiating changes in anticipation of expected opportunities, and providing interpretations of the rapid, dynamic changes that surround postindustrial organizations. The practical importance of change to managers and society at large is apparent.

In this book, change also captures the attention of organization scientists. The authors present new perspectives on organizational change and redesign that reflect their research and several years of stimulating interaction on the research project that led to this book.[1] They identify a variety of important factors that managers can control to improve the performance and survivability of organizations facing dynamic, unpredictable environments. Many managers (and academics) were undoubtedly surprised both (1) to read about the range of factors that executives must manage simultaneously in dynamic, unpredictable environments and (2) to learn that some common beliefs about how organizations should design or redesign in fast-changing, turbulent environments are mistaken, and can actually lead to lower performance.

This final chapter addresses the question, "*What* are the most important and recurrent managerial lessons that were learned about organization change and redesign?" Viewing the chapters as a set, the most important and recurrent lessons for managers can be rephrased and summarized as four central lessons:

1. Even change, itself, is changing.
2. Organizational success and survival depend on continuous and discontinuous improvements.
3. Increasing volumes and varieties of information processing and analysis are the norm for successful organizations.
4. Teamwork and shared values are critical for managing change and enhancing organizational performance.

EVEN CHANGE, ITSELF, IS CHANGING

Chapter 1 starts with the argument that rapidly accelerating improvements in information technology and transportation technology are leading to globalization. These changes contribute to ever-increasing environmental complexity and turbulence and, consequently, to a rapid rise in organizational change. Taken together, these phenomena are causing organizations to radically reduce their cycle times for decision making, implementation, and information acquisition.

Nonlinear, Unpredictable Changes

Even the trend toward increasing change is not constant, as Meyer, Goes, and Brooks (Chapter 3) demonstrate most forcefully. "Change isn't what it used to be" (Meyer et al., Chapter 3, page 98). Change is no longer linear, constant, or predictable. Both the rate and form of change are changing frequently. Small changes are precipitating larger effects. Past trends are disappearing more quickly. Seemingly distant and unimportant changes are severely crippling entire industries despite long histories of profitability and positive projections. The process of creating and implementing novel changes "does not unfold in a simple linear sequence of stages and substages. Instead, it proliferates into complex bundles of innovation ideas and divergent paths of activities by different organizational units" (Van de Ven, Chapter 8, page 275).

Weick (Chapter 11) argues that managers' ability to interpret and make sense of these changes will significantly determine the effectiveness of the organization. By carefully developing and managing interpretations of new changes, top managers can have the greatest impact on organizational actions. Unfortunately, both academics and managers are often at a loss for words when it comes to describing the nature of changes. Monge (Chapter 10) partially addresses this problem with a careful consideration of six temporal characteristics of change: magnitude, trend, continuity, rate of change, duration, and cyclicity. His clear message is that unidimensional descriptions of change are inadequate. We must enrich our language for describing and understanding change.

Long Chains of Changes

Changes from both internal and external sources are creating long chains of organizational changes. Huber, Sutcliffe, Miller, and Glick (Chapter 7) show how internal changes in technology, processes, and structure, which are designed to improve performance, often stimulate further changes in staffing, organizational form, and strategy. Cameron, Freeman, and Mishra (Chapter 2) report that once an organization starts the downsizing process, a series of cascading changes is set in motion. O'Reilly, Snyder, and Boothe (Chapter 5) observe that changes in the composition of the upper-echelon team improve team dynamics and, consequently, increase the frequency of adaptive changes. Further, Glick, Miller, and Huber (Chapter 6) describe how changes in the composition of the upper echelon also increase the comprehensiveness of decision making, cohesion, and organizational profitability. Daft, Bettenhausen, and Tyler (Chapter 4) link changes in information technology to the creation of new opportunities for structuring strategic decision making.

Meyer and his colleagues (Chapter 3) observe that changes among competitors, suppliers, and customers require strategic reorientations. Reorientations are particularly important when hyperturbulence in the industry leads to the creation of social enclaves of networked organizations that span multiple industries. Although most organizations in the social enclave thrive, isolated organizations outside of the favored networks often fall into social vortices where resources are uncertain and scarce. Rather than forming larger and larger organizations to control these changes, organizations are disaggregating and affiliating with loosely coupled members of an interorganizational network. Slocum and Lei (Chapter 9) extend this logic to note that the rapid improvements in information technology and transportation technology are changing the economics of global strategic alliances and creating many new opportunities for organizational learning and internal organizational changes. Change begets change.

Facing the constantly changing rate and nature of changes, managing organizational change and redesign is increasingly difficult. Managers are in need of new metaphors, terminology, and conceptual tools to describe, anticipate, and look for the increasing variety and consequences of changes. The preceding chapters partially address this need through several approaches. At one extreme, the folly of theorizing before gathering all of the evidence is illustrated in the reflective chapter by Meyer and his colleagues. The nature and pace of changes in the hospital industry could not have been anticipated. At the other extreme, Monge provides critical terminology to enable us to observe more clearly the multiple characteristics of change. Thus, these chapters provide both inductively and deductively derived ways of describing changes. They contribute to our understanding of change, and they illustrate our ignorance by opening new research streams focused on understanding the contexts, consequences, and prevalence of the different types of changes.

Beyond recognizing the increasingly difficult task of managing change, managers can learn more about describing and conceptualizing change from these chapters. Further, managers can benefit directly from the three remaining central lessons learned from this project.

CHANGE REQUIRES CONTINUOUS AND DISCONTINUOUS IMPROVEMENTS

In a world of constant change, complacency leads to obsolescence. Organizations in dynamic, globalized environments must be continually improving just to stay afloat. Further, to gain industry leadership, discontinuous, breakthrough changes are often necessary. Incremental changes may be sufficient only for follower strategies. Two major stimulants to continuous and discontinuous improvements that are examined in the prior chapters are executive leadership and organizational redesign.

Executive Leadership

Continuous and discontinuous improvements can be fostered and encouraged by executive actions. Chapter 1 describes how top managers can instigate improvements by communicating values, cultivating supportive ideologies, allocating rewards, taking leadership positions, and carefully managing organizational learning. When such actions are needed but not present, it may be necessary to stimulate organizational change by personnel shifts at the top. O'Reilly and his colleagues (Chapter 5) report that positive team dynamics and more frequent adaptive changes follow the creation of upper-echelon teams that are homogeneous with regard to the tenure of the executives.

Executive tenure also plays a key role in the results of Chapter 7, where Huber and his colleagues find that the frequency of organizational changes is much greater at the beginning of the top manager's tenure. New managers are often brought in, or promoted, with a mandate for change. They start off amid great expectations and support for change during a honeymoon period. After several years in office, the top manager often turns to defending, rather than challenging, the status quo. This idea suggests that organizations facing rapidly changing, turbulent environments might limit the tenure of the top manager and develop a policy of bringing in new top managers. Given the difficulties in creating and sustaining deep cultural changes, however, decreasing executive tenure may be detrimental. The alternative is continuous rejuvenation of the top managers and their organizations.

The key conclusion in Chapter 2, by Cameron and his colleagues, is that continuous improvement must be ingrained into the organization's culture. Managers should adopt the perspective that change creates opportunities for improvement, not just problems to solve. Further, managers should take responsibility for encouraging everyone in the organization to take this proactive view. These researchers conclude that everyone in the organization should be trained and motivated to find the root causes that can lead to improvements. Continuous improvement is based on focusing attention on opportunities for improvement and change, rather than assigning blame for problems. This encourages a proactive, positive mode of operations, rather than a destructive, reactive mode. Adoption of a creative quality culture focused on quality, innovation, continuous improvement, and gradual incremental changes is an important predictor of successful downsizing efforts.

Chapter 3, by Meyer and his associates, makes vivid the argument that successful organizations cannot rest on their laurels. Being successful yesterday may provide an organization with the resources to drive change today, but too often past successes promote rigidity, complacency, and resistance to change. Too much success can be very detrimental if it leads the organization to miss opportunities for organizational learning (Sitkin, 1992). A little failure can induce enough humility to drive out the "not invented here" syndrome and encourage experimentation. In periods of discontinuous environmental change, managers will have to overcome the fear of failure by pushing continuous improvement *and* encouraging breakthrough, frame-breaking changes. Rather than blaming departments and individuals for failures, managers need to develop organizational capacities to examine and improve processes. This puts the blame on the process, not the individual, and it facilitates the adaptability and flexibility necessary for dealing with unexpected events in the future.

Van de Ven in Chapter 8 describes the innovation process as a "cumulative synthesis of numerous events performed by many different people over an extended period of time" (page 275). Innovation cannot be attributed to "the discrete acts of a single entrepreneur on a particular date and at a particular place" (page 275). Change and innovation must be continuous, not segregated as a passing event.

Organizational Redesign

Continuous and discontinuous improvement can also be fostered by redesigning the organization. For example, Slocum and Lei (Chapter 9) examine several different approaches to rejuvenate both top management teams and their organizations through creating global strategic alliances. Alliances can be viewed as learning opportunities that stimulate either focused short-term changes or broad long-term changes. Licensing agreements are relatively simple to manage and keep strategic partners at a distance. They are best suited to one-shot learning and limited change. Joint ventures and consortia provide opportunities for more complex, continuous learning. By using a series of different alliances, each incrementally more complex than the preceding alliance, top managers can stimulate organizational learning while minimizing disruptions and perception of a loss of control. These alliances, however, should be approached with some caution and a great deal of curiosity. Many of the strategic alliances are relatively new, experimental forms of organizational design. Some failures should be anticipated and used as learning experiences.

Both Monge (Chapter 10) and Weick (Chapter 11) use architecture as a point of departure for reframing organizational design as a fluid, dynamic process rather than a static characteristic of an organization. Monge (Chapter 10) adopts Alexander's (1964) approach to architectural design through the identification of misfits between functional specifications and current design, but adds the novel twist of placing this static approach in a dynamic framework. Rather than etching an organizational design in stone, Monge argues for a "flexible, dynamic process for creating forms and for continually adapting them to changing context requirements" (page 330). He also develops a recipe for dynamic organizational design that emphasizes the importance of monitoring systems for constant feedback and continuous improvement.

Weick (Chapter 11) is skeptical about the common use of static architectural metaphors for organizational design and develops improvisational theater as an alternative. Thinking of organizational design as a static outcome of an intentional decision making process by a single individual in isolation impedes managers' abilities to improve organizational performance. Weick argues for thinking about organizational redesign as a fluid, social process of interpretation. Through interpretations, top managers influence actions, organizational design, and the distribution of resources. Organization design should be a dynamic, fluid process aimed at both continuous and discontinuous improvement. Improvisation and bricolage (making do with the resources that are available) are effective techniques for stimulating breakthrough, discontinuous changes.

Regardless of the mechanism for stimulating continuous and discontinuous improvements, all of the chapters attest to the importance and variety of improvement efforts in effective organizations. In the book's epilogue, Lewin and Stephens underscore this message with their characterization of the emerging forms of organization as fluid and flexible with permeable boundaries and empowered individuals and groups implementing concepts of continuous learning and cross-functional teams. In this context, they also suggest that organization scientists should be playing a much stronger role in facilitating continuous improvement in organizations, both by accurately describing new organizational forms and by providing conceptual metaphors and typologies to help managers make sense of the new forms. They argue that by supporting continuous improvements in organization design through descriptions of new organizational forms, organization scientists can help rebuild the traditional strength of U.S. business in the design and management of organizations. Of particular importance for future research is the investigation and description of organizational designs and practices that facilitate continuous and breakthrough changes. Can executives stimulate continuous and discontinuous changes through improvisation and bricolage?

CHANGE REQUIRES MORE INFORMATION PROCESSING AND ANALYSIS

In Chapter 1, the analysis of the fundamental causes of environmental change facing organizations leads to the conclusion that organizational change requires the acquisition and analysis of greater amounts and varieties of information in order to remain competitive. For example, the chapter sets forth the idea that increasing amounts, speed, and availability of knowledge and the increases in environmental complexity and turbulence require faster and faster decision making, implementation, information acquisition, and environmental scanning. To keep up with the competition, organizations must develop systems and procedures for faster processing of more information from more sources using more modalities than ever before, and they must analyze information faster and more comprehensively.

Processing More Information Faster

Organizations can process more information faster by purchasing advanced information technologies, or they can try to make do with the resources already available by redesigning their information processing. As one example of how the latter can be done, Huber and his colleagues in Chapter 7 suggest that separate procedures be established to handle routine and nonroutine messages, so that nonroutine messages about important, fast-breaking changes can move quickly and reliably without being lost in a sea of routine messages.

Daft and his coauthors in Chapter 4 provide a much closer look at how organizations process these ever-increasing amounts and types of information. They find that the choice of communication media depends on the nature of the firm's strategy and environment. Firms that adopt a low cost strategy tend to rely on leaner communication media and direct their communications externally to implement their strategy. Firms that engage in a differentiation strategy use a greater mix of information media for both collecting and disseminating information. Similarly, higher levels of environmental turbulence and ambiguity contribute to a greater reliance on a greater variety of communication media.

Analyzing Information Faster and More Comprehensively

Effective change requires systematic analysis and management by facts. Cameron and his associates report in Chapter 2 that in order to support a culture of continuous improvement, current performance must be measured and evaluated at multiple stages in the production process. In Chapter 10, Monge presents a very useful framework for conceptualizing and analyzing dynamic processes. Too many of our conceptual and analytical tools are based on static comparisons that oversimplify dynamic processes. Effective organizational redesign in a dynamic, turbulent environment will require the types of detailed, longitudinal information gathering and analyses that Monge describes.

Although shooting from the hip may lead to fast action, Glick and his associates (Chapter 6) observe that comprehensiveness of decision making in the upper echelon of the organization is positively related to profitability in most environments, particularly in highly turbulent ones. Their work resolves an important debate in the academic literature concerning whether the relationship between comprehensiveness of decision making and profitability is positive or negative (see Chapter 6 for a discussion of the debate). The results clearly indicate that executives who disdain comprehensive decision making processes in fast-paced environments may be making fast decisions, but they are also making mistakes. In the highly turbulent and competitive organizational environments of the future, profitability is most likely to be associated with attempts to be more exhaustive and inclusive in making strategic decisions. Thus, executive teams must become more adept at comprehensively processing information rapidly.

In Chapter 11, Weick challenges the assumptions that the purpose of design is to facilitate decision making and that decisions determine effectiveness. As alternative assumptions, he advances the ideas that interpretations determine effectiveness and that the purpose of design is to facilitate interpretation. This implies that interpretive analysis, rather than data transmission or numerical calculations, is the crucial component in information processing in postindustrial organizations. Future performance and strategic actions are profoundly affected by the way in which managers make sense of their organization's environment and of prior organizational actions.

The bottom line of these chapters is that faster, more efficient, and more comprehensive systems and procedures for processing information are necessary for successfully handling the increasing volumes, types, sources, and destinations of information. The chapters provide some answers and open many questions regarding organizational approaches to accomplishing these goals.

CHANGE REQUIRES TEAMWORK AND SHARED VALUES

The importance of teamwork and shared values is possibly the strongest message from this program of research. Despite differences in foci, organizations interviewed, and theoretical frameworks, almost all of the researchers involved in this project conclude that teamwork and shared values are critical for managing change and increasing organizational performance, particularly in highly turbulent, rapidly changing environments.

Teamwork

Chief executive officers are key contributors to change in organizations, but they cannot change their organization by their efforts alone. Weick is most forceful in exploding the myth of the individual manager acting in isolation in Chapter 11. Management is a group phenomenon, even when it may appear that a manager is acting in isolation. "Any act by an 'individual manager' is actually an act by a representative, whose stature and membership are on the line" (page 360). The individual manager is selected, trained, and developed in a particular organizational culture. When that individual is promoted or hired into the chief executive office, he or she is confronted with the unique pattern of behaviors and roles that have been defined as acceptable or unacceptable in that organizational culture. In postindustrial organizations, continuous communication and direct supervision are less important as control mechanisms because shared beliefs and values will be needed to guide individual actions and create positive team dynamics.

O'Reilly and his coauthors in Chapter 5 report empirical evidence showing that within the upper echelon, positive team dynamics appear to increase the frequency of adaptive changes and to reduce seemingly politically motivated changes. Similarly, in Chapter 6, Glick and his colleagues describe their findings that shared values concerning human resource goals and system maintenance goals improved cohesion of the upper-echelon team.

The boundaries of teamwork, however, extend beyond the confines of the management team. For example, in Chapter 2, Cameron and his associates demonstrate that teamwork and the involvement of everyone very often makes the difference between successful and unsuccessful attempts at downsizing. Contrary to the typical view of executives as primarily decision makers, Daft and his colleagues show in Chapter 4 that top managers spend as much time communicating strategic decisions *to others* as they spend gathering information for making the decisions. These communications to others are directed at obtaining cooperation for strategy implementation—in other words, half of their communications are directed at creating a team effort. Further, those top managers who communicate most effectively in this context are also the highest performing.

The boundaries of teamwork extend even beyond the confines of the formal organization. In addition to the involvement of everyone in the organization, Cameron and his coauthors of Chapter 2 observe that involving customers and suppliers in the downsizing process greatly enhances organizational effectiveness. In Chapter 4, Daft and his associates report that top managers communicate extensively to people outside of their organization in attempts to gain acceptance and cooperation in strategy implementation. Meyer and his coauthors of Chapter 3 also conclude that a very effective strategy is to disaggregate into smaller organizations and then affiliate with other organizations. Through the formation of transorganizational networks, teams of organizations are able to gain economies of scale, while maintaining the flexibility that is required in hyperturbulent environments. Finally, Slocum and Lei explicitly focus on extending alliances to the global arena in Chapter 9, but note that these alliances fail if the interorganizational dynamics are not well managed.

Shared Values

The effective management of teamwork involves both communication (discussed above) and shared values. We noted in Chapter 1 that top managers can either instigate or impede organizational change through values, ideologies, and cause-effect maps. Top managers influence interpretations of environmental changes and help create many of those changes. Current managers can learn and change their belief structures, and new managers can challenge old assumptions in order to develop a shared set of beliefs and values.

Meyer and his colleagues conclude in Chapter 3 that shared values about goals and strategies are important for coping with change because they provide a basis for commitment, cooperation, and tolerance. When organizational members share similar values, they are more likely to endorse actions by others because it is assumed that the actions were made in good faith. Thus, during periods of rapid change, shared values will provide critical support for the independent, decisive actions that are often required.

In Chapter 2, Cameron, Freeman, and Mishra describe the best practices for downsizing, including an active, aggressive, and accessible leadership that is pursuing an advanced quality culture. By providing a vision and consistently communicating a quality culture, managers are able to instill overarching values to guide behavior in the face of ambiguity. This focus on shared values and culture exemplifies the systemic strategy of downsizing that drives for the long-term payoffs from continuous improvement.

CONCLUSION: NEW ENVIRONMENTS AND NEW ORGANIZATIONAL OPTIONS

The explosion of information, globalization of many markets, rapid technological change, and discontinuities in previously predictable patterns of change create both threats and opportunities for organizations. With all of this bustling, buzzing confusion in the environment, some managers may despair. The positive conclusion to be drawn from the chapters in this book is that these new environments are rich with opportunities for positive organizational changes. Further, many managers are taking advantage of these opportunities by creating new and efficacious organizational forms and designs.

In the Epilogue to this book, Lewin and Stephens describe the disconcerting gulf between managers and academics concerned with organization design. Academics have not always provided managers with useful, relevant knowledge, and managers have not always understood the nature of the academic enterprise. As an approach to resolving these issues, Lewin and Stephens argue that the critical challenge for organization science is to help managers learn about new organizational forms: What are the new forms? Which of these forms are most effective? When are they effective? How can organizations adopt these forms? And, most importantly, why are these new organizational forms effective?

In this book, academics make an important step toward meeting this challenge. They describe diverse, novel, and/or untested organizational designs and practices. These new organizational options are both intellectually stimulating and show great promise for managerial application. The lessons learned about organizational change and redesign can best be summarized as a need for postindustrial organizations (1) to encourage continuous and discontinuous improvements, (2) to increase information processing and analysis, and (3) to foster teamwork and shared values.

NOTES

1. The research reported in this book was supported in part by a grant from the Army Research Institute for the Behavioral and Social Sciences (Contract no. MDA-903-85-K-0404) to George P. Huber (Principal Investigator) and William H. Glick (Co-Principal Investigator).

REFERENCES

Alexander, C. 1964. *Notes on the synthesis of form.* Cambridge, MA: Harvard University Press.
Sitkin, S. 1992. Learning through failure: the strategy of small losses. In Staw, B. M., and Cummings, L. L. (Eds.), *Research in organizational behavior,* Vol. 14 (pp. 231–266). Greenwich, CT: JAI Press.

Epilogue

Designing Postindustrial Organizations: Combining Theory and Practice

ARIE Y. LEWIN and CARROLL U. STEPHENS

> The future ain't what it used to be.   Yogi Berra

> I am interested in the future because I will spend the rest of my life there.
>   C. F. Kettering, *Seeds for Thought*

In the late 1950s, science writer Arthur Clarke (1963/1958) portrayed a fantastic vision of the year 2000, complete with manned colonies on Mars, control over weather, and human immortality just a few years away. Of course, as 2000 approaches, this scenario has not been realized. However, Clarke's predictions for the role of computing technology in the organization of the twenty-first century have been almost prescient:

> When you wish to send an urgent message, you will purchase a standard letter form on which you will write or type whatever you have to say. At the local office the form will be fed into a machine which scans the marks on the paper and converts them into electrical signals. These will be . . . picked up at the destination where they are reproduced on a blank form identical with the one you inscribed. . . . We will be able to conjure up, from central libraries and information centers, copies of any document we desire. . . . The captains of industry in the 21st century may live where they please, running their affairs through computer keyboards and information-handling machines in their homes. (Clarke, 1963: 194–195)

Obviously, Clarke was describing the now-ubiquitous fax, e-mail, on-line computer search, and personal computer. He concluded that these technologies would render "administrative and executive skills . . . independent of geography," thus enabling the development of boundary-less, transglobal organizations.

Clarke's technological predictions have come to pass, and so have demographic changes he failed to presage. In tandem, the technological and sociological shifts of the late twentieth century have had profound impact on the form and nature of organizations. These changes provide the field of organization theory not only with the fascinating challenge of addressing how to design the new forms of organizations in the future, but also with an opportunity to definitively establish the relevance of organization design to management practice.[1]

This relevance, currently, is open to question. Scholars such as Schoonhoven

(1981), Beyer (1982), Miles and Snow (1986), and Daft and Lewin (1990) have noted that very little mutual influencing appears to take place between organization theorists and the general managers who routinely—albeit intuitively—practice actual organization design and redesign. For instance, the notion of total quality management (TQM) or continuously improving organizational performance has achieved enormous popularity in management circles, but has received little attention from organization scientists. It is as if the questions that researchers see as pertinent are not those that managers view as consequential, and thus organization science findings do not frequently inform managerial practice.

Organization design even seems to be, metaphorically speaking, the unwanted stepchild of the management sciences. Although a human resources management function is virtually certain to be present on the organization chart of any corporation other than the very smallest ones, organization design is rarely,—if ever—, represented as a formal management function in mission statements or job descriptions. Corporations recruit functional specialists at business schools, but they do not recruit organization design specialists; business schools do not even train such specialists. In short, there are no career tracks in business for organization design professionals.

In this epilogue we argue that the illusion that organization science and management practice operate entirely independently may exist because questions of the relationship between the two spheres have been improperly framed. As this volume illustrates, organization science has a great deal to offer managers. Moreover, major organizations throughout the world are currently engaged in exciting and innovative redesign efforts. We believe that the practice of organization design as well as the state of organization science could be greatly enhanced by nurturing a dialogue between organization theorists and management practitioners, thus diffusing the sometimes rigid boundary between management and academia. Furthermore, we see the panoply of issues and challenges facing turn-of-the-millennium organizations as an extraordinarily fertile environment in which to further this interface, and also as a powerful motivation for academics and practitioners to seek each others' counsel.

Until quite recently the irrelevance of organization theory and design research to management practice had been taken as a given. However, the best-seller status of practitioner-oriented books on management such as *In Search of Excellence* (Peters and Waterman, 1982), *The Change Masters* (Kanter, 1983), *Reinventing the Corporation* (Naisbitt and Aburdene, 1985), and *Thriving on Chaos* (Peters, 1987) indicates the increased interest that managers have in new forms of organizations and the extent to which concern with the structuring and management of organizations has come to permeate the business culture.

Consider two illustrations. First, managers at Corning Inc., from upper echelons to staff to line, see their organization's competitive advantage as lying in its design. This past decade, Corning has moved from a classic divisionalized bureaucratic form to one characterized by flexibility, very low levels of hierarchy, and strong, shared values. "We don't succeed on the basis of technology," a top Corning executive told us.[2] "The structuring of our plants, and of our company as a whole, is the key to our performance. Our most valuable asset is our workforce, and our organization design is what enables us to get the most out of our people's capabilities." Second, human resource professionals in a variety of companies, including Corning, Upjohn, and Philip Morris, have recently been called on by top management to provide advice on organization design. In order to amass more information on the topic, which has not traditionally fallen under their area of expertise, some of these human resource managers have formed a group called Association for the Management of Organization Design, which allows human resource professionals who work in the design arena as well as general managers to share ideas with each other and with organization theorists from universities. This association now has 450 members, including internally based practitioners of organization design, external consultants, and top managers (including CEOs).

The widespread recognition of the functional areas of management as academic disciplines came about in the 1950s, because of technological and environmental transformations in our society. As the tasks and functions of the organization became increasingly more complex, the seat-of-the-pants approach that practitioners historically had taken was no longer good enough. The functional areas of marketing, operations, finance and accounting, and, later, human resource management, information systems, and strategic planning, came to be seen as strategic determinants of competitive advantage for individual firms and perhaps the U.S. economy as a whole. These advances were associated with academic developments in management that contributed to the professionalization of these functional-area specialties. As a result, corporations became consumers of functional area research and established career tracks for functional specialists, thus recognizing the relevance of these applied management disciplines. However, this recognition did not extend to organization design.

Chandler (1990: 263) observes with irony that, just as marketing, financial, and other functional specialists were gaining ascendancy in this country following World War II, American business began to neglect the area that had been one of its crucial strengths, namely, the design and management of organizations. By the late 1950s, Chandler (1990) says, as a consequence of post–World War II dominance, American management and organization design practices were still considered to be the most advanced in the world. At the time, American companies, almost without exception, focused on single industries and on maximizing output of goods to satisfy pent-up demand globally and in the United States. Beginning in the mid 1960s, however, American managers began to devote resources to endless mergers and conglomerations, leveraged buyouts, and other variants of paper entrepreneurship (Reich, 1982, 1991; Chandler, 1990). According to Chandler's analysis, American business became more concerned with selling products and overseeing diversification than with processes of product engineering, manufacturing, and improvement. American businesses lost sight of the organization and of the management process as a source of competitive strength. When troubled operations lost market share, when products become obsolete, when manufacturing processes become inefficient, the characteristic response of American managers was to divest rather than to invest resources in order to address the underlying problem. Meanwhile, Germany and Japan, having rebuilt their industries after World War II and evolving new ones, and having learned American management methods, were paying close attention to the basic issue of how the organization should be designed and how to build organization capabilities. It is as a direct result of U.S. business's inattention to management and organization design, Chandler (1990) says, that the United States has lost ground as a competitive leader in the global economy.

What do organization scientists have to offer to managers? Why have managers up until recently been so seemingly uninterested in the wide body of knowledge that organization theory has to offer? And will this state of affairs, in which organization theory and management practice often appear to operate independently of each other, persist into the twenty-first century? In this epilogue to the volume, we consider each of these questions in turn. Our conclusion is that, because of massive environmental shifts, the design of the organization itself is being recognized as a key strategic variable. Because organization itself is becoming a source of sustained competitive advantage and a critical success factor, seat-of-the-pants organization design as a management practice will become a liability in the twenty-first century, just as seat-of-the-pants human resources, financial, and marketing approaches did in the mid-twentieth century. Furthermore, we believe that fundamental alterations in the nature of organizational forms are emerging in response to changes of a magnitude that have not been seen since the Industrial Revolution and the consequent emergence of bureaucracy. The challenge for organization theory is to exploit this historic opportunity to aid management practice. The challenge for managers is to seek out the knowledge that organization scientists can bring to bear on the task of designing organizations that can thrive in a post-industrial environment.

ORGANIZATION THEORY AND MANAGEMENT PRACTICE

It is fashionable both to note the cataclysmic changes on the organizational landscape and also to conclude that the body of knowledge published in academic journals and summarized in textbooks has practically no audience in the practice of management (e.g., Porter and McKibbin, 1988; Dubin, 1976). Schoonhoven (1981) has suggested that organization theory, as a field, is inconclusive and often contradictory, and hence not amenable to utilization by managers. We argue that, in contrast and despite some shortcomings, organization theory has in fact accumulated a substantial body of coherent, pragmatic knowledge. Most notably, important and cohesive findings have emerged regarding the appropriate "fit" among an organization's structure or design and its environment, strategy, task, and technology. In broad terms, for example, organization scholars agree that when conditions are unstable, complex, and unpredictable, organizations should be relatively unstructured and that when conditions are stable, simple, and predictable, organizations should be relatively structured. Further, there should be congruence among an organization's environment, and its strategy, technology, and structure—, that is, the level of centralization, formalization, specialization, and standardization. Whether organic or mechanistic (Burns and Stalker, 1961) (i.e., less structured or more structured), all of these organizational properties are some variant on Weber's (1978/1910) bureaucracy.

These general observations are based on a large number of studies and a voluminous amount of data. Taken together, these works can be drawn upon by organization scholars to provide quite-detailed recommendations to managers about appropriate designs for their organizations. Many textbooks have distilled this body of knowledge comprehensively. As a strong example of the potential to distill knowledge about organization design, Baligh, Burton, and Obel (1990) have demonstrated how organization theory recommendations regarding design can be presented in a pragmatic form that is utilizable by managers. These researchers have developed a PC-based, interactive expert system that uses contingency theory prescriptions and if-then logic to make specific recommendations about organization design, based on information elicited from the manager/user.

Of course, there are theoretical and empirically based disagreements in the literature as to the importance of many contingency variables. For instance, organization theorists (e.g., Blau and Schoenherr, 1971; Pugh, Hickson, Hinings, and Turner, 1969; Pugh, Hickson, and Hinings, 1969; Aldrich, 1972) disagree about the importance of size as a determinant of structure. Furthermore, organizations often face conflicting contingencies (Gresov, 1989) that may cancel each other out. For example, task uncertainty may dictate one type of structure and environmental uncertainty another. Nonetheless, many textbooks that distill the organization theory literature, and the expert system developed by Baligh et al. (1990), provide evidence that organization design prescriptions *can* be synthesized in a format that *is* accessible to managers, with real potential for utilization.

MANAGERS' ATTITUDES TOWARD ORGANIZATION THEORY

Despite our strong contention that organization theory has relevance for management practice, few managers have been breaking down the office doors of organization theorists for advice. Although executives at Corning and members of the Association for the Management of Organization Design are noteworthy and prophetic exceptions, many practitioners of management appear to be either ignorant of organization theory or scornful of it. Before we consider how to address this situation, we must ask how it has come about. We see four reasons, three perceptual and one substantive.

The first plausible explanation calls to mind Shakespeare's timeless quote "What's in a name? A rose by any other name would smell as sweet." It seems to us that much is in a name and that organization theory by some other name might be more acceptable and accessible to nonacademics. Organizational behavior, strategy, human resources management—all are organizational sciences and all are based on theory, but the name *organization theory* is reserved for the study of organization design and structure. As Beyer (1982) says, this label imbues the field with a rarefied aura, and thus managers may perceive organization theory as being at the opposite end of the spectrum of the management sciences from those that are applied. Perhaps Thompson's (1956) call that the then-nascent field of organization theory be distinguished from other management sciences by its level of abstraction has had negative as well as undeniably positive ramifications.

The second reason that practitioners might not seek out organization theory to use as a basis for organization design is that they may believe it to contain nothing that they do not already know. This is not surprising since much of organization theory is based in description of what organizations are doing (e.g., Woodward, 1965; Burns and Stalker, 1961; Chandler, 1962, 1977, 1990; Lawrence and Lorsch, 1967) and reflects a distillation from the experience of practitioners (e.g., Barnard, 1938). What is surprising is the lack of utilization of the primary contribution that organization scientists have made involving the codification and evaluation of management practices and the derivation of prescriptive theories. Managers may be seeing themselves on the forefront of practicing and inventing organization design and therefore behave as if the body of knowledge of organization science is of no value. In other words, they perceive the field to relay back to managers their own practices and ignore or are unable to discern the prescriptive content or engineering value of organization science.

The descriptive role of organization science is actually, we believe, quite reasonable, and may indeed *enhance* the utility of organization theory to practitioners. It is not at all surprising that managers have sometimes developed effective organization designs by means of a seat-of-the-pants approach. A central concept in organization theory is "fit." What "fits" maps very closely on what is "appropriate" and "natural." This suggests that managers can possibly arrive at the normatively prescribed organization design via a trial-and-error process by making successive adaptations to the existing organization and/or, almost intuitively, via a Gestalt process. Certain dimensions of organization design simply do not go together. For instance, high standardization and high formalization together constitute crucial underpinnings of the machine bureaucracy (Weber, 1978/1910; Burns and Stalker, 1961). However, there is no normative suggestion anywhere in organization theory that high formalization should ever be coupled with low standardization. Since formalization is itself a codification of standards—one possible means of maintaining standardization—coupling high formalization with low standardization is a logical and practical impossibility, and managers can arrive at this conclusion as well as organization theorists can.

The third perceptual reason relates to managerial preferences. Lewin and Stephens (1990) suggest that when general managers have the opportunity and discretion to shape organization design, their design preferences often spring from their individual properties—including their attitudes, past experiences, and demographics. For example, if a CEO has high need for power, he or she is very likely to prefer a centralized structure, characterized by high control intensity. If the CEO's choice of design fits the organization's contingencies, performance can be expected to be high; if not, performance can be expected to suffer. In either event, the design is likely to be consistent with the CEO's preferences (although not necessarily consistent with contingency prescriptions), and the CEO will have arrived at the design specification independently, without the counsel of organization theorists. In the case of fit, practitioners will see themselves as having intuitively made the right choice. In the case of misfit, we believe that managers are likely to persist in their preferences, despite the findings of organization scientists. Therefore, managers may have no *cognitive or affective felt need* for advice from organization theorists: managers may believe they would either receive no new information, or information that is inconsistent with their preferences. However, simply because a need is not perceived does not mean that it does not exist nor is not being fulfilled.

As we noted earlier, many practioners do not realize that much research on organizations involves the evaluation and interpretation of management practices in different contexts and the subsequent derivation of prescriptive theories for various situations. Astley and Zammuto (1992), have proposed an additional role. They make the case that the rightful role of organization theorists has nothing to do with being "engineers offering technical advice to managers," but rather with providing "conceptual and symbolic language for use in organizational discourse." Unlike Dubin (1976) who laments that the *goals* of management scholars and management practitioners are antithetical, we argue instead that the *roles* of academics and practitioners vis-à-vis the practice of management are distinct. To ask whether organization theorists are informing the nuts-and-bolts, day-to-day operations of business is to confound the two roles, and therefore to arrive at the mistaken perception that organization theory is irrelevant to management practice. Organization theorists do and are able to generalize, abstract, distill, codify, and evaluate the empirical realities of business practice, thus assigning meaning to data. "It is at the abstract, ideational level, rather than at the level of specific tools and techniques, where much of the knowledge transfer between scientific and practitioner domains occurs," say Astley and Zammuto (1992).

The above deals with three perceptual reasons that practioners do not utilize organization theory as a basis for their organization design efforts. We turn now to a substantive reason. Even though the discussion so far on the contributions of organization theory to management practice makes us more sanguine than many other commentators, we believe that there is a serious, substantive shortcoming in the ability of management scholars to continue to address questions of consequence. Because organization theory has been locked into a paradigm of Weberian (1978/1910) bureaucracy and its variants, it has not been addressing the dimensions of design that are becoming most important to managers, and to organizational viability and prosperity. This is, we believe, largely a result of the intellectual heritage of the field. In the early 1960s, two schools of thought received equal attention and respect. The Aston group (Pugh, Hickson, and Hinings, 1969; Pugh, Hickson, Hinings, and Turner, 1968, 1969; Pugh, Hickson, Macdonald, Turner, and Lupton, 1963; Inkson, Pugh, and Hickson, 1970) focused on "hard" measures that captured formal architecture of the organization. The second school of thought (Hall, 1963; Hage and Aiken, 1967) included "softer," more processual dimensions in the definition of organization structure. The Aston approach became dominant, most likely because at that time all of the management sciences were reaching for increased rigor and quantification—what Daft and Lewin (1990) call the "normal-science straitjacket." Thus, the processual dimensions of organization design—particularly the facilitation and management of workflow, which Mackenzie (1991) labels task processes—was largely overlooked until relatively recently.

The stability of many observed variations of organization designs suggests that design is to organization as personality is to individual—that is, any fairly enduring property that is relatively stable across time and situation. Such a specification accommodates the evolution and coexistence of a huge variety of organizational forms, not merely forms embodying different levels of structural variables such as centralization. As the next section illustrates, the organization theory issues facing contemporary managers are much better addressed under the organization design construct (see Note 1) than by the traditional rubric of structure. Organization science, under this updated perspective, has a crucial opportunity to inform management practice at a time when many new organization design and redesign experiments are being attempted.

ENVIRONMENT OF POSTINDUSTRIAL ORGANIZATIONS

According to Max Weber (1978/1910), particular forms of organization arise at particular times in history, within particular sets of social and technological conditions. Bureaucracy, still the predominant type of formal organization and the bedrock of organization theory assumptions in the late twentieth century, evolved in response to post-enlightenment rational thought, the weakening of primary institutions such as family and church, and the technological advances of the Industrial Revolution (Weber, 1978/1910). Chandler (1962, 1977, 1990) notes the prominent role that railroads, telegraphs, and telephones played in the development of the large, complex modern organization. The development of the transportation and communications industries required the ability to manage across wide geographic areas and the capacity for differentiation, integration, and coordination to support their goals. These industries also provided the technology that permitted businesses in other fields—manufacturing and retailing, for example—to manage across time and space. Thus the technologies of the nineteenth century facilitated emergence of the bureaucratic organization with its focus on standardization and mass production (Chandler, 1990: 1).

Weber (1978/1910) emphasized that organization forms are not static. As technologies and social conditions shift, so does the nature of organization. Bureaucracy is ideally suited to mass production, mass markets, relatively stable environments, and purely economic goals—in other words, the conditions of industrialization. The design hallmarks of the bureaucratic organization are standardization, homogeneity, and hierarchy, all geared to the ends of economic efficiency. Since these conditions increasingly tend not to characterize the social-economic landscape, bureaucracy becomes no longer the appropriate form of organization, and the emergence of new organizational forms can be expected (Coleman, 1990; Etzioni, 1988). A crucial question for organization theory is what form or forms might characterize organizations in the emerging post-industrial age.

Much has been written about the transformations taking place in our post-industrial society (Galbraith, 1967; Marcuse, 1968; Bell, 1973; Huber, 1984; Reich, 1991). Some commonly mentioned trends include globalization, heightened turbulence, the emergence of extraeconomic goals for business organizations, demassification, and quantum changes in technology. Each of these transformations implies postbureaucratic organizational forms, which organization researchers have yet to address in detail.

An interdependent global economy—*globalization* (Bartlett and Ghoshal, 1989; Omae, 1990; Slocum and Lei, Chapter 9 in this volume)—is forcing many multinational companies in almost every business sector to reexamine the appropriateness of their management philosophies and organization designs. Bartlett and Ghoshal (1989) have researched the attempts of various companies across diverse industries in their quest to transform themselves into transnational organizations. While it is premature to determine whether any transnational organizational form will emerge as prototypical, it is clear that multinational corporations are trying to determine when, where, and how to localize activities, how to build and integrate cadres of global managers, how to facilitate cross-national organizational learning, and how to manage cross-culturally diverse employees. In this new global environment, the traditional managerial functions of planning, coordination, and control require new organizational solutions.

Toffler (1980) argues that business will be facing *heightened turbulence* in terms of rapid changes in the rules governing the conduct of business and economic competition, an increased rate of crises faced by managers, and increased pressures for time-based competition. *Demographic changes* further contribute to the forces of change associated with heightened turbulence. These involve aging of the population in all the developed countries, increased diversity of the workforce (e.g., a rise in the participation of women and other minorities, cross-cultural diversity) and (in the United States) a declining educated and skilled workforce. Currently accepted human resources practices are incressingly being recognized as incompatible with these demographic changes. Heightened turbulence highlights the need for extremely flexible, adaptive, continually improving and evolving organization designs.

Business is also facing profoundly expanded mandates to address *extraeconomic goals* (Keeley, 1988; Meyer and Gustafson, 1988). Strictly economic, instrumental rationalities no longer prevail (Coleman, 1990; Etzioni, 1988). Instead, the public is increasingly demanding that business organizations take extraeconomic values into account when establishing both goals and means. This is so, Etzioni (1988) argues, because in recent years business has become the predominant institution in the social landscape, eclipsing family, polity, community, and church in importance. Thus many people have grown concerned about the negative externalities that business has imposed on society, and they are insisting that business take on the broad goals of social responsibility beyond the narrow goals of economic efficiency. Thus, for example, stakeholders such as employees and environmentalists are insisting that business address concerns involving justice and ecological stewardship.

The shift from mass markets to short-lived, narrowly specialized niches, from large-scale standardized production to customized, flexible, batch production represents another fundamental environmental change (Reich, 1982). Toffler (1980) referred to this phenomenon as the *demassification* of economy. This segmentation of markets creates new organizational challenges for coordination and integration of marketing, product development, and manufacturing, as well as for continually innovating and improving these processes and products.

The shift from standardized to flexible manufacturing has been enabled by *quantum changes in technology,* such as computer-integrated manufacturing systems and computer-aided design. In addition, advances in computer-mediated communication technology—the integration of telecommunications, office automation, data processing, and video technologies (Culnan and Markus, 1987; Huber, 1990; Tesler, 1991)—have given managers new options for designing their organizations. For example, Malone and Rockart (1991) discuss how computer-mediated communications technology enable companies to integrate markets into their hierarchies or to implement equally effective centralized or decentralized decision making structures.

Taken as a whole, these transformations suggest that post-industrial organizational forms will be fundamentally different from the bureaucratic form that the Industrial Age spawned. In addition to the need to address extra-economic goals, it is clear that standardized processes and markets are becoming increasingly obsolete. Standardization is not a viable response to turbulence, since what the standards are from day to day becomes unknowable. Furthermore, a "demassified" society suggests that standards vary from group to group even at any given point in time. Finally, as Clarke (1963/1958) predicted, sophisticated technologies are now in place that we believe are as distinct from the technologies of the mid-twentieth century as the railroads and telegraphs of the late nineteenth century were from the wagon trains and Wells Fargo Express of the early 1800s.

DESIGNING POSTINDUSTRIAL ORGANIZATIONS

In the face of these transformations, managers and organization scholars have begun to recognize that in many contexts, especially in the world of business, traditional institutional arrangements and forms of organizations are no longer appropriate (Hage, 1988; Rose, 1990; Dumaine, 1991). In this section, we provide a distilled description of some of the new forms that are arising.

There has been an accompanying proliferation of popular business articles and books (e.g., Naisbitt and Aburdene, 1985; Mills, 1991; Peters, 1987) whose common denominator is to pitch quick-fix organization redesign solutions. The primary value of these books to managers derives from the books' accounts of various companies' experiences in redesigning their organizations, thus creating among managers a shared implicit mental model of the changing environment and of "legitimate" approaches to restructuring their organization (Astley and Zammuto, 1992). A *Fortune* article entitled "The Bureaucracy Busters" (Dumaine, 1991) exemplifies this type of reporting to managers. The article describes the drastic redesign efforts of several top managers, including Xerox's Paul Allaire, Becton Dickinson's Raymond Gilmartin, Levi Strauss's Bill Eaton, and GE's Jack Welch. Our preliminary content analysis of these stories about organization redesign experiments under way in corporations seems to suggest that corporate leaders share certain ideas regarding effectiveness criteria of post-industrial organizations, and that common features exist in these redesigned organizations.

The competing-values model of organization effectiveness (Quinn and Rohrbaugh, 1983) holds that organizations strive to achieve four *simultaneous* goals—economic efficiency, internal integration and coordination, adaptivity and responsiveness to the external environment, and utilization of human capital—all to the ends of achieving economic profit. In this view the various effectiveness dimensions are not prioritized. However, according to Lewin and Minton (1986), concern with economic efficiency, integration, and coordination seems to be operative in every organization regardless of the prioritization of any other effectiveness criteria.

Because "bureaucracy busters" are primarily focused on the imperatives of heightened turbulence, demassification, and quantum changes in technology, they put a high priority on designing organizations that are *hyperflexible, adaptive,* and *continually improving and innovative.* In addition, they recognize that their organizations must be *global* and *stakeholder focused.* To achieve flexibility, adaptivity, and continual innovation, the "bureaucracy busters" *flatten* the hierarchy of their organizations by delayering levels of management and decentralizing decision making. They create *permeable boundaries* for their organization by breaking internal boundaries [in the words of GE's Jack Welch, creating a "boundaryless organization—no hierarchical boundaries vertically, no functional boundaries horizontally" (Rose, 1990)] and by blurring their external boundaries (often through the application of computer-mediated communications technology). Their human resource strategy strives to design jobs that increase the *empowerment* of individuals and groups by implementing concepts of *worker self-control, self-responsibility, cross training,* and *continuous learning.* These top managers recognize that their own roles will have to change too; they are challenged by such concepts as *leadership without control,* which involves a shift from planning, directing, evaluating, rewarding, and organizing to establishing values, facilitating, structuring processes, communicating, and networking.

Advances in computer-mediated communications technologies have made it possible for managers to experiment with new organization designs. Thus, for example, a major consumer packaged-goods company and a major national retailer[3] are experimenting with a bridge organization (half inside each company) whose responsibilities are to manage all transactions between the two companies. Information technology provides the means for integrating the producer's product promotion strategies with the store promotion strategies of the retailer. Information technology also makes it possible for the producer to implement a continual inventory replenishment process at the retailer level, eliminating the need for purchase orders: computer networks provide an electronic link to the relevant scanner product-sales data from each store. The linking of the two companies electronically within the bridge organization also streamlines their respective accounting systems by eliminating, for example, the costly and time-consuming process of matching invoices with purchase orders and of reconciling the mismatches.

This experiment with a bridge organization is a concrete example of blurred boundaries between producer and retailer and of the instrumental role of information technology in producing this result. Both companies have plans for replicating the bridge-organization concept with hundreds of key customers and vendors. However, both recognize the challenge of managing a network of bridge organizations in which each embodies some unique attributes of the two parties to the relationship.

Another example of creating internally and externally permeable boundaries is provided by Hagström (1990), who describes the strategic deployment of information technology by SKF, a Swedish ball-bearing company. Information technology has enabled the creation of a community of users at SKF: not only can a major customer enter an order electronically, but, if the item is out of stock, the customer can electronically initiate production. The same customer can also electronically modify specifications for an existing product and then initiate its production. These processes bypass the traditional transactions between buyer and marketing representative or between product designer and design engineers. Similarly, SKF has empowered its workers and given them self-responsibility; for example, by allowing them to electronically order consumables and supplies directly from vendors, thus restructuring traditional purchasing and control functions.

The central objective of the various ongoing attempts at organization redesign is focused on flexibility rather than stability. These organization redesign experiments are characterized by permeability of boundaries, fluid, ever-evolving structures, and continually changing (and improving) processes. The redesign efforts also involve restructuring the employment relationship and the design of work flows by emphasizing self-organization of work teams and multiple approaches to accomplishing similar tasks. The permeability and adaptiveness of such organizations are rendered possible by advances in information processing and communication technologies that overcome the constraints that time, space, and hierarchy impose on organizational decision making and structure.

These new organizational forms have been variously labeled "networks" (Miles and Snow, 1986), "clusters" (Mills, 1991), and "perpetual matrices" (Bartlett and Ghoshal, 1989). Although a consensus does seem to be emerging about attributes of the new organizational forms (see Table E.1), there is no comprehensive theory of the new organization forms, and no ideal-type description of the sort that Weber (1978/1910) formulated for bureaucracy.

THE CHALLENGE TO ORGANIZATION SCIENCE

The last time that a fundamental shift in management practice and organization design occurred was at the end of the nineteenth century, with the development of the modern bureaucratic organization. At the time, no discipline of organization science

Table E.1. Attributes of Effective Postindustrial Organizations

---

Overall Effectiveness Attributes

Global
Hyberflexible and adaptive
Continuously improving and innovative
Stakeholder focused, just
Tolerance for uncertainty

Structural Characteristics

Flatter
Decentralized
- Networked
- Self-organizing
- Control through culture and values
Permeable boundaries
- Internally "boundary-less"
- Blurred external boundaries
- Fit between structure and task processes

Information Processing

Virtual electronic organizations
Integration of telecommunications, office automation, data processing, and video technologies
Integration of planning and flow processes of work

Job Design

Individual/group empowerment
- Self-control and self-designed responsibility
- Intraentrepreneurship
- Multiple organization memberships
Cross-functional
- Continuous learning
- Cross training

Management

Leadership without control
- Less demanding, directing, evaluating, or organizing
- More facilitating, communicating, and networking
- Tolerance for ambiguity
- Trust in people
- Cosmopolitan

---

existed to analyze and interpret the changes or to inform management practice. This time around as the transformation of the postbureaucratic society takes shape, organization scholars have the opportunity to influence managerial practice and the new developments in organization science in several ways. First, at a preparadigm stage, organization scientists as well as popular business writers can provide conceptual metaphors and typologies that serve both to create shared mental models for managers and to legitimate new approaches to organization problems. Thus, for example, the concepts of network organizations (Miles and Snow, 1986), cluster organizations (Mills, 1991), perpetual matrix organizations (Bartlett and Ghoshal, 1989), and self-designing organizations (Nonaka, 1988) have all served to create and reinforce new organizational metaphors of the flexible, fluid, and continually evolving organizations. These new organizational metaphors, coupled with the transformations facing the management profession, have also forced organization scholars to reconsider theories and to search for new frameworks, theoretical concepts, and paradigms.[4]

In the immediate term, organization scientists need to determine the contingencies for which "network" organizations are particularly effective and, more importantly, identify the steady-state requirements for operating continually improving and evolving organizations. Although the conditions for the emergence of a new ideal-type theory of network organizations are propitious, the precise timing of such a development cannot be predicted. However, organization scholars can accelerate the process of theory building by undertaking careful case studies of organization redesign endeavors initiated by practitioners (viz. Cameron et al., Chapter 2 in this volume). The role of organization scholars in the process will be to identify and sort out the more innovative and more creative managerial practices, to analyze underlying similarities in seemingly disparate practices, and to generate new practice-oriented theories from these observations (Glaser and Strauss, 1967; Eisenhardt, 1989). For instance, Bartlett and Ghoshal (1989) credit the effective implementation of perpetual matrix design at Lever Bros. as the primary cause of the company's ability to continuously effect organizational adaptations to environmental discontinuities. We believe that more and more organization scholars will find that their research questions are shaped by real-world management problems (viz. Cameron et al., Chapter 2, Meyer et al., Chapter 3, and O'Reilly et al., Chapter 5 in this volume).

Organization scientists must stretch the boundaries of the topics that they address. Keeley's (1988) contention that organization theory is stultified by an almost exclusive focus on division of labor for economic efficiency is extremely germane. In the new forms of organization, division of labor will be changing continuously and often will be decided upon by work-group members themselves. Satisficing behavior (if it ain't broke don't fix it) and the quest for standard operating procedures will no longer be the norm. Issues that will come to the fore include (1) designing for stakeholder justice as well as for economic efficiency (Sheppard, Lewicki, and Minton, 1992; Stephens and Lewin, 1992); (2) creating organizations that span national and cultural boundaries (Slocum and Lei, Chapter 9 in this volume); and (3) managing empowered organizations—that is, defining leadership in a profoundly different sense, not on the basis of control or power (Tichy and Devanna, 1986; Trice and Beyer, 1991).

In particular, the extensive body of knowledge on participative management, job design, total employee involvement, and gain sharing can provide the basis for new human resource strategies appropriate for network organizations. For example, new selection, compensation, performance appraisal, and succession planning systems are needed to fit self-organizing work units, team work, continous learning, and control through culture and shared values.

Finally, as we have already noted, the transformations taking place in the environment of business render established management practice and organization theories obsolete. It is evident that organization science faces a historic opportunity to articulate for the emerging forms of network organizations what Weber (1978/1910) did for bureaucracy. This entails building an *ideal type theory* of network organizations. The theory should precisely delineate the attributes of the form, differentiate it from other organizational forms, and link its attributes to organizational effectiveness, not only along the new criteria of the post-industrial society but also along such traditional and inevitable managerial functions as planning, coordinating, organizing, and control.

CONCLUSION

Given the profound social and technological shifts now taking place, it seems highly likely that concomitant changes in organizational forms will occur on a widespread level. Anecdotal evidence (e.g., Dumaine, 1991) strongly suggests that managers already recognize that they are "pushing the limits of the envelope" by continuing to rely solely on intuition, imitation, and trial and error in redesigning their organizations. A Corning executive told us: "As it is now, there are really no guidelines for us. We try it one way, nd if that doesn't work, we revise." As the design of organizations is increasingly viewed as a source of competitive advantage, the interaction and mutual influencing between practitioners and organization theorists will broaden and intensify, and the field of organization theory and design will emerge as a functional discipline. Even though much work remains to be done on developing a comprehensive theory of the new organizational forms, the current body of knowledge continues to be of immediate relevance to practitioners who seek to redesign their organizations. Organization science can currently enhance management practice on specific organization design issues such as work-unit design of self-organizing groups, continuously improving organization, leadership without control, building global alliances, and leveraging computer-mediated communication technology.

Just as the industrial revolution led to the emergence of the bureaucratic organization and spawned a large body of research on structuring organizations for economic efficiency, we expect that the transformations of the twenty-first century and the accompanying postbureaucratic forms will rejuvenate both the field of organization theory and the practice of organization design.

NOTES

The authors wish to especially acknowledge the editors of this volume, George P. Huber and William H. Glick, for their insightful comments and many editorial suggestions.

1. The term *organization design* is more encompassing than the traditional concept of *organization structure* (e.g., Pugh, Hickson, and Hinings, 1969). It goes beyond the traditional domain of organization theory. As used here and increasingly in the literature, organization design embraces the formal architecture of the organization, its culture, processes, decision mak-

ing norms, information processing, structure of employment relationship, and values (Daft and Lewin, 1990).

2. Interviews with Corning managers took place as part of the research for the second author's dissertation.

3. The case is being researched by the first author, but both companies requested anonymity.

4. The concept of self-designing organizations was first proposed by Hedberg, Nystrom, and Starbuck (1976). However, the metaphors did not inform management practice or influence organization theory research, most likely because the unequivocal conditions of the postindustrial society apparent in the 1990s were not yet compelling in the 1970s.

REFERENCES

Aldrich, H. 1972. Technology and organizational structure: a reexamination of the findings of the Aston group. *Administrative Science Quarterly,* 17: 26–43.

Astley, W. G., and Zammuto, R. 1992. Organization science, managers, and language games. *Organization Science 3,* 00: 00–00.

Baligh, H., Burton, R., and Obel, B. 1990. Devising expert systems in organization theory: putting "design" into organizational design. In Masuch, M. (Ed.), *Organization, management, and expert systems,* (pp. 59–77). Berlin: Walter DeGruyter.

Barnard, C. 1938. *The functions of the executive.* Cambridge, MA: Harvard University Press.

Bartlett, C. A., and Ghoshal, S. 1989. *Managing across borders: the transnational solution.* Boston: Harvard Business School Press.

Bell, D. 1973. *The coming of postindustrial society: a venture in social forecasting.* New York: Basic Books.

Beyer, J. 1982. The utilization of organizational research: introduction to special issue, Part I. *Administrative Science Quarterly,* 27: 588–590.

Blau, P., and Schoenherr, R. 1971. *The structure of organizations.* New York: Wiley.

Burns, T., and Stalker, G. 1961. *The management of innovation.* London: Tavistock.

Chandler, A. D. 1962. *Strategy and structure: chapters in the history of the American industrial enterprise.* Cambridge, MA: MIT Press.

Chandler, A. D. 1977. *The visible hand: the managerial revolution in American business.* Cambridge, MA: Belknap Press.

Chandler, A. D. 1990. *Scale and scope: the dynamics of industrial capitalism.* Cambridge, MA: Belknap Press.

Clarke, A. K. 1963/1958. *Profiles of the future.* New York: Harper and Row.

Coleman, J. 1990. *Foundations of social theory.* Cambridge, MA: Belknap Press.

Culnan, M., and Markus, M. 1987. *Information Technologies.* In Jablin, F., L. Putnam, K. Roberts, and L. Porter (Eds.), *Handbook of organizational communication: an interdisciplinary perspective* (pp. 420–443). Newbury Park, CA: Sage.

Daft, R., and Lewin, A. 1990. Can organization studies begin to break out of the normal science straitjacket? An editorial essay. *Organization Science,* 1: 1–9.

Dubin, R. 1976. Theory building in applied areas. In Dunnette, M. (Ed.), *Handbook of industrial and organizational psychology* (pp. 17–39). Chicago: Rand.

Dumaine, B. 1991. The bureaucracy busters. *Fortune,* June 17, pp. 36–51.

Eisenhardt, K. M. 1989. Building theories from case study research. *Academy of Management Review,* 14: 532–550.

Etzioni, A. 1988. *The moral dimension: toward a new economics.* New York: Free Press.

Galbraith, J. K. 1967. *The new industrial state.* Boston: Houghton Mifflin.

Glaser, B., and Strauss, A. 1967. *The discovery of grounded theory.* Chicago: Aldine.

Gresov, C. 1989. Exploring fit and misfit with multiple contingencies. *Administrative Science Quarterly,* 34: 431–453.

Hage, J. 1988. *Futures of organizations: innovating to adapt strategy and human resources to rapid technological change.* Lexington, MA: Lexington Books.

Hage, J., and Aiken, M. 1967. Programmed change and organization properties: a comparative analysis. *American Journal of Sociology,* 72: 267–272.

Hagström, P. 1990. New information systems and the changing structure of MNCs. In Bartlett, C., Y. Doz, and G. Hedlund (Eds.), *Managing the global firm:* (pp. 164–185). London: Routledge.

Hall, R. 1963. The concept of bureaucracy: an empirical assessment. *American Journal of Sociology,* 69: 32–40.

Hedberg, B., Nystrom, P., and Starbuck, W. 1976. Camping on seesaws: prescriptions for a self-designing organization. *Administrative Science Quarterly,* 21: 41–65.

Huber, G. P. 1984. The nature and design of post-industrial organizations. *Management Science,* 30(8): 928–951.

Huber, G. P. 1990. A theory of the effects of advanced information technologies on organizational design intelligence and decision making. *Academy of Management Review,* 15: 47–71.

Inkson, J., Pugh, D., and Hickson, D. 1970. Organizational context and structure: an abbreviated replication. *Administrative Science Quarterly,* 15: 318–329.

Kanter, R. M. 1983. *The change masters: innovations for productivity in the American corporation.* New York: Simon and Schuster.

Keeley, M. 1988. *A social-contract theory of organizations.* Notre Dame, IN: University of Notre Dame Press.

Lawrence, P. R., and Lorsch, J. W. 1967. *Organization and environment: managing differentiation and integration.* Boston: Harvard University, Graduate School of Business Administration.

Lewin, A. Y., and Minton, J. W. 1986. Determining organizational effectiveness: another look and an agenda for research. *Management Science,* 32: 514–538.

Lewin, A., and Stephens, C. U. 1990. Individual properties of the CEO as determinants of organization design. Paper presented at the Academy of Management Meeting, San Francisco.

Mackenzie, K. 1991. *The organizational hologram: the effective management of organizational change.* Dordrecht: Kluwer Academic Publishers.

Malone, T., and Rockart, J. 1991. Computers, networks, and the organization. *Scientific American,* September: 128–137.

Marcuse, H. 1968. *Negations: essays in critical theory.* London: Penguin Publishers.

Meyer, J., and Gustafson, J. 1988. *The U. S. business corporation: an institution in transition.* Cambridge, MA: Ballinger.

Miles, R. E., and Snow, C. C. 1978. *Organizational strategy, structure, and process.* New York: McGraw-Hill.

Miles, R. E., and Snow, C. C. 1986. Organizations: new concepts for new forms. *California Management Review,* 28(3): 62–73.

Mills, D. 1991. *Rebirth of the corporation.* New York: Wiley.

Monge, P., and Eisenberg, E. 1987. Emergent communication networks. In Jablin, F., L. Putnam, K. Roberts, and L. Porter (Eds.), *Handbook of organizational communication* (pp. 304–342). Newbury Park: Sage.

Naisbitt, J., and Aburdene, P. 1985. Reinventing the corporation: transforming your job and your company for the new information society. New York: Warner Books.

Nonaka, I. 1988. Creating organizational order out of chaos: self-renewal in Japanese firms. *California Management Review,* 30: 57–73.

Omae, K. 1990. *The borderless world: power and strategy in the interlinked world economy.* New York: Harper Business.

Peters, T. 1987. *Thriving on chaos: handbook for a management revolution.* New York: Knopf.

Peters, T. J., and Waterman, R. H. 1982. *In search of excellence: lessons from America's best-run companies.* New York: Harper and Row.

Porter, L., and McKibbin, L. 1988. *Management education and development: drift or thrust into the 21st century?* New York: McGraw-Hill.

Pugh, D., Hickson, D., and Hinings, C. 1969. An empirical taxonomy of work organizations. *Administrative Science Quarterly,* 14: 115–16.

Pugh, D., Hickson, D., Hinings, C., and Turner, C. 1968. Dimensions of organizational structure. *Administrative Science Quarterly,* 13: 65–105.

Pugh, D., Hickson, D., Hinings, C., and Turner, C. 1969. The context of organizational structures. *Administrative Science Quarterly,* 14: 9–114.

Pugh, D., Hickson, D., Macdonald K., Turner C., and Lupton, D. 1963. A conceptual scheme for organizational analysis. *Administrative Science Quarterly,* 8: 289–315.

Quinn, R. E., and Rohrbaugh, J. 1983. A spatial model of effectiveness criteria: towards a competing values approach to organizational analysis. *Management Science,* 29: 363–377.

Reich, R. 1982. *Minding America's business: the decline and rise of the American economy.* New York: Vintage Books.

Reich, R. 1991. *The work of nations: Preparing ourselves for 21st-century capitalism.* New York: Knopf.

Rogers, E. 1988. Information technologies: how organizations are changing. In Goldhaber, G., and Barnet, G. (Eds.), *Handbook of organizational communication* (pp. 437–452). Norwood, NJ: Ablex.

Rose, F. 1990. A new age for business? *Fortune,* October 8, pp. 156–164.

Schoonhoven, C. 1981. Problem with contingency theory: testing assumptions hidden within the language of contingency "theory." *Administrative Science Quarterly,* 26: 349–377.

Sheppard, B., Lewicki, R., and Minton J. 1992. *Organizational justice.* Lexington, MA: Lexington Press.

Steinfield, C., and Fulk, J. 1990. The theory imperative. In Fulk, J., and Steinfield, C. (Eds.), *Organizations and communication technology* (pp. 13–26). Newbury Park: Sage.

Stephens, C. U., and Lewin, A. Y. 1992. *Bounded morality: a cross-level model of the determinants of ethical choice in organizations.* In D. Ludwig and K. Paul (Eds.), Contemporary Issues in the Business Environment, pp. 1–20. Lewiston, NY: Edwin Mellen Press.

Tesler, L. 1991. Networked computing in the 1990s. *Scientific American,* September 1: 86–93.

Thompson, J. D. 1956. On building an administrative science. *Administrative Science Quarterly,* 1: 102–111.

Thompson, J. D. 1967. *Organizations in action: social science bases of administrative theory.* New York: McGraw-Hill.

Tichy, N. M., and Devanna, M. A. 1986. *The transformational leader.* New York: Wiley.

Toffler, A. 1980. *The third wave.* New York: Morrow.

Trice, H. M., and Beyer, J. M. 1991. Cultural leadership in organizations. *Organization Science,* 2: 149–169.

Walton, R. 1989. *Up and running: integrating information technology and the organization.* Boston: Harvard University Business School Press.

Weber, M. 1978/1910. *Economy and society.* G. Roth and C. Wittich (Trs.). Berkeley: University of California Press.

Woodward, J. 1965. *Industrial organization: theory and practice.* New York: Oxford University Press.

Appendix: Studying Changes in Organizational Design and Effectiveness: Retrospective Event Histories and Periodic Assessments*

WILLIAM H. GLICK,[1] GEORGE P. HUBER,[1] C. CHET MILLER,[2]
D. HAROLD DOTY,[3] and KATHLEEN M. SUTCLIFFE[4]

[1]*Graduate School of Business, University of Texas, Austin, Texas 78712*
[2]*Hankamer School of Business, Baylor University, Waco, Texas 76798*
[3]*Department of Management, University of Arkansas, Fayetteville, Arkansas 72701*
[4]*Carlson School of Management, University of Minnesota, Minneapolis, Minnesota, 55455*

This paper describes assumptions, rationale, and trade-offs involved in designing the research methodology used in a longitudinal study of the relationships among changes in organizational contexts, designs, and effectiveness. The basic research question concerns when, how, and why do different types of organizational change occur. Given this research question and a desire to develop and test generalizable theory about changes in organizational design and effectiveness, we conducted a longitudinal study of over 100 organizations. Data concerning the changes were obtained through four interviews spaced six months apart with the top manager in each organization. Each interview provided a short-term retrospective event history over the preceding 6-month interval. In aggregate, the four interviews provided a 24-month event history for each organization. Additionally, periodic assessments of the state of the organization's context, design, and effectiveness were collected with two questionnaires spaced one year apart. Finally, in each organization, the top manager's personal characteristics were assessed after all other data were obtained. This paper examines the alternatives, advantages, and disadvantages of the research design decisions. With some hindsight, we also offer some suggestions for future researchers with similar goals of developing and testing generalizable explanations of change processes in organizations. (ORGANIZATION THEORY; ORGANIZATIONAL DESIGN; RESEARCH METHODS; ORGANIZATIONAL CHANGE; ORGANIZATIONAL EFFECTIVENESS)

*From *Organization Science* 1(3): 293–312. Copyright © 1990, The Institute of Management Sciences. Reprinted by permission.

Top managers are preoccupied by change, both the changes that they must react to, such as new and important threats and opportunities, and the changes that they initiate as a result of their values and aspirations. To increase effectiveness, improve efficiency, gain market share, or simplify the organizational design, managers are constantly creating new programs, streamlining procedures, evaluating proposed courses of action, and encountering new opportunities in their organizations' environments. All of these activities involve change.

The research methodology described in this paper was designed to aid in our investigation of changes in organizations, particularly the important changes that grasp the attention of the organization's top manager. What types of changes occur? What types of changes occur most frequently? When and how do these different types of changes occur? In other words, what are the antecedent conditions, causes, and consequences of changes across a variety of organizational forms, contexts, and internal processes? The goal of our investigation was both to build and to test theories to answer these research questions. The overall research program chosen to achieve this goal was a multi-investigator set of longitudinal studies of Changes in Organizational Design and Effectiveness (CODE). This paper focuses on the central study in the program. The dependent variables of primary interest in the central CODE study were attributes of changes (e.g., types of changes and frequency of changes) and attributes of change processes (e.g., causes of changes, consequences of changes, and sequences of changes). To understand more fully these attributes of changes and change processes, we investigated their relationships with characteristics of the organization, such as its environment, performance, technology, strategy, and design.

The primary purposes of the paper are (1) to describe the research methodology for the central study; (2) to discuss the trade-offs that shaped the methodology; and (3) to evaluate these choices with the advantage of some hindsight. Each of these purposes is addressed in the four major sections of the paper. These sections are organized around the key features of the methodology: (1) the management and conduct of the overall research program and the central study; (2) the field sites; (3) the retrospective event histories; and (4) the assessments of organizational, contextual, and top manager characteristics.

MANAGEMENT AND CONDUCT OF THE CODE RESEARCH PROGRAM

Trade-offs Decided Prior to Funding

Thorngate (1976, p. 126) and Weick (1979, pp. 35–42) note that it is impossible for a theory to be "simultaneously accurate, general, and simple." Given the basic research questions, our biases, and the interests of the funding agency, the focus of the research was on developing and testing *generalizable theory* about the changes that are likely to affect or occur in any organization. This focus obviously precluded addressing alternative research questions, such as questions about the rich details of the processes related to one or a few types of organizational changes (cf., Barley 1990, Leonard-Barton 1990, Van de Ven and Poole 1990). The resultant relatively positivist focus and research question also precluded research designs involving very intensive examination of a limited number of cases. Thus, even before submitting the research proposal, we made the first trade-off that shaped the methodology, sacrificing some depth in order to gain breadth.

Another major issue that had to be resolved prior to submitting the research proposal was the matter of choosing a design that would be satisfactory with respect to the following criteria: (1) the efficiency of data collection techniques; (2) the time span of the data; (3) the efficiency and ease of coordinating the research project; (4) the need to recruit and maintain participation of a large number of field sites; (5) the desire to discover new types of changes, antecedents, and consequences; and (6) the desire to develop new theory about the antecedents and consequences of different types of change in different contexts. The first two criteria argue for archival data collection over a long period of time to capture both rapid and evolutionary changes in organizational design and effectiveness. The last two criteria, however, prevented complete reliance on archival or survey data collection techniques because of the need for richer, more detailed information. Because theory development often can be facilitated by the interaction of multiple, independent researchers, and because the use of multiple researchers also facilitates the recruitment and maintenance of multiple field sites, the last three criteria argued for the inclusion of multiple researchers. The inherent difficulties of coordinating among multiple researchers, however, obviously runs counter to the third criterion.

After considering the trade-offs among these criteria, we adopted a design that emphasizes a series of interviews in a large number of field sites by several researchers. Four additional researchers at different universities collaborated in the research program. All collaborators took responsibility for theory development for their local studies and data collection for both their local studies and the central study. (The central study is hereafter referred to simply as the study.) Each local study reflected the respective collaborator's research interest, but was required to be related also to the central study theme of organizational change. In order to draw upon an even larger base of methodological and substantive expertise, six consultants also were included in the research program (see Figure A.1).

Choices Made During the Study

The overall CODE research program was scheduled for five years beginning September 1, 1985. During the first year, the principal investigators initiated literature reviews and theory-building efforts to guide the subsequent empirical research. The products of these efforts include Daft and Huber (1987), Huber (1990, 1991), Huber and Daft (1987), Huber and McDaniel (1986), and Huber, Miller and Glick (1990). This work identified many variables relevant to changes in organizational design and effectiveness that would be of interest to both the research and practitioner communities. These reviews also revealed a lack of maturity in the field's understanding of change. Thus, we decided that in addition to addressing some a priori issues, the research would be designed to develop a data base that could be used in the future to develop post hoc theories about the relationships among many dimensions of change, design, and effectiveness.

During the second year, we designed the central study and conducted pretests of the interview instrument, the interview administration and coding procedures, and the organizational assessment questionnaire. Also during year two, the collaborating

Dr. George P. Huber, Principal Investigator
University of Texas at Austin

Dr. William H. Glick, Co-Principal Investigator
University of Texas at Austin

Collaborating Researchers

Dr. Kim S. Cameron, University of Michigan
Dr. Richard L. Daft, Texas A & M University*
Dr. Kenneth Bettanhausen, Texas A & M University[1]
Dr. Alan D. Meyer, University of Oregon
Dr. Charles A. O'Reilly, University of California

Consultants

Dr. William W. Cooper, University of Texas at Austin
Dr. Arie Y. Lewin, Duke University
Dr. Peter S. Monge, University of Southern California
Dr. John W. Slocum, Southern Methodist University
Dr. Andrew Van de Ven, University of Minnesota
Dr. Karl E. Weick, University of Texas at Austin*

Research Associates

Joan Boothe, University of California-Berkeley
Geoffrey Brooks, University of Oregon
D. Harold Doty, University of Texas at Austin*
Sarah Freeman, University of Michigan*
James B. Goes, University of Oregon*
C. Chet Miller, University of Texas at Austin*

Aneil Mishra, University of Michigan
Doug Orton, University of Michigan*
Richard Snyder, University of California-Berkeley
Kathleen M. Sutcliffe, University of Texas at Austin
Beverly B. Tyler, Texas A & M University*

*Affiliations shown are at the time the contributor joined the research study. Those with new affiliations are asterisked.
[1] Added after the study began.

Figure A.1 CODE Research program contributors.

researchers began designing their studies and establishing their field sites. All central study instruments and the respective protocols for administering them were circulated among the researchers and consultants for feedback before being finalized.

A trade-off unique to large-scale research projects involves reaching a compromise between encouraging each collaborator to do something unique versus insisting on uniform adoption of a single theoretical model. This trade-off stimulated a lively debate during the second year of our project. Arguing in favor of greater consensus on theoretical perspectives are the criteria of: economies of scale; standardization; ease of identifying the main contribution of the research project; the potential to stimulate a very creative theory-building process among a group of collaborators; and the potential to make a single, large research contribution. The advantages of encouraging multiple perspectives are: greater diversity of final theories; reduced need for coordination; more contributions; each collaborator can pursue his or her own interests; and established researchers with interesting research agendas can be enlisted in the collaborative project. Given the field's limited understanding of change processes in organizations and the geographic dispersion of the collaborators, we decided against adopting a unified theoretical perspective for the project.

During the third, fourth, and fifth years, the four interviews were conducted, and all questionnaires were administered. The interview data suggested that detailed information was also needed about the top manager. Thus, an additional questionnaire was designed and administered during this period. Also during the fifth year, additional data coding schemes were developed and employed, and all researchers focused on interpreting their results and publishing the result of their studies.

In addition to frequent coordination contacts by telephone and electronic and postal mail, the researchers, consultants, and some research associates met annually for a one-day coordination meeting. Many of the ideas discussed in this paper were brought into sharper perspective through informal exchanges at these meetings and subsequent interactions. A myriad of problems were preempted or solved using these coordination procedures. Nevertheless, despite our coordination efforts, lack of uniformity crept into data collection procedures and resulted in the need to discard and replace some data. In retrospect, additional efforts at coordination probably would have reduced this problem. Our insufficient coordination was the result of our partially incorrect beliefs that protocols and related communications would provide sufficient training for all interviewers and that all researchers would adhere tightly to the protocol. Also, we believed that more frequent coordination meetings would detract from the time and enthusiasm directed at developing and testing theories. Consequently, although we seriously considered additional meetings for focusing the research questions, interviewer training, and final discussion of the research design, we decided against them. Hindsight suggests that additional coordination, especially meetings related to interviewer training, should have been undertaken.

FIELD SITE SELECTION AND RETENTION

Number of Field Sites

Data were collected from 153 diverse organizations. Complete data sets, i.e., four interviews, two organizational/context questionnaires, and the top manager characteristics questionnaire, were collected from over 100 organizations.[1] Two related arguments contributed to the decision to study this relatively large number of field sites rather than focus on a limited number of case studies. First, as indicated earlier, the goal of the research was to develop theories that would be generalizable across a variety of organizational forms, contexts, and processes. Given this goal, statistical power considerations suggested a bare minimum of 15 observations to detect very large effects with better than a 50-50 probability (Cohen 1988). Tests of more complex contingency hypotheses required sample sizes in excess of 100 (Cohen 1988, Drasgow and Kang 1984).

A second reason for studying a large number of field sites was the underlying assumption that any change in organizational design and effectiveness is likely to be determined by a plethora of factors (Katz and Kahn 1978, Weick 1979). Multiple processes and events may increase the probability of a change, but any single event or process may fail to have the expected effect due to countervailing forces. Thus, given an overdetermined system, it is impossible to specify the necessary and sufficient conditions for any change in organizational design and effectiveness (Markus and Robey 1988, Mohr 1982). Antecedents could be necessary *or* sufficient, but might not be both. In addition, the marginal impact of any process or effect is often a function of the levels or changes in other factors, levels or changes that may not be known or recognized for their importance. Thus, causal determinants of change are not wholly pre-

---

[1] At the time of this writing, additional data still are being collected. The completed data set will have complete information on approximately 120 organizations.

dictable in their effects because other unmeasured determinants of change might be changing simultaneously.

There are two possible ways to handle the methodological complications implied by overdetermination and the consequent inability to fully specify the necessary and sufficient conditions for changes in organizations. The first approach is very idiographic and emphasizes context-dependent descriptions of the processes of change (Markus and Robey 1988, Mohr 1982). The second approach is more nomothetic and treats all causal explanations as probabilistic rather than deterministic statements. This approach is based on the assumptions that (1) changes and outcomes of changes in organizations are overdetermined; (2) countervailing forces may obscure a true effect; and (3) countervailing forces occur at random. Thus, any causal effect is a probabilistic rather than deterministic event. Given our nomothetic research goals, we adopted the second approach. The methodological implication of adopting this approach is that inferences should be based on large samples and statistical criteria rather than detailed observations of a single case.

Variation among Field Sites

The focus of the study was on understanding the nature of a broad variety of changes and change processes that might occur in a variety of organizations. This focus is based on the nomothetic assumption that many of the antecedents and consequences of organizational change are important across a broad variety of organizations. Thus, we chose to study a heterogeneous set of field sites. The set of field sites includes organizations ranging in size from 16 to 6000 employees, with a mean of 1024 and median of 304, and includes multiple industries in both the service and manufacturing sectors. Heterogeneity was constrained only by the requirement that each organization (1) have primary responsibility for its strategy and design; (2) include at least two managerial levels; and (3) have an external constituency independent of any parent organization.

Despite our general acceptance of the nomothetic assumption of generalizability, however, we included homogeneous clusters of organizations in the set of field sites. The homogeneous clusters enable development of limited domain or middle-range theories (Pinder and Moore 1980, Weick 1974). The study includes (for example) sizable clusters of hospitals, electronics manufacturers, financial services, business schools, new organizations, organizations in declining manufacturing industries, profit-oriented organizations, and not-for-profit organizations.

This combination of overall heterogeneity and within-cluster homogeneity allows us to test both nomothetic and idiographic assumptions (Duncan 1972, Hambrick 1982). A limited domain theory developed or initially validated within one cluster can be tested further in the larger, heterogeneous set of organizations or in other clusters from the larger set. To the extent that theories developed in one context generalize across clusters or to other clusters, it will be possible to support more nomothetic, less idiographic assumptions. Alternatively, a theory developed or initially validated in the heterogeneous set of organizations can be tested within clusters to examine the assumption that the theory can be generalized to specific homogeneous clusters.

This decision to use field sites that in aggregate were heterogeneous but clustered into homogeneous sets involved a trade-off. First, it resulted in losing an opportunity to sample randomly from a *theoretically* defined and *theoretically* relevant population of organizations. This loss is important because it weakens the generalizability of the results to an unknown degree. We believe, however, that the final set of field sites is sufficiently heterogeneous and representative of the population of organizations to support most assertions of generalizability. Second, this trade-off created several problems in developing instruments useful in a variety of contexts. Simple terms such as customers, financial backers, or organizational performance are interpreted differently in different contexts such as banks, hospitals, business schools, and manufacturers. (In one religious organization the main criterion of performance was the number of souls saved.) Despite these disadvantages, the considerations above led to an early decision to study field sites that were heterogeneous overall, but homogeneous within clusters.

Selecting and Recruiting Field Sites

To assure maximal generalizability of results, field sites should be randomly sampled from a known population of organizations. Further, the boundaries of the population should be defined based on theoretical considerations. In addition to generalizability, however, researchers also must contend with the two practical considerations of limited resources and potentially unwilling participants.

To make the greatest use of travel and time budgets, we and our collaborators selected and recruited field-site organizations that were located in nearby geographical areas, typically in cities near our universities. If the researcher had a good rapport with the contact person at the field site after one or two face-to-face interviews, telephone interviews were used occasionally to conserve additional time and travel expenses.

Besides the matter of limited travel and time budgets, a second practical consideration was that each organization's top manager had to be willing to commit to multiple interviews and questionnaires over a two-year period. By using nearby field sites, we increased the likelihood that the top managers would participate in the research because we could interview face-to-face and because they were helping researchers from a local university rather than a distant rival. The final set of field sites was geographically dispersed throughout the United States, with large clusters in central California, the San Francisco Bay area, central Texas, southeast Texas, Virginia, and parts of the midwestern states of Michigan, Ohio, and Illinois.

The purposeful selection of field sites resulted in some loss of generalizability of the results due to the lack of random sampling from a theoretically defined population. We believe, however, that the loss in generalizability is limited by the heterogeneity of the total set and the ability to test assumptions of generalizability across clusters. The heterogeneity of the field sites reflects more closely the population of strategic business units that are the focus of most organizational theories than do the more homogeneous sets of field sites used in most empirical organizational research.

Retaining Field Sites

Unlike participants in cross-sectional interview studies, the key informants were required to provide four interviews over an 18-month time period, to complete two seven-page questionnaires spaced a year apart, and one one-page questionnaire at the end of the 18 months. Believing that whatever motivations led to initial cooperation would likely diminish across time, we worked to retain as many of the organizations as possible across the entire study. We cultivated the informant at each field site by one or more of the following: (1) making it easy for the informant to participate by scheduling interviews at his or her convenience; (2) asking for and using a limited amount of the informant's time; (3) guaranteeing confidentiality; (4) maintaining a personal relationship through phone calls, letters, and personal visits; (5) promising (and providing) clear rewards to the informant such as personalized feedback and copies of the papers and book at the end of the project; (6) focusing the fixed amount of researcher time and energy on a limited number of informants; (7) using semi-personalized letters describing the relevance of the study to the practice of management before the first interview and again with each organizational profile assessment questionnaire; (8) developing personal rapport with each participant by engaging in "common interest" conversation before the interview began; and (9) personally mailing journal articles or other materials of professional interest. (When such mailings occurred, care was taken so that their content was unlikely to affect data provided by the informant in the future.) These procedures seem to be effective; we estimate at this time that attrition due to controllable causes will be less than 10%, that attrition due to uncontrollable causes (such as acquisition and bankruptcy) will be 10%, and that attrition due to turnover of the key informant (and subsequent noninterest of the new top manager) will also be 10%.

Summary

Field site organizations were selected to reflect the heterogeneous population of organizations by including a heterogeneous set of homogeneous clusters. This approach was used in order to obtain variety in the nature and antecedents of change and thereby to develop interpretations of organizational actions that were both contextually valid within clusters and generalizable across clusters. Each cluster of organizations within a single domain provides specificity for validating explanations related strictly to that domain. The heterogeneity of the total set is compatible with more nomothetic assumptions about the phenomena of interest, and yet allows us to test more specific, idiographic assumptions about the limits of generalizability.

RETROSPECTIVE EVENT HISTORIES

The primary methodology for obtaining information about the changes in the field sites organizations was to develop a 24-month retrospective event history (Tuma and Hannan 1984) obtained from a series of four structured interviews with the top manager in each organization. The interview procedure focused the top manager's attention on relevant changes by soliciting the retrospective report after reviewing two lists entitled "generic examples of organizational design changes" and "generic examples of nondesign organizational changes" (see Figure A.2).[2] The top manager was placed in the role of key informant (Bagozzi and Phillips 1982, Phillips 1981, Seidler 1974)

---

[2]The interview instruments, protocols, and coding instructions are described in CODE Study Technical Reports 01, 05, 10, and 11 and are available from the first author.

Design Changes

(a) Important changes in the responsibility or resources of top management team members, (i.e., of the CEO or of any manager who reports to either the CEO or to the chief operating officer).

(b) Important changes in responsibility or resources at the other levels in the organization.

(c) Important additions or eliminations of a major organizational unit.

(d) Important changes in the way that your organization interacts with its customers, clients, or parent organization, such as introducing electronic funds transfer or the solicitation of orders by phone.

(e) Important changes in the way that you produce your product or service, such as a change in equipment, techniques, or sequencing of activities.

(f) Important changes in administrative procedures such as changing control or incentive systems.

(g) Important changes in internal coordination or communication procedures, such as introducing electronic mail or teleconferencing.

Nondesign Changes

(a) Important changes in the performance of either the whole organization or an important subunit (e.g., changes in costs, client complaints, personnel turnover, sales).

(b) Important changes in the organization's external environment (e.g., changes in competitors, regulators, or suppliers).

(c) Important changes in the organization's externally-directed strategy (e.g., changes in products, markets, emphases, relations with important outsiders).

(d) Important changes in the organization's internally-directed goals, philosophy, or culture (e.g., the decision to focus on human resource development, cost control, employee participation).

(e) Important changes in specific personnel or in staffing levels (e.g., additions, deletions, transfers, reassignments) not mentioned previously.

Figure A.2   Generic examples of organizational changes.

and asked to take 10 to 20 minutes to briefly describe the important design and nondesign changes that occurred at his or her organization during the six months preceding the interview. Example changes included the departure of specific, key personnel, a doubling in sales volume, addition of new product lines, major reorganizations or reassignments of people and resources, and change in governmental regulations. The manager was also asked to identify the dates that these changes occurred, unless the changes were actually ongoing processes, such as a demographic trend, in which case he or she was asked the date when a critical level of change was noted, or, if this was not possible, to label the change as "ongoing."

After listing the changes, the manager was asked to identify the three most important design and three most important nondesign changes and the factors leading to these six important changes. Although different top managers may have used different criteria in assigning importance, we felt that the interviewers would be less qualified to make this assessment than would the top manager. The disadvantage of this protocol design is that some of the variation across organizations may be attributed to the differences in criteria applied by the top managers rather than any real differences in importance of the different types of changes.

This retrospective event history methodology reflected a series of trade-offs. The three most important judgment calls were (1) selecting the method to assess change; (2) using the organization's top manager as the sole key informant about the organization; and (3) defining the characteristics of the change to be coded. The following sections describe alternative methodologies, the nature of the trade-offs, and the alternative that we selected in each of these judgment calls.

Selecting the Method to Assess Change

Researchers interested in organizational change are very often absent when important changes occur. Thus, a major challenge when studying organizational change and change processes is to get data consistently on events and processes that may occur while the researcher is not present.

Alternative Methodologies to Assess Change

We considered four alternative methods to assess change: (1) direct observation; (2) records compiled by organizational members; (3) panel designs; and (4) retrospective reports. One approach for investigating change requires researchers to be immersed in the organizations in order to be more likely to observe changes directly. Given the obvious time demands, this approach is most compatible with small sample research. Change processes that occur either *simultaneously* or *unpredictably* in different organizational subunits cannot be studied using direct observation unless multiple observers are used in each organization. Our interest in understanding a broad variety of changes, including unpredictable changes that may occur simultaneously, precluded the use of this approach.

A second approach to studying change is to rely on an organizational member to make the observations and record the data as changes occur, or shortly thereafter. The records can be compiled in a special log provided by the researcher or in archival sources that are regularly used by the organization. Logs are useful techniques for capturing change processes, but many top managers are not willing to keep a log of changes for research purposes across an extended period of time (such as two years). Archival sources are also useful for studying change, but these sources are rarely sufficiently detailed or consistent across time or organizations to fulfill our research goal.

A third approach to examining change is analogous to time-lapse photography; change processes can be inferred by looking for differences across a series of snapshots taken at fixed time intervals. For example, panel designs assess change processes by estimating change between static assessments. They do not capture directly the critical change events. Panel designs are most effective when the time lapse between the static assessments is very short. The shortened time interval loses less information about the sequencing of events and improves the continuous time estimates of dynamic processes (Tuma and Hannan 1984). Panel designs are very useful in many organizational contexts (Monge 1990), but if any of the causal processes occur faster than the interval between panels of data collection, it is impossible to estimate accurately the relationships among the variables (Cook and Campbell 1979, Monge, Farace, Eisenberg, Miller, and White 1984). Given the fast pace of many changes in organizational design and effectiveness, a panel design would have required weekly or monthly interviews. This would have been prohibitively expensive, given our decision to study a large number of organizations, and would have caused many top managers to refuse to participate across the period of the study.

Retrospective reports from key informants, a fourth approach to capturing change, was adopted as the primary method for obtaining information about important events and processes. Every six months the top manager was asked to report the important changes that occurred over the previous six months and the dates that these changes occurred. The factors that led to the six most important of these listed changes were also elicited in the interview and, in the subsequent interview six months later, the consequences of these six most important changes were elicited. This series of four interviews provided retrospectively reported changes for a retrospective event history spanning 24 months. The sequencing of these reported changes and the open-ended nature of the retrospective reports provided a rich base of data and stimulated insights into the unique changes in each organization.

Advantages and Disadvantages of Retrospective Reports

A key advantage of the retrospective reports is that the time intervals between events are much shorter than the intervals between interviews. It is important to recognize that the data from the four interviews are not analogous to four snapshots of static conditions at six-month intervals, but rather they are four reasonably fresh and timely reports of events and their causes and consequences across a 24-month period. The actual dates of changes are obtained with direct questions rather than being a consequence of the frequency and timing of data collection, as would be the case in a panel design.

A second advantage of retrospective reports is that the top manager describes directly the key events and processes of change. Organizational participants often attend to different characteristics of organizations and describe these characteristics and their relationships using terms different from those used by organizational scientists (Blackburn and Cummings 1982, McGuire 1986). We involved organizational participants in the theory development process (as recommended by Beyer and Trice 1982) by relying on open-ended retrospective reports. The top managers described the important changes and their antecedents in their own terminology. Thus, we expect our theory development to be more grounded in the experiences and terminology of top managers.

A disadvantage of asking open-ended questions and relying on the top managers' terminology is that their terminology may be imprecise or may be inconsistent across top managers. Thus, our interpretations of their open-ended responses may be inaccurate or depend on the verbal skills of the top managers. This creates problems as the open-ended responses are recorded and then coded by the interviewer and other researchers using the data. As we discovered new types of changes or later decided to code additional characteristics of the changes, the open-ended responses had to be reinterpreted by someone who had never visited any of the field sites. Given our reliance on the top managers' terminology, the validity of our coding interpretations undoubtedly suffered, particularly when the coder did not have all of the rich cues that are available in the actual interview.

A second disadvantage of asking open-ended questions about recent changes is that the responses may be associated with errors of recall, e.g., informants may selectively neglect some events that are important or focus on trends that are actually unimportant but temporarily conspicuous to the informant. If too many truly important events are omitted, the theoretical explanations will be inaccurate and lack descriptive relevance. If nonimportant events are included, they may be falsely accepted as important possible antecedents of other changes in organizational design and effectiveness.

Errors of recall can result from strong cognitive processes such as rationalization, self-presentation, simplification, attribution, or simple lapses of memory (Wolfe and Jackson 1987). And, of course, more recent changes are more likely to be recalled. Although errors of recall are important problems with retrospective event histories, the magnitude of these problems was minimized in the study by the following procedural safeguards: (1) the interview was explicitly focused on "important" changes that tend to be recalled more reliably; (2) all key informants were top managers who, by virtue of their positions, tended to be involved with or close observers of the important events and processes about which they reported; and (3) the questions were restricted to changes that occurred relatively recently (within the previous six months). Each of these safeguards tends to minimize errors of recall (Huber 1985, Huber and Power 1985) and was used in the interviews.

Selecting the Key Informant(s)

A second judgment call in the retrospective event history methodology involved selecting the person(s) to provide the event history from each organization. Using retrospective reports implied that the interviewee should be placed in the role of key informant supplying descriptive information about the organization rather than in the role of a respondent reacting to questions about his or her perceptions (Glick 1985, Houston and Sudman 1975, Phillips 1981, Seidler 1974). This key informant role was most appropriate given the research questions.

The top full-time manager in each organization was selected as the single key informant for describing changes in that organization.[3] Choosing the top full-time manager to be the sole key informant was based on (1) criteria for selecting informants; and (2) criteria for choosing to use single versus multiple informants.

Criteria for Selecting Key Informants

The main criteria used to select key informants were (1) the expected validity of their descriptions and assessments of the phenomena; and (2) the anticipated extent of cooperation in providing these data across the duration of the study. These criteria implied that the best key informants for the study would be (1) knowledgeable about the widest possible variety of important changes and their relative importance; (2) knowledgeable about the antecedents and consequences of these changes; (3) able to articulate the important changes and their antecedents accurately; and (4) willing to report accurately (cf., Glick 1985, Houston and Sudman 1975, Huber and Power 1985, Phillips 1981, Seidler, 1974).

Any organizational member was a potential key informant because of his or her knowledge about some events. Every organizational member, however, was also relatively ignorant about other events due to the reward structure, the pattern of specialized information flows in organizations, and individual and organizational limits in information processing. Of the potential informants, the top manager was the most

---

[3]In roughly 10% of the organizations, the top position on the organizational chart was occupied by an individual with substantial or primary responsibilities in nonadministrative capacities, and most administrative issues were handled by a full-time professional administrator. In these cases, we interviewed the professional administrator. In several cases, the CEO explicitly told us that the professional administrator was the most knowledgeable individual for our study.

likely to be knowledgeable about a broad variety of important changes both within and outside the organization as argued by Snow and Hrebiniak (1980) and Zajac and Shortell (1989) and as found by Hambrick (1981) (also see Aguilar 1967, Mintzberg 1975, Zajonc and Wolfe 1966). The top manager also was most likely to be able to assess the relative importance of changes from an organizational point of view and, therefore, to report only the changes that were most important to the organization. Other informants in more specialized product or functional positions were likely to emphasize changes that were primarily relevant to their positions (Dearborn and Simon 1958, Ireland, Hitt, Bettis, and DePorras 1987). Selective perception and exposure to different information lead more specialized or less central managers to report more peripheral events (cf., Houston and Sudman 1975, Phillips 1981). Finally, variations in knowledge about the intentions of change initiators (Hax and Majluf 1988) were also likely to result in different reported antecedents if informants holding a variety of organizational positions were used. By selecting the top manager as the sole key informant, we avoided these threats to the validity of the reports, but by doing so we undoubtedly obtained data that is biased in the direction of an over-reporting of factors linked to the top manager.

Given the attributes of desirable key informants, one alternative to selecting the top manager as the key informant in all organizations was to select the most knowledgeable, articulate, and cooperative informant from each organization, regardless of position. Although in some organizations this selection rule might provide better informants than the top manager, we believed that it would be difficult to apply across a large number of organizations. We also believed that it would result in the introduction of different biases associated with the informant's position (Dearborn and Simon 1958, Ireland et al. 1987, Zajonc and Wolfe 1966). Thus, this selection rule would confound real differences among organizations with the biases associated with the informants.

It is important to note that by consistently selecting the top manager as the key informant from the same position in each organization, we controlled for the several biases that are associated with the top manager position (Glick 1985, Seidler 1974). That is, report biases that are associated with the top manager position are present in all of the reports and, therefore, are not a source of cross-organizational variance in reports concerning changes and their antecedents and consequences.

Choosing Between Single Versus Multiple Informants

Although our treatment of the top manager as a key informant was consistent with obtaining the most valid retrospective reports possible, the use of a single key informant did not respond to frequent calls for multiple informants (Bagozzi and Phillips 1982, Huber and Power 1985, Phillips 1981, Seidler 1974, Williams, Cote, and Buckley 1989). An important advantage of using multiple informants is that the validity of information provided by any informant can be checked against that provided by the other informants. By selecting a single informant, we traded off the opportunity to test the validity of the reports.

A second, more important, advantage of using multiple informants is that the validity of the data used by the researcher can be enhanced by resolving discrepancies among different informants' reports. Discrepancies typically are resolved by using a heuristic to compute a composite score for the organization or by face-to-face discussions among the informants (Wolfe and Jackson 1987). With continuous or equal-interval level data, the most common heuristic is a simple averaging across informants. With categorical data, such as the types of reported changes and their antecedents, discrepancies must be resolved by more elaborate heuristics, such as ignoring any changes mentioned by less than two informants.

But using multiple informants rather than a single informant also has important disadvantages: (1) organizations tend to decline to participate or to continue participating in the study because they incur greater costs—especially when asked to volunteer the time of multiple informants to supply seemingly redundant factual information as a validity check on the most informed informant's report; (2) informants tend to decline to participate, or to put forth substandard efforts, as one of several informants rather than as the special key informant; (3) informants decline to participate or they withhold information for fear of breaches of confidentiality in subsequent interviews with other informants; (4) the researchers' time and other resources are absorbed with the additional interviews rather than being employed to access additional single informant field sites; and, most importantly, (5) the larger the number of informants, the less well-qualified is the average informant. Given the importance of generalizability to our study, the potential self-selection and loss of organizations and informants were also important.

After considering all of these issues and considering our prior decision to study a large number of organizations, we made the judgment call to use the top manager as the sole key informant from each organization.

Defining the Attributes of Changes to Be Coded

The third major judgment call involved the process of reducing open-ended descriptions of changes into a parsimonious set of attributes for theory testing and building. The retrospective reports of recent changes were solicited with open-ended questions that encouraged top managers to describe the changes in their own words. Some of the attributes to be coded were defined a priori, while others were developed and applied post hoc. The diverse descriptions of changes from the top managers provided an extremely rich data set for both deductive and inductive theory development. Four examples of the attributes that have been coded are described below.

Nominal Type of Change.

Top managers were asked to describe recent design and nondesign changes for their organizations. These two types of changes were separated in the interview by providing the top manager with separate lists of generic design and nondesign changes (Figure 2) and asking first for descriptions of design changes and then for descriptions of nondesign changes. Occasionally, the informants described nondesign changes when the interviewer was recording design changes, and vice versa. The initial coding of the changes identified each change as a design or nondesign change. Changes were subsequently coded into the subcategories suggested in the lists of generic examples (Figure 2).[4] This coding system was applied both to the reported changes and to the reported antecedents of the most important changes.

[4]These subcategories are defined more precisely in CODE Technical Reports 01 and 05 and are available from the first author.

Reaction Versus Proaction as Impetus for Change

In accord with the "reactive" system-structure paradigm (Astley and Van de Ven 1983), we initially expected antecedents of the most important changes to be other recent or expected design or nondesign changes. We did not anticipate that many of the reported antecedents would reflect a proactive nature of organizations. Early in our interviewing efforts, however, we discovered that many of these antecedents were long-standing aspirations or changes in aspiration levels rather than actual or expected changes. For example, some top managers reported that recent changes were changes that they had always wanted to introduce, but were unable to pursue or accomplish until recently. Other top managers reported that recent changes were the consequence of their attention and action on an existing, well-known opportunity. In some cases, these change-inducing shifts in aspiration levels were prompted by ideas from consultants, professional meetings, or reading of management literature.

Given a large number of these proactive changes, after the first round of interviews we had the interviewers code all factors leading to changes either as (1) an actual, observable change that had occurred or that, at the time of the decision to make the change, was expected to occur, or as (2) an increase or decrease in aspiration level or a long-standing aspiration or policy that was not satisfied. This distinction between reactive and proactive changes is supported in Hrebiniak and Joyce's (1985) theoretical model of the causes of strategic actions.

Distinguishing Discrete Events from Ongoing Processes

At the extreme, changes can occur either as discrete events or as relatively ongoing dynamic processes. For changes that occur as discrete events, observers can date the event and examine the sequencing of changes to learn about the causal processes connecting different types of changes. Ongoing dynamic processes, however, are more difficult to locate in a temporal sequencing, and intertwined causes and effects render causal inference problematic (Meyer 1982). For example, the AIDS epidemic is having profound effects on health care providers, but these effects cannot be linked to specific events or critical junctures. Further, the causation is circular because health care providers are undertaking changes designed to control the AIDS epidemic.[5]

Between the extremes of very discrete events and ongoing processes, change also may occur as a moderately discrete event. For example, change may occur as an accelerating process with a clear inflection point in the trend line. Change may occur as a slow process that evolves over months or years, rather than minutes. The speed of a change may also vary across time. Alternatively, an ongoing change may reach a specific threshold level that triggers a decision point for a top manager. The length and intensity of a change process can vary considerably. Thus, to distinguish accurately among the variety of changes, research methodologies must represent each change as a series of observations to capture the complete trend line with inflection points, fluctuations in speed, threshold levels, and absolute beginning and end points of the change process. Although accuracy is enhanced, simplicity is ignored by this much detail.

[5]This vivid example of the difficulty of disentangling causal effects from ongoing processes was provided by Alan Meyer, one of the collaborators on this study.

Our approach to representing change and distilling the change sequences strongly favors simplicity by classifying each change as either a relatively discrete event or as an ongoing process. Relatively discrete events were dated by the month in which they were first observed or crossed a threshold level. If we had decided to study fewer organizations or fewer changes for each organization, we would have preferred a more fine-grained assessment of the trend line of the change processes.

Relative Importance of Changes

Some key informants listed changes that appeared to be relatively unimportant, or at least of a nature that the key informants in other organizations did not list. For example, when a major shift in organizational structure was made, some informants listed changes about reporting relationships of lower-level personnel. Other informants did not bother to mention these lower-level changes. In some cases, we suspected that this omission of lower-level changes was an artifact of the interview protocol limiting the description of design and nondesign changes to a maximum of 20 minutes. In very dynamic organizations, time limits caused the informant not to have time to get to the lower-level changes. In more stable organizations, informants had plenty of time to describe mundane, lower-level changes. To control for these apparent differences in reporting behaviors, all 1110 changes from the first round interviews were coded by two people as "strategically important," "important, but not strategically important," and "not important." Interrater reliabilities are 0.74 and 0.85 for single or multiple raters, respectively [ICC(1, 1) and ICC(1, k); Shrout and Fleiss 1979].[6] Subsequent interview rounds were coded by a single rater. By coding the relative importance of changes, we controlled for differences in reporting behaviors by deleting unimportant changes or by differentially treating changes based on their relative strategic importance. Thus, we can avoid testing theories of important or strategic change with data about less-strategic changes.

Summary

After considering many trade-offs, we selected retrospective reports by the top manager as the primary method for developing and testing theories about the nature and antecedents of important changes. We attempted to minimize the errors of recall by interviewing the top managers every six months and asking about recent, important changes. Our decision to use the top manager as the sole key informant was based on the belief that the top manager was the person most knowledgeable about the broad variety of changes that occur within and across the organization.

The outcome of the four interviews was a 24-month event history for each of well over 100 organizations with comparable data on thousands of important organizational changes. The open-ended descriptions of these changes were coded with mul-

---

[6]The interrater reliability of a single rater, ICC(1, 1) (Glick 1985, Shrout and Fleiss 1979), is analogous to an item reliability statistic, while the interrater reliability of the mean, ICC(1, k), is similar to an inter-item scale reliability statistic, such as Cronbach's alpha. ICC(1, k) is an estimate of the interrater reliability of the *average* of the two raters for each coded change. ICC(1, 1) is an estimate of the interrater reliability of the rating from a *single* rater randomly selected from the pair of actual raters. Both ICC(1, k) and ICC(1, 1) are functions of the within and between coded change variances and the number of informants (raters) per coded change. Given an acceptable individual rater reliability for the coding task (0.74), only a single rater coded the subsequent changes.

tiple coding schemes to characterize the nature of changes and their antecedents. To further understand these changes and develop theories about change processes we collected additional information about these organizations concerning their designs, contexts, and leaders, as described below.

ASSESSMENTS OF ORGANIZATIONAL, CONTEXTUAL, AND TOP MANAGER CHARACTERISTICS

To enhance our understanding of reported changes, we assessed a large number of organizational and contextual variables for each organization after both the first and third retrospective event history interviews.[7] These variables were related to multiple dimensions of structure, process, technology, strategy, environment, and performance. We also assessed the characteristics of the top manager of each organization after the final retrospective event history interview.[8] These characteristics included demographic variables, work histories, and personality variables. The organization, contextual, and top manager characteristics were assessed with questionnaires that were hand-delivered or mailed to the key informant. Completed questionnaires were returned by mail to the researcher.

Selecting the Key Informant for the Questionnaire

The top manager was selected to complete both types of questionnaires for all of the same reasons described above in the selection of the key informant for the retrospective event history, especially the expectation that the top manager would be the most knowledgeable and qualified informant (Hambrick 1981, Snow and Hrebiniak 1980, Zajac and Shortell 1989). It also was easier to continue using the top manager after we had developed a good rapport during the interviews. This decision to again use the top manager as the key informant was not without cost. A consequence of the decision is that data from the interviews would be more correlated with data from the questionnaires than if different key informants had provided the two types of data (Glick, Jenkins, and Gupta 1986). The problem with the single informant procedure is that top managers may provide answers on the various data-collecting media that are cognitively consistent and reflect their own cognitive map of how organizations operate. To the extent that the cognitive maps of most top managers overemphasize some causal connections, the common methods variance may bias the relationships between variables assessed in the interviews and variables assessed with the questionnaires.

We attempted to minimize the problem of common methods variance by employing different methods for collecting information from the informant. Specifically, the methods for obtaining the retrospective report data and the questionnaire data differed in three ways: (1) the interview questions were open-ended (e.g., "please list . . ."), whereas the mailed questionnaire items were close-ended (e.g., "to what extent is . . .,"

[7]The questionnaires to assess organizational and contextual variables are included with full documentation in CODE Study Technical Reports 02 and 06. They are available from the first author.

[8]The questionnaire to assess top manager characteristics is included with full documentation in CODE Study Technical Report 09. It is available from the first author.

with forced choice or numeric responses); (2) the interview response mode was oral in a social context, while the questionnaire response mode was written in private; and (3) the time interval between the interview and completion of the questionnaire was long enough for informants to forget the specifics of the interview before completing the questionnaire, with an expected procedural minimum of one week and an allowed maximum of three months. The mean interval was approximately one month. Despite these efforts to minimize common methods variance, however, the top managers' cognitive maps may have influenced the observed patterns of relationships to some unknown degree. In retrospect, we believe that choosing to use a single informant for the retrospective reports was a good decision. On the other hand, it would have been useful to have sent the organizational assessment questionnaires to multiple informants in order to have collected more independent measures of the consequences of changes, and of the effectiveness of the organizations with the questionnaires. Although the top manager was the best informant for assessing the changes and most other information, in retrospect we believe that multiple informants should have been used for some outcome measures to eliminate single source bias in predicted relationships.

Characteristics Assessed in the Questionnaires

The main purpose of the questionnaire about organizational and contextual characteristics was to enhance our understanding of changes in organizational design and effectiveness. For example, they asked for information about the organization's effectiveness, external environment, strategy, internal functioning, goals, technology, and size. The specific variables and measures used in the questionnaires were identified through reviews of theoretical and empirical literatures, as noted earlier.

A variety of empirical studies (cf., Gupta and Govindarajan 1984, Meyer and Goes 1988, Miller, Kets de Vries, and Toulouse 1982) have demonstrated that the top manager's characteristics are important determinants of organizational change or effectiveness. After the last of the four interviews, each of our key informants completed a questionnaire on which he or she provided information on age, education, work history, and six personality characteristics.

Validity and Reliability of CODE Study Questionnaire Measures

The validity and reliability of the questionnaire measures are partial consequences of four critical judgment calls described earlier: (1) the key informant, the top manager, was selected as the most knowledgeable about his or her organization; (2) a single informant was questioned rather than multiple informants; (3) the set of field sites was selected to be heterogeneous in terms of the key variables in the study; and (4) the questionnaires were designed to assess these variables in terminology that is meaningful to top managers in a broad variety of organizations. To the extent that these judgment calls were appropriate, we expected the factor analyses and reliability statistics to support our a priori measures. After deleting a few of the a priori measures due to disconfirming evidence from one or more of the analyses, the mean Cronbach's alpha inter-item scale reliability for the first round organizational assessment questionnaire was 0.72. Following revision of the questionnaire for the second round, the mean reliability was 0.74. The mean reliability for the top manager questionnaire also was 0.61. Overall, these results support the validity and reliability of our measures and the four judgment calls above.

As a further assessment of these judgment calls, in the 36 organizations selected by The University of Texas research group, multiple informants were asked four of the same organizational effectiveness questions that were asked of the top manager. These additional informants were members of the top management team who reported to the top manager or chief operating officer. Averaging across all informants within each organization provided a reliable organization-level score. The mean rater reliabilities [ICC(1,k); see Glick 1985, Shrout and Fleiss 1979] for the four items were 0.71, 0.68, 0.74, and 0.63, respectively.[9] These mean rater reliabilities indicated that the average scores varied substantially across organizations on all four dimensions of effectiveness. This supports our belief that the set of organizations in The University of Texas local study were moderately heterogeneous. Heterogeneity was even greater among the set of field sites in the overall study.

Our decision to question the top manager as the sole key informant in most field sites is more difficult to evaluate. Although we can estimate the interrater reliability of a single rater with ICC(1, 1),[10] this estimate applies to the reliability of an informant randomly selected from the set of actual informants. As argued earlier, the top manager is a more qualified informant than the other members of the top management team. The multiple informants from The University of Texas local study occupied diverse positions with different functional and product line responsibilities that expose them to different information, reward structures, etc. Thus, our estimates of the interrater reliability of a single rater can only be interpreted as lower bound estimates of the accuracy of the top managers' assessments. In our local study of 36 organizations, the interrater reliabilities for a single randomly selected top management team member, ICC(1, 1) (Glick 1985, Shrout and Fleiss 1979), are 0.30, 0.26, 0.33, and 0.23 on the four dimensions of effectiveness. These values indicated that randomly selecting a single informant from the top management team would not provide reliable measures of effectiveness.

In addition to the distinction between the top manager versus other top management team members, it is likely that even stronger positional effects are associated with the dramatic differences among top management team members' job titles. We cannot separate, however, the differences among these other positions because the titles vary considerably across organizations. Therefore, we can conclude that the top managers will be more accurate than suggested by the reported ICC(1, 1), but we cannot determine how much more accurate. Selecting the key informant from a single position controls for all systematic differences among positions. By consistently selecting the top manager from each organization as the key informant, we control for the moderate positional effects that we estimated above, and for an undetermined amount of variance associated with differences among other top management team positions.

---

[9] As described in footnote 6, interrater reliability of the mean, ICC(1, k), is analogous to an inter-item scale reliability statistic, such as Cronbach's alpha (Glick 1985, Shrout and Fleiss 1979). In The University of Texas local study, there were an average of 5.9 key informants for each of the 36 field sites.

[10] As described in footnote 6, the interrater reliability of a single rater, ICC(1, 1), is analogous to an item reliability statistic (Glick 1985, Shrout and Fleiss 1979).

SUMMARY AND CONCLUSION

The goal of the CODE study was to understand better the nature, frequency, antecedents, and consequences of a broad variety of changes in organizations, particularly as these changes affect organizational effectiveness. This relatively positivist goal had several implications that led us to adopt a methodology that involved more independent observations than used in the other longitudinal studies described in this special issue.

To learn about the variety of ways in which organizational designs, contexts, and leaders can affect how and when different types of changes occur, numerous trade-offs were required. First, despite the potential for coordination problems, top-grade researchers from several universities were included as collaborators to contribute data, insights, and theory. Second, rather than focus on a small number of changes or organizations, data about a large number of changes were collected in each of more than 100 organizations. This set of organizations was heterogeneous, yet clustered in subsets that are relevant to our theories. The heterogeneous clusters allow development of middle-range theories within clusters as well as tests of generalizability across the heterogeneous set. Third, retrospective reports of the most important, recent changes were obtained in semi-annual interviews. These reports provide retrospective event histories that include information on the timing of changes in much greater detail than possible with a panel design. Fourth, the top manager was selected as the key informant from each organization. The top manager is likely to be more knowledgeable about a broader variety of changes than other informants. By consistently selecting an informant from the same position in each organization, we controlled for a number of report biases that are likely to be associated with an informant's position in the organization due to specialized information flows and biased information processing. Fifth, only one key informant was used in each organization. This minimized the loss of field sites (and thus compromising generalizability) and avoided including reports from less knowledgeable informants. As a consequence, however, we do not gain the potential advantages of multiple informants, such as reducing common methods variance, testing reliability, and increasing validity by resolving discrepancies among multiple reports. Sixth, multiple attributes of the reported changes were coded to distill the diverse descriptions of specific changes into relatively simple and general (Weick 1979) descriptions of the changes. Seventh, assessments of organizational, contextual, and top manager characteristics were obtained with questionnaires completed by the top manager. By using the same informant for the interview and the questionnaires, our results might be confounded with common methods variance, but this potential confounding is limited by using different methods for collecting information from the informant and collecting the different types of data at different occasions. The threat to internal validity due to common methods variance from a single informant was accepted as a trade-off to avoid the reductions in internal and external validity that would result from using less knowledgeable informants or from losing field sites that would not provide multiple informants.

All research methodologies reflect necessary trade-offs among the desirable theory characteristics of generality, accuracy, and simplicity (Thorngate 1976, Weick 1979). Some methodologies, however, achieve lower scores on all characteristics, while stronger methodologies achieve higher aggregate scores across all three dimensions. In the CODE study methodology, *generality* was sought by acquiring and using data from a relatively large variety of organizations and organizational contexts. *Accuracy* was sought by developing and comparing theories created within and for specific contexts or domains, i.e., specific industries and environments. Accuracy also was sought by obtaining data on a variety of contingency variables. Finally, *simplicity* was sought by creating a data base sufficiently large that events and variables that might possibly be antecedents, causes, or consequences of organizational change and change processes can be tested for inclusion using inferential statistics. Less important and nonsignificant factors can be dropped to develop simplicity in the final theories. Still, trade-offs were made with the result that the CODE study methodology provides more generality, but less accuracy, than do the more ethnographic methods typically used to study organizational changes and change processes.

ACKNOWLEDGMENTS

This research was supported by a research contract from the Basic Research Office of the Army Research Institute for the Behavioral and Social Sciences to the first two authors. The authors thank Alan Meyer and Andrew Van de Ven for their helpful comments on earlier drafts of the manuscript, and the helpful comments on our presentation from participants in the National Science Foundation Conference on Longitudinal Field Research Methods for Studying Organizational Processes, Austin Texas, September, 1988.

REFERENCES

Aguilar, F. J. (1967), *Scanning the Business Environment,* New York: Macmillan.

Astley, W. G. and A. Van de Ven (1983), "Central Perspectives and Debates in Organization Theory," *Administrative Science Quarterly,* 28, 245–273.

Bagozzi, R. P. and L. W. Phillips (1982), "Representing and Testing Organizational Theories: A Holistic Construal Process," *Administrative Science Quarterly,* 27, 459–489.

Barley, S. R. (1990), "Images of Imaging: Notes on Doing Longitudinal Field Work," *Organization Science,* 1, 3, 220–247.

Beyer, J. and H. Trice (1982), "The Utilization Process: A Conceptual Framework and Synthesis of Empirical Literature," *Administrative Science Quarterly,* 27, 591–622.

Blackburn, R. and L. L. Cummings (1982), "Cognitions of Work Unit Structure," *Academy of Management Journal,* 25, 836–854.

Cohen, J. (1988), *Statistical Power Analysis for the Behavioral Sciences* (2nd ed.), Hillsdale, NJ: Lawrence Erlbaum.

Cook, T. D. and D. T. Campbell (1979), *Quasi-experimentation: Design and Analysis Issues for Field Settings,* Chicago: Rand McNally.

Daft, R. L. and G. P. Huber (1987), "How Organizations Learn: A Communication Framework," in S. B. Bacharach and N. DiTomaso (Eds.), *Research in the Sociology of Organizations—Vol. 5,* 1–36, London: JAI Press.

Dearborn, D. C. and H. A. Simon (1958), "Selective Perception: A Note on the Departmental Identifications of Executives," *Sociometry,* 21, 140–144.

Drasgow, F. and T. Kang (1984), "Statistical Power of Differential Validity and Differential Prediction Analyses for Detecting Measurement Nonequivalence," *Journal of Applied Psychology,* 69, 498–508.

Duncan, R. B. (1972), "The Characteristics of Organizational Environments and Perceived Environmental Uncertainty," *Administrative Science Quarterly,* 17, 313–326.

Glick, W. H. (1985), "Conceptualizing and Measuring Organizational and Psychological Climate: Pitfalls in Multi-level Research," *Academy of Management Review,* 10, 601–616.

Glick, W. H., G. D. Jenkins, Jr. and N. Gupta (1986), "Method versus Substance: How Strong Are Underlying Relationships between Job Characteristics and Attitudinal Outcomes?" *Academy of Management Journal,* 29, 441–464.

Gupta, A. K. and V. Govindarajan (1984), "Business Unit Strategy, Managerial Characteristics, and Business Unit Effectiveness at Strategy Implementation," *Academy of Management Journal,* 27, 25–41.

Hambrick, D. C. (1981), "Strategic Awareness within Top Management Teams," *Strategic Management Journal,* 2, 263–279.

Hambrick, D. C. (1982), "Environmental Scanning and Organizational Strategy," *Strategic Management Journal,* 3, 159–174.

Hax, A. C. and N. S. Majluf (1988), "The Concept of Strategy and the Strategy Formation Process," *Interfaces,* 18 (May-June), 99–109. Prentice-Hall.

Houston, M. J. and S. Sudman (1975), "A Methodological Assessment of the Use of Key Informants," *Social Science Research,* 4, 151–164.

Hrebiniak, L. G. and W. F. Joyce (1985), "Organizational Adaptation: Strategic Choice and Environmental Determinism," *Administrative Science Quarterly,* 30, 336–349.

Huber, G. P. (1985), "Temporal Stability and Response-Order Biases in Participant Descriptions of Organizational Decisions," *Academy of Management Journal,* 28, 943–950.

Huber, G. P. (1990), "A Theory of the Effects of Advanced Information Technologies on Organizational Design, Intelligence, and Decision Making," *Academy of Management Review,* 15, 47–71.

Huber, G. P. (1991), "Organizational Learning: An Examination of the Contributing Processes and a Review of the Literatures," *Organization Science* (in press).

Huber, G. P. and R. L. Daft (1987), "The Information Environments of Organizations," in F. M. Jablin, L. L. Putnam, K. H. Roberts and L. W. Porter (Eds.), *Handbook of Organizational Communication,* 130–164, Beverly Hills: Sage Publications.

Huber, G. P. and R. R. McDaniel (1986), "The Decision Making Paradigm of Organizational Design" *Management Science,* 32, 572–589.

Huber, G. P., C. C. Miller and W. H. Glick (1990), "Developing More Encompassing Theories about Organizations: The Centralization-Effectiveness Relationship as an Example," *Organization Science,* 1, 11–40.

Huber, G. P. and D. J. Power (1985), "Retrospective Reports of Strategic-Level Managers: Guidelines for Increasing Their Accuracy," *Strategic Management Journal,* 6, 171–180.

Ireland, R. D., M. A. Hitt, R. A. Bettis and D. A. DePorras (1987), "Strategy Formulation Processes: Differences in Perceptions of Strength and Weakness Indicators and Environmental Uncertainty by Managerial Level," *Strategic Management Journal,* 8, 467–485.

Katz, D. and R. L. Kahn (1978), *The Social Psychology of Organizations* (2nd ed.), New York: Wiley.

Leonard-Barton, D. (1990), "A Dual Methodology for Case Studies: Synergistic Use of a Longitudinal Single Site with Replicated Multiple Sites," *Organization Science,* 1, 3, 248–266.

Markus, M. L. and D. Robey (1988), "Information Technology and Organizational Change: Causal Structure in Theory and Research," *Management Science,* 34, 583–598.

McGuire, J. B. (1986), "Management and Research Methodology," *Journal of Management,* 12, 5–17.

Meyer, A. D. (1982), "Adapting to Environmental Jolts," *Administrative Science Quarterly,* 27, 515–537.

Meyer, A. D. and J. B. Goes (1988), "Organizational Assimilation of Innovations: A Multilevel, Contextual Analysis," *Academy of Management Journal,* 31, 897–923.

Miller, D., M. E. R. Kets de Vries and J. Toulouse (1982), "Top Executive Locus of Control and Its Relationship to Strategy-making, Structure, and Environment," *Academy of Management Journal,* 25, 237–253.

Mintzberg, H. (1975), "The Manager's Job: Folklore and Fact," *Harvard Business Review,* 53, 49–61.

Mohr, L. B. (1982), *Explaining Organizational Behavior,* San Francisco: Jossey-Bass.

Monge, P. R. (1990), "Theoretical and Analytical Issues in Studying Organizational Processes," *Organization Science,* 1, 4.

Monge, P. R., R. V. Farace, E. M. Eisenberg, K. I. Miller and L. L. White (1984), "The Process of Studying Process in Organizational Communication," *Journal of Communications,* 34, 1, 22–43.

Phillips, L. A. (1981), "Assessing Measurement Error in Key Informant Reports: A Methodological Note on Organizational Analysis in Marketing," *Journal of Marketing Research,* XVIII, 395–415.

Pinder, C. C. and Moore, L. F. (1980), "The Inevitability of Multiple Paradigms and the Resultant Need for Middle-range Analysis in Organizational Theory," in C. C. Pinder and L. F. Moore (Eds.), *Middle Range Theory and the Study of Organizations,* 87–100. Boston: Martinus Nijhoff.

Seidler, J. (1974), "On Using Informants: A Technique for Collecting Quantitative Data and Controlling Measurement Error in Organization Analysis," *American Sociological Review,* 39, 816–831.

Shrout, P. E. and J. L. Fleiss (1979), "Intraclass Correlations: Uses in Assessing Rater Reliability," *Psychological Bulletin,* 86, 420–428.

Snow, C. C. and L. G. Hrebiniak (1980), "Strategy, Distinctive Competence, and Organizational Performance," *Administrative Science Quarterly,* 25, 317–336.

Thorngate, W. (1976), "Possible Limits on a Science of Social Behavior," in L. H. Strickland, F. E. Aboud and K. J. Gergen (Eds.), *Social Psychology in Transition,* 121–139, New York: Plenum.

Tuma, N. B. and M. Hannan (1984), *Social Dynamics: Models and Methods,* New York: Academic.

Van de Ven, A. H. and M. S. Poole (1990), "Methods for Studying Innovation Development in the Minnesota Innovation Research Program," *Organization Science,* 1, 3, 313–335.

Weick, K. E. (1974), "Middle Range Theories of Social Systems," *Behavioral Science,* 19, 357–367.

Weick, K. E. (1979), *The Social Psychology of Organizations* (2nd ed.), Reading, MA: Addison-Wesley.

Williams, L. J., J. A. Cote and M. R. Buckley (1989), "Lack of Method Variance in Self-reported Affect and Perceptions at Work: Reality or Artifact?" *Journal of Applied Psychology,* 74, 462–468.

Wolfe, J. and C. Jackson (1987), "Creating Models of the Strategic Decision Making Process via Participant Recall: A Free Simulation Examination," *Journal of Management,* 13, 123–134.

Zajac, E. J. and S. M. Shortell (1989), "Changing Generic Strategies: Likelihood, Direction, and Performance Implications," *Strategic Management Journal,* 10, 413–430.

Zajonc, R. and D. Wolfe (1966), "Cognitive Consequences of a Person's Position in a Formal Organization," *Human Relations,* 19, 139–150.

NAME INDEX

SUBJECT INDEX